P9-BJU-815

5816

YALE PUBLICATIONS IN AMERICAN STUDIES, 4

DAVID HORNE, Editor

Published under the direction of the American Studies Program

ARMY EXPLORATION IN THE AMERICAN WEST 1803-1863

by William H. Goetzmann

New Haven: YALE UNIVERSITY PRESS, 1959

Set in Baskerville type and
printed in the United States of America by
Vail-Ballou Press, Inc., Binghamton, N.Y.

Library of Congress catalog card number: 59-12694

TO MY MOTHER AND MY FATHER

The present is emphatically the age of discovery. At no period since the days of Columbus and Cortez has the thirst for exploration been more active and universal than now. One by one the outposts of barbarism are stormed and carried, advanced parallels are thrown up, and the besieging lines of knowledge, which when once established can never be retaken, are gradually closing around the yet unconquered mysteries of the globe. Modern exploration is intelligent, and its results are therefore positive and permanent. The traveller no longer wanders bewildered in a cloud of fables prepared to see marvels, and but too ready to create them. He tests every step of his way by the sure light of science and his pioneer trail becomes a plain and easy path to those who follow. The pencil, the compass, the barometer, and the sextant are his aids; and by these helps and appliances his single brain achieves results now which it would once have required an armed force to win.

—*Washington National Intelligencer, Oct. 12, 1855.*

PREFACE

THE AIM of this study is to describe, analyze, and evaluate the role played by the U. S. Army in exploring the trans-Mississippi West, and in particular the role of the Topographical Engineers between the years 1838 and 1863—a time span that covers the entire independent life of that Corps. In studying their activities, I have sought to view the West not as an isolated region but as an integral part of the continental nation whose destiny was of the utmost importance to the other sections of the country; and the Corps itself as an American, rather than a western, institution. This seems appropriate first because as a branch of the Army the Corps was by definition representative of the whole nation; secondly, because the scientific activities of the Topographical Engineers had utility and meaning for the country as a whole, and at the same time contributed to a total body of knowledge that was the property of both American and Western European cultures.

A sincere attempt has been made to record the Corps' western activities as completely and definitively as possible, and to do full justice to their exploits. The Topographical Engineers performed heroic deeds, and in spite of the anonymity of their army "blues," they were as colorful and as human as any group of explorers whose deeds history is likely to record. The Portuguese in the Indies, the Conquistadors in the New World, and the legendary mountain men have all had their chroniclers; it seems but just that the men of the Topographical Corps should have their hearing as well, particularly because the highly colored and romanticized chronicles of the mountain men have all but obscured the achievements of the Engineers, who came after them.

To put oneself beside Lieutenant Emory as he rode westward along the Gila River to California in 1846 or to stand with Captain Macomb on a peak overlooking the Colorado Plateau and the junction of the Green and Grand rivers is to appreciate the problems faced by these men, the extent of their own knowledge, and the impact of discovery upon their minds. Only in this way is it possible to assess the true significance of their achievements in the light of their own age. The study of their scientific endeavors thus becomes the study of the human mind in the act of comprehension. This applies to the individuals involved and, as the new knowledge accumulated, to the collective mind of America as well. For the learning process itself, in all its dramatic aspects, was one of the most characteristic activities of Americans in the mid-nineteenth century, when infinite possibilities for progress stretched out before the people.

Originally submitted as a doctoral dissertation to the American Studies Program of the Yale University Graduate School, where it was awarded the John Addison Porter Prize for 1957, this book, characteristically, is the labor of many. To my director, David M. Potter, must go double thanks, first for calling attention to the William Hemsley Emory Papers when they were acquired by the Yale Collection of Western Americana, and secondly, of course, for his extensive critical labors. Special thanks are also due Archibald Hanna, Curator of the Yale Collection of Western Americana, and to his staff, who made the resources of this collection available to me. Zara Jones Powers, then Curator of the Yale Historical Manuscripts Collection, provided her usual valuable aid and also made me realize the importance of *The American Journal of Science* to my study. Howard R. Lamar, John Morton Blum, Edmund S. Morgan, Ralph Henry Gabriel, Rollin G. Osterweis, and Norman Holmes Pearson of the Yale History and American Studies departments read the manuscript either in whole or in part and made important critical suggestions. John E. Smith of the Yale Philosophy Department contributed advice concerning materials relating romanticism and science. Thomas Manning of Texas Technological College and Jerry E. Patterson of Edward Eberstadt and Sons allowed me to read their respective unpublished works. In addition I benefited immensely from Manning's searching criticism of my own ideas and methods. John Muldowny of the Yale Graduate School called my attention to several details which I might otherwise have overlooked. Edward S. Wallace, a pioneer student of the Corps of Topographical Engineers, contributed much sound advice and, most of all, his very genuine appreciation and enthusiasm for the people of the 1840's and '50's. The late Robert Glass Clelland graciously allowed me the use of various materials that he was using in his own studies. Stanley Pargellis of the Newberry Library made available the drawings of F. W. von Egloffstein, which he had just purchased in an uncommon stroke of good fortune. Charles Coulston Gillispie of Princeton University gave me important advice in matters pertaining to the history of science. Nathan Reingold of the National Archives contributed information on the resources of the archives, and Herman Friis and his assistant Joseph F. Winkler of the Cartographic Records Section furnished me with a rare copy of their catalogue of the National Archives Exhibition of *Geographical Exploration and Topographic Mapping by the United States Government*.

Henry Borger of Clark University, whose own dissertation was on the Lake surveys of the Topographical Corps, also provided aid and encouragement. Franklin Bache Abert of Rockville, Maryland, told me all he knew of the papers of his great grandfather, Col. John James Abert. Col. L. H. Hewitt, the present United States Commissioner of the International Boundary and Water Commission of the United States and Mexico, followed this project with considerable interest and made valuable suggestions. Miss Emily B. Warren of Newport, Rhode Island, daughter of Gen. G. K. Warren, was extremely helpful in granting me permission to use her father's papers.

The staffs of the many libraries and historical societies where I have worked or to which inquiries have been sent also deserve special thanks: the National Archives, especially in the State Department, Interior Department, Cartographic Records, Still Pictures, and Old Army sections; the Library of Congress; the Pennsylvania State Historical Society; the John Carter Brown Library; the New York State Museum; the New York State Library; the New York Public Library; the New York Historical Society; the Torrey Botanical Gardens; the Huntington Library; the Bancroft Library; the Barker Memorial Library of the Texas State Historical Society; the Denver Public Library; the Panhandle-Plains Historical Museum; the Arizona Pioneers Historical Library; the Rosenberg Library in Galveston, Texas; the Houston Public Library; the Oklahoma State Historical Society; the West Point Museum; and the Newberry Library of Chicago.

Parts of this book have appeared in altered form in *The South-*

western Historical Quarterly, The Password of the El Paso Historical Society, and *The New York Westerner's Brand Book,* to which acknowledgments are due.

My typist Marie Avitable, provided literary criticism and encouragement as well as uncounted hours of tedious labor far beyond the call of duty.

A special debt of gratitude is due the Provost of Yale University, who provided a travel grant that made it possible for me to retrace many trails taken by the Topographical Engineers. I am grateful also to the trustees of the Andrew W. Moorhouse Fund, the Executive Committee of the American Studies Department, and the Fund for Young Scholars of Yale University for providing financial assistance which made the project and its publication possible.

Finally, of course, something more than gratitude is due my wife, Mewes, who was always with me as we went in spirit, "down the edges, through the passes, up the mountains steep."

W.H.G.

New Haven, Conn.
January 1959

Note on the Explorer's Maps

Perhaps the most valuable insight into the achievements of the explorers in this period can be gained from the maps they produced. Reproductions of the hitherto unknown map by Jim Baker and the monumental works of Frémont, Preuss, Warren, and von Egloffstein, first discussed in the text on pages 24, 95, 105, 315, and 393 respectively, have been included in a pocket on the back cover.

CONTENTS

CONTENTS

ILLUSTRATIONS

Pictured on the jacket is the Lt. Joseph Christmas Ives expedition ascending the Colorado River in 1857 aboard the home-made steamboat *U. S. Explorer*. The original drawing is by John J. Young from a sketch by the German artist, H. B. Möllhausen, who accompanied the expedition. It appears in Ives, *Report upon the Colorado River of the West,* 36th Cong. 1st Sess., *Sen. Exec. Doc.* (unnumbered), Washington, 1861.

Illustrations on the part-title pages are adapted from original pencil sketches by F. W. von Egloffstein now in the Newberry Library, Chicago, Illinois. See pages 1, 63, 339.

The illustrations listed below will be found in a section preceding the index.

18. Examples of scientific data published in the *Pacific Railroad Reports*, 1853–59.

19. Camp Floyd, Utah, headquarters of the United States Army in the Mormon War. Drawn by Joseph Heger. Original in the Yale Collection of Western Americana.

20. Yellow Creek Camp of the United States Army in the Mormon War. Drawn by Joseph Heger. Original in the Yale Collection of Western Americana.

21. Capt. James Hervey Simpson's expedition setting out westward across the Great Basin in 1859. Painted by John J. Young. Original in the National Archives, Washington, D.C.

22. Capt. James Hervey Simpson's expedition arriving at Genoa, a Mormon settlement on the eastern slopes of the Sierra Nevadas near Lake Tahoe. Drawn by John J. Young. Original in the National Archives, Washington, D.C.

23. Earliest known view of the Grand Canyon, drawn by F. W. von Egloffstein in 1857, from the floor of the Canyon near Diamond Creek. Yale University Library.

24. Capt. W. F. Raynolds' Yellowstone expedition of 1859, sketched by the artist, Antoine Schoenborn. Original in Yale Collection of Western Americana.

25. Part of the United States Northwest Boundary Commission Camp on San Juan Island, Nov. 4, 1859. Photographer unknown. Original in Yale Collection of Western Americana.

26. A Topographical Engineer at work: Capt. Darrah of the Royal Engineers taking a sighting with his Zenith telescope. Northwest Boundary Survey. Photographer unknown. Original in Yale Collection of Western Americana.

27. Cutting a swath through the forest to mark the Northwest Boundary near the Moofie River. Photographer unknown. Original in Yale Collection of Western Americana.

MAPS

ROUTES AND BOUNDARIES

EXPLORER'S MAPS *back cover*

MAPS

[illegible] AND SKETCH MAPS

[illegible] MAPS [illegible]

ABBREVIATIONS AND SHORT TITLES

BES 48, 77
Bureau of Explorations and Surveys, Record Group 48 (or 77), National Archives.

Chittenden, *Fur Trade*
Hiram Martin Chittenden, *The American Fur Trade of the Far West,* 2 vols. New York, 1902.

Emory, *Notes*
W. H. Emory, *Notes of a Military Reconnaissance from Fort Leavenworth, in Missouri to San Diego in California, Including Parts of the Arkansas, Del Norte, and Gila Rivers,* 30th Cong., 1st Sess., Sen. Exec. Doc. 7, 1848.

Emory, *Report*
W. H. Emory, *Report on the United States and Mexican Boundary Survey,* 34th Cong., 1st Sess., H. R. Exec. Doc. 135, 1857.

EP
William H. Emory Papers, Yale Collection of Western Americana, Sterling Memorial Library.

Frémont, *Exploration*
John C. Frémont, *A Report on an Exploration of the Country Lying between the Missouri River and the Rocky Mountains on the Line of the Kansas and Great Platte Rivers,* Derby ed., Buffalo, 1851.

Frémont, *Memoirs*
John C. Frémont, *Memoirs of My Life,* New York, 1887.

Frémont, *Report, 1843–44*
John C. Frémont, *Report of the Exploring Expedition to the Rocky Mountains in the Year 1842, and to Oregon and North California in the Years 1843–44,* Derby ed., Buffalo, 1851.

Jackson, *Wagon Roads*
William Turrentine Jackson, *Wagon Roads West,* Berkeley, 1952.

LS, LR
Letters Sent, Letters Received.

Meisel, *Bibliography.*
Max Meisel, *A Bibliography of American Natural History* (3 vols. New York, 1926), Vol. *3.*

MVHR
Mississippi Valley Historical Review.

Moore, *Buchanan*
John Bassett Moore, ed., *The Works of James Buchanan* (Phila., 1909), *7,* 1846–48.

Pacific Railroad Reports
33d Cong., 2d Sess., Senate Exec. Doc. 78, 1855.

Russel, *Improvement of Communication*
Robert R. Russel, *Improvement of Communication with the Pacific Coast as an Issue in American Politics, 1783–1864,* Cedar Rapids, 1948.

TE 77
Manuscript of the Corps of Topographical Engineers, Record Group 77, National Archives.

Warren, *Memoir*
Gouverneur Kemble Warren, *Memoir to Accompany the Map of the Territory of the United States from the Mississippi to the Pacific Ocean* . . . 33d Cong., 2d Sess., Sen. Exec. Doc. 78, 1859.

Wheat, "Mapping the American West"
Carl I. Wheat, "Mapping the American West, 1540–1857," *Proceedings of the American Antiquarian Society, 64* (1954), 19–194.

PART ONE
1776–1842

1. A NEW KIND OF EXPLORER

AMERICANS have traditionally viewed the settlement of the western frontier as a struggle between the individual and the wilderness environment. In his famous essay *The Significance of the Frontier in American History*,[1] Frederick Jackson Turner went so far as to designate it the very source of American individualism. Beyond the edge of civilization, where the struggle was more elemental, inventiveness, practicality, and nervous energy were dominant traits. Each man carved out his destiny in his own particular way, and with the passage of years these hardy settlers came to be celebrated as ideal types, symbolic of the winning of the West. Turner himself indicated the principal figures. "Stand at Cumberland Gap," he bade his readers, "and watch the procession of civilization marching single file—the buffalo following the trail to the salt springs, the Indian, the fur trader, the hunter, the cattle raiser, the pioneer farmer—and the frontier has passed by." He continued, "Stand at the South Pass in the Rockies a century later and see the same procession with wider intervals between." [2]

Of all these rugged types none has been so celebrated in recent years as the "mountain man" who functioned variously as trapper, hunter, and scout. Ranging far out ahead of the march of settlement, he was the first to pit his skill against the dangers of the western wilderness. His life stood for the freedom and individualism that have become traditional American values. According to the historian Hiram M. Chittenden, the mountain man was a virtual knight-errant clearing a way for the course of empire in the West: "It was the roving trader and the solitary trapper who first sought out these inhospitable wilds, traced the streams to their sources, scaled the mountain passes, and explored a boundless expanse of territory where the foot of the white man had never trodden before." Chittenden insisted, with a firmness that has to the present day called forth no denial, that "*They* were the

1. (New York, 1920), p. 37.
2. Ibid., p. 12.

'pathfinders' of the West, and not those later official explorers whom posterity so recognizes."[3]

As a result of this and similar statements by historians and expansionist spokesmen of the 1840's and '50's, one important phase of western development has been largely ignored and the cast of western heroes deprived of what should be one of its principal archetypes. The phase ignored was the era of official exploration which began about 1840. The missing archetype is the United States Army's Topographical Engineer.

From the year 1838 down to the Civil War, there existed a small but highly significant branch of the Army called the Corps of Topographical Engineers. Its total complement at any one time was thirty-six officers. Though it followed in the shadow of those larger-than-life heroes, the mountain men, no other group of comparable size contributed so much to the exploration and development of the American West. Its task was essentially different from that of the mountain man, and geographical discovery was only one of its functions. The Engineers were concerned with recording all of the western phenomena as accurately as possible, whether main-traveled roads or uncharted wilderness. As Army officers they represented the direct concern of the national government for the settling of the West. As an expression of what could be called the "collective will," in contrast to the individualism of the wild-western citizens, the Topographical Engineer, even one who could be rugged and individualistic in his own right, seemed less free, less eligible for the pantheon of western heroes and almost an alien to the frontier.

Nevertheless, the Corps of Topographical Engineers was a central institution of Manifest Destiny, and in the years before the Civil War its officers made explorations which resulted in the first scientific mapping of the West. They laid out national boundaries and directly promoted the advance of settlement by locating and constructing wagon roads, improving rivers and harbors, even performing experiments for the location of subsurface water in the arid regions. In short, they functioned as a department of public works for the West—and indeed for the whole nation, since the operations of the Corps extended to every state and territory of the United States.

3. Chittenden, *Fur Trade, 1,* viii, ix.

The work of the Corps in the West had still broader significance. Since a major part of its work was to assemble scientific information in the form of maps, pictures, statistics, and narrative reports about the West, it contributed importantly to the compilation of scientific knowledge about the interior of the North American Continent. The Topographical Engineers were sophisticated men of their time who worked closely with the foremost scholars in American and European centers of learning. Scientists and artists of all nationalities accompanied their expeditions as partners and co-workers. The Army Topographer considered himself by schooling and profession as one of a company of savants. By virtue of his West Point training and status he was an engineer, something above the ordinary field officer, whose duties were confined usually to strictly military tasks. As a Topographical Engineer he on occasion might address the American Association for the Advancement of Science. He probably subscribed to Silliman's *American Journal of Science* and he was a pillar of the Smithsonian Institution.

The Topographical Corps had to satisfy numerous demands while avoiding the pressures and pitfalls created by local and national factions. It was, first of all, a military unit, and as such it had to serve as part of the fighting force. But it was also an agency of civilian development, of public works, so that it was responsible to the demands of settlers and their Congressional representatives. This anomalous status on occasion threatened to bring about the dissolution of the Corps. Even more difficult was its strange role as both a purveyor of practical benefits and an instrument for advancing theoretical science. Frequently the practical and theoretical aspects of its duties seemed incompatible, and all too often it was subjected to criticism by western spokesmen for neglecting the one for the other.

Equally often, however, the multiplicity of its roles was used to advantage by the government. Under the guise of a scientific expedition, a topographical survey could serve a series of political ends. At the same time, under the camouflage of military appropriations, internal improvements and various scientific subsidies could be attached to the annual Army bill. But whichever role the Corps played, whether a pawn of politics or an instrument of science, it had to run the gantlet of Congressional scrutiny, at times yielding to pressures but frequently wielding great influence. Yet this anomalous role of the Corps was hardly surprising; it reflected the federal government itself during the early years of the Republic, in that the government, too, had no precedents to follow, was susceptible to the influence of personal leadership, and above all was faced with the ever-mounting problems of national growth.

The formal creation of a Corps of Topographical Engineers was achieved by the act of July 5, 1838, which provided that such a Corps "shall be organized and increased by regular promotions in the same, so that said corps shall consist of one colonel, one lieutenant-colonel, four majors, ten captains, ten first lieutenants, and ten second lieutenants." [4] This gave the Topographical Engineers status equal to the regular Corps of Engineers in the hierarchy of military command. It made its first chief, Colonel John James Abert, equal to the other heads of service departments, such as the Medical Corps and the Department of Ordnance, and thus gave him an importance as a member of the Army's general staff.

Although the Topographical Corps was not granted its independence until 1838, its origins extend back to the American Revolution, when General Washington, on July 25, 1777, appointed Robert Erskine of New Jersey the first geographer and surveyor in the Continental Army. His duties were "to take sketches of the country and the seat of the war." When he died in 1780 he was succeeded by his assistant, Simeon DeWitt, and in the same year Thomas Hutchins received a similar appointment in the southern wing of the American Army. Both men received the title "Geographer of the United States of America." The most significant fact about these appointments was that they created a distinct branch of the Army entirely separate from that of the military engineers, headed by the French General Louis du Portail.[5]

After the war, when the Army disbanded, DeWitt became the Surveyor of the State of New York, while Hutchins managed to

4. Raphael P. Thian, *Legislative History of the General Staff of the United States from 1775 to 1901* (Wash., 1901), pp. 488, 492–93.

5. Ibid.

retain his title as the "Geographer of the United States." [6] Hutchins' primary task in the postwar years was the laying out of the first seven "ranges" of public lands in the West, in execution of the Land Ordinance of 1785.[7] Other than this, with the war over, there seemed to be little use for a trained topographer on the rolls of the government. The tasks of Lewis and Clark and Zebulon Pike were, of course, similar to those of professional geographers, as were Dunbar's and Hunter's assignments in the Louisiana Territory.

The War of 1812 saw the creation of a full-fledged topographical engineer unit, which consisted of sixteen officers holding the ranks of brevet captains and majors. Among the men selected for positions as topographers were Isaac Roberdeau and John James Abert, who were eventually to serve as leaders of the Corps during most of its lifetime. The sixteen officers were divided between the northern and southern wings of the Army, and lengthy orders were formulated to define their duties while in the field. The order of March 3, 1813, provided a guide for all future operations of Topographical Engineers in time of war and as such is an important document. The engineers were

> To make such surveys and exhibit such delineations of these as the commanding general shall direct; to make plans of all military positions (which the Army may occupy) and of their respective vicinities, indicating the various roads, rivers, creeks, ravines, hills, woods and villages to be found therein; to accompany all reconnoitering parties sent out to obtain intelligence of the movements of the enemy or of his position, etc.; to make sketches of their route, accompanied by written notes of everything worthy of observation thereon; to keep a journal of every day's movements when the army is on the march, noticing the varieties of ground, of buildings, of culture, and the distances and state of the road between given points throughout the march of the day, and, lastly, to exhibit the positions of contending armies on fields of

6. *DAB.*

7. Edward Burr, "Historical Sketch of the Corps of Engineers, United States Army," *Occasional Papers, The Engineer School, United States Army, 71* (Wash., 1939), 34.

battle, and the disposition made whether for attack or defense.[8]

When the War of 1812 was over, all but two topographical officers were honorably discharged, and these two, John Anderson and Isaac Roberdeau, were retained to make a survey of Lake Champlain and the Northwest frontier.[9] The result of their efforts was a report submitted to Secretary of War William H. Crawford on January 16, 1816, which recommended "the completion of a frontier military survey of the whole interior and exterior of the United States." [10] Because of this report the number of Topographical Engineers was increased to ten, and though they were attached as subordinate units to the northern and southern field divisions, considerable progress was made in laying out seacoast fortifications and locating forts on the inland frontier.[11] The work of Major Stephen H. Long in establishing Fort Smith in Arkansas Territory and Fort Snelling in Minnesota during this period is representative of the kinds of assignments given them.

As the migration began into the Old Northwest, the question of internal improvements became all important. In April 1824 the passage of an act providing for the establishment of a Board of Engineers for Internal Improvements signified an official interest in western development.[12] The following year found the duties of the small unit of Topographical Engineers greatly increased.[13] They made a series of reconnaissances of routes between New Orleans and Washington for a national road. They worked on the construction of the Chesapeake and Ohio Canal, made surveys of Nantucket and Marblehead, supervised the removal of snags from the Ohio and Mississippi rivers, superintended the work on the Cumberland Road, and sponsored the survey of the

8. Ibid., p. 499.

9. Henry Putney Beers, "A History of the U. S. Topographical Engineers, 1813–1863," *Military Engineer, 34* (1942), 287.

10. Burr, p. 38.

11. Beers, p. 287.

12. Ibid., p. 288.

13. *Report of the Operations of the Engineer Department, during the Year Ending on the 30th of Sept., 1825* . . . in *Annual Report of the Secretary of War, Dec. 1, 1825,* 19th Cong., 1st Sess., Sen. Exec. Doc. 2 (Dec. 6, 1825), 56–60.

Santa Fe Trail. It was clear that during the initial stages of expansion the services of trained topographers and engineers were vitally needed.

Soon new duties, such as work on the Coast Survey and the Lighthouse Board, competed with demands from the West for their talents. In 1822 Major Roberdeau, acting chief of the Topographical Bureau, declared in his annual report that "No other country in the world feels the want of professional character of this kind [engineers] as does the United States; nor is there a nation in the world whose prosperity and improvement so much depends upon the establishment of some system by which this deficiency may be supplied." [14] His solution was to detail qualified West Point cadets for work as apprentices on "Public Civil Works of a State or Territory, or of an individual association, when in the opinion of the President, it may not interfere with the ordinary duties of service." In this way he hoped to keep his engineer officers from resigning in favor of lucrative positions in civilian life. "It is truly a matter of much concern," he wrote, "to all who are interested in the promotion of internal improvements."

The accession of Andrew Jackson to the presidency did very little to halt the enthusiasm for internal improvements, though it forced the engineer officers to proceed with caution. Old Hickory's dislike of the West Point élite was a lesson to the ambitious staff officers, particularly when the brilliant Colonel Sylvanus Thayer was forced to resign his post as head of the Academy.

In the year 1829, upon the death of Major Roberdeau, John James Abert became chief of the Topographical Bureau.[15] One of the early graduates of West Point, a part-time lawyer, and an assistant to Ferdinand Hassler on the Coast Survey, Abert had had a busy career up to this time. He was a stern, upright man, a bluff soldier of the old school whose enthusiasm for horse races and out-of-door living belied his learning and political shrewdness.[16] Besides his thorough grounding in science, he possessed

14. Isaac Roberdeau to Thomas Newton, Dec. 25, 1822, LS, TE 77.

15. *DAB.*

16. *DAB.* See also the correspondence between Abert and Daniel Parker, ca. 1830 (Daniel Parker Papers, Box 35, Pennsylvania Historical Society,

a certain political adroitness that enabled him to enhance the prestige of his Bureau, until in 1838 he saw it become a full-fledged Corps. With the utmost tact he gained the support of such important men as Joel Poinsett and James Barbour, so that little by little he gained autonomy. In February 1829 he was appointed special assistant to the Chief Engineer.[17] In 1831 the Topographical Bureau was made an independent office of the War Department, which moved it out from under the jurisdiction of the Chief of Engineers, though it still retained a lesser status.[18] At the same time Abert, with an eye on the official Jacksonian aversion to internal improvements, made certain that his Bureau would be known as a military rather than a civilian-oriented unit. This was in contrast to Roberdeau's outspoken espousal of the cause of internal improvements. Abert even went so far as to engage in a lengthy dispute with General Totten of the Engineers over the right of the Topographers to use the title "military engineers." [19] It is a certain sign of Abert's political skill that he was able to induce both Lewis Cass, Jackson's Secretary of War, and Joel Poinsett, his successor under Van Buren, to advocate an increase in size and status for the Corps.[20]

Meanwhile, the most obvious aid to Abert's efforts on behalf of the Topographical Bureau was the ever-mounting demand for the services of the Army topographers. In addition to duties with the Coast Survey and Lighthouse Board, the engineers found that the operations of the Seminole War made an additional and extraordinary bid for their limited manpower. Then, too, with settlement reaching out beyond the Mississippi such work as Featherstonehaugh's survey of the Ozark Plateau and Long's labors in clearing the Red River of its raft of logs created still

---

Phila.), consisting of approximately fifty informal letters; it is the only extensive personal correspondence of Colonel Abert that I have been able to find. The letters cover such topics as the social climate of Georgetown and the prospects for Abert's racing horse. Brief insight into his politics is afforded by a letter of Dec. 12, 1830, to Parker, which reads: "He says also that Judge Clark tells him all the west will go for Mr. Clay. I sincerely hope it may, although it is quite problematical whether his success will ever benefit me or mine."

17. Ibid. See also Beers, "History," p. 289.

18. Beers, p. 289.

19. Abert to Poinsett, March 31, 1840, LS, TE 77.

20. Beers, p. 290.

another demand not to be overlooked by a politically alert administration.

It was not surprising, then, that in the Army Reorganization Act of 1838 provision for expanding the Bureau and raising its status was included. After twenty years of operation from a subordinate position, the Topographical Engineers were at last equal to the regular Corps of Engineers. As a Corps they could maintain exclusive control over their own policies, subject only to the Secretary of War, and they could have a much larger voice in the direct formation of national policies. As head of a Corps, Colonel Abert could deal directly with the Secretary of War. This was important politically as a means of bringing expert technical opinion to bear on questions of national importance.

Within the Corps itself the outlook was also improved. There was a broader chance for promotion and there was an opportunity to work steadily at topographical engineering as a profession. Previously the younger officers of the Bureau, temporarily detached for duty from the artillery or infantry, had by this been virtually penalized, in that their devotion to the essentially civilian duties of the Corps detracted from their chances for military advancement. After 1838 a professional pride developed. The new officers supplied by West Point improved in quality, and Colonel Abert instituted an exchange of professional papers among them, encouraging mutual criticism.

Under the reorganization the operations of the Corps multiplied rapidly. A long series of explorations beyond the Mississippi was begun. In the 1840's extensive surveys of the Great Lakes were inaugurated and later coordinated under the Board of Engineers for Lake Harbors and Western Rivers. This involved a mammoth project of geodetic mapping, as well as the improvement of the harbors on the Lakes at a time when such services were an important aid to the rapidly expanding inland commerce. The work on western rivers continued, with operations focused on the Ohio, the Upper Mississippi, the Tennessee, and the Lower Mississippi. In connection with the latter project Capt. A. A. Humphreys and his assistant, Lt. Henry L. Abbott, produced the monumental *Report upon the Physics and Hydraulics of the Mississippi River* (1861), which took its place among the classic works of hydraulic science. At this time, too, the Corps engaged in public works in the city of Washington, such as the construction of the Georgetown aqueduct, the paving of Pennsylvania Avenue, and the erection of the Washington Monument. Meanwhile, out on the edge of civilization, an assemblage of Topographical Engineers headed by Major James Duncan Graham and assisted by the civilian engineer George Gordon Meade was cooperating with a Texan commission under Memmucan Hunt in the laying out of the Sabine River boundary line between the United States and Texas.[21] Thus by the beginning of the Manifest Destiny period the Corps was already established as an effective instrument of public works, and its officers were experienced in an infinite variety of undertakings.

The education and training of the Topographical Engineer was the result of three major influences—his West Point years, contact with the leading American scientists of the day, and the study of European ideas and techniques by means of travel abroad and the exchange of correspondence.

Seventy-two officers served as Topographical Engineers between 1838 and 1863, and of these all but eight graduated from the Military Academy at West Point.[22] Of these eight, who were by no means the least accomplished of the Corps, two had attended West Point and left before graduation to work in civilian life. One, Stephen H. Long, was a Dartmouth graduate, though he served an apprenticeship as a young instructor at the Military Academy. Another, John C. Frémont, gained his education through experience in the field and through the careful tutoring of the scientists Joseph N. Nicollet and Ferdinand Hassler.[23] Six of the eight nonacademy officers—Stephen H. Long, John C. Frémont, Walter B. Guion, George W. Hughes, Howard Stansbury, and Joseph D. Webster—served with distinction on the

21. 27th Cong., 2d Sess., Sen. Exec. Doc. 199 (1841–42), 68.

22. See below, Appendix A, for a complete roster of all Topographical Engineers, based on Beers, "History," p. 291, and supplemented by data from George W. Cullum, *Biographical Register of the Officers and Graduates of the U. S. Military Academy at West Point* . . . New York, 1891; Francis B. Heitman, *Historical Register and Dictionary of the United States Army* . . . 2 vols. Wash., 1903; and the *DAB*.

23. Frémont, *Memoirs,* p. 56.

trans-Mississippi frontier. Hughes later acted as construction engineer for the first railroad across the Isthmus of Panama.[24] Of these officers only Frémont had occasion to resent the existence of a West Point clique which appeared to dominate the Army.

Sixty-four of the officers who served in the Corps, or over 85 per cent, were West Point trained. From its beginning in 1802 the Academy had been under the direction of the Engineer Corps, and its entire curriculum had been oriented toward the education of engineer-soldiers. Colonel Thayer, its most important commandant, had seen to it that liberal arts played little part in its course of study. Even Latin and Greek, those two major hallmarks of the 19th-century gentleman, were omitted, and the accent was upon the practical. In 1830 the Board of Visitors at West Point concluded that one of the important aims of the Academy's training was "to furnish science for exploring the hidden treasures of our mountains and ameliorating the agriculture of our valleys." [25]

Thus West Point was a new type of school in the United States. Education was directly geared to the fulfillment of national aims, and the core of its curriculum, engineering, was designed to implement this function. Until the establishment of a full-fledged course of engineering at Rensselaer Polytechnical Institute in 1829, the Academy was the only institution that offered instruction in civil engineering. After 1845 Annapolis began to offer a course in mechanical engineering. In that same year Union College and the Polytechnical Institute of Brooklyn followed suit. The Lawrence Scientific School at Harvard opened its doors in 1846, while by 1847 Yale had established its Sheffield Scientific School.[26] Graduates of West Point were the pioneer instructors in civil engineering at both these latter schools.[27] Because of the profound influence of Louis Agassiz and Benjamin Silliman, however, both Harvard and Yale leaned more strongly toward the

24. *DAB.*

25. Quoted in Sidney Foreman, *West Point* (New York, 1950), p. 81.

26. A. Riedler, *American Technological Schools,* in *Report of the Commissioner of Education to the Sec. of the Interior,* 53d Cong., 2d Sess. H. R. Exec. Doc. 1, Pt. V (1895), 661. Charles R. Mann, *A Study of Engineering Education* (New York, 1918), passim.

27. Foreman, p. 88.

natural sciences of zoology, chemistry, and geology than toward the practical studies of engineering.[28] Thus West Point stood nearly alone, in the years before the Civil War, as the source of formally trained engineers in America.

If its curriculum was directly related to American progress, it reflected, most of all, the French spirit and technique of instruction. The only foreign language taught was French, universally acknowledged as the language of science. The great bulk of the Academy's library was composed of French books. Even the librarian, Claudius Berard, was of French extraction.[29] Both in the texts used and in the persons of the ranking instructors, the influence of the Ecole Polytechnique was all important. This institution, born of the revolutionist's dislike of aristocratic privilege and perfected under the archnationalist Napoleon, was a perfect prototype for any school that wished to combine national dedication, military instruction, and practical education.[30] It was designed for a nation impatient of anything that did not contribute directly to national progress. The important difference in the American adaptation of this plan of education was, characteristically, that instead of immediate specialization, with advanced training in particular military branches, West Point aimed at a more general training in the various fields of practical endeavor.

The man most responsible for the establishment of a sound engineering course at West Point was Claudius Crozet, a graduate of the school of "Ponts et Chaussée" in Paris, and a veteran of the Military School of Engineers and Artillerists at Metz. Dedicated to Napoleon, he had fought through all his leader's battles, from Wagram to Waterloo, and in 1816 had fled to America where, thanks to the influence of General Simon Bernard (an expatriate French general in the American Army) he secured a post at West Point. Crozet began with the fundamentals of mathematics and analytical geometry, depending for texts upon the works of his former mentors at the school of "Ponts et Chausée." Vernon's three-volume translation *Treatise on the Science of War and Fortifications,* Sganzin's *Program d'un course de construction,*

28. Riedler, p. 661.
29. Foreman, p. 52.
30. William Couper, *Claudius Crozet* (Charlottesville, Va., 1936), pp. 7–8.

and Hachette's *Traité des machines* were used as standard works. Later Crozet wrote his own treatise on descriptive geometry. He was among the first teachers in America to make extensive use of the blackboard as a means of communication.[31]

Other important instructors, like William H. C. Bartlett, who taught natural philosophy (physics), used Francoeur's *Traité de mécanique* and Farrar's treatises on electricity, magnetism, optics, and astronomy.[32] Bartlett had toured Europe in 1840 studying the latest methods of technical instruction.[33] West Point's own prodigy, Dennis Hart Mahan, had also been to Europe in 1826, where he spent four years traveling and studying.[34] Fortifications, gun foundries, canals, railroads, bridges—everything interested him, and he mastered the two-year course at the Military School at Metz in one year, carrying its details back to America in his head. Mahan's book, *An Elementary Course of Civil Engineering*, published in 1837, combined all he had learned abroad with his years of experience in teaching at West Point. It became the standard text in America for nearly half a century;[35] with its various topics—building materials, masonry, framing, bridges, roads, railways, canals, rivers, and sea-coast fortifications—it became a guidebook for all engineers engaged in public works.[36] As late as 1866 it was still being revised. Other works by Mahan were more closely related to military tactics, and they served both Union and Confederate officers during the Civil War.

In addition to their engineering training, the fledgling officers also received instruction in several other fields that had important bearing on their work in the trans-Mississippi West. They studied drawing with Robert Walker Weir, once "boon companion" of Horatio Greenough and friend of Washington Irving, Samuel Morse, Washington Allston, and Rembrandt Peale.[37] It was Weir who trained the cadets' eyes for the observation of the details

31. Ibid., pp. 25, 28.

32. Foreman, p. 56.

33. Ibid., p. 83.

34. Ernest Dupuy, *Where They Have Trod* (New York, 1940), pp. 189 n., 197 n.

35. Foreman, p. 82.

36. See D. H. Mahan, *An Elementary Course of Civil Engineering for the Use of Cadets of the United States Military Academy*, New York, 1852.

37. Irene Weir, *Robert Walker Weir, Artist* (New York, 1947), p. 19.

of landscape. He taught them the important skill of topographic sketching. John Torrey and later Jacob Bailey conducted classes in chemistry and mineralogy in which Parker Cleaveland's *Mineralogy* was the standard text.[38] This, too, was an important book, because it was the first American work to make its classification of rocks on the basis of their chemical content.[39] Torrey, who was the foremost botanist of his day, and Bailey, a specialist in the study of fresh-water algae and the techniques of microscopy, provided whatever grounding the cadets received in natural science. Judging from their later enthusiasm for the subject, the influence of both Torrey and Bailey must have been considerable.

The training received at West Point was not all the officers acquired, however, nor was it their only contact with European learning. Andrew A. Humphreys toured the European Continent from 1851 to 1854, where he examined the various methods of river control.[40] The work in the Po Valley was particularly impressive to him. In 1856 the Crimean Commission, composed of the three brightest younger officers of the Army, McClellan, Delafield, and Mordecai, journeyed to the Crimean front to observe the latest in ordnance and fortifications in action and under fire. The McClellan saddle was one of the innovations they introduced upon their return.[41]

Other officers, like John C. Frémont, maintained direct correspondence with European scientists.[42] William H. Emory was in touch with such men as Airy at the Greenwich Royal Observatory; Hooker, the botanist and curator of Kew Gardens; Des Caisne at Paris Gardens; Fleugel at Leipzig; and Humboldt at

38. Foreman, p. 56. Andrew D. Rodgers, 3d, *John Torrey* (Princeton, 1942), pp. 70–71, 76, 125–26.

39. Foreman, p. 58. See also the review of Cleaveland's book in the *American Journal of Science, 1* (1818), 35–52.

40. Henry H. Humphreys, *Andrew Atkinson Humphreys* (Phila., 1924), pp. 141–45. Also *DAB*.

41. John K. Herr and Edward S. Wallace, *The Story of the U. S. Cavalry* (Boston, 1953), p. 78. See also the *Report* by George B. McClellan, 34th Cong., Spec. Sess., Sen. Exec. Doc. 1 (1857), passim. I am indebted to John Muldowny for first calling my attention to this commission, which is the subject of his own unpublished, more detailed study.

42. Allan Nevins, *Frémont, Pathmarker of the West* (New York, 1939), p. 346.

Potsdam.[43] Amiel Weeks Whipple, though only a junior officer, on occasion received advice from the great Alexander von Humboldt.[44] Foreign scientists like Agassiz and Lyell and Möllhausen also exchanged ideas with the soldier-scientists.

At the same time the important American figures, such as John Torrey and Asa Gray and Spencer F. Baird, worked as closely as possible with the War Department. Thus when George Englemann, the St. Louis botanist, went to Europe for study, he acted as an agent for the War Department and its engineers as well as for his own colleagues in the world of pure science.[45] This constant contact with European ideas kept the United States remarkably close in scientific and technical development to the Old World. Within ten years after the founding of the Ecole Polytechnique, America had in West Point a similar institution. Her military leaders were trained in the latest European methods. Scientific specimens and learned papers were exchanged. Mutual visiting was a commonplace. For all practical purposes a common scientific community existed, in which the Topographical Engineers played the part of an advance guard as they collected and assembled an ever-mounting number of facts about a little-known area of the world.

The Corps acted as a focus for national enthusiasms in still another way. It was the expression of a general spirit of Romanticism that both governed its purpose and prescribed its methods. In the first place it was an instrument of self-conscious nationalism. Each of its projects was related to the development of the nation, and its work in the West was part of a grandiose urge toward continental fulfillment. These nationalistic aims, so perfectly expressed by the phrase "Manifest Destiny," might properly be seen as an American version of the current European strivings so often expressed by writers like Herder and Michelet. The Corps, as the agent of a democratic collective will, was aiding

43. EP, passim.

44. For example, see A. W. Whipple, *Report of Explorations and Surveys to Ascertain the Most Practicable and Economical Route for a Railroad from the Mississippi River to the Pacific Ocean* . . . 33d Cong., 2d Sess., Sen. Exec. Doc. 78 (1856), 130–31.

45. See EP for correspondence between Emory, Torrey, and Englemann during this period.

the yeoman and the cattle raiser and the storekeeper to take proper possession of his fee-simple empire in the unspoiled West.

At the same time the spirit of Romanticism influenced the scientific orientation of the Corps. It posited at the outset a theory of knowledge that reacted against a narrow selectivity in the gathering of data or erecting of hypotheses. In the words of Arthur B. Lovejoy, for Romantics "One thing alone is needful: Everything." [46] Certain characteristics of the scientific work of the Corps therefore seem more intelligible if regarded as manifestations of this spirit. The first is the essentially cosmic approach to the West that was assumed. All data was somehow related, part of a great organic system which, if it was not, as Louis Agassiz believed, "the work of thought, the production of intelligence carried out according to plan . . . the thoughts of the Creator," [47] was at least similar to the system that Humboldt envisaged in his *Cosmos*.[48] The task of the scientist, it was thought, was not merely to determine limited relationships like that of plant growth to altitude, but to erect grand structures of classified data which eventually would enable man to know all of nature.

American scientists implicitly accepted the idea of an ordered universe, but it was a universe so vast and complex as to make any mathematical description appear too simple. Instead they came to appreciate the cosmos as a thing of grandeur and mystery, stretching to infinity.

Another characteristic, in part an aspect of the first, was the urge toward diversity. Romanticism itself, defined historically, involved a reaction against the clear-cut and the classical, demanding that the mind be opened, the gaze broadened to include the widest possible range of experience. To the scientifically oriented Engineer everything was relevant, everything important. The trivial and the obvious had to be observed and recorded, though

46. Quoted in Rollin G. Osterweis, *Romanticism and Nationalism in the Old South* (New Haven, 1949), appendix, p. 236.

47. Agassiz, *Methods of Study in Natural History* (17th ed. Boston, 1886, first published 1863), p. 14.

48. Alexander von Humboldt, *Cosmos, a Sketch of a Physical Description of the Universe* (5 vols. and atlas, London, 1845–61), passim. See also the comment on Humboldt by James H. Simpson, *Report of Explorations across the Great Basin of the Territory of Utah . . .* (Wash., 1876), p. 69 n.

Frémont carried this to extreme when he climbed what he thought was the highest peak in the Wind River Mountains and commented chiefly upon the habits of a bumble bee he found buzzing there.[49] The exotic was all-important; and the West was an exotic place, both in space and in time. Here could be found stupendous canyons, breathtaking evidences of erosion, immense lakes of undetermined origin, strange tribes primitive as the stone age, and evidences of past civilizations and their mysteriously vanished glories. The results of this fascination for novelty and for the exotic were twofold: the field investigator was spurred on to one of the most rapid and complete inventories ever made of any portion of the globe, and the best scientific minds of this country were so busy recording the mass of data that they had little time to formulate hypotheses about the meaning and utility of it all. American abundance was never better expressed than in the tidal wave of specimens of rocks and plants and animals that were thrust upon the scientists from out of the western wilderness.

Finally, there was a noticeable kinship between science and art. Many of the Topographical reports, like those of Frémont and Joseph C. Ives and William F. Raynolds, read like self-conscious literary compositions. Incidents were selected, episodes heightened, characters drawn, and exotic background sketched in, so that often the scientific report read like a draft of Walter Scott or Francis Parkman. What lay at the very heart of this artistic approach to science was the desire not only to measure but to get at the *quality* of the new-found data. Like true Romantics they associated themselves with it intuitively. At their best they were able to express the West in qualitative terms. Perhaps the best evidence for this instinct is to be found in the lithograph drawings made by the artists who accompanied the expeditions. In these, very often, realism in the sense of faithful reproduction of the scene is nowhere present. They have a style, an interpretation, however crude, and the form itself competes with the phenomenon portrayed. At times what is unseen is more important than the objects depicted. It was hardly great art, nor were the Topographical reports great literature, but like the travel books of John Lloyd Stevens and the drawings of Frederick Catherwood,

49. Frémont, *Exploring Expedition,* p. 103.

they conveyed a certain emotion over and above the simple facts.[50]

The history of the scientist and the artist during this period has a still further parallel, expressed in part by the experience of the topographical surveys. The artist, when actually confronted with the spectacle of rugged Western nature, was overwhelmed. As one topographer remarked, the sublimity was almost painful.[51] For a moment the imagination was "stunned." [52]

The artist reacted by narrowing his vision from nature to the ways of perceiving nature. And for the scientist, by mid-century, with the tremendous increase in new data, the difficulty of pursuing the inductive method while at the same time maintaining a unified view of the cosmos was becoming increasingly apparent; more and more the scientist began to specialize and to shift from unity to complexity, from the general to the particular. This is the drift of scientific investigation which can be discovered in the long series of Topographical reports from that of the Stephen H. Long expedition of 1819 to F. V. Hayden's report on the Yellowstone expedition of 1859. The Civil War, however, soon diverted attention from this general scientific development, and the work of the Corps, which was ended in that war, ceased before it was possible to note the final chapter in this progression. Darwin's hypothesis, confirmed, in one instance, by such a carefully limited piece of evidence as O. C. Marsh's paleontological horse cycle, eventually brought a new generalization to science which provided the order that the earlier generation had been seeking as they moved ever farther afield. But this story belongs to a later era than that of the Topographical Engineer.

It was thus as a complex institution having a political, a military, a scientific and even a Romantic significance that the Corps of Topographical Engineers entered the West. Its officers were

50. See John Lloyd Stephens, *Incidents of Travel in Central America, Chiapas and Yucatan* (New York, 1841), and esp. the illustrations by Frederick Catherwood.

51. Joseph Christmas Ives, *Report upon the Colorado River of the West*, 36th Cong., 1st Sess., H. R. Exec. Doc. 90 (1861), 86.

52. This term belongs to Wallace Stegner, who used it to characterize F. W. von Egloffstein's first drawings of the Grand Canyon. See Stegner, *Beyond the Hundredth Meridian* (Boston, 1954), plate 2, following p. 92.

a new type of explorer, self-consciously carrying the burden of civilization to the wilderness and the lessons of the wilderness back into civilization. They were not rivals of the mountain men, whose aim was very different, yet they have been obscured in favor of those buckskin "knight-errants." It seems just, then, to give the Topographical Engineer his hearing; to let his own achievements determine what place he shall have in the history of the trans-Mississippi West.

2. INTO THE MOUNTAIN MAN'S WEST

> A little 'bacca, ef its a plew a plug, an' Dupont an' G'lena, a Green River or so, an' he leaves for the Bayou Salade. Darn the white diggins while thar's buffler in the mountains.—*John Hatcher, mountain man*

THE ERA of the Topographical Engineer in the Far West began with Lieutenant John C. Frémont's first expedition to the Rocky Mountains in 1842. From this date onward, exploration in the trans-Mississippi West took on a different character. The whole region became the object of a closer scientific scrutiny, more complete in scope and more refined in techniques and objectives. Beginning in 1842 and continuing down to the Civil War, the Engineers, in close collaboration with the leading scientists of the day, conducted expedition after expedition in the western region. Taken together, they constitute, in the words of one recent writer, "The Great Reconnaissance." [1]

If, however, the scientific inventory began in 1842, it nevertheless had forty years of previous American exploration, and before that nearly three centuries of European efforts, upon which to depend. The year after Frémont's first trip to the Rockies a grizzled veteran of mountain exploration built himself a fort on the emigrant route and settled down in semiretirement. Jim Bridger's construction of an emigrant station was symbolic of the passing of the free trapper's day. It denoted the end of a period in the exploration of the West. Lt. John W. Gunnison called attention some years later to the peculiar ability of Bridger and those of his kind:

> The builder of Fort Bridger is one of the hardy race of mountain trappers who are now disappearing from the continent, being enclosed in a wave of civilization. . . . His graphic sketches are delightful romances. With a buffalo-skin and a piece of charcoal, he will map out any portion of this immense region, and delineate mountains, streams,

1. Edward S. Wallace, *The Great Reconnaissance,* Boston, 1955.

> and the circular valleys called "holes" with wonderful accuracy . . .[2]

Insofar as basic geographical information and magnitude of actual discovery is concerned, the achievements of such men as these, from 1803 to 1843, rival those of the Topographical Engineers, and a review of their deeds should provide a background and some perspective for judging the relative merits of the work of the Army explorers.

At the outset we should understand how the mountain man transmitted his geographical lore.

> Meanwhile in 1833 on any street corner in St. Louis you could ask a bystander how to get to Lyonesse and be told. Several hundred men left the Missouri frontier every spring for Santa Fe, the Yellowstone, South Pass, the Green, the Columbia. They did not resemble Achilles, but they were prepared to meet several hundred others on the day appointed and at the place assigned, and did not care if the geographers had moved it a full ten degrees. They went about the blank spaces of the map like men going to the barn. The Great American Desert was their back yard.[3]

Information about the West was everywhere available to settlers in 1833. It was, as De Voto indicates, street-corner parley, barbershop gossip, a common language among men whose reasons for being in St. Louis in 1833 invariably had something to do with the Far West. Knowledge of this type traveled by word of mouth. It was advice, it was admonition, it was rumor, and it could often be fact. Such advice, it is worth noting, often steered the greenhorn traveler in the wrong direction: for many of the forty-niners the "back yard" turned out to be a desert grave. But this was not the responsibility of the mountain men who did the exploring. For the most part they knew what they were doing, because it was their business to know. They knew the whereabouts of beaver streams, passes, sheltered grassy meadows among the mountains, routes across the deserts, edible plants, and game. Survival depended upon it. But like a man with a good fishing

2. John W. Gunnison, *The Mormons or Latter-Day Saints in the Valley of the Great Salt Lake* (Phila., 1852), p. 151.

3. Bernard De Voto, *Across the Wide Missouri* (Boston, 1947), p. 5.

hole, they were often reticent about where they had been, and when they did talk they could be as misleading as Baron La hontan, that notorious explorer who never saw the mountains at all.

Mountain men occasionally left journals and letters which were published, often in newspapers. Jedediah Smith's account of his first trip across the Great Basin, written in a letter to General William Clark, was printed in the Missouri *Republican* of October 11, 1827.[4] James Ohio Pattie wrote a vivid personal narrative, part fact and part fiction, of his incredible adventures in traversing most of the West from the Gila River and the western desert to the Yellowstone and the Upper Missouri. It included the first American account of the Grand Canyon of the Colorado. Timothy Flint edited it in Cincinnati in 1831.[5] John B. Wyeth told spiteful tales of his cousin's expedition to Oregon.[6] The Astorians (below pp. 29–31) had their chronicler in the incomparable Washington Irving, whose classic account of their activities was published in 1836.[7] And Irving's *Adventures of Captain Bonneville,* which came out in 1837, included two of the most important maps of the West ever published, in that they imparted for the first time to a wide audience some idea of the Great Basin.[8]

Maps, therefore, were another method of communication, though one seldom resorted to by mountain men. Jedediah Smith is said to have sketched a few, but they were lost.[9] His cartographic information appeared where it would not be widely circulated, in Gallatin's *Map of the Indian Tribes of North America,* published as a part of the *Transactions of the Amer-*

4. Henry R. Wagner, *The Plains and the Rockies* (San Francisco, 1921), p. 24.
5. Ibid., pp. 27–28.
6. De Voto, p. 182.
7. Washington Irving, *Astoria, or Anecdotes of an Enterprise beyond the Rocky Mountains,* 2 vols. Phila., 1836.
8. Washington Irving, *The Rocky Mountains; or, Scenes, Incidents, and Adventures in the Far West; Digested from the Journal of Capt. B. L. E. Bonneville, of the Army of the United States* . . . 2 vols. Phila., 1837; see maps, Vols. *1, 2.*
9. Wheat, "Mapping the American West," p. 78. For a more extended consideration of Smith's maps see Dale L. Morgan and Carl I. Wheat, *Jedediah Smith and His Maps of the American West,* San Francisco, 1954.

ican Antiquarian Society in 1836. Other maps were drawn by George Drouillard, a mountain man killed by the Blackfeet Indians in 1810. His work, consisting of the first sketches of the Yellowstone-Bighorn country, is said to have been used by William Clark in compiling his own map. William Kittson, a member of Peter Skene Ogden's expedition of 1824–25, which came upon the Great Salt Lake, also made a map, which remained in the archives of the Hudson's Bay Company.[10] Later sketch maps showing the Yellowstone country drawn by Alexander Culbertson, Jim Baker, and other trappers, in 1854, also exist.[11] Their particular importance lies in the fact that they were drawn by request for Lt. G. K. Warren while he was making his Dakota Survey, as part of the basis for his over-all map of the West. But this was the extent of their work; and in general, it can be concluded, the actual map-making activities of the mountain men were relatively meager, and what they did rarely came to light. Instead, the mountain men made maps, like those by Bridger, with charcoal and a piece of buffalo hide, in response to an outside demand, for they had no need of maps themselves. The country was all written in their heads as part of their special lore.

They did serve often as guides, and in the course of their duties educated their charges. Frémont learned most of what he knew about the West in this manner, and all of the Topographical Engineers owed debts to the trappers and guides who frequently accompanied them. Jim Bridger personally guided the Stansbury expedition to the Great Salt Lake in 1850 and Captain Raynold's Yellowstone expedition of 1859.[12] Governor William Clark, too, passed on data acquired from the mountain men to students like Albert Gallatin, back in New York, buried in his studies of Indian ethnology.

Others besides trappers at this time saw the country for themselves. The Santa Fe traders and adventurous scholars, like Thomas Nuttall, the Philadelphia botanist, went West and

10. Wheat, "Mapping the American West," pp. 68 and n., 78, 83.

11. MS maps, Gouverneur Kemble Warren Papers, New York State Library, Albany, N.Y.

12. Howard Stansbury, *Exploration and Survey of the Valley of the Great Salt Lake of Utah,* 32d Cong., Spec. Sess., Sen. Exec. Doc. 3 (1851), 299. William F. Raynolds, *Report on the Exploration of the Yellowstone and the Country Drained by That River,* 40th Cong., 2d Sess., Sen. Exec. Doc. 77 (1868), 38.

brought back important information.[13] Missionaries and sportsmen, Whitman and Stewart and Ruxton of the Rockies all had their tales to tell, for the most part accurate but hardly admissible as data for the scientist. Prince Maximilian of Wied, another European sportsman, took the artist Carl Bodmer up the Missouri River with him, and this artist presented the world with faithful paintings of the fur-trade country, both of the landscape and of the inhabitants.[14] Artists like George Catlin and Alfred Jacob Miller played an important part in the transmission of knowledge about the West. Under their pencil and colors previously unknown phenomena were interpreted in vivid and accurate terms. Catlin's Indian Gallery brought the West to the foot of Capitol Hill in Washington.[15] Missionaries like Marcus Whitman and Samuel Parker personally carried back information about the Oregon Country and the routes by which it could be reached. Father De Smet was undoubtedly the best geographer among these western missionaries. His maps, incorporating data given him by Jim Bridger, are said to be among the most accurately sketched representations of the mountain area.[16] He, himself, however, noted their limitations. Describing his general map of 1851 to officials of the Interior Department, he added, "In my humble opinion therefore, it can be of very little service for your purposes, in which accuracy of instrumental measurements and observations seem to be absolutely necessary." [17]

Still another channel of knowledge was through Mexican or Spanish observations, which for a long time represented the all-important medium of information about California and the

13. Thomas Nuttall, *A Journal of Travels into the Arkansas Territory, during the Year 1819, with Occasional Observations on the Manners of the Aborigines,* ed. R. G. Thwaites, Early Western Travels, 1748–1846, No. 13, Cleveland, 1905–07.

14. Maximilian of Wied, *Travels in the Interior of North America,* ed. R. G. Thwaites, Early Western Travels, 1748–1846, Nos. 22–24, Cleveland, 1905–07. For Bodmer's drawings see original folio, Yale Collection of Western Americana.

15. Lloyd Haberly, *Pursuit of the Horizon* (New York, 1948), pp. 109–10.

16. Merrill Mattes, "Behind the Legend of Colter's Hell," *MVHR, 36* (1949–50), 278.

17. Ibid., p. 278.

Southwest. Finally, of course, the efforts of sea captains, such as Gray and Cook and Wilkes, must not be overlooked, as they charted the Northwest Coast. These are the ways information concerning the West could spread, before the government began publishing its official reports of explorations.

The Northwest

How much was actually learned of the West between the time the mountain men first entered it and the time Frémont began his explorations in the western mountains? When Lewis and Clark came back down the Missouri River in 1806 from their epic journey, they found that the fur traders were already pushing up the river into what was for the traders still unknown territory. Not until 1814 was Lewis and Clark's report published and their map widely distributed (though before that, others had had access to their information).[18] Their expedition solved the first problem of western geography: it showed the width of the Continent, and thereby underscored the magnitude of the effort that was required to cross it. Mackenzie's report of his journey across the Canadian Rockies had failed to bring this home to geographers, because they were still hoping that a Missouri-Columbia River route might be found which would facilitate a water transit to Cathay, thereby shrinking the Continent in human terms. In addition to this fundamental discovery, President Jefferson's explorers were able to fill in enough details of the Northwest to present a picture of the varied character of the topography, with its complex systems of rivers and mountains. They also called to the attention of geographers and explorers at least five passes through the mountains: Lemhi Pass in the Beaverhead Range, Bozeman Pass, Gibbon Pass, Lewis and Clark Pass, and Lolo Pass around the northern end of the Bitterroot Mountains. By means of these one could get from the Missouri

18. One source of information about their trip by a member of the expedition, available before 1814, was Patrick Gass' *A Journal of the Voyages and Travels of a Corps of Discovery, under the Command of Capt. Lewis and Capt. Clarke of the Army of the United States, from the Mouth of the River Missouri through the Interior Parts of North America to the Pacific Ocean, during the Years 1804, 1805 & 1806* . . . Pittsburgh, 1807.

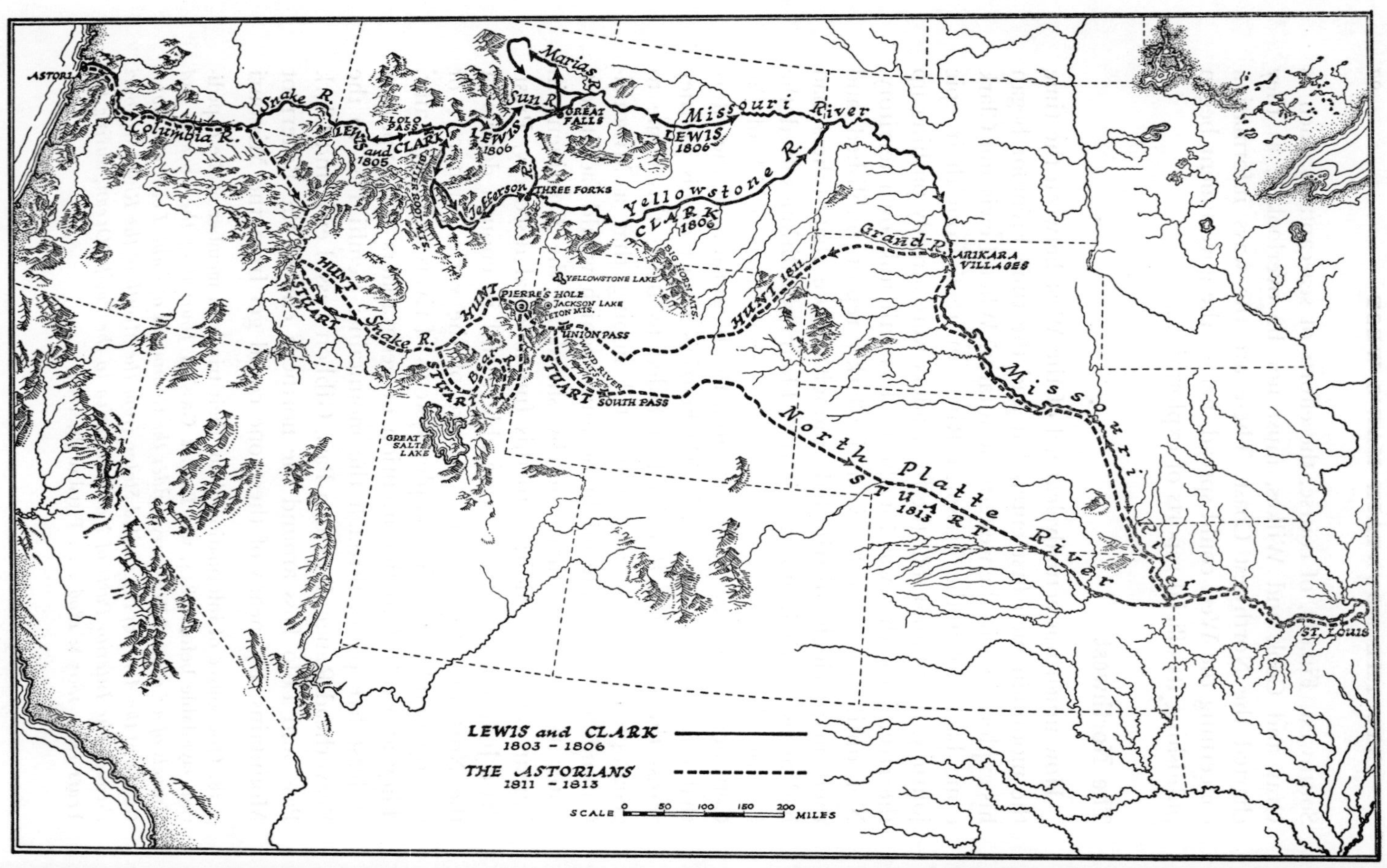
ASTORIA
Columbia R.
Snake R.
LOLO PASS
LEWIS and CLARK 1805
BITTER ROOT MTS.
LEWIS 1806
Sun R.
Marias R.
GREAT FALLS
Jefferson R.
THREE FORKS
Missouri River
LEWIS 1806
Yellowstone R.
CLARK 1806
BIG HORN MTS.
YELLOWSTONE LAKE
Grand R.
ARIKARA VILLAGES
HUNT 1811
HUNT
STUART
Snake R.
PIERRE'S HOLE
JACKSON LAKE
TETON MTS.
UNION PASS
WIND RIVER MTS.
Bear R.
STUART
SOUTH PASS
GREAT SALT LAKE
North Platte River
STUART 1813
Missouri River
ST. LOUIS
LEWIS and CLARK
1803 - 1806
THE ASTORIANS
1811 - 1813
SCALE 0 50 100 150 200 MILES

or the Yellowstone to the Snake and the Columbia Basins, hence to the Pacific. They also ventured up the Marias River north of the Missouri.

Once Lewis and Clark had laid the groundwork, subsequent discoveries in the North could be charted with reference to these already existing basic landmarks. When their map was published in 1814, it was quickly copied by Aaron Arrowsmith in England and Brué in Paris, and these editions commanded widespread attention.[19]

Despite such important achievements and despite their marked influence upon mapmakers of the time, much of their work, cartographically speaking, was primitive.

Six months after Lewis and Clark returned from their trek, Manuel Lisa, a shrewd Spanish fur trader from St. Louis, established a fort at the mouth of the Big Horn River. Lisa sent John Colter, one of Clark's men, south toward what is now the Yellowstone Park area, down as far as Jackson's Hole and over the Tetons to Pierre's Hole.[20] After this expedition Colter returned to Lisa's fort with news of the good beaver country he had traversed, and he afterward described some of nature's miracles that he witnessed: burning lakes, small geysers, and warm bubbling springs.

Andrew Henry, one of Lisa's partners in the newly formed Missouri Fur Company, went up the Missouri River to its headwaters at the Three Forks, where he established another fur-trading post in 1810. The Blackfeet Indians soon forced him to abandon the fort, and he then crossed over to the north branch of the Snake River to spend the winter.[21]

The next step in the exploration of the Northwest was the far-flung operation of John Jacob Astor's Pacific Fur Company. Backed by New York capital and unofficial government support, Astor sent two expeditions into the Far West.[22] One founded Fort Astoria. It went by sea on the ship *Tonquin,* leaving New

19. Wheat, "Mapping the American West," p. 69.

20. Mattes, passim. For other accounts see De Voto, *Across the Wide Missouri,* p. 387; and E. W. Gilbert, *The Exploration of Western America, 1800–1850* (Cambridge, 1933), p. 124.

21. Gilbert, pp. 124–25.

22. Ibid., pp. 127–28.

York in September 1810 and arriving at the mouth of the Columbia River on May 25, 1811. A few months after the landing, the Canadian David Thompson worked his way down the Columbia River to find the Americans already there ahead of him.[23]

The other half of Astor's operation was an overland expedition under the command of Wilson Price Hunt of Trenton, New Jersey, a man with little experience in frontier exploration but a veteran of years of service in the fur-trading houses of St. Louis. His second in command was Donald McKenzie, described by Irving as a man who "had been ten years in the interior, in the service of the Northwest Company," and who "valued himself on his knowledge of 'woodcraft,' and the strategy of Indian trade and Indian warfare."[24] Hunt and McKenzie left St. Louis in March 1811 and went up the Missouri, where they arrived at the Arikara villages on June 12. On the way up the river they were accompanied by Manuel Lisa and three of Andrew Henry's men. According to Irving's map they left the Missouri just north of the Arikara villages and crossed the Big Horn Mountains and then the Wind River Mountains somewhere near Union Pass. When they reached the Green River they went over the divide to Henry's Fork of the Snake River, and down the Snake to Cauldron Linn, where they left the river and proceeded overland, reaching the Columbia at approximately the site of Fort Walla-Walla, whence they proceeded along the Columbia to Astoria. This was the fourth crossing of the North American Continent and the second by an American. Union Pass, where they crossed the divide between the Wind River and the Green, was in later years given its name by Captain Raynolds of the Topographical Corps.[25]

Even more important was the return journey led by Robert Stuart, which began on June 29, 1812.[26] Stuart's expedition followed the Snake River south to Bear River, north to the Henry branch of the Snake, and then over to the Green River. In crossing the Continental Divide, Stuart skirted the southern edge of

23. Bernard De Voto, *The Course of Empire* (Boston, 1952), p. 538.

24. Irving, *Astoria,* p. 40.

25. Chittenden, *Fur Trade, I,* 198.

26. This account is based upon Irving, *Astoria,* passim, and Gilbert, *Exploration,* pp. 130–31.

the Wind River Mountains instead of crossing by way of Union Pass at the northern extreme; hence he came close to the most important geographic gateway in all western North America, the South Pass. On his way home he followed what was to be the immigrant trail, down the Sweetwater, the Platte, and the Missouri, to St. Louis, where he arrived on April 30, 1813.

With Stuart's return expedition American exploration in the Northwest regions reached a culmination point. The entire Snake River System, as well as the Columbia and Upper Missouri, were by this time (1813) reasonably well known, at least among the fur traders. It was only much later with the publication of Clark's map, however, that the public at large began to comprehend the geography of the Northwest and Stuart's near discovery of South Pass had to wait for Irving's chronicle in 1839 before it received its just due. So uncertain was Stuart's route in the eyes of the country, however, that today some still argue that he actually traversed the South Pass.[27] The mountain men, too, seemed oblivious to the implications of Stuart's journey, and it was not until the rediscovery of the South Pass by Jedediah Smith in 1824 that it came into general use by the fur hunters.

With the surrender of Astoria to the British in 1813 all further exploring activities by the Astorians necessarily ceased. Some of Astor's men, like Donald McKenzie, joined the British Hudson's Bay Company. In 1819 McKenzie went down the Snake River Valley and Bear River to Bear Lake in Northern Utah, the deepest southern penetration into the interior basin made by a mountain man up to that time.[28] Another British trader, Alexander Ross, explored the upper tributaries of the Salmon River in Idaho. But it was Peter Skene Ogden who really dominated British explorations during this period. In the words of Dale L. Morgan, "Ogden stands second only to Jedediah Smith among the field captains of the fur trade in this decade [1820–1830]." [29] Ogden, for years a member of the Northwestern Fur Company, became one of the most talented leaders for the Hudson's Bay Company after the government-enforced merger of the two companies in 1821. In May 1825, while leading a trapping expedition down

27. Gilbert, pp. 140–41.
28. Ibid., p. 132.
29. *Jedediah Smith* (New York and Indianapolis, 1953), p. 131.

the Bear River, his party came upon the Great Salt Lake. He was not the first to discover the lake; Jim Bridger had seen it in the late fall of 1824, or early spring of 1825, also while on a trapping excursion. Etienne Provost, another mountain man, is said by Morgan to have, "laid eyes on the Great Salt Lake as early as the fall of 1825." [30] Historical knowledge of their exact movements is so uncertain, however, that some doubt still exists as to priority between Provost and Bridger. Ogden, with no concern for the role of discoverer, continued his widespread explorations in search of beaver. In 1825–26 he went up the Deschutes tributary of the Columbia to the sources of John Day's River. In 1827 he visited the Klamath River and Mount Shasta, and, in 1828–29 he returned and explored the north side of Great Salt Lake, which is when he gained his first actual sight of the Lake.[31] On this same hunt he came upon an even more significant find, the Mary's River, later renamed by Frémont the Humboldt. This was to be, within a few years, the main-traveled emigrant route to California. Most important in connection with Ogden's discoveries is the fact that they were made known to the cartographer Aaron Arrowsmith of London, who used them as data in the maps he drew for the Hudson's Bay Company.[32]

The Southwest

Alexander Von Humboldt's "Carte Generale du Royaume de la Nouvelle Espagne," published in the atlas to his monumental *Essai sur Nouvelle Espagne* in 1811, proved to be the most important compendium of knowledge concerning the Southwest. Combining most of the data of the important Spanish explorers, Humboldt's map presented a reasonably accurate idea of the relationship between the Colorado, the Gila, and the Rio Grande rivers. In addition, he included two interior lakes, the Timpanogos and one other south of it, beside which he wrote on the map, "Les limites occidentale de ce Lac Sale sont inconnues." [33] The

30. Ibid., p. 131.
31. Ibid., pp. 183–84.
32. Gilbert, p. 133.
33. See atlas to Alexander von Humboldt, *Essai politique sur le royaume de la Nouvelle Espagne,* 4 vols. Paris, 1811.

source of his information concerning these lakes he stated to be Father Escalante, who in 1776 made the first penetration by a white man into the Great Basin area, going as far north as Utah Lake in central Utah.[34] Almost certainly, Humboldt used secondary accounts of Escalante's *Journal* and Miera's accompanying map, which could be found in the Mexico City archives. Other data, notably on the territory west of the Colorado River, he derived from the work of Father Pedro Font, a Spanish explorer and map maker.[35] His picture of Sonora included the frontier towns of "Tubson" (Tucson), and San Xavier del Bac. Northward across the Gila he correctly located the Pima tribes, and even the "Moquis" (Hopi). In addition, Humboldt speculated that Lake Timpanogos might be the same lake beside which the Aztecs were said to have passed on their way southward to the Gila and into Mexico.[36] His surmises in this respect became a foundation for continued speculation as to the Aztec origin of the ruined pueblos which were found along the Gila, the Puerco, and the Rio Grande.

As in the Northwest, the gathering of precise information by Americans on the Southwest was initiated by Thomas Jefferson and carried out in large measure by men who were acting as agents of the United States government. On July 15, 1803, Jefferson sent a list of seventeen basic questions concerning the laws, geography, population, and extent of the recently acquired Territory of Louisiana to Ephraim Kirby, special commissioner of the Spanish Boundary.[37] He also sent copies of the questions to Daniel Clark, United States Consul at New Orleans, William Dunbar, a scientist from Natchez, and W. C. C. Claiborne, the new governor of the Louisiana Territory.[38] In a letter he explained to Dunbar the reason for his queries, which was to provide information to Congress as a basis on which to "ask from the people an amendment of the Constitution authorizing their

34. De Voto, *The Course of Empire,* p. 293.

35. C. Gregory Crampton, "Humboldt's Utah, 1811," *Utah Historical Quarterly, 26* (1958), 273–74.

36. Humboldt, atlas.

37. Paul Leicester Ford, *The Writings of Thomas Jefferson, 8* (New York, 1897), 252–53.

38. Isaac J. Cox, "The Exploration of the Louisiana Frontier, 1803–1806," *American Historical Review,* Annual Report (1904), p. 152.

receiving the province [Louisiana] into the Union and providing for its government."[39] This first request by Jefferson for information concerning the Southwest was of vital importance in deciding its destiny.

A reply was forwarded to Jefferson by Clark, and included information contributed by Dunbar and Claiborne, and probably by John Sibley, a physician who had moved from Natchez to Natchitochez in March 1803.[40] Since the information told little about the western boundaries of Louisiana, Jefferson determined to send an exploring expedition up the Red River, which ran toward the West.

The first of these expeditions was financed by Congress and included as its members William Dunbar and Dr. George Hunter, a chemist from Philadelphia. They were accompanied by Dr. Hunter's son, a sergeant, and twelve enlisted men, plus Dunbar's Negro servant. They left on an autumn afternoon, October 16, 1804, from St. Catherine's Landing near Dunbar's Natchez plantation.[41] Their course took them up the Red River to the Washita, up the latter river to its source near the Hot Springs, and then back downstream. The trip took four months in all, and the observations made were included by Jefferson in his message to Congress on February 19, 1806, which dealt also with the preliminary results of the Lewis and Clark expedition as ascertained from the party that returned from Fort Mandan in the spring of 1805. The message included a further report by Dr. Sibley on the laws and resources of Louisiana, and it was accompanied by several maps drawn by Nicholas King, one of which showed Lewis and Clark's accurate sketch of the Missouri River, and another of which was taken from Dunbar's and Hunter's description of the Washita River.[42]

The following year Jefferson secured $5,000 from Congress to

39. Ford, p. 255.

40. Cox, p. 152.

41. Ibid., p. 156 n. The account is also based on Thomas Jefferson, *Message from the President of the United States Communicating Discoveries Made in Exploring the Missouri, Red River and Washita by Captains Lewis and Clark, Doctor Sibley and Mr. Dunbar; with a Statistical Account of the Countries Adjacent. February 19, 1806,* Wash., 1806.

42. Jefferson, *Message of the President.* Wheat, "Mapping the American West," pp. 64–65.

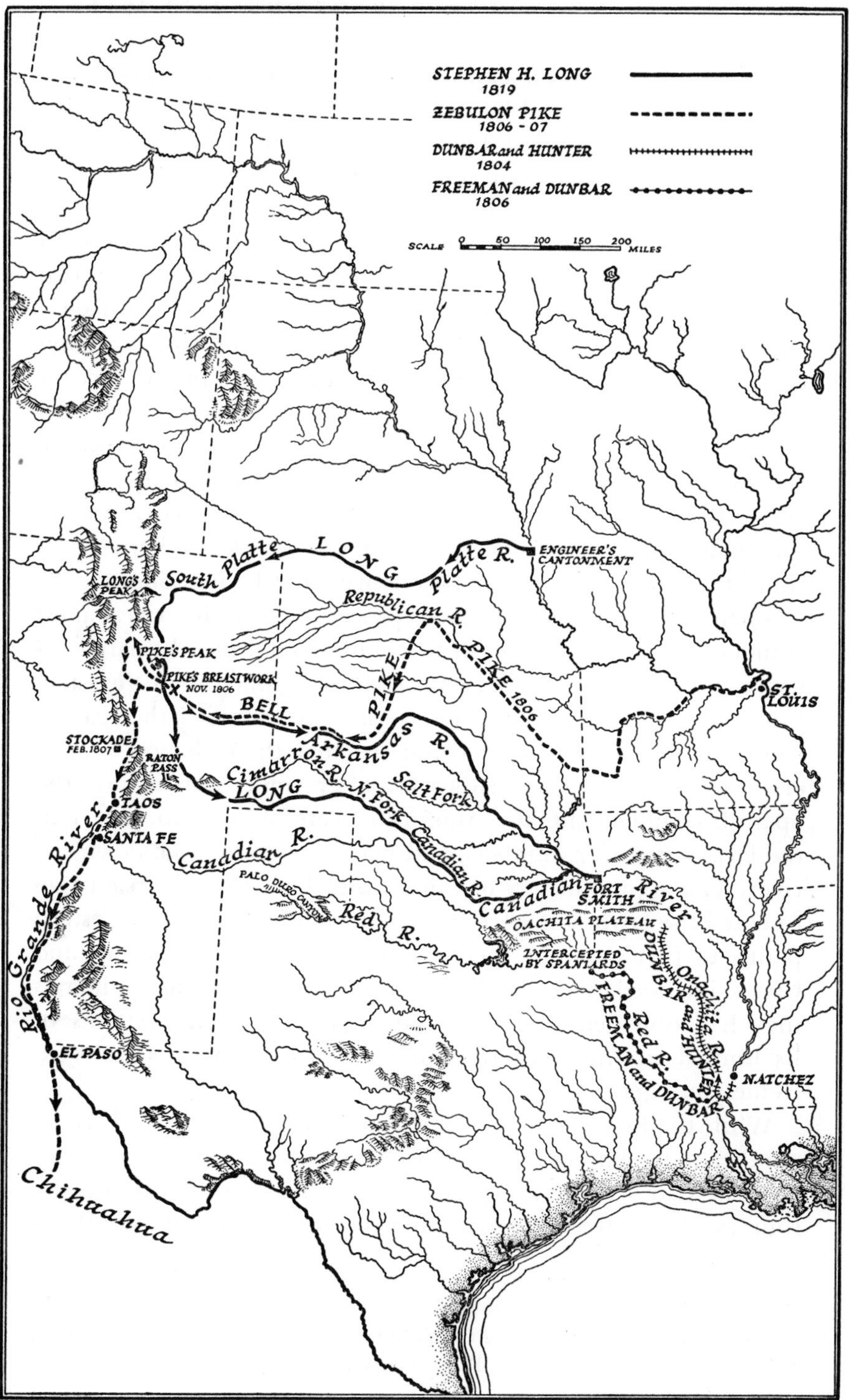
STEPHEN H. LONG
1819
ZEBULON PIKE
1806 - 07
DUNBAR and HUNTER
1804
FREEMAN and DUNBAR
1806
SCALE 0 50 100 150 200 MILES
ENGINEER'S CANTONMENT
LONG
Platte R.
South Platte
LONG'S PEAK
Republican R.
PIKE'S PEAK
PIKE'S BREASTWORK
NOV. 1806
PIKE
PIKE 1806
BELL
ST. LOUIS
STOCKADE
FEB. 1807
Arkansas R.
RATON PASS
Cimarron R.
Salt Fork
LONG
N. Fork
TAOS
SANTA FE
Canadian R.
Canadian R.
Rio Grande River
PALO DURO CANYON
Red R.
Canadian
FORT SMITH
River
OACHITA PLATEAU
INTERCEPTED BY SPANIARDS
DUNBAR
Oachita R.
and HUNTER
Red R.
FREEMAN and DUNBAR
NATCHEZ
EL PASO
Chihuahua

MAP 2

launch another scientific expedition to continue the explorations of the western lands and borders of the Louisiana purchase. This expedition was organized by Dunbar, but it actually consisted of Thomas Freeman, a surveyor, "who was furnished with the requisite instruments for determining geographical portions by astronomical observations"; Dr. Peter Custis, a botanist; Captain Sparks, the nominal commander; Lieutenant Humphreys; two noncommissioned officers; seventeen privates; and a Negro servant.[43] They left Fort Adams on the Mississippi on the afternoon of April 19 in two barges and a dugout canoe. In the face of possible Spanish objections the expedition continued up the Red River, around the great raft which was to cause so much trouble for so many years, to a backwoods Coashutta Indian village, where they presented the chief with an American flag. Freeman, following Jefferson's instructions, encouraged the Indians at all times to maintain friendly relations with the United States.

Then Freeman and his men proceeded up the river amid rumors of a pursuing Spanish force, until on July 28 a large detachment of Spanish soldiers was sighted. Crouched in the canebrake, the Americans prepared to resist whatever attack the Spanish would mount, though they could see that their chances of success were slim, indeed. However, after some words with the Spanish commandant, the Americans were allowed to depart in the face of superior numbers, and made their way back down the river. The approximately 635 miles they had gone upstream represented the farthest American penetration into the southwestern plains to that date. In their report to Jefferson, Freeman and Custis included scientific lists of animals, plants, and minerals they had observed along the way. However, even in terms of its limited frontier objectives, the expedition's results were extremely meager.

While the Freeman party was still proceeding up the Red River, another more important expedition got under way. Lt. Zebulon N. Pike had left St. Louis and was on his way to explore the sources of the Red River as they lay hidden in the Southern

43. Unless otherwise stated, this account is based on Thomas Freeman and Peter Custis, *An Account of the Red River in Louisiana Drawn Up from the Returns of Messrs. Freeman and Custis to the War Office of the United States, Who Explored the Same in the Year 1806,* Wash., 1807.

Rockies. He had sailed away from the landing on July 15, 1806, with a party of twenty-three men.[44] Floating first up the Missouri River, and then following the Osage, they reached the Osage Indian villages in late August, where they camped nearby at a trading post established by Manuel Lisa. While at the villages, Pike ascertained his correct position with the use of a theodolite and other instruments with which he had come equipped. On September they left the villages and marched first southward and then westward, until then reached the Smokeyhill Fork of the Kansas River, which they crossed, heading northwest. They continued onward to the Republican Fork of the Kansas, where they went into encampment. It was shortly before this that Pike first learned that a large Spanish force was already on the prairies with the twin object of intercepting both his expedition and that of Thomas Freeman, should he get by Captain Viana's blockades on the Red River. The Spanish expedition was described by Pike, with a note of pride, as "the most important ever carried on by the province of New Spain" (p. 410). Commanding the force was Don Facundo Malgares, an officer who, according to Pike, "had distinguished himself in several long expeditions against the Apaches and other Indian nations with whom the Spaniards were at war" (p. 413).

Leaving the Pawnee villages on the Republican, Pike continued his trek southward until he reached the Arkansas River near the future site of Bent's Fort. There, on October 28, he detached Lieutenant Wilkinson and four men with orders to descend the Arkansas while he himself intended to search out the sources of the Red River wherever they lay, in the "Mexican Mountains." With this objective he went up the Arkansas River accompanied by the remainder of the expedition until he saw the Rocky Mountains. Some days later they constructed a temporary breastwork as protection from the Indians. On November 27, ill-equipped and lightly clad, they climbed what is now Pike's Peak to a height of 9,000 feet. The next few months were spent searching for the sources of the Red River (sources which were destined to elude

44. Unless otherwise stated, the account is based on Zebulon M. Pike, *Expedition to the Headwaters of the Mississippi River, through Louisiana Territory, and in New Spain during the Years 1805–6–7,* ed. Elliot Coues, New York, 1895.

explorers for many years to come, being finally tracked down by Capt. Randolph B. Marcy in 1852). Pike's party suffered great hardships as it marched northward again into the mountains near the headwaters of the Arkansas. By early January 1807 the party, forced to turn south again, had built a blockhouse for shelter and was slowly starving to death in the Sangre de Christo Mountains of Southern Colorado. In desperation, leaving two men behind with frozen feet, Pike marched southward through a mountain pass and built another stockade on the banks of the Rio Grande, where on February 26 he and his men were taken into custody by a large body of Spanish Cavalry. The Spanish officers at first offered to supply them with mules, conduct them to the head of the Red River, and set them on the way home. This suggests that if the sources of the Red River had been known to the Spaniards, they were not the primary object of Pike's expedition, since he refused the offer. Indeed, the fact that Pike had received his orders from General James Wilkinson has led some students to see a broader and more ambitious design in his expedition than a hunt for the sources of the Red River.[45]

The role of Dr. James Robinson, the expedition's scientist and later a brigadier general in the Mexican revolutionary army, remains somewhat mysterious.[46] In 1810, before the results of Lewis and Clark's expedition were officially published, Pike's report and maps were printed and widely read. They showed the rivers as they cut across the great plains and demonstrated their relationship to one another. In his *Memoir* of 1857 Lt. G. K. Warren gave Pike credit for discovering the sources of the Grand River (which Pike had mistakenly called the Yellowstone) and for being the second American explorer to cross the Continental Divide.[47] Lieutenant Pike held, however, to one erroneous theory, that all the great rivers of the West had a common source. "I have no hesitation," he declared, "in asserting that I can take a position in the mountains from whence I can visit the sources of any of those rivers in one day." [48] By "those rivers" he meant the Arkansas, the Yellowstone [actually the Grand], the Platte, the Colorado, and the Rio Grande. Pike's geographical vision

45. Gilbert, *Exploration of Western America,* p. 155.
46. Wheat, "Mapping the American West," p. 71.
47. Warren, *Memoir,* p. 21.
48. Wheat, "Mapping the American West," p. 60.

enabled him to see, somewhere in the heart of the Rockies, a "Grand reservoir of snows and fountains." [49] But despite his errors, Pike's report and map were important. As Carl Wheat concludes, "Even after the publication in 1814 of the first reasonably accurate map of Lewis and Clark's discoveries, these maps of Pike and Humboldt continued to provide the cartographic basis for wide areas not visited by Lewis and Clark." [50]

In 1818 Major Isaac Roberdeau and William Rector of the Topographical Corps made a compilation of most of the data concerning the West that was then available.[51] But since it contained no new discoveries concerning the trans-Mississippi region, it was really no advance over other maps of the time. One year later the Topographical Bureau entered the field of western exploration on a larger scale as it sponsored the scientific operations of the Army's grandly conceived campaign up the Missouri known as the Yellowstone expedition.[52] The primary objective of the expedition, which was composed of nearly 1,000 men commanded by Gen. Henry W. Atkinson, was to proceed upriver to the Mandan villages near the mouth of Yellowstone River and there establish a fort which would serve as a bivouac for a large force of troops. It was hoped that such a show of strength would fill the Indians with awe and respect while at the same time discouraging the British traders, who from their Canadian posts were in virtual domination of the entire northwest fur trade.[53] Expressing his official aims, as Secretary of War, Calhoun explicitly stated: "The expedition ordered to the mouth of the Yellowstone, or rather to the Mandan village, is a part of a system of measures which has for its objects the protection of our northwestern frontier and the greater extension of our fur trade" (Chittenden, p. 561). The troops were to be transported upriver in five steamboats. A sixth, the *Western Engineer,* was to be placed at the disposal of the scientific corps. It was the first time steam transportation had been used on the Missouri River.

49. Ibid.

50. Ibid., p. 62.

51. Ibid., p. 71; see also Warren, *Memoir,* plate 2, for reproduction of the Rector-Roberdeau map.

52. Unless otherwise stated, the account is based on Chittenden, *Fur Trade,* 2, 560–83.

53. Henry P. Beers, *The Western Military Frontier, 1815–1846* (Phila., 1935), p. 41. Chittenden, *Fur Trade,* 2, 561.

As it was conceived by Calhoun, with President Monroe's enthusiastic support, the project embodied Jefferson's technique as well as his plan. It had military, commercial, diplomatic, and scientific aspects, and was a grandly conceived, far-flung project. At least one observer had his imagination captured by the expedition:

> See those vessels, with the agency of steam, advancing against the powerful currents of the Mississippi and the Missouri! Their course is marked by volumes of smoke and fire, which the civilized man observes with admiration, and the savage with astonishment. Botanists, mineralogists, chemists, artisans, cultivators, scholars, soldiers; the love of peace, the capacity for war: philosophical apparatus and military supplies; telescopes and cannon, garden seeds and gunpowder; the arts of civil life and the force to defend them—all are seen aboard. The banner of freedom which waves over the whole proclaims the character and protective power of the United States [pp. 563–64].

Such a scene would be more characteristic of the later era of the Topographical Engineers.

Commanding the scientific party was Major Stephen H. Long of the Topographical Bureau. A graduate of Dartmouth College, Long belonged to that older group of army engineers who had entered the service without benefit of previous West Point training. He had gained experience in frontier surveying and exploring in his expeditions to the Falls of St. Anthony, where he had laid out Fort Snelling. In the winter of 1817–18 he also helped to construct Fort Smith in the Arkansas territory.[54] The others who made up the scientific party were Major John Biddle; Dr. William Baldwin, physician and botanist; Dr. Thomas Say, zoologist; Augustus E. Jessup, geologist; Titian R. Peale, assistant naturalist (a globetrotter, and occasional painter); Samuel Seymour, a painter; and Lt. James Duncan Graham and Cadet William H. Swift, assistant topographers.[55]

54. *DAB.*

55. Edwin James, *Account of an Expedition from Pittsburgh to the Rocky Mountains, Performed in the Years 1819 and '20 . . .* ed. R. G. Thwaites, Early Western Travels, 1748–1846, No. 14 (Cleveland, 1904–07), 11.

The military half of the expedition, which got under way up the Missouri somewhat before the party of scientists left St. Louis, progressed only as far as Council Bluffs, because of the failure of the steamboats provided for their transportation. In almost every case the boats drew more water than the shallow Missouri was able to provide. By September the army group had established a bivouac at Council Bluffs and was awaiting the coming of winter. But the logistics problem was not well handled and the men came down with scurvy, which made further operations on a grand scale virtually impossible.

Long's scientific corps fared somewhat better. They left St. Louis on June 21 in the steamer *Western Engineer* which, being of shallower draft than the other boats, was able to provide slow but steady transportation up the river. One of the side excursions undertaken by a party under Dr. Say lost its horses and equipment to marauding Pawnee Indians, and Say and Jessup became ill, delaying the progress of the expedition. By the time the party reached Franklin on the Missouri, Dr. Baldwin, the botanist, had also been taken seriously ill and was left behind; he died there on August 31.[56] On September 17 the scientific party went into winter quarters near Council Bluffs.

That winter Long and Jessup returned to the East, the former to get married and the latter to retire permanently from exploring operations.[57] Meanwhile, the rest of the party spent their time at the cantonment collecting data on the geology and natural history of the region and studying the customs of the aborigines. Also during that winter Congress, having lost enthusiasm for the project, decided to abandon the show of force on the upper Missouri. Moreover, it decided to cut the expenses of the scientific excursion as far as possible, while sending it in a different direction across the prairies toward the headwaters of the Platte, Arkansas, and Red rivers. Concerning the retrenchment plans, James commented:

> Detestable parsimony! The only country but one in the world, that has not been reduced to an avowed or virtual

56. Ibid., p. 12. Supplementary details for this part of the expedition can be found in Titian R. Peale, "Journal," Library of Congress; and in Chittenden, *Fur Trade, 2,* 569.

57. James, p. 12. Also *DAB.*

> bankruptcy; the country which has grown and is growing in wealth and prosperity beyond any other and beyond all nations, too poor to pay a few gentlemen and soldiers for exploring its mighty rivers, and taking possession of the empires, which Providence has called it to govern.[58]

This perhaps explains the carelessness and apparent lack of enthusiasm of the members of the expedition when they embarked on their exploration under Long the following spring. They journeyed westward along the north bank of the Platte and on reaching the forks, crossed over to the southern bank of the South Fork and continued onward until they reached the Rocky Mountains, which they first sighted on June 30. After locating Long's Peak, one of their few discoveries, the party proceeded southward along the wall of the Rockies toward the headwaters of the Arkansas River. Upon reaching Pike's Peak, Dr. James and two others made the first ascent to the top, though many hunters and Indians, including Pike himself, had previously made the attempt.[59] Lieutenant Swift measured the altitude of the mountain above the surrounding plain but misjudging the altitude of the base plain above sea level, he failed to give its true height, an error that would be avoided by later expeditions using barometric measures for distance above sea level. He also made observations for longitude and latitude. Leaving Pike's Peak, the expedition reached the Arkansas River, where after a half-hearted attempt to ascend the Royal Gorge at the point where the river enters the mountains, they turned downstream again. On July 24 they divided forces; one party under Captain Bell went down the Arkansas in a trek that turned out to be aimless wandering rather than meaningful scientific exploration. Moreover, they traversed country already familiar to hunters and to those who had followed the fortunes of Lieutenants Pike and Wilkinson some fourteen years previously.

Long, with a party that included James and Titian Peale, continued his march southward until he struck what he took to be the upper Red River. Again like Pike, when confronted with the immediate possibility of discovering the source of this river, he manifested a lack of interest in it. Instead, he turned

58. James, p. 23 n.
59. James, p. 14.

downstream toward civilization. It was with some amazement that the party discovered that the supposed branch of the Red River which they had been following flowed into the Arkansas River, hence turned out to be not the Red at all but another stream, the Canadian. Because of his mistake, Long must be given credit for changing the ideas of map makers concerning the river systems of the southwest plains.

Historical commentary on this expedition has largely been restricted to criticism directed toward its careless and seemingly cavalier interest in actual discovery.[60] The failure to ascend to its source, the Platte or the Arkansas or the Canadian, has seemed almost inexcusable. Furthermore, in his *General Description of the Country Traversed by the Exploring Expedition,* Long became the author of the "Great American Desert" myth, which caused people to consider the West as a desert and for which midwestern agrarians and historians in general have never forgiven him, despite confirmations of his assertions by his contemporaries and calamitous experiences since that time which have, in large measure, provided a vindication of his views:

> In regard to this extensive section of country, I do not hesitate in giving the opinion, that it is almost wholly unfit for cultivation, and of course, uninhabitable by a people depending upon agriculture for their subsistence. Although tracts of fertile land considerably extensive are occasionally to be met with, yet the scarcity of wood and water, almost uniformly prevalent, will prove an insuperable obstacle in the way of settling the country. This objection rests not only against the section immediately under consideration, but applies with equal propriety to a much larger portion of the country. The whole of this region seems peculiarly adapted as a range for buffalos, wild goats, and other wild game; incalculable multitudes of which find ample pasturage and subsistence upon it.[61]

He found some advantage in the discouraging outlook for agriculture which might have curbed the fears of man like Calhoun and Jefferson who were so much aware of the danger to the new

60. Chittenden, *Fur Trade,* 2, 580–87.
61. James, *Account,* pp. 147–48.

Republic of too rapid an expansion across the continent. "This region, however, viewed as frontier, may prove of infinite importance to the United States inasmuch as it is calculated to serve as a barrier to prevent too great an extension of our population westward, and secure us against the machinations or incursions of an enemy that might otherwise be disposed to annoy us in that part of our frontier." [62] A final evaluation of the Yellowstone expedition was given by Hiram M. Chittenden, who declared it to be "an unqualified failure if not a huge fiasco" that "had been smothered in elaboration of method." [63]

In defense of Long it may be remarked that there was at least a preliminary attempt at scientific investigation by experts whose qualifications were the best available and by military engineers of unquestioned ability. New species of plants and animals were found, and extensive notes and specimens were taken, many of which were unfortunately lost in the desertion of three men from Major Bell's party which was carrying the notes and collections back to civilization. Limitations on the amount of new data were undoubtedly set by the lack of techniques for investigation. A scant ten years later, geology and botany would be more highly developed, as would the techniques for mathematical measurement. But even allowing for these limitations, men like Long, Graham, and, especially, Edwin James, who had been trained by Amos Eaton and John Torrey, should have been expected to produce better results.

As for the failure to make new geographical discoveries beyond Long's Peak and the Canadian River, it may be observed that Long's party was composed of scientists intent upon making a survey of the whole plains region; their mission did not necessarily entail following one river wherever it led into the mountains or, for all they knew, even to the South Seas.

Long's description of the "Great American Desert" seems to have been an honest and significant assessment of the plains area as it appeared to his generation and those which followed down to the Civil War. Walter P. Webb, in his study of the Great Plains, quotes two travelers of the 1850's, Captain Randolph B. Marcy, who termed the country "arid and destitute of timber," and

62. Ibid.

63. Chittenden, *Fur Trade, 2,* 570.

Horace Greeley, who in 1859 after a tour across the plains remarked that they offered "little sustenance and less shelter to man" and that "Wood and water—the prime necessities of the traveler as of the settler—are in adequate though not abundant supply."[64] Besides quoting these accounts which tend to substantiate Long's impressions of the plains, Webb's whole study is directed toward presenting the discovery of techniques for settlement on the plains that made water more available or provided substitutes for wood. This implies that for a society such as Long represented, which still depended upon timber and surface water, a sober evaluation such as his was not only prudent but necessary. Actual settlement of the plains area had to wait for these new techniques, which, for the most part, came into prominent use after Long's generation had passed away.

The narrative of James Ohio Pattie, published by Timothy Flint in 1831, is on the borderline between romantic fiction and slightly colored fact. Nevertheless, it helped to reveal much of the unknown Southwest. Pattie and his father set out from Missouri in 1823 on a fur-trading expedition up the Missouri River.[65] When they were turned back for not having trapping licenses, they headed south for Santa Fe. In a series of adventures which involved Indian clashes and the rescue of the beautiful Spanish daughter of a New Mexican grandee they made their way to Santa Fe. Between 1821 and 1828 they explored the Gila River country as well as the Colorado River and the whole interior of western North America.

In 1826 the younger Pattie went down the Gila River to the Colorado and north along that river, where he became the first white man since Garces in 1775 to approach the Grand Canyon of the Colorado. He continued northward across the central plateau area to the South Pass, and on to the Big Horn River and the Yellowstone. This part of his odyssey finally terminated with his return to Santa Fe in November 1826, where he visited his father, who was managing the Santa Rita del Cobre copper mines in the midst of the savage Apache country. Because he was

64. Walter P. Webb, *The Great Plains* (New York, 1931), pp. 158–59.

65. Unless otherwise stated, the account is based on James Pattie, *The Personal Narrative of James Ohio Pattie* . . . ed. R. G. Thwaites, Early Western Travels, 1748–1846, No. 18, Cleveland, 1905.

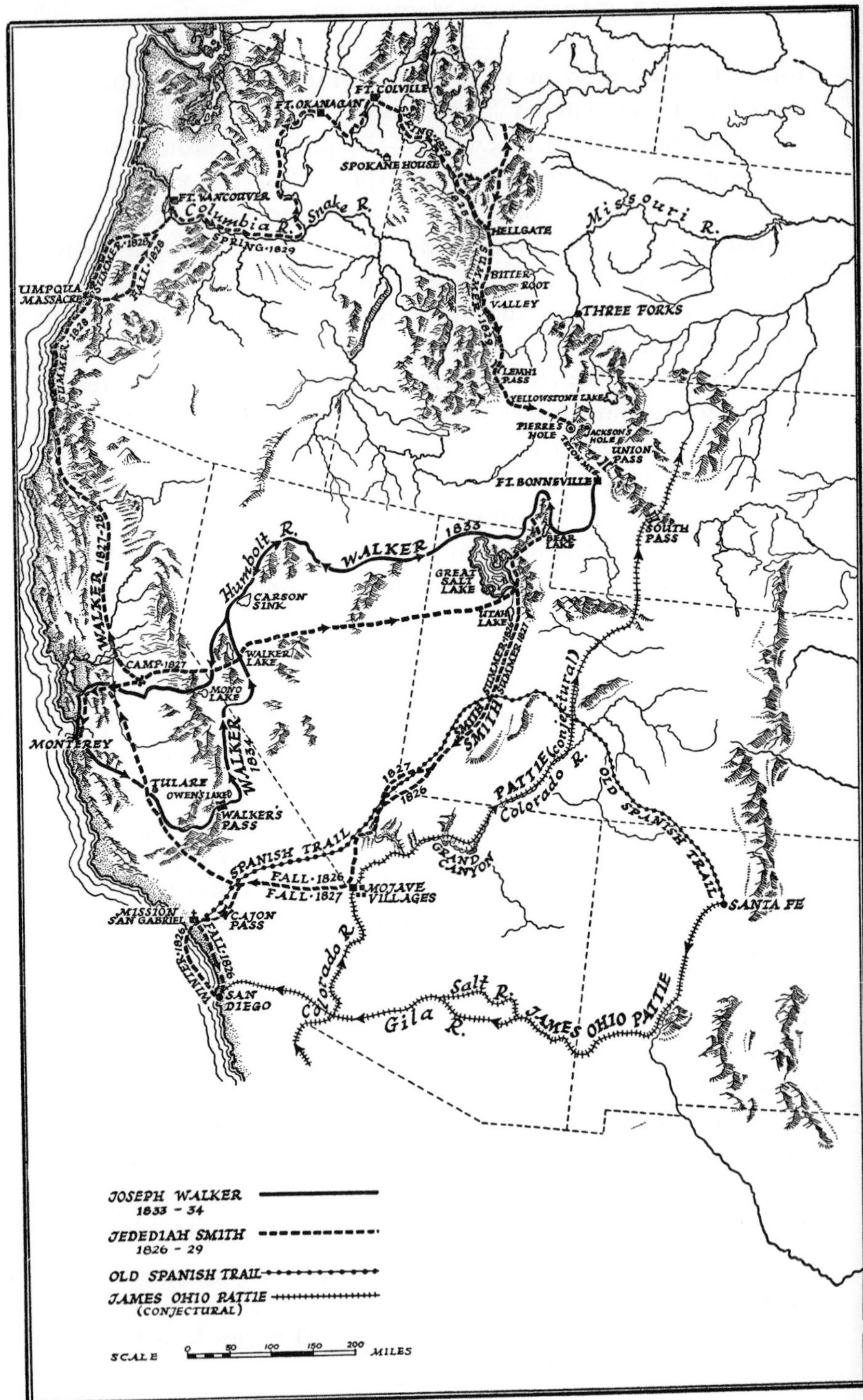

FT. COLVILLE
FT. OKANAGAN
SPOKANE HOUSE
FT. VANCOUVER
Columbia R.
Snake R.
SPRING·1829
SUMMER·1828
FALL·1828
UMPQUA MASSACRE
HELLGATE
Missouri R.
BITTER ROOT
V. ALLEY
THREE FORKS
LEMHI PASS
YELLOWSTONE LAKE
PIERRE'S HOLE
JACKSON'S HOLE
UNION PASS
FT. BONNEVILLE
SOUTH PASS
BEAR LAKE
WALKER
1833
Humbolt R.
GREAT SALT LAKE
UTAH LAKE
CARSON SINK
WALKER LAKE
CAMP·1827
MONO LAKE
WALKER 1827-28
MONTEREY
TULARE
OWEN'S LAKE
WALKER'S PASS
WALKER 1834
SMITH
PATTIE (conjectural)
Colorado R.
OLD SPANISH TRAIL
1827
1826
SPANISH TRAIL
GRAND CANYON
FALL·1826
FALL·1827
MOJAVE VILLAGES
MISSION SAN GABRIEL
CAJON PASS
SANTA FE
WINTER·1826
FALL·1826
SAN DIEGO
Colorado R.
Salt R.
Gila R.
JAMES OHIO PATTIE
JOSEPH WALKER 1833 - 34
JEDEDIAH SMITH 1826 - 29
OLD SPANISH TRAIL
JAMES OHIO PATTIE (CONJECTURAL)
SCALE 0 50 100 150 200 MILES

MAP

not a Mexican, Sylvester Pattie had been allowed by the Apaches to reopen the mines. In 1827, however, one of Pattie's subordinates absconded with the funds from the mine, forcing father and son to recoup their losses by a fur-trapping expedition through the comparatively virgin beaver country along the Gila River. They went downstream until they reached the Colorado River, and this time floated *down* the Colorado to its mouth. Again they had been preceded by the Spaniards, Garces by land and Ulloa by sea, but they were the first Americans to come upon this new and strategic outlet. Starving and thirst-maddened, they buried their furs and made their way across the Southern California deserts into San Diego, where they arrived on March 27, 1828. They were immediately put into prison by the Mexican governor, and while in captivity Sylvester Pattie died. James Ohio lived to continue his travels north to San Francisco Bay and the Vallejo estancias, and he even visited the mysterious Russians at Fort Ross. Then he returned to the south, and eventually went to Mexico City to obtain redress of his grievances, but instead was robbed by highwaymen and arrived back in Cincinnati on August 30, 1830, penniless and "broken in health and spirit" (p. 17). The most important practical result of his expedition was that for the first time a transcontinental route from Missouri to Santa Fe and down the Gila to California was brought into the realm of possibility. It had been done by trappers; why not by others—soldiers, settlers, scientists, perhaps even horse thieves? This latter group, headed by the mountain man Old Bill Williams, attempted something of the sort a few years later as it hurried a remuda of stolen California horses eastward into New Mexico.[66]

The final important discovery in the Southwest, that of the route known as "The Old Spanish Trail," connecting New Mexico with California, has been credited to the efforts on one William Wolfskill, who led a group of trappers out of Taos in September 1830 and headed northwest across Colorado, crossing first the Grand River and then the Green, through country characterized by fantastic eroded arches and huge monoliths standing out on broken plateaus or towering over sheer canyons.[67] Making their

66. David Lavender, *Bent's Fort* (New York, 1954), pp. 153–54.

67. Gilbert, *Exploration of Western America*, p. 168.

way westward, the party passed through the rugged mountains of central Utah and reached the Sevier River, which they followed in a southwest direction to the Virgin River. This route led them to the Mojave Desert, over which they crossed, passing just south of the present limits of Death Valley National Park. Cajon Pass was their gateway to California and Los Angeles, where they arrived in February 1831. The route followed by Wolfskill, though far from direct, and traversing some of the most forbidding country in western North America, became frequently traveled. Many of the forty-niners as well as later explorers, fur hunters, and Mexican traders used the Old Spanish Trail. On his second expedition in 1844 John C. Frémont, returning from California, followed this trail far into the Central Rockies, eventually crossing over to the South Park, whence he made his way across the plains to St. Louis and home.[68]

There is evidence to indicate, however, that previous to Wolfskill's expedition in 1831, Richard Campbell, a fur trader out of Santa Fe, traveled to San Diego with a group of Mexican traders.[69] This was in 1827 shortly after Jedediah Smith's first crossing of the Basin area from Salt Lake. A careful student of the Southwest has termed this "perhaps the first trip from Santa Fe across the fearful deserts of California to the Pacific Coast." The route followed was similar to that of Wolfskill, though it was not that which later became the Spanish Trail.

The Basin and Range Country

While the trappers and Mexican traders were searching out and exploring the Southwest for its beaver streams or for trails over which trains of burros laden with goods could travel between California and Santa Fe, other expeditions were afoot which filled in the required knowledge concerning the Central Basin area from the Wasatch Mountains to the Sierra Nevadas. Of these operations, two stand out as more significant than all

68. Frémont, *Report, 1843–44,* p. 374.

69. Lavender, p. 81. It should also be noted that the merchant Antonio Armijo led a caravan out of Santa Fe on Nov. 7, 1829, and proceeded overland to California on a route that was similar but not identical to the Old Spanish Trail.

the rest; Jedediah Smith's two crossings to California, and Joseph Walker's expedition under the direction of Capt. Benjamin L. E. Bonneville. An intelligent man who understood the significance of his travels, as well as a trail-breaker and discoverer, Jedediah Smith is a most important western figure.

In addition to making the all-important rediscovery of the South Pass, Smith made a crossing from Great Salt Lake to California and thus became the first American to have some idea of the extent of the Great Basin. On August 16, 1826, he and fourteen men left the annual rendezvous at Cache Valley and rode southward toward the Great Salt Lake and Utah Valley.[70] From there he continued onward until he struck the Sevier River, which he followed in a southwestwardly direction. Leaving the Sevier, he followed the rim of the Basin until he came upon a river, which he named Adams after President John Quincy Adams (it was later renamed the Virgin River). At the mouth of this river he crossed the Colorado and followed down its left, or eastern bank. Somewhere near the point where the State of Nevada comes to a point against the Arizona State line, Smith and his party of trappers left the Colorado and struck out across the Mojave Desert. They reached California by way of Cajon Pass, thus preceding William Wolfskill's party by a good five years. It was on November 26, 1826, that Smith and his party came down from the Cajon Pass into the San Bernadino Valley of California. It had taken them sixteen days to cross the desert country from the Colorado River.

After a delay in California due to the fact that the governor was suspicious of all Americans coming into that territory, the party set out northward through the Tehachapi Pass, passed the Tulare Lakes, and continued all the way to the Stanislaus River, where because of snows in the passes the whole party, laden as it was with beaver, was not able to cross the Sierra Nevadas. Taking two men and promising to return, Smith made the mountain crossing. With infinite hardship he and his two companions, Gobel and Evans, crossed directly over the deserts of central Nevada and the Great Salt Lake Desert. On June 26, 1827, they finally sighted the Salt Lake. Smith rejoined his partners for the

70. Unless otherwise stated, the account of Jedediah Smith's travels is based on Morgan, *Jedediah Smith*.

rendezvous of 1827 considerably richer in information, but the real object of his heroic trek, beaver pelts, was still cached out in California in great quantity.

Smith's newly acquired knowledge went far toward filling one of the few remaining blank spots on the mountain man's mental map of the Far West. He recognized the importance of his explorations, but his first interest was in beaver, so he set out again in July, after the rendezvous had broken up, and followed a similar though not identical trail southwest to the Mojave Indian villages on the Colorado River near where he had left the river and turned westward into the desert. This time his party consisted of eighteen men well equipped for the journey, whose hardship Smith could now anticipate. However, the Mojave Indians were unfriendly, and catching the party unawares while making the hazardous crossing of the Colorado they massacred ten of Smith's men and captured two squaws who had accompanied the party. With only five guns and few supplies, the survivors fought off their pursuers and crossed the desert once more to throw themselves on the generosity of the Californians. They made the San Bernadino Valley by August 28, 1827. Leaving two men behind at San Bernadino, Smith rejoined his men at the Stanislaus River on September 18.

The rest of Smith's journey carried him northward out of California along the upper Sacramento River. He swung westward toward the Trinity River and eventually reached the Pacific Ocean at Point St. George, a few miles from today's Oregon-California state line. The trappers then followed the coastline until they reached the Umpqua River, where Indians set upon the camp and murdered all but one man, who escaped to Fort Vancouver. Smith and two other companions who had been off on a hunting trip, also escaped the massacre and hurried to Fort Vancouver. Though he returned to the site with a party of the Hudson's Bay men to reclaim his furs and chastise the Indians, Smith was unable to accomplish either objective satisfactorily. In the spring and summer of 1829 he returned to Pierre's Hole by way of the upper Columbia and Bitterroot rivers and the Lemhi Pass, having visited Forts Okanagan and Colville and penetrated as far north as the present Canadian border before joining his partner, David Jackson, somewhere north of Flathead Lake in what is now northern Idaho.

Smith's significance lies in more than his own personal love of adventure or in his geographical imagination. The data he gained was expressed on at least three maps compiled shortly after his death, two by the firm of A. H. Brué in Paris, in 1833 and 1834 respectively, which were based upon Smith's letter to William Clark reprinted in the *Nouvelles Annales des Voyages* in 1828; and a third in Albert Gallatin's map of 1836 to accompany his *Synopsis of the Indian Tribes of North America*, previously mentioned.[71] If Gallatin's map was not widely known, neither was a later map of 1839 compiled by David H. Burr, geographer to the House of Representatives, from actual sketches by Smith.[72] It is assumed that a map drawn by Smith was loaned to Burr, at some time between 1831 and 1837, by General Ashley, retired fur trader, friend, and onetime employer of Smith, who served as congressman from the State of Missouri during this period.[73] The Burr map containing Smith's discoveries was followed in 1841 by a map of the Oregon country based upon explorations conducted by Lts. George F. Emmons and Henry Eld of the Wilkes expedition, whose personal sketches laid the foundation of their map. This map included many of Smith's place names, which suggests that a manuscript map done by Smith had been deposited at Fort Vancouver, a fact to which George Gibbs, the Oregon naturalist, attested.[74] Finally, as recently as 1953, still another evidence of Smith's influence was found in the Frémont-Gibbs-Smith map, discovered by Dale L. Morgan and Carl I. Wheat. This map is a Frémont map of 1844 with Smith's data added at a later date, presumably by Gibbs. The significance of all of these reappearances of the findings of Jedediah Smith is that they provide some insight into the extent to which the important geographical discoveries by these lonely mountain men were transmitted among their fellow trappers and even to the centers of civilization. It indicates also that such discoveries

71. Morgan and Wheat, *Jedediah Smith* (above, n. 9), pp. 18–19.
72. Ibid., pp. 20–23.
73. Ibid., p. 20.
74. Ibid., p. 24.

could be part of the general knowledge for a few years and then sink, like one of Smith's "Inconstant Rivers," into the sands of oblivion and be lost and buried for years. This is particularly true of the data which remained in private hands, for if it was government produce, it was generally preserved in Washington and consulted by professional map makers, such as Lieutenant Warren, and commercial cartographers, like Disturnell or Mitchell.

The last major expedition that made an original discovery before 1842 was conducted by Major B. L. E. Bonneville, an officer of the United States Army on leave of absence for two years, beginning in 1832. Bonneville, who had been a protégé of General Lafayette, received special permission to visit the Rocky Mountain area, at his own expense, and explore the possibilities of the fur trade. Such an undertaking was not without precedent: English officers, like Sir William Drummond Steward and Lt. George F. Ruxton, became conspicuous figures in the Far West.

It was not Bonneville himself who made the important discoveries, though he ever afterward claimed the credit was due him as the commander who sent the trapper, Joseph Walker, on his way. Walker was a mountain man. He was primarily interested in furs when he headed west from Salt Lake in 1833 under Bonneville's orders. The expedition, composed of forty men, came upon the Humboldt River and followed it southwest across the Basin until it faded into the Carson Sinks.[75] Here they went west, past Carson Lake and across the Sierras, to the Merced tributary of the San Joaquin. On the return trek, they skirted the southern end of the Sierras and crossed over them at Walker's Pass. Then they headed northward along the eastern wall of the mountains until they again sighted the Humboldt, which they followed back across the Basin to Salt Lake. In this way Joseph Walker and his men traversed what became the most important emigrant route to California.

When Bonneville's story was told by Washington Irving in 1837, two years after the Captain had returned from the wilderness, it included a map which gave some indication of the nature of the Basin, with its Salt Lake having no outlet to the Pacific Ocean. Hiram M. Chittenden has declared that these maps were

75. Chittenden, *Fur Trade, I,* 408.

the "one really valuable result of Captain Bonneville's expedition so far as he alone is concerned."[76] He added, however: "Nearly all of the valuable features appeared on Gallatin's map of the year before and were further brought to public notice by Gallatin's memoir accompanying the map." General Chittenden lamented the fact that Bonneville's map received wide publicity

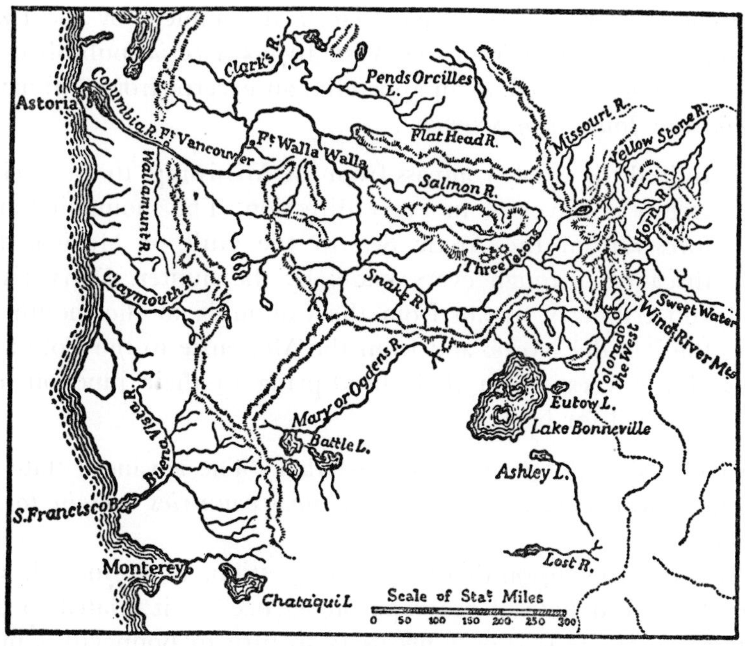

Map B. Benjamin Bonneville's 1837 map.

while Gallatin's lanquished unread by the experts and even overlooked by Lieutenant Warren in his *Memoir.* Although this is true, it fails to do justice to the fact that Bonneville, without benefit of Jedediah Smith's data but by means of an expedition conceived and sent out under his orders had accumulated enough knowledge of the Basin and Range area to form a general but substantially correct conception of its nature. Furthermore, he secured wide distribution for his map, which has been used many times. What he did was the same as Gallatin had done, except that Bonneville had explored much of the region himself, and had received his information as the result of his direct orders,

76. Ibid., pp. 423–24.

and not by chance. The real irony of the matter lies in the fact that Frémont, six years later, spent most of a year looking for the Rio Buenaventura, when any avid reader of Irving's romance could have told him it didn't really exist, in the Great Basin or anywhere else.

Because of the efforts of the fur hunters and the comparatively few expeditions sent out by the federal government, the exploration of Western North America seemed complete by the time Bonneville returned from the West. In his *Astoria,* published in 1836, Irving included, as an appendix, an excerpt from Silliman's *American Journal of Science,*

> Indeed the whole compass from the Mississippi to the Pacific Ocean is traversed in every direction. The mountains and forests from the Arctic Sea to the Gulf of Mexico, are threaded, through every maze, by the hunter. Every river and tributary stream from the Columbia to the mouth of the Rio del Norte, and from the McKenzie to the Colorado of the West, from their headspring to their junction are searched for beaver.

In conclusion the *Journal* asserted that "The advanced state of geographical science shows that *no new countries remain to be explored.*" [77]

It is this conclusion that raises the question. What, indeed, was the "advanced state of geographical science" as it related to the American West? It is only necessary to turn to Bonneville's map to get a clue; or even to Gallatin's map. True enough, in Bonneville's map an idea of a vast, sandy plain bounded by mountains and containing within its area a large lake with no outlet to the sea is conveyed. But this is all, and it is hardly correct beyond the limits of the idea. No range borders the Great Basin continuously on its northern flank; instead it fades into the Columbia Plateau and isolated mountain spurs. Bonneville's Sierra Nevadas, or California Mountains, are only a single narrow chain, and there is no coast range at all. Even San Francisco Bay, by this time explored and presumably familiar to ship captains if not to fur traders like the Patties, is incorrectly drawn. And in addition to the vaguely drawn landmarks, Bonneville's map

77. Irving, *Astoria,* appendix, pp. 270, 274.

lacks still another requirement which the scientific geographer would demand. It is nowhere based upon astronomical observations for positions of latitude and longitude, and though generally the data is well placed, precise measurement is the hallmark of scientific cartography. Bonneville was an untrained amateur map maker, which, perhaps, accounts for the poor technical quality of his production. He and his expedition remain significant for his idea alone.

What of Gallatin and his map of 1836? Though it embodied Jedediah Smith's data, showed the course of the Rocky Moun-

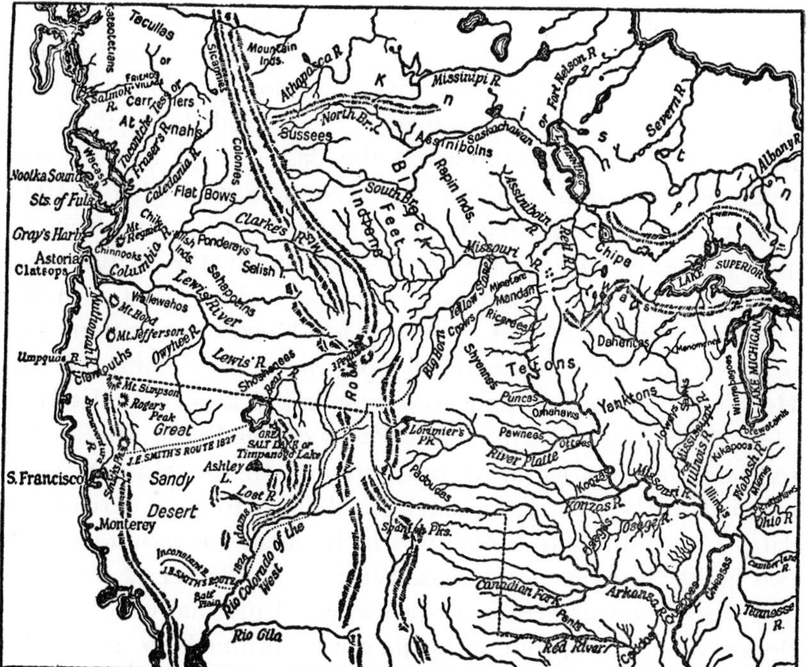

Map. C. Albert Gallatin's 1836 map, showing the route taken by Jedediah Smith in his first crossing of the Great Basin in 1827.

tains, included a California range, and had the Basin area, labeled "Great Sandy Desert," it, too, was far from a precise picture. Though he had access to Humboldt's atlas, and even to Escalante's journal and map in the library of Colonel Peter Force in Washington, Gallatin's whole Southwest remains, for the most part, devoid of details and full of faulty information. Prominent examples of the latter are the Gila River, which flows directly into the Gulf of California, and the Rio del Norte, which has too great a north-south orientation in relation to the Gila and Colorado. Thus Gallatin's map presents an *idea* of the West based largely on reports of explorers and on sketch maps drawn without the use of accurate instruments for recording positions. It gives merely a hazy view, like an underexposed film. Some of the important objects are in their places, but the outlines are not sharply defined or accurately discernible.

In 1837 a professional entered the field. He was Washington Hood, Captain, United States Topographical Engineers. On his map one might expect to find the latest and most accurate data concerning the West, since he was a trained topographer and map maker. On his 1838 map of Oregon, however, Hood showed the Great Salt Lake as a *rectangle*.[78] He revived the myth of the Rio Buenaventura flowing across the Basin, failed to show correctly both the Basin and the Sierra Nevadas, and left out Utah Lake completely. Apparently Hood had copied his map from an atlas published in 1834 by Aaron Arrowsmith, the British commercial cartographer, particularly the part which dealt with the Oregon Territory.[79] Unfortunately for Hood's reputation, this part was the only one with any pretension to accuracy at all. Hood's map seems, perhaps, the most imprecise of all. His later *Map, Exhibiting the Practicable Passes of the Rocky Mountains,* compiled in 1839 while he was stationed on the Missouri frontier, is equally incorrect, though he claimed to have derived his data "from information obtained in frequent conversations with two highly intelligent trappers, William A. Walker of Virginia, and Mr. Coates of Missouri who belonged originally to Captain Bonneville's party, but subsequently continued to roam the mountains as free trappers during six consecutive years" and "from others, who were connected with surveys and expeditions as far to the westward as Santa Fe and Taos." [80] Ironically,

78. Washington Hood, *Map of the United States Territory of Oregon, West of the Rocky Mountains,* 25th Cong., 3d Sess., H. R. Rep. 101 (1838), facing p. 1.

79. Wheat, "Mapping the American West," p. 87.

80. Washington Hood, "Map, Exhibiting the Practicable Passes of the Rocky Mountains," Cartographic Records Section, National Archives; see map legend.

Hood's map of 1839, along with the Lewis and Clark maps and those of Pike, were thought to represent the furthest advance of geographical science before the era of the "Great Reconnaissance" by the Army Topographical Engineers. If an interested person in Washington wished to learn of the geography of the central mountain region, he could do no better, by 1840, than to refer to Hood's map. He could do no better, that is, short of going to the West to see for himself. By 1842 he could add to this the atlas of Commander Wilkes' United States Exploring Expedition for accurate data on California and Oregon. Lieutenants Eld and Emmons of this expedition made careful observations for position, which were kept in their field notebooks and journals.[81] This was perhaps the beginning of accurate western cartography.

If the geography of the West was well known though unmapped, the same applied to the flora and fauna. The nutritiousness of buffalo grass, the potable liquid of the cactus, the habits of the beaver, and the fierceness of the grizzly bear were all lessons to be learned by rote for the mountain man. They were learned merely as part of his immediate response to the environment, and such knowledge was passed on from master to apprentice as part of the craft. The mountain men rarely if ever gathered data on the plants and animals of the West for a purpose which remained, by intention, undesignated. They had no idea of the value of collections of institutionalized information.

On the other hand, when making their reconnaissances the Army explorers looked for different things, oftentimes, than had those of previous generations. Their conception of what constituted important national resources was greatly enlarged. They took stock of the geological formations, for example, an inventory not easily taken beyond the level of superficial description

81. For specimens of their field work see Henry Eld, "Journal of an Expedition to Survey Gray's Harbor and Shoalwater Bay, Aug. 11 to Sept. 7, 1841," accompanied by three sketchbooks with his original topographic drawings, Yale Collection of Western Americana; also George F. Emmons, three journals kept while on board the U. S. Sloop of War *Peacock,* Aug. 12, 1838—June 10, 1842, particularly Vol. *3,* which includes an account of the Emmons-Eld overland journey from Oregon to California, Aug.–Oct. 1841, Yale Collection of Western Americana. Still another account is in Peale, "Journal" (above, n. 56).

before the rapid advance in the science of geology in the United States which began about 1830. Such a basic technique as stratigraphic correlation by means of fossils was not generally recognized in this country, though Thomas Say, the naturalist on the Long expedition, had insisted upon its value in an article in 1818 in the first issue of the *American Journal of Science.*[82] The idea was only partially accepted after S. G. Morton again suggested it ten years later, in a paper before the American Academy of Science in which he used the method to compare the American Cretaceous strata with that of Europe.[83] Even Alexander von Humboldt in his *Political Essay on the Kingdom of New Spain,* 1811, which contained the famous cross-section from Vera Cruz to Mexico City, was unaware of the inaccuracies that would result from correlations of strata which ignored fossil data.[84] Though America had in *The American Journal of Science* a first-rate scientific journal, and though there were American textbooks of geology beginning with Amos Eaton's *Index to the Geology of the Northern States,* also published first in 1818, it was not until after 1830, with the experience gained in the various state surveys, that detailed and reasonably accurate geological reconnaissances based on advanced techniques of stratigraphy and paleontology could be undertaken in the West.

Likewise, other new techniques, such as the observation for latitude with a 46-inch Zenith telescope, developed by Captain Talcott of the Engineer Corps in the Ohio State surveys of 1835,[85] and the determination of altitudes by barometric measurement, used by Humboldt in 1810 [86] but first employed in the United States by J. N. Nicollet in 1838 in his Dakota surveys,[87]

82. Thomas Say, "Observations on Some Species of Zoophytes, Shells etc. Principally Fossils," art. 12, *American Journal of Science, 1* (1818), 382.

83. George P. Merrill, *The First One Hundred Years of American Geology* (New Haven, 1924), p. 117.

84. See the atlas to Humboldt (above, n. 33). Also Helmut de Terra, *Humboldt* (New York, 1955), p. 167.

85. Charles W. Raymond, *Notes in Relation to Surveys in the Western Territories of the United States,* 43d Cong., 2d Sess., H. R. Exec. Doc. 109 (Jan. 1876), 34.

86. Humboldt (above, n. 84), barometric profile in the atlas.

87. J. N. Nicollet, *Report Intended to Illustrate a Map of the Hydrographical Basin of the Upper Mississippi River,* 26th Cong., 2d Sess., Sen. Exec. Doc. 237 (1840–41), 93 n.

enabled the Army engineer-explorer to measure what he saw with a new degree of accuracy. Such techniques as these led to what may well be the most important achievement of this period of scientific and utilitarian reconnoitering: the drafting of the first comprehensive outline map of the trans-Mississippi West by Lt. Gouverneur Kemble Warren.

There were men before 1842 who were interested in science—that is, the collection and organization of knowledge for its own sake, and among these were the Army explorers, like Lewis and Clark, and Major Long with his retinue of experts. This group also included Thomas Nuttall of Philadelphia and Harvard, and William Dunbar, the naturalist of Louisiana. But they were ahead of their time. A more basic geographic vocabulary had to be built up first. This was true in terms of the absolute need for generalized information concerning the West, such as the width of the Continent, the extent of the mountains, the location and flow of the rivers, and the fierceness of the Indians. It was also true in terms of the need to develop new techniques for ascertaining, classifying, and evaluating the newly acquired facts. Microscopes and telescopes and new systems of classification had to be perfected. Institutions like the Smithsonian were needed to process the data. Schools of science and engineering had to have time to develop advanced students with a degree of sophistication in matters of science. Therefore the difference between exploration in the West before 1842 and that which developed afterward is one of expansion, growth, and, above all, new ideas. In a sense it is this difference in approach that distinguishes the periods of exploration before and after 1842.

Schoolcraft prefaced his *Narrative Journal of Travels from Detroit, Northwest through the Great Chain of American Lakes to the Sources of the Mississippi in the Year 1820* by saying:

> American geography may be said to have had three important problems to solve in modern times. The first and second of these related to the Columbia. Both were substantially resolved by the expedition of Lewis and Clark under the administration of Jefferson. . . . The true source of the Mississippi which forms the third topic of inquiry was brought into discussion at the same period.[88]

88. Quoted in Warren, *Memoir* (above, n. 51), p. 30.

Looking backward at Schoolcraft's pronouncement from his vantage point in 1859, Lieutenant Warren voiced his objections, those of a larger perspective,

> But if these were the *great* problems of modern American geography, surely there were more than three. The sources of the Rio Grande del Norte, of the Yellowstone, of the Great Colorado of the West, might have been considered of equal importance, and the discovery, since, of large lakes of salt water, of large basins and long rivers with no outlets to the ocean, show that the field was not yet deprived of objects of great geographical interest.[89]

Here, in a symbolic sense, is the difference, a changing horizon of knowledge which saw new problems. The new age depended upon the old, but it raised new questions. It sought a refinement of information for different purposes, and it saw new possibilities. As river travel became impractical, a railroad spanning the vast spaces of the Continent became an accepted eventuality. Just as, twenty years before, General Ashley had created a revolution in the fur business by leaving the Missouri River and striking out overland with a string of pack mules to carry his trade goods, so, too, with the building of railroads explorers ceased to devote all their attention to the rivers and began to look for passes through the mountain barrier that were not too steep to admit the iron horse. This, in its own way, was also a revolution.

When they saw new possibilities, the western explorers were only keeping in step with their time. Whether it is called the Era of Manifest Destiny or not, the keynote of the age was expansion. National expansion was obvious. To contemporaries, intellectual expansion was also evident, in Emerson's spiritual journeys into Indian and German philosophy, in Melville's creation of his great vision of the whaling world, based upon his experiences from Typee to the Galapagos. Clipper ships were having their heyday on the run to San Francisco, and fast packet boats conducted passengers regularly to Liverpool and the Continent. Travelers from America constantly made pilgrimages to the Holy Land, and tramped all over the forbidden regions of the Near East. Newspapermen like Bayard Taylor became internationally

89. Ibid.

famous globetrotters. The travel book was in vogue. One writer of such books, John Lloyd Stephens, turned United States Consul, disappeared into the Central American jungles and reappeared as the discoverer of the entire lost civilization of the Mayas.[90] Another United States Consul, Ephraim George Squier, also produced a first-rate book on Central America.[91] Many others aspired to these heights. The United States Navy, too, was active in all parts of the world, and the feats of the Topographical Engineers were more than matched by Perry's expedition to Japan, by the Rodgers and Ringgold North Pacific expedition, by Wilkes' spectacular Antarctic and South Sea explorations, by Lieutenant Lynch's survey of the Dead Sea, and by Lieutenant Gilliss' astronomical expedition to Chili. Elisha Kent Kane searched out the remains of Sir John Franklin's exploring expedition near the North Pole and became the hero of the hour. Lt. Matthew Fontaine Maury produced the most significant of all works on oceanography, with his study of the winds and currents. When Lieutenants Herndon and Gibbon published their official accounts of their trip down the mysterious Amazon, a young man named Clemens from Hannibal, Missouri, set off down the Mississippi, his imagination fired to be a coffee planter in Brazil. Short on capital, by the time he reached New Orleans he had been befriended by a kindly riverboat Captain named Bixby and became a steamboat pilot instead.

The age, therefore, was somehow different, the horizon broader, the demands greater, the tempo increased; knowledge was fuller, and the government, which was, after all, of the people, went right along with the times. And so, beginning in 1842, the United States Topographical Engineers, specially trained in the new scientific techniques, went out into the West asking new questions.

90. Stephens, *Incidents of Travel* (above, p. oo, n. oo). See also Victor W. Van Hagen, *Maya Explorer* (Norman, Okla., 1947), esp. pp. 97–119.
91. *DAB*.

PART TWO
1842–1854

3. JOHN C. FRÉMONT

> It is said that Lieutenant Frémont has been appointed to the Survey of the Oregon Territory. We are heartily glad of it. He will be sure to do his work well, and if our topographical engineers labor in the same style and spirit, we may reckon on obtaining, through their joint efforts, an accurate knowledge of that country, so that we may be able to calculate, on safe grounds, the exact amount of blood and treasure which may be prudently expended in the conquest of it.—*London Athenaeum, March 1844.*

MOST FAMOUS of all the Topographical Engineers was John C. Frémont, who became a national hero in his own lifetime. However, the least remembered fact about his career was that he achieved his initial fame as a member of the Topographical Corps. That his official role was ignored was due in part to his association with the free trappers, but more particularly to the efforts of his political mentor, Senator Thomas Hart Benton of Missouri, the foremost advocate of westward expansion. In his later life the Senator was fond of emphasizing the importance of the western pioneer and minimizing the contributions of the Army. "It was not an act of government leading the people and protecting them," he declared, "but like all the other great emigrations and settlements of that race [Anglo-Saxon] on our continent, it was the act of the people going forward without government aid or countenance, establishing their possession and compelling the government to follow with its shield and spread it over them." [1] Specifically he insisted that "connected with this emigration and auxiliary to it, was the first expedition of Lieutenant Frémont to the Rocky Mountains . . . undertaken and completed in the summer of 1842—upon its outside view the conception of the government, but, in fact conceived without its knowledge, and executed upon solicited orders, of which the design was unknown." [2] In part what the Senator said was true.

1. Thomas Hart Benton, *Thirty Years' View; or, a History of the Working of the American Government for Thirty Years, from 1820 to 1850* (2 vols. New York, 1854–56), *1*, 468–69.
2. Ibid., p. 478.

But at the same time Benton obscured the fact that when it provided funds, and virtual *carte blanche* orders for Lieutenant Frémont, the Topographical Corps was knowingly performing a special service for the people of the West. In listening to the demands of Benton as an informed western spokesman, and in providing one of the Corps' best officers for a mission designed to fulfill those western demands, Colonel John J. Abert, the commandant of the Corps, was doing what he could for the cause of expansion. Since the Topographical Corps, with its thirty-six officers, had been established in 1838 as a branch of the Executive designed to perform duties assigned by the President and the Congress, Abert could not, as did Senator Benton, intrigue on behalf of a special policy of imperial aggrandizement, nor could he initiate a legislative policy for the West. In 1842 when the Corps began its work in the West, this limitation was clearly drawn. Consequently, it was Frémont, backed by the influence of the western senators, who appeared to initiate the important work of the Army in exploring the West. Regardless of his own designs, Colonel Abert was forced by his position to allow the Senator from Missouri and the subordinate lieutenant, John C. Frémont, to assume credit for first suggesting the official exploration of the West.

But though Colonel Abert allowed Frémont a wide latitude, he still saw him as a member of the Corps, subject to its authority. In 1843 it was Abert who wrote an irate letter to Frémont demanding to know who gave him authority to take a howitzer on his reputed "scientific" expedition.[3] When Benton assumed the role of Frémont's protector, Colonel Abert did not back down, as historians have implied.[4] Instead, he asserted his authority in a letter to the powerful Senator, declaring,

> The error of Lieutenant Frémont was that he kept the authority to which he was responsible, and from which he should have sought advice and direction . . . entirely uninformed of his proceedings, wants, or views. . . . Now as the

3. J. J. Abert to John C. Frémont, May 22, 1843, LS, TE 77.

4. See Frémont, *Memoirs,* p. 168, for the original source of this interpretation. It is generally accepted by Frémont's biographer, Allan Nevins. See esp. Frémont, *Narratives of Exploration and Adventure,* ed. Nevins (New York, 1956), p. 254, n. 5.

> equipment of his party contemplated a serious change in the character of the expedition under his command, one that might involve the Government in Indian hostility, I have no doubt you will admit it to have been a negligence deserving some reproach that he did not seek the advice and orders of the Department. The Department might, under such anticipations, have prohibited the expedition, or it might have made it adequate successfully to have encountered the contemplated emergency.[5]

Despite the encounters with Benton, however, Colonel Abert was pleased with Frémont as a Topographical Engineer. As late as October 27, 1851, Abert severely reprimanded Lt. John Pope for disparaging Frémont's earlier work.[6] Shortly after the publication of Frémont's first report in 1843, Abert had written him an unprecedented personal note which said,

> It appears to be no more than a just tribute to your exertions that I should express my great personal pleasure as well as official satisfaction with your report which has now been printed reflecting credit alike upon your good taste as well as intelligence. It is by efforts like these that officers elevate their own character while they also render eminent public services; and . . . contribute to the standing and usefulness of their particular branch of the service.[7]

It was natural that Abert should be pleased with Frémont's work because it brought recognition to the Corps. At the same time the Colonel, as his commanding officer, was in a position to observe Frémont's genuine talent and enthusiasm for the profession of topographical engineering. In Washington he could note the officer's fascination with the intricate, detailed work involved in putting together thousands of astronomical calculations and topographical sketches into a map of the western regions.[8] From his friend Joseph N. Nicollet the Colonel could hear of Frémont's love of the western life with its "grand simplicity," of his ability to adjust himself to the greatest hardships, and to com-

5. Abert to Benton, July 10, 1843, LS, TE 77.
6. Abert to John Pope, Oct. 24, 1851, ibid.
7. Abert to Frémont, April 26, 1843, ibid.
8. Frémont, *Memoirs,* p. 64.

mand the respect of even the wildest mountain man. Thus he saw Frémont's better side; and valuing his talent, the Colonel could, perhaps, all the more appreciate his boundless ambition.

But Frémont was soon caught up in the spirit of Manifest Destiny. As a young and promising officer of the Corps he came under the influence of Senator Benton. When the Senator from Missouri unfolded his own grandiose visions of a western empire, the Lieutenant became a part of the visions, both in spirit and as a practical instrument for achieving them. After one of his first meetings with Benton, Frémont was elated. "In this interview," he wrote, "my mind had been quick to see a larger field and differing and greater results. It would be travel over a part of the world which still remained the new—the opening up of unknown lands; the making unknown countries known; and the study without books—the learning at first hand from nature herself; the drinking first at her unknown springs—became a source of never-ending delight to me." [9] Thus it was that the Lieutenant of the Topographical Corps assumed his larger role and, backed by the higher authority of the powerful Senator, cut himself loose, in spirit at least, from the restraints of the Corps. In his next expeditions he wrote his own orders, ignored any reasons Colonel Abert might have had for sending him to the West, and led his men where he pleased. Only Benton knew the needs of the West, and his word was enough to justify changing the entire scope of his missions, proceeding to California when he was ordered back to Missouri via the Oregon Trail, even finally exchanging his commission as a Topographical Engineer for that of a lieutenant colonel of the Mounted Rifles so that he could follow the fortunes of Manifest Destiny in the Bear Flag Revolt.

Frémont's career as an Army explorer, therefore, illustrates the curious dual position of the Topographical Engineer, indeed of the whole Corps. The Corps occupied a difficult position as an executive agency in which it always ran the danger of becoming too closely involved with particular factions or current enthusiasms. Almost to a man, for example, the officers of the Corps were in accord with the policy of Manifest Destiny. On certain crucial occasions they would come to ally themselves with forces similar in spirit to that represented by Benton which promised

9. Ibid., p. 65.

to advance the cause of national destiny. This would prove to be a severe limitation upon the Corps' usefulness as a national institution, just as it ended Frémont's effectiveness as a scientific observer in the West. Because his career combines, and even exaggerates, this whole complex of talents, enthusiasms, and ambitions, Frémont can be considered an archetypal figure of the Topographical Engineer. He was actually imitated by his colleagues, and at various times they saw themselves as competitors for his fame.

The foundation of Frémont's fame rests upon his two exploring expeditions of 1842 and 1843–44. A closer evaluation of these expeditions as scientific reconnaissances can perhaps best serve to indicate his contributions to the work of the Corps and at the same time indicate its achievements in the West during this period.

Though the year 1842 marks the first real attempt by the Topographical Corps to penetrate the mountain region, there had been several expeditions to the plains region west of the Mississippi between 1838 and 1842. It was on these plains expeditions that Frémont got his first actual experience in the West. Before that, his only contact with a frontier environment came as a result of his reconnaissance of the Cherokee country of Georgia, North Carolina, and Tennessee in 1836–37, under the direction of Captain William G. Williams of the Topographical Engineers.[10] But in 1835, while Frémont was in Georgia, Joseph N. Nicollet, an immigrant French scientist, backed by Pierre Chouteau of the American Fur Company, set out on his first trip up the Mississippi with the object of mapping its upper reaches. When he came back down the river he had his scientific data, and he had also located a stream flowing into Lake Itasca which was the true source of the Mississippi.[11] Nicollet's data was important, and Secretary of War Joel Poinsett called the French scientist to Washington so that he might work more closely with the Topographical Bureau.[12] The formation of the Corps came

10. Ibid., pp. 24–25; see also Nevins, *Frémont, Pathmarker of the West* (above, p. 16, n. 42), pp. 24–27.

11. *DAB.*

12. Frémont, *Memoirs,* 30–31.

in the same year that Nicollet was sent west again, this time with government backing. His second expedition was under the auspices of the new Corps, and his assistant was Poinsett's protégé, Lt. John C. Frémont.[13] The two-year expedition with Nicollet and the subsequent labors on the report of that expedition proved to be Frémont's "Yale College and his Harvard."

The summer of 1838 they spent on a trek westward from Fort Snelling to the Red Pipestone Quarry just east of the present Minnesota-South Dakota border.[14] It was a significant terminal point because there they made contact with the Couteau des Missouri, the extensive escarpment marking the eastern edge of the great upland region stretching westward to the Missouri River. On this expedition the important scientific field work was done by Nicollet and Frémont, assisted by Charles Geyer, an adventurous German botanist. Frémont was impressed with the prairie sights as they marched north toward Renville's Fur Station and the Lac qui Parle, but his romantic feeling for the landscape and the picturesque Indians and Red River traders was in contrast to the scientific preoccupation of Nicollet. "In all this stir of frontier life," Frémont wrote in his *Memoirs,* "Mr. Nicollet felt no interest and took no share; horse and dog were nothing to him. His manner of life had never brought him into their companionship, and the congenial work he now had in charge engrossed his attention and excited his imagination. His mind dwelt continually upon the geography of the country, the Indian names of lakes and rivers, and their signification, and upon whatever tradition might reveal of former travels by early French explorers" (p. 33).

The party returned via the Minnesota River, pausing for a side trip to examine the Mankato or Blue Earth region. Frémont and Nicollet spent the winter in Washington and Baltimore. The following spring they headed a more elaborate expedition up the Missouri River to Fort Pierre. Among the personnel of the party were the mountain voyageurs Louison Frenière, William Dixon, and Etienne Provost. Louis Zindel, a Prussian artillerist, also went along. From Fort Pierre their course took

13. Ibid., pp. 30, 31.

14. Unless otherwise stated, this account is based on Frémont, *Memoirs,* pp. 31–54.

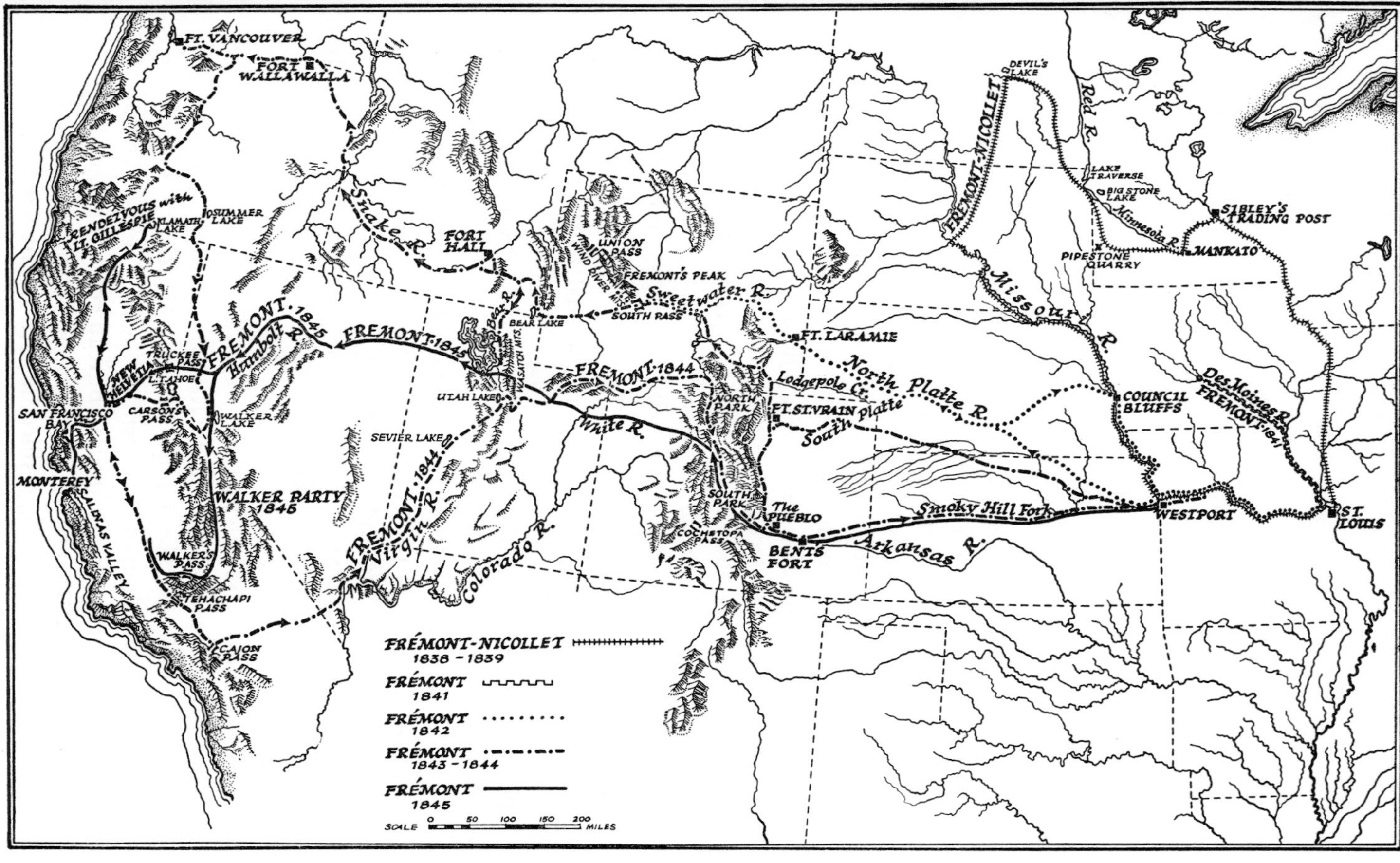

FT. VANCOUVER
FORT WALLAWALLA
Snake R.
FORT HALL
RENDEZVOUS with LT. GILLESPIE
KLAMATH LAKE
SUMMER LAKE
UNION PASS
WIND RIVER MTS.
FREMONT'S PEAK
Sweetwater R.
SOUTH PASS
BEAR LAKE
Bear R.
FT. LARAMIE
FREMONT 1845
Humboldt R.
FREMONT 1845
TRUCKEE PASS
NEW HELVETIA
L. TAHOE
FREMONT 1844
WASATCH MTS.
UTAH LAKE
CARSON'S PASS
WALKER LAKE
SAN FRANCISCO BAY
SEVIER LAKE
White R.
NORTH PARK
FT. ST. VRAIN
Lodgepole Cr.
North Platte R.
South Platte
MONTEREY
SALINAS VALLEY
WALKER PARTY 1845
FREMONT 1844
Virgin R.
Colorado R.
SOUTH PARK
The PUEBLO
COCHETOPA PASS
BENTS FORT
Smoky Hill Fork
Arkansas R.
WALKER'S PASS
TEHACHAPI PASS
CAJON PASS
DEVIL'S LAKE
FREMONT-NICOLLET
Red R.
LAKE TRAVERSE
BIG STONE LAKE
SIBLEY'S TRADING POST
Minnesota R.
MANKATO
PIPESTONE QUARRY
Missouri R.
COUNCIL BLUFFS
Des Moines R.
FREMONT 1841
WESTPORT
ST. LOUIS
FRÉMONT-NICOLLET 1838 - 1839
FRÉMONT 1841
FRÉMONT 1842
FRÉMONT 1843 - 1844
FRÉMONT 1845
SCALE 0 50 100 150 200 MILES

MAP 4

them across the James and Cheyenne rivers and northward to Devil's Lake in present day North Dakota, where they stopped to make extensive scientific investigations. Almost immediately Frémont began learning of the ways of the West. He took part in a buffalo hunt, racing over the rolling prairies; got lost and spent the night alone in Indian country; lived with the Sioux on their annual "surround," and, in short, experienced the free life of a prairie hunter and voyageur. Frémont enthusiastically described this phase of his education:

> Whatever the object may be—whether horseman or antelope or buffalo—that breaks the distant outline of the prairie, the surrounding circumstances are of necessity always such as to give it special interest. The horseman may prove to be enemy or friend, but the always existing uncertainty has its charm of excitement in the one case, and the joy of the chase in the other. There is always the suspense of the interval needed to verify the strange object, and long before the common man decides anything, the practised eye has reached certainty. This was the kind of lore in which Frenière was skilled, and with him my prairie education continued under a master [p. 44].

From Devil's Lake they crossed to the Red River and marched southward to revisit the fur baronage of Renville at Lac qui Parle. Then they followed the Minnesota to Prairie du Chien, where they missed the last steamer for St. Louis and were forced to make a winter's march overland to that city. Nicollet had finished his work in the West, and there remained only the task of analyzing the data and constructing the great map of the upper Mississippi. Frémont had finished his apprenticeship. His next excursion into the West would be an independent command.

The results of Nicollet's three expeditions were incorporated in his brief *Report Intended to Illustrate a Map of the Hydrographical Basin of the Upper Mississippi River.* They represented the first important scientific achievement west of the Mississippi by the Topographical Bureau since the Long expedition of 1819–20. Nicollet's report was published posthumously as a Senate document in 1843, since he died in the summer of that year, "in the night and alone at a hotel" according to Frémont.[15]

The importance of Nicollet's work was best expressed by his own statement of intention. His point of view, somewhat similar to that of Henry Adams toward his scientific history, was that "In the philosophical study of nature, where we seek to determine the *laws* that govern progressive and variable phenomena which are continually presenting themselves, we want chiefly *points of departure,* well fixed, and observations made with care to show us the vicissitudes of the phenomena, so as to connect the present and the past by numerical comparisons of determinate epochs." [16] For an example he quoted Humboldt, who had written, "If only in every thousand years the mean temperature of the atmosphere and of the earth in different latitudes could have been determined . . . we should know in what ratio the heat of different climates has increased or diminished, and if any change has taken place in the height of the atmosphere." [17]

True to his own canons, Nicollet made his report a "point of departure" for further geographical surveys in the trans-Mississippi country. His map was the most important, of course. It was as mathematically accurate as he could make it. All of the observations on which it was based—those for latitude and longitude in determination of various positions, from the Natchez lighthouse to Schoolcraft's Island in Lake Itasca, plus those for the altitude above sea level—taken together, were estimated, by Nicollet, to amount to some 90,000 readings.[18] Three hundred and twenty-six distinct positions along the Mississippi alone, complete as to latitude, longitude, and altitude, were included in an appendix.[19] These were supplements to his cartographic picture of the Northwest country.

Perhaps the most noteworthy technical accomplishment in connection with the map was his use of the barometer in determining the altitude above sea level. Though the method was well known in Europe, it had never been successfully employed in America. Prior to this time, the only recorded attempt had

15. Ibid., p. 412.
16. Nicollet (above, p. 58, n. 87), p. 95.
17. Ibid.
18. Ibid., p. 106.
19. This is my own calculation, from Nicollet, appendix.

been by Stephen H. Long in 1819–20, but in that expedition the barometers were broken before they could be used. In assessing his own cartographic achievements Nicollet wrote: "There remains, then, nothing indeterminate but the form and dimensions of detail objects, such as lakes, the detours and sinuosities of rivers; things of which we can only come to have precise knowledge by systematic surveys which it will be the business of civilized men to establish in proportion as they people the country." [20] Among the sincerest tributes to Nicollet's map was Lt. John Pope's report on Minnesota in 1849, which included a map boldly plagiarized from Nicollet's work.[21]

In the field of natural science, Nicollet discovered Cretaceous fossils along the Missouri, which he was able to link with the specimens discovered by S. G. Morton in New Jersey, and commented upon by him before the Philadelphia Academy of Natural Sciences.[22] Nicollet's researches added weight to the arguments advanced by leading scientists, like Thomas Say, John Finch, Lardner Vanuxem, and S. G. Morton, on behalf of employing fossil correlation as the indispensable tool of the geologist.[23] He himself regarded the hypothesis as already proven by the work of Sir Roderick Murchison on the Devonian rocks of the Boulonais.[24]

Also included in Nicollet's report was a list of fossils and plant specimens collected by Geyer and classified by Torrey. With this his report closed. It was a dry, slim volume for a life's work, but it was an important beginning for others. Nicollet's reputation grew much larger than the printed page, and among his accomplishments not the least were the lessons taught to Frémont that gave scientific meaning to his later adventures in the Rocky Mountains.

It was when they returned to Washington from the 1838 expedition and began work on the map that Frémont came under the influence of Thomas Hart Benton. Between that year (1838)

20. Ibid., p. 107.

21. Abert to Pope, Oct. 2, 1851, LS, TE 77.

22. Nicollet, p. 37.

23. See Merrill, *The First One Hundred Years* (above, p. 00, n. 00), pp. 117–18, for the opinions of Finch, Vanuxem, and Morton in 1828. But as early as 1818 Thomas Say had the same idea: *American Journal of Science, 1* (1818), 382.

24. Nicollet, p. 31.

and 1842 Lieutenant Frémont was sent on only one expedition by the Topographical Bureau. This was a hurried survey of the Des Moines River, which he carried out in the late summer of 1841, less than a year after Capt. W. B. Guion of the Topographical Corps had performed that duty.[25] Though his work had important bearing on the state boundary between Iowa and Missouri, the young Lieutenant always believed he was sent to the West at the behest of Mrs. Benton, who objected to his attentions to her daughter, Jessie.[26]

Nevertheless, when Frémont returned, he married Jessie. The powerful rhetoric of Senator Benton had already attracted Frémont to the cause of Manifest Destiny, and now his romantic feelings had drawn the young Lieutenant even closer to the Benton household. But it was not his marriage to Jessie that caused Frémont to follow Benton. Like most of the Topographical Engineers, he was particularly susceptible to projects for national aggrandizement. They worked as part of an institution dedicated to that cause, and in an atmosphere of romantic optimism and absolute belief in the nation's potential. Most of the officers, and, indeed, the Corps as a whole, were eager to demonstrate their particular usefulness to the cause of national development. Senator Benton's interest offered Frémont his chance to do so, a chance that few officers could have resisted. The marriage to Jessie really only assured Frémont of Benton's continued support, and thus allowed him greater freedom for his projects. Such powerful backing made him a hero in the cause of Manifest Destiny.

If the rhetoric of the "western" men like Benton and his colleague Senator Lewis F. Linn was grandiose and ill-defined, their plans for the West were much more concrete and practical. Since 1818, when Benton had been editor of the St. Louis *Enquirer,* he had worked to secure Oregon for the United States. He believed that Britain possessed no legitimate claim below the 49th parallel, and that the government should terminate its joint occupation agreement and move settlers into its fertile valleys and strategic harbors.[27] Benton, Linn, and John B. Floyd of

25. Frémont to Abert, April 12, 1842, and W. B. Guion to Abert, Oct. 9, 1841; LR, TE 77.
26. Frémont, *Memoirs,* pp. 68–69.
27. Ibid., pp. 59–62.

Virginia offered bills repeatedly in the Senate for the granting of land to Oregon settlers and the extension of federal protection to them. They all failed, though Andrew Jackson was interested enough to send a personal agent to Oregon in search of information about its value.[28] But statistics alone could not secure Oregon, and Benton, searching for ways to aid his cause, saw the possibilities inherent in a much-publicized Rocky Mountain reconnaissance by his son-in-law Frémont. An ardent admirer of Jefferson, Benton undoubtedly remembered the Virginian's skillful employment of Lewis and Clark as an instrument of public policy.[29] The Senator actually believed that he was fulfilling Jefferson's intent when he worked to secure Oregon, and the dispatch of another "scientific" expedition to lead the way was thus all the more appropriate. Like Jefferson, too, Benton was really eager to obtain scientific information about the West. However, he valued the scientific data in a pragmatic sense. It would help him to help his constituents in their conquest of the West.

The actual details of the way in which the western politicians secured an appropriation and persuaded Colonel Abert to send Frémont to the Rocky Mountains have been obscured. All that exists in the way of information is contained in Frémont's *Memoirs*. He describes the extreme secrecy employed to prevent the true political object of the expedition from becoming known. "The amount appropriated was small," he wrote, and "in obtaining this it was necessary to use great caution in order to avoid the opposition which, for various reasons, might be expected." [30] Almost certainly, President Tyler would have resented any move which threatened to disrupt the spirit of Anglo-American harmony existing over the crucial question of the Northeastern Boundary. There is no way of telling what Colonel Abert thought about the expedition, or even whether he realized its implications. Thus at the outset the Corps of Topographical Engineers was committed to a kind of activity in the West that

28. See William A. Slacum, *Report on the Territory of Oregon to Accompany H. R. Bill No. 976,* 25th Cong., 3d Sess., H. R. Rep. 101 (1839), and supplement.

29. Frémont, *Memoirs,* p. 59.

30. Ibid., p. 71.

was neither sanctioned by the chief executive nor clear in its implications for future policy.

Frémont's first expedition to the mountains began in an air of secrecy and restrained excitement. He left Washington on the second of May 1842, and by the twenty-second he was in St. Louis. There he paused only long enough to make arrangements with Pierre Chouteau for his outfit and the procurement of a guide. With him in St. Louis was a tall, red-faced, blond-haired German named Charles Preuss, who was Frémont's topographer and the man destined to make some of the more important maps of the western regions.

On the steamboat heading up the Missouri, Frémont met the second of his two greatest friends, Kit Carson. Of this first meeting Frémont wrote, "I was pleased with him and his manner of address. . . . He was a man of medium height, broad-shouldered and deep chested, with a clear, steady, blue eye and frank speech and address; quiet and unassuming." [31] When Frémont met him, Carson was a veteran of the Rocky Mountain fur trade, well known among his fellow trappers, and much traveled over the mountain and plains region. He did not become a national hero, however, until his exploits became known through Frémont's writings.

At Chouteau's station, up the Missouri, Frémont spent twenty days carefully assembling and equipping his party. Hawkin rifles, ammunition, blankets, cooking kettles, packsaddles, mules, presents for the Indians, and even a patented new inflatable India-rubber boat made up the equipment of the exploring party. Most of the personnel were French voyageurs hired in St. Louis. There was Lucien Maxwell, the hunter, nephew to the famous merchant of Santa Fe, Carlos Beaubien, and others—Basil Lajeunesse, Clement Lambert, Baptiste Bernier, and François La Tulipe—who would become better known as the result of their exertions on the various Frémont expeditions. Of these, Lajeunesse possessed outstanding qualities of daring and skill and courage that made him one of Frémont's favorites.

On the tenth of June the party began its march.[32] A routine

31. Ibid., p. 74.

32. Unless otherwise stated, this account is based on Frémont, *Exploration,* pp. 5–122.

was quickly established. At daybreak the camp was roused and the animals turned out to graze. By seven o'clock the mules were packed, breakfast eaten, and the party on the march. They would stop at noon for an hour or two to rest the animals and then march until nearly sundown. When the evening camp was made, caution was always exercised for fear of Indian attacks. The carts were assembled in a defensive ring, with the horses picketed close by. Three men were on watch at all times during the night. It was obvious that Frémont's expedition was organized down to the last detail.

By day the monotony of the flat country was broken in numerous ways: by problems like the difficulty of fording the swollen Kansas River, where even the mighty Carson caught cold from an untimely fall in the water; by the close observation of nature's details, such as a snake attacking the nests of swallows in a riverbank; by the collection of plants and other kinds of scientific specimens; by meetings with nomad bands of Indians; and by that exciting sport of the plains, the chase after buffalo. In the buffalo hunt sensation was the thing, and with it a feeling for style. Nothing was more appreciated than a good performance in the chase—a clean, one-shot kill made from a racing horse in the midst of a wildly stampeding buffalo herd. "Mounted on a horse, without a saddle, and scouring bareheaded over the prairies," wrote Frémont, "Kit [Carson] was one of the finest pictures of a horseman I have ever seen." [33] It was perhaps the secret of Frémont's success with the crude mountain men that he appreciated to such a degree the joys of their way of life. It was natural for him to adjust to their values without altering his own more purposeful course.

The exploring party followed the regular Oregon Trail across the plains along the Platte, heading straight for the mountains. Several days ahead of them was the emigrant caravan of Elijah White, and every day news drifted back of new calamities, of sickness and death, families wiped out, men turning back in discouragement. It was easy to follow their trail, with its discarded accouterments of civilization.

At the forks of the Platte, Frémont divided his party. Lambert led the main group along the regular trail to Fort Laramie, while

33. Frémont, *Memoirs*, p. 82.

Frémont, Preuss, and four others took the South Fork, heading toward Long's Peak and Fort St. Vrain. Frémont recorded his reason for detouring south:

> In a military point of view, I was desirous to form some opinion of the country relative to the establishment of posts on a line connecting the settlements with the south pass of the Rocky Mountains by way of the Arkansas and the South and Laramie Forks of the Platte. Crossing the country northwestwardly from St. Vrain's Fort to the American [Fur] Company's fort at the mouth of the Laramie would give me some acquaintance with the affluents which head in the mountains between the two.[34]

The South Fork route took them through huge herds of buffaloes, a wild, confused Indian surround, and finally into a large village of Arapaho and Cheyenne Indians, which lay like some feudal encampment on the field of honor. As they rode into the village, almost the first thing Frémont noticed were birchwood racks displaying the warriors' weapons, "scrupulously clean," the spear-heads "burnished bright," and the shield "white and stainless." "It reminded me of the days of feudal chivalry," Frémont wrote, "and when as I rode by, I yielded to the passing impulse and touched one of the spotless shields with the muzzle of my gun, I almost expected a grim warrior to start from the lodge and resent my challenge." [35]

The immediate objective of their march, St. Vrain's Fort, was reached on the tenth of July. It was situated on the South Fork of the Platte about seventeen miles east of Long's Peak, which towered above it. St. Vrain's Fort was an important point because it was the northernmost outpost of Bent, St. Vrain, and Company, whose operations reached as far south as Chihuahua in Mexico. It was on the fur traders' route east of the mountains between Santa Fe and Fort Laramie. Ceran St. Vrain himself was there to assist them in taking on supplies.

From St. Vrain's Fort they marched due north along the mountain escarpment, crossing Lodgepole Creek and heading for the North Platte. In five days they reached Fort Laramie,

34. Ibid., p. 92.

35. Frémont, *Exploration,* pp. 38–39.

most famous of all the fur traders' outposts in the West. Frémont described its setting almost in painter's terms, "A cluster of lodges, which the language told us belonged to the Sioux Indians, was pitched under the walls; and with the fine background of the Black hills and the prominent peak of Laramie mountain strongly drawn in the clear, bright light of the western sky, where the sun had already set, the whole formed at the moment, a strikingly beautiful picture" (p. 49).

When he rejoined his main party, Frémont learned of Indian danger ahead along the Sweetwater River. No less an authority than Jim Bridger had ridden into camp with the news of an uprising by the Oglalla band of the Sioux. Frémont did not hesitate, however. He determined to push on to the South Pass. In a scene that resembled nothing so much as Pizarro confronting his band of Peruvian conquistadors, Frémont drew the men up before him and announced his determination to go on to their destination. Those who "were disposed to cowardice and anxious to return," he said, "had but to come forward at once and state their desire" (p. 61). There was only one man who did, and he was ridiculed by the rest. However, the veteran mountain men soon turned to the serious business of making out their last will and testament.

When they moved out of Fort Laramie, the trail led up the Platte and the Sweetwater via the Red Buttes, Independence Rock, and the Devil's Gate. The Indian danger faded before them as the Oglallas split up into small bands and disappeared into the Wind River Mountains to raid the Crows to the north. Only two painted braves were sighted, and these were promptly captured and questioned. When they were released, the crestfallen warriors rode off a short distance and then shot one of their own horses as a gesture of their bad humor.

On the eighth of August the party reached the South Pass, where they found the summit a disappointing spot between two low hills, fifty or sixty feet high. In visible elevation it seemed no higher to Frémont than Capitol Hill in Washington, and it did not at all resemble the famous passes of the European Alps. The moment of recognition at the summit of the Pass was so unimpressive to Frémont that he failed to make any observations for its exact longitude and latitude. Instead he moved his party eight miles farther and camped on the Little Sandy River, where he then made his calculations for exact position. It must be said, however, that he was only three miles off in his estimate of its distance west from Kansas City, according to the figures derived from the United States Geological Survey cited by Chittenden in 1901.[36]

From the South Pass they turned to the investigation of the Wind River Mountains, finally settling upon a plan to scale what they took to be the highest peak in the chain. It was a time for enshrining one's name in the western wilderness, and the thought of placing "Frémont" on some prominent peak, along with the names of Pike and Long, must certainly have appealed to the young lieutenant's romanticism if not his vanity. As they entered the mountains, the scenery changed from a rolling champagne country to the breath-taking world of Albert Bierstadt. Again, though he remarked the existence of granite rocks, Frémont's reaction was that of an artist rather than a scientist. Nicollet would probably never have written, as did Frémont,

> Here a view of the utmost magnificence and grandeur burst upon our eyes. With nothing between us and their feet to lessen the effect of the whole height, a grand bed of snow-capped mountains rose before us, pile upon pile, glowing in the bright light of an August day. Immediately below them lay the lake, between two ridges, covered with dark pines which swept down from the main chain to the spot where we stood. Here, where the lake glittered in the open sunlight, its banks of yellow sand and the light foliage of aspen leaves contrasted well with the gloomy pines [p. 90].

Making their way past the glittering mountain lakes, they approached the loftiest peak in sight. But before they could begin the climb, Frémont had to turn his ingenuity to the repair of the expedition's last barometer, which had suddenly broken. What seems like a trivial crisis was of the greatest importance, because never before had anyone attempted to measure the altitude of an American mountain with a barometer. Nicollet's ex-

36. Frederick S. Dellenbaugh, *Frémont and '49* (New York, 1914), p. 82.

periments had been on the prairies, and Lieutenant Swift's calculations on the Long expedition had been made by means of mathematical triangulation.

After establishing a base camp, Frémont and a chosen party of eight men began the ascent. Only four of these men besides Frémont actually climbed to the top. Once on the summit, a narrow icy crag, the Pathfinder made his supreme romantic gesture. Standing bareheaded in the cold mountain wind he raised a special American flag with thirteen stripes and a field bearing a triumphant American eagle clasping a bundle of arrows and a pipe of peace in his claws, and surrounded by two banks of stars.[37] It was an impulsive, boyish gesture that captured the imagination of young America. Destiny's screaming eagle had replaced the fabled god Terminus so often referred to by Senator Benton in his public addresses.

Besides his gesture, Frémont's observations, too, were interesting. Standing astride the continental spine he had a panoramic view. Turning in a circle he saw on one side the tributaries "of the Colorado of the Gulf of California," and on the other the Wind River Valley, which he believed to be the source of the Yellowstone. Far to the north were the Grand Tetons, source of the Missouri and the Columbia; to the South were the headwaters of the Platte. "Around us," he wrote, "the whole scene had one main striking feature, which was that of terrible convulsion" (p. 104). His other view was of a bumblebee, which, with a true romantic's eye for the trivia of nature, he noticed in the midst of his moment of sublimity. Like the raising of the flag, Frémont's description of the bee was a romantic gesture so exquisite to his readers that it was remembered long after his description of the geography was forgotten. Significant, also, is the omission of any details of measuring the altitude of the mountain with his barometer.

After the descent from the mountain, the party turned immediately for home. But on the Sweetwater River, Frémont risked his collections in an experiment with his India-rubber boat, and ruined them all when the boat capsized; much of the scientific value of the expedition was lost by his foolhardy gamble. But when he reached St. Louis and civilization, the loss did not seem

37. An illustration of the flag appears in Frémont, *Memoirs,* facing p. 152.

irreparable. He determined to take to the field again the next summer and make even better collections. Meanwhile, he wrote in his journal, "We had climbed the loftiest peak of the Rocky mountains and looked down upon the snow a thousand feet below; and standing where never human foot had stood before, felt the exultation of first explorers" (p. 105).

Frémont, with his wife writing from dictation, assembled his official report as quickly as possible. It passed through the Topographical Bureau and was placed before the Senate on March 2, 1843. One thousand additional copies were ordered printed.[38] The report consisted of Frémont's narrative, a catalogue of the surviving plant specimens by John Torrey, a table of astronomical data which included sixty-eight observations for longitude and latitude, a table of over 600 meteorological readings, and a map of the area from Fort Laramie to the Wind River Mountains. James Dwight Dana, of Yale College, had assisted in making brief geological descriptions of the region by means of the specimens collected and observed. In scientific terms, however, the expedition could hardly be called a success. Professor Torrey's list of plants included only a few new species, although he noted that several descriptions had been omitted because of the anxiety of Benton and the western men to rush the report into print.[39] This in itself suggests the basic purpose of the expedition. In addition, Preuss' map had only limited utility for westbound emigrants, since it had few details which would indicate water holes or timber stands, all-important information to the overland traveler. Moreover, since the map covered only the area between Fort Laramie and Frémont's peak, it was no help for the most difficult part of the journey on the far side of the South Pass. There were correctable errors in the longitude and latitude calculations, and the altitude of Frémont's peak was underestimated by 180 feet.[40]

But if the scientific value of this first official trip into the Rocky Mountains was negligible, its broader impact made up for the deficit. Another Oregon bill was launched to coincide

38. 27th Cong., 3d Sess., Sen. Exec. Doc. 243 (1842–43), introductory resolution.

39. Ibid., p. 81.

40. Dellenbaugh, p. 87.

with Frémont's return; and though the House failed to vote forts or land grants or anything else to the Oregon settlers, the signs for eventual passage were more encouraging than previously.[41] Even more important was the impression that Frémont made on the public mind. His feats as an explorer were the perfect expression of individual heroism as it represented the romantic vision of a grand national destiny. The best description of the report's impact was given years later by Joaquin Miller. He described in his autobiography how he felt as his father read Frémont's report to the family by candlelight in their Ohio farm:

> I never was so fascinated. I never grew so fast in my life. Every scene and circumstance in the narrative was painted in my mind to last and to last forever. . . . I fancied I could see Frémont's men, hauling the cannon up the savage battlements of the Rocky Mountains, flags in the air, Frémont at the head, waving his sword, his horse neighing wildly in the mountain wind, with unknown and unnamed empires on every hand. It touched my heart when he told how a weary little brown bee tried to make its way from a valley of flowers far below across a spur of snow, where he sat resting for a moment with his men; how the bee rested on his knee till it was strong enough to go on to another field of flowers beyond the snow; and how he waited a bit for it to go at its will.
>
> I was no longer a boy . . . now I began to be inflamed with a love for action, adventure, glory, and great deeds away out yonder under the path of the setting sun.[42]

To the people of the time, as to Miller, exact details seemed to matter little. Episodes and impressions conveying emotion were all that was important. What did the public at large care for precise knowledge when it had such noble deeds to contemplate, and such heroes to worship? And yet, on closer examination, there was a disappointing hollowness about Frémont's work.

41. Frémont, *Memoirs,* p. 165.

42. Joaquin Miller, *Overland in a Covered Wagon,* ed. Sidney G. Firman (New York, 1930), pp. 42–43.

He had been wrong, for example, when he claimed to have climbed the "highest peak of the Rocky Mountains." There were at least twenty others taller, even one in the Wind River chain itself.[43] He was probably not even the first to scale that peak: Captain Bonneville, according to Irving's account, had done it in 1835.[44] It becomes difficult, too, to account for his failure to pinpoint the exact location of South Pass, which was the main scientific excuse for the expedition. Thus despite Colonel Abert's emphatic approval the results of Frémont's 1842 expedition were of little value to science, while at the same time the Topographical Bureau had been committed to activities that ventured far beyond the realm of science into that of national politics.

The Great Reconnaissance of 1843–44

In the early spring of 1843 Colonel Abert wrote to Senator Benton: "I have the honor to acknowledge the receipt of your letter of the seventh inst., and to thank you for your suggestions in reference to the survey now required in the vicinity of the Rocky Mountains. Be assured that they will receive the greatest attention. A sketch embracing your views has been enclosed to Mr. Frémont in order to obtain from him the customary estimate." [45] Thus was outlined the precise manner in which Frémont's project for 1843 was formulated. The Topographical Bureau, while it assumed the responsibility for Frémont's expeditions, in reality served merely as a clearing house for Benton's ventures in western exploration.[46]

The orders drawn up by Colonel Abert directed Frémont "to connect the reconnaissance of 1842 with the surveys of Commander Wilkes on the coast of the Pacific Ocean, so as to give a connected survey of the interior of our continent." [47] In 1841–42 Commander Wilkes had made a reconnaissance in Oregon as far

43. Dellenbaugh, p. 87.

44. Ibid.

45. Abert to Benton, March 10, 1843, LS, TE 77.

46. Ibid. See also enclosed sketch of Frémont's duties based upon Benton's suggestions.

47. Frémont, *Report, 1843–44,* p. 123.

as Fort Walla Walla.[48] He also sent the Emmons-Eld party south into California, and from these field surveys a reliable map of the Northwest was compiled. The plans of the Topographical Bureau and of Benton now called for Frémont to link his explorations with those of Wilkes. He was to return from Oregon by way of the regular Oregon Trail.[49] Again the political purpose was obvious. Publicity resulting from the expedition would serve to point up the importance of Oregon, as well as California.

Frémont's 1843–44 expedition was above everything else a chronicle of heroic adventure. In this quality lay its value as a means of inspiring western emigration and settlement, as well as capturing national attention. Also, with a year's experience in commanding his own expedition, Frémont paid closer attention to the details of science, with more impressive results. However, in the last analysis his great expedition must be viewed in his own romantic terms. Again, as in 1842, he saw the West with the eye of an artist, and his narrative reveals the emotional quality of his experience in first penetrating the mountainous wilderness. For this reason a mere listing of his achievements fails to get at what Frémont was really doing in the West. To understand his importance it is necessary to follow along with him in his adventurous march.

Frémont began his expedition of 1843–44 by incurring the displeasure of Colonel Abert, as noted above, over his inclusion of a howitzer as part of the scientific equipment. But thanks to his wife, Jessie, the Pathfinder was well on his way before anything could be done to halt the expedition.[50] His party consisted of thirty-nine men, partly recruited in St. Louis and the rest signed on at the Kansas Landing. It included French voyageurs, mountain men, and a few green hands who had drifted west from the frontier farming communities. The legendary mountain veteran Tom "Broken Hand" Fitzpatrick was the guide. Lucien Maxwell was the hunter. Also along as a kind of supercargo were three tenderfeet, Theodore Talbot of Wash-

48. See Charles Wilkes, *Narrative of the United States Exploring Expedition during the Years 1838, 1839, 1840, 1841, 1842*, 5 vols. and atlas, Phila., 1844.

49. See sketch referred to in Abert to Benton, March 10, 1843, LS, TE 77, which was enclosed as part of Frémont's instructions.

50. Frémont, *Memoirs*, pp. 167–68.

ington, Frederick Dwight of Springfield, Massachusetts, and Jacob Dodson, a young Negro servant of the Benton household. Charles Preuss represented the interests of professional science. His duties were to collect specimens, help with the astronomical observations, take care of the fragile scientific instruments, and made topographical sketches of the landscape. That Preuss and Frémont were the only scientifically trained men on the expedition is a measure of the extent of its scientific objectives.

Even the amount of scientific equipment was surprisingly meager. There was one refracting telescope by Frauenhofer, one reflecting circle by Gambey, two sextants by Troughton, one pocket chronometer by Goffe and Falmouth and another by Brockbank, six thermometers, and a number of small compasses.[51] Despite the experience of the previous year, they carried only *two* barometers, one syphon type and one cistern type. For an extended expedition the scientific equipment was totally inadequate, though it was probably sufficient for a rapid reconnaissance of the type Frémont actually carried out.

The early spring of 1843 was a difficult one in which to outfit an expedition. It was the year of the "great migration" to Oregon, when over a thousand settlers filed through the passes to the valleys of the Columbia and Willamette. Some were already heading for California. Missionaries, too, were in evidence. Two Belgian priests were starting out for Father De Smet's vineyard in the Flathead country. Most colorful of all was the hunting cavalcade being formed by the British officer Sir William Drummond Stewart. Himself a veteran of the Rocky Mountains, Stewart was making one last hunt in the grand manner before settling down to the dull life in an old English castle.[52] For him, a hunt along the Seeds-kee-dee with his old friends the mountain men was the only proper sport in the world. When they met, the English sportsman suggested that Frémont join forces with him as far as the Green River, but the Pathfinder refused. Perhaps his inherent distrust of the English led him to

51. Ibid., p. 170.

52. Theodore Talbot, *The Journals of Theodore Talbot,* ed. Charles H. Corey (Portland, Ore., 1931), p. 5. For a more colorful account of Stewart's excursion see Alvin M. Josephy, Jr., "First 'Dude Ranch' Trip to the Untamed West," *American Heritage,* 7 (Feb., 1956), 8–15.

suspect that sport was not the only objective of Stewart's lavish excursion.

Because of the difficulty over the howitzer Frémont quickly terminated his preparations and moved out on his way. They followed the Oregon Trail for a time but eventually turned south of the regular route to explore the line of the Kansas River. Trains of wagons were constantly in sight, giving the road an almost populous appearance. At Elm Grove they overtook the J. B. Chiles party bound for California. At this point, too, Manifest Destiny in the person of William Gilpin joined Frémont's party. Gilpin, a Philadelphian transformed by the bustling frontier, was a politician without a constituency, ever ready to serve the westward march in some capacity. At the time, he was on his way to Oregon, the frontier of the moment. He was also a philosopher. With ideas mostly copied from Humboldt, he could see a grand geopolitical destiny for America in which the settlers moving westward along Humboldt's carefully determined line of world population migrations would inevitably make the valley of the Mississippi and the western plains the heartland of an American Empire.[53] Though he was to ride with Doniphan on his epic march across Mexico, all most people could remember of Gilpin was his unfortunate experience with a mule that had departed with all his equipment, leaving him a chastened figure alone in the dusty main street of Independence, Missouri. Gilpin's mule, but never Gilpin, gained renown on the frontier.

In a sense it was fitting that those two colorful personalities the pathfinder and the politician should journey west together in 1843. They were similar in many respects—in energy, in their possession of a certain erratic brilliance—but most of all in their frantic—often unseemly—struggles to gain public recognition. Both men appeared always on the verge of greatness, but there remained more than a touch of the comic about their lives, a distortion that caused them to fall humiliatingly just short of the mark they had set for themselves.

53. William Gilpin, *Mission of the North American People, Geographical, Social, and Political. Illustrated by Six Charts Delineating the Physical Architecture and Termal Laws of All the Continents*, Phila., 1873. See also Hubert Howe Bancroft, *History of the Life of William Gilpin . . .* (San Francisco, 1889) for general biographical details.

Following the line of the Kansas, the party reached the Big Timbers on June 16.[54] Here they split into two divisions, with Fitzpatrick leading the main group of twelve wagons northward to the emigrant route on the Platte. Frémont and fifteen men continued straight ahead in a more rapid survey. The plan was to meet at St. Vrain's Fort. After the separation, Frémont's men found themselves on a high level prairie, where buffalo appeared in immense herds and prairie dog communities were scattered everywhere underfoot. After ten days of traveling, the scenery changed to bare sand hills and gently rolling terrain. The climate was dry, and the sluggish rivers struggled along through treeless banks.

At St. Vrain's Fort they paused to celebrate the Fourth of July and then departed southward to the Fontaine-qui-Bouille (Fountain Creek) on the upper Arkansas, where there was a rude furtrader's settlement called the Pueblo. It was at this point that Kit Carson joined the party. At the same time Lucien Maxwell, who had ridden south to Taos for fresh mules, was prevented from rejoining his comrades by an Indian uprising. Without Maxwell and the mules, the party headed north to where Frémont was to attempt the tracing of a new route through the mountains. They followed the Cache de la Poudre River, a tributary of the South Platte, into the Laramie Mountains. Despite the long experience of Carson and Fitzpatrick, there was no one in the party who knew the region. It was never a promising place for taking beaver, and few mountain men had ventured to explore it. Those who did, according to Frémont, had "dwindled to a few scattered individuals—some one or two of whom are regularly killed in the course of each year by the Indians" (p. 147). This was one difficulty with the specialized geographical knowledge which the mountain man possessed: it could die with them.

Finally, however, the party secured the services of Alexis Godey, one of the most skillful of the mountain men. Then Frémont led a picked party of thirteen men up the Cache de la Poudre, while Fitzpatrick again took the main force along the Sweetwater emigrant route. The exploring party never found the pass they

54. Unless otherwise stated, the account that follows is based on Frémont, *Report, 1843–44*.

were looking for. Instead they were forced to pick their way over the broken and rocky country and through the mountains to the Laramie Plains on the western side. Eventually the original plan was abandoned and they turned northward to the Sweetwater, crossing the mountains via the South Pass.

When they crossed the Green River, Frémont remembered looking southward down its beautiful valleys, which had served so often as summer rendezvous for the mountain men. He also recalled that much of the river was still enshrouded in mystery. "The Indians have strange stories of beautiful valleys abounding with beaver, shut up among inaccessible walls of rock in the lower cañons of the river; and to which the neighboring Indians in their occasional wars with the Spaniards and among themselves drive their herds of cattle and flocks of sheep, leaving them to pasture in perfect security" (p. 163). No trapper had ever undertaken a voyage down the river, though James Ohio Pattie had probably followed along the rim of its canyons as far back as 1822.[55]

On the Muddy Fork of the Ham River Frémont found coal deposits and fossil specimens that seemed to resemble those appearing in the famous stratigraphic sections of Europe. Thanks to his tutoring under Nicollet, he was able to identify them and recognize their value.

Presently they reached the Bear River—which runs north, then south, into the Great Salt Lake—and they felt elated at being so near one of the primary objectives of the expedition, the mysterious inland sea of the West.

> Hitherto [Frémont wrote] the lake had been seen only by trappers who were wandering through the country in search of new beaver streams, caring very little for geography; its islands had never been visited, and none were found who had entirely made the circuit of its shores; and no instrumental observations or geographical survey of any description had ever been made anywhere in the neighboring region. It was generally supposed that it had no visible outlet; but among the trappers, including those in my own camp, were many who believed that somewhere on the surface was

55. Pattie, *Personal Narrative* (above, p. 45, n. 65), pp. 137–38.

> a terrible whirlpool, through which its waters found their way to the ocean by some subterranean communication [p. 168].

On September 6, after weeks of groping down the valley of the Bear River and across miles of marshy bottom land, they were finally rewarded. From the top of a small butte they could see the Great Salt Lake: "the object of our anxious search—the waters of the inland sea, stretching in still and solitary grandeur far beyond the limits of our vision." Frémont added, "I am doubtful if the followers of Balboa felt more enthusiasm when, from the heights of the Andes, they saw the great Western Ocean" (p. 198). The party made camp on the banks of the Weber River, which flows into the lake from the east. On the following morning Frémont, Preuss, Carson, Bernier, and Basil Lajeunesse dragged the inflated rubber boat over the mud flats to the lake and embarked on a marine reconnaissance. They attempted no systematic survey of the lake because of damage suffered by their boat. Instead, they paddled to a large island, set up camp, and scanned the horizon with their telescopes. Frémont noted in his report: "We felt pleasure also in remembering that we were the first who, in the traditional annals of the country, had visited the islands and broken with the sound of human voices, the long solitude of the place" (p. 205). However, he did not know that in 1826 Jim Bridger and a party of trappers had paddled around most of the lake in improvised bull boats.[56]

They spent only a few days in the vicinity of the lake, collecting plants and rock specimens and making astronomical observations to fix its exact location on future maps. The exploration was too rapid to be more than a superficial survey, and perhaps the most important result was Frémont's general evaluation of the country around the lake and in the vicinity of the Bear and Weber rivers. He believed it formed "a natural resting and recruiting station for travelers, now, and in all time to come" (p. 217). In his report he termed the bottom land "extensive," the water "excellent," the timber "sufficient," and the soil "good and well-adapted to grains and grasses suited to such an elevated region." In his view, it was "truly a bucolic region" (p. 213). He

56. Cecil J. Alter, *James Bridger* (Salt Lake City, 1925), pp. 71–72.

recommended the establishment of a military post at some point near the lake. It was Frémont's report with its glowing descriptions that persuaded Brigham Young that the Great Salt Lake was, indeed, the place for his people to settle.[57]

Fort Hall, the Hudson's Bay station on the Oregon Trail, was the explorer's next stop. Here the whole party was assembled for the first time since they had parted at Fort St. Vrain. The reunion was short-lived, however, as eleven of the explorers turned back for civilization. The post itself irritated Frémont, because it represented a foreign claim to what was, in his mind, American soil. He recommended that here, too, an American military post be constructed. "Such a post," he asserted, "would naturally form the *nucleus* of a settlement" (p. 217).

From Fort Hall the now consolidated exploring party went up the Snake River past Fort Boise and out onto the Columbia Plateau. Frémont's journal describes it as "a melancholy and strange-looking country—one of fracture and violence and fire" (p. 224). Their route took them, via the Grand Ronde, to Marcus Whitman's mission at Walla Walla. When they reached this point, they could see, straight ahead in the distance, the white shadow of Mount Hood, 180 miles away. After leaving Walla Walla, they followed the Columbia to the Dalles. Along the way they passed the famous emigrant Jesse Applegate and his men, poling flatboats down the river on the last leg of their journey to Oregon. At the Dalles, Frémont made his base camp; and leaving his men to rest after their long journey, he went on alone to Fort Vancouver to meet Doctor McLoughlin. From his observations he was able to form an optimistic impression of the prosperity of the settlers and the prospects for its becoming American territory in the future. Significantly, in terms of Benton's plans for Oregon, Frémont did not bother to examine the harbor facilities at the mouth of the Columbia but concentrating on the agricultural settlement, he was more impressed by the sound of a sawmill working late into the night and with the number of new American settlers pouring into the country every day.

With his arrival at Fort Vancouver, Frémont had carried out his official orders. Having surveyed the Oregon Trail and revealed

57. Young in an interview for the New York *Times,* quoted in Frémont, *Memoirs,* pp. 415–16.

the mysteries of the Great Salt Lake, he had only to retrace his steps to the Mississippi Valley. It was true he had located no new pass or any new route to Oregon, but he had at least obtained a general idea of the western geography. He had also made clear the potential value of the whole region, and the needs of the incoming settlers. For a whole generation of people his report and map were to serve as guides for their trek to the promised empire on the Pacific.

Once he had run his survey as far as that covered in the Wilkes report, Frémont's official duty was done. But instead of making an immediate return, he looked to a further set of objectives beyond the scope of his orders. On the homeward journey, he proposed to march his men in a great arc toward the Southwest, which would give him an idea of that imperfectly known region of mesa and desert and canyon. He had three immediate objectives: an examination of the Klamath Lake area, which he believed formed a table land between the heads of the Des Chutes River and the Sacramento; a search for the legendary Buenaventura River, which was said to flow westward from the Rocky Mountains to the Pacific; and a survey of the Rockies near the headwaters of the Arkansas and Colorado rivers.[58] The first of these was based on the idea that Klamath Lake might be the outlet of a water passage from the Great Basin to the sea. If this idea proved to be true, it would be important to know whether the outlet lay above the 42nd parallel in territory claimed by the United States.

It has been pointed out by historians that Frémont had only to look at Gallatin's map of 1836 or Bonneville's maps of 1837 to find that there was no truth to the legend of the Buenaventura.[59] Moreover, he might have had access to Jedediah Smith's data, through Doctor McLoughlin at Fort Vancouver, which would have proved the nonexistence of the fabled river.[60] This latter contention seems debatable, however, for it must be based solely on Frémont's references to Smith's unfortunate experiences in the Klamath country in 1827,[61] and Benton's assertion in *Thirty*

58. Frémont, *Memoirs,* pp. 285–86.

59. Dellenbaugh, *Frémont and '49,* pp. 177–78.

60. Frémont met and talked with Dr. McLoughlin when he visited Fort Vancouver: *Report, 1843–44,* pp. 262–63.

61. Ibid., pp. 286–87.

Years' View that Doctor McLoughlin had given Frémont faulty information.[62] In any event the criticism is not really fair to Frémont. What officer or scientist with access to what were supposedly the most advanced maps of his time would set out on an exploring expedition, totally ignoring them in favor of a map of demonstrable vagueness appearing in a popular romance? How was he to judge the validity of the Bonneville-Irving map against those he saw in the Topographical Bureau, which included the River? How could he be sure of Bonneville's competence as a map maker, or even that Joseph Walker's march, from which the relevant portions of the maps were derived, was not such as to make him turn west into California far enough north so that he would have missed the river on his outgoing trek; or that, following the Humboldt on his way home, Walker had not turned east into the Great Basin just south of where the Buenaventura ran? Both the Bonneville and the Gallatin maps were obviously the work of amateurs, and the latter was so obscure that, as has been previously noted, Lieutenant Warren even overlooked it in his memoir on western exploration.

As for the question of Jedediah Smith's data, it seems likely that the only thing Frémont knew for certain of Smith was that he had traversed the country and had suffered a frightful disaster near Klamath Lake. This much he could have learned from men in his own employ. There is no certainty that he actually saw a Smith map or that Doctor McLoughlin even knew what Smith had learned about the country. If Frémont had been told of Smith's findings by someone at Fort Vancouver, it seems logical to conclude that he would not have risked having his men search for a river he knew was not there, and he would have mentioned this startling information in his journal, particularly since he greatly admired the mountain men.

In any case, as a scientist he would have been justified in going south to check these important theories for himself rather than accepting dubious authority. This was the real achievement of the Topographical Corps: they brought the element of trustworthiness inherent in the scientific method to the making of western maps where only the uncertain perpetuation of myth, resting on dubious authority, existed before. Though they made

62. Vol. 2, p. 560.

relatively few major geographical discoveries, their account of what they did see had a much greater factor of dependability.

In considering Frémont's three objectives, perhaps it is not too ingenious to speculate that he might have been looking for a water route across the far-western country that connected the Klamath by way of the Buenaventura to the headwaters of the Arkansas. If such a route did happen to exist below the 42nd parallel, a revision of American policy directed toward the acquisition of California might become necessary. In his report he said nothing about such an idea, however, but instead dwelt upon the prospects for unlimited scientific discovery in that *terra incognita.*

With a party of twenty-five men, Frémont started southward on a course paralleling the Des Chutes River.[63] Mount Hood stood out on their right and provided a guide which indicated the rate of their daily progress. On December 10 they reached the marshes on the eastern border of Klamath Lake that formed its overflow basin. Three days later the explorers stumbled upon the Klamath River, mistaking it in a blinding snowstorm for the Sacramento. The mistaken discovery caused great exultation because it was thus believed that the Sacramento had its source in American territory.

Toward noon on December 16 they rode out onto a rocky precipice and looked down at a view one thousand feet below. They saw " a green prairie country with a beautiful lake . . . its shores bordered with green grass." "And just then," Frémont remembered, "the sun broke out among the clouds and illuminated the country below, while around us the storm raged fiercely. . . . the glow of the sun in the valley below brightened up our hearts with sudden pleasure; and we made the woods ring with joyful shouts to those behind" (pp. 289–90). What they were seeing, far below them, was part of the Great Basin that extended eastward as far as the Wasatch Mountains on the other side of the Great Salt Lake. Frémont's conceptualization of the great depression between the Sierras and the Wasatch was particularly striking. Across the large empty space on his map he arched the resounding descriptive legend: "The Great Basin; diameter 11°

63. Unless otherwise stated, the acount is based on Frémont, *Report, 1843–44.*

of latitude, 10° of longitude: elevation above the sea between 4 and 5,000 feet: surrounded by lofty mountains: contents almost unknown, but believed to be filled with rivers and lakes which have no communication with the sea, deserts and oases which have never been explored, and savage tribes which no traveler has seen or described." [64]

Descending from the rim of the Basin, the party made its way southward paralleling the Sierra Nevadas. The month of December passed and half of January, but still they had found no sign of the Rio Buenaventura. They had even missed the Humboldt River. On January 19 Frémont decided to turn westward and cross the Sierras into California. Coming upon a substantial stream which seemed to issue from these mountains, the party followed its course in a westward direction. Soon there were Indians circling all around them on snowshoes, "skimming about like birds" (p. 318). They held a parley with one group of these people to determine how far the settlements in California lay to the West, and also to secure a guide. The Indians were reluctant to act as guides because, as they said, it was six days of ordinary travel over the mountains, and in winter, when the snow was over their heads, it was impossible. They advised the party to winter on the shores of Lake Tahoe, one day's march to the north. But Frémont impressed several of the Indians as guides, and on February first began a winter assault on the Sierra Nevadas. The temperature was near zero, and snow fell steadily all day and all night. The Indian guide shook his head and pointed to the mountain towering directly above them.

Almost immediately they were plunged into deep snow. For four days they marched, taking turns in breaking a trail through the snow for those who followed. Whenever they could, they kept to the exposed hillsides, where the wind blew the snow thin and scattered tufts of exposed grass provided food for the horses. On the night of February 4 two local Indians came into camp and told them more news of what lay ahead. "Rock upon rock, rock upon rock, snow upon snow," they said (p. 329). Even a Chinook boy from Fort Vancouver, who belonged to the party, looked around into the gloomy forest and the cold night and then gave

64. See map accompanying 28th Cong., 2d Sess., Sen. Exec. Doc. 174, 1844–45.

up hope. He pulled his blanket over his head and cried. That night the last of the captive guides deserted.

Two days later they ascended a slight promontory, and Kit Carson recognized, far ahead, dimmed by the distance, a low range of mountains he had seen once fifteen years before. When they reached these mountains (actually the Coast Range), they would be in California. But to reach the valley of the Sacramento they still had to cross the Sierras dead ahead. Already the snow had reached depths up to twenty feet. The altitude was 8,050 feet, over 1,000 feet higher than the South Pass. The depth of the snow continued to increase, and for five more days they flailed and plunged their way ahead, until finally the horses began to flounder helplessly in the snow. The men then took mauls and shovels and dug out a road. Frémont's advance party worked backward toward Fitzpatrick's main group which they could see three miles away, digging its way forward. Besides the cold and the snow and the almost impossible exertions demanded of them, hunger, too, began its assault as the supplies ran low. Their common fare consisted of pea soup, mule meat, and dog.

By February 20 they had reached the summit of the pass, 9,338 feet high. Here was a range of mountains, as Frémont remarked, "still higher than the great Rocky Mountains themselves" (p. 336). From the summit the way was downhill, but the toughest road was still ahead. The weather turned warmer, but just enough to melt the snow crust, so that men and animals sank deep into the drifts. Once Frémont fell into an ice-cold mountain stream, but Carson plunged in to the rescue, and even his rifle was saved. At the end of that harrowing day, as the weary men sat around the campfires, Frémont remembered, "Many of the men looked badly; and some this evening were giving out" (p. 339).

Two days later they had descended to approximately 4,000 feet, and the stream they were following became a river. On the first day of March one of the men lost his mind and went for a swim in the roaring ice-cold torrent just as if it were summer, and the river a placid pond. Another man came into camp, sat by the fire, and commenced to have hallucinations. Before the adventure was over, he was destined to wander off into the mountains, never to be seen again. At this point even Frémont had to admit that "The times were severe when stout men lost their minds" (p. 344). The only encouragement was that the snow was beginning to disappear and they were fast approaching the warmer climate of the valley below. When they reached the foothills, Charles Preuss spent three days lost without food or firearms. He solved his problem by placing his hand in a large nest of ants, and then licked them off his hand. According to Frémont whose information was second hand, they "had an agreeable acid taste" (p. 349). When Preuss finally caught up with the advance party, it was March 5 and they had reached the springtime lands on the valley floor. It was not long before they met some California Indians, and a vaquero in the service of Captain John Sutter. The vaquero told them they were on the American River and that Sutter's Ranch was just over the hill.

Meanwhile, the rest of the party straggled, man by man and mule by mule, down from the mountain pass. It had been a fantastic test of their endurance and courage. Somewhere back on the mountain, however, they had lost the mule carrying all of the plant specimens, when it tumbled off an icy precipice into a mountain river far below. A good part of the expedition's scientific value had gone with it. But at least, as Frémont had said once before after the Nicollet expedition, they "had made an experience."

Sutter's Ranch was a perfect illustration of California's abundant promise. Frémont's glowing descriptions of the fertile land and the extensive gardens, as well as of the industrious citizens spinning wool and making other commodities, helped to call the attention of western emigrants to California. Sutter's Fort Frémont described as "a quadrangular adobe structure mounting twelve pieces of artillery . . . and capable of admitting a garrison of a thousand men. . . . The inner wall is formed into buildings, comprising the common quarters, with blacksmith and other workshops; the dwelling house, with a large distillery house, and other buildings, occupying more the center of the area" (p. 354). It was obvious that Captain Sutter lived like some feudal baron in his self-sufficient adobe castle, with his serfs and his men-at-arms. There were even two vessels belonging to the Captain, which rode at anchor in the river while they were being loaded for a voyage to Fort Vancouver. While they were at Sutter's Fort, Frémont again met J. B. Chiles, whose California caravan they had left at Elm Grove. Like two modern American tourists they discussed the trials and triumphs of the outward journey.

On March 24 Frémont's party, re-outfitted and ready to march, left Sutter's hospitality, heading down the Sacramento to the San Joaquin, which they hoped to follow to Walker's Pass, and the southern route back to the Mississippi Valley. They were aiming for the regular Spanish trail across the Mojave Desert and into Santa Fe. Along the way they marveled at green pastures and fresh-flowing streams. Herds of animals—elk and wild horses—were continually in evidence. Grizzly bear tracks abounded. The whole country seemed fresh and promising and alive. It was no wonder that Frémont's descriptions inspired people to take the trail to California.

Riding southward, they crossed over the San Joaquin where it curves down from the Sierras and passed by the Tulare Lakes. Soon they had reached the foot of the great interior valley of California. Near the site of present-day Bakersfield they turned southeast and entered the Tehachapi Pass, mistaking it for Walker's Pass, which was further north. As they left California, Frémont reviewed his geographic achievements. They had become acquainted with the Sierra Nevadas, established their connection with the Cascade Range, and pointed up the existence of a separate coastal range. Most important of all, he could declare confidently, "No river from the interior does, or can, cross the Sierra Nevada—itself more lofty than the Rocky Mountains" (p. 369). This led him to a further conclusion in the realm of geopolitics: "thus, this want of interior communication from the San Francisco Bay, now fully ascertained, gives great additional value to the Columbia which leads from the ocean to the Rocky Mountains, and opens a line of communication from the sea to the valley of the Mississippi" (p. 370).

From the Tehachapi Pass they rode southeastward, until on April 18 near Cajon Pass they struck the Spanish Trail. Ahead lay the broad desert, and then the Colorado River. Six days later, in the dry country, a Mexican man and boy ran into their camp. They were the sole survivors of an Indian raid upon their horse caravan bound for Sonora. Carson and Godey, alone, rode off in pursuit of the Indians, determined to recapture the horses and exact vengeance. The next afternoon, with a war whoop, the two mountain men returned to the caravan, driving the horses and dangling two bloody scalps from a gun. They had ridden most of the day and part of the night. At daylight they surprised the Indian camp in a bold two-man charge. Carson related the details of the battle. They "fired their rifles upon a steady aim, and rushed in, two Indians were stretched upon the ground, fatally pierced with bullets: the rest fled, except a little lad who was captured. The scalps of the fallen were instantly stripped off; but in the process, one of them, who had two balls through his body, sprang to his feet, the blood streaming from his skinned head, and uttered a hideous howl. . . . they did what humanity required, and quickly terminated the agonies of the gory savage" (p. 381). They were masters of the camp, and as they surveyed their conquest they couldn't help noticing the remarkable stoicism of their small captive, who sat quietly gnawing at his food, a horse's head, unmoved by the misfortunes of the others. Abandoning the boy, the hunters rode as rapidly as possible back to the main expedition, where they made their triumphant return. When, several days later, they reached the Mexican camp site and set about the task of burying the massacred victims, "all compunction for the scalped alive Indian ceased and we rejoiced that Carson and Godey had been able to give so useful a lesson to these American Arabs who lie in wait to murder and plunder the innocent traveller" (p. 384). After Carson's and Godey's skirmish, large bands of Utah Indians began to menace the party, and one careless voyageur fell victim to the Indian revenge.

They reached the camping ground at Las Vegas and then continued north along the Sevier River. One day they were joined by the great mountain man Joseph Walker, who had ridden alone through the hostile Indians to reach them. He became the guide, and Frémont was able to compare impressions of the Great Basin with him. In his journal Frémont wrote, "Mr. Joseph Walker, our guide . . . has more knowledge of these parts than any man I know" (p. 395). They followed the Sevier River to Utah Lake, and here, despite the help of Walker, Frémont made his greatest geographical blunder, which eventually led to a long dispute with Brigham Young. He declared the Utah to be the southern arm of the Great Salt Lake. This assertion was repeated at least twice in his journal, so there is no mistaking the faultiness of his assertion (pp. 398–99). In making the claim, the Pathfinder ought certainly to have noticed the impropriety of terming a freshwater lake part of the Great Salt Lake. But he had no time for an extensive survey, and the error, while obvious, seems minor in comparison with his total achievement.

From Utah Lake they marched almost due east along the Duchesne Fork and the White River across northern Utah into Colorado. On the way they visited the ill-fated Uinta Mountain trading post of Antoine Robideau, which was wiped out not many weeks after they left it. Their course continued eastward via Brown's Hole, Vermillion Creek, and St. Vrain's Fork of the Green River, till on June 13 they ascended a mountain and saw spread out before them "the valley of the Platte, with the pass of the Medicine Butte beyond" (p. 411). They were back in familiar country. An eastward course led directly home, but instead Frémont turned southward to explore the three central "parks" of Colorado. After narrowly escaping an Indian war in one of the parks the explorers trudged into the little settlement of Pueblo on June 29. Two days later, when they reached Bent's Fort, they were saluted by "a display of the national flag and repeated discharges from the guns of the fort" (p. 422). Here the party disbanded, with Walker and Carson remaining behind while Frémont and the rest of the men continued on to St. Louis. Though the balance of the trek was over relatively familiar ground, it still proved eventful. They ran into Arapaho and Pawnee warriors ready for battle, and, worst of all, on the night of July 10 the Kansas River overflowed and washed away most of the expedition's supplies. Again, the plant specimens were lost.

Eventually the expedition came to an end; around midnight on August 6, 1844, Frémont jumped ashore in St. Louis from a small steamboat that had taken him downstream from Kansas Landing. He had led successfully the most spectacular official reconnaissance of the American West since Lewis and Clark, and its results would be a definite aid to American settlement.

The Significance of Frémont's Work

Frémont returned to Washington in triumph. More than anything else, his remarkable exploration had been a supreme gesture for its time. To the people at large his adventure struck a classic pose in the romantic imagination. As such, it served admirably its original political purpose of calling the nation's attention to the potentialities of Oregon and California. Even his soberer scientific reflections were tinted with larger-than-life sublimity which has obscured the precise limits of his achievement down to the present day.

As soon as he could, Frémont set to work on the twin tasks of compiling his scientific report and spreading the word about the trans-Mississippi country among those who counted in the councils of state. In his *Memoirs* [65] he recalled his enthusiasm for these tasks: "To me in drawing these results into visible form, there was the impelling gratification of bringing into clear view the different face which our examination had given to the regions explored; their many points of general interest; their unexpected resources and capacities for population and trade; thus vindicating the West in the importance which they attached to that territory."

In March he went with Senator Benton to visit President Polk. The President was cautious. Even when Frémont produced his maps proving the Columbia to be the only river that led from the Rockies to the Pacific, he refused to be stampeded into any commitment on Oregon. In disappointment Frémont recalled that "The President seemed, for the moment, skeptical about the exactness of my information and disposed to be conservative. He evidently 'respected that ancient chaos' of the western geography as it existed on the old maps. Like the Secretary [of War] he found me 'young,' and said something of the 'impulsiveness of young men,' and was not at all satisfied in his own mind that those three rivers were not running there as laid down." [66]

Daniel Webster invited the young lieutenant to dine with him and "talk about California." In the course of their discussion two attitudes toward the value of the western country became apparent. "I found," Frémont wrote, "that his mind was specially fixed upon the Bay of San Francisco and the commanding advantage it would give us for war and commerce. He drew his line, however, at the coast. Coming, as he did, from a part of our

65. Page 414.
66. Ibid., p. 419.

country where grass contends with rocks for possession of the fields, it was difficult to make him realize the wonderful fertility of the unobstructed soil of California, where wild oats make unbroken fields from valley to mountain top." [67]

It is difficult to measure Frémont's actual success in the councils of state. By implication, in his *Memoirs,* he claimed much, but he also admitted that Polk had taken office with an already "fixed determination to acquire California." George Bancroft, the Secretary of the Navy, had also been interested in this project from the beginning. Thus Frémont's most important influence was not upon the governmental officials. Rather, it was upon the public at large, and perhaps his report properly deserves to be classified in American literature as a political pamphlet designed to appeal not so much to the public in common sense terms as to those grandiose national urges so characteristic of the times.

If Frémont's political contributions were ambiguous, the precise value of his contributions to the body of knowledge have also remained far from clear. His expedition as a whole made a certain spectacular contribution to the appreciation of the West, but analyzed in detail his scientific findings seem either inconclusive or anticipated by others. Some observers have been unwilling even to grant him the title of "Pathfinder." [68] Everywhere he went, it seems, someone had been there before, sometimes even official explorers. Emigrants were already filing over the trail to Oregon. Bonneville and numerous trappers had seen, and even navigated, the Great Salt Lake. Jedediah Smith and Joseph Walker, among others, had traversed the Great Basin. J. B. Chiles had found an easy way into California. Wilkes had mapped the Pacific harbors, and had noted the existence of a coastal mountain range. Almost every mountain man had trapped for beaver in the three parks of present-day Colorado. Moreover, when completed, Frémont's own map contained some noticeable errors. Wherein, then, lay his contribution to geographical knowledge?

He could not claim primacy of discovery. Rather, his contributions derived from three aspects of his type of exploration: its comprehensiveness, its manner of presentation, and the relative trustworthiness of the authority upon which it rested. The au-

67. Ibid., p. 420.
68. Chittenden, *Fur Trade, I,* ix.

thoritativeness of Frémont's work resulted from his devotion to science. Though he was a romantic believer in Manifest Destiny, he was also a carefully trained scientific observer. His experience with Nicollet and under the eyes of his superiors in the Topographical Corps had made him see the wilderness in practical scientific terms as well as those of the artist and the visionary. He paused every day to make observations and calculations for his correct position. He patiently collected plant and mineral specimens, and recognized the importance of the fossil remains that he found. Though his was necessarily a hurried reconnaissance, with mixed purposes, the spirit of contemporary science was present on every page of his final report. Nine thousand feet high, in the wintry Sierras, when the issue of life was in doubt and even the Indians had sung their death songs, Frémont calmly turned his attention to the observation of the great masses of "white micaceous granite" that formed the mineralogical content of the mountain.[69] He went into the West for several reasons, but one of the most important of these was to collect data and make a beginning toward the absolute measurement of its surface topography.

For presenting his geographical data, he created perhaps the most important map of the decade, one which remained among the most significant down to the Civil War. Drawn by Charles Preuss from computations made by Frémont and Joseph C. Hubbard of the Coast Survey, the map derived much of its value from the fact that it portrayed only the country actually traversed by the expedition, or data secured from relaible surveys like that of the Wilkes expedition.[70] There was one departure from this practice which resulted in Frémont's blunder in describing Utah Lake and its connection with the Great Salt Lake. Otherwise, he had gone out to see the country for himself, and afterward had drawn his map, something no other trained observer had done since Stephen H. Long. Bonneville had been forced to depend to a large extent on Walker's descriptions. Albert Gallatin never left New York. Their maps, when compared with Frémont's, show the difference. Though Bonneville claimed in 1857, "It was from my explorations and those of my party alone that

69. Frémont, *Report, 1843–44,* p. 329.
70. Map (above, n. 64).

it was ascertained that this lake [Great Salt Lake] had no outlet; the California range *basined* all the waters of its eastern slope without further outlet; that the Buenaventura [Sacramento] and all the California streams drained only the western slope,"[71] his map represents these facts so crudely as to raise real doubt that he knew just what he was doing. He distributed mountain chains all over the West where none existed at all, and he left the southern and western parts of the Basin area blank, indicating that he knew nothing, one way or the other, of a possible outlet to the sea in that direction. The Great Salt Lake was inaccurately drawn, and Utah Lake was not in correct relation to it. In Bonneville's California, one looks in vain for any sign of the Coast Range. The Bay of Monterey dwarfs that of San Francisco. All that remained of real value on this map was the indication that the Great Salt Lake had no outlet to the sea. It represented good guesswork but was without any obvious foundation.

Gallatin's map, the other one which rivals Frémont's, was of value chiefly because it incorporated Jedediah Smith's routes on it. But this map, too, was extremely vague and amateurish. The mountains were isolated cones distributed at random over its face, and the Basin area was merely labeled "sandy plains," not really the connotative equivalent of "Great Basin." Moreover, this map also suggested that the Kern River linked with the Inconstant, or Mojave, River, crossing the Sierras and providing an outlet for the "sandy plains." It is obvious that though no Rio Buenaventura appeared on Gallatin's map, he also lacked any true idea of the Great Basin. This concept rightfully belongs to Frémont, though like many important ideas it had antecedents that could lay partial claim to its achievement. Based upon thousands of careful observations for longitude and latitude, Frémont's map of 1845, which accompanied his report to the country, was the first of a series of scientific mappings of the western country which has continued down to the present. As such, it is a landmark in the progress of geographical knowledge.

In 1846 another important map was published by the government from Frémont's field notes and journal. Drawn by Preuss, its title was *Topographical Map of the Road from Missouri to Oregon Commencing at the Mouth of the Kansas in the Missouri*

71. Quoted in Warren, *Memoir,* p. 33.

River and Ending at the Mouth of the Wallah-Wallah in the Columbia.[72] It was in seven sections, extremely detailed, which outlined the Oregon Trail in clear fashion for prospective emigrants. The scale was ten miles to the inch, and printed over the face of the map were excerpts from Frémont's *Report* describing strategic places along the trail. There was also, on each sheet, a series of notations concerning the following topics: the distance from Westport Landing, game, grass, fuel, and Indians. The first sheet declared typically under the latter heading, "Sioux Indians are not to be trusted." Section two showed clearly the Indian war grounds and advised vigilance and caution. On the fifth section, which portrayed the Great Salt Lake country, the map included Frémont's evaluation of the area as a "bucolic region." Each sheet also contained a meteorological chart for its particular area. This authoritative map, well drawn, detailed, and aimed at the wants of the emigrants, was one of Frémont's (and Preuss') greatest contributions to the development of the West. It was widely used by western travelers.

Later, in 1848, Preuss drew another map for Frémont, which gave a larger portrait of the West, with many of the blank spaces filled in from reference to other works, like Lt. William H. Emory's map of the Gila River country.[73] This map, too, was highly significant in that it presented an over-all view of the West, showing clearly for the first time the relationships between the various basins, rivers, and ranges. It must be observed, however, that since it attempted to present the whole picture, its accuracy suffered somewhat, most notably in the inclusion of parallel ranges marking the northern and southern borders of the Great Basin, which do not, of course, exist.

If the cartographic achievements of Frémont's expedition were comprehensive, in geology the results were almost the opposite. Only the most tentative guesses could be made from the few important fossil specimens brought back. Perhaps the specimens

72. Charles Preuss, *Topographical Map of the Road from Missouri to Oregon . . . in VII Sections . . . from the Field Notes and Journal of Captain J. C. Frémont . . . by Order of the Senate of the United States,* Baltimore, 1846.

73. Map accompanying John C. Frémont, *Geographical Memoir upon Upper California in Illustration of His Map of Oregon and California,* 30th Cong., 1st Sess., Sen. Misc. Doc. 148, 1848.

from the Cretaceous beds and from the coal measures were the most meaningful to scientists, hence the most important. James Hall of Albany, the State Paleontologist of New York, described the coal measure fossils as being important because they "show us the wide extent and nature of the vegetation of this modern coal period." [74] By way of a general summary of the geological results of the expedition Hall declared, "Although we are far from being able to fix the minute or detailed geology, this collection presents us with sufficient materials to form some probable conclusions regarding the whole region from this side of the Rocky Mountains, westward to the mouth of the Columbia River." [75]

Frémont's contributions to botany were severely limited by the loss of his collections in the Kansas River flood. Some specimens did, however, survive, and when Frémont's returns from his third expedition in 1845 arrived at Doctor Torrey's herbarium in Princeton, the Doctor was able to put them all together into a monumental final report.[76] It was a particularly important source of information on the plants of California.

Also included in Frémont's official report were twenty-two pages of meteorological data, important for indicating the existence of cultivable land and for providing a factual footnote to any conclusions about the Great American Desert. In addition to the weather, Frémont paid close attention to the habits, distribution, and physical appearance of the numerous Indian tribes with which he came in contact. He was not aware of the advanced linguistic techniques in ethnology and thus failed to bring back the vocabularies of Indian languages that were so characteristic of later scientific explorations. He did, however, provide a description of the Pawnees, Sioux, Delaware, Kansas, Arapaho, Cheyenne, Snakes, Utes, Pai-utes, Nez Perce, Chinook, Klamath, Digueños, and Mojaves, with some index of their attitudes toward white settlement, at a time when many of these tribes were virtually unknown.

74. Quoted in Sen. Exec. Doc. 174 (above, n. 64), 299.

75. Quoted ibid., p. 295.

76. John Torrey, "Plantae Fremontianae, or Descriptions of Plants Collected by Colonel J. C. Frémont in California," *Smithsonian Contributions to Knowledge, 6* (Wash., 1854), art. 2.

Taken altogether, Frémont's contributions were extensive, though not particularly profound in any one field. They were a tentative beginning in many directions. His help to the west-bound emigrants was even more significant. There were many instances of emigrant parties who depended upon Frémont's data to guide them. Among these, for example, was Sarah Royce, mother of the philosopher Josiah Royce, who recalled that her westward trek to California had been "guided only by the light of Frémont's *Travels*." [77] Countless others depended upon his maps or memorized his advice in preparation for their trip. There were at least six American printings of his works, and two English printings.[78] Abroad, the Pathfinder's prestige was enhanced by Humboldt's lavish praise of the "talent, courage, industry and enterprize" demonstrated by his *Report*.[79] Humboldt went even further and gave special mention to Frémont's findings in his own new edition of *Aspects of Nature,* published in 1849.[80] Thus, though Frémont's expeditions were politically conceived and oriented toward practical objectives, as a Topographical Engineer his scientific work added a cubit to the national stature. And, in terms of the age, what other single set of exploits could rival his for a classic expression of Romantic values? With the coming of the Mexican War there would be more Topographical Engineers to take up the task of exploring the West. But though they would consciously model their careers after Frémont, and even contribute more significant scientific results, none would replace the Pathfinder in the popular imagination.

77. Sarah Royce, *A Frontier Lady,* ed. Ralph H. Gabriel (New Haven, 1932), p. 3.

78. Joseph Sabin, *A Dictionary of Books Relating to America* (29 vols. New York, 1875), 7, 51–53.

79. Quoted in 30th Cong., 1st Sess., Sen. Exec. Doc. 226 (1848), 6–7 n.

80. Alexander von Humboldt, *Aspects of Nature,* trans. Elizabeth J. Sabine (Phila., 1849), pp. 51, 219.

4. THE MEXICAN WAR RECONNAISSANCE

Not but what abstract war is horrid,
I sign to thet with all my heart,
But civlyzation doos git forrid
Sometimes upon a powder-cart . . .
—*James Russell Lowell*

In the year 1845 the progress of American expansion stood opposed by Mexico's steadfast refusal to acknowledge the independence of Texas and the legality of its annexation by the United States. Far to the north, in Oregon, another crisis continued to mount, in this instance with Great Britain. Thus when James K. Polk assumed the presidency of the United States, he was immediately faced with the unpleasant prospect of a war on two widely separated fronts and with two different enemies. The obvious course of action was that of diplomatic negotiation. With Britain this was readily accomplished, but with Mexico it was not to be; though Polk tried on repeated occasions to establish diplomatic contact with Mexico, he eventually came to believe that it might be necessary to resort to arms in order to maintain the border of Texas at the Rio Grande. Such a military policy would be unfortunate because it would upset all plans for purchasing California from Mexico. On the other hand it would, of course, offer an almost certain opportunity for acquiring that province. Thus with the possibility of war imminent, Polk issued orders that called for the concentration of the Army, under Zachary Taylor at Fort Jessup, on the Louisiana frontier.[1]

An important preliminary to the launching of any campaign against Mexico was the necessity for acquiring some accurate idea of the country in which operations would have to be conducted. In 1845 the American general staff was singularly ignorant of Southwestern geography. When asked by Representative Brinkerhoff, in July of that year, what he considered the present boundaries of Mexico, Colonel Abert referred the Con-

1. Justin Smith, *The War with Mexico* (2 vols. New York, 1919), *I*, 140.

gressman to Tanner's *American Atlas* of 1839, a commercial map of questionable accuracy.[2] Actually, the Topographical Bureau possessed a better map than Tanner's, but it was unpublished. Drawn in 1844 by Lt. William H. Emory, it was a map of Texas compiled from the latest authorities.[3] On one of the two copies filed in the Topographical Bureau was marked the tentative outline of Texan claims as far as the Rio Grande. Unlike most of the later maps made by Topographical Engineers, however, this one depended not on original scientific data but on various authorities (Humboldt's Atlas, Brown's survey of the Santa Fe Trail, Kennedy's *Texas,* Folsom's *Mexico in 1842,* Commodore Moore's survey of the Gulf Coast for the Texas Navy, Kendall's narrative of the Santa Fe expedition, Mitchell's commercial map of 1843, and the field maps of the United States-Texas Boundary Commission), hence it could not furnish truly reliable information on the country in question.[4] As much as anything else, Emory's map indicated just how inadequate the sources of geographical data on the Southwest actually were. Across the barren Llano Estacado of Texas the Lieutenant naively printed, "according to Arrowsmith, this tract of country was explored by Le Grand in 1833, and is naturally fertile, well-wooded, and with a fair proportion of water." [5] By all odds the best single work on the Southwest was Josiah Gregg's 1844 *Commerce of the Prairies.*[6] Gregg was a careful observer who used instruments in making his maps.[7] But beyond the works of Emory and Tanner

2. Abert to I. Brinkerhoff, July 13, 1845, LS, TE 77.

3. William H. Emory, "Map of Texas and the Country Adjacent" (1844), Cartographic Records Section, National Archives.

4. Ibid. Emory listed sixteen sources in all, but he does not appear to have seen Josiah Gregg's map drawn for Col. John Garland about 1842, which portrays the Santa Fe Trail, nor did he use Gregg's final map published in 1844 with Gregg, *Commerce of the Prairies* (below). A MS copy of the 1842 map by Gregg is in the Headquarters Map File of the Office of the Chief of Engineers, Record Group 77.

5. Ibid. See map legend.

6. Josiah Gregg, *Commerce of the Prairies: Or the Journal of a Santa Fe Trader, during Eight Expeditions across the Great Western Prairies, and a Residence of Nearly Nine Years in Northern Mexico* (1844), ed. Max Moorhead, Norman, Okla., 1954.

7. Maurice G. Fulton, ed., *Diary and Letters of Josiah Gregg* (2 vols. Norman, Okla., 1941), 2, 199.

and Gregg, the military strategist would have to either guess or depend on the services of local guides.

It was in partial awareness of this situation that three trans-Mississippi expeditions were launched in the spring of 1845. They were all related to the diplomatic crisis, though they turned their primary attention to the gathering of scientific information about the western country. This data proved useful for military strategists and settlers alike. The first of the expeditions, Colonel Stephen W. Kearny's dragoon reconnaissance, headed out along the Oregon Trail to the South Pass, then swung southward along the mountain wall to Bent's Fort. Its purpose was to keep open the emigrant road to Oregon by impressing the Indians with American military power.[8] It also made a survey of the country and functioned as a model experiment in the use of cavalry in plains operations. Lieutenant W. B. Franklin of the Topographical Corps was specially detailed as the expedition's topographer and map maker.[9] The second expedition was Frémont's march from Bent's Fort through the Rocky Mountains to California. As in his two previous excursions, the true purpose of this one was known only to himself and Senator Benton, and the Pathfinder again felt free to depart at will from Colonel Abert's orders. The third expedition was led by Lieutenant James W. Abert, the Colonel's son, and it explored the Comanche country along the Canadian River. Two of these ventures of 1845 introduced officers of the Topographical Corps into the West as auxiliaries to what were essentially military operations; the third, Frémont's, seemed oriented more toward international politics and science. But they all serve to illustrate the dual nature of the Topographical Engineer's work in the West, since their results had implications for science and settlement as well as for politics and war. They can be considered as the beginning of those later reconnaissances of the Mexican War which brought for the first time to the American people a scientific awareness of southwestern geography.

8. Henry J. Carleton, *The Prairie Logbooks: Dragoon Campaigns to the Pawnee Villages in 1844, and to the Rocky Mountains in 1845*, ed. Louis Pelzer (Chicago, 1943), p. 157.

9. Stephen W. Kearney, *Report of a Summer Campaign to the Rocky Mountains . . . in 1845*, 29th Cong., 1st Sess., Sen. Exec. Doc. 1 (1846), 211.

Kearny's Plains Reconnaissance

Colonel Stephen Watts Kearny's expedition to the Rocky Mountains was composed of five companies of the First Dragoons, one of two cavalry regiments in the United States Army. Other elements of the First Dragoons were scattered along the frontier from the Indian country along the Arkansas and Washita rivers to the Red River of the North, making it difficult to mobilize more than half of the regiment.[10] Five companies, however, were enough to make the demonstration of force required to deter the Indians from any outbursts in the event of war with England or Mexico.

Specifically, Kearny's command was to gather information on the plains country, protect the emigrants on the Oregon Trail as far as the South Pass, and then swing southward to Bent's Fort so as to convoy the traders' caravans moving from Santa Fe to Saint Louis. He was also ordered to persuade the Indians to refrain from attacking the emigrant trains, by words if possible and by convincing demonstrations of military prowess if necessary.[11] In this sense the dragoon reconnaissance was an experiment to test the value of occasional cavalry forays as a means of keeping peace among the Indians as well as an attempt to find an alternative to the chain of forts recommended by Frémont as nucleii for settlement and stepping stones for continental expansion. A patrol in force representing strictly military considerations was the policy advocated by a number of professional soldiers, including Kearny himself. It followed the example of the French Army in Algeria, which was concentrated in the large population centers, leaving the hills and desert to the native tribes, except when caravans passed through. The contrast between the points of view of Kearny and Frémont was representative not only of the different objectives of military and civilian occupation but also of the fundamental difference between Frémont's optimistic view of the West as a garden inviting settlement and Kearny's pessimistic view of it as an uninhabitable desert.

10. Carleton, p. 155.
11. Ibid., p. 157.

Lieutenant William B. Franklin, the Topographical Engineer attached to the party, was fresh from West Point, where he had been first in the class of 1843.[12] He joined Kearny's command ten days out of Fort Leavenworth with the necessary instruments to make his scientific reconnaissance.[13]

The course followed by the soldiers was clearly marked by the wagon ruts of the emigrants bound for Oregon.[14] They crossed the Little Blue, followed the Platte to Fort Laramie, and continued on through Indian country to the South Pass, where they turned back. At Fort Laramie, on a cold, drizzling morning, with the rain turning to sleet, Kearny held a grand parley with the Brulé and Oglalla bands of the Sioux. Despite the inclement weather, it was a successful pageant with colorful costumes, flags flying, and much loud firing of ceremonial cannons. After an impressive speech by Kearny, the Indians agreed to refrain from attacks on emigrant trains.

Then the dragoon column swung southward along the Chugwater branch of the Laramie Fork on the eastern side of the mountain ranges. Another Indian council was held with the Cheyenne and Arapaho, and afterward the march continued via Cherry Creek and the Arkansas River to Bent's Fort, which was reached on July 20. Kearny wasted no time there, however, and left the next day on a rapid march for the regimental headquarters at Fort Leavenworth.

The dragoon reconnaissance was remarkable for having covered so much territory in so short a time. With considerable pride, Kearny reported that the column had been absent 99 days and had ridden at least 2,200 miles through the Indian country, carrying its own provisions, with the horses sustaining themselves on prairie grass (p. 211). In his estimation, the summer campaign had conclusively demonstrated the utility of mounted troops. It was a lesson not fully comprehended by the War Department until Jefferson Davis became Secretary of War in 1852. But though the cavalry had proved its ability to range far out

12. *DAB.* See also Cullum, *Biographical Register* (above, p. 12, n. 22), 2, 152–54.

13. Carleton, p. 195.

14. Unless otherwise stated, this account is based on Kearny, *Report of a Summer Campaign* (above, n. 9).

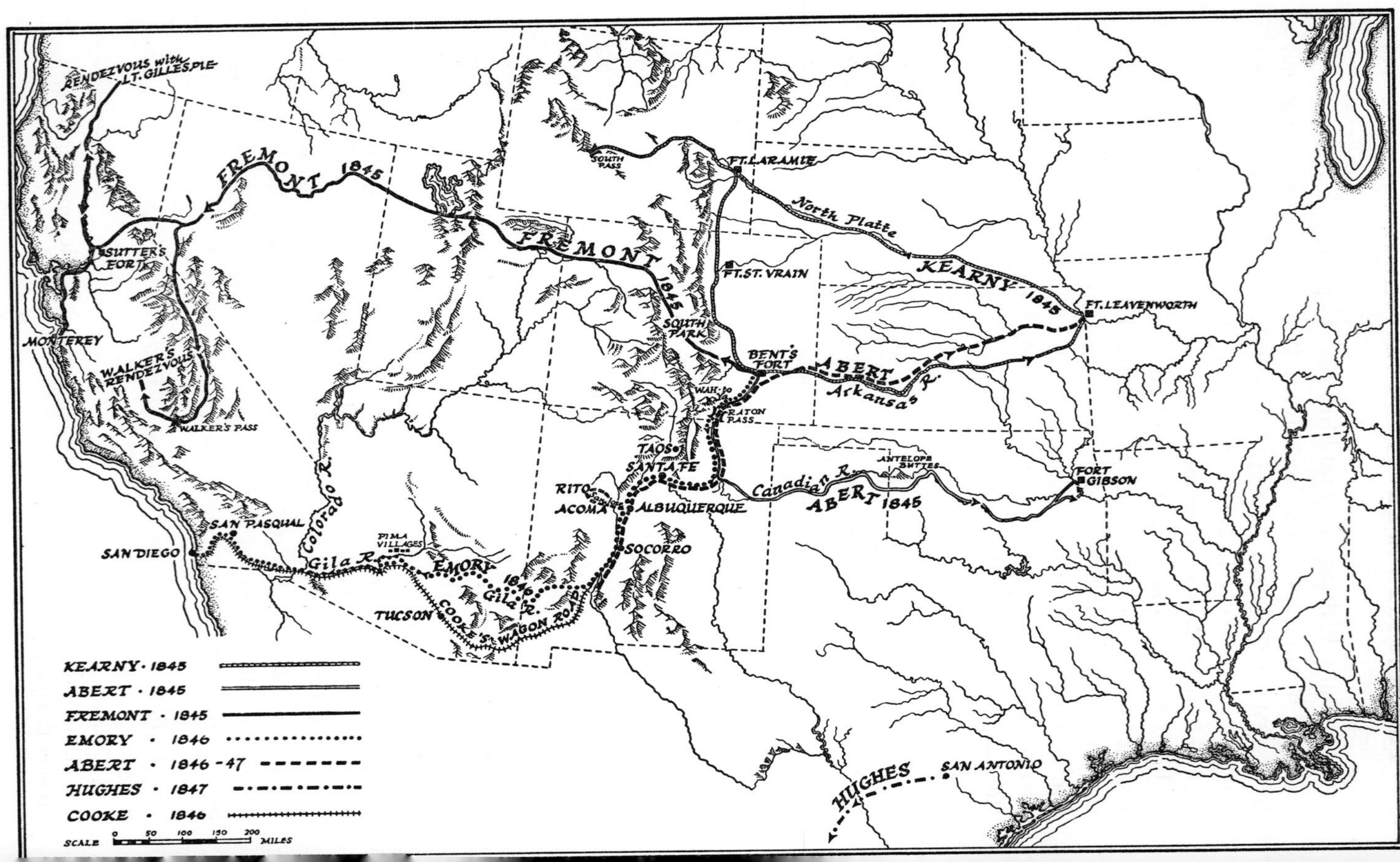
RENDEZVOUS with LT. GILLESPIE
FREMONT 1845
FREMONT 1845
SUTTER'S FORT
MONTEREY
WALKER'S RENDEZVOUS
WALKER'S PASS
SOUTH PASS
FT. LARAMIE
North Platte
FT. ST. VRAIN
KEARNY 1845
FT. LEAVENWORTH
SOUTH PARK
BENT'S FORT
ABERT
Arkansas R.
WAH-to
RATON PASS
TAOS
SANTA FE
RITO
ACOMA
ALBUQUERQUE
Canadian R.
ANTELOPE BUTTES
ABERT 1845
FORT GIBSON
SOCORRO
Colorado R.
SAN PASQUAL
SAN DIEGO
PIMA VILLAGES
Gila R.
EMORY 1846
Gila R.
TUCSON
COOKE'S WAGON ROAD
HUGHES
SAN ANTONIO
KEARNY · 1845
ABERT · 1845
FREMONT · 1845
EMORY · 1846
ABERT · 1846-47
HUGHES · 1847
COOKE · 1846
SCALE 0 50 100 150 200 MILES

over the plains country carrying its own supplies, Kearny had overestimated its impact on the Indians. Though they were temporarily awed, the various tribes soon reverted to what Captain Philip St. George Cooke called, "their morbid inclinations for internal agression." [15]

Another important lesson which Kearny drew from his experience seemed directly aimed at Frémont. He wrote, "It has been suggested by some persons that a military post should be established near Fort Laramie, or above there for the protection of the Oregon emigrants, and as a connecting link with the Oregon Territory. I am of the opinion that the establishment of a post there at this time would be very injudicious." To reinforce this assertion, he pointed to the "enormous" expense involved in supplying and maintaining such a post. Instead, he proposed a military expedition similar to his own which should be made "every two or three years." [16] More than merely emphasizing the significance of his own endeavor, the Colonel was thereby representing the professional military view of the West, which focused on frontier defense rather than on the spreading of settlement. Keeping the Indians peaceful was all the Army needed to do. Let the traders and storekeepers form the future settlements. As for using military posts to establish legal claims to doubtful territory, he had no opinions at all. His report was that of the old-line soldier and seemed slightly contemptuous of using the Army otherwise than as a potential combat force.

Lieutenant Franklin, as Topographical Engineer to the expedition, contributed a carefully drawn map of the country traversed.[17] In part it duplicated the work of Frémont in 1843–44, and Franklin acknowledged the Frémont map as his source for the area between the Platte River and the South Pass. Franklin's map added new data, however, on the country between the Platte and the Arkansas. Also on his map was the suggestion that the Grand River flowed westward from the vicinity of Long's Peak into the Green River.[18] Though only a vague guess, this

15. Philip St. George Cooke, *Scenes and Adventures in the Army* (Phila., 1857), p. 223.
16. Kearny, p. 212.
17. Ibid. The map accompanies the report.
18. This was pointed out by Wheat, "Mapping the American West," p. 107.

was a significant advance toward the understanding of the Colorado River system. Only one page of geologic conclusions was presented by Franklin, and none of these was important. It was clear from the final report of the Dragoon Reconnaissance that in this case science was definitely subordinated to military concerns.

Frémont in 1845

Both the Frémont and the Abert expeditions of 1845 were broader in scope than that of Franklin. Though these expeditions had a certain military purpose, the Topographical Engineers rather than the line officers were the commanders. It was understood that they were to take time to collect scientific data on the country they passed through. As long ago as the previous summer of 1844, shortly after his return from the West, Frémont had written to the botanist John Torrey at Princeton telling him in confidence of his plans to return to California to recoup some of his scientific losses. "I have 60 or 70 fine mules and horses at pasture on the frontier," he wrote, "and shall immediately commence my preparations so as to leave the frontier early in April." [19]

Two months later Frémont wrote again, describing his scientific preparations for the projected trip: "The arrangements for our expedition go on handsomely, I am having excellent instruments made, and [am] myself engaged in hard study, among other things, descriptive botany." He added earnestly, "We must have the geological formation, geographical position and elevation above the sea for all our plants. This, with the colored figures of the new specimens, will make a solid work." [20] Beyond the insight they afford into Frémont's enthusiasm for science, it is clear from these letters that even before the War Department had decided or before Colonel Abert had issued any orders, Frémont had launched his expedition to California.

Colonel Abert's plans for Frémont were somewhat different.

19. Frémont to Torrey, Sept. 15, 1844, Torrey Papers, New York Botanical Gardens.

20. Ibid., Nov. 21, 1844.

In an order of February 12, 1845, Abert ordered Frémont to lead an expedition that would

> strike the Arkansas as soon as practicable, survey that river, and if practicable, survey the Red River within our boundary line, noting particularly the navigable properties of each, and [he] will determine as near as practicable, the points at which the boundary line of the United States, the 100th degree of longitude west of Greenwich, strikes the Arkansas and the Red River. It is also important that the Arkansas should be accurately determined. Long journies [*sic*] to determine isolated geographical points are scarcely worth the time and expense which they occasion; the efforts of Captain Frémont will therefore be more particularly directed to the geography of the localities within reasonable distance of Bent's Fort, and of the streams which run east from the Rocky Mountains, and he will so time his operations that his party will come in during the present year.[21]

Between this order and the next came the joint resolution that annexed Texas and provoked the Mexican ambassador into calling for his passports. Accordingly, the Colonel modified his instructions to Frémont, but adhered to their original scope. On April 10, 1845, he wrote, "On arriving at Bent's Fort, if you find it desirable, you will detach a lieutenant and party to explore the Southern Rocky Mountains and the regions south of the Arkansas under such instructions as your experience shall suggest. . . . It is extremely desirable that you should be in before the adjournment of the next session of Congress in order that if operations should be required in that country the information obtained may be at command." [22]

Colonel Abert detailed his own son, Lieutenant J. W. Abert, as Frémont's assistant for the projected auxiliary expedition.[23] Nowhere, however, is there any evidence to suggest that the Colonel contemplated sending a transcontinental expedition to California. This project, like the previous ones, represented a

21. Abert to Frémont, Feb. 12, 1845, LS, TE 77.
22. Ibid., April 10, 1845.
23. J. J. Abert to J. W. Abert, March 5, 1845, LS, TE 77.

direct violation of official orders by Frémont. Thanks to Benton's powerful backing, he seemed entirely immune from the rigors of military discipline.

Delayed by the printing of the report on his previous expedition, it was not until the middle of June that Frémont began outfitting a party for his projected continental expedition.[24] With the possible exception of the replacement for Fitzpatrick, who was scouting with Kearny, and for Charles Preuss, who remained behind in Washington, the personnel of the third expedition exceeded in quality that of the previous ones. The party included Joseph Walker, Alexis Godey, Basil Lajeunesse, Lucien Maxwell, Theodore Talbot, Lieutenants Abert and Peck, and, a little later, an exotic escort of twelve Delaware Indians. To replace Preuss as his topographic assistant, Frémont took along Edward M. Kern, a young Philadelphia artist and naturalist.

On June 20 they set out on a rapid march for Bent's Fort. The first day out, Frémont read the provisions of martial law under which the expedition was to be conducted, and thirteen of the men hastily turned back for St. Louis.[25] The remaining company followed the Santa Fe Trail to Bent's Fort, as Frémont intended to waste no effort in exploring the plains. On the second day of August they reached their destination at the Arkansas River outpost. At this point the Delawares, under Chief Sagundai, joined the party, and they paused for two weeks to wait for Kit Carson, who was bringing his partner, Dick Owens, up from their ranch on the Little Cimarron to join the expedition.[26]

On August 16, after two weeks of outfitting, Frémont led his company out of Bent's Fort and up the Arkansas River. They were sixty or so well-armed men, led by the giants of the West, Frémont, Carson, Walker, Godey, and Maxwell, and they were headed straight for California on a mission of unspecified purpose. Their course took them around the Royal Gorge of the Arkansas, to the Tennessee Pass, and across the Continental

24. Thomas Salathiel Martin, "Narrative of John C. Frémont's Expedition to California in 1845–46, and Subsequent Events in California Down to 1853, Including Frémont's Exploring Expedition of 1848," dictated to E. F. Murray (Sept. 5, 1878), Bancroft Library, Berkeley, California.

25. Ibid., p. 3.

26. Lavender, *Bent's Fort* (above, p. 47, n. 66), p. 245.

Divide. Frémont was fully aware that his expedition was proceeding entirely within Mexican territory, and he was unconcerned. If this was Mexican territory, "so," as he later wrote, "was all of the Salt Lake Valley" where he had proposed the establishment of an American settlement.[27] His party managed a crossing of the Grand River near the headwaters of the White and followed the latter river westward across the eroded plateau country of western Colorado and eastern Utah. Eventually they crossed the Green River and struck the Duchesne as it flowed through a valley cut into the badlands bordering the Wasatch Plateau. On their right were the Uinta Mountains. By a descent of the Timpanogos River they came down from the Wasatch Mountains into the Great Basin near Utah Lake. By this time summer was over and it was October 10. Three days later they reached the southern shore of the Great Salt Lake and remained there, making a detailed survey of its southern shores, collecting specimens of plants and animals, and refreshing their horses for an attempted crossing of the great desert that stretched away to the West.

When the horses were fit again, Frémont gave the order to strike out across the Great Salt Desert toward California. "The route I wished to take," he wrote, "lay over a flat plain covered with sage-brush. The country looked dry, and of my own men none knew anything of it; neither Walker nor Carson. The Indians declared to us that no one had ever been known to cross the plain which was a desert; so far as any of them had ventured no water had been found." [28] This indicates that the news of Jedediah Smith's crossing in 1827 apparently remained as unknown among the mountain men as it did in Frémont's official circles.

Carson, Archambeau, and Maxwell were sent ahead to find a way across the desert, while Frémont followed with the main contingent. Their course led them to Pilot Peak, where in spite of the dire warnings they found a supply of water. Then they turned southwest to Whitten's Springs in the Humboldt River Mountains. This desert route gained later notoriety among the emigrants as the Hastings Cutoff used by the Donner Party (those

27. Frémont, *Memoirs,* p. 430.

28. Ibid., p. 432. Unless otherwise stated, the account is based on this work.

heroic emigrants who all but perished in the wintry Sierras in 1846).[29] At Whitten's Springs the party split, with Frémont taking ten men directly across the remaining desert to the southwest while Walker led the larger party along the familiar Humboldt River route to a rendezvous at Walker Lake. Theodore Talbot was the official commander of this latter group, with Ned Kern as topographer.[30]

On November 24 both parties met at Walker Lake, only to split up again. Talbot, Walker, and Kern proceeded with the main party southward to Walker Pass over the Sierras to another proposed rendezvous at the Tulare Lakes. Frémont and a smaller group of fifteen picked men crossed over the mountains via the Donner Pass and made their way southward to the American River, which they reached on December 9. This route took them through the area which, within three years, would be the El Dorado of the California gold rush, but according to Frémont the precious metal was overlooked because the explorers were more interested in "a clear cold spring of running water, or a good camp, big game, or fossils embedded in rock" (p. 449). In a letter to Jessie he indicated what he considered to be the expedition's primary achievement: "By the route I have explored, I can ride in thirty-five days from the Fontaine-qui-Bouille River [above Bent's Fort on the Arkansas] to Captain Sutter's; and for wagons the road is decidedly better" (p. 452). However, before the next winter was over there would be those among the survivors of the Donner party who would have occasion to disagree with the Pathfinder. The desert of the Hastings Cutoff and the severity of winter in the mountain pass combined to produce their epic disaster, which would seem to cast a strong shadow on Frémont's proclaimed achievement.

When the Frémont party reached the rendezvous at the Tulare

29. Ray Allen Billington, *The Far Western Frontier, 1830–1860* (New York, 1956), p. 111.

30. Dellenbaugh, *Frémont and '49*, p. 296. Frémont states in his *Memoirs*, p. 434, that Kern was placed in charge of the party. Both Martin ("Narrative," p. 10) and E. M. Kern ("Journal of an Exploration of Mary's or Humboldt River, Carson Lake, and Owens River and Lake in 1845," appendix to J. H. Simpson, *Report of Explorations across the Great Basin of the Territory of Utah . . . in 1859*, Washington, 1876, p. 477) imply that Talbot, not Kern, was in command of the party.

Lake Fork of the Kern River, the rest of the men were not to be found. There was nothing to do but winter at Sutter's Fort and await their arrival. During the month of January, Frémont visited Leidesdorff, the American counsul at San Francisco, as well as Larkin, the American representative at Monterey (p. 454). While making an official visit to Gen. Don José Castro and ex-Governor Alvarado of Monterey, he informed the suspicious Mexicans that his expedition "was made in the interests of science and commerce, and that the men composing the party were citizens and not soldiers" (p. 454). To the Mexican officials, particularly after Commodore Jones' seizure of Monterey in '42, Frémont's party of mountain sharpshooters must have looked like anything but scientists. Shortly after Castro had granted Frémont permission to resupply, Carson and Owens located the rest of the expedition and the whole party was reunited. They were headed up the Salinas Valley when the Mexican officials issued an order for their detention. For several days they defied the Mexicans from a fort constructed in the foothills of the Gabilon Mountains. Frémont and his men then moved northward to Lassen's Meadows, heading for the Klamath country. It was while Frémont was on his way to Oregon that Lieutenant Gillespie of the United States Marines arrived from Washington and started Frémont southward into the War with Mexico. At this point his duties as a Topographical Engineer ceased. He became, officially, a lieutenant-colonel in the Mounted Rifles.[31] More significantly, all thought of scientific labors became subordinated to the spirit of war.

No one can say precisely what the motives were that directed Frémont to California. His own conflicting stories suggest that at the time and for years afterward a confusion existed in his own mind as to the exact reason, political, military, or scientific, that he so far exceeded the scope of his orders on his third expedition. The simple desire to enhance his reputation as a geographer and explorer must figure strongly in any attempt to assess these motives. In March of 1847, with the war in California still smoldering, Jessie Benton Frémont wrote to Torrey concerning her husband's point of view: "I have no sympathy for the war nor has Mr. Frémont. Fighting is not his aim, and though he threw all

31. Heitman, *Historical Register* (above, p. 12, n. 22), *1*, 436.

his energy into the affair last July and August, yet it was as if revenging a personal insult *for he knew nothing of the war*."[32] In a candid moment, Jessie Frémont had, perhaps, revealed the true limits of Frémont's knowledge of the American government's plans for California. What Jessie's letter suggests is that the orders Frémont received from Lieutenant Gillespie at Klamath Lake were far less extensive than the Pathfinder later claimed, for they did not even inform him of the state of war then existing between the United States and Mexico. According to Mrs. Frémont, the Pathfinder's return to California had little to do with international politics but was motivated by personal reasons—reasons that were, nevertheless, to have surprising consequences for the history of California, since Frémont soon helped to launch the Bear Flag Revolt.

Whatever its political and military results, Frémont's third expedition had important implications for American geography. In crossing the Great Basin he proved that the desert was not as formidable as previously supposed, and he indicated a probable new route for overland communications. He also managed to collect a number of plants which, as previously mentioned, appeared as "Plantae Fremontianae" in *The Smithsonian Contributions to Knowledge*.[33] Much of the value of his reconnaissance was lost, however, when Congress tabled a measure to provide for the publication of a narrative describing his scientific labors.[34] Instead, belatedly in 1848, the Thirtieth Congress published twenty thousand copies of his brief but significant *Geographical Memoir upon Upper California,* which accompanied Preuss' important map.[35] This memoir was not in the form of a journal, but it broadly described the natural characteristics of the country from New Mexico to the Pacific. Its chief shortcoming as far as contemporaries were concerned was its failure to include data on the gold regions. A year's delay might have considerably altered its orientation.

The California expedition concluded Frémont's career as a

32. Jessie B. Frémont to Torrey, March 21, 1847, Torrey Papers. Italics added.

33. John Torrey, "Plantae Fremontianae" (above, p. 107, n. 76).

34. *Sen. Jour.*, 30th Cong., 2d Sess. (1849), p. 55.

35. Frémont (above, p. 106, n. 73), p. 2.

Topographical Engineer. While wearing the uniform of the United States Army, he had distinguished himself as geographer, scientific collector, and explorer. His prestige in the centers of learning rivaled his popularity before the people at large. The new information he acquired, together with his own geographic conceptions, formed the major part of the official body of knowledge of the trans-Mississippi West prior to the Mexican War. Through Senator Benton this information was effectively used to implement a western-oriented national policy.

Frémont's glamorous career served as a model toward which other officers could aspire. And though, historically, his exploits have obscured those who followed him, his passing from the scene actually opened the way for others of his Corps who possessed talents equal, if not superior, to his own. Jessie Benton Frémont, only twenty-two and loyal to her husband, as always, had the faintest of praise for the first of these new pretenders. She wrote Professor Torrey, "Young Abert's report accompanies this—perhaps it may be of some interest, although he seems unskilled in exploration." [36]

Abert in the Comanche Country

On August 9, 1845, at Bent's Fort, Lt. James W. Abert of the Topographical Corps assumed his first independent command by order of Captain Frémont.[37] He was to make a reconnaissance southward and eastward along the Canadian River through the country of the Kiowa and the Comanche. This meant that he was to execute that survey of the Texas border country that had been the original object in ordering Frémont into the field, while the Pathfinder himself led his own unauthorized expedition away toward California.

During the two-week interval of outfitting at Bent's Fort, Frémont instructed Lieutenant Abert and his assistant, Lt. William G. Peck, also a Topographical Engineer, in the correct use of the instruments employed in topographic exploration.[38] Iron-

36. Jessie B. Frémont to John Torrey, March 21, 1847, Torrey Papers.

37. James W. Abert, *Journal of Lieutenant James A. Abert, from Bent's Fort to St. Louis in 1845*, 29th Cong., 1st Sess., Sen. Exec. Doc. 438 (1846), 2.

38. See Abert's instructions to Frémont, April 10, 1845, LS, TE 77.

ically enough, however, when Abert and Peck set out on their own for the Canadian River, they were equipped with only a sextant and chronometer, while Frémont took the newer, more elaborate instruments himself. Even so, *both* of the parties felt seriously the shortage of such obviously indispensable instruments as barometers.

On August twelfth, four days before Frémont left Bent's Fort to go up the Arkansas River, Lieutenant Abert led his men downstream.[39] The young lieutenant was well provided with assistance, for Tom Fitzpatrick went along as his guide. The brilliant Lt. William G. Peck (Topographical Corps), served as assistant topographical officer. Peck was possessed of outstanding mathematical ability, and had ranked first in his West Point class, in contrast to Abert's fifty-fifth position in a class of fifty-six cadets.[40] For hunters, the expedition hired two veteran mountain men, Caleb Greenwood and John Hatcher. Hatcher, short, ugly, almost comical, was a refugee from Wapakoneta, Ohio, who had drifted to the frontier and become one of its most colorful citizens. Termed by Lewis H. Garrard "the beau ideal of a Rocky Mountain man," he was a teller of tall tales, a dead shot, and absolutely fearless.[41] In all, the party numbered thirty-three men, only two of whom were soldiers.[42]

Initially, their course was down the Purgatory River (Rio des las Animas), but soon they swung westward along the regular trail to Santa Fe, which passed in the shadow of the twin peaks of the Wah-to-Yah and led over the Raton Pass to the headwaters of the Canadian River.

Along the way, both of the Army topographers gathered geological data and made collections of flora and fauna. Very often their scientific detachment was tempered by a romantic appreciation of nature for its intrinsic beauty. One passage in Abert's journal recorded: "Although sheltered from the sun, when we gazed upward, we beheld the flicker, with golden wings, gliding

39. Abert, *Journal*, p. 6.

40. Cullum (above, p. 12, n. 22), 2, 151, 192.

41. L. H. Garrard, *Wah-to-Yah and the Taos Trail*, ed. Ralph Bieber, Southwestern Trails Series, 6 (Glendale, 1938), 219 and n.

42. Abert, *Journal*, p. 7. Unless otherwise stated, the following account is based on this work.

above and glistening in its brilliant rays" (p. 16). Another time Abert hastily consulted his bird manual to identify a "falco borealis" or a "corvus ultramarinus" in less romantic but more scientific terms. The mineral resources of the country also commanded his attention, and though he discounted Hatcher's yarns about Indians trading handfuls of gold dust for lead bullets, Abert noted in his report that New Mexico was "a great mineral country" (p. 18).

By September 2 they had entered Comanche territory on the northern edge of the Llano Estacado which stretched from New Mexico into West Texas. From that point on, the Indians were dangerous and unpredictable. The exploring party was fortunate, however, in that Greenwood and Hatcher were adopted members of the Kiowa tribe, which afforded the whole party a measure of protection. It was several days before they made contact with the Comanches, whom Abert termed merely "dirty and mean" (p. 38). All along the line of march Indians observed them from crags and promontories, and the constant sound of war drums announcing an excursion against the Pawnees caused the explorers the greatest anxiety.

Abert also had a good opportunity to observe the habits of the Kiowas, and the impressions he formed were important. The Kiowas were a key tribe, and the Lieutenant was satisfied of their importance, as a "people excelling the Comanches in every respect," who, "though far inferior to them [the Comanches] in numbers . . . yet exercise control over them" (p. 42).

On September 15 Greenwood and Hatcher turned back toward Bent's Fort, and the exploring party went south onto the Llano Estacado toward the head of the False Washita River. They followed this small river for a week across the otherwise desert-dry country called the Sand Hills. Indian signs were as abundant as mirages, and when Indians did appear, Abert described them in the same terms: "An Indian mounted now appeared, and as he swept along the horizon, looked a very giant; another and another burst upon our view, on every side, which led us to believe we were surrounded" (p. 49). But despite the constant Indian menace the party was never attacked. Soon they reached the Canadian River again and as rapidly as possible, proceeded downstream, leaving the hostile Indian country behind. When they reached the Cross Timbers they were nearing civilization, as evidenced by the Creek Indians they saw peacefully building permanent cabins. By October 21 the whole party had reached Fort Gibson in the Arkansas Territory, and the expedition was officially ended.

The chief scientific results were geographic. Abert's carefully drawn map provided authoritative information about the North Texas country. Though he had admittedly borrowed from the earlier maps of Lieutenant Franklin, Captain Frémont, and Josiah Gregg, his map was important because it was the first trustworthy representation of the Canadian River region, although Long's expedition had discovered the river more than twenty years earlier.[43]

Abert's written report served to supplement his map. It filled in with qualitative description what the map could only represent in terms of distance, direction, and altitude. Such data as that on the whereabouts of water holes and timber stands was important for any plans for settlement in the region. Most of the information, however, had primarily a military value, since few people at this time would be inclined to brave the danger of hostile Indians to plant a settlement in such a dry, unpromising country.

Abert's descriptions of Indians, both pictorially and in the text of his report, provided another kind of valuable information. It was the first time the federal government had access to any data on the Kiowas and Comanches from one of its own agents. His descriptions of the hostile Comanches and Kiowas, if they discouraged settlement, served a practical purpose.

As a scientific observer, Abert had his limitations. He was not a specialist in any particular field, a fact which held true for most of the Topographical Engineers. The notes he made on the wild life were little more than raw material for the zoologist, since he confined his activities to merely observing and collecting data. Others, more expert, could analyze his report for whatever reasons they chose. But to describe his limitations is not to imply that he was unqualified for the tasks of a field scientist. He had a special interest in birds and was familiar with the works of John James Audubon and Alexander Wilson. Besides his intense

43. Abert, *Journal,* p. 49; see the accompanying map.

interest in zoology, Abert had kept abreast of the latest works in travel and geography. For example, he was familiar with the data in Kendall's *The Texan Santa Fe Expedition* (1842) and Gregg's *Commerce of the Prairies* (1844).[44] In addition, he brought to his western survey a kind of enlightened, almost pragmatic, common sense, in that he noted the regional geography with an eye to everything that would contribute toward the possible solution of the problem of settlement and national development in the particular area. This point of view was typical of all the Topographical Engineers, from Frémont with his grand surveys to Warren's meticulous researches in the Dakotas. By the time he submitted his report, however, the question of settlement had yielded to the preoccupation with war, and Abert's information could be put to immediate practical use in the military campaigns in the Southwest.

Emory's March to the Pacific

When President Polk ordered General Kearny to extend his conquest of New Mexico onward to California, it provided the Topographical Bureau with an opportunity for important original exploration. Though the Spaniards, the Indians, and the mountain men had traversed the country between the Rio Grande and the Pacific, an accurate knowledge of the whole area did not exist. There were no dependable maps, and it was difficult even to visualize a line of communication through the Southwest to the Pacific. Yet such a route had become, in 1846, a military necessity for maintaining a supply line to California. With the acquisition of the southwestern region, an overland communication route would become even more vital for the defense of the border against Indian and Mexican attacks.

When the "Army of the West" took the field, Kearny and his officers were issued Tanner's new map of 1846 and Mitchell's map of the same year, both compiled from Frémont's California data and from that collected by the Wilkes Expedition.[45] These

44. Ibid., p. 26; for Gregg, see acknowledgment on Abert's map.

45. *Report from the Sec. of War, Communicating . . . a copy of the Official Journal of Lieutenant-Colonel Philip St. George Cooke from Santa Fe to San Diego etc.,* 30th Cong., Spec. Sess., Sen. Exec. Doc. 2 (1849), 59.

were mere commercial maps, and since neither Frémont nor Wilkes had penetrated the Southwest, even as far as the Gila River, it is not surprising that the Tanner and Mitchell maps were vague on that all-important region.[46] The immediate need for a new cartographic representation of the area was acute. Thus, in many ways, the activities of the topographical party attached to the "Army of the West" presented a classic example of the varied uses, both civilian and military, of the Corps in developing the trans-Mississippi West.

The man selected to be Kearny's topographer was First Lt. William Hemsley Emory, a Topographical Engineer who looked more like a veteran cavalryman than anything else. His picturesque language, flamboyant red whiskers, and haughty grace all proclaimed him the perfect image of the romantic frontier soldier. But his outward appearance belied the scientist and man of practical intelligence that he really was. As a western explorer, Emory soon became the rival of Frémont himself.

Like Frémont, he was not without an impressive background. Even a brief consideration of his family and friends serves to illustrate, as it does in the case of Frémont, just how an ordinary officer of the Topographical Corps could wield an influence upon national decisions far out of proportion to his rank. The scion of a tidewater Maryland family that went back to the colonial days of proprietorship, Emory belonged to the American equivalent of landed aristocracy.[47] His grandfather had fought in the Revolution and his father in the War of 1812. In peacetime they cultivated the acres of Poplar Grove, the family plantation in Queen Anne County on the eastern shore of Maryland. It is indicative of his southern connections that Emory owed his appointment at West Point to the friendly offices of John C. Calhoun.[48] The appointment was tendered in 1823, when he was eleven years old.[49]

46. See S. Augustus Mitchell, *A New Map of Texas, Oregon and California with the Regions Adjoining,* Phila., 1846. H. S. Tanner, *A Map of the United States of Mexico,* 3d ed. Phila., 1846.

47. *DAB.*

48. W. H. Emory to John C. Calhoun, May 28, 1823 (acknowledging his appointment to West Point and sending his acceptance), EP.

49. Ibid. The calculations for Emory's age were made by Dale L. Morgan, cataloguer of EP, and his statement accompanies the manuscript.

At the Academy, where he was a member of the class of 1831, his best friends and constant companions were Jefferson Davis, Joseph E. Johnston, and Henry Clay, Jr. Years later Jefferson Davis, writing on Emory's behalf, recalled that "From our boyhood, Major Emory and myself have been intimate friends." [50] Indeed, since their boyhood summers in Kentucky they had been the closest of friends. There, along with the younger Henry Clay, they became expert riders and judges of fine horseflesh in the best Southern tradition.[51] Like Frémont, these three enjoyed a youth that was filled with "splendid outdoor days." In the years before the Mexican War the Emorys shipped their blooded Maryland horses to the Clays for transport down the Mississippi and eventual sale at New Orleans. It was from these friends that Emory received the lifelong chivalrous nickname of "Bold Emory." [52]

When he married, it was with an eye to family. His wife was Matilda Wilkins Bache, the great granddaughter of Benjamin Franklin once described by Mary Boykin Chestnut as "one of the stiff-necked, stiff-kneed Franklin race." [53] More important for Emory, she was a member of the powerful Bache family of Philadelphia.[54] Through this marriage connection Emory became associated with one of the prominent political families of the time. It included George M. Dallas, Polk's vice-president, who along with Buchanan represented the political power of the strategic state of Pennsylvania. Emory's brother-in-law was Robert J. Walker, the outspoken imperialist and master politician of the "new" Democratic party. It was Walker who later helped launch the political career of Jefferson Davis, and it was he too who helped to secure the election of Polk in 1844.[55] Matilda's

50. Jefferson Davis to John B. Floyd, Wash., June 15, 1859, fair copy to Emory, EP.

51. Henry Clay, Jr., to Emory, Dec. 29, 1842, EP.

52. *DAB.*

53. Mary Boykin Chestnut, *Diary from Dixie,* ed. Isabella D. Martin and Myrta Lockett Avary (New York, 1929), pp. 61, 352.

54. Albert Gleaves, ed., *The Life of an American Sailor: Rear Admiral William Hemsley Emory, United States Navy, from His Letters and Memoirs* (New York, 1923), pp. 12–13.

55. William E. Dodd, *Robert J. Walker, Imperialist* (Chicago, 1914), pp. 22–23.

father was A. D. Bache, the eminent successor to Ferdinand Hassler as director of the Coast and Geodetic Survey.[56]

Once in the Corps, Emory's professional interests were directed toward science, and he began building up a circle of friendships among the chief astronomers, mathematicians, and geologists of the country. William C. Bond at Harvard, John Torrey at Princeton, Louis Agassiz, Asa Grey, George Engelmann, Spencer F. Baird, Charles Girard, and Joseph Henry of the Smithsonian Institution were numbered among his close friends. Whenever he was able, he attended the yearly conclaves of the American Association for the Advancement of Science. In large part, it was through Emory and his friend James Alfred Pearce, Whig Senator from Maryland, that the scientists as a group made their presence felt in Washington. His previous topographical duties had included work under Major James D. Graham on the Northeast Boundary Survey in 1843–44 and the compiling of his map of Texas in 1844.[57]

When Emory was ordered to join Kearny's Army, he was given just twenty-four hours to assemble his scientific equipment, a time, according to the Lieutenant, "sufficient for all the objects appertaining directly to our military wants, but insufficient for the organization and outfit of a party intended for exploration."[58] Nevertheless, his supply of instruments included two large box chronometers, two Gambey's eight and one-half inch sextants, and a Bunten syphon barometer.[59] In addition, his property returns show that he took along two copies of Frémont's *Report* of 1843–44; Mitchell's Map of Texas, Oregon, and California; four copies of his own map of Texas; one copy of Lieutenant Abert's map; Gregg's *Commerce of the Prairies;* two sets of Hasswell's tables; and two nautical almanacs.[60]

Included as members of his party were the experienced Lieutenants Abert and Peck and First Lt. William H. Warner. Two civilians of note were also attached to the topographical section:

56. Gleaves, pp. 12–13.
57. Cullum, *1*, 481.
58. Emory, *Notes,* p. 8.
59. Ibid., pp. 8–9.
60. Emory, "Memorandum of Property Received from the Topographical Bureau, 'To Be Used in Surveys West of the Mississippi River,' " 1846, EP.

Norman Bestor, a statistician, and John Mix Stanley, an important landscape painter.[61]

Emory and his assistants joined Kearny's command at Fort Leavenworth. The total force of the western Army was only 1,700 men, consisting of the First Dragoons, the First Missouri Cavalry, two batteries of artillery, and two companies of infantry. In addition, there was a force of nearly 100 mounted plainsmen from St. Louis called the Laclede Rangers, who were accompanied by fifty Delaware and Shawnee scouts.[62]

On the twenty-eighth of June the last of the troops filed out of the Leavenworth quadrangle and started down the trail to Santa Fe. In his report, Emory did not even deem this part of the route sufficiently novel to merit a topographical description.

The advanced elements of the Army reached Bent's Fort on July 29 and went into camp on the meadows some miles below the Fort. Emory began the important part of his journal on the morning of August 2 when the Army of the West started on its march south from Bent's Fort on the Arkansas River.[63]

As the column rode southward over the Raton Pass and across Vermejo Creek, Emory observed little that was favorable for a farming settlement in that dry country. He was able, however, to confirm Abert's discovery of bituminous coal deposits along the trail. When he speculated on the geologic history of the country, he judged the whole area to have been a plateau, level with the tops of the surrounding hills, which had been eroded away into valleys by some "denuding process" which only the hard volcanic rock had resisted.[64] He was unwilling to attribute this erosion solely to water, and for this reason his generalization was more cautious than Abert's had been.

Though today such speculation over the power of erosion

61. Emory, *Notes,* p. 45. For biographical details on Stanley see David I. Bushnell, Jr., "John Mix Stanley, Artist-Explorer," *Annual Report, Smithsonian Institution* (1925), pp. 507–12. See also Robert Taft, *Artists and Illustrators of the Old West* (New York, 1953), pp. 269–76.

62. Justin Smith, *The War with Mexico, 1,* 287–88.

63. Emory, *Notes,* p. 15. He published another, slightly different, version of his reconnaissance, which also began at this point. See W. H. Emory, "Extracts from His Journal while with the Army of the West," *Niles National Register, 71* (Oct. 31, 1846), 138.

64. Emory, *Notes,* p. 23.

seems elementary, it was not so in Emory's day. Barely fifty years before, scientists had been occupied by the classic debate over the aqueous or igneous origin of the earth's crust. In the 1840's and '50's the doctrine of catastrophism and special creation was still accepted. That he saw the shaping of the western land forms by a continuous process, like erosion, places Emory among the advanced scientific thinkers of his time.

As the Army advanced, William Bent's company of mountain men acted as scouts and hovered about the flanks of the marching column. Every day they brought in Mexican prisoners—soldiers, alcaldes, sheep tenders, padres—anybody who might belong to the enemy force. The appearance of these prisoners was so pathetic that once Kearny was moved to remark, "Emory, if I have to fire a round of grape into such men I shall think of it with remorse all my life." [65]

When the Army reached the pueblo of Las Vegas, Kearny delivered the first of his speeches of conciliation from a rooftop on the main square. While making the crestfallen city officials swear an oath of allegiance to the United States, he also guaranteed the protection of the towns from the Apaches and Navahoes as well as the protection of their churches from desecration. Then he and his staff, which included Emory, climbed down a rickety ladder, mounted their horses, and rode off toward the canyon reported to have been fortified by the Mexican General Armijo. With pennons flying and sabres cutting the air, the first elements of cavalry rode into the canyon—to find it empty. After passing this last strongpoint, the way was clear to Santa Fe. When the Army occupied the capital on August 18, it was obvious that Kearny's efforts had been more than adequate. Armijo and his assistant, Archuleta, had fled.

The ancient town of Pecos aroused Emory's interests, and at this point in his narrative he began his description of the peoples and antiquities of the Southwest. Emory's report marked the crude beginning of American anthropological and archeological studies in the West. The most impressive sight in the town of Pecos was the ruined church which stood on a promontory overlooking the town. Emory noted that it represented the grafting of Spanish Catholicism upon the primitive Indian religion.

65. Emory, "Extracts," p. 189.

At one end of the temple the Mass was celebrated; at the other end a perpetual fire to Montezuma had once burned.

When he examined these ruined towns Emory had before him the visions of Aztec and Mayan civilizations as described by Prescott in his *The Conquest of Mexico* (1843) and John Lloyd Stephens in his *Incidents of Travel in Central America, Chiapas and Yucatan* (1841). These books, best-sellers of their time, were typical products of the romantic age that helped to inspire both a popular and a professional enthusiasm for the exotic study of vanished Indian civilizations to which Emory's new-found data became an additional contribution.

It was characteristic of the encyclopedic nature of the duties of a Topographical Engineer, however, that when Emory reached Santa Fe he was kept busy selecting and surveying the site of Fort Marcy and making observations upon the contemporary economic, social, political, and religious life of the Mexican community. He also launched into the construction of a map of the route followed by the American Army, observing that "It was rather a bold undertaking to compress in[to] a few days, the work of months," but "We all worked day and night, and with the assistance of several gentlemen of the volunteers, I succeeded in accomplishing the work, not, however, in a very satisfactory manner." [66]

As for natural resources, he was not impressed by the fertility of the soil or the potential yield of precious metals in New Mexico. Instead, he hailed the grape, which, he declared, would make the whole area a center of wine production. The vintage products of El Paso were already famous on the frontier. In summary he concluded, "New Mexico was in a commercial and military aspect an all-important military possession for the United States," and "The road from Santa Fe to Fort Leavenworth presents few obstacles for a railway, and if it continues as good to the Pacific, will be one of the routes to be considered over which the United States will pass immense quantities of merchandise into what may become, in time, the rich and populous States of Sonora, Durango, and Southern California." [67] All of these considerations, from the practical to the theoretical,

66. Emory, *Notes*, p. 32.
67. Ibid., pp. 35–36.

were related in Emory's mind as factors governing the eventual patterns of settlement in the area.

On September 25 Kearny set out for California with a force of 300 Dragoons, Emory's fourteen-man topographical unit, and a few veteran scouts. As an adjunct to Kearny's column, Capt. Philip St. George Cooke was detailed to command a Mormon Battalion, equipped with wagons, which would follow a more southern route, south of the mountains and the Gila River. Cooke's battalion was not a combat unit but was organized as a supply train for the purpose of blazing a wagon trail.[68]

Emory's assistants were Lt. William Warner (Topographical Corps) and Bestor and Stanley. Lieutenants Peck and Abert were left at Santa Fe with orders, upon their recovery from illness, to make a careful map and survey of the entire province of New Mexico.[69]

The cavalry column rode down the valley of the Rio Grande, past Albuquerque, Valencia, and Socorro. Just before they reached Valverde, on October 6, Kit Carson rode up to the column with the news that California had surrendered. "The American flag floated in every port." [70] He had been sent across country from California by Frémont. Upon receiving this news, Kearny divided his force, sending Major Sumner and 200 Dragoons back to Santa Fe while he pushed on with the remaining one hundred men and the topographical unit. Carson, despite his protests, was pressed into service as a guide. Captain Cooke and his column, following behind, were guided by Antoine Leroux and Pauline Weaver, mountain trappers and veterans of the Gila River country.[71]

The first landmark reached by the truncated Army of the West was the deserted copper mine Santa Rita del Cobre, which had last been worked by Sylvester Pattie and his son James Ohio back in 1827. In 1846 it was a ghost town, the particular domain of the notorious Apache chieftain Mangus Colorado. At the Cop-

68. Philip St. George Cooke, W. H. C. Whiting, and Francis X. Aubrey, *Exploring Southwestern Trails, 1846–1854,* ed. Ralph P. Bieber and A. B. Bender, Southwestern Trails Series, 7 (Glendale, 1938), 26.

69. Emory, *Notes,* p. 45.

70. Ibid., p. 53.

71. Cooke, *Report* (above, n. 45), pp. 3, 12.

per Mine General Kearny held a meeting with Mangus Colorado and his fellow chieftains at which the Apaches all swore allegiance to the United States and offered to make war on Mexico. They were somewhat disappointed when the General declined their aid. To Emory the pow-wow was an impressive sight, with the Indians looking like helmeted "antique Greek warriors." Kit Carson, who knew them better than anyone else, was less impressed, and observed that he "would not trust one of them." [72] When the short meeting had ended, the military column moved on, leaving Mangus Colorado still in command of the copper mines, a possession he was to hold in fief for years to come.

The following day the column struck the Gila River, which ran through pulverized volcanic dust and hard layers of rocky basalt. For Emory the country assumed a greater interest as they came upon a series of ruined pueblos, abandoned water acequias, piles of broken pottery, and boulders inscribed with hieroglyphics of antique origin. He was inclined in his first enthusiasm to identify most of those remains with the Aztec cultures of Mexico. Upon later reflection he saw them as products of a distinct culture, forerunners of the pueblos in the Rio Grande Valley.[73] While he located traces of at least twelve aboriginal towns along the Gila, the most significant find was the Casa Grande, or Casa Montezuma as it was called by the natives. With its pink adobe walls still largely intact after four centuries, the Casa Grande provided Emory with some idea of the nature of the primitive architecture and the way of life of the former inhabitants. He was the first explorer to examine the ruin since Padres Pedro Font and Francisco Garces in 1776.[74] He concluded that most of the ruins he saw were not only vestiges of a unique culture but remains left by the forerunners of the inhabitants of his own day. He saw the modern tribes as an example of cultural regression in which the people had lost the skills of previous generations. In a letter to Albert Gallatin he also described the location of seven ruined towns on the Rio del San Jose, which he believed to be Coronado's original Seven Cities of Cibola. (Mod-

72. Emory, *Notes,* pp. 60, 61.

73. Ibid., pp. 131–34.

74. H. H. Bancroft, *History of Arizona and New Mexico* (San Francisco, 1889), pp. 623–25.

ern research has designated the pueblos at Zuñi as the actual site of Coronado's conquest.)[75]

At one site Emory found some bits of shells and obsidian which he linked with the Aztec sacrificial ceremonies described by William Hickling Prescott. He continued to speculate about the vanished inhabitants of the pueblo towns. "Who were they?" he wrote, "And where have they gone? Tradition among the Indians and Spaniards does not reach them."[76] Though more than three centuries had passed since Coronado's march, and the age of science was rapidly advancing, the old southwestern legends proved irresistible to explorers and conquistadors—even those in Army blue.

Not many days later, just after they had finished inspecting one of the ruins, they met a lone Maricopa Indian who led them to his village on the Gila near its confluence with the Salt River. Here the soldiers remained, trading with the Maricopas and their friendly neighbors the Pimas. Emory viewed these Indians with some astonishment: "To us it was a rare sight to be thrown in the midst of a large nation of what is termed wild Indians, surpassing many of the Christian nations in agriculture, little behind them in the useful arts, and immeasureably before them in honesty and virtue" (p. 84). The Pimas and Maricopas were skillful farmers who planted their corn and cotton crops near the river bottoms in order that they might irrigate with the overflow, much as did the ancient Egyptians along the Nile. Though living in the midst of the Apache stronghold, neither the Pimas nor the Maricopas were troubled by their warlike neighbors. In nearly every previous encounter the Apaches had been bested; consequently, they preferred to turn their aggressions toward the more docile Mexicans.

From the Pima villages the route led through a sandy country interspersed with dismal promontories, and extending as far as the junction of the Gila and Colorado rivers. Here Emory paused to determine the position of the junction with his astronomical

75. Paul Horgan, *Great River* (2 vols. New York, 1954), *1*, 109–13. Herbert E. Bolton, *Coronado on the Turquoise Trail, a Knight of Pueblo and Plains* (Albuquerque, 1949), map.

76. Emory, *Notes*, p. 68. Unless otherwise stated, the account is based on this work.

instruments. Near the crossing of the Colorado he discovered the trail of a large party that had recently passed northward from Sonora. The Lieutenant led a reconnoitering patrol which happened upon a Mexican camp, where they captured a colonel and several soldiers with a herd of 1,000 horses. The next day Emory surprised a Mexican courier carrying despatches from California to Sonora which told of the uprising under Flores and the subsequent recapture of Santa Barbara and Los Angeles (pp. 94–95). It then became imperative to push on to California as rapidly as possible, so as to throw the 114 men of the Army of the West upon the enemy from an unexpected quarter.

Before describing the Army's passage of the desert from the Colorado to California, Emory took time in his report to make two important observations concerning the country recently traversed. "In no part of this vast tract can the rains from Heaven be relied upon, to any extent, for the cultivation of the soil. . . . The cultivation of the earth is therefore confined to the narrow strips of land which are within the level of the waters of the streams and wherever practised in a community with any success, or to any extent, involves a degree of subordination and absolute obedience to a chief, repugnant to the habits of our people" (p. 98). Thus he recognized and stated the essential problem of arid lands settlement as it was to be formulated by John Wesley Powell some thirty-two years later.[77] He saw the need for a new kind of settlement pattern, related to water instead of land, and he saw that such a settlement required a cooperative agreement for water control that seemed to conflict with the traditional exploitative and individualistic settler values. The free settler could never be harnessed to a system of planned distribution, even where there was scarcity. Only the Mormons, by means of their religious sanction for communitarianism, were successful in creating a planned society adapted to the geographical realities of the Great Basin region. Even then, there were those who objected to such an authoritarian compact.

Emory also added another conclusion of fundamental significance for its time. Speaking, perhaps, from his Maryland plantation experience, he declared: "No one who has ever visited

77. See John Wesley Powell, *Report on the Lands of the Arid Region of the United States* (Wash., 1878), passim.

this country and who is acquainted with the character and value of slave labor in the United States would ever think of bringing his own slaves here with any view to profit, much less would he purchase slaves for such a purpose. Their labor here, if they could be retained as slaves among peons nearly of their own color, would never repay the cost of transportation, much less the additional purchase money." [78] Was it this conclusion, so explicit on the question of slavery and the new territories, that guided Webster in his all-important speech for the Compromise of 1850? It was the voice of a hard-thinking, practical Southern man of experience, and it must have caused serious thought among his contemporaries in the North and South alike.

From the Colorado River to Warner's Ranch at the base of the Sierra Madres was eight days' journey over a sahara country. Only with extreme difficulty was General Kearny able to bring his party across it intact. It was the first of December before they completed the *jornada* and stood in command of the pass between Sonora and California which lay across the supply line of the Mexican Army. When Emory finished taking the latitude and longitude of the Ranch, his work as a scientist was drawing to a close and his work as a soldier was approaching its climax.

San Pascual and San Diego

The Californians under General Flores had risen from defeat to recapture most of Southern California, including Santa Barbara and the Pueblo de los Angeles. When they learned that Kearny's bedraggled force of dragoons was advancing on the rear along the lifeline from Sonora, Don Andreas Pico and several squadrons of mounted lancers were sent to meet the threat. By the morning of December 4 they were bivouacked in the crude mud huts of an Indian village at San Pascual which stood on one of the two roads leading to San Diego.[79] They had a vague idea that Kearny's dragoons were camped at Warner's Ranch, but they had no certain knowledge of his whereabouts until an American reconnaissance patrol inadvertently crashed into the

78. Emory, *Notes*, p. 99.

79. Arthur Woodward, *Lancers at San Pascual* (San Francisco, 1948), p. 20.

outskirts of their camp.[80] Warned of an impending attack, they collected their mounts, sharpened their lances, and prepared for battle.

General Kearny was eager for combat. Ignoring the fact that his dragoons were worn-out and ill-mounted, he prepared for an all-out cavalry charge in the classic manner. The predawn morning of December 6, 1846, was cold, wet, and foggy, but before daybreak the Army of the West was in the saddle and moving forward. The General sent the howitzers to the rear, along with a small reinforcement that had come out under Captain Gillespie from the Pacific Squadron, and prepared to make his supreme cavalry gesture with cold steel. He chivalrously invited Emory and Warner to join him at the head of the main column, while Captain Johnston and twelve men formed the advance guard.[81] Through the haze they sighted the Mexicans waiting—scattered, disorganized, and armed mainly with lances. The General ordered a trot, and then a charge, and the battle began like a medieval encounter, with both sides disdaining tactics in favor of the headlong charge and hand-to-hand clash of arms. Johnston's men, far ahead of the rest, met the enemy first. Soon after, the main body of troops made contact, and as Emory later wrote, "we found ourselves in hand-to-hand conflict with a largely superior force."[82] Individual skirmishes were strung out for half a mile along the road. Captain Johnston fell with the first volley, pierced through the brain by a musket ball fired from an ancient flintlock. Captain Moore, Emory's closest friend on the march, was lanced to death by an obscure Mexican named Leandro Osuna. Lieutenant Hammond fell at his side. Captain Gillespie was solely pressed on all sides, the object of the special hatred of the Mexicans because of his part in the first conquest of California. He escaped with his lung pierced, his mouth torn open, his teeth smashed, and a lance thrust through him just above the heart.[83]

80. Emory, *Notes,* p. 108. Woodward, p. 27.
81. Emory, *Notes,* p. 108.
82. Ibid.
83. The account is based on Woodward, pp. 30–36; Edwin L. Sabin, *Kit Carson Days* (2 vols. New York, 1935), *2,* 529; Emory, *Notes,* p. 108.

One trooper guarding the howitzers was beset by two lancers. He tried desperately to make himself smaller by hiding under the gun carriage, but he was slaughtered just the same. Early in the fight Kit Carson fell from his horse and broke his rifle. It was as much as he could do to crawl from under the jousting horses and secure another gun. General Kearny himself was wounded in the arm and buttocks, the latter wound perhaps the result of some overenthusiastic swipe by the saber of a fellow officer. Lieutenant Warner suffered three wounds. Emory became the hero of the battle when he saved Kearny's life and killed a lancer who was just about to finish the General. This lancer was one of two Mexicans killed in the skirmish. Soon the swirls and eddies of combat became smaller, and the clash of arms less frequent. Suddenly the Mexicans retired from the field. The Army of the West had triumphed only by the merest technicality, since its losses were eighteen killed and thirteen wounded, with one-third of the officers among the casualties. The Mexicans suffered two killed and several wounded. The Battle of San Pascual, by the end of the first day, was the least glorious American victory of the Mexican War.

That night the Americans buried their dead under a willow tree amid the howling of ravenous coyotes. The wounded demanded attention, rendering the force immobile, and the General had lost consciousness. All the while Mexican horsemen hovered about the edges of the battlefield. The survivors, nearly all of them wounded, lay all night on their arms.

"Day dawned," Emory remembered, "on the most tattered and ill-fed detachment of men that ever the United States mustered under colors." [84] All that day they marched, dragging the wounded on crude travois made by the mountain men. When night fell, they had driven the Mexicans off a small hill west of Snooks Ranch and fortified themselves for a last stand. Four men under Alexis Godey, previously sent for help, had been captured and the outlook was dim. But on the night of December 8 Kit Carson, Lt. Edward Fitzgerald Beale, and an Indian scout crawled through the Mexican lines and made their way to San Diego twenty-nine miles away. The dragoons held out through the 10th and that night 180 sailors and marines under Lieutenant A. V. F. Gray

84. Emory, *Notes,* p. 109.

arrived to turn the balance in favor of the Americans. The Mexicans were dispersed and General Kearny advanced successfully to the Pacific. For Emory the reconnaissance was completed, and as he stood at the end of his journey and looked out to the ocean, he heard a mountain man exclaim in ignorant wonder, "Lord! There is a great prairie without a tree!" [85] It was thus he realized that on his march through the Southwest he had seen what few other Americans and no American scientist had ever seen.

Kearny's small force had spanned the entire trans-Mississippi Southwest. In doing so they had taken a route previously known only to occasional fur trappers and parties of Apache raiders. They had dragged their small cannon across another route to the Pacific in a latitude where weather conditions would permit year-round emigration and where, perhaps, it might prove feasible to construct the first transcontinental railroad. So well was Emory's survey performed that it influenced Topographical Bureau activities and national policy for the next ten years.

But though Emory considered the Gila route along the 32nd parallel practicable for a railroad, it had certain disadvantages —the broken and rocky nature of the country along the river itself, the ninety-mile desert *jornada* west of the Colorado River, the difficult river crossing itself, and the mountainous country between San Diego and the desert. Captain Cooke's Mormon Battalion helped solve some of these problems. It followed a southern route around the lower extremity of the Sierra Mimbres mountains of New Mexico, and across the playas, or dry lake beds, to the Guadalupe Pass, and thence westward to the town of Tucson, which was captured, by gentleman's agreement, from its Mexican garrison.[86] From this point they headed north to the Pima villages on the Gila, thence west in Kearny's footsteps. It was a route which at least avoided the rugged stretches of country along the Gila, and the fact that wagons had made the journey did much to confirm the opinions of those who deemed it suitable for a transcontinental road. Cooke saw his route as connecting at some point on the Rio Grande with Josiah Gregg's route from Van Buren, Arkansas, across North Texas. According to Cooke, "Emigrants could very cheaply supply themselves with cattle,

85. Ibid., pp. 112–13.
86. Cooke, *Report,* pp. 41–42.

mules, and sheep in New Mexico. If their destination was Southern California, there could be no question as to the best route." [87]

It was with these considerations in mind that Emory personally advised Secretary of State Buchanan to demand a national boundary line at 32° north latitude in the negotiations with Mexico.[88] He believed that this would include the transcontinental route, whether for wagons or railroads, and that the securing of this route was vital for controlling Indian raids and marching troops to California, as well as for the economic development of the newly acquired territories.

Though Emory's reconnaissance was a rapid one in which military objectives predominated, it was nevertheless an outstanding addition to scientific geography. His map was the first accurately drawn one of the whole area.[89] It corrected the errors in Humboldt's Atlas, modified Frémont's map of 1845, and rendered the new commercial maps of Mitchell and Tanner immediately obsolete. In compiling his map Emory was, in most cases, careful not to include anything that he or his subordinates did not actually observe, so that his map was with some exceptions a trustworthy view of the Gila River region. It changed the entire conception of southwestern geography, and it came into wide use in 1849 when California gold-seekers moved west along the southern route. Compiled from more than 2,000 astronomical observations and supplemented by an altitude profile based on 357 separate barometric observations, it was the final major piece needed to complete the early outline of trans-Mississippi geography. It remains one of the landmarks in western American cartography.

With the map as the geographic base of his official report, Emory was able to add descriptions of the topography, lists of the animals and plants of the region, and some commentary on the geology and fossil remains characteristic of the various strata.

87. Ibid., p. 51.

88. See Buchanan to Trist, Wash., July 19, 1847, in Moore, *Buchanan,* pp. 368–69.

89. In Emory, *Report, 1,* 17, Emory admits that the bend of the Gila was laid down on his map from conjecture, and he also admits that, as A. W. Whipple, A. B. Gray, and J. R. Bartlett point out in their later reports, his map is in error on this point. He declared, "It is a small affair, subtended by a chord of thirty or forty miles."

In the course of his observations he also touched upon the potential mineral resources of the country, though like Frémont he did not consider this a primary objective of his investigations.

John Torrey made a detailed study of the plant specimens sent back from the expedition, and when Emory's report was published, the cautious botanist listed eighteen new species and one new genus as Emory's discoveries.[90] One of the plants he named *Querus Emoryi* in the Lieutenant's honor.

A special report on the cactus specimens was contributed by Dr. George Engelmann of St. Louis, the leading authority on such plants. Fifteen species were identified, and the *Cereus Giganteus*, or giant cactus, was described for the first time in a scientific report. Emory even included an illustration of that now-familiar plant in his report. As late as 1856 the botanical returns from this wartime reconnaissance were still the object of analysis. In that year Engelmann read his "Synopsis of Cactacae" before the American Academy of Arts and Sciences.[91]

The study of Indian ethnology through archeological remains was also pioneered in the Southwest by Emory's reconnaissance. Though Gregg's *Commerce of the Prairies* contained an account of the Pueblo Bonito,[92] Emory's searches through ruined townsites like the Casa Grande proved to be an important first step in the serious study of the pueblo tribes and their mysterious past.[93] His findings were made available through Albert Gallatin to the American Ethnological Society, which the ex-Secretary of the Treasury had helped to found in 1842.[94] An idea of Emory's role as a pioneer in these studies is afforded when one remembers that the first volume of the Society's proceedings was only published in 1845, and the monumental study by two of its members, E. G. Squier and E. H. Davis, on "The Ancient Monuments of the Mississippi Valley" appeared in 1847, in the *Smithsonian Contributions to Knowledge*. Though the science of man was a relatively

90. Emory, *Notes*, pp. 137–55; the number of new species has been calculated by me.

91. Meisel, *Bibliography*, p. 17.

92. Vol. *1*, 284–85.

93. Justin Winsor, *Narrative and Critical History of America* (8 vols. Boston, 1889), *1*, 396.

94. John Russell Bartlett, "Autobiography" (Bartlett Papers, John Carter Brown Library, Brown University), pp. 32–33.

new discipline,[95] it was natural that it should attract the attention of the Army topographers in the Southwest, because it was part of their duty to study the habits and customs of the Indian inhabitants.

The living Indian tribes were closely scrutinized by Emory, and his data on the Pimas and Maricopas was preceded by only one other study.[96] His descriptions of the Apaches also were authoritative, being made at first hand.

Viewed generally, Emory's *Report* was a noteworthy work of geographical observation. On a smaller scale, it was the kind of many-sided survey conducted by Humboldt in Mexico, though it suffered from the same defects. Time prevented Emory from going far in any direction, for he was taking part in a military campaign in the midst of enemy territory. But he had made a beginning, and he could feel justified in leaving later generations to question nature more closely.

Abert and Peck in New Mexico

Lieutenant Emory's reconnaissance was not the only important wartime survey to produce scientific results. Lt. James W. Abert's work in New Mexico and Capt. George W. Hughes' report on General Wool's march to Saltillo also contributed to the public knowledge of western geography. They served to give Americans a better acquaintance with the nature of the whole southwestern region, of which New Mexico and Arizona were only a part. Any observer who passed over the plateau country of the North Mexican provinces and saw the way of life of the people, the extent of Indian depredations, and the limitations imposed upon economic and cultural development by the natural surroundings, could not help being wiser in advising his own country on its plans for the Southwest. At the same time, though not a primary object, the purely military achievements of the Corps should not be overlooked. They helped to win those large areas of the West toward which so much attention was later to be directed.

The original complement of the topographical unit attached

95. Carl Ritter's *Erdkunde* was first published in 2 vols. 1817–18, and a second edition of 21 vols. appeared 1822–59.

96. Namely Josiah Gregg's examination of the Pueblo Bonito, published in 1844 in his *Commerce of the Prairies*. See Winsor, *1*, 396.

to the Army of the West had included four officers. Of these only two, Lieutenants Emory and Warner, made the trip to California. The other two, Lieutenants Abert and Peck, being ill, were left behind, Abert at Bent's Fort and Peck at Santa Fe. Their orders were, upon their recovery, to join forces and carry out a thorough survey of the conquered province of New Mexico.[97] Their primary duty, of course, was to construct an accurate map of the whole region. This would provide a starting point for the location of resources, towns, and Indian tribes.

From July 30 to September 9 Lieutenant Abert lay stricken with fever at Bent's Fort. But even though sick, he continued his studies in natural science and ethnology, building up a collection of specimens, sketching the Indians, and compiling tribal vocabularies (pp. 11–13).

When he was well enough to travel, Abert made his way to Santa Fe where he met Lieutenant Peck, now also recovered from fever. While waiting for Abert's arrival, Peck had made a reconnaissance of Taos and its vicinity and had also constructed a sketch map of the area,[98] made in conjunction with Lieutenant Warner, which was immediately forwarded by Emory to the Topographical Bureau in Washington.[99] It represented little original information but it did provide a confirmation of the many unofficial accounts of Taos.

Impatient to get into action, the two lieutenants, Abert and Peck, began a swing southward on September 29. Their immediate destination was the gold-mining region south of Santa Fe along Galisteo Creek. There they saw various kinds of mines. Some were primitive operations where ragged peons scratched the earth with pieces of iron; in others, more advanced, the rock was dumped into a mill that was really a pit where two burros circled round and round dragging huge stones over a flat, stone crushing-floor. The ore itself was found in small veins running through

97. *Report of the Secretary of War, Communicating in Answer to a Resolution of the Senate, a Report and Map of the Examination of New Mexico, Made by Lieutenant J. W. Abert, of the Topographical Corps,* Feb. 10, 1848, 30th Cong., 1st Sess., Sen. Exec. Doc. 23 (1848), 32. Unless otherwise stated, the following account is based on this work.

98. Emory to Abert, Sept. 25, 1846, LR, TE 77. Two sketch maps are enclosed.

99. Ibid.

quartz, and to dig it out often necessitated tunneling straight down into the earth. Most of the mines they visited were owned by Americans. Of the mining operations in general Abert concluded: "The value of the mines cannot very well be estimated now as there have been many improvements in the methods of working gold, which, when adopted at the mines, may produce a great increase in their annual yield. At present, none of the owners of these gold mines have ever become wealthy by the mining operations, and I have met several who have sunk all they had in searching for gold" (p. 36).

Another project of the two topographers was to search for the Seven Cities of Cibola. It was, to some extent, Abert's data that Emory used in his report on the cities, but he differed sharply in his conclusions. Abert and Peck crossed the Rio Grande opposite Albuquerque and headed into the Navaho country up the Puerco River. When they reached the San Jose River, which flowed into the Puerco, they began encountering the first of the cities. There was Cibolleta, Moquino, Pajuate, Covero, Laguna, Rito, and Acoma, and they seemed to fit the description of Aztec cities made by the Spanish authorities Clavigero and de Solis, to which Lieutenant Abert constantly referred. Most of the actual pueblos were a disappointment to the explorers. Rito was a pile of moldering adobe ruins rapidly returning to the earth. The other towns consisted of one- and two-story adobe pueblos filled with Indians practicing their primitive agriculture similar to those east of the Rio Grande. Only Acoma, high on a lofty rock of limestone, lived up to their expectations. It was reached by a narrow winding stairway cut from the rock face of the cliff. Once on top of the mesa, one saw the large blocks of pueblos and the square adobe church that formed the town proper. Lieutenant Abert found the inhabitants "quiet and generous" and engaged in their everyday tasks of processing the village food supply (p. 55).

When he came to reflect upon these cities of the San Jose Valley, Abert saw a clear connection between them and the Aztec culture (pp. 73–75). He was correct when he traced Coronado's march to these villages.[100] However, when he cited Francisco Javier Clavigero's description of the Aztec migrations southward

100. Winsor, 2, 487. A detachment was sent to these villages by Coronado, and the battle of Acoma Pueblo resulted. The battle is best described in Horgan, *Great River, 1,* 203–9.

from the Colorado to the Gila and saw the San Jose cities as way stations on their march, he was on less certain ground. Finally, when he agreed that proof was supplied by Torquemada and Betancourt, who found the pueblos speaking the Mexican language, the Lieutenant could be accused of entering the realm of fancy. In these conclusions he was adopting a position opposite to that of Emory and Albert Gallatin, who maintained that the ancient pueblos were the forerunners of the present Pueblo Indians rather than vestiges of the Aztecs.[101] Nevertheless, Abert's conclusion was in line with that of Humboldt, who also upheld the Aztec theory and who specified on his 1811 map their various resting places on the southward trek into Mexico.[102] Despite the researches of modern anthropologists and the discovery of some Aztec artifacts, the question remains an intriguing one even today.

In their survey Abert and Peck also collected important data on the population and political organization of the province. They included in their journal an official census report from the records of Santa Fe which had been compiled in 1844 and gave the population of New Mexico as 100,064 people. It divided the province into Northern, Central, and Southern districts, with capitals at Las Luceras, Santa Fe, and Valencia respectively (pp. 61–63).

When the survey of New Mexico was completed, Abert was ordered to Washington to report first hand on conditions in New Mexico and to construct his maps with the proper instruments. Peck remained in Santa Fe for a while longer, then he too marched East with a party that included Kit Carson and others recently returned from California. It seems an oversight on the part of Colonel Abert that no Topographical Engineer was attached to Alexander W. Doniphan's column moving south into Chihuahua. Major William Gilpin was the only member of that force who was at all scientifically educated until the Americans liberated a curious St. Louis German named Adolph Wislizenus from the calaboose of the city of Chihuahua.[103]

101. Emory, *Notes,* pp. 127–34.

102. Von Humboldt, *Essai politique* (above, p. 32, n. 33), atlas. See notation on the map.

103. F. A. Wislizenus, *Memoir of a Tour to Northern Mexico, Connected with Colonel Doniphan's Expedition, in 1846 and 1847,* 30th Cong., 1st Sess., Sen. Misc. Doc. 26 (1848), passim.

The return journey of Lieutenant Abert proved to be a fantastic ordeal. When he and his party started for Bent's Fort it was the end of December, but it took him until March to reach civilization in the valley of the Mississippi. By January the men had begun to experience the freezing cold of the prairie winter, and the snow was five feet deep in Raton Pass. The mules continually lost their footing, and men and wagons were plunged into ice-cold streams or sent sprawling across the iced-over surface. Seven men came down with measles. Two couldn't walk. Teamsters suffered frostbite if they rode on the wagon box, so they were forced to trudge through the snow drifts. When they reached Bent's Fort, their trial was only beginning. Both the Arapahos and the Pawnees were on the warpath, and they lay in wait between the Big Timbers and the Pawnee Fork for wagon trains floundering along the Santa Fe Trail. Abert's small party was tempting bait.

Soon after leaving the Big Timbers, they met the Arapahos, but when the Indians noted that the Lieutenant was on his guard, they offered friendship and proceeded to steal what they wanted. A few days later, snowstorms began. All day on February 12 the snow fell, and the men stayed in their buffalo robes to keep warm. One man had hysterics, and crouching at Abert's feet implored him, "O Lieutenant, take me to a house! I shall freeze to death! I'm freezing I'm freezing!" Abert remembered, "I took the poor fellow and put him in my own bed and covered him with blankets and buffalo robes; it was all I could do" (p. 115). That night three mules froze to death. The next day a man went blind. While the others were busy breaking camp, the blind man, resting by the fire listening to the ravens and magpies, felt a slight tug at his buffalo robe, and heard the sound of panting wolves by his side. With his last reserve of strength he frightened them away.

When the party's fortunes seemed at their nadir, a band of Pawnees stampeded their mules, leaving them with two worn-out oxen to pull the train of wagons. It was then that the determination that goes with disaster arose in the men. They placed the sick in one of the wagons and harnessed themselves as beasts of burden. Abert recalled: "We now started amid the loud exalting cheers of the men as they thus triumphed over our difficulties when we seemed to have reached the 'ne plus ultra' of misfortune" (p. 119). The Pawnees still hung about, tempting them with their own mules and threatening attack in an unguarded moment. Abert was hard put to restrain his men. Even then the worst was not past. On the night of February 23 a heavy snow fell, and on the following morning when they arose two men were missing. Somewhere under the drifts they lay buried alive. After moments of frantic digging, the rescuers found a boot, then a robe, and then, finally, five feet down, one of the men still breathing, hysterical with joy at being redeemed from the dead. Beside him, under the snow, lay his weaker bedfellow who had slowly suffocated to death (p. 127).

The next day they reached the prairie groves, and their ordeal was at last nearing its end. By March 1 they were out of the cold, and they saw the sun come up over the Kansas River. Abert wrote what was to be his farewell impression as an explorer: "There was a majesty in the lofty groves which now surrounded us, and a music in the plash of the wild duck as it lit upon the bosom of the river; there was music even in the scream of the parraquette that swept over our heads; there was a charm in everything, for we now really felt that our trials were at an end" (p. 130).

With Wool to Saltillo

In September 1846, while Kearny's dragoons were preparing for their march to the Pacific and Lieutenant Abert was making his way over the Raton Pass to Santa Fe, Captain George W. Hughes commanded another detachment of Topographical Engineers which assembled for a march with General Wool's Army into the heart of Mexico.[104] Performing functions similar to that of the unit headed by Emory, Hughes and his men led the Army of Occupation via Presidio del Rio Grande, Santa Rosa, and Monclova to Parras, a strategic road hub between Chihuahua and Monterey. The country traversed was known only in the vaguest

104. George W. Hughes, *Report of the Secretary of War, Communicating . . . a Map Showing the Operations of the Army of the United States in Texas and the Adjacent Mexican States on the Rio Grande; Accompanied by Astronomical Observations, and Descriptive and Military Memoirs of the Country, March 1, 1849,* 31st Cong., 1st Sess., Sen. Exec. Doc. 32, 1850.

terms, and Hughes' main contribution consisted in the large map of his route drawn by Lts. Lorenzo Sitgreaves and Willian B. Franklin, his subordinates. They were assisted in their work by Josiah Gregg the famous prairie traveler, who accompanied the expedition.[105] Unlike the expeditions of Emory and Abert, however, the Hughes party made no lasting scientific contribution other than its map. Hughes made no collections, and established no liaison with scientists in the centers of learning on the eastern seaboard. Instead, he offered a few practical comments and suggestions for promoting future development of the regions he had traversed. They sounded more like the military strategist than the scientist. As the first step in the reclamation of the Indian-devastated areas, Hughes believed the federal government should build a line of forts along the newly surveyed "road" from San Antonio to Presidio Rio Grande for the protection of settlers. He believed that at least one regiment of mounted troops would be needed, and that four posts ought to be set up: at San Antonio, on the Quihi River, on the Leona, and at the Rio Grande Crossing.[106] It is interesting to note that before 1850 his suggestions were being followed virtually to the letter, and the so-called "inner ring" of forts was established in western Texas.[107] At the same time, Hughes also thought this would be but a temporary expedient. He declared, "there can be no question that the protection which they [the troops] would afford would be the means of rapidly settling the country with a population that soon would be able to defend itself." [108] In Hughes' mind the Army was the only possible spearhead of settlement in that area of hostile plains Indians. In some respects, this army-convoyed mode of settlement was similar to that of the older Spanish system of presidios, or garrisons, except that here the emphasis was upon mounted troops rather than local garrisons of foot soldiers.

When it came to the Indians, Hughes was very realistic, if somewhat callous: "it must be obvious to even the most super-

105. Ibid., p. 8 n. See also Fulton, *Diary and Letters of Josiah Gregg,* pp. 251–99.

106. Ibid., p. 35.

107. The Texas defense system is described in Averam B. Bender, *The March of Empire* (Lawrence, Kan., 1952), pp. 33–37.

108. Hughes, *Report,* p. 35.

ficial observer that hostilities with the Comanches and Lipans, the most warlike of the native tribes, are neither remote nor contingent. I regard it as inevitable, and I believe we shall never establish cordial relations with them until they have been severely punished—an affair, by-the-by, not easy of accomplishment." [109] By comparison with Emory's expedition, Hughes' results seem less spectacular, but it is significant that in the midst of a military campaign his thoughts were focused on some concrete expression of the Manifest Destiny of the United States in the western regions which were not yet securely conquered from the enemy.

The actual combat duties of the Topographical Engineers are only distantly related to their role in the development of the West. Even their mapping was carried on mostly in Mexican territory, where it would be of use only as an aid to later historians of the war itself. But by virtue of the fact that they did accompany the armies into the lands of Mexico, they learned of a whole new geographical area, and helped to bring it to public attention. Their reports, partially released in the newspapers and published in full as Senate and House documents, underscored the potential of all these new western lands. Moreover, in their marches the topographers gained practical experience in dealing with the problems that arose in that previously unfamiliar environment. It gave them a sense of the importance of natural facts, stimulated their accumulation, and caused the evaluation of this new data in response to the needs of their own expanding culture. What conditions did the environment impose on man, and how could it best be utilized—these were the questions always implicit in their inquiry. If they had learned only the simple importance of water and nothing more, it would have been a valuable lesson for any later federal plans concerning the trans-Mississippi West.

Though it may be difficult to see a precise connection between armed combat and the accumulation of knowledge for peaceful pursuits, this was the task of the Army topographers during the Mexican War. Emory wielding a saber at San Pascual, Meade scouting under the very walls of Monterey, Derby wounded at Cerro Gordo after making a crucial reconnaissance of the Mexican right flank, William G. Williams, Frémont's first instructor, dead at Monterey, Hughes fighting guerillas on the road to Jalapa

109. Ibid.

—all were somehow attuned to the quest for kowledge, and the Corps as a whole was acquiring that geographical information so valuable to those who would be working in similar lands and among similar people in the American West.

The theme was epitomized when the victorious American armies battered down the gates of Mexico City to storm the Halls of Montezuma. There, on the height of Chapultepec, in the ruins of the military academy, Lt. Edmund L. F. Hardcastle, Topographical Corps, laid down his saber to pick up the very instruments used by Humboldt himself in mapping the Valley of Mexico.[110] Together with Lt. M. L. Smith, also of the Corps, Hardcastle spent the succeeding weeks retracing Humboldt's footsteps, making a new survey of the valley. His map supplanted that of the great geographer, but it was made for a very different reason—to portray the final American conquest of the city. Both men, Humboldt and Hardcastle, were gatherers of knowledge, scientists, but their work, once completed, did not amount to the same thing. Humboldt's data remained in the realm of pure knowledge, while Hardcastle's report descended to the market place of hard political reality to be used for good or evil. When it came to be published among the Senate Documents, there were those who viewed it, as they did the work of all the Topographical Engineers, in only the political sense. It was an excuse, they said, merely part of some sinister presidential plan to annex all Mexico, and nothing more.[111]

110. H. L. F. Hardcastle and M. L. Smith, *In Further Compliance with the Resolution of the Senate of August 3, 1848, Calling for a Map of the Valley of Mexico, by Lieutenants Smith and Hardcastle,* Jan. 29, 1849, 30th Cong., 2d Sess., Sen. Exec. Doc. 19 (1848–49), 9.

111. *Cong. Globe,* 31st Cong., 1st Sess., *19* (1849–50), 391. See also Brantz Mayer to James Alfred Pearce, Baltimore, March 22, 1850, in Bernard C. Steiner, ed., "Some Letters from the Correspondence of James Alfred Pearce," *Maryland Historical Magazine, 16* (1921), 157–58, for a plea by a prominent American intellectual on behalf of the publication of Hardcastle's report and map.

5. THE BOUNDARY SURVEY

> There is another topic, one too, which possesses a deeper interest for the American People and the whole civilized world than those to which I have alluded. This is the adaptation of the country explored by the Boundary Commission for the purposes of a railway.—*John Russell Bartlett*

THE SURVEY of the boundary between the United States and Mexico was the first large-scale project undertaken by the Topographical Corps in the trans-Mississippi West. It required the Topographical Engineers assigned to the survey commission to play an exacting dual role. They were, first of all, scientific technicians and subordinate administrators who would see to the actual details of running and marking the boundary line. At the same time, since the negotiations for the proper location of the line depended on a knowledge of geography and cartography, they were called upon to offer opinions in these matters which in turn brought them to their second major role of diplomat and national policy adviser. They were thus carried far beyond the duties of routine soldiering and placed in the difficult position of helping to formulate an international policy that had crucial implications in terms of the mounting sectional rivalries within the United States itself.

The Boundary Commission proper was a mixed commission composed of civilian and military officers operating under the orders of the Department of State. It was an improvisation based upon the exigencies of the moment, and with a prominent politician serving as Commissioner it was virtually certain to generate friction between the civilian workers and the proud officers of the Topographical Corps. The friction generated, the wounded vanities, the blasted reputations, and even the acts of quiet common sense—in short, the very workings of the bureaucracy, as it were—form an important part of the whole story of the Boundary Survey.

Two themes were inextricably bound together. Viewed in one

way, the history of the Survey is an important chapter in the diplomatic annals of the United States and Mexico. In another way, it is a case history of the role played by a military corps engaged in public works when the federal government itself had no clearly devised plan for its extensive operations in the far-flung territories of the New West.

On February 2, 1848, Nicholas P. Trist put signature to his masterpiece, the Treaty of Guadalupe Hidalgo, and thus brought an end to the war with Mexico. The section of the Treaty which described the boundary between the two republics, Article V, had undergone extensive revisions as both countries argued over the exact amount of territory to be ceded by Mexico to the United States. With such a vast domain, including California, New Mexico, and part of Texas, changing hands, a difference in minutes of latitude might seem trivial except that a number of points of strategic importance were located near the proposed boundaries. The Port of San Diego lay somewhere near the southern extreme of Upper California, and it was important to the United States to ensure its being north of the proposed border. An outlet to the Gulf of California was also desirable, so as to prevent a possible recurrence on the Colorado River of a deposit dispute of the kind that had occurred on the Mississippi at New Orleans. It was imperative, furthermore, that "the town called Paso" remain Mexican, since it was the northern outpost of the state of Chihuahua, which would not consent to any treaty that ceded one foot of its soil.[1] Finally, behind all the deliberations, lay the desire on the part of the United States government to acquire the southwestern route for a transcontinental railroad that Lieutenant Emory in 1847 had reported as existing somewhere along the Gila River. All of these objectives commanded Trist's serious attention, for as he believed, upon their fulfillment depended the cessation of hostilities.[2]

Article V of the Treaty declared that the boundary line should run from a point three leagues out in the Gulf of Mexico up the Rio Grande along its deepest channel to the point where the river

1. This town of El Paso should not be confused with present-day El Paso. It was situated where the town of Juarez now stands.

2. William R. Manning, *Diplomatic Correspondence of the United States,* Inter-American Affairs, 8, Mexico (Wash., 1937), 1044–49 n.

struck the southern boundary of New Mexico. From this point it ran westwardly along the whole southern boundary of New Mexico, "which runs north of the town called Paso," to its western termination, and thence northward along the western line of New Mexico until it intersected the first branch of the Gila River, or to the point on the line nearest such branch, and then down that branch to the Gila, down the Gila, and across the Colorado River to the Pacific Ocean. The terminal point on the Pacific Ocean was to be one marine league south of the southernmost point of the Port of San Diego, as laid down in the 1782 map of Don Juan Pantoja,[3] second sailing master of the Spanish fleet.

The southern and western limits of New Mexico were those specified in J. Disturnell's *Map of the United Mexican States, as Organized and Defined by Various Acts of the Congress of Said Republic and Constructed According to the Best Authorities.*[4] This map was known at the time to be inaccurate but was nevertheless included as an arbitrary definition of the limits of New Mexico.[5] Even the two copies of the map attached to the treaties were not identical, the American copy being the seventh edition and the Mexican copy the twelfth edition.[6] All versions of Disturnell's map were based upon a plagiarism in 1828 by White, Gallaher, and White of Tanner's 1825 map of Mexico.[7] The only changes made by Disturnell had been the incorporation of some new data in the northern areas.[8] And though it was probably the best commercial map of the Southwest then available, its errors were to provide a basis for extensive diplomatic controversy over the position of the boundary line.

In deriving the line, Trist had gone to considerable trouble to search for a proper set of cartographic authorities on which to base his treaty *projét.* During the negotiations, Captain Robert

3. *The Treaty betwen the United States and Mexico* . . . 30th Cong., 1st Sess., Sen. Exec. Doc. 52 (1848), 43–45.

4. Revised edition published in New York in 1847.

5. Emory, *Report, I,* 21; also Nicholas P. Trist, draft of a letter to the New York *Evening Post,* n.d., Nicholas P. Trist Papers, Vol. 34 (June 20, 1849—Feb. 23, 1853), Library of Congress.

6. Laurence Martin, *Disturnell's Map* (Wash., 1937), p. 353.

7. Ibid., p. 343.

8. Wheat, "Mapping the American West," p. 109 n.

E. Lee furnished him with a geographical memorandum of Mexican and other foreign versions of the country in question.[9] It included, among other things, a notation which quoted Moscaro on the latitude of El Paso del Norte, placing it at 32° 9′—that is, within eleven minutes of the position accorded it on Disturnell's map.[10] Other authorities on this point were J. S. Escudero, *Noticias Estadisticos del Estado de Chihuahua,* which had El Paso at 32° 50′, and a work entitled *Ojado sobre Nueva Mexico formada por el licenciado Antonio Barriero* . . . in which the town was at 32° 40′. All of these were known to be inaccurate, and Trist himself wrote a memorandum attached to the compilation which indicated his awareness of these errors. It read: "All these geographical notes are replete with errors; for nothing is positively known, and the only basis for them consists of ill-formed conjectures and worse information." [11]

Some accurate information was supplied to Trist by Secretary of State Buchanan. In a despatch of July 19, 1847, he sent Emory's recently determined latitude of San Diego.[12] But since neither Emory nor Abert had gone to El Paso, and since the Topographical Bureau had sent no officer with Doniphan's column, an accurate latitude of that city was not available to Trist. He was thus forced to depend upon his admittedly erroneous sources. For this reason neither Trist nor the Mexicans knew exactly where to place the boundary with respect to latitude so that it would be certain to leave El Paso a Mexican town. Instead, they compromised by introducing Disturnell's map as an arbitrary guide that would furnish a pictorial description of the line's location, and the words "which runs north of the town called Paso" were inserted into the Treaty, further describing the southern boundary of New Mexico for the protection of the Mexican interests.[13] As it stood, then, in the Treaty, the boundary was based upon (1) an exact initial point on the Pacific, (2) an arbitrary line dividing upper and lower California, extending from the initial

9. Nicholas P. Trist, Memorandum, Jan. 1848, Trist Papers, Vol. 29, Jan. 28–Feb. 13, 1848.

10. Ibid.

11. Ibid.

12. Moore, *Buchanan,* p. 369.

13. Trist (n. 5 above).

point on the Pacific to the junction of the Gila and Colorado, (3) two rivers, the Gila and the Rio Grande, (4) a notoriously erroneous map, and (5) a specific reference to the geographical point of El Paso. Quite obviously, the officials appointed to "run and mark" the line would have an important role in determining just what these provisions, in fact, meant.

Article V of the Treaty also specified the appointment by each of the two governments of a commissioner and surveyor who were to meet at San Diego within one year of the Treaty's ratification and "proceed to run and mark the said boundary in its whole course to the mouth of the Rio Bravo del Norte." [14] It declared that "the result agreed upon by them shall be deemed a part of this Treaty, and shall have the same force as if it were inserted therein." [15] Thus the relatively extensive powers of the commissioner and surveyor were incorporated into the Treaty itself. The men chosen by the United States to execute this important commission would seemingly have to be men of wide experience in diplomacy and topographical and geodetic work, and have the ability to organize and control a large party engaged in extensive operations in an unknown country, among hostile tribes, in cooperation with a nation ever on the alert to salvage even a minor victory from its recent humiliating defeat.

The composition of the American commission was a mixture of civilians and officers of the Corps of Topographical Engineers. First choice of President Polk for commissioner was A. H. Sevier, a former senator from Arkansas, appointed on December 12, 1848. Before Sevier's appointment could be confirmed by the Senate, he died.[16] On the same day, January 16, 1849, John B. Weller of Ohio received the post of boundary commissioner.[17] Weller was by training a lawyer, but his active profession was politics. After having served one term as Democratic Congressman from Ohio, he had been narrowly defeated in the previous (1848) election for governor of that state.[18] The commissioner's

14. Above (n. 3), p. 44.
15. Ibid.
16. Paul Neff Garber, *The Gadsden Treaty* (Phila., 1923), p. 11.
17. Ibid., p. 12.
18. *DAB*.

appointment was, of course, his reward for faithful party service. Because of the late date of the appointment, less than a month before the end of Polk's term, the Whigs looked upon Weller as something of a midnight appointee.[19]

For the post of surveyor, Polk selected Andrew B. Gray of Texas, a topographer of limited experience who had served under Memmucan Hunt as the Texan representative on the United States–Texas Sabine River Boundary Survey in 1840.[20] Gray was in sympathy with those Texas interests who were working to secure a transcontinental railroad through the Southwest.[21]

Representing the military was William Hemsley Emory, now a brevet major. His title on the Commission was "Chief Astronomer and Commander of the Escort." [22] Lt. Amiel Weeks Whipple of Portsmouth, New Hampshire, and Lt. Edmund L. F. Hardcastle, the Marylander who had surveyed the valley of Mexico, were Emory's assistants. Both were Topographical Engineers. From the beginning the precise limits of the duties and authority of the civilians and military were imperfectly defined, except that all acknowledged Weller's leadership.

The total personnel of the Commission numbered thirty-nine men, plus an Army escort of one infantry and one cavalry company (approximately 105 soldiers). Included among the civilians were a physician and surgeon, a quartermaster, a draughtsman, several surveyors, a carpenter, a laundress, an interpreter, four servants, and the respective brothers of Weller and Emory.[23]

19. *Cong. Globe,* 31st Cong., 2d Sess., *20* (Dec. 18, 1850), 78–84. Lewis P. Lesley, "The International Boundary Survey from San Diego to the Gila River, 1849–50," *California Historical Society Quarterly, 9* (1930), 4.

20. *Message of the President Communicating . . . the Proceedings of the Commissioner Appointed to Run the Boundary Line between the United States and the Republic of Texas,* 27th Cong., 2d Sess., Sen. Exec. Doc. 199 (1842), 61.

21. The best indication of this is that he later made a private railroad survey for the Texan interests. See A. B. Gray, *Southern Pacific Railroad. Survey of a Route for the Southern Pacific R. R. on the Thirty-Second Parallel by A. B. Gray, for the Texas Western R. R. Company,* Cincinnati, 1856; see also A. B. Gray, *Report and Map, Relative to the Mexican Boundary,* 33d Cong., 2d Sess., Sen. Exec. Doc. 55 (1855), 27.

22. Emory, *Report, 1,* 1.

23. Weller to Emory, April 1, 1850, list of employees of the Boundary Survey, MS, Letters, Jan.–Dec. 1850, EP. Also Emory, *Report, 1,* 3.

Once appointed, Weller lost no time in embarking for San Diego, where according to the Treaty he was required to meet the Mexican Commissioner by May 30, 1849, exactly one year from the date of ratification of the Treaty. By the twenty-eighth of February he had completed his preliminary arrangements and set sail for Panama. On the twelfth of March he was in Chagres. The Whigs later asserted that this speedy departure was due less to efficiency than to Weller's desire to be beyond the reach of any possible recall by the new administration.[24] Indeed, the organization of his commission was somewhat less than perfect, indicating perhaps some undue haste in its formation. Weller had failed to make previous arrangements with Aspinwall and Company for through passage to San Diego, and the sudden flood of gold-seekers so taxed the company's facilities that the Commission was left stranded in Panama to await transportation whenever it should become available.[25]

The rest of the Commission was scattered in numerous places, all in various stages of progress toward San Diego. Lieutenant Hardcastle sailed around Cape Horn with the heaviest instruments. Lieutenant Whipple was delayed at Cambridge for some months testing the instruments collected from the Northeastern Boundary Survey, West Point, and the Smithsonian Institution. Major Emory and several assistants had gone with Weller on the steamer *Panama,* while A. B. Gray, with another group including Frederick Emory, went via the rivers to New Orleans, where they hopefully awaited passage to Panama.

Despite their initial haste, it was not until May 13 that the first party was able to leave the Isthmus, and even then it was a select force which included only Weller, Gray, Emory, and some of the technicians; Whipple and the rest of the men staying behind to wait for the next steamer.[26] The long wait at the Isthmus

24. *Cong. Globe* (above, n. 19).

25. Emory, *Report, 1,* 2–3.

26. Weller to Captain Stout, agent for Aspinwall and Company, Panama, New Grenada, May 14, 1849, in Thomas Ewing, *Report of the Secretary of the Interior . . . in Relation to the Operations of the Commission Appointed to Run and Mark the Boundary between the United States and Mexico,* 31st Cong., 1st Sess., Sen. Exec. Doc. 34 (1850), 8. Weller's list of passengers does not include Emory, but see Emory, *Report, 1,* 3, which indicates he, too, sailed north on the steamer *Panama.*

was not entirely wasted, however, as Major Emory used the time to make extensive scientific observations which could be used as the basis for a map of that strategic area. They were sent to Professor William C. Bond at Harvard, who saw to their publication in the *Memoirs of the American Academy of Arts and Sciences.*[27]

Eventually, after a series of bitter disputes between the civilian and military officials of the party, the last of the Commission reached San Diego. As slow as their progress was, they still arrived well ahead of the Mexican Commission. It was not until July 3 that the frigate *Caroline,* carrying the Mexican Commission, dropped anchor in San Diego harbor, where they were received with considerable ceremony by the entire American Commission.[28]

The Mexican Commission was headed by General Pedro Garcia Conde, former military commander of Chihuahua. His assistant was José Salazar Ylarregui, who served as surveyor. There were, in addition, two first class engineers, two second class engineers, and Felipe de Iturbide, son of the emperor, who served as official interpreter and translator.[29] An escort of soldiers was to be sent from Sonora under the redoubtable Indian fighter General Carrasco.

By July 7 the survey operations had begun. The Mexicans, because of their inferior instruments, were forced to depend somewhat on the services of the American engineers.[30] Emory organized three field parties, each headed by an Army topographer.[31] He set up a camp and began making observations from which the

27. William H. Emory, "Observations, Astronomical, Magnetic, and Meteorological, Made at Chagres and Gorgona, Isthmus of Darien, and at the City of Panama, New Grenada," *Memoirs of the American Academy of Arts and Sciences,* new ser. 5 (1850), 1–25. Also Emory to J. M. Clayton, Panama, May 9, 1849, EP.

28. José Salazar Ylarregui, *Datos de los trabajos astronomicos y topograficos despuestos en forma de diario. Practicados durante el ano de 1849 y principio de 1850 par la Comision de limites Mexicana en la linea que divide esta republica de la de los Estados-Unidos, por el geometra de dicha comision, Jose Salazar Ylarregui . . .* (Mexico, 1850), p. 12.

29. Ibid., p. 8.

30. Ibid., p. 13.

31. Emory, *Report, 1,* 4.

initial point on the Pacific could be defined. A. B. Gray surveyed the Port of San Diego. Lieutenant Whipple, accompanied by a cavalry escort under Lieutenant Cave J. Couts, set out into the desert to establish the exact point of confluence of the Gila and Colorado rivers. Hardcastle had the job of exploring the barren country between these points and connecting them by means of flash signals observed through surveying instruments.[32] On each of these operations a Mexican engineer was on hand to verify the results by means of his own observations. The essential task lay in determining the two initial points by means of elaborate astronomical observations and then simply laying out and marking the azimuth, or straight line along the earth's curvature, which ran between them. The astronomical work called for scientific attainments of the highest character.

Almost immediately numerous problems arose. The California gold rush proved a temptation to desertion, and since rising prices caused by the boom rapidly used up the Commission's supply of money, Weller had to wait for another appropriation from Washington.[33] Meanwhile, the workers in the field received little or no pay and the necessities of life proved harder and harder to acquire. In addition, there arose disputes within the Army between Whipple and Couts out on the Gila,[34] and then between Couts and Lieutenant Beckwith of the artillery, who came westward along Cooke's wagon road escorting the Collector for the Port of San Francisco.[35] Two men, a major and a lieutenant, engaged in a brawl in the public square at San Diego over the honor of another man's California sweetheart.[36] There arose a deep grievance because the cavalry escort was not large enough to suit the commissioner.[37] The surveyor, Gray, received a severe reprimand because he abandoned his own line of survey to lead the Collier

32. Ibid., p. 4. Also Weller to Clayton, San Diego, Jan. 3, 1850, in Ewing, *Report* (above, n. 26), p. 38.

33. Weller to Emory, San Diego, Jan. 9, 1850, EP.

34. Cave J. Couts to Emory, Camp Calhoun, opposite the Gila, Oct. 10, 1849, EP. See also Couts quoted in Arthur Woodward, *Feud on the Colorado* (Los Angeles, 1955), p. 75.

35. Couts to Emory, Camp Calhoun, Calif., Oct. 24, 1849, LR, EP.

36. J. McKinstry to Emory, San Diego, Sept. 2, 1849, contemporary copy; George F. Evans to Emory, San Diego, Sept. 2, 1849, contemporary copy, EP.

37. Weller to Emory, San Diego, June 16, 1849, LR, EP.

party into San Diego and thus never reached the Gila-Colorado junction to verify Whipple's establishment of that point.[38] When Gray, nevertheless, endeavored to claim credit for having run the entire survey from San Diego to the Gila, he naturally aroused the ire of Lieutenant Whipple and Major Emory.[39] All the while, a torrent of gold-seekers poured across the southern route to California in various states of unpreparedness, demanding food and succor from whatever Army force they saw.[40] The son of John James Audubon was one of these settlers who wrote to Lieutenant Couts, "If you do not get the means of supplying the cravings, *and that speedily,* of the *starving* who must pass your post this winter, I would not be in your position for any consideration."[41] In addition, the Yuma Indians who controlled the ferry across the Gila were becoming openly hostile toward the emigrants. Lieutenant Couts had to depose the green-goggled, sword-carrying Yuma leader, Pablo, and conduct a democratic election for a new and more kindly disposed chief.[42] Outlaw gangs congregated at the Gila-Colorado junction, and the notorious Glanton gang was known to be on the rampage.[43]

Difficulties of a diplomatic nature also arose. As noted, the Treaty specified that the initial point of the line on the Pacific should be located one marine league south of the southernmost point of the Port of San Diego. But since there was no accepted standard length for a marine league, surveyors Gray and Salazar had to compromise on an arbitrary length of 5,564.6 meters.[44] In addition General Conde, with his eye on the Port of San Diego, pointed out that Trist had previously offered an amount of coastline on the Pacific for a small stretch of land along the left bank of the Colorado River below its junction with the Gila. In order to carry out the spirit of the Treaty, Conde suggested

38. Weller to Gray, San Diego, Nov. 9, 1849, in Ewing, *Report,* p. 47.

39. Gray to Clayton, San Diego, Nov. 17, 1849, ibid., p. 44.

40. Couts to Emory, Camp Calhoun, Oct. 19, 1849, LR, EP.

41. J. W. Audubon to Couts, four miles below Camp Calhoun, Colorado River, Oct. 16, 1849, LR, EP.

42. Couts to Emory, Camp Calhoun, opposite the mouth of the Gila, Oct. 10, 1849, LR, EP.

43. For the story of this gang see Woodward, *Feud on the Colorado,* pp. 20–30.

44. Gray to Weller, San Diego, Oct. 4, 1849, in Ewing, *Report,* p. 30.

that the two governments ought to leave the question for further negotiation, implying that the trade should be made.[45] When it became known to Weller that the Colorado River flowed northwest after leaving the Gila, and that by the present terms of the Treaty the United States already possessed more than two leagues on the right and left banks, the Commissioner refused to view Trist's offer as still binding, and insisted upon the confluence of the Gila and the Colorado as the terminal point on the eastern end of the California line.[46] Compared to later questions involving geography and diplomacy these were minor skirmishes. But the negotiations were significant because they were indicative of the type of complicated geographic problem that could arise in carrying out the Treaty provisions. It also seemed to demonstrate a certain willingness on the part of General Conde to capitalize on any advantage he might gain through his understanding of the local geography.

The greatest obstacle to the successful completion of the Weller Survey was the Whig administration in Washington. From the time of Weller's appointment, the Whigs had been hostile toward him, and on June 20, 1849, he was officially replaced by John Charles Frémont.[47] The circumstances of this action indicate that the removal of Weller was prompted by partisan political considerations, though Secretary of State Clayton had technically correct reasons for his action. The charges were (1) that Weller had been extravagant, (2) that he had failed to get on with the work, (3) that he had neglected to render his quarterly accounts, (4) that he had failed to send in a list of his employees, and (5) that his Commission was full of dissension and badly organized.[48] It was true that Weller was somewhat delinquent in his accounts and had furnished the State Department with no list of his employees. It was not true that he had been unduly extravagant,

45. *Report of the Secretary of the Interior Made in Compliance with a Resolution of the Senate Calling for Information in Relation to the Commission Appointed to Run and Mark the Boundary between the United States and Mexico,* 32d Cong., 1st Sess., Sen. Exec. Doc. 119 (1852), 61.

46. Ibid.

47. Clayton to John C. Frémont, Wash., June 20, 1849, in Ewing, *Report,* p. 9.

48. Ibid. The charges are specified in more detail in *Cong. Globe* (above, n. 19).

and the work itself was proceeding well in spite of the unusual difficulties presented. Moreover, Weller had been skillful in his diplomatic relations with General Conde and staunch in upholding American rights. The dissension in the Commission could hardly have been laid to his charge. Rather, it was the fault of Congress in appointing such a mixed body for the job. It was also due to the unusual conditions present in booming California. In addition, the date of Weller's recall, June 26, scarcely gave him time to reach San Diego. In fact, it was actually issued before the Mexicans had even arrived in the field at all.[49] Weller's defenders also insisted that his returns were not required until the end of the quarter and that when his returns arrived the next day, June 27, no order was sent out to reinstate him.[50]

Frémont's appointment was inconvenient for several reasons. He was given Weller's letter of recall and told not to deliver it until he was about to "enter upon the duties of the office." [51] When Frémont arrived in California, he did not deliver the order to Weller. Instead, he waited, deliberating whether he should seek to become Senator from California or take the boundary commissioner's job.[52] Unofficial rumors of Weller's impending replacement were common, though it was not certain if Frémont or Emory was to become commissioner.[53] Because of the rumors, Weller was unable to cash a draft on the government, and the various work parties were in serious need of supplies. Emory had to "borrow" from the local Army posts to maintain his troops.[54] With Frémont's help, Weller negotiated a $10,000 draft in San Francisco, but when the draft was protested the bankers seized Weller's private property and he was financially ruined.[55] Finally, Frémont

49. Note that Frémont was appointed on June 20, but Clayton's recall of Weller was dated June 26, Clayton to Frémont, Wash., June 20, 1849, and Clayton to Weller, Wash., June 26, 1849, in Ewing, *Report,* p. 9. The Mexican Commission arrived on July 3, 1849 (above, n. 28).

50. *Cong. Globe* (above, n. 19).

51. Clayton to Frémont, Wash., June 28, 1849, in Ewing, *Report,* p. 10.

52. *Cong. Globe* (above, n. 19). See also Couts to Emory, San Diego, Calif., Sept. 5, 1849 (EP), which implies that Frémont actually delivered the recall to Weller. The *Globe* version is here preferred because Couts' assertion appears to be based on hearsay.

53. Couts to Emory, San Diego, Sept. 5, 1849, EP.

54. Emory, *Report, 1,* 5–6.

55. Ibid., p. 5.

declined the commissioner's post for the senatorial seat. Weller continued to remain at his post. As one senator put it, "Mordecai still sat at the King's gate." [56] He was still the boundary commissioner because Frémont had failed to hand him his official removal, but he could not draw funds to carry on the work. Emory's military connection alone sustained the parties in the field, but even so the men had to work without pay in a country where everyone else had a chance for easy wealth.

Frémont's course of action placed the Whigs in an uncomfortable position. Either they had to sanction Weller's continuance at his post or they had to bear the responsibility of replacing him when the grounds for his removal (he had now rendered his accounts) were considerably less impressive than before. To escape this dilemma, the jurisdiction of the Boundary Survey was passed from the State Department to the Interior Department.[57] On December 18, 1849, nearly seven months after the first move to suspend him, Weller received notice of his dismissal from his old political rival, Thomas Ewing of Ohio, now Secretary of the Interior.[58] He was to turn over all books and property to Emory, who remained as astronomer.[59] Senator Gwin, in an address to the Senate gave his own version in vivid terms of the maneuvers that led to Weller's dismissal: "The Secretary of State was sick and tired of his vain attempts to butcher this official incumbent. He was handed over to more skillful and experienced hands." [60] Weller wrote to Ewing, pointing out how "fortunate" it was for the government to recall him after he had virtually finished the work at his own expense, and how "unfortunate" it was for him, since he could not get his money back, or any credit for his work.[61]

Frémont's appointment as commissioner was also an insult to Emory, who had been General Kearny's chief witness against the Pathfinder in his famous court-martial trial following the Mexican War.[62] Upon hearing of Frémont's appointment, Emory re-

56. *Cong. Globe* (above, n. 19).
57. Ibid.
58. Ewing to Weller, Wash., Dec. 18, 1849, EP.
59. Ibid.
60. *Cong. Globe* (above, n. 19).
61. Weller to Ewing, San Francisco, March 1, 1850 (above, n. 45).
62. *Message of the President . . . Communicating the Proceedings of the*

quested immediate release from his post as astronomer. However, Secretary of War George Crawford refused to relieve him, on the grounds that such a move might start a precedent.[63] The entire Maryland delegation in Congress protested the action, and Senator James Alfred Pearce, Emory's particular friend, went all the way to President Taylor himself, but the President upheld Crawford's action.[64] It was Colonel Abert who broke the deadlock with a bit of elementary psychology. He provided Crawford with a way out of his uncomfortable position by declaring that "Major Emory being engaged upon the part [of the boundary survey] between the Pacific and the Gila, should, I think, be required to complete this duty before he is relieved." [65] This enabled Crawford seemingly to punish Emory at the same time he gave in to his demand. Crawford complied, but with one perverse addition; he assigned Emory to General Riley's command in California after the completion of the boundary survey.[66] This would reduce his duties to that of an ordinary lieutenant with no exalted command or brevet major status. It was even more intolerable than the first course, and Emory prepared to resign from the Army. Once again his friends, James Alfred Pearce, Jefferson Davis, Henry Stuart Foote, James Shields, George W. Jones of Iowa, and Pierre Soulé applied what political pressure they could.[67] The question was again finally resolved by Abert, who wrote to Crawford that the Interior Department was entitled to order Emory to Washington if it chose to do so, but after these duties were finished, he pointed out, "Major

Court Martial in the Trial of Lieutenant Colonel Frémont, 30th Cong., 1st Sess., Sen. Exec. Doc. 33 (1848), 163–67 and passim. John C. Frémont was court-martialed in 1847 for refusing to obey the order of General S. W. Kearny removing him as military governor of California. He was found guilty, but the sentence was commuted by President Polk.

63. Emory to Clayton, Sept. 15, 1849; see also Clayton to Emory, Nov. 28, 1849: EP.

64. J. A. Pearce to Emory, Wash., Dec. 5, 1849, EP.

65. Abert to G. W. Crawford, Dec. 10, 1849, contemporary copy; see also J. J. Abert to Emory, Wash., Dec. 11, 1849: EP.

66. Abert to Emory, Dec. 14, 1849, EP.

67. Matilda W. Emory to Emory, Wash., Jan. 11, 1849, EP. This letter is a general discussion of the affair by Mrs. Emory and reveals the Major's attitude as well as describing the political situation in Washington. See also Emory to Ewing, San Diego, April 2, 1850, draft, EP.

Emory having terminated his services with the Department of the Interior would then fall under the directions of General Order #57, December 13, 1849 [which ordered Emory to Riley's command]. But this will allow ample time for the reconsideration of that order." [68] Thus, with the question only partially resolved, Emory finished the work on the San Diego–Gila boundary section. Then, leaving Lieutenant Hardcastle to supervise the placing of the monuments, he returned to Washington to finish the official survey maps.

Despite the political interference and other difficulties, the western section of the boundary line had been completed. The officers of the Topographical Corps worked together with a minimum of friction, and they provided the element of stability that eventually accomplished the work. Weller did not interfere in the actual surveying operations, which thereby aided the work materially. The status of the civilian surveyor, A. B. Gray, continued to rankle the Topographical officers, however, since he had undeniable authority according to the Treaty, but he was their marked inferior in ability. The first phase of the survey ended with Gray and the Army in virtually an open conflict.[69] When the Commission adjourned, it was agreed by both the Americans and the Mexicans that they would meet next at El Paso on the first Monday in November of 1850.[70] By that date there was to be a new American commissioner and a new astronomer, and even a new set of difficulties confronting all concerned.

The new boundary commissioner was appointed by President Zachary Taylor on May 4, 1850, even before the California parties had finished operations on the western end of the line.[71] The appointment of a Whig promised a complete reorganization of the Boundary Survey, though it was, nevertheless, to remain

68. Abert to Crawford, Wash., June 22, 1850, contemporary copy, EP.

69. Whipple to Emory, Portsmouth, N.H., June 13, 1850; also Gray to Emory, San Diego, July 15, 1850: EP.

70. Weller to Emory, San Diego, Feb. 17, 1850, EP.

71. W. W. J. Bliss, Sec. to Pres. Taylor, to John Russell Bartlett, May 14, 1850, Letter Book 1, May–July 1850, Bartlett Papers, John Carter Brown Library.

under civilian command. John Russell Bartlett, a prominent bibliophile and amateur ethnologist from Providence, Rhode Island, was the man selected for the Commissioner's post. A spare, serious little man with a face like James K. Polk, Bartlett had lived since 1836 in New York, where in partnership with Charles Welford he ran a bookstore and publishing house on the ground floor of the Astor Hotel, specializing in foreign books and travel accounts. It became the center of a unique literary group similar to that associated with the *Knickerbocker Magazine* or the publishing house of Duyckinck. It included such men as Ephraim George Squier, John Lloyd Stephens, George Folsom, Doctor F. S. Hawks, Henry Schoolcraft, Albert Gallatin, and, on occasion, Edgar Allan Poe.[72] Together with the aged Gallatin, Bartlett had founded the American Ethnological Society, which along with the American Antiquarian Society provided an early focal point for anthropological studies in the United States. Of this group, both Stephens and Squier had been afforded an opportunity to make spectacular explorations of Central America by means of diplomatic appointments tendered by the United States government.[73] Another friend from Baltimore, Brantz Mayer, had served as United States consul to Mexico in 1842, and his sojourn resulted in a successful travel book, *Mexico as It Was and as It Is*.[74] It was, perhaps, with these, his more famous friends in mind, that Bartlett sought the commissioner's job. Undoubtedly he envisioned himself as an explorer of exotic and unknown regions rather than as a practical administrator engaged in a monotonous survey through barren and dangerous country. He wrote in his unpublished autobiography:

> Although my life and pursuits had always been of a sedentary character I always had a great desire for travel, and particularly for exploring unknown regions. I had also ever felt a deep interest in the Indians, and was glad of an opportunity to be thrown among the wild tribes of the interior. I saw, too, that there would be a wide field for new explora-

72. Bartlett, "Autobiography" (above, p. 143, n. 94), pp. 32–33, 59.
73. Ibid., pp. 38–39; also *DAB*.
74. Jerry E. Patterson, introduction to MS "Journal of Brantz Mayer," Yale Collection of Western Americana. See also *DAB*.

tion and that if the government would permit these, I would prefer the office of Commissioner to that of any other.[75]

Out of the avalanche of applications for positions on the newly formed Commission, Bartlett formed a large and luxuriously equipped party which included a detachment of Topographical Engineers, a contingent of civilian surveyors, a force of fifty mechanics, a platoon of field scientists sponsored by the learned societies, a collection of personal friends and relatives, and a small navy, commanded by his "publicity agent," the volatile Lt. Issac G. Strain, U.S.N.[76] The chief Topographical Engineer was Brevet Lt. Col. John McClellan, a veteran of both the Florida and Mexican campaigns.[77]

On the third of August 1850 the main party embarked on the steamer *Galveston* from New York City bound for Indianola on the Gulf Coast of Texas. Commissioner Bartlett and a small party followed ten days later. Even before the *Galveston* was out of New York harbor an unseemly friction began to develop between the various military and civilian officers of the Commission. Bartlett's provision for the mechanics aroused the ire of Colonel McClellan. He particularly objected to their being forced to eat from tubs of food placed at various points around the deck.[78] At Key West, Lieutenant Strain, who was in nominal command while on the high seas, led the men ashore for a sailor's bacchanal which terminated abruptly upon their return to the ship, where Lieutenant Strain ordered one man thrown overboard and two others to be bound and locked in their cabins. Again Colonel McClellan stepped in to rescue the men.[79] Fric-

75. Bartlett, "Autobiography," pp. 50–51.

76. I. G. Strain to Bartlett, Astor House, New York, May 17, 1850; Strain to Bartlett, May 18, 1850, Strain to Bartlett, May 23, 1850: Bartlett Papers.

77. John Russell Bartlett, *Personal Narrative of Explorations and Incidents in Texas, New Mexico, California, Sonora and Chihuahua, Connected with the United States and Mexican Boundary Commission during the Years, 1850, '51, '52, and '53* (2 vols. New York, 1854), *1*, 6. See also Cullum, *Biographical Register* (above, p. 12, n. 22), *1*, 367.

78. *Report of the Secretary of the Interior, Communicating . . . a Copy of the Charges Preferred against the Present Commissioner Appointed to Run and Mark the Boundary Line between the United States and Mexico,* 32d Cong., 1st Sess., Sen. Exec. Doc. 60 (1851–52), 53.

79. Ibid., pp. 52–53. Note that the versions of this affair vary only slightly between Edward Doran and John M. Bigelow.

tion mounted when the ship reached New Orleans, where according to sworn testimony the men were compelled to go ashore to be quartered in a house of prostitution. One deponent asserted that when the ship reached Indianola Bay he saw Lieutenant Strain down "not less than one dozen glasses of brandy" between the time the ship passed the sand bar and the time it dropped anchor.[80]

Once ashore, the party started for San Antonio in two groups. At the outset the men were attired in natty uniforms consisting of red or blue flannel shirts, dark trousers, and broad-brimmed white felt hats.[81] But aside from the uniforms there was no semblance of discipline or efficiency. It took nearly a month to cover the 165 miles to San Antonio, and it was a month of constant quarreling. One of the teamsters casually shot a local citizen, and Bartlett, almost as casually, satisfied the family with an indemnity of $100.[82]

When they finally reached San Antonio, Bartlett decided to push on ahead to El Paso with a small advance party so that he could meet the Mexican commissioner on the day appointed. Accordingly he set out with a party of twenty-four civilians along Lieutenant F. T. Bryan's newly surveyed northern route, via the Horsehead Crossing of the Pecos River. Commissioner Bartlett and his friend, Doctor Webb, rode in style across the wild Edwards Plateau country of West Texas, in a four-horse rockaway carriage, armed with one double-barreled gun, one Sharp's repeating rifle, two Colt's six-shooters strapped to the doors, plus two pair of Colt's five-shooters strapped to the two passengers and a pair of Derringers issued to the driver. Bartlett proudly declared, "We were thus enabled in case of necessity, to discharge a round of 37 shots without reloading; besides which, Sharp's rifle could be fired at least six times in a minute." [83]

The main force was left behind under divided and unspecified authority. Orders were issued to the supply train to follow Bartlett's party some weeks later over the southern route to El Paso. Even before it left San Antonio, one teamster had mur-

80. Ibid., pp. 53–54. The New Orleans episode is on p. 53.
81. Bartlett, *Personal Narrative, I,* 20.
82. Ibid., p. 32.
83. Ibid., p. 48.

dered another and successfully escaped. Once on the trail, a continuous dispute flared between quartermaster James Myers and Colonel McClellan over the choice of campsites, protection of the livestock, and issuing of supplies.[84] Meanwhile, Lieutenant Strain had left the expedition and hurried to Washington, where he preferred charges against Colonel McClellan before the Secretary of the Interior.[85] Mishaps continued all the way to El Paso. Captain Dobbins of the Colonel's party shot the wagonmaster, Mr. Wakeman, and then, in turn, committed suicide while a hastily assembled jury was acquitting him on self-defense.[86] The wagonmaster lay with two bullets in his leg for ten days before he died, and his words cast a sad reflection upon the logistics of the expedition, "I am in much misery," he dictated to a friend, "and a sorry chance of recovery: and the doctor has no instruments to work at me with." [87]

Ultimately, the dissension in the expedition became official when Commissioner Bartlett asked Colonel McClellan to resign or be faced with charges of "habitual drunkenness and conduct unbecoming an officer." [88] The Colonel, in reply, demanded a court martial and leveled an impressive series of charges at Bartlett, declaring that George F. Bartlett, the commissioner's brother, had transported trade goods out to the frontier at government expense and then sold them for exorbitant private gain to the workers on the Commission. He further charged the commissioner with keeping Quartermaster Myers at his post even though he knew him to be defrauding the government. Furthermore, the Colonel objected to being placed under the orders of any civilian quartermaster.[89] He answered the charges of Bartlett and Strain with testimony which included statements by the trustworthy Doctor Bigelow, the chief mechanic Mr. Chamberlain, and a proven scoundrel named Edward Caffee.[90] Secretary of the Interior A. H. H. Stuart was not in a position to decide

84. Above (n. 78), pp. 16–18.
85. Ibid., pp. 50–51.
86. Above (n. 45), pp. 390, 396.
87. Ibid., p. 497.
88. Ibid., pp. 28, 30.
89. Above (n. 78), pp. 3, 4.
90. Ibid., pp. 42–43, 51–52.

which party was right, but he backed the Whig commissioner, Bartlett, as far as he dared. McClellan was recalled, though not reprimanded, and placed in charge of the Tennessee River surveys.[91] Lieutenant Strain was also placed on other duties.[92] Quartermaster Myers was dismissed, and George F. Bartlett was removed from the command of the commissary to a less sensitive but equally lucrative position on the Commission.[93] Thus nearly all concerned had both lost and saved their reputations. Eventually the expedition struggled into El Paso, where many of the unruly teamsters could be summarily dismissed and left to their own deserts.

This latter action proved unwise, for scarcely had the work begun near the town of Socorro when another rash of murders broke out, all committed by the recently discharged teamsters. The most prominent casualty was Edward Clarke, the youthful son of Senator John Clarke of Rhode Island, Bartlett's political sponsor. Earlier on the fatal day the outlaw teamsters had shot and killed an inoffensive barkeep and then carefully laid out his corpse, all the while shouting and reveling in advanced stages of inebriation. That night they cornered young Clarke at a fandango and stabbed him to death before the assembled guests, at the same time shooting a man who came to his rescue.[94] The only authority at Socorro was a United States judge and a Mexican justice of the peace, and the military could spare no troops for police duty, so the Commission itself undertook to maintain justice. The culprits, except the leader, had made no attempt to leave town but instead attempted to terrorize all the civilians present. They were therefore readily available for trial, which

91. Cullum, p. 367.

92. *DAB.*

93. *Report of the Secretary of the Interior Made in Compliance with a Resolution of the Senate Calling for Information whether any Steps Were Taken to Investigate the Charges Preferred by Col. McClellan against the Commissioner to Run and Mark the Boundary between the United States and Mexico,* 32d Cong., 1st Sess., Sen. Exec. Doc. 89 (1851–52), 2.

94. Bartlett, *Personal Narrative, I,* 157–58. See also other versions of the affair in clippings from the New Orleans *Picayune* (date unknown) and Providence *Journal* (date unknown) in Bartlett's own scrapbook, Bartlett Papers. The version in the Providence *Journal* is by George Thurber. It is extremely lurid and in places at factual odds with Bartlett's version.

they were forthwith given. The local judge presided; the jury, composed of local citizens and employees of the Commission, duly convicted three of the prisoners of murder and they were taken to the edge of town and hanged.[95] Some weeks later the leader of the gang, Alexander Young, was also caught, convicted, and hanged.[96] Thus with frontier justice improvised and positively administered, Bartlett was left with the unpleasant task of communicating the sad news of Clarke's death to his father, the senator. In addition he was left with an indifferently organized, unruly Commission, in the heart of the Apache country, with the further exacting duty of deciding, in joint conference with the Mexican Commissioner, just where the boundary line should be drawn.

The first meeting between Commissioner Bartlett and General Conde took place on December 3, 1850, at El Paso.[97] In this and subsequent meetings they discussed the practical measures necessary for correctly and legally dividing their two countries. Most pressing of all their problems was one involving the exact location of the southern boundary of New Mexico as laid down on Disturnell's map of 1847. A comparison of astronomically determined geographical points with Disturnell's map indicated that it embodied two major errors: the Rio Grande River was laid down on the map two degrees too far West; and the crucial landmark, El Paso, was placed nearly 40 minutes of latitude (approximately 30 miles) too far to the North. The entire southwestern region suffered from this distortion: it was all too far to the north and west with respect to the grid pattern of longitude and latitude on the map. Both sides, American and Mexican, nevertheless insisted upon using the Disturnell maps as a definition of the southern boundary of New Mexico.[98]

General Conde maintained that the line should be laid down with strict reference to its orientation *vis-à-vis* the lines of latitude and longitude on the map. Thus the boundary would begin

95. Bartlett, *Personal Narrative, 1*, 163.
96. Ibid., p. 164.
97. Ibid., p. 151; *Report of the Sec. of the Interior . . .* , 32d Cong., 2d Sess., Sen. Exec. Doc. 41 (1853), 2.
98. Above (n. 45), pp. 146–48, 278.

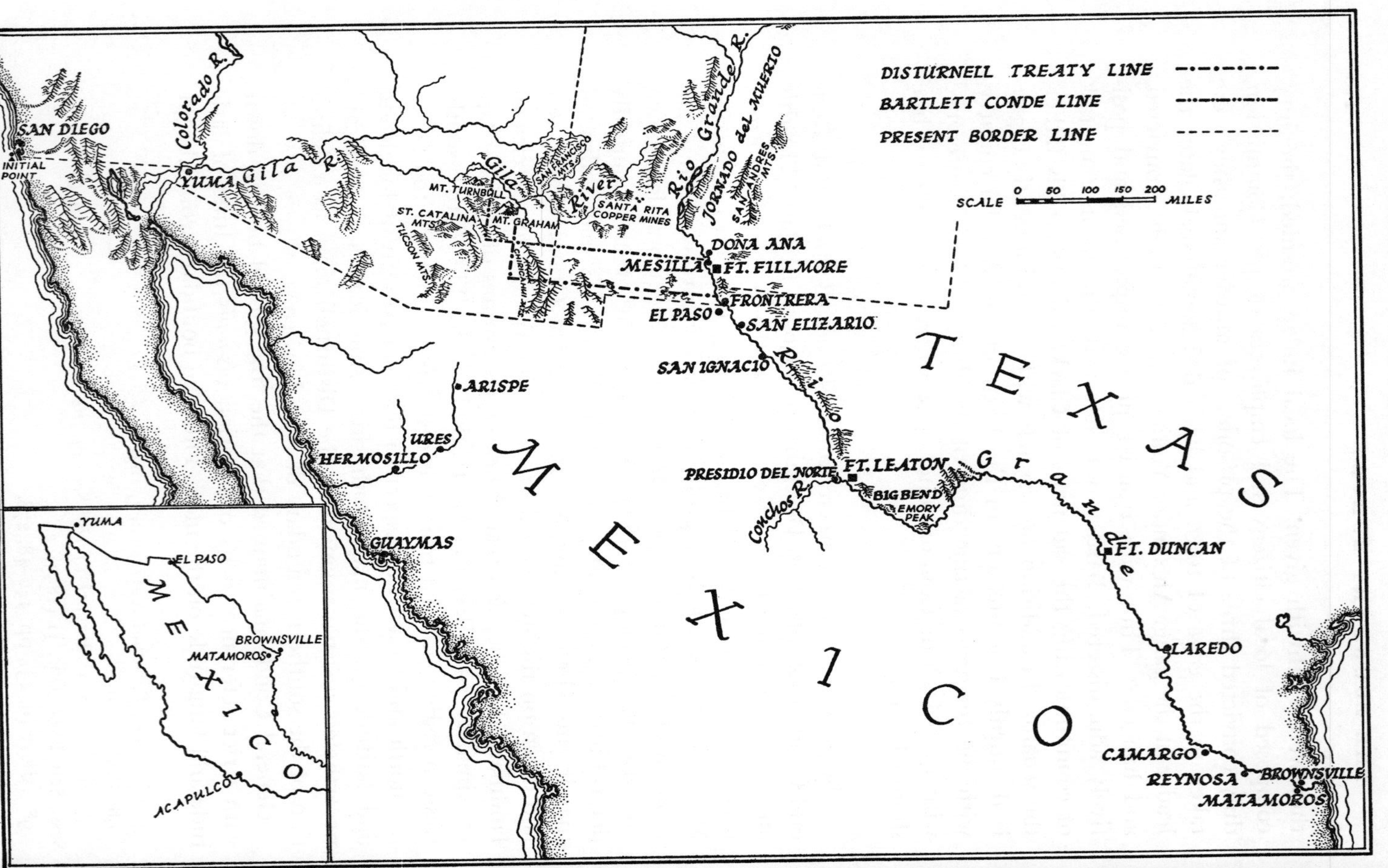
DISTURNELL TREATY LINE
BARTLETT CONDE LINE
PRESENT BORDER LINE
SCALE 0 50 100 150 200 MILES
SAN DIEGO
INITIAL POINT
Colorado R.
YUMA
Gila R.
Gila River
SAN FRANCISCO MTS.
MT. TURNBULL
ST. CATALINA MTS.
MT. GRAHAM
TUCSON MTS.
SANTA RITA COPPER MINES
Rio Grande R.
JORNADO del MUERTO
SAN ANDRES MTS.
DOÑA ANA
MESILLA
FT. FILLMORE
FRONTRERA
EL PASO
SAN ELIZARIO
SAN IGNACIO
Rio Grande
ARISPE
URES
HERMOSILLO
GUAYMAS
PRESIDIO DEL NORTE
FT. LEATON
Conchos R.
BIG BEND
EMORY PEAK
FT. DUNCAN
LAREDO
CAMARGO
REYNOSA
BROWNSVILLE
MATAMOROS
TEXAS
MEXICO
YUMA
EL PASO
MEXICO
BROWNSVILLE
MATAMOROS
ACAPULCO

at a point on the Rio Grande some thirty miles north of El Paso and continue west for one degree of longitude, thence north to the first tributary of the Gila River. Such a line would give Mexico the potential riches of the Santa Rita del Cobre mines and the Mesilla Valley.

Commissioner Bartlett assumed that such a line had not been Trist's intention, but upon reference to the map he was forced to admit the strength of Conde's position. He remembered, too, his instructions, which were to maintain a conciliatory attitude toward Mexico. Thus he was prepared to be more than fair. There were, however, two discrepancies on the map which were irreconcilable with Conde's position: the southern boundary of New Mexico was plainly indicated as extending westward not one, but three degrees beyond the Rio Grande; and the town of El Paso, by the scale on the map, was located only eight miles south of the line as shown on the map. Bartlett argued that Trist had surely meant the southern boundary of New Mexico to extend farther than one league westward, and he pointed to the map for support. After much discussion, the two commissioners compromised. General Conde agreed that the boundary should run as pictured on the map, three degrees west of the Rio Grande, regardless of the River's true position. Bartlett, in turn, conceded that the initial point on the Rio Grande should be at 32° 22′ north latitude and not eight miles north of El Paso, which was really located further south at 31° 45′.[99] He thus freely interpreted the clause in the Treaty which specified that the boundary should run "north of the town called Paso" to mean any distance north of El Paso. The formal agreement was made and signed by the two commissioners and the Mexican surveyor, Salazar Ylarregui. Lieutenant Whipple, the acting United States surveyor in the absence of A. B. Gray, signed the document too, though he registered a protest with Bartlett concerning the northern location of the initial point.[100] By April 24 the observations had been made, and in a brief ceremony a great stone marker was placed on the Rio Grande at 32° 22′. Conde

99. Ibid., map which accompanies the *Report*. See also Bartlett, *Personal Narrative, 1,* 201–3.

100. Whipple to Bartlett, El Paso, Dec. 12, 1850, in Sen. Exec. Doc. 119 (above, n. 45), p. 247.

and Bartlett then ordered their surveyors into the field west of the Rio Grande.[101] Headquarters were established at the Santa Rita Copper Mines, where, surrounded by Apaches and Navahos who ran off the horses and mules and boldly pilfered the camp's supplies, both commissioners somehow managed to keep parties at work on the survey.[102]

On July 19, 1851, the official American surveyor, A. B. Gray, arrived at the copper mines from Texas, where he had been convalescing from a severe illness. One look at the Bartlett-Conde agreement convinced him that the United States had been duped. He stopped all surveying work on the line until a new conference with Conde could be held which would set matters right.[103] Shortly before Gray arrived at the mines, Lt. Col. James Duncan Graham of the Topographical Engineers had also arrived at El Paso ready to begin his work as "chief astronomer and head of the scientific corps" of the Boundary Commission. He subsequently ordered Lieutenant Whipple to report to him at El Paso,[104] which of course insured the suspension of all American surveying activity west of the Rio Grande. After a conference with Whipple, Colonel Graham also protested the Bartlett-Conde agreement, for substantially the same reason that had prompted Gray to do so.[105]

The three scientific men of the Commission, Gray, Graham, and Whipple, were thus aligned in opposition to Bartlett's interpretation of the Treaty with respect to the location of the initial point on the Rio Grande. Their argument, like that of the Mexicans, demanded a rigid adherence to the Treaty map, but they emphasized different aspects of the map. They pointed to the fact that the Treaty had made no reference to longitude and latitude, and, in fact, had made only one specific geographical reference, that the line should run north of the "town called Paso." The boundary must, therefore, have been deliberately

101. Bartlett, *Personal Narrative, 1*, 181.

102. Ibid., p. 346.

103. A. B. Gray, *Report and Map, Relative to the Mexican Boundary*, 33d Cong., 2d Sess., Sen. Exec. Doc. 55 (1855), 21–23. See also J. D. Graham, *Report on the Subject of the Boundary Line between the United States and Mexico*, 32d Cong., 1st Sess., Sen. Exec. Doc. 121 (1852), 59.

104. Above (n. 45), p. 114.

105. Graham, *Report*, pp. 11–12, 17.

drawn eight miles north of the town rather than the town's having been placed on the map after the line had been marked out.[106] They insisted, then, that latitude and longitude should be discounted, and the line placed on the earth in the same relation with the town of El Paso that it had on the map, namely eight miles to the north of the plaza. This position posited an interesting dilemma in cartographic perception: were the lines of latitude and longitude the important determinants, or was the geographical picture drawn on them, with its own logic of relationships, the most important? Article V of the Treaty, aside from its ambiguous reference to "the town called Paso," left the problem completely without a solution.

What made this initial-point controversy so significant was that both Gray and Graham believed the area between 31° 45′ north latitude to contain the only practicable route for a railroad across the Southwest to the Pacific.[107] The security of California demanded more than a tortuous emigrant trail through the Rocky Mountains as a link with the rest of the country, and another year-round route, free of ice and snow, was unknown at the time. Indeed, to most expansionists the loss of the southwestern trail endangered the whole grand design of continental destiny.

The southwestern railroad route also had another importance. By Article XI of the Treaty the United States had assumed the responsibility for preventing Indian raids from Texas, New Mexico, and Arizona into the North Mexican States. It was considered impossible to stop these raids without some means of rapid communication between points along the southern border.[108] Meanwhile, Mexican claims for indemnification could reach fantastic proportions.

Surveyor Gray remained adamant in his refusal to sanction the Bartlett-Conde agreement, and his position caused the Whig administration no little distress. On October 3, 1851, the Secretary of the Interior officially ordered Gray to sign the agreement and authenticate the maps which portrayed the initial point.[109]

106. The best exposition of their arguments is in Gray, *Report and Map*, pp. 6–12.

107. Ibid., p. 27. Graham, p. 61.

108. Emory to Volney Howard, near El Paso, Dec. 18, 1851, contemporary copy, EP.

109. Above (n. 45), p. 118.

Before Gray could refuse, he was removed from office by Stuart, and once more Major William H. Emory was sent out to the Southwest, this time in the dual role of surveyor and chief astronomer.[110]

The dispute over the location of the boundary line was further complicated at the outset by a dispute over the extent of their respective authority between Colonel Graham and the civilian officials, Bartlett and Gray.[111] Graham considered his rank next to that of the commissioner and superior to that of Gray, since his instructions placed him in charge of the scientific corps. Moreover, when the Colonel arrived at El Paso, he brought with him Lieutenants Tillinghast and Burnside, who were to assume command of the commissary and quartermaster supplies, replacing George Bartlett and James Myers. Thus the Corps of Topographical Engineers, in the person of Colonel Graham, attempted to take over virtually all the scientific and administrative duties of the Commission.

Surveyor Gray objected to this usurpation of his authority, as he had when Major Emory had tried a similar exercise of command at the California end of the survey.[112] Commissioner Bartlett backed Gray in the matter and refused to allow Colonel Graham to attend any conferences that might be held with the Mexican commissioner on the grounds that only the commissioner and surveyor were designated as negotiators in the Treaty.[113] Colonel Graham retaliated by ordering Lieutenant Burnside to refuse supplies to Bartlett, which was done in a manner calculated to ruffle rather than soothe injured feelings. The Colonel refused to perform any duty himself, or to allow his subordinates to perform any, until Bartlett acknowledged his authority. Inevitably, Bartlett protested to Secretary Stuart, who promptly saw to the removal of Graham and Gray almost at the same time, although for different reasons.[114] The quarrel between the arrogant colonel and the long-suffering surveyor for a time tended to obscure the more serious initial-point dispute.

110. Emory, *Report,* p. 10.
111. Above (n. 45), pp. 457–59.
112. Whipple to Emory, Portsmouth, N.H., Jan. 13, 1850, EP.
113. Above (n. 45), pp. 211–12.
114. Ibid., pp. 114, 225–27.

Ultimately, however, it created two powerful groups of adversaries for Secretary Stuart and the Whigs—the Army and the western expansionist Democrats who supported Gray. The entire Texas delegation in Congress, including Sam Houston, Thomas Rusk, and Volney Howard, demanded an explanation of the Bartlett-Conde agreement from Secretary Stuart.[115] They soon joined forces with the Army political supporters and along with Senator Weller from California began an all-out denunciation of the Whig Boundary Commission.

Despite the annoyance caused by these various conflicts, Commissioner Bartlett continued to conduct business as usual out on the boundary line. At his headquarters near the Santa Rita Copper Mines he held frequent parleys with the Apache war chiefs, Mangus Colorado, Ponce, and Delgadito, hoping to educate them in the ways of peace. On occasion he patiently sent parties out to reclaim his stolen livestock from these same Indians. Once the Commission was unable to mount an escort for the surveying parties because the Indians had stolen all the available horses and the soldiers were out chasing them on foot.[116] Between May 16 and June 17 the Commissioner led an expedition into Mexico as far as Arispe, a distance of over 200 miles. The object of the trip was to examine Cooke's wagon road, secure supplies, and stimulate trade with the Copper Mines. On the way they also conferred with the Mexican Indian fighter General Carrasco, at Frontreras. When they returned to the Copper Mines, the Apache chieftain, Mangus Colorado, gravely warned them of the risk in taking such jaunts, and of the "many bad Indians prone to theft and murder in the country through which he passed" (*I*, 353).

On June 27 Bartlett began an engagement in knight-errantry that was to determine his activities for nearly a year. He purchased a young Mexican girl, Inez Gonzales, from three Indian traders out of Santa Fe. She was, by his description, "quite young, artless, and interesting in appearance, prepossessing in her manners, and by her deportment gave evidence that she had

115. Russel, *Improvement of Communication*, p. 135.

116. Bartlett, *Personal Narrative*, *I*, 353. Except as noted, the following account is based on this work.

been carefully brought up" (*I*, 306). He deemed it his duty to "extend over her the protection of the laws of the United States, and to see that, until delivered in safety to her parents, she should be treated with the utmost hospitality that our position would allow." To these considerations General Conde gave his warm approval (*I*, 353).

On August 27 Commissioner Bartlett and a party of fifty-seven men took the recent captive, Inez Gonzales, and set out toward the country south of the Gila River to meet with General Conde and discuss the initial-point difficulties. Included in the party were A. B. Gray and Lt. A. W. Whipple. Col. J. D. Graham, full of suspicion, took thirteen men and followed the main party. After several days of wandering in the desert country, they found the Mexican commissioner, who had also been on the move, but in a direction away from them. A meeting of the joint Commission was held on September 6, and Gray registered his protest against the initial-point. All agreed to continue the survey of the Gila and Rio Grande, but Conde refused to concede on the crucial point (*I*, 376). After the meeting Lieutenant Whipple and Surveyor Gray went back to work on the Gila line, while Colonel Graham returned to El Paso and protested his nonadmittance to the Commissioners' meeting. Bartlett, with a party of fourteen—including his friends Doctor Webb, Messrs. Thurber and Cremony, and the artist Henry Pratt—continued onward to Santa Cruz to return the captive Inez to her parents. The beneficent Commissioner described the reunion with great satisfaction, "Tears of joy burst from all; and the sun-burnt and brawny men, in whom the finer feelings of our nature are wrongly supposed not to exist, wept like children as they looked with astonishment on the rescued girl" (*I*, 399).

From Santa Cruz, Bartlett set out for Magdelena, seventy-five miles to the south, in search of mules and provisions. Finding no supplies, he continued his excursion to Ures, ninety miles deeper into Mexico. Here he came down with typhoid fever and remained, attended by his faithful friend Doctor Webb, until December 15, when Doctor Webb and the five others of the party departed for the Pima villages on the Gila River with the intention of meeting Lieutenant Whipple (*I*, 435, 437). Bartlett stayed in Ures convalescing and studying the Yaqui and Tonori

Indians until the twenty-ninth, when he left for Guayamos. While at Ures he learned of the death of General Conde, from typhus, on December 19. By the first week in January the convalescent Commissioner had gone from Guayamos to Mazatlan, and on the 31st he dined sumptuously with a Mr. Quanachu, a Chinese merchant of Acapulco, over 1,000 miles south of the border. It was at this city that he finally boarded the steamer *Oregon* bound for San Diego. In eight days he was reunited with Lieutenant Whipple and the escort at San Diego (*1*, 505). Three days later, on February 11, Doctor Webb and his party staggered into San Diego after having made a difficult and useless trek across the deserts of Sonora and Southern California (2, 1).

Because of the lack of supplies, Lieutenant Whipple had been forced to abandon the survey of the Gila before it was completed. He planned to finish this work on the return to El Paso, but the return was again somewhat delayed while Bartlett explored California as far north as San Francisco, making copious notes on the aborigines, the gold seekers, and the geysers (2, 26, 34, 44, 57–58). Finally, by the end of May, he was ready to march for El Paso. His party set out under the expert guidance of the veteran mountain man Antoine Leroux. Along the way Colonel Craig, who was commanding the escort, was foully murdered by two deserters and left in the desert west of the Colorado River (2, 137–38). When the Commission reached the Gila, Lieutenant Whipple and a party were detached to complete the survey, while the main force went on with an escort (2, 186). Turning south, the commissioner visited Tubac (Tucson) and there, he related, "To our infinite astonishment and regret, we learned that Senorita Inez Gonzales, the Mexican girl whom we had liberated and restored to her parents at Santa Cruz in September was living at this place with the officer just named [one Captain Gomez]" (2, 303). They did not pause again to return the girl to her home, but they did lodge a vigorous puritan protest with the local padre (2, 316). After a further march across northern Mexico, the roving Commission reached El Paso on August 17, 1852. It was like coming home. Bartlett, erring greatly on the side of modesty, proudly recorded that he had traveled *eleven hundred miles* (2, 378). During this time the Commission had expended over $200,000 and had accomplished little besides

Lieutenant Whipple's survey of the Gila River portion of the boundary.

In September 1851, even before Gray received his dismissal, Secretary Stuart had appointed Emory the chief astronomer and surveyor.[117] By the twenty-fifth of that month the Major had embarked from New Orleans for Indianola with a small corps of experts to add to those already present on the Rio Grande. His principal assistant was Lt. Nathaniel Michler of the Topographical Corps, and he also took along Arthur Schott, a German protégé of the Princeton botanist John Torrey, who was employed as a special scientific collector.[118] Before Emory even reached the scene of activity, he was given a special communiqué from Secretary Stuart ordering him to authenticate the Bartlett-Conde agreement in his new capacity as official surveyor.[119]

It was late in November when Emory arrived in El Paso, to find that the commissioner had disappeared somewhere in Mexico leaving behind only a disbursing agent who had no money and no idea of the commissioner's whereabouts.[120] Emory later described the situation: "On my arrival here I found things more complicated than I had expected, a large party, half with Colonel Graham at this place, and the other half with Mr. Bartlett God-knows-where, the whole numbering one hundred and upwards, no money, no credit, subdivided amongst themselves and the bitterest feeling between the different parties. Little or no work has been done, and yet the appropriation is all gone and that of next year anticipated." [121] Though unexpected, it was a familiar situation for Emory, and he immediately set about organizing parties for field service, depending upon his friend James Magoffin for a loan of money and upon the various military garrisons in Texas for supplies.[122] "I have taken a different course from Colonel Graham," he wrote, "he stood still until he could get things fixed to his liking. I have taken the means at hand and pressed the work to the utmost [limits], in-

117. Emory, *Report, I,* 10.

118. Torrey to Emory, Princeton, July 12, 1851, EP. See also ibid., Aug. 4, 1851; and Emory to Arthur Schott, New York, Sept. 16, 1851, ibid.

119. A. H. H. Stuart to Emory, Nov. 4, 1851, EP

120. Emory to James A. Pearce, ca. Jan. 15, 1852, draft, EP.

121. Ibid.

122. Emory to James Magoffin, Frontrera, Dec. 29, 1851, draft, EP.

deed beyond them, and intend when a stop takes place to put the saddle on the right horse." [123]

In order to achieve maximum efficiency, Emory speedily discharged the incompetent employees and organized the remainder into several parties that could all work at different sections of the line simultaneously. Lt. Nathaniel Michler was sent with his party to Fort Duncan, near Eagle Pass, whence he was to run the line south to Laredo. Another assistant surveyed the country immediately south of El Paso, between San Ignacio and Presidio del Norte, while Lt. W. F. Smith of the Topographical Corps established a temporary observatory at San Elizario and began making celestial observations to determine the exact longitude. Emory set up his own headquarters at Frontrera, near El Paso, and endeavored to secure supplies for his men, make astronomical observations of his own, and discover the whereabouts of the missing commissioner.[124]

The diplomatic outlook was not promising. In mid-December Emory appraised the situation for an irate congressman from Texas and concluded that there was little hope of persuading Conde to recede from the Bartlett-Conde agreement. He wrote: "It is a great source of glorification for him, and after the attack made on him by Colonel Carrasco for yielding too much on the Pacific line, he will sacrifice his commission and everything else before receding from what he considers the act of the Joint Commission." [125] A new treaty seemed the only possible way to rectify the situation. Later, even after Conde's death, Emory wrote that his successor, Salazar, was equally "inflexible" on the initial-point question, and he expressed the opinion that the American Commission had irrevocably committed itself.[126] The series of reports which they received caused the Texan delegation to make a solemn protest to Secretary Stuart over Bartlett's action, which promised to bring the fight onto the floors of Congress.[127] These political rumblings soon placed Emory in a

123. Emory to Pearce, ca. Jan. 15, 1852, EP.

124. Emory to Magoffin, Frontrera, Dec. 29, 1851, EP.

125. Emory to Volney Howard, near El Paso, Dec. 18, 1851, contemporary copy, EP.

126. Emory to Howard, San Elizario, June 1, 1852, draft, EP.

127. A. D. Bache to Emory, Wash., Sept. 1, 1852, EP.

delicate position. He was required by Secretary Stuart's orders to authenticate the Bartlett-Conde agreement, but if he did so, he closed the last loophole for re-opening the boundary negotiations, for the Democrats maintained that the agreement was not binding without the surveyor's signature and were rapidly rallying Congressional strength around this stand. To obey the Stuart order meant removal and disgrace for Emory, and it is no wonder he lamented his connections with the Boundary Survey, adding that he had shared "the fate of everyone who throws a stone into a nest of rotten eggs," and had thus "become a little spattered by the explosion." [128] Fortunately for Emory, his friends in the Capital kept him informed on the Washington situation, so that he was able to come about with the political wind.[129] Thus when he met the Mexican commissioner, Salazar, on August 26 and 27 of 1852, he was able to avoid the trap of confirming the initial-point agreement: he signed the maps with the reservation that he was merely witnessing the previous agreement of the two commissioners.[130] By this expedient Stuart's order had been obeyed, the Mexican commissioner was satisfied, the Democrats still had their loophole, and his own career was saved.

Meanwhile, on August 18, 1852, Commissioner Bartlett arrived at El Paso and sent a messenger to Emory suggesting a meeting within a month's time.[131] Then he blithely proceeded to commandeer the escort and leave the field parties without protection from the numerous Indian war parties. In addition, there was no money forthcoming, despite repeated drafts from Bartlett. When the commissioner finally decided to join Emory, the Major had moved to Camargo further down on the Rio Grande.[132] This news determined Bartlett to take the route via Chihuahua, Parras, Saltillo, and Monterey, to avoid the Indians, and to take advantage of Colonel Emilio Langberg's escort of

128. Emory to Howard, San Elizario, June 1, 1852, EP.

129. E. L. F. Hardcastle to Emory, Wash., July 29, 1852, EP. See also the accompanying note by Dale L. Morgan.

130. Emory and José Salazar Ylarregui, Minutes of their official meeting at Presidio del Norte, Aug. 26, 27, 1852, EP.

131. Bartlett to Emory, El Paso, Aug. 18, 1852, EP.

132. Emory to A. H. H. Stuart, Camargo, Nov. 30, 1852, contemporary copy, EP.

Mexican lancers.[133] Emory could not conceal his disgust at this further jaunt as he wrote Lieutenant Michler, "The pretext for this second trip of pleasure is the danger of passing along the road without an escort. Now the Indians in Mexico are worse then they are on the road in question, and two trains have passed along the road since Mr. Bartlett's arrival with either of which my assistants could have come and the commissioner himself if he had chosen." [134] Emory's disgust seemed all the more appropriate when Bartlett's party suffered the only all-out Indian attack during the entire Survey. The Commissioner fortunately escaped, but Doctor Thurber, out collecting plants, was almost caught by an Apache lance before he reached the safety of the caravan.[135]

As if to counterbalance Bartlett's excess caution, other members of the Boundary Commission under the leadership of W. M. T. Chandler, the son of a Whig congressman, carried out an heroic exploration in the trackless canyons of the Big Bend country.[136] It was the first scientific exploration and survey of the Rio Grande. Only Colonel Langberg, a Swedish soldier of fortune commanding the Mexican Militia and Border Patrol, had attempted a survey of the country prior to this, and his sketch map helped guide the explorers part way.[137] The men of Chandler's expedition were clad in rags and some had no shoes. Their food supply was meager, and even the boats upon which they depended were leaky and fragile craft. In addition, the main Apache-Comanche war trail crossed the Rio Grande in this country, and they were continually under the eyes of hostile Indians. One of the men, Charles Abbot, made the trip through the

133. Bartlett to Emory, El Paso, Oct. 5, 1852, EP.

134. Emory to Michler, Fort Duncan, Oct. 26, 1852, draft, EP.

135. Charles Radziminski to Emory, Saltillo, Dec. 10, 1852, EP. Bartlett, *Personal Narrative*, 2, 412–14.

136. Emory to Duff Green, Presidio, Aug. 30, 1852, draft; Thomas Thompson to M. T. W. Chandler, Camp near San Carlos, Oct. 1, 1852, contemporary copy; Arthur Schott to Emory, Camp on the Rayo [*sic*] San Felipe, Oct. 1, 1852; Chandler to Emory, Camp on Rio Grande, Nov. 4, 1852: EP.

137. Emory to Duff Green, Presidio, Aug. 30, 1852, draft, EP. Emory furnished Chandler with a map drawn by Langberg, who had made a previous exploration of the Big Bend country. See also M. T. W. Chandler to Emory, Fort Duncan, Nov. 25, 1852, EP.

nearly impassable canyons in an India-rubber boat and drew a crude sketch of the country as he passed by, which helped Arthur Schott to plot and map the entire area.[138] Though most of the party remained anonymous, their achievement deserves to be ranked alongside those later, more famous, explorations of the canyons of the Colorado.

On June 28, 1852, while Bartlett was making his way toward El Paso and Emory was directing the surveys of the Upper Rio Grande, John B. Weller, now a newly elected senator from California, arrived in Washington and began a debate in the Senate which led to a review of the whole Boundary Survey, and ultimately to the suspension of its activity. Weller considered himself a victim of political assassination, and he was primarily interested in vindicating his own reputation and gaining revenge on the Whigs. Both of these ends were achieved in a lengthy speech delivered by the senator on July 6, wherein he reviewed the history of the Boundary Survey to date and called into question Bartlett's current prosecution of the survey.[139] His personal assault provided a rallying point for other groups who were both opposed to the Whigs and interested in expansion. During the exchange between Weller and Senator Clarke, following the Californian's speech, Rusk of Texas interjected a comment which shifted the focus away from Weller and onto the Bartlett-Conde agreement. He declared emphatically, "I do not intend to vote another dollar to this boundary commission—so far from it, I mean to resist the appropriation of any more money until we have some assurance that the Treaty of Guadalupe-Hidalgo and not the negotiations between the commissioners is to settle the initial point of the line upon the Rio Grande." [140] Senator Rusk spoke for a determined group of southwestern men from Texas, Arkansas, Louisiana, and Mississippi, who were especially concerned over the possible loss of the southern railroad route to California. Since 1844, when Asa Whitney had proposed his Pacific railroad plan, a complicated set of local and sectional

138. Arthur Schott to Emory, n.d [before Nov. 25], EP. See also Chandler to Emory, Fort Duncan, Nov. 25, 1852, EP.

139. *Cong. Globe,* 32d Cong., 1st Sess., *24* (July 6, 1852), 1660.

140. Ibid.

economic rivalries had deadlocked the Congress over the question of a proper location for the transcontinental road. Numerous explorations by the Corps of Topographical Engineers, of which the most prominent had been the one conducted by Lieutenant Emory during the Mexican War, indicated that a route across Texas, through El Paso, and along the Gila River was the best route for the national railroad. In public letters to the St. Louis railroad convention of 1849 and to the 1851 convention in New Orleans, Colonel Abert had wholeheartedly endorsed the southern route.[141] Thus, with the prospect of victory within their grasp, the southwestern men were resolved not to countenance any diplomatic blunder that would lose them the right of way along the Gila River. Initially, they were inclined to accept the Bartlett-Conde agreement as a *fait accompli,* and they immediately proposed a new treaty to purchase the land needed for the right-of-way.[142] But after hearing Surveyor Gray's arguments, the Rusk faction saw a more effective way to accomplish their purpose. They supported Gray and termed the Bartlett-Conde agreement null and void, since it did not bear the signature of the official American surveyor.[143] To save his own reputation, Major Emory was finally forced to explain that he had done nothing to alter Gray's refusal to authenticate the initial-point agreement by his witnessing of the official maps.[144]

Another group which joined in the assault on the Whigs was the delegation from Virginia led by Senator Mason. They were primarily interested in vindicating the aggrieved Colonel Graham, who was a distinguished citizen of that state.[145] In their stand they were joined by the defenders of Colonel McClellan and ultimately, though not immediately, by those who supported Major Emory, so that viewed in one sense the conflict was between the Army technicians and the civilian commissioner. Mason's actions had a telling effect. As chairman of the Committee on Foreign Relations he delivered a report on the bound-

141. Abert to J. Loughborough, St. Louis, Sept. 24, 1849, copy, LS, TE 77. Abert to Glendy Burke Esq., New Orleans, Dec. 17, 1851, copy, ibid.

142. Russel, Improvement of Communication, p. 135.

143. Ibid., p. 136.

144. Emory to Mason, Wash., Feb. 16, 1853, draft, EP.

145. *Cong. Globe* (above, n. 139), p. 1660.

ary situation which disagreed in every respect with Secretary Stuart's evaluation of the situation. It concluded with resolutions which (1) forbade the commissioners and surveyors to "alter, vary, or modify" the boundaries in the treaty; (2) declared the commissioner and surveyor to have equal and joint powers *only;* and (3) declared that the action of Commissioner Bartlett was a departure from the treaty.[146] On August 27 Mason provided a finishing stroke when he moved to attach a proviso to the crucial Deficiency bill which included an appropriation of $120,000 for completing the Survey. It specified "that no part of this appropriation shall be used or expended until it shall be made satisfactorily to appear to the President of the United States, that the southern boundary of New Mexico is not established by the Commissioner and Surveyor of the United States further north of the town called Paso than the same is laid down on Disturnell's map which is attached to the treaty."[147] This provision meant the virtual cessation of all activities in the field.

While the Democrats had good patriotic and economic reasons for attacking the Bartlett-Conde agreement, the language of their speeches also indicates that they were not unmindful of its value as a campaign issue for the coming elections three months hence.[148]

The Whigs were on the defensive. President Fillmore's message to the second session of the Thirty-Second Congress, along with Secretary Stuart's report, attached to the same message, were weak rebuttals. Fillmore lamented the inevitable cessation of field activities, while Stuart merely denied Gray's right to protest the Bartlett-Conde agreement. He refused, however, to consider the real point at issue, which was whether the Bartlett-Conde agreement correctly fulfilled the provisions of the Treaty.[149] The Whigs were thus easily labeled the party of the great land give-away and an obstacle in the path of Manifest Destiny.

146. 32d Cong., 1st Sess., Sen. Com. Rep. 41, 1849–50.

147. *Cong. Globe* (above, n. 139).

148. Ibid., esp. Weller's speeches.

149. *Message of the President,* 32d Cong., 2d Sess., Sen. Exec. Doc. 1 (1852–53), 50–55.

The Whigs received their best support from the popular press, particularly from the administration organs in Washington and the commercial presses in New York and throughout New England.[150] Papers in Newark, Philadelphia, and Columbus, Ohio, staunchly defended Bartlett, and as early as February 1852 the San Diego *Herald* had described all the disputes as stemming from the jealousy of the Army topographers. Its editor wrote: "From some unaccountable influence exercised at home, one or two prominent officers of the Topographical Corps, while they have been at the bottom of most of the disputes without doing any of the labor, have managed to appropriate all the honors connected with the survey of the United States and Mexican Boundary Survey."[151] This was essentially the Whig defense: an all-out attack upon the military who were associated in the popular mind with the Mexican War and with expansion at any cost. The Providence *Journal,* adhering to this line, declared, "the epaulettes rule in Washington."[152] Inevitably, then, the lines of conflict were drawn over the issue of expansion, with one side pictured as unpatriotic and backward, the other side as superpatriotic, demagogic, and militaristic. Personalities were prime targets, and as late as 1858 a few last parting shots were fired at Major Emory by the Providence *Journal.* It ridiculed the idea of naming a peak after Emory, and predicted that when the next volume of his report was issued, "we shall expect to find pictured 'Emory toads' and 'Emory vipers.'"[153]

In all the heat of conflict no one thought to turn to the obvious source to find what the treaty-makers had meant when they composed Article V. The actual negotiator, Nicholas P. Trist, was at the time a resident lawyer in Washington, D.C., but apparently no one consulted him. It was not until after Governor William Carr Lane's bold proclamation of American jurisdiction over the disputed Mesilla Valley that Trist was moved to speak out. Among his personal papers is the draft of an interminable

150. This assertion is based on a survey of newspaper clippings in Bartlett's Scrapbook, Bartlett Papers.

151. Ibid.; see esp. the San Diego *Herald,* Feb. 14, 1852.

152. Ibid., Providence *Journal,* n.d. (clipping only).

153. Ibid., July 14, 1858.

letter to the New York *Evening Post* in which he emphatically scorned the idea that there was any boundary question at all.[154] He termed the "pretended" boundary dispute merely a vote-getting device for the Democratic Party and then launched into a tirade on how it had betrayed American principles and Jeffersonian ideals. He also managed to explain the basis upon which the boundary line and the map ought to be interpreted. "What was this map?" he asked,

> and what is it now? Let all geographers answer. Let the little boys and girls of the geography classes in the ward schools of this city answer: for not one of them who has become accurately and distinctively possessed of the fundamental notions of the science will be at a loss for the reply. . . . in a word, it is to be regarded as a large sheet of *blank* paper with scales of latitude and longitude engraved upon its edges and having *that line* [the southern border of New Mexico] traced upon it; that one line and *nothing else.* Its eastern extremity rests on a river bank, namely that of the Rio Grande.

He continued warmly, "in order to the marking out [*sic*] upon the ground the limits which shall geographically correspond to the representations made of them on the map, what then is to be done consists in going upon the right bank of the Rio Grande and there finding the point of beginning, 'laid down on the map', that is the spot whose latitude is 32° 22′ 30″."

The words "north of the town called Paso" were dismissed as having been inserted to ensure the "good faith" of the United States to Mexico. Only the uncertainty of the *length* of the boundary west of the river was left unresolved, for if it depended upon the coordinate positions, then the three-degrees length as drawn by Trist was impossible. He himself appeared confused on that point. But for Governor Lane, the Army, and the expansionists he had a curious, emphatic message, "A war began [*sic*] for the Mesilla Valley might last an age until at length our Eagle, our most democratic and truly Christian Eagle, perching

154. Trist to the New York *Evening Post,* draft, Vol. 32, 1848 misc., and Vol. 34, June 20, 1849—Feb. 23, 1853 (the two parts of the letter are separated in the Library of Congress Letter volumes), Trist Papers, Library of Congress.

herself upon the southernmost cliff of Cape Horn, should begin to weep after the fashion that eagles are used to weep, at there being nothing more left to civilize." [155]

With the aid of the Trist letter, it is now possible to resolve the dilemma of Disturnell's map and thus determine the exact meaning of Article V of the Treaty. In order to avoid merely specifying a line of latitude, Trist and his Mexican counterparts drew a line on Disturnell's map where they had agreed the boundary should run, and apparently recognizing that the map was incorrect, they guaranteed that the line would run "north of the town called Paso." Commissioner Bartlett had thus correctly interpreted Trist's meaning with respect to the initial point, and his compromise with General Conde over the *length* of the Southern boundary of New Mexico provided an intelligent answer to the question Trist had left unresolved.

Conceivably Trist himself had erred in making the Treaty; perhaps he had not secured all the territory to which the United States was legitimately entitled. Was it not clear that when the scientific parties arrived in the field they saw, as Trist had not, that the traditional boundary of New Mexico was, in fact, "A line touching the northern limit of the town of Paso del Norte 'with the jurisdiction it had always possessed' "? [156] and that that jurisdiction, as Gray pointed out, "extended to El Paso del Norte, the point at which the Rio Grande breaks through the mountains, a natural frontier about eight miles above the central part of 'the town called Paso' "? This argument, actually directed at Bartlett by Gray in his report to Congress, was a powerful one. It rested on the authority of trained scientific observers, upon the reputation of celebrated soldier-engineers who had every reason to be objective. Nevertheless, they were all in the wrong. The disputed Mesilla Valley had been colonized by Mexican settlers from Chihuahua, and the land had been granted under authority from Chihuahua. One of the Mexican officials involved in making the grant testified in 1873:

> the lands embraced in the limits of this grant to the colony known as the civil colony of Mesilla are situate in the pres-

155. Ibid., *32*, 1, and n. 3.
156. Gray (above, n. 103), p. 6.

> ent limits of the county of Doña Ana. . . . At the time this grant was made said lands were within the limits of the State of Chihuahua, Republic of Mexico. At the time this grant was made, the grantees immediately entered into possession of same without molestation and have continued in possession ever since. . . . My acts as commissioner aforesaid were approved by the general government of the Republic of Mexico; also by the officials of the State of Chihuahua, and have been recognized as legal and binding by everyone.[157]

Moreover, anyone wishing to familiarize himself with the New Mexico of that time could have had recourse to Josiah Gregg's classic description in his *Commerce of the Prairies*. Had he done so, he would have seen that the unusually conscientious observer Gregg had placed the southern boundary of New Mexico "not far north of Robledo" which was on the Jornado del Muerto sixty-eight miles north of El Paso del Norte.[158] It is hard to believe that the Topographical Engineers, Emory, Graham, and Whipple, had not been aware of Gregg's allusion to that traditional boundary. This significant omission can perhaps be seen as part of a larger pattern of evidence which indicates the part played by the Topographical Engineers in attempting to secure the railroad route for the United States. On April 2, 1849, Emory had written to Secretary of State Buchanan proposing that the survey of the Boundary line be made from east to west, rather than vice versa, because it would then strike a tributary of the Gila River far enough south to secure the railroad route. He also added that if the Commissioners negotiated a line at the 32nd parallel, the desired route would also be secured.[159] Later he admitted that he had written the letter "in the hope that the United States Commissioner might succeed in torturing the Treaty of Guadalupe Hidalgo to embrace a practicable [railroad] route." [160] Thus Emory, at least, was willing to use questionable methods to gain the desired national ends. Still later, when he

157. Quoted in Ralph Emerson Twitchell, *The Leading Facts of New Mexican History* (5 vols. Cedar Rapids, Iowa, 1917), *3*, 198–99.

158. Gregg, *Commerce of the Prairies* (above, p. 110, n. 6), p. 271.

159. Emory, *Report, 1*, 20–21.

160. Ibid., p. 51.

despaired of securing the route, he advocated taking it by force.[161] It is difficult to say just how closely he was working with the Texan expansionists because his views on the proper location for the route were extremely vacillating, and often inconsistent with those of the expansionists. In his 1846 reconnaissance he had explored the Gila River and declared a route to exist in its vicinity. This had resulted in Trist's securing of a provision in the Treaty of Guadalupe-Hidalgo for the laying out of a railroad route within one league on either side of the Gila.[162] Later Emory saw the 32nd parallel as a boundary that would secure the route for the United States.[163] Yet when A. B. Gray insisted on a boundary south of that line, a boundary which the expansionists earnestly desired, Emory declared that it was still not far enough south to secure the route.[164] This stand placed him decidedly out of favor with the Rusk faction, and when he saw the Bartlett-Conde agreement as a *fait accompli,* like Bartlett he was definitely an obstacle in the way of expansion.[165] Therefore, while it is possible to conclude that Emory and the Topographical Corps favored the 32nd parallel route and were ready to "torture the Treaty" to secure it, it is not at all certain that they adopted this stand on behalf of sectional, rather than national, interests.

In the actual course of events Trist's explanation of the proper boundary line went unheeded. The expansionists succeeded in making the Whigs appear as a party of anti-expansionists and blunderers. Mason's proviso was confirmed, and on December 22, 1852, the Boundary Commission was disbanded.[166] Bartlett and Emory left for Washington, where they arrived by February 1, 1853.[167] In the meantime, Senator Mason had agreed to break the boundary deadlock by pushing through

161. Emory to Volney Howard, Fort Duncan, Nov. 7, 1852, draft, EP.

162. Above (n. 3), p. 45. See also Moore, *Buchanan,* p. 365.

163. Above (n. 3), pp. 368–69. Emory, *Report, 1,* 21.

164. Emory to Howard, Fort Duncan, Nov. 7, 1852, draft, EP.

165. Emory to Howard, near El Paso, Dec. 18, 1851, contemporary copy; also James, A. Pearce to Emory, Wash., Dec. 14, 1852: EP.

166. Bartlett to Emory, Ringgold Barracks, Dec. 21, 1852, EP. The final order came on Dec. 23, 1852; see Bartlett to Emory, Ringgold Barracks, Dec. 23, 1852, EP.

167. Emory to Abert, Wash., Feb. 1, 1853, contemporary copy. EP.

Congress a revision of his proviso which permitted the survey of the Rio Grande below the disputed area to be concluded.[168] Early in May 1853 a new Commission headed by Gen. Robert Blair Campbell of Alabama took the field to finish the survey of the river from Laredo to the Gulf. Major Emory was again the chief astronomer and surveyor, and it was he who for all practical purposes directed the entire survey; [169] Campbell made the journey to the Rio Grande, but he merely supplied authority to Emory's initiative. Under this arrangement the work proceeded speedily, with parties led by Lieutenant Michler and Messrs. Schott, Radziminski, and Gardner surveying alternate sections of the river boundary.[170] The Coast and Geodetic Survey, in collaboration with assistant surveyor Clinton Gardner, sounded the mouth of the Rio Grande and carried the line the required three leagues out to sea. Though the Mexican revolutionary Luis Carvajal was active in the North Mexican provinces, only minor incidents occurred between the Mexicans and the American surveyors. The matter of the initial point remained in abeyance, however, with neither field party pushing the issue. By September 1853 the river survey was virtually concluded, and Major Emory, after leaving the usual skeleton crew to place the boundary markers, sailed for Washington.[171]

The Gadsden Treaty of December 30, 1853, provided a solution to the problems arising out of the previous Treaty of Guadalupe-Hidalgo. It resolved the initial-point controversy by the purchase of enough territory for a railroad route, and it also caused the abrogation of Article XI of the previous treaty, which made the United States responsible for the Indian raids into Mexico. Though the purchase raised considerable opposition,[172] the way for its eventual acceptance was undoubtedly prepared by the long and painful boundary dispute and the possibility of war over the Mesilla Valley suggested by the actions of Governor Lane. For if Lane's direct measures had made peaceful purchase

168. Pearce to Emory, Wash., Dec. 14, 1852, EP.

169. Emory to R. B. Campbell, n.d., "Preliminary Progress Report," draft, EP. This is a sample of the tasks performed by Emory and of his relationship to Campbell.

170. Emory to Campbell, mouth of the Rio Bravo, Aug. [31], 1853, draft, EP.

171. G. Clinton Gardner to Emory, Sept. 20, 1853, EP.

172. Garber, *The Gadsden Treaty* (above, n. 16), p. 103.

more acceptable than war, the existence of a scapegoat in the person of the Whig appointee, Bartlett, made the whole purchase seem merely an effort to rectify an unfortunate mistake by the opposition party.

The actual survey of the Gadsden Boundary provided a sharp contrast to the inefficient operation presided over by Commissioner Bartlett. Major William H. Emory accepted the post as Commissioner and Chief Astronomer on August 16, 1854,[173] and immediately put his experience to work in selecting an accomplished party for field service. The new Commission was divided into two parties, one under Emory that was to work its way west from the Rio Grande, and one under Lieutenant Michler that was to proceed via San Diego to the Colorado River, and thence eastward to the 111th meridian. Emory was assisted by one Topographical officer, Lieutenant Turnbull, while Michler had the efficient artist, surveyor, and collector Arthur Schott as his aide. In all, Emory's party numbered eleven skilled men of officer status, and Michler's numbered four such men, including himself.[174]

By the end of November 1854 Emory had arrived at El Paso after passing safely through a great coastal hurricane and a yellow fever epidemic. The first week in December he met with the new Mexican Commissioner, Salazar, to agree upon a method of procedure. By this time Emory and his Mexican counterpart were old friends, so they were able to reach a plan of action in a short while. There was no attempt to score a diplomatic victory by either side, merely an earnest desire to see the end of that task which had occupied both of them for so long.[175] Moreover, the Mexican government, anxious to receive the final payment of the $3,000,000 required at the completion of the Survey, was even moved to concede Emory the right of making *ex parte* surveys to which it would later agree.[176]

173. Emory to Robert McClelland, Sec. of the Interior, Aug. 16, 1854, draft, EP.

174. Emory to McClelland, Castroville, Texas, Oct. 24, 1854, EP.

175. Emory to Salazar, San Elizario, Nov. 30, 1854, draft, and Emory to McClelland, El Paso, Dec. 8, 1854, draft: EP.

176. Harland Aspinwall to Emory, New York, Dec. 21, 1854, EP.

The surveying operation itself was for the most part merely routine. It was interrupted only when the Mexican Commissioner was thrown into prison by his government, which was temporarily suspicious of his political affiliations with the deposed Santa Anna.[177] He was released within a month's time, however, and allowed to proceed with the survey, although no government appropriation was forthcoming.

Emory's party experienced no difficulty at all in running the line west from the Rio Grande. He was forced to operate in the midst of the Apache country, but his experience guided him in avoiding Indian trouble. "I never trusted them," he later wrote, "and during the last year of experience with them I gave orders to permit none to come into my camp . . . and to kill them on sight." [178] He did not hate the Indians as such, however. In another instance he was moved to plead with the Departmental military commander on behalf of the land and water rights of the peaceful Pima and Maricopa tribes of the Gila River country.[179]

There was a noticeable absence of dissension on the Commission; no murder, no thievery, no brawling took place. This can perhaps be accounted for by the simple, uncomplicated chain of authority, the experience and competence of the men, and the constant attendance of the commissioner to his duty. The only dispute occurred when Emory reached the junction of the 111th meridian and the parallel of 31° 20′ north latitude, where he was supposed to meet Lieutenant Michler. The Major's quick temper was aroused over Michler's failure to reach the rendezvous, and he ordered him to come to his headquarters at Nogales, "bringing all papers relative to public property under his charge." [180] Fortunately, the Lieutenant was able to explain his delay satisfactorily, and in conjunction with Captain Jimenez of the Mexican Commission he finished the western half of the survey on October 14, 1855.[181] At long last, the line was marked upon the earth, and there remained only the business of completing and signing the official maps and then of publishing the federal re-

177. Emory to McClelland, Aug. 9, 1855, draft, EP.
178. Emory, *Report, I,* 88.
179. Emory to General Garland, Fort Bliss, Aug. 11, 1855, draft, EP.
180. Emory to Michler, Santa Cruz, June 1, 1855, draft, EP.
181. Michler to Salazar, Janos, Oct. 14, 1855, fair copy, EP.

port before Congress. In a letter to Secretary of Interior McClellan, written from New Orleans on the way home, Emory advised a final cautious policy:

> I suggest to you, the policy of resisting the payment of one cent of this money until the Mexican Commission has completed and signed the maps representing the Boundary.
>
> This is required by the treaty, and, if the three million is paid before it is done, we will have nothing in hand to coerce the Mexican Government and Commission to a conclusion of the labors of the Commission according to the stipulation of the Treaty.[182]

His policy was heeded, and by January 1857 the field records of the Mexican Boundary Survey could at long last be officially closed. For the Topographical Corps this marked the end of a long and unpleasant duty, their largest project in the West up to that time. Before it was finally over, Major Emory had transferred to the cavalry, Colonel Graham had turned his talents to the Great Lakes Surveys, and Colonel McClellan had died while on duty on the Tennessee River.[183] The status of the Topographical Corps itself had also been changed. It had been forced to ally itself openly with the forces of expansion, thus moving it into the mainstream of sectional politics.

In addition to their duties as surveyors, the Topographical Engineers introduced the scientific study of geography into the Mexican Boundary Survey. Both Major Emory and Colonel Graham intended to produce a scientific description of the entire Southwest as a physical region, beginning with an accurate outline map to which would be added the findings of scientists in all the other disciplines, including ethnology. Their aim was only partially utilitarian, since much of the data accumulated had no direct bearing on such of the problems at hand, as the location of the transcontinental railroad. Through their project they became part of the main trend of nineteenth-century geographical investigation, which was characterized by the system-

182. Emory to McClelland, New Orleans, Nov. 4, 1855, draft, EP.
183. Cullum (above, p. 12, n. 22), p. 367.

atic exploration of the interiors of all the great continents.[184] Their concentration upon physical more than upon human data related them to Humboldt, and like most of the other western publications of the Topographical Engineers the *Report of the Mexican Boundary Survey* was a compendium in this important tradition.

The final *Report* was published in three large quarto volumes as an Executive Document by the Thirty-Fourth Congress. There were 10,000 copies of the first, or narrative, volume ordered to be printed on August 15, 1856.[185] But by the time the second and third volumes were ready for publication, Congress had become alarmed over the vast sums spent for illustrated scientific books and at Emory's suggestion had authorized the publication of only 3,000 copies of the botanical and zoological reports for distribution among the centers of learning.[186] Because it reflected upon rival publications, Emory agreed to the curtailment, for he termed most of the other reports besides his own "trashy swindles got up for the benefit of author and public printers." [187] It was not until 1859 that his final volumes appeared in print. By that time much of the new-found data had been anticipated in separate papers read before the various learned societies.[188]

In organization and style of writing, Emory's *Report* was much inferior to that of his rival, Frémont. Following the Humboldt example, Emory conceived of his subject in chapters which were topical essays, thus including much that was repetitious. His own narrative of the boundary operations was brief and confined to an unsystematic account of his labors and an inappropriate castigation of the behavior of Commissioner Bartlett (pp. 16–18). One chapter was a general description of the country. Also included were narrative accounts by Lieutenant Michler of his work while separated from Major Emory (pp. 74–92, 101–29). The result of this method of organization produced no really

184. R. E. Dickinson and J. R. Howarth, *The Making of Geography* (Oxford, 1933), p. 125.

185. Emory, *Report,* 2, printing resolution.

186. Emory to Jacob Thompson, Wash., Oct. 7, 1857, draft, EP. Emory recommended the publication of 1,000 copies, but 3,000 were printed. See n. 185, above.

187. Emory to George Engelmann, Wash., April 8, 1856, draft, EP.

188. Meisel, *Bibliography,* pp. 103–5.

clear picture of the operation of the survey itself. Such a picture remained buried among the archives of the Commission. The scientific content of the *Report,* however, was of the greatest significance, and it equalled the findings of Frémont.

Emory's important contributions to the *Report* were primarily cartographic, though he supplemented his map with a series of random comments that were often striking and astute. With respect to the cartography, he made most of the thousands of astronomical observations from which were derived 208 separate points of latitude and longitude from the Gulf of Mexico to the Pacific.[189] He also supervised the making of a barometric profile showing the variations in altitude all along the line. To this profile Dr. Parry, the field geologist, added data showing the various geologic strata. Several pages of the *Report* were devoted to a determination of eight points of declination, dip, and horizontal intensity of the field of terrestrial magnetism. A similar study by Humboldt had resulted in his law of declining magnetic intensity between the poles. Emory's conclusions perhaps added a modicum of weight to this generalization.[190]

Most of this information was related to the master map of the entire trans-Mississippi West which was made to accompany the Boundary Survey *Report.* Emory's map was drawn to a scale of 1:6,000,000, just half the size of Lieutenant G. K. Warren's monumental trans-Mississippi map intended as a supplement to the Pacific railroad surveys. In one of his letters Emory confided that he had exchanged data with Captain A. A. Humphreys, who supervised the making of Warren's map, and thus they were similar productions.[191] They are not, however, identical in detail, as Warren's map includes a complete picture of the Oregon country, most of which Emory left blank. In addition, Warren's map shows a crucial railroad pass through the Chiricahua Mountains above the 32nd parallel, which Emory neglected to include. Of the two maps, cartographers generally consider Warren's the more important, and a comparison of them bears out this verdict.[192] Nevertheless, Emory's version of the trans-Mississippi

189. My calculation, based on Emory's tables.

190. Helmut de Terra, *Humboldt* (New York, 1955), p. 376.

191. Emory to James Hall, Jan. 15, 1857, contemporary copy, EP.

192. This is the judgment of, e.g., Wheat, "Mapping the American West," p. 161.

country was only the second (after Frémont's) important attempt to portray the region as a whole and a clear advance over the previous work of Preuss and Frémont. It was obscured only by the rapid march of events. Besides the large master map, three other groups of maps were made but not published—four military maps, fifty-three sectional maps of great detail, and a series representing islands and special localities.[193]

In the text accompanying the maps, Emory included a personal account of the operations of the survey itself, as well as a general description of the country. Most striking of his topographical observations was his description of a great continental depression along the 32nd parallel area. He wrote:

> . . . if the sea were to rise 4,000 feet above its present level, the navigator could cross the continent near the 32nd parallel of latitude. He would be on soundings of uniform depth from the Gulf of California to the Pecos River. He would see to the north and south prominent peaks and sierras, and at times, his passage would be narrow and intricate. At El Paso he would be within gun-shot of both shores [p. 41].

The Major's comments on the relation of the arid lands to settlement, like those of his 1846 *Report,* foreshadowed John Wesley Powell's study made two decades later. "Whatever may be said to the contrary," Emory wrote, "these plains west of the 100th meridian are wholly unsusceptible of sustaining an agricultural population, until you reach sufficiently far south to encounter the rains from the tropics" (p. 47). He added: "The country must be settled by a mining and pastoral or wine-making population; and the whole legislation of Congress directed heretofore so successfully towards the settlement of lands east of the 100th meridian must be remodeled and reorganized to suit the new phase which life must assume under conditions so different from those to which we are accustomed" (p. 49).

With respect to the railroad route through the Southwest, Emory repeated his argument that neither Bartlett's nor Gray's line would have secured the road (p. 20). Drawing upon the

193. Emory, *Report, 1,* xiv.

Pacific railroad surveys, he asserted that Lt. J. G. Parke's survey had confirmed his theory that the San Pedro Valley was the only route south from the Gila River to the table lands west of the Rio Grande (p. xiv). Warren's map, however, shows this route above the 32nd parallel.[194] It was Cooke's wagon route through Tucson that ran far south of the Bartlett-Conde line.

The most significant scientific contributions were made by the scientists who examined the collections in detail back in the eastern centers of learning. Of these, the geological report deserves the most prominence, for it was the first attempt by reputable scientists to construct an over-all version of the trans-Mississippi geology. In addition to this, the three geologists—Parry, Schott, and Hall—attempted to derive causal principles from the mass of observed data and thus to reconstruct the geologic history of the region. Their reconstructions were general and often superficial, but they included an acceptance of surprisingly advanced theories, so that even today they are for the most part still valid. To their remarks must also be added those of Lieutenant Michler, who, when observing the arroyos and canyons draining laterally into the Rio Grande from the Llano Estacado, concluded, "they are but miniature creations of the same power which forced a passage for the Rio Grande," [195] thus implicitly accepting the doctrine of uniformitarianism as opposed to catastrophism.

Doctor Parry and Arthur Schott made geologic reports on different sections of the line. Nevertheless, a general picture of vast areas of aqueous or sedimentary deposits pierced by igneous intrusions emerges from both versions. Parry's most interesting contribution was his theory of mountain-making and continental uplift. He wrote, "Now it is well known that all extended continental ranges are due to a line of internal disturbance of varying intensity at different points, but in all alike characterized by the protrusion of various igneous products, together with the uplifting of adjacent stratified deposits." [196] His explanation of a broad area of igneous intrusion resulting in general elevation previewed G. C. Gilbert's later discoveries of the "Laccolite" or

194. Cf. Warren, *Memoir,* general map.
195. Emory, *Report, 1,* 78.
196. Ibid., *1,* Pt. II, 15.

laccolith formation of the Henry Mountains.[197] In this explanation of mountain-making, Parry was also in substantial agreement with James Hall of Albany,[198] but Dana's geosyncline and anticline explanation with its implied horizontal displacement, published in his *Manual of Geology,* superseded these theories.[199]

Schott attempted to reconstruct the periods of inundation by the great coastal seas. He noted various Cretaceous deposits which indicated the ebb and flow of several inundations. This was also substantiated by his discovery of "various cretaceous terraces of the lower Rio Bravo [Grande] basin, placed as they are one above the other . . . as so many antediluvial tidemarks of that vast sea." By means of the fossil deposits he was able to envisage several distinct horizons. At the same time he linked some of these fossils with those in the Cretaceous chalk formations of New Jersey earlier described by the paleontologists Morton and Conrad. Even beyond this he found that some of the new specimens were analogous to those of southern Europe, which suggested a similar geologic horizon. This need not, of course, have existed at the same time. Other Cretaceous specimens were indigenous to Texas only,[200] thus helping to substantiate the hypothesis that not one but several periods of inundation had occurred in the Southwest.

Schott also saw evidence of vast inland seas in the deserts on both sides of the Colorado and Gila similar to Lake Bonneville further north, and he added perceptively, "Since the water has receded, an ocean of a more subtle character sweeps over this area. Aerial currents are now driving the shifting sand from place to place as the waters of the sea once did" (pp. 63–64).

Along with the sedimentary deposits Schott, like Parry, found abundant evidence of igneous intrusion in dikes, mountains, and even in the volcanic cores, standing out like the chimneys of burned-down houses, in the midst of the barren deserts (p. 47). He also had his own curious theory of mountain-making, which included the action of electro-magnetism on volcanic flows. In

197. Stegner, *Beyond the Hundredth Meridian* (above, p. 20, n. 52), p. 156.

198. James Hall, "Memorandum on Mountain-Making," n.d., Hall Papers, New York State Museum, Albany, N.Y.

199. James Dwight Dana, *Manual of Geology,* Phila., 1863.

200. Emory, *Report,* 2, Pt. II, 46–47.

explanation he stated, somewhat ambiguously: "To the stratification, lamination, and cleavage, of the sedimentary rocks, as determining the subsequent direction of volcanic forces we may ascribe the formation of the catenary mountain ranges and dykes and the cellular system of their intermediate bases" (p. 65). By way of final conclusion to his report, like Lieutenant Michler he expressed himself in favor of uniformitarianism over catastrophism:

> Considering such facts, we cannot doubt that the regions here spoken of have not yet passed through all the phases of their destiny. We do not, however, believe any general and violent catastrophe indispensable for further geological developments. A long continuance and perhaps imperceptible rising of the country, a simple increase of elevation . . . would aid the torrents of the mountains and the sweep of aerial currents to clear the surface of the country from its desert burden [p. 77].

James Hall of Albany approached the regional geology from the paleontologist's point of view and attempted to locate various strata formations on his master geological map of the trans-Mississippi country. He was most successful in correlating the various Cretaceous outcroppings discovered by Nicollet, Frémont, Abert, and Stansbury with those found on the Boundary Survey. The common factor was a fossil appropriately named *Inoceramus Problematicus,* which enabled Hall to deduce the existence of the "same geological horizon for the strata of these localities from the Kansas River to New Mexico." [201]

The comparative ages of the mountain ranges was another subject that occupied Hall. After first correctly deducing that the Sierra Nevadas, Coast Ranges, and Rockies were not the same age, Hall went on to conclude, curiously, that the rugged Sierra Nevadas were about the same age as the worn-down Appalachians (pp. 120–21). It would take another generation of geologists to disprove Hall's assertion.

As a supplement to Schott's findings, Hall also located fossil evidence of another southwestern sea during the later coal periods (p. 125). What these geological conclusions represented was the

201. Ibid., *I,* Pt. I, 117.

first groping attempt in the trans-Mississippi West to derive principles of scientific causality from the newly discovered data. The collection and classification persisted, but these essays marked the beginning of a long process of scientific reasoning about the West which is unfinished even today. It was thus in its own time an important advance in scientific thinking.

The botanical report was primarily the work of John Torrey, who classified the 2,648 [202] species of plants brought back by the field collectors. According to Asa Gray, who reviewed it in the *American Journal of Science,* the "Botany of the Boundary" deserved to be "ranked as the most important publication of the kind that has ever appeared." [203] It was in the form of an immense list that systematized not only all of the new and old species collected by the Boundary Survey collectors—Parry, Schott, Wright, Thurber, and Bigelow—but also those assembled by free-lance collectors like Berlandier, Lindheimer, Fendler, and Lt. J. M. Couch.[204] Torrey's report, taken together with Engelmann's separate discussion of the cactacae, was the largest survey of plants undertaken in the United States up to that time.[205]

There was virtually no attempt at generalization beyond that implicit in Torrey's scheme of classification, except for an introduction by Parry which related the plants to the various topographic and geologic regions.[206] This was done in two ways, by lateral area and also by altitude. The result was a characterization of different plant regions within the larger Southwest region. Parry also speculated on the possibilities of agriculture and concluded that climate, not soil fertility, was the chief obstacle, and that it was such a serious one as to make it extremely doubtful that an agricultural community of any size could survive.[207] This, of course, bore out Emory's own generalization.

The classification of the zoological specimens was done by the team of Spencer F. Baird and Charles F. Girard of the Smith-

202. My calculation, based on a count of the species in Emory, *Report, 2,* Pt. III.

203. Quoted in Rodgers, *John Torrey* (above, p. 16, n. 38), p. 227.

204. See Samuel Woods Geiser, *Naturalists of the Frontier* (Dallas, 1937) for a description of the work of these botanists.

205. A. B. Gray, as quoted in Rodgers, p. 227.

206. Emory, *Report, 2,* Pt. III, 9–26.

207. Ibid., pp. 15–16.

sonian Institution. It was divided into sections on mammals, birds, and reptiles, for which Baird was responsible, and a section of fishes, which was the special province of Girard. Baird classified 311 [208] different species, and his report was purely descriptive, without even an attempt at correlation between the animal and the geographic locale.

Among the most significant contributions to knowledge were numerous illustrations accompanying the various sections of narrative reports. Arthur Schott made colored illustrations of the Yumas, Co-Co-Pas, Digueños, Lipans, Papagos, and other characteristic Indian tribes of the region, which contributed a great deal more information than an abstract description in words. There were other views—of San Antonio, Brownsville, the Rio de San Pedro, and one striking illustration of a *Cereus Giganticus* cactus. Most of these engravings were made from the work of three artists: Schott; an Austrian emigrant named John Weyss; and an eccentric Louisiana Frenchmen, A. De Vaudricourt. Weyss also drew a series of outline sketches that portrayed the entire length of the boundary line, so that even if the stone markers should be removed, some idea of their location would remain. His outline drawings also presented an excellent idea of the topography and characteristic vegetation. All of these various elements taken together—the narrative, the scientific reports, and the pictures—made Emory's production an overwhelming contribution of factual knowledge concerning the American Southwest.

Still another source of information on the southwestern region was John Russell Bartlett's *Personal Narrative of Explorations and Incidents in Texas, New Mexico, California, Sonora and Chihuahua,* a travel book obviously modeled after the successful work of his friend John Lloyd Stephens, *Incidents of Travel in Central America, Chiapas and Yucatan.* Bartlett's book included a running account of his extensive travels over northern Mexico, California, and the southwestern United States, as the title indicates. The Commissioner considered himself a scientist, and he collected a great amount of data on the Indian languages which he left out of his *Narrative,* lest it mar the literary quality.[209] As

208. My figure, computed from Emory's *Report,* 2, Pt. IV.
209. Bartlett, *Personal Narrative,* p. vi.

a piece of narrative writing about the American West, Bartlett's book ranks alongside those of Frémont, Parkman, and Gregg as a classic. Within its pages is contained a panoramic view of the way of life of an entire region previously known only to a few. It was to be of little use to scientists, but for many a hammock reader at Saratoga or Newport it opened up an exciting America and helped create an image of the exotic West.

The Mexican Boundary Survey was thus an important event in the history of American expansion—both politically and intellectually—as well as in the history of the Topographical Engineers. As a controversy, it represented the desperate struggle of the expansionists to secure what was regarded at the time as the only practicable year-round line of communication with California. But the dispute with Mexico, like the whole issue of national expansion, became enmeshed in the mounting political and sectional differences within the United States. The result of the diplomatic struggle, General Gadsden's Purchase, seemed clearly a favor to the aggressive Southwestern faction, whom many already blamed for instigating the Mexican War. In terms of potential economic development, the securing of the railroad route by federal purchase appeared to have given the Southwest (or the South) a vital advantage which threatened the economic development of the Northern and Central cities.

Within this complex of economic and political rivalries stood the Topographical Engineers. As an institution committed to the task of national development, part of the Corps' job was to seek a communication route to the Pacific Coast wherever it existed in the national domain. Since a large force was already committed to surveying operations in the southwestern region, their discovery and aggressive campaign on behalf of a railroad line in that area was undoubtedly a normal reaction to the situation in which they were placed. As yet, no one had located another practicable route, and it seemed vital to the national interest to secure the one at hand, not only to ensure the proper defense of California but to facilitate the defense of the entire southwestern border against devastating raids by hostile Indians. Significantly enough, such bitter enemies as Colonel Graham and A. B. Gray found themselves in agreement on the necessity for securing the southwestern right-of-way. Thus, as the architects and engineers of national development, the Topographical officers were all convinced of the value of an aggressive policy on the Rio Grande.

This commitment, however, irrevocably allied them with the expansionists. It gave a sectional tint to their expressions of opinion on the subject of national development and therefore depreciated their scientific judgments. Since they were a branch of the government, perhaps this was inevitable, because a judgment by one of a number of factions is almost certain to be unpopular with the others. Like the unfortunate Commissioner Bartlett, the officers of the Topographical Corps came under fire from powerful factions in the North and West.[210] Bartlett could retire from the scene to the hilltop library of his patron, John Carter Brown, but the Topographical Engineers had to remain under public scrutiny for the rest of the decade.

They had suffered some indignity, too, in being placed in a position subordinate to inexpert political appointees. Colonels Graham and McClellan never fully recovered their reputations. Major Emory eventually transferred to the cavalry by a special appointment from Jefferson Davis.[211] Clearly, the makeshift arrangement of a mixed commission with dual loyalties to the State Department and the Army was in large measure responsible for the sorry administrative spectacle the Survey presented. There was little coordination between the various elements of the Survey: Bartlett disappeared into Mexico; Whipple was isolated on the Gila River; Emory fumed in helpless frustration at El Paso with no money and a near mutiny on his hands. Lieutenant Strain of the Navy and Colonel McClellan of the Army were, of course, subject to entirely different authority. At one point there were even four botanists on the Commission busily collecting the same specimens in competition with one another. Absurd and even tragic, the spectacle might be considered a reflection of the national government itself. It represented an Executive in which bureaus and functions were added in makeshift fashion, where a naval officer might easily find himself with a command on the Llano Estacado, or even shepherding a herd of camels on

210. See esp. the attack by Thomas Hart Benton in *Cong. Globe,* 33d Cong., 1st Sess., 23 (1854), pp. 1031–36.

211. Emory to Jefferson Davis, San Antonio, Sept. 25, 1855, draft, EP.

the Arabian deserts.[212] There were few precedents to guide the president and his cabinet officials, and many new problems to solve; so accidental drift and improvisation rather than a system of rational planning prevailed. The same phenomenon had characterized the English colonial experience; the curious division of authority among the royal governor, the local assembly, the governor's council, the Board of Trade and Plantations, and the Privy Council had historically arisen in the same unplanned, accidental fashion.

In summarizing the achievements of the Corps on the Mexican Boundary Survey, one may say they were instrumental in promoting the Gadsden Purchase, they provided the elements of skill and stability that eventually resulted in the completion of the project, and they made striking contributions toward a scientific knowledge of the American West. Of these, only the latter merits further word. In both original exploration and in pure science the Corps performed notable service. The maps, the reports, and the long series of learned papers that resulted were the brightest lights in that somber adventure along the Rio Grande.

212. See, e.g., the experience of Lt. Edward Fitzgerald Beale, in Wallace, *The Great Reconnaissance* (above, p. 22, n. 1), pp. 235–66.

6. EXPLORING THE NEW DOMAIN, 1848–1853

> Our *cortège* passing along Kearny Street attracted much attention from the natives . . . First came the cart, bearing our instruments; then a cart containing Lieut Zero with a level, with which he constantly noted the changes of grade that might occur; then one hundred and fifty men, four abreast, armed to the teeth, each wheeling before him his personal property and a mountain howitzer; then the *savans,* each with notebook and pencil, constantly jotting down some object of interest . . . and finally, the Chief Professor, walking arm in arm with Dr. Dunshunner, and gazing from side to side, with an air of ineffable blandness and dignity, brought up the rear.—*George Horatio Derby,* "Official Report of Professor John Phoenix, a.m."

LIEUTENANT EMORY'S REPORT of his military reconnaissance across the Southwest with General Kearny's Army of the West had a profound effect upon the postwar plans of the Corps of Topographical Engineers. The report underscored the all-important problem of communications in the newly acquired country, and it offered the prospect of a practicable route through the Southwest as a solution to this problem. With the publication of Cooke's report as a supplement to Emory's, it seemed clear that, at the very least, a wagon road existed between the Santa Fe settlements and California. Thus it became the main objective of the Topographical Bureau during the postwar years to locate suitable routes across the Southwest which could eventually be used to join the Mississippi River with the Pacific provinces by a transcontinental railroad.

"The consequences of such a road are immense," wrote Colonel Abert in the spring of 1849 in a letter to Francis Markoe of the State Department, and he added, "they probably involve the integrity of the Union. Unless some easy, cheap, and rapid means of communicating with these distant provinces be accomplished, there is danger, great danger, that they will not constitute parts of our Union. Then what will become of our great moral power, our great commerce, our infinite resources . . . ? We shall sink into two second rate governments if we are even able to maintain as good a position as that of second rate." [1]

To urge his point, the Colonel wrote long letters to the St. Louis Railroad Convention of 1849 and the New Orleans Convention of 1851, enclosing copies of the letter to Markoe, which contained a detailed exposition of his plan. He scorned the Isthmian canal projects as mere "temporary expedients" and again and again repeated his argument that the only really sound project was to be found "in a continuous Railroad route from the Mississippi to the Pacific within our own jurisdiction." [2] The route he had in mind was, of course, based upon Emory's report. It was the same route that caused such consternation over the Bartlett-Conde agreement of the Mexican Boundary Survey. That road would start from San Diego and follow Emory's track along the Gila River to the Rio Grande below Santa Fe. Here it would make contact with steamboats coming up the river "for military as well as commercial reasons." Then the road was to pass southeastward across Texas through San Antonio, Bastrop or La Grange, and Washington, to Nacogdoches. Abert observed, "By this route the road will pass through a highly valuable part of Texas and communicate with the principal rivers of that state at boatable points from which it will have access to the ports of this state on the Gulf by means of these rivers or by branch roads." [3]

At Nacogdoches the road was to split into two branches, one to course northward across the Red River to Little Rock. St. Louis, Pittsburgh, and points east; the other, a southern route, to strike the Mississippi near Vicksburg and connect with Savannah, Charleston, Wilmington, Norfolk, and Washington.[4] It was to be, in Abert's mind, a national project, designed to bind the Far West to the whole Union east of the Mississippi as far as the northern and southern Atlantic seaboards. Moreover, it looked toward the economic development of the new southwestern region by the efficient exploitation of its natural river arteries, its belt of fertile soil along the headwaters of its rivers, and the

1. Abert to Francis Markoe, May 18, 1849, LS, TE 77.

2. Abert to J. Loughborough, St. Louis, Sept. 24, 1849; and to Glendy Burke, New Orleans, Dec. 17, 1851: ibid.

3. Abert to Markoe, May 18, 1849, ibid.

4. Ibid.

adaptability of its flat topography for any sort of local overland communications. These objectives formed a backdrop for the operations of the Corps in the new lands of Texas, New Mexico, Utah, and California. It was the nearest approach to federal planning for the development of the trans-Mississippi region that existed, and it had arisen out of the military necessity of binding the political Union closer together and the desire to facilitate the exploitation of the gold deposits in California.

At the same time, other needs of an even more immediate practicality became apparent in the Southwest. The problem of frontier defense against the Comanches, Apaches, and Navahos preoccupied every secretary of war from George Crawford to Jefferson Davis. Article XI of the Treaty of Guadalupe Hidalgo added a diplomatic urgency to this need. Forts had to be constructed, roads built between them, rivers surveyed as avenues of supply, and the intricate system of Indian trails sought out and mapped. Because of the Indian barrier, the southwestern frontier from San Antonio to Fort Yuma became a military frontier. The best part of the American Army was stationed between these points, and the Topographical Engineers provided most of whatever reconnoitering service was needed for its operations.

If it was first a military frontier, it soon became a settler's frontier in Texas, and after 1848 a miner's frontier in California. Thus a number of new tasks, such as harbor surveying and wagon road building, were added to the purely military activities of the Corps. The relationship between the projects for military use and those for civilian use was such as to make them very often identical. The policy of frontier defense went hand in hand with the aggressive, positive advance of commercial settlement. This relationship was the key to settlement in much of the vast environs of the Southwest. It was a process of stimulus and response, of settler's petition or adjutant general's request, and the subsequent assignment of an engineer officer. Thus in January 1849, in response to petitions submitted by Senators Benton of Missouri, Borland of Arkansas, and Houston of Texas,[5] a Senate Committee on Military Affairs, headed by Jefferson Davis, recommended the appropriation of $50,000 for surveys in Nebraska, California, New Mexico, and Texas, declaring:

5. *Sen. Jour.*, 30th Cong., 2d Sess. (1848–49), pp. 109–10.

> The establishment of posts must be preceded by the construction of military roads, and these roads and posts, giving facility, inducement and protection to emigrants will be followed by settlements, which will remove the necessity for the maintenance of garrisons, unite the regions on opposite sides of the mountain ridge which divides the continent, by successive links of farms and villages, lead to the construction of commercial roads, and bind the whole country by constant intercourse and common interest durably together.[6]

When the House Military Committee concurred, the appropriation was granted.[7]

What emerges, then, in the postwar period, is a concentration of activity by the Topographical Engineers in the Southwest—activity of extremely varied nature serving long-range as well as immediate ends, paralleling and abetting national enthusiasms such as those for gold, land, and increased transportation facilities. At all times the Corps stood ready to supply whatever technical aid was needed for the protection and advancement of the American people as they took full possession of their immense new domain, from the Rio Grande to the Coast of California.

The most ambitious overland reconnaissances of the year 1849 undertaken by the Corps of Topographical Engineers were in direct response to resolutions offered by senators representing western states. Even before the news of the gold discovery in California had reached the citizens of Fort Smith, Arkansas, they had petitioned the federal government for aid in laying out an emigrant road across Texas to Santa Fe.[8] Remembering Josiah

6. Ibid., Sen. Com. Rep. 276 (1848–49), 3. Cf. J. J. Abert's statement, ibid., Sen. Exec. Doc. 1 (1848–49), 327, which reads: "These distant military posts and military roads are the pioneers of civilization and of wealth, by the protection they afford to remote settlements, the value they give to public lands, the encouragement to civilization by the consumption of produce, and by the intelligence and good habits diffused by such a nucleus of well-informed and orderly persons of both sexes as generally constitute the population of our garrisons."

7. *Select Committee on a Canal or Railroad between the Atlantic and Pacific Oceans*, 30th Cong., 2d Sess., H. R. Rep. 145, 1847–48. Grant Foreman, *Marcy and the Gold-Seekers* (Norman, Okla., 1939), p. 121.

8. Foreman, pp. 118–19.

Gregg's trail of 1839 along the Canadian River to Santa Fe, the citizens of the young Arkansas metropolis saw an opportunity to make their town a hub of commerce where the river network made contact with the best prairie route. In their plans, Fort Smith could well become the *entrepôt* for any stream of emigration and commerce directed overland through the Southwest.[9] For these reasons, as early as June 26, 1848, Senator Borland of Arkansas offered the first resolution for an overland reconnaissance to California.[10] He also petitioned the Secretary of War directly for an officer to survey the Fort Smith—Santa Fe route.[11] Accordingly, on April 2, 1849, Colonel Arbuckle, commandant of the Seventh Military District, ordered Capt. Randolph B. Marcy of the Fifth Infantry to escort a large train of emigrant wagons from Fort Smith to Santa Fe along a route following the south bank of the Canadian River. He was to ascertain the best overland route to New Mexico and California, to aid the emigrants in whatever manner possible, and do his best to placate any Comanche Indians they might meet along the way.[12]

The reconnaissance was to be in force, and Marcy, a comparatively youthful veteran of frontier garrison duty and a lowly infantryman besides, had under his command one company of the First Dragoons, headed by Lt. James Buford, and two companies of the Fifth Infantry led by Lts. M. P. Harrison and J. Updegraff.[13] In addition, Colonel Abert, taking advantage of the appropriation charged to the Seventh Military District, sent Lt. James H. Simpson of the Topographical Corps, one of his best young officers, to act as topographer and assistant to Captain Marcy.[14]

Lieutenant Simpson arrived at Fort Smith on April 7 aboard the river steamer *Sally Anderson,* along with ninety eager goldseekers, with orders to proceed with the emigrant train all the

9. Ibid., pp. 14–15.

10. Ibid., pp. 118–19.

11. Solon Borland to Abert, Feb. 23, 1852, LS, TE 77.

12. Randolph B. Marcy, *Report of a Route from Fort Smith to Santa Fe,* 31st Cong., 1st Sess., Sen. Exec. Doc. 64 (1850), 169.

13. Ibid.

14. James Harvey Simpson, *Report and Map of the Route from Fort Smith, Arkansas, to Santa Fe, New Mexico,* 31st Cong., 1st Sess., Sen. Exec. Doc. 12 (1850), 1–2.

way to California.[15] Marcy and the rest of the military force had already left on April 4, and even before Simpson could catch up to the train, his orders were changed so as to cause him to stop when he reached Santa Fe and forward his report to Washington, where it was eagerly awaited. He was further advised that he was to make a reconnaissance out of Santa Fe, along the "caravan route," north through Abiquiu and St. Joseph's Spring, to Los Angeles. This was the route commonly called the Old Spanish Trail.[16]

The main military party was twenty-six miles out of Fort Smith when Simpson overtook it and proceeded with it through the difficult terrain of the Cross Timbers to Edwards Trading Post, where they made a rendezvous with an advance party led by Captain Dent.

On May 8 Marcy's command reached Chouteau's Fort, site of an abandoned military post, Old Fort Holmes. Here they waited until the 17th for the emigrant train to catch up before venturing out beyond the Cross Timbers along the prairie divide between the Washita and Canadian rivers. Once they started, they found the roadway smooth and a perfect natural highway, so much so that the usually restrained Lieutenant Simpson was led to report, "Indeed, so superior was it that I scarcely ever got on it from my explorations to the right and left without involuntarily wishing that I had a fleet horse and a light buggy that I might skim over it to my satisfaction." [17]

Their route led them past the Antelope Hills or Boundary Buttes, and in comparing them with Lieutenant Abert's drawings, made in 1845, Simpson found them exactly as represented (p. 9). All along the way he was able to compare notes with Abert's report, since the fledging Lieutenant had followed approximately the same route on his earlier reconnaissance in 1845. Besides referring to Abert's report Simpson also made observations of his own. Of particular interest was his speculation as to the origin of the volcanic cores standing out alone on the prairie. He saw them as the sole surviving elements of formations that had been eroded away by the "Noachic deluge," and from this period he

15. Foreman, p. 28.
16. Simpson, p. 2.
17. Ibid.

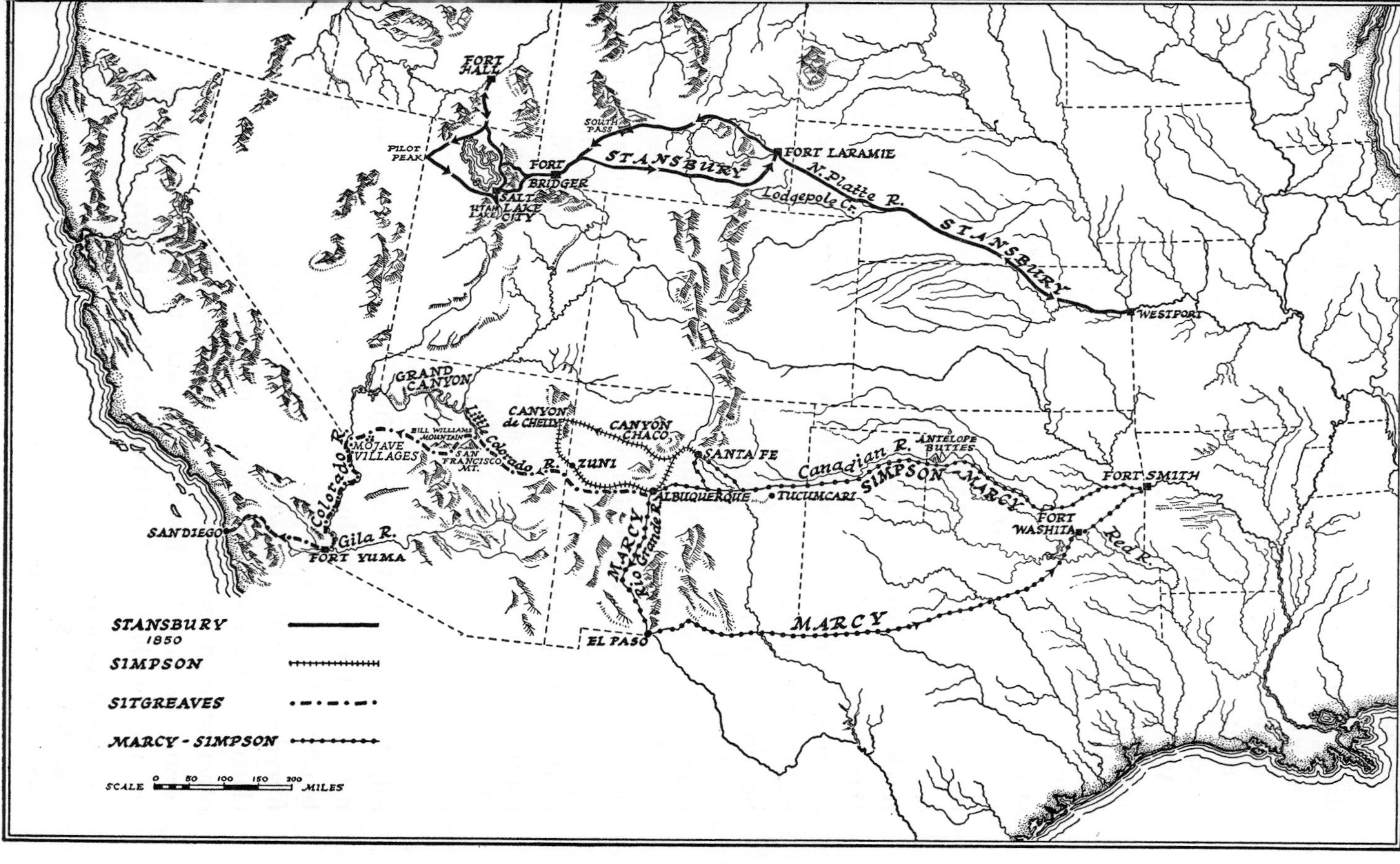
FORT HALL
PILOT PEAK
SOUTH PASS
FORT LARAMIE
STANSBURY
FORT BRIDGER
SALT LAKE CITY
UTAH LAKE
N. Platte R.
Lodgepole Cr.
STANSBURY
WESTPORT
GRAND CANYON
CANYON de CHELLY
CANYON CHACO
BILL WILLIAMS MOUNTAIN
MOJAVE VILLAGES
SAN FRANCISCO MT.
Little Colorado R.
ZUNI
SANTA FE
Canadian R.
ANTELOPE BUTTES
SIMPSON
MARCY
FORT SMITH
ALBUQUERQUE
TUCUMCARI
FORT WASHITA
Red R.
Colorado R.
SANDIEGO
Gila R.
FORT YUMA
MARCY
Rio Grande R.
MARCY
EL PASO
STANSBURY 1850
SIMPSON
SITGREAVES
MARCY - SIMPSON
SCALE 0 50 100 150 200 MILES
MAP 7

dated their origin (p. 11). His acceptance of biblical-catastrophic geology was in contrast to Lieutenant Michler's more modern uniformitarian generalizations along the Rio Grande,[18] and it illustrates that the advanced scientific theories had by no means been universally accepted.

When the party ascended the high table lands of the Llano Estacado, Captain Marcy described them as "a vast illimitable expanse of desert prairie . . . the great Zahara [*sic*] of North America." He added that "even the savages dare not venture to cross it except at two or three places where they know water can be found." [19] On June 16 they sighted the Cerro Tucumcari, and they overtook some emigrants proceeding alone with a team of oxen at the rapid rate of thirty-eight miles per day. They reached the Pecos River town of Anton Chico on Saint John's Day, June 24, and stopped to replenish their supplies and enjoy a municipal celebration of the feast day. At 4 P.M. on the twenty-eighth of June they rode down the trail into Santa Fe, completing the most important stage of their reconnaissance.

"The route we have travelled," wrote Marcy, ". . . is 819½ miles; and for so long a distance, I have never passed over a country where wagons could move along with as much ease and facility, without the expenditure of any labor in making a road, as upon this route." He added enthusiastically, "I am, therefore, of the opinion that but few localities could be found upon the continent which (for as great a distance) would present as few obstacles to the construction of a railway as upon this route" (pp. 191–92).

Simpson was more conservative. He deemed the route "practicable" for a railroad because of its freedom from snow, the level nature of the topography, the abundance of timber, coal, and building stone, and the fact that it ran parallel to but was never forced to cross the two great rivers of the region. "But," he declared, "to my mind the time has not yet come when this or any other railroad can be built over this continent." [20] Among the reasons he gave for this assertion were the vast distance to be covered and the lack of centers of population to furnish labor and

18. See above, p. 201.
19. Marcy, p. 185.
20. Simpson, pp. 21–22.

markets for produce. In conclusion, he soberly maintained in the face of popular enthusiasms that "the order of means in respect to the establishment of this railroad is, first, the creation of centers of population wherever along the road they can be created; second the development of the resources of these several points by this population; and third, the taking advantage of these resources to aid in the prosecution of the road.[21] For most of his outstanding career Simpson remained a "wagon road man," but his conservative view of the feasibility of a transcontinental railroad cannot be entirely overlooked, particularly when his prediction that such a railroad would not be built for twenty years proved to be exactly correct. It was the Topographical Engineer's job to render a considered judgment in these matters, and a comparison of the engineer's report with that of the enthusiastic infantryman Marcy reveals something of the unique value of the trained army topographers in the work of western development.

At Santa Fe, Simpson took up his duties in the Ninth Military Department under Lt. Col. John M. Washington. Marcy proceeded down the Rio Grande to Doña Ana, a town just north of El Paso, and then turned eastward with the intention of blazing a trail across Texas that would form a more direct connection with Cooke's wagon route which headed west from Doña Ana.[22] His route took him through the Organ, Sacramento, and Guadalupe mountains to the Pecos River, and thence down the Pecos, across it, and across the southern rim of the Llano Estacado to Big Spring, a favorite resort of the Comanche raiders. Near the Big Spring, one of Marcy's aides, Lieutenant Harrison, was murdered by a wandering band of Kiowas.[23] From this point the explorer's route proceeded across the upper Brazos and thence to Preston on the Red River and north to Fort Washita. Marcy, quite justifiably, deemed his return route even better than his outgoing route because it provided a more direct link with the road to California west of the Rio Grande and passed through a well-watered and well-timbered country. It proved to be of considerable value to later outgoing parties of California emigrants; it was also in line with Colonel Abert's projected plan for a rail-

21. Ibid., pp. 22–23.
22. Marcy, p. 196.
23. Ibid., p. 210.

road across Texas cutting close to the heads of navigation of the principal rivers flowing into the Gulf. The over-all results of the Marcy-Simpson reconnaissances were an important contribution to overland transportation and to an understanding of the geography of the Oklahoma-Texas border country. In addition, careful maps of the route were constructed, which filled a gap in the knowledge of western geography.

Throughout the early months of 1849 sentiment for the federal improvement of the central or Oregon Trail route to California received expression in the form of memorials presented to the Senate by Benton and Atchison of Missouri and Douglas and Breese of Illinois. Those petitions made no explicit reference to geography, but when they called for military escorts on the route to California, and for the establishment of a post "at some point convenient to the gold region," [24] it was clear that they were concerned with securing for the Central route the same federal attention that was advocated for the Southwestern route. The series of Senate memorials marked the emergence on a national level of what was essentially a frontier struggle between the states and cities of the Mississippi Valley. It was believed that whichever group succeeded in promoting enough improvement on the transcontinental route that ran through its locality would make its city the "future great city of the world." This was true because the railroad, key to commercial prosperity, appeared certain to be built upon the most improved, practicable, and heavily populated route.

The Memphis Railroad Convention met in October 1849 and declared itself in favor of a route that would pass across Texas to the Pacific.[25] Most of the Southern states approved of the route, and Lieutenant Matthew F. Maury, U.S.N., of Virginia, made a long speech in favor of it. Only Arkansas among the Southern states was opposed, possibly because the route would make Memphis, not Fort Smith, the terminus of the road.[26] In St. Louis another convention was held, at which Senator Benton supplied the rhetoric, "Let us beseech the national legislature to build

24. *Sen. Jour.* (above, n. 5), pp. 205, 220.
25. Foreman, p. 121.
26. Ibid.

a great road upon the great national line which unites Europe and Asia—the line which will find on our continent the Bay of San Francisco at one end, St. Louis in the middle, the National metropolis and great commercial emporium at the other end." [27] A system of commercial rivalries had thus developed which made every reconnaissance in the West a skirmish in the battle. No longer was the safety of the emigrants the primary aim; instead the possibilities for future economic promotion stood uppermost in the minds of the representative statesmen.

Because it was the federal agency responsible for exploration and development beyond the Mississippi, the Corps of Topographical Engineers stood in the midst of these struggles for commercial power, and though Colonel Abert believed the Southwestern route to be the most advantageous, he had also to look to the satisfaction of the other regional demands. Accordingly, he ordered an experienced engineer, Capt. Howard Stansbury, to accompany Col. William Wing Loring's regiment of Mounted Rifles along the Oregon Trail as far as Fort Hall, where he was to begin a detailed survey for a military post to help the emigrants prepare for the desert crossing to California.[28] It was a project previously urged by Frémont.[29] Stansbury was given further extensive instructions which required him to survey the entire valley of the Great Salt Lake, making a study of the Indian tribes and Mormon cities. He was to map the lakes and locate a supply route from the Mormon settlement to the emigrant trail, and he was to take note of all potential resources, such as timber and coal. In short, he was to make a thorough, comprehensive study of the whole region from the geologic formations to the local religious customs, and in addition to collect general information on the Mormons. At the same time Colonel Abert still kept in mind the idea of a southwestern trail, and Stansbury was ordered to return home along the Old Spanish Trail to Santa Fe.[30]

Captain Stansbury and his assistant, Lt. John W. Gunnison,

27. Ibid., p. 122. This speech concluded with the famous flourish, "There is the East—there is India."

28. Abert to Stansbury, April 11, 1849, LS, TE 77.

29. See above, Chap. 3. Stansbury also carried a copy of Frémont's *Report, 1843–44,* with him.

30. Abert to Stansbury, April 11, 1849, LS, TE 77.

also of the Topographical Corps, did not reach Fort Leavenworth in time to start with Colonel Loring's detachment, so they formed their own party of eighteen men, five wagons, and forty-six horses and mules, and in company with an emigrant train set out along the clearly marked Oregon Trail.[31] Their force consisted of "experienced voyageurs" led by a veteran of Frémont's expeditions, Archambeau. As they proceeded along the trail, the Pathfinder himself would probably have been astonished at the change. Emigrant parties were everywhere, and long trains of empty government supply wagons were headed eastward with the mail from Salt Lake City along with groups of disgruntled deserters from the various parties of California Argonauts. On June 19 they reached Fort Kearny, a new fort on the Platte River consisting of low adobe buildings, scattered stables and workshops, and tents for the accommodation of the soldiers. It was commanded by Col. B. L. E. Bonneville, the aging veteran of the days of the fur traders. Once, near Scott's Bluff, they passed a blacksmith's shop set up out on the prairie along the route. Another time they noted the deserted lodges of a band of Sioux caught by the cholera. Chimney Rock had broken off in a thunderstorm, and Independence Rock had become a virtual tourist attraction covered with a thousand meaningless names. After they had passed through Fort Laramie, they paid two dollars per wagon to cross the Platte in a ferryboat run by a newly arrived entrepreneur. All along the trail one could pick up guns, gold pans, pickaxes, sunbonnets, hope chests, bean bags, furniture, tools, ammunition, and even food, discarded by the onrushing gold-seekers. It was by no means the same trail that Jedediah Smith had followed to the South Pass in search of beaver and satisfaction for his natural curiosity twenty-five years before.

On August 11 they came upon Fort Bridger, where they met Jim Bridger himself and secured his services as a guide to Salt Lake. Captain Stansbury was looking for a route from Fort Bridger direct to the north shore of Salt Lake which would be an improvement over the standard trail that led north to Soda Springs and Fort Hall and then south again to the Humboldt River. Lieutenant Gunnison took the wagon train by the regular

31. Stansbury, *Exploration* (above, p. 25, n. 12), p. 14. Unless otherwise noted, the following account is based on this work.

trail to Salt Lake City, while Stansbury and Bridger with a picked party of voyageurs explored the country to the east of the Wasatch Mountains along the valley of the Bear River, past Medicine Butte to the Red Chimney Fork and Ogden's Hole. They passed Ogden's Creek through a canyoned passage in the Wasatch Mountains and emerged on the Mormon Road along the eastern edge of the Salt Lake, about three miles from Brown's settlement, the site of the future city of Ogden. Stansbury concluded that a good road could be found between Fort Bridger and the Salt Lake but that it must run farther to the north, through Cache Valley and Blacksmith's Fork (p. 84).

When the expedition arrived at the Mormon settlements it was met with suspicion and hostility, because an attaché of General Wilson, the Indian agent of California, had spread the rumor that the government was preparing to expell the Mormons. It took a long conference with Brigham Young to dispel this notion. (Eventually, however, the Mormons aided the Topographical Engineers in the work of the survey.)

On September 12 the Captain journeyed to Fort Hall in fulfillment of his instructions from Colonel Abert. After making his short reconnaissance, he was able to report "the entire practicability of obtaining an excellent wagon-road from Fort Hall to the Mormon settlement on the Great Salt Lake" (p. 93). In addition he surveyed Cache Valley, once the site of the American Fur Company's annual rendezvous, concluding that the severity of the winter climate made it an unlikely spot for a military post (p. 94).

Next he set out, on October 19, on an exploration around the western side of the Salt Lake. No one had ever traversed the arid western shores of the lake, and Stansbury, with a touch of pride, recorded: "By the old mountain-men such a reconnaissance was considered not only hazardous in the highest degree, but absolutely impracticable, especially at so late a season of the year" (p. 97). The reconnaissance proved to be a difficult one because of the barrenness and desert-like characteristics of the Basin area. As he passed on his way through the great silent Basin, he inevitably paused to speculate on the probable geologic history of the region. "There must," he guessed, "have been here at some former period a vast *inland* sea, extending for hundreds of miles;

and the isolated mountains which now tower from the flats forming its western and southern shores, were doubtless huge islands, similar to those which now rise from the diminished waters of the lake" (p. 105). It was not until years later that this inland sea received its present geologic name of Lake Bonneville.[32] After a difficult march, during which they were without water for nearly forty hours and consequently lost a number of mules, the explorers reached Pilot Peak. It marked the point where Frémont had made his successful crossing of the Great Basin in 1845. The final leg of their trek required them to cross another seventy miles of desert before they reached the Jordan River and Salt Lake City on the far shore. It had been a daring feat of exploration, succeeding where the mountain men had all failed, and by means of his map of the western portion of the lake Stansbury had painted at least one more bold stroke into the unfinished portrait of the national landscape.

Lieutenant Gunnison, meanwhile, had been operating in the south, near Utah Lake. He had laid down the astronomical base line from which a network of triangles could be constructed that would enable them to make an accurate map of the whole valley. He had also surveyed Utah Lake, and erected fourteen triangulation stations in preparation for the mapping operation the following spring. Then, during the height of the winter, field operations were suspended, and the officers and men engaged in the construction of boats and the close study of the Mormon community. Both officers admired the Mormon communitarian experiment. Stansbury had particular occasion to praise its legal system when it delivered a judgment in favor of him over the expedition's geologist, Blake, who had attempted to appropriate all of the scientific specimens and field notes of the expedition for himself.[33] Moreover, Blake was ostracized from the city and forced to flee to California. Lieutenant Gunnison from his observations and researches, was able to write one of the few im-

32. So named by G. C. Gilbert of the United States Geological Survey in his *Lake Bonneville,* United States Geological Survey Monographs, *1*, Wash., 1890.

33. Stansbury to Abert, Jan. 17, 1851, LS, TE 77. He encloses depositions by Albert Carrington, a Mormon scout, and Lt. John W. Gunnison, attesting to the truth of his account.

partial books of the time on the Mormons.[34] It was published in 1852, just one year before Gunnison's tragic death in an Indian massacre near Utah Lake.

With the coming of spring the Topographers, assisted by the Mormon scout Albert Carrington, began an extensive survey of the Great Salt Lake, which lasted until June 27. It was the basis for their map of the entire region of 5,000 square miles. When this last long task was completed, they could look back upon an impressive achievement in terms of the scientific measurement of the earth. They had laid down an astronomical base line six miles in length. They had surveyed Utah Lake, the Great Salt Lake, and the River Jordan, plus all of the islands in the lakes. It was a thorough job, and the boundaries of the long-mysterious lake now stood revealed.

On the way home Stansbury was determined to search out still another central overland route south of the regular trail through South Pass. He was thus ignoring Colonel Abert's instructions to return via the Spanish Trail, but the results of the trip undoubtedly justified this decision to the Colonel's satisfaction. The route they followed was from the Jordan River due east to the Weber River, striking it just above Camas Prairie, then along that river to Echo Creek, and across to the Bear River, Muddy River, and Fort Bridger. From this point their guide, the famous Bridger himself, led them over the valley of the Green River and along Bitter Creek, then across the sage desert and the Indian war grounds of south central Wyoming. They passed through Bridger's Pass, the Medicine Bow Mountains, Laramie Basin, and Cheyenne Pass, to the upper reaches of the Chugwater River, where Captain Stansbury was injured in a fall from his horse, causing the sudden termination of the year's exploration. The return trail blazed by the Stansbury-Gunnison party was one of its most important achievements, for it was the most direct and efficient route located thus far to the Salt Lake. Stansbury reported "that a practicable route exists through the chain of the Rocky Mountains, at a point 60 miles south of that now pursued and in a course as much more direct as the chord of an arc is

34. John W. Gunnison, *The Mormons or Latter Day Saints in the Valley of the Great Salt Lake, a History of Their Rise and Progress, Peculiar Doctrines, Present Conditions and Projects,* Phila., 1852.

to the arc itself" (p. 261). He added that it meant a saving of 61 miles between Fort Laramie and the Mormon settlements. The Stansbury trail was in approximately the same spot where Frémont had sought to breach the Rocky Mountains on his way to the Salt Lake in 1843, but the Pathfinder in going up the Cache-de-la-Poudre Creek to its source had somehow missed the Cheyenne Pass.[35] The lasting effects on the history of transportation wrought by Stansbury's survey were thus considerable. The Overland Stage, the Pony Express, and the Union Pacific all followed part way along the trail he had blazed.[36]

As a scientific document, Stansbury's *Report* was the most ambitious one submitted before the publication of the *Pacific Railroad Reports.* It was issued first as a Senate Executive Document in March of 1851 and subsequently in commercial editions by Lippincott, Grambo of Philadelphia in 1852 and by Johnson and Company of Philadelphia in 1855. It was popular in Europe as well: there was a London printing in 1852 and one in Stuttgart in 1854.[37] The enthusiastic scientific promoter Spencer F. Baird declared in an appendix to the book that "no government expedition since the days of Major Long's visit to the Missouri has ever presented such important additions to natural history . . ."[38] In this judgment he was perhaps a bit too enthusiastic, for although Stansbury did bring back extensive collections of animals and plants, the lack of a trained and dedicated field scientist hampered him considerably. The Report had seven scientific appendices, including tables of distances and astronomical positions, a minute examination of the zoological and etymological specimens, a description of the plants, a geological analysis, a chemical analysis of the lake waters, and a meteorological report.

The tables of distances and astronomical positions, together with the maps, made up the geographical basis of the *Report.* Professor Hall's geological study was in the form of a long letter

35. Frémont, *Report, 1843–44,* pp. 150–51. Frémont found only a very rugged route through a pass which he termed "rough and difficult," though "an excellent road may be made with a little labor."

36. Jackson, *Wagon Roads,* p. 34.

37. F. V. Colville, "Three Editions of Stansbury's Report," *Torrey Botanical Club Bulletin, 23* (1896), 137–39.

38. Stansbury, *Exploration,* p. 307.

which characterized the various strata along the route but purposely made no attempt at a comprehensive survey of the region. It is interesting principally because of his early reference to the words "syncline" and "anticline" in connection with mountain-making (p. 406), indicating that perhaps his own theory made use of these important concepts. But he did not elaborate on them, as did Dana's *Manual* of 1862. Torrey's plants were again his standard Linnean list, and included no new species.

The *Zoological Report* was the most impressive, though it was padded with the results of other expeditions, including James W. Abert's bird and mammal collections from his New Mexican reconnaissance and a complete list of all the trans-Mississippi birds not included in Audubon's *American Ornithology* (p. 308). The zoologists, Baird and Girard, noted the discovery of thirteen new species of reptiles and several new mammals and birds (pp. 336–65). Professor Haldeman contributed a description of the legendary grasshopper of Salt Lake, and Titian R. Peale commented on the insect larvae that littered the Lake (pp. 371, 379).

Compared to the later reports of the Mexican Boundary and the Pacific railroad surveys, Stansbury's work was not particularly impressive, but for its time it gathered together between its covers a respectable amount of geographic data of all descriptions, and it revealed the hitherto mysterious Great Basin country to the men of science. Furthermore, the text, along with the thirty-five illustrations, provided a matchless picture of the Mormon community and the environmental conditions which governed its existence.

The operations of the Corps of Topographical Engineers in Texas represent, in a sense, the perfect expression of the military-commercial partnership in the trans-Mississippi West. It is significant that Texas came into the Union as an already organized state whose citizens were well aware of its economic potential. Thus with a good idea of what was needed to implement the advance of settlement, they were not loath to petition the federal government for the required services. Its representatives in Congress, particularly Sam Houston and Thomas Rusk, were among the most active of all the western statesmen in calling federal attention to their needs. It was Houston who, early in 1849, called for a transcontinental survey,[39] and it was Houston, too, who followed up this request with a bill to authorize the Galveston and Pacific Railroad Company "to construct and extend a railroad to the coast of the Pacific Ocean in California." [40] Such important personages as Robert J. Walker, formerly Polk's Secretary of the Treasury, and General Gadsden, the later treaty-maker, were interested in Texas railroad projects.[41] The vigorous efforts of Thomas Rusk and Volney Howard to secure the railroad route through the Mesilla Valley to California by a tortured interpretation of the Treaty of Guadalupe-Hidalgo have already been observed.[42] Their efforts were rewarded, of course, by the Gadsden Purchase. All of this political activity emphasized the needs of Texas and indicated its strategic value to the rest of the country.

Colonel Abert's plan for the development of Texas included besides the building of a railroad from its eastern border to El Paso a subsequent improvement of the numerous streams which ran toward the Gulf, so that steamboats could come upriver to the railroad centers. He also proposed, in 1849, an exploration of the Red River, from Natchitoches to Old Fort Washita, so that supplies could be sent upriver to ports in the Comanche country. These forts were to be connected with the Rio Grande by means of a military road.[43]

In addition to the obvious commercial opportunities presented in Texas, the defense against the Indians who dominated West Texas from the Canadian River to the Big Bend of the Rio Grande was an all-important problem in securing federal attention.[44] This was heightened by the increased tide of emigration and settlement caused by the overland migrations of 1849.

With these considerations in mind, Colonel Abert detailed

39. *Sen. Jour.* (above, n. 5), pp. 109–10.

40. Ibid., p. 227.

41. Russel, *Improvement of Communication,* pp. 13, 96–97.

42. Ibid., pp. 135–36, 145, 147. See also above, pp. 000.

43. Abert to Joseph E. Johnston, June 12, 1849, LS, TE 77.

44. In all the reports of the secretaries of war from George W. Crawford to Jefferson Davis this question was given primary consideration. See, e.g., George W. Crawford, *Report of the Sec. of War,* 31st Cong., 1st Sess., Sen. Exec. Doc. 1 (1849–50), 93–94; and Jefferson Davis, *Report of the Sec. of War,* 34th Cong., 1st Sess., H. R. Exec. Doc. 1 (1855–56), 5.

one of his outstanding officers for service in Texas under Gen. William J. Worth commanding the Eighth Military District. He was Brevet Lt. Col. Joseph E. Johnston, one of the heroes of the Mexican War and later an important Confederate general. Colonel Johnston had under his command, at various times, four lieutenants of the Topographical Corps whom he kept busy making river surveys and exploring routes for wagon roads to supply the frontier garrisons. Johnston himself was interested in the proposed railroad across Texas, and during the years from 1850 to 1852 he sent numerous inquiries to Colonel Abert concerning the technical details of railroad construction.[45] Judging from this correspondence, the actual launching of a joint military-civilian project for a railroad across Texas seemed imminent,[46] and the numerous reports of good routes to the West made it seem certain of accomplishment.

The first efforts toward the exploration for roads between the Texas settlements and those of the Rio Grande originated in the commercial aspirations of the citizens of San Antonio, who collected $800 for a road survey designed to divert the Chihuahua trade away from New Mexico. John Coffee Hays and Capt. Samuel Highsmith, with a party of thirty-five Texas Rangers and Indian guides, set out from San Antonio on August 27, 1848.[47] They marched northward through the German settlement of Fredericksburg toward the Llano River, and then westward to the headwaters of the San Saba on the Edwards Plateau. From this point they wandered southward to Las Moras Creek, a tributary of the Rio Grande, and then back again to the northwest across the San Pedro River and the Pecos. After that their course followed roughly along the great northward curve of the Rio Grande through a rugged, forbidding country previously left to the domination of the Comanches. When they reached the

45. Abert to Johnston, Jan. 12, 1852, LS; and Johnston to Abert, Feb. 29, 1852, and Dec. 1, 1851, LR: TE 77.

46. Abert to Johnston, Jan. 12, 1852, LS, TE 77. Johnston's inquiries had already reached the point where he was asking where railroad equipment could be purchased, and which kinds of equipment would be best to buy.

47. Jackson, *Wagon Roads,* pp. 36–37. See also A. B. Bender, "Opening Routes across West Texas, 1848–1850," *Southwestern Historical Quarterly, 37* 1933–34), 119. The description of the Hays expedition here given is based on these accounts.

Big Bend, they avoided its canyons by crossing to the Mexican side of the river, where, in search of food, they made for the tiny frontier settlement of San Carlos. After replenishing their supplies, the rangers moved up the Mexican side of the river to Presidio del Norte, at which point they recrossed the river and went into camp at Fort Leaton, the American trading post nearby.

The rangers had located no practicable road to Chihuahua and they were too exhausted to continue to El Paso, so Hays decided to lead them back to San Antonio. His return route was scarcely more direct than the outgoing trail. It led for 150 miles across barren country to the Pecos River, and then down that desert river to Pecos Springs, the San Pedro River, and an eventual junction with the outgoing trail near Las Moras Creek. Though both Hays and Highsmith reported the discovery of a wagon route through to Presidio del Norte, their trip must be accounted a fiasco. They had merely wandered about through the West Texas badlands, and their trail hardly constituted a road. Nevertheless, their expedition did serve an important purpose.

As a result of this exploration, Gen. William Jenkins Worth authorized the first survey involving Topographical Engineers on February 9, 1849.[48] It was commanded by Lt. W. H. C. Whiting, then only twenty-three years of age. His assistant was Lt. W. F. Smith of the Topographical Corps, a Yankee from St. Albans, Vermont.[49] Their orders were to resurvey the Hays-Highsmith trail to Presidio del Norte and then proceed on to El Paso. If their outgoing route was unsatisfactory, they were to blaze another trail, via the Pecos and San Saba rivers, to San Antonio. The two young lieutenants were guided by R. A. Howard, a Texan scout, as they rode west out of Fredericksburg on their important mission.[50] When they reached the San Saba, they ascended the high tablelands, where they rode for three days and four nights without water before they struck the Live Oak Creek, a tributary of the Pecos. They crossed over the Pecos and proceeded through the Davis Mountains to Presidio del Norte and then along the Rio Grande to El Paso.

48. Jackson, *Wagon Roads,* p. 39.

49. *DAB.*

50. W. F. Smith, *Report . . . of Routes from San Antonio to El Paso,* 31st Cong., 1st Sess., Sen. Exec. Doc. 64 (1850), 4–7.

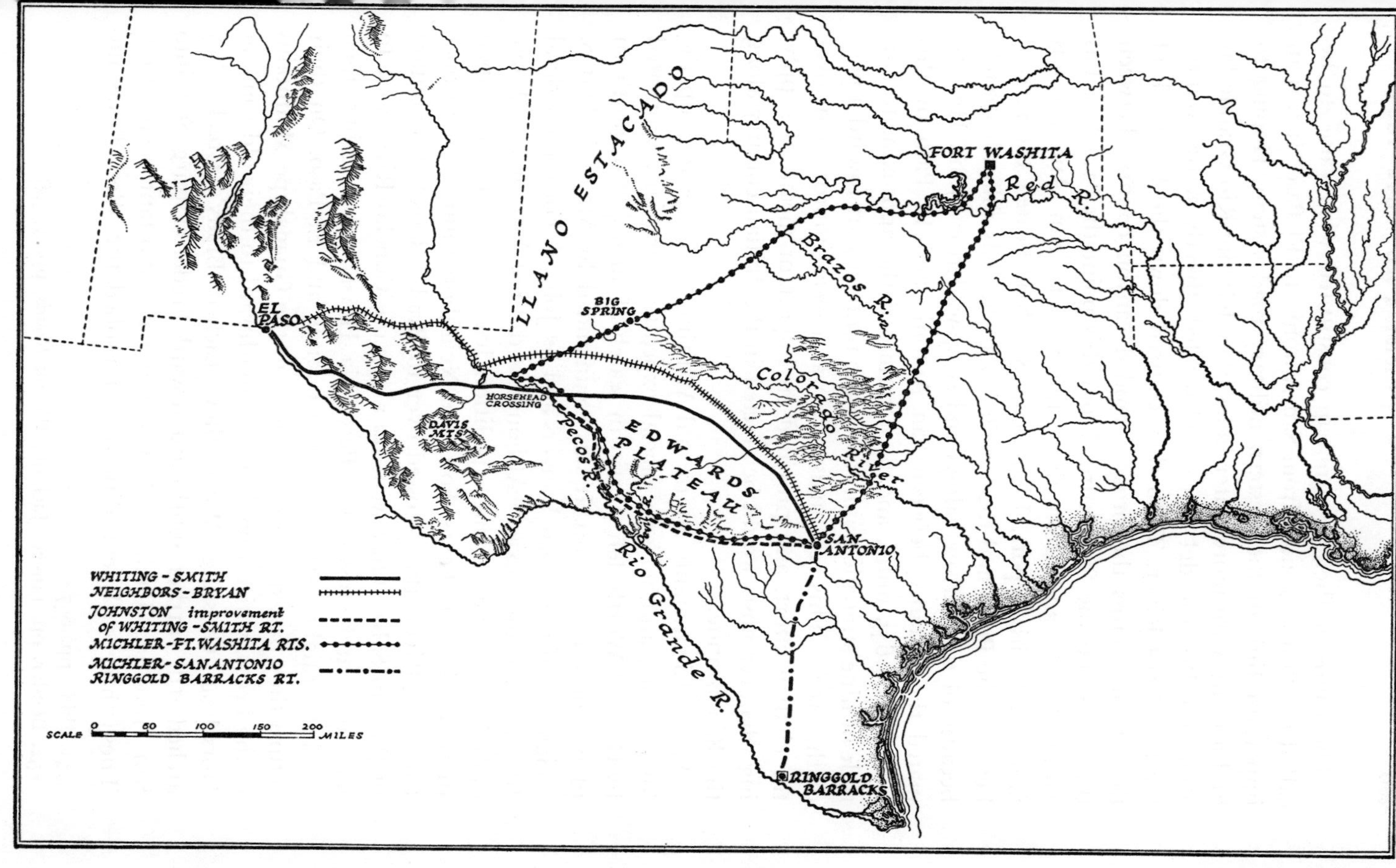

FORT WASHITA
Red R.
LLANO ESTACADO
Brazos R.
BIG SPRING
EL PASO
Colorado River
HORSEHEAD CROSSING
DAVIS MTS.
EDWARDS PLATEAU
Pecos R.
SAN ANTONIO
Rio Grande R.
RINGGOLD BARRACKS
WHITING - SMITH
NEIGHBORS - BRYAN
JOHNSTON improvement of WHITING - SMITH RT.
MICHLER - FT. WASHITA RTS.
MICHLER - SAN ANTONIO RINGGOLD BARRACKS RT.
SCALE 0 50 100 150 200 MILES

MAP 8

The route of their return trip constituted what came to be called the "lower route" from San Antonio to El Paso. It was an important link in the western military road system. Hoping to find a route with more water holes, they left the Rio Grande far above the Presidio del Norte and headed directly across country for the Pecos River. Then they coursed down the left bank of that stream across the broken, eroded canyon country between the Pecos and the San Pedro. From this point they reached Las Moras Creek, and from there the way to San Antonio was familiar. In his report, Lieutenant Smith indicated the section between the Pecos and the San Pedro as the only difficult stretch, because of the narrow valleys and steep-walled canyons. He estimated the distance between San Antonio and El Paso by this route to be 645 miles, and he determined the approximate latitude of nine strategic points along the route, a start toward a map of the area.[51] This reconnaissance was a clear improvement over the civilian effort, and provided an important means of supplying whatever posts would be erected in the Indian country along the Rio Grande.

While Lieutenants Smith and Whiting were opening up the lower route, another semi-official expedition, partially sponsored by General Worth, left Austin in search of an upper or northern plains route to El Paso. It was commanded by Major Robert S. Neighbors of the Texas Rangers and by John S. Ford, the federal Indian agent for Texas.[52] Although it did not include any Topographical Engineers, the expedition had a direct bearing upon their activities in Texas. Ford and Neighbors followed the upper Colorado River, then crossed over to Brady's Creek, a tributary of the San Saba. They went up along the Concho River west to its source and crossed the Pecos via Horsehead Crossing, then headed straight west to the Rio Grande and El Paso. On their return they passed northward through the Guadalupe Mountains to the Pecos, which they followed southward to their old route at Horsehead Crossing. When they reached Brady's Creek, they arched still further southward toward Fredericksburg and into San Antonio. Their trail was another important route west. These three early expeditions that probed the West Texas un-

51. Ibid., pp. 6–7.

52. Bender, pp. 119–20. Jackson, *Wagon Roads,* pp. 37–38.

known involved the whole range of local and federal cooperation in solving the problems confronting the frontier state. The results indicated that federal aid and trained engineers had been indispensable factors in discovering the main transportation trails west from San Antonio.

Before the first Army expedition had even returned, the new commandant of the Eighth Military District, Brig. Gen. W. S. Harney, had ordered Colonel Johnston to organize two engineer parties for further reconnaissances of the upper and lower routes to El Paso.[53] One party, to be led by Lt. Francis T. Bryan of the Topographical Corps, was to retrace the Ford-Neighbors route and confirm its practicability for wagons. The other unit was to be led by Colonel Johnston himself, assisted by Lt. W. F. Smith, who had just arrived from El Paso. They were to serve as a reconnoitering party for Major Jefferson Van Horn's battalion of the Third Infantry and a long train of supply wagons headed for El Paso. The arrival in San Antonio of Lieutenants Whiting and Smith with the news of a lower route to El Paso had determined Colonel Johnston to follow their new road, using Lieutenant Smith and R. A. Howard as his guides.[54] Their course followed Wool's road west out of San Antonio, eventually diverging northward toward Las Moras Creek, the San Pedro, and the Pecos. Captain French of the Quartermaster Department maintained a detail all along the road to make the necessary improvements for safe traveling. In his own report he gave a graphic idea of the work of the Topographical Engineers as they ranged far ahead scouting the difficult terrain: "It was not enough to know that a road could be made up one valley, or that a range of mountains could be passed, but it became necessary to explore the country further beyond, to definitive points, before the opening of the route. When the nature of the country is seen by those who may hereafter pass over the road, it may excite surprise; but it will not be that so practicable a route has been found, but rather that any was found at all." [55]

Only two departures from the Whiting-Smith route were

53. Joseph E. Johnston, in Smith, *Report* (above, n. 50), p. 26.

54. Ibid., pp. 26–29. The account is based on this report. See also S. G. French, in Smith, *Report,* pp. 40–54, esp. p. 40.

55. Smith, *Report,* p. 49.

made, one between the lower ford of the San Pedro and the Pecos, the other in avoiding the mountains in the approach to the Rio Grande. The successful arrival of the train and Major Van Horn's command in El Paso, on September 3, provided a confirmation of the existence of a practicable road. Colonel Johnston, however, was not satisfied and proposed, in the spring, a series of reconnaissances to shorten the route by straightening its meanderings across the lower Rio Grande country.[56] It was Captain French, however, who gave expression to what might well have been the thoughts of those interested in transcontinental routes in the Southwest:

> El Paso, from its geographical position, presents itself as a resting-place on one of the great overland routes between the seaports of the Atlantic on one side and those of the Pacific on the other. . . . a little further to the north and west are the head-waters of the Gila: and should the route from El Paso to the seaboard on the west present no more difficulties than that from the East, there can easily be established between the Atlantic States and those that have so suddenly sprung into existence in the West—and which are destined to change, perhaps, the political institutions and commercial relations of half the world—a connexion that will strengthen the bonds of union by free and constant intercourse. The government has been a pioneer in the enterprise, and the little labor bestowed may not be lost to the public weal.[57]

While the mule teams were being recruited for the return march, Colonel Johnston ordered his subaltern, Lieutenant Smith, to make a reconnaissance of the Sacramento Mountains to the north and east of El Paso, which he carried out between September 21 and October 3, 1849.[58] On October 11 Johnston, with a party of twenty-five men and two Delaware Indian scouts, began a return march over the northern route.[59] Cold weather caused them to turn southward when they reached the Pecos,

56. Johnston, *Report,* p. 27.
57. Smith, *Report,* p. 50.
58. Ibid., pp. 13–14.
59. Johnston, *Report,* p. 27.

and they made the rest of the homeward journey along the lower route. One side reconnaissance was made by the Colonel and R. A. Howard eastward from the head of the San Pedro to the Nueces, but they found the country destitute of water and recommended the regular route as superior despite its disadvantages. By means of this extended reconnaissance the chief Topographical Engineer in Texas had been able personally to survey what was to be the most important supply route for the outer chain of frontier defense posts, and he had also been able to gain some idea of the suitability of the terrain for a railroad.

Lieutenant Bryan, meanwhile, had resurveyed the northern route and pronounced it fit for the easy passage of wagons. He reported: "Grass and water may be had every day, within marches of twenty-five miles, except from the head of the Concho to the Pecos—a distance of sixty-eight miles, which is entirely without permanent water at present. The character of the country is such, however, as to leave no doubt of the success of attempts to find water by means of wells, sunk at proper intervals." [60] He further suggested that the road could be shortened in three places, between Fredericksburg and the San Saba, between the San Saba and Brady's Creek, and between the Pecos and the Guadalupe Mountains, if wells were sunk between the specified places.[61] Lieutenant Bryan's survey, like that of Colonel Johnston, had provided official confirmation of a route across West Texas. These routes remained for years the main lines of communication for soldier, settler, and gold seeker alike. When the railroads were built through Texas, the Texas Pacific followed generally along Bryan's trail and the Southern Pacific followed part way along the lower road.[62]

Also important was the series of surveys carried out in the summer and fall of 1849 by Lt. Nathaniel Michler, of the Topographical Corps, prior to his assignment to the Mexican Boundary Survey. In January 1849, together with Lieutenant Bryan, Michler explored the country in the vicinity of Aransas Pass and Corpus Christi for an army depot and laid out a road to

60. F. Z. Bryan, in Smith, *Report,* p. 23.
61. Ibid.
62. Jackson, *Wagon Roads,* p. 43.

San Antonio.[63] This proved to be a valuable survey for the government because it enabled Colonel Johnston to detect the fallacy of a locally proposed scheme for government improvement of the Guadalupe River to Seguin as a means of supplying San Antonio.[64] The early summer of 1849 saw the intrepid Michler again south of San Antonio running a road from Port Lavaca to that city.[65] Later, in June and July, he surveyed a route from Corpus Christi to Fort Inge on the Leona River. In addition he made a reconnaissance of the Frio and Nueces rivers.[66] His most important service was a road survey from Fort Washita, in what is now Oklahoma, to the Pecos River, following part way along Marcy's return route from Doña Ana.[67] This was an execution of Colonel Abert's plan to connect the Red River forts with the settlements on the Rio Grande by an overland trail, for which the Colonel had issued specific orders to Johnston. On this expedition Lieutenant Michler left Fort Washita on November 9, after having previously conferred with Captain Marcy about the nature of the trail across Texas. The route led through the Cross Timbers along the Red River and thence to the main fork of the Brazos, via the divide between the Big and Little Witchita rivers. Concerning this stretch of the route Michler was moved to comment that "a more beautiful country for roads of any kind cannot be found" (p. 34). Along the way he met with numerous bands of Shawnees, Delawares, Tongues, and Comanches, but found them all peacefully inclined and more interested in their buffalo hunt than the exploring party.

The last road-surveying assignment carried out by Lieutenant Michler was part of his duty with the Mexican Boundary Survey. In September 1850 he collaborated with Lt. M. L. Smith of the Topographical Corps in tracing a road from San Antonio to Ringgold Barracks, the most important military depot on the lower Rio Grande. This survey was meant to provide a link with that other important phase of western communication which proceeded via the great rivers.[68]

63. Warren, *Memoir,* p. 61. See also N. Michler, in Smith, *Report,* pp. 7–13.

64. Johnston to Abert, Sept. 11, 1850, LR, TE 77.

65. Warren, *Memoir,* p. 62.

66. Ibid.

67. The account is based on Michler, *Report,* pp. 29–39.

68. Warren, *Memoir,* p. 62. One other important expedition in Texas deserves special mention here, that of Capt. Randolph B. Marcy to the sources

Almost from the beginning, the Army as well as the local citizens realized that surveys of the rivers in Texas would be nearly as important a factor in promoting communication and settlement as would that of the road surveys. Most of the local petitions received by the Secretary of War and the Chief of Topographical Engineers called explicitly for the survey and improvement of the series of Texas rivers that joined the interior with the Gulf. Though the West stood on the threshold of the railroad age, it had not yet abandoned the idea of river travel, which was much cheaper than the current alternative of the freight wagon and the pack mule. Colonel Johnston, in his reports to the Topographical Bureau, repeatedly emphasized the economy that would result from the opening up of the Rio Grande to navigation. His remarks merely confirmed the contentions of many of the local citizens.[69] Typical of the Texan petitions was a request submitted to the Topographical Bureau in April 1850 by G. M. Saluman which underscored the close relationship existing between the establishment of a military base on the upper Trinity River and the benefits that would be conferred on the local inhabitants by an improvement of river communication with that base.[70] This letter was followed by a more impressive petition two months later in which Senators Houston and Rusk and Congressmen Howard and Kaufman demanded a survey of the Trinity similar to that which had been performed on the Colorado.[71] In this case the request went unheeded by the Topographical Bureau for reasons of expediency. But though not all such demands were answered, at least two river surveys were carried out in Texas during this period which could be regarded as a service to the military and civilian interests alike.

Since the days of the Republic, the citizens of Austin, anxious to enhance their city commercially and to secure for it the state capitol, had financed surveys for the improvement of the Colo-

of the Red River in 1852. This expedition was instigated by Senator Borland of Arkansas, and included Capt. George B. McClellen, Corps of Engineers, as Marcy's assistant. (For a modern account see W. Eugene Hollon, *Beyond the Cross Timbers,* Norman, Okla., 1955.) See Randolph B. Marcy, *Exploration of the Red River of Louisiana, in the Year 1852,* 32d Cong., 2d Sess., Sen. Exec. Doc. 54, 1853.

69. Johnston to Abert, Jan. 7, 1851, and Jan. 10, 1851: LS, TE 77.

70. G. M. Salumen to Abert, April 3, 1850, LR, TE 77.

71. Sam Houston to the Secretary of War, June 5, 1850, copy, LR, TE 77.

rado River.[72] By 1849 enthusiasm for the removal of the raft of logs and other debris which obstructed the river had reached a high point. The first river steamer to reach Austin, the *Kate Ward,* had indicated the possible prosperity that would come with the complete opening of the river as far as Matagorda Bay on the Gulf of Mexico. A private firm soon began work on the raft. This drew the attention of the federal government. In the winter of 1850 Colonel Johnston ordered Lt. W. F. Smith to accompany Capt. Henry Cheatham, of the Corps of Engineers, in a reconnaissance of the river. They were primarily interested in the availability of the river as a means of military supply to the interior chain of forts, but their work also served to supply information to the civilian groups. On March 3, 1850, Captain Cheatham wrote a letter to the Texas *State Gazette* pronouncing the river above the raft "a fine river for boats capable of carrying a burden of four hundred bales of cotton." He urged the procurement of a stout steamboat to remove the raft, a project which must certainly have occurred to the citizens but which, of course, reinforced their conviction with authoritative testimony.

Lieutenant Smith's report, submitted in April, was more explicit.[73] He described the existence of fifty-four clusters of snags stretching out over a distance of seven miles. In an accompanying table he estimated the cost of improvement—based upon the figures of the civilian engineer already employed in making the actual improvements—at $50,000. He added that the government could save $20,000 per year in transporting its supplies up the improved river. In conclusion, he made explicit the possible basis of a military-civilian partnership in the project: "Should the government remove the raft, the inhabitants of the valley of the Colorado would probably complete the opening of the river. More than $20,000 has been subscribed for that service." [74] It was the Corps of Enginers, however, who finally undertook to provide assistance to this project.[75] Lt. W. H. C. Whiting had charge of an operation that dug a channel around the raft, using

72. Comer Clay, "The Colorado River Raft," *Southwestern Historical Quarterly,* 52 (1948–49), 410. The account that follows is based on pp. 410–18.

73. Smith, *Report,* pp. 39–40.

74. Ibid., p. 40.

75. Clay, p. 421.

the old *Kate Ward* as their dredge boat. By 1855, however, Congress lost interest in the work and the raft was left to grow past the outlet of the artificial channel, thus again closing navigation.[76] After that date the problem remained exclusively the property of the State of Texas.

The other important river survey took place in the summer and fall of 1850 on the Rio Grande. It was made in cooperation with the Mexican Boundary Survey, since at this time Lts. M. L. Smith, W. F. Smith, and Nathaniel Michler were also assigned to duty with Emory's scientific party. The orders for the survey, however, came directly from Colonel Abert himself.[77] Lt. W. F. Smith led one party south along the river from El Paso on June 15. He proceeded downstream by means of flatboats while his colleague, Lieutenant Bryan, took the main party overland along the river. After a difficult trip in which two of the boats sank, Lieutenant Smith abandoned the survey at Presidio del Norte after having located several of the main Indian trails into Mexico and a site for a fort which would command them.[78]

On August 25 Lt. Martin Luther Smith, later chief Confederate engineer at Vicksburg, led a party upstream. He was accompanied by Lieutenant Michler.[79] They poled their flatboats up the river from Ringgold Barracks, near Camargo, to a point eighty miles above the mouth of the Pecos River some 470 miles from their starting point. In his report Lieutenant Smith recommended the improvement of the river to a point 120 miles above Ringgold Barracks at Isleta, eight miles below Woll's Ford at Presidio del Rio Grande. He directly contradicted Dragoon Captain Love, whose report of his previous survey over the same distance had declared the river navigable for 230 miles above Isleta.[80] Smith asserted that above Fort Duncan (Eagle Pass) the river was but ten inches deep, and he pointed for proof of this contention to insurmountable sandstone formations across the river where the San Rodriguez joined the Rio Grande.

76. Ibid., p. 422.

77. Johnston to Abert, Jan. 7, 1851, LR, TE 77. Johnston has reference to Abert's instructions in this matter.

78. W. F. Smith to Johnston, Oct. 26, 1850, LR, TE 77.

79. M. L. Smith to Johnston, Jan. 6, 1851, LR, TE 77.

80. Ibid. See also Major W. W. Chapman, *Report of Sept. 5, 1850*, 31st Cong., 2d Sess., Sen. Exec. Doc. 1, Pt. II (1849–50), 324–29.

In recommending federal improvements of the river to Presidio del Rio Grande, Lieutenant Smith again emphasized the mixture of civilian and military motives which warranted the expense. "In truth," he declared, "the Rio Grande has already become a public highway in which interests belonging to various sections of our country are interested." [81] Colonel Johnston, whose own party had gone by wagon along the river for 130 miles between the two surveys, seconded his remarks, adding that the river improvement was indispensable for maintaining a supply route to the forts at Laredo and Eagle Pass. As a final argument Lieutenant Smith cited the role of the rivers in promoting population as an effective means of clearing away the Indian menace, for it would create "a country busy with a population and the constant communication in every direction which necessarily results in no place for the savage." [82]

Throughout the postwar years the Topographical Bureau continued to be bombarded with petitions for improvement of the Sabine, the Trinity, the Brazos, the Guadalupe, and other Texas rivers, but most of these were too far behind the Indian frontier to justify either the erection of a military post or the expenditure of Army appropriations on the surveying of the channels of communication. In most cases Colonel Abert concentrated on the areas where military defense and the advancement of settlement went hand-in-hand, legitimately dependent on one another. He therefore resisted the lure of the pork barrel.

In 1853 interest in the Pacific railroad route became institutionalized in the Pacific railroad surveys conducted by the Corps of Topographical Engineers. There was, thus, no need for a Lieutenant Colonel in Texas, so Johnston was transferred to the western river improvements projects in the Mississippi Valley. Lieutenants Michler and the two Smiths were also re-assigned to the Boundary Survey and the Great Lakes Surveys. New officers were assigned to Texas, but the work was confined to local road surveys and the testing of camels for service in the Davis Mountains. In this sense, 1853 marked the termination of one period of Topographical exploration in Texas.

In evaluating the efforts of the Topographical Engineers in Texas during this period it must be observed that their task was

81. Ibid.
82. Ibid.

usually one of making routine surveys under a military department, hence was oriented entirely toward the practical. Though they contributed a map of the relatively unknown and by-passed frontier area of West Texas, it was virtually their only scientific contribution. On the other hand, they did promote transportation and settlement, and they did their part toward solving the difficult problem of frontier defense. To analyze their projects is to study the progress of settlement in this area. At the same time, their often monotonous reconnaissances through arroyo and canyon and across mesa and desert had a place in the national scene. In that they were consciously furthering Southern plans for a transcontinental railroad route, they were playing an important role in stimulating the sectional rivalry over the spoils of the West.

The operations of the Corps of Topographical Engineers in New Mexico were even more closely related to the needs of the local military department than were those in Texas. Because of the vulnerability of the settlements to raids by the Apaches, Navahos, and Utes, the problem of defense was acute. In the postwar years it overshadowed all civil projects in the territory except the comprehensive explorations of the Mexican Boundary Survey in the country south of the Gila and Mimbres rivers. However, in comparison with Texas, New Mexico had less need of extensive topographical projects. There were fewer navigable rivers and shorter distances to be spanned. Moreover, Colonel Abert was confident that the Topographical Bureau already had a good general idea from the Emory-Cooke *Report* of the routes to the Pacific west of the Rio Grande. Nor had New Mexico an effective governmental organization, as had the State of Texas; consequently it was far less persuasive in Congress. During the immediate postwar years it had a military governor, Lt. Col. John M. Washington; hence for the Washington policy-makers it took on the character of a military frontier.

The only Topographical Engineer attached to the Ninth Military Department (New Mexico) was Lt. James Hervey Simpson, who had been detached from Marcy's command at Sante Fe by special order of Colonel Abert.[83] Simpson's duty was to answer to the immediate needs of the military governor, Lieutenant Colo-

83. Abert to Simpson, May 4, 1849, copy, LS, TE 77.

nel Washington, and, if possible, see his way clear to exploring the Spanish caravan route from Abiquiu and St. Joseph's Springs north across Colorado to Los Angeles. Almost immediately the long-range task was scrapped and Simpson marched out of Santa Fe on August 15, 1849, as part of Colonel Washington's punitive raid into the Navaho country.[84] The entire command was made up of four companies of infantry and two of artillery, plus a detachment of mounted Mexican and Indian volunteers. As the topographical staff officer, Simpson had three assistants, T. A. P. Champlin and the Kern brothers, Richard and Edward, who made sketches and assisted in the topographic work.

Once out of Santa Fe the command marched due west past the populated pueblo of Santo Domingo, across the Rio Grande, to a temporary bivouac at the Jemez pueblo on that river. Here Simpson had a chance to study at close range the way of life of the pueblo people. Hosta, the so-called "governor" of Jemez, described the customs and history of the Jemez Indians, and he filled in with tribal myths when there was no history to relate. Hosta was afforded ample opportunity to instruct Simpson, as he guided the expedition for most of the way out of Jemez. The Kerns were meanwhile occupied in making sketches of the buildings, of Hosta and his wife, and of the mysterious religious drawings that covered the walls of the "estufa" which was the characteristic circular meeting room of all pueblo tribes.

When they left Jemez, they marched across the headwaters of the Puerco River through a desert country studded with mesas which Simpson compared with Prescott's descriptions of southern Mexico. Their course took them to the upper reaches of the Chaco River near the 36th degree of north latitude, where they headed into a canyon country, with evidences of ruined and lost pueblo civilizations everywhere at hand. The first ruin they examined was called by chief Hosta the Pueblo Pintado, and he declared it to be the temporary abode of Montezuma when he

84. The account is based on J. H. Simpson, *Journal of a Military Reconnaissance from Santa Fe, New Mexico to the Navajo County Made with the Troops under Command of Brevet Lieutenant-Colonel John M. Washington, Chief of the Ninth Military Department and Governor of New Mexico*, 31st Cong., 1st Sess., Sen. Exec. Doc. 64 (1850), 55–168. See May 7, above, p. 215.

was leading his people southward into Mexico. In all, they discovered ten ruined townsites as Simpson led a detached reconnoitering party through the length of the canyon. It was one of the most important archaeological finds made in America up to that time, and Lieutenant Simpson included in his report his own idea of the vanished inhabitants of the pueblos. He noted their similarity of construction, out of stone rather than adobe, and concluded that these, instead of the Casas Grandes discovered by Lieutenant Emory on the Gila River, were of Aztec origin. "It is not at all improbable," he speculated, "that they are the identical ruins to which Humboldt has referred" (p. 83). Of great value were R. H. Kern's diagrams and sketches of the ruins, which, besides indicating their dimensions, placed them in their proper setting in the landscape and indicated their state of preservation in 1849. His reconstructed version of the Pueblo "Hungo Pavie" embodied Simpson's idea that these pueblos presented one solid wall to the outside on three sides, while the inner side faced a courtyard and was tiered with a series of step-back terraces of houses. While it was necessarily a hasty reconnaissance made in the line of military duty, Simpson's work in the Chaco Canyon was of lasting importance for the study of Indian antiquities.

From the Chaco the command marched westward to the foothills of the Chuska mountains, where they at last made contact with the Navahos. There ensued a short skirmish in which Colonel Washington employed his artillery, Lieutenant Simpson recalling that "Major Peck . . . threw among them [the Indians] very handsomely much to their terror . . . a couple of round shot" (p. 91). The only casualties were six Indians, including a decrepit chieftain named Norbona, but the desired effect was achieved when the Indians were impressed by the consequences of hostility, and Colonel Washington's command was able to march unmolested through the mountain passes into the very citadel of the Navahos, the Chelly Canyon. They were the first Americans to visit this tribal stronghold, and Lieutenant Simpson recalled his exhilaration upon their approach to the canyon. "It was somewhat exciting to observe, as we approached the valley of Chelly, the huts of the enemy one after another springing up into smoke and flame, and their owners scampering off in flight" (p. 100). The Colonel succeeded in making peace with the chastened Navaho chieftain, Martinez, and it was comparatively safe for Simpson to reconnoiter the previously unknown canyon fortress. With an escort of sixty men he proceeded down the canyon, observing the conical Navaho huts and the Indians themselves, jumping and gesticulating among the high crags, or scampering nimbly along the seemingly sheer cliff walls. They also found a number of spectacular ruined pueblos. One was nestled under a tremendous overhanging rock like the ruins at Mesa Verde. The scientific party collected numerous specimens of potsherds, some of which Richard Kern later reproduced in Simpson's *Report*. The usual scenes and diagrams were also made, and again the Simpson party had made a spectacular contribution to scientific knowledge. While they were on their reconnaissance, they met a Moqui Indian and learned of the existence of more pueblos to the west, which they were unfortunately unable to visit.

The return home was by way of Canyon Bonito, the future site of Fort Defiance and also the site of past ruins, one room of which was carefully described by Surgeon Hammond of the expedition and included in Simpson's *Report*. The Lieutenant also looked to his practical topographical duties and, with an eye to solving future military supply problems, reviewed the possibilities for a wagon route from the Canyon Bonito to the Rio Grande settlements. On September 15 they crossed a treeless plain covered with corn fields and approached the friendly and historic village of Zuñi. Again they were afforded an opportunity to study the Indians closely. Zuñi was part of a unique group of pueblos located on lava beds in the shadow of a mesa which the Spaniards Fray Marcos and Coronado had called the Seven Cities of Cibola. It was thus an important culture for historical as well as archaeological reasons. The men of Doniphan's Navaho expedition of 1846 had preceded Simpson in this region, but the report submitted was far from accurate and the best previous report on these pueblos, that of Josiah Gregg, was actually compiled from hearsay.[85]

85. Ibid., p. 114. See also Gregg, *Commerce of the Prairies* (above, p. 110, n. 6), pp. 197–98; and Adolph F. Bandelier, "Final Report of Investigations among the Indians of the Southwestern United States, Carried On Mainly

A short distance to the east was Inscription Rock, a high mesa which had been a Spanish landmark. It was covered with names and dates in Spanish and Latin, extending back to 1606. Here Simpson's party spent several days making an accurate copy of all the inscriptions they could distinguish. These, too, were of value to ethnologists and historians, particularly after several of the inscriptions were effaced after 1849. The guide described two ruins on top of the mesa, and Simpson climbed up to examine them, making his way from a spring on one side of the rock up through a cleft to the top. Years later the great ethnologist, Bandelier, made a similar exploration of Inscription Rock and confirmed all that Simpson had seen, except for the spring of which he found no trace at all.

From Inscription Rock the trail led through the pueblo towns of the Puerco Valley, which Lieutenant Abert had mistaken for the Cities of Cibola in his 1846 reconnaissance of New Mexico.[86] At this point Lieutenant Simpson recommended the establishment of a fort to guard the western approaches to the Rio Grande settlements from the expected Navaho raids. There were, in addition, other topographical results of Simpson's expedition, most important of which was his recommendation that an expedition be sent due west from Zuñi in search of a reported wagon road to California. Simpson based his idea upon a conversation with Richard Campbell, a mountain man who claimed to have made the trip in 1827, though the other trappers saw the canyons of the Colorado as an insurmountable obstacle. Such a road, if it did exist, would have been on a nearly direct line between Fort Smith, Santa Fe, Cajon Pass, and Los Angeles, and consequently a much better route than the Spanish Trail to the north or the Emory-Cooke trails far to the south.

It was in the interests of science that Simpson really made his lasting mark. His discovery of the spectacular ruined pueblos of Chaco and Chelly canyons and his accurate reporting of what he saw were his most impressive contribution. But his over-all

in the Years from 1880 to 1885," *Papers on the Archaeological Institute of America,* American Series, *4,* Pt. II (Cambridge, Mass., 1892), 336. This is supported by Neil M. Judd, "The Material Culture of Pueblo Bonito," *Smithsonian Miscellaneous Collections, 124* (Dec. 29, 1954), 6.

86. See Abert (above, p. 145, n. 97), pp. 73–75.

survey of the New Mexican Indian civilizations and his comparative vocabulary, which stressed the existence of six different linguistic groups, were also important. He was the first American to make an accurate eyewitness survey of the region west of the Rio Grande past the Puerco and to penetrate the northern canyons. As such, his report was the forerunner of the later works by Morgan and Bandelier. No work on these pueblos is complete without reference to Simpson's researches.[87] Another Topographical Engineer had helped effect the scientific opening of the Southwest.

In September 1851 Capt. Lorenzo Sitgreaves, recently detailed to the Department of New Mexico, began a reconnaissance west of Zuñi in search of the wagon route described by Simpson.[88] His expedition formed part of Col. Edwin Vose Sumner's diversion against the Navahos, and he took along, as part of his command, an escort of fifty infantrymen. Lt. John G. Parke, also of the Topographical Corps, was his assistant, while S. W. Woodhouse, R. H. Kern, and Antoine Leroux served as naturalist, draughtsman, and guide respectively. After spending nearly a month at Zuñi, the expedition started down the barely flowing Zuñi River and followed it to its confluence with the Little Colorado River. When they reached that river, they followed its course northward through the country of the Moquis and the Yampais Apaches, to the San Francisco Mountains near present-day Flagstaff, Arizona. Along the way they had several brushes with the Yampais. They reached the lower canyon of the Little Colorado near the San Francisco Mountains, and Leroux advised Sitgreaves that to follow the river any longer would bring them out in the Great Canyon of the Colorado. Because of the poor condition of his pack animals and the dwindling supply of food, the Captain decided to leave the river and march due west so as to strike the Colorado below the Great Canyon. Thus they

87. The latest researches on the Pueblo Bonito of the Chaco Canyon include repeated reference to Simpson's exploration of the Canyon and its ruins. See Judd, pp. 4, 6, esp. p. 6: "Simpson was the first to publish a personal impression of the Chaco ruins."

88. The account is based on Lorenzo Sitgreaves, *Report of an Expedition Down the Zuñi and Colorado Rivers,* 32d Cong., 2d Sess., Sen. Exec. Doc. 59, 1853. See Map 7, above, p. 215.

crossed over the San Francisco Mountains, turned past Bill Williams Peak, and headed west to the Colorado. The way lay across high tablelands covered with lava and almost entirely devoid of water.

On the 30th of October they camped on a small creek, which Sitgreaves named the Yampais. The next day they had a skirmish with a band of Cosnino Indians who had designs on their mules. It was the first of a series of small ambushes which eventually resulted in the disabling of Leroux, the guide, for the rest of the difficult journey. By the 5th of November they had laboriously crossed the last mountain barrier and looked down upon the Colorado River, winding far below through a broad valley. Sitgreaves related: "The smoke of numerous fires in the valley gave evidence of a large Indian population, and the sight brought a spontaneous cheer from the men who believed that this was to be the end of their privations and of the labors and anxieties of the journey" (p. 16). This hope was not destined to be rewarded; for after Sitgreaves reached the river he turned southward and continued the march through country inhabited by the warlike Mojaves, the same tribe that had attacked Jedediah Smith's party in 1827. The landscape itself appeared hostile. According to Sitgreaves it presented "the most perfect picture of desolation I have ever beheld, as if some sirocco had passed over the land withering and scorching everything to crispness" (p. 16). The march down the Colorado was made in the face of repeated attacks, first by the Mojaves and then by the Yumas. The former succeeded in wounding Doctor Woodhouse, and the latter dispatched a straggling infantryman with their war clubs. Food also was scarce, and as the mules died of exhaustion they afforded the only source of fresh provisions. But the 30th of November, when they reached Fort Yuma, marked the end of their tribulations. Here they obtained supplies and a temporary respite. From Fort Yuma the command eventually proceeded overland to San Diego, thus completing the trek from Santa Fe to the Pacific, but not on the direct line necessary for a transcontinental road. Because of this, Sitgreaves' exploration, though it had penetrated the hitherto imperfectly known regions of Arizona, was of less significance in the history of exploration than it might have been. His report was likewise somewhat disappointing. There was no attempt at scientific generalization about the country traversed, either in geology or in geography; instead, there was a catalogue of the scientific specimens collected by Doctor Woodhouse, who had actually traversed the continent all the way from Philadelphia. He had crossed Texas with Colonel Johnston, and New Mexico and Arizona with Captain Sitgreaves. His collections, however, included only a few new species, and Doctor Torrey, who examined the plants, did not place a high value on the materials collected in New Mexico and Arizona (p. 175). Woodhouse's botanical report would undoubtedly have been more impressive had he published the results of his extensive collections in Texas as well as those from New Mexico. But he graciously stepped aside to allow Asa Gray and Charles Wright to gain priority for this region with the publication of *Plantae Wrightae* under Smithsonian auspices. Ironically, this production itself was an unethical attempt to anticipate the findings of the Mexican Boundary Survey by one of its staff of four botanical collectors.[89]

The importance of Sitgreaves' exploration lies in the fact that it was a careful reconnaissance of a hitherto forbidding and imperfectly known country. Though he had not been able to explore the Grand Canyon or push a trail across the Mohave Desert to California, Sitgreaves had at least presented an informed picture, by means of his map, of the country through which a great part of the trail could pass as far as the Colorado River. The Santa Fe Railroad follows his route today. Beyond the Colorado, however, his map was based on guesswork and the stories of Leroux and Campbell, and was consequently unscientific and untrustworthy.

A final important result of the expedition were the drawings of Richard Kern, which presented views of the unique Indian tribes, like the Yampais and the Cosninos, never before known to ethnologists. These and his landscape views of the Arizona topography added another dimension to the knowledge of the West.

Not all of the Topographical Engineers assigned to the Ninth Military Department performed heroic service. Brevet Capt.

89. Emory to Torrey, Wash., Sept. 28, 1853, draft, and Torrey to Emory, New York, Nov. 3, 1853: EP.

John M. Pope, who in the seven years he had served with the Corps had become somewhat of a problem, was also assigned to duty under Colonel Sumner. He had just finished a report on his reconnaissance in Minnesota which, Colonel Abert pointed out, was largely plagiarized from Nicollet's 1838 report.[90] Before that he had received a reprimand from his superior, Colonel Graham, for misconduct and inefficiency on the Northeastern Boundary Survey.[91] In addition, Joseph Johnston declined the offer of Pope's services in his own command.[92] Pope, however, was irrepressible. Displaying the same outrageous bravado that emanated from "headquarters in the saddle" at the Second Manasses, he had arrived in New Mexico, petitioning for a subaltern so that he might return along a "new" Santa Fe trail to Fort Leavenworth.[93] He was next heard from in the pleasanter environs of St. Louis, where he had arrived after his survey across the plains, declaring in characteristic fashion, "I have been successful beyond my most sanguine expectations." [94] After deftly condemning Frémont's "inaccurate and useless map," he went on to describe his own survey, which, as it turned out, was largely based on conversations with the Indians, since all his horses and mules had been stampeded by Arapahoes at the Smokeyhill Fork of the Kansas River.[95] When Colonel Abert indignantly demanded to know what he was doing in St. Louis,[96] Pope, in an equally indignant tone, produced orders from Colonel Sumner which conflicted with Abert's.[97] In answer to Abert's jaundiced review of his career Pope coolly replied, "the complaints or censuries of any officer of the Corps are alike indifferent to me." [98]

By the following spring he had returned to New Mexico,

90. Abert to Pope, Oct. 2, 1851, copy, LS, TE 77. See also John Pope, *Report of an Expedition to the Territory of Minnesota,* 31st Cong., 1st Sess., Sen. Exec. Doc. 42, 1850.

91. Abert to Pope, Oct. 2, 1851, copy, LS, TE 77.

92. Johnston to Abert, Feb. 17, 1851, LS, TE 77.

93. Pope to Abert, Aug. 12, 1851, LR, TE 77.

94. Ibid., Sept. 18, 1851, LR, TE 77.

95. Ibid.

96. Abert to Pope, Oct. 2, 1851, copy, LS, TE 77.

97. Pope to Abert, St. Louis, Oct. 11, 1851, LR, TE 77.

98. Ibid.

where he performed routine reconnaissances to Acoma, along the Rio Grande, and into the Navaho country. He also accompanied Colonel Sumner to Fort Webster on the lower Rio Grande.[99] In October, again backed by Sumner, Pope wrote a private letter directly to J. S. Phelps, a congressman from Springfield, Missouri, expressing his views on the Pacific railroad question. He recommended a road along the Zuñi, the Little Colorado, and the Mojave River to California as the best route, allegedly basing his opinion on data gained from Carson, Hatcher, and Leroux. As an afterthought he mentioned the Sitgreaves expedition, which had already traversed most of the route, and acknowledged the fact that Leroux had been Sitgreaves' guide.[100] Colonel Sumner loyally recommended Pope for the Zuñi Survey, declaring, "There is nothing to be done in this department by the officers of your corps to compare in importance with the proposed exploration from this to the Pacific." [101] Whatever may have been his motives, Colonel Sumner succeeded in getting Pope attached to another command, as the "headquarters in the saddle" became part of the staff of the Pacific railroad surveys assigned to the 32nd parallel route.[102] His services in the Department of New Mexico had added little to the reputation of the Topographical Corps. He had managed, however, to convince Congressman Phelps, who campaigned strenuously for a railroad route along the 35th parallel (Pope's route), which would pass through Springfield. As such, he steadfastly opposed Senator Benton's demands for a 38th parallel route intended to "glorify" St. Louis.[103]

One of the most important results of the military reconnaissances in New Mexico was Lt. John G. Parke's basic map of the

99. Ibid., Oct. 29, 1852, report, LR, TE 77.

100. Pope to Phelps, Oct. 28, 1852 (enclosed in above report to Abert), LR, TE 77.

101. E. V. Sumner to Abert, Oct. 27, 1852 (enclosed in above report to Abert), LR, TE 77.

102. See John Pope, Letter of Transmittal for his *Report of Exploration of a Route for the Pacific Railroad Near the Thirty-Second Parallel of North Latitude from the Red River to the Rio Grande,* 33d Cong., 2d Sess., Sen. Exec. Doc. 78, 1855.

103. For the important role played by Phelps of Missouri see Russel, *Improvement of Communication,* 185, 194.

region from Pike's Peak to Cooke's wagon road in Sonora. It was drawn in 1851 by Richard Kern under Parke's supervision and finished before they left on the Zuñi expedition with Sitgreaves.[104] Parke's map replaced Lt. J. W. Abert's as the basic compilation of geographical information on New Mexico. It drew upon the work of Frémont, Simpson, and Abert as well as upon the less reliable data furnished by Old Bill Williams, John Hatcher, Antoine Leroux, and other local inhabitants.[105] The original map was sent to the War Department, where it was printed and distributed among the officers of the government heading for that frontier region, and also among citizens interested enough to request a copy.[106] Soon the military commander could add the results of other surveys, by Lt. Henry B. Judd of the Artillery and Capt. James Henry Carleton of the Dragoons,[107] to the base map, and the picture thus became more complete with time.

These surveys represent the total postwar achievements of the Topographical Corps in New Mexico. They had conducted, as part of their regular military duties, just enough surveys to lay the groundwork for further projects. What the combined efforts of Simpson and Sitgreaves and of Parke and Pope amounted to was a beginning—the beginning of geographical knowledge concerning this obscure region and the beginning of ethnological knowledge concerning its obscure and romantic Indian peoples.

In California the manifold duties performed by the Topographical Engineers afforded a microcosmic picture of nearly all of the services performed by the Corps in the West. Their postwar projects in the Tenth Military Department included railroad, wagon road, and harbor surveys; reconnaissances for fort sites, military reservations, and emigrant trails; observation of

104. The approximate date of the completion of this map is deduced from the fact that Pope requested a copy of the map in a letter to Abert of Aug. 12, 1851; see Pope to Abert (above, n. 93).

105. Wheat, "Mapping the American West," pp. 131–32.

106. Pope to Abert, Aug. 12, 1851, and Oct. 29, 1852, LR, TE 77. Pope implies that the map was printed and distributed throughout New Mexico. Wheat, p. 132, points out that the Bartlett Boundary Commission was furnished a copy of this map when it took the field.

107. Bender, *The March of Empire*, pp. 98–99.

Indian habits, mining practices, and the location of mineral deposits; as well as river explorations and modest efforts at public works. All these duties they carried out in the midst of a fantastic gold-rush environment of booming prices and fabulous opportunities for wealth, where tent cities prospered and paper towns abounded, while 300 settlers a day filed over the Sierras past Lassen's Peak to the ever-widening gold fields. San Francisco harbor was choked with deserted ships whose captains would never return for another load of passengers. Temptations of every kind were nearly overpowering for the poorly paid soldiers, and with officers like Joseph Hooker, who lived in scandalous luxury, to show them the way,[108] it is no wonder that desertion, next to drunkenness, was the Army's most constant headache. Even generals faced up to this problem, and in 1849 when Brig. Gen. Bennett Riley inspected the gold fields, he included only officers in his modest escort, lest the "weaker" private soldiers succumb to the lure of easy gold.[109]

It was into this situation that Colonel Abert had ordered two of his younger Topographical officers, Second Lts. George Horatio Derby and Robert S. Williamson, in February 1849.[110] They were to serve as assistants to the Chief Topographical Engineer of the Department, Capt. William H. Warner, who had been detached from Kearny's army following the conquest of California. Warner had put in a long tour of duty on the remote frontier, and he had petitioned Colonel Abert for a transfer back to the East. The Colonel was forced to refuse [111] because Warner's experienced services were needed in California, particularly when Major Emory threatened to resign rather than serve in that department. Immediately after the war ended, Warner's job was to help construct a map of the principal battles in the conquest as a supplement to the official reports submitted by General Kearny. Then he made preliminary reconnaissances of the area around

108. George R. Stewart, *John Phoenix, Esq.* (New York, 1937), p. 85. Here Hooker is described as "drinking hard, living openly with a mulatto mistress, and in other ways also conducting himself unlike an officer and a gentleman."

109. Bennett Riley, *Report of a Reconnaissance of a Portion of the San Joaquin and Sacramento Valleys,* 31st Cong., 1st Sess., H. R. Exec. Doc. 17 (1850), 941–43. See also Stewart, p. 60.

110. Abert to Derby and Williamson, Feb. 5, 1849, copy, LR, TE 77.

111. Abert to Warner, June 22, 1849, copy, LR, TE 77.

the harbor of San Francisco and extensive surveys for military roads connecting strategic points along the coast. His road survey from Monterey to San Luis Obispo was typical of the kind of routine tasks he was called on to perform.[112]

When Lieutenants Derby and Williamson arrived on the scene, Warner was able to embark on a project of somewhat greater significance. On June 27, 1849, he received orders from the headquarters of the Pacific Division to lead an expedition from the Upper Sacramento River across the Sierra Nevada Range to the Humboldt River—"the main object of the expedition," so the orders read, "being to discover a railroad route through that section of the country." [113] His work, therefore, was to have an obvious connection with that of Stansbury working out on the eastern rim of the Great Basin along the central route.

By August 11 Warner had begun his march from Benecia up the Sacramento River.[114] His work party consisted of himself and Lieutenant Williamson plus eleven civilians, including François Bercier, a former Hudson's Bay man, who served as guide. Eighty troopers and four officers formed his escort, since the region they were to explore lay dangerously close to the Klamath country, where both Frémont and Jedediah Smith had suffered severely at the hands of the Indians. The first stop was Lassen's Rancho on Deer Creek, where they paused for a few days to discuss the trail with its discoverer, Lassen, and to lay in a stock of supplies. On the advice of Lassen, they turned up Deer Creek and followed it into the Sierras, where the trail almost immediately became impractical for a railroad route and the going unnecessarily difficult for a large body of men. Accordingly, most of the escort was left behind while Warner with a reduced force struck out northward toward the Pit River, at

112. See reference to Warner's road survey in the orders issued to Derby by E. R. S. Canby, April 9, 1850, in Francis P. Farquhar, ed., "The Topographical Reports of Lieutenant George H. Derby," Pt. II, *California Historical Society Quarterly, 11* (1932), 247.

113. R. S. Williamson, *Report of a Reconnaissance of a Route through the Sierra Nevadas by the Upper Sacramento,* 31st Cong., 1st Sess., Pt. II, Sen. Exec. Doc. 47 (1849–50), 17.

114. The account is based on Williamson, p. 17.

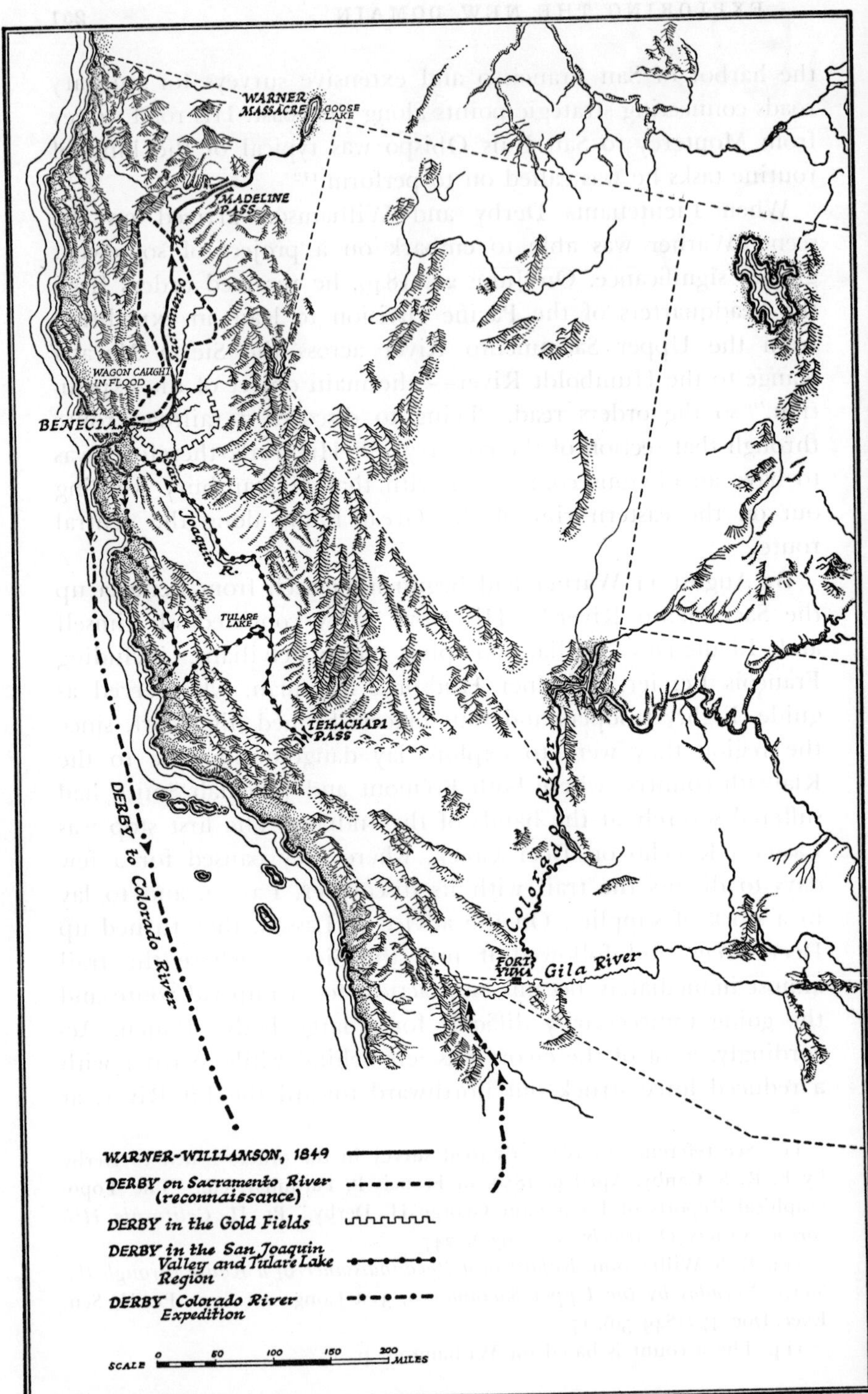
WARNER MASSACRE
GOOSE LAKE
MADELINE PASS
Sacramento R.
WAGON CAUGHT IN FLOOD
BENECIA
San Joaquin R.
TULARE LAKE
TEHACHAPI PASS
DERBY to Colorado River
Colorado River
FORT YUMA
Gila River
WARNER-WILLIAMSON, 1849
DERBY on Sacramento River (reconnaissance)
DERBY in the Gold Fields
DERBY in the San Joaquin Valley and Tulare Lake Region
DERBY Colorado River Expedition
SCALE 0 50 100 150 200 MILES

MAP 9

the head of which he hoped to find a pass over the mountains. Lassen's route with its grade of 50° had proven practicable for wagons, as witnessed by the flood of emigrants they met coming over the trail, but it would not do for a railroad, and this is what determined Warner to turn north to the Pit River. On September 20 he left Lieutenant Williamson behind with a party of sick men and pushed on seventy miles to the vicinity of Goose Lake, where he found his pass at last. But at the very hour of his triumph disaster struck. They were ambushed by a party of twenty-five Pit River Indians who suddenly fired a volley of arrows into the party, killing Captain Warner outright and mortally wounding two others. Lieutenant Williamson later reported:

> The Captain's mule turned with him and plunged down the hill; and having been carried about two hundred yards, he fell from the animal, dead. The guide dismounted and prepared to fire, but finding he could not aim his rifle he succeeded in remounting and retiring down the hill. He died the next morning. The party was thrown into confusion and retreated at once. Two men, George Cave and Henry A. Barling were badly wounded. Cave died before reaching the valley, while Barling . . . now has nearly recovered [p. 20].

Lieutenant Williamson prudently led the remainder of the command out of the mountains and back to Benecia. He had managed to recover Captain Warner's notes from his body; hence he was able to compile a report of the new pass over the Sierras, so that Warner's sacrifice in the line of duty was not in vain. The Warner Range in northeastern California, the site of the massacre, stands as his memorial today.

There were four other expeditions of importance carried out under orders from the Tenth Military Department during the postwar period, all of which were commanded by Second Lt. George Horatio Derby. A madcap of the first order as well as an accomplished soldier-engineer, Derby managed, in the years he served in California, to become one of its legendary characters as well as its most active engineer. Originally from Medford,

Massachusetts, he was the protégé of John Quincy Adams at West Point. Like many of the soldiers of his day, he had a certain gift for literary expression and some skill as an artist. But in Derby's case these talents were irrevocably committed to a wry sense of humor which soon caused him to be known throughout the Army as a wag who was only incidentally an engineer. It was when he reached the Pacific province, however, that he really found an atmosphere congenial to his antics. There he joined the literary circle at Barry and Patten's Saloon in San Francisco and exchanged salvos of wit and practical jokes with a group of prominent publishers, editors, and critics who formed whatever culture was to be found on that commercially-minded frontier. When he was stationed in San Diego, he contributed humorous sketches to the *Herald* under the names of Squibob and John Phoenix that made it, for a brief time, a world-famous publication. Once, for two weeks, he filled in for John Judson Ames, its arch-Democrat editor, and completely reversed the policy of the paper. Yet it was the same editor, Ames, who collected Derby's sketches together in his first book, *Phoenixiana,* published in 1855, which went through twenty-six editions in England and America.[115] The pretensions of a frontier, where any collection of adobe huts called itself a metropolis, were his prime targets, and his attentions usually were directed toward evidences of the absurd cultural aspirations that he found there. The Ladies' Relief Society, the San Francisco Antiquarian Society, the California Academy of Arts and Sciences, musical reviews, lectures on astronomy, the illustrated newspapers, and the Pacific railroad surveys were all satirized.[116] The Army, too, came in for its share. Derby was most incensed at the new uniform ordered by Jefferson Davis, which was adapted from the French Army. He made a series of sketches of the high shako cap and the tentlike cape, suggesting more appropriate uses for them as well as some changes, such as a hook on the seat of the trousers for dragoon soldiers. Then he sent the sketches and suggestions to Davis himself. It was rumored that only because Derby's dis-

115. Stewart, *John Phoenix, Esq.*, pp. 3, 22–23, 73, 123–30, 141, 170–71, 197, 201.

116. George Horatio Derby (pseud. John Phoenix), *Phoenixiana, or Sketches and Burlesques,* New York, 1856.

missal would make public his comic salvos was the outraged Davis deterred from calling a court-martial on the spot.[117] Whether in cartoons, burlesques, parodies, or practical jokes, Derby kept up a running fire of humor during his tour in California that was perhaps, in a unique way, also a contribution toward the "development" of the trans-Mississippi region. And while unique in themselves, his works can serve to call attention to the numerous literary and artistic efforts of the frontier soldiers which have been largely overlooked. Derby's influence was great. It touched Mark Twain, impressed Lewis Gaylord Clark of the *Knickerbocker Magazine,* and caused Thackeray, so it was said, to term him "America's first wit." [118]

The first of Derby's topographical expeditions took place at the same time that Warner and Williamson were exploring the Pit River. He served as aid and chief topographer to Brig. Gen. Bennet Riley, who made a rapid survey of the San Joaquin and Sacramento valleys in June and July of 1849.[119] The object of the reconnaissance was to locate strategic points in the interior for military posts that would afford protection for and from the Indians and keep peace among the gold miners. The command marched from the lower San Joaquin near the mouth of the Merced River across the Toulumne and Stanislaus rivers, past the gold regions on the Calaveras and Mokelumne rivers, to a point on the south fork of the American River, and then back again to San Francisco. One pass, Pacheco, had been verified as a suitable military supply route from the coast to the interior by General Riley, who recommended further surveys for routes from Monterey and San Miguel into the upper end of the San Joaquin Valley near the Tulare Lakes. The most important result of the brief excursion was Derby's map of the Gold Regions, which was printed and distributed in large numbers among the civilians and the military.[120]

On September 5, 1849, Derby was ordered to accompany Major Kingsbury of the Second Infantry to establish a military

117. Ben Perley Poore, *Perley's Reminiscences of Sixty Years in the National Metropolis* (2 vols. Phila., 1886), *1,* 492–93.

118. Stewart, p. 201.

119. Ibid., p. 60.

120. Ibid., p. 201.

reservation on Bear Creek, a tributary of the Feather River.[121] He was also to make a general reconnaissance of the country traversed, noting the resources, means of communication, and number and kinds of Indians. He was to extend his survey northward past Deer Creek as far as 39° 20′, or "the mouth of Butte River" where it joined the Sacramento River. This was Derby's first independent command, and his force consisted of an assistant, three rodmen, a teamster, a servant, and an adventurer named Kemp who volunteered for the mission.[122]

At 2 P.M. on the twenty-second of September they marched out of Sacramento City, and at 5 P.M. reached the American River, "having made," Derby reported with a straight face, "a distance of nearly two miles in three hours" (p. 107). With much labor, they crossed the American River and followed the road north through Nicholas' Rancho to the destination near Johnson's Rancho on Bear Creek. There they made camp and surveyed the reservation. It was so placed as to command both the Truckee emigrant route coming over the mountains from a point north of west, and Lassen's route coming down from the Pit River Country far to the north. In addition, the post was in the heart of the gold region, with a little stream nearby where the unemployed soldiers might indulge in the "healthy and profitable recreation" of gold panning. Undoubtedly it was with a smile that Derby predicted this would probably "be the occasion of preventing many desertions that might otherwise occur" (pp. 110–11).

It was while they were near the gold diggings that Derby's servant, Manuel, deserted, taking $425 in public funds, numerous personal possessions of the Lieutenant, and the best horse in camp. The adventurer Kemp immediately volunteered to go after him. Unfortunately, he was likewise never heard from again, much to the fledgling Lieutenant's "surprise and consternation" (p. 111).

When the reservation survey was completed, Derby proceeded northward, surveyed part of Lassen's route, which he pronounced an "extremely good road," and reached the northern limits of his reconnaissance at Butte Creek. There he turned south again

121. The order is quoted in Farquhar (above, n. 112), p. 105.

122. Ibid. The account is based on this work unless otherwise stated.

toward Sacramento. His report on the northern valley was a general commentary on the Indians and the resources. His map included a detailed if somewhat inexpert sketch of the local topography of the valley region. Before the expedition was finally terminated, however, misfortune again struck Derby. While proceeding against previous advice between Sacramento and Benecia by way of the direct road across the flats, a flash flood engulfed his wagon, forcing him to abandon it, along with the less portable instruments and equipment. Derby called it an unavoidable accident, while the quartermaster, remembering the previous advice, charged it to his account (pp. 122–23). Colonel Abert solemnly directed him to recover the property or make it good.[123] The data gained on this ill-fated reconnaissance formed part of Tyson's *Report on the Geology and Topography of California,* which was published as a Senate Document in 1850.[124] Its initial printing was 5,000 copies, most of which were undoubtedly read with excitement by prospective gold-seekers.

In April 1850, after he had recovered the lost instrument wagon, Derby ventured forth on another expedition, this time south to the Tulare Valley. His objectives were to (1) locate a fort site between San Miguel and San Luis Obispo covering the road from the coast to the Tulare Lakes, (2) examine the passes between San Miguel and the Tulare Lakes for a wagon road into the interior, (3) explore the country east of the Tulare Lakes for a military post, and (4) locate a route of supply for such a post. He was warned by Adjutant Canby to beware of Indians.[125]

Derby began his reconnaissance from Monterey and resurveyed the road south to San Luis Obispo. Then he carefully surveyed the country east of San Luis from Santa Margarita to San Miguel. He located a suitable wagon route and suggested a fort be located at Estrella, so named because of its strategic location where four interior valleys met. These duties completed, the Lieutenant and his escort crossed eastward to the south shore

123. Abert to Derby, Feb. 16, 1850, copy, LS, TE 77.

124. Derby, *Topographical Memoir Accompanying Maps of the Sacramento Valley* . . . 31st Cong., 1st Sess., Sen. Exec. Doc. 47 (1850), 2–16.

125. Farquhar, p. 247. The account is based on Derby's report as reprinted in Farquhar, unless otherwise noted.

of Tache Lake, the largest expanse of water in the valley. A few days later he left his escort camped on Moore's Creek (the present Deer Creek), and proceeded southward to Buena Vista Lake at the head of the valley, not far from where Walker's Pass leads into California. The trip was far from pleasant because of the "venemous mosquitos" and the fact that Derby had neglected to bring along the food supply. For nearly three days their diet was hardtack and water.

Upon their return to Moore's Creek, Derby sent the escort back to Monterey and continued his march up the valley to the east of Tache Lake, crossing the series of rivers that flow down from the mountains into the lake. All along the route he noted the presence of various tribes of Indians, some evidently hostile, others decidedly friendly. Ultimately, they crossed the Sanjon (Fresno Slough) to the north of the lake, and from this point surveyed a road to Monterey. In his report Derby found the valley "little better than a desert," and concluded that the only feasible place for a post was east of the lake on the River Francis. He submitted a table of geographical positions and a map of the valley. The Indian population he estimated at 4,000. Though he had had a few minor misfortunes, this, Derby's second independent command, was a decided improvement over his first effort. He had been able to supply the commanding general with a critical evaluation of an important geographical region, and he had performed the practical tasks of road surveying and fort location in an area where civilian settlement had not yet penetrated.

The most important of Derby's reconnaissances in the Southwest was his exploration of the lower Colorado River in search of a suitable supply route to Fort Yuma at the confluence of the Gila and Colorado. Previously, the only exploration of this area that had utility for midcentury geographers and policy-makers was that conducted in 1826 by Lt. R. W. H. Hardy, an officer on leave from the Royal Navy.[126] The map which accompanied his book, *Travels in the Interior of Mexico, in 1825, 1826, 1827, and 1828,* along with that drawn by Von Humboldt in 1806, was probably the source of the United States-Mexican difficulties concerning the international boundary as it crossed the lower Colo-

126. Wallace, *The Great Reconnaissance* (above, p. 22, n. 1), p. 173.

rado, for it showed the Gila running into the Colorado only a short distance above the mouth of that river. Thus Hardy's book, while it was of considerable merit, had not resulted in a reliable picture of the lower stretches of the great Colorado River. It was Derby's job to remedy this deficiency, and to test the navigability of the river to Fort Yuma.

On November 1, 1850, the Lieutenant and one assistant set sail aboard the schooner *Invincible,* bound for Fort Yuma via the Gulf of California, and as far up the Colorado as they could get. The ship was commanded by Capt. A. H. Wilcox and carried 10,000 rations for the desert garrison. By November 28 they had rounded the tip of Southern California and put in for provisions at Guayamas on the western coast of Mexico. The local officials at this point warned Derby of hostile Indians at the head of the Gulf, causing him to increase the number of his crew to twelve and the ship's armament by two swivel cannons and eight carbines before resuming his trip. On the way northward they passed the forbidding island of Tiburon, said to be inhabited by fierce Ceres Indians, whose poisoned arrows guarded rich gold mines. Derby, however, was skeptical, and noted in his report, "but as no one is ever known to have landed there, it is difficult to understand how the fact was ascertained" (p. 370).

It was Christmas day of 1850 when the party landed on Montague Island at the mouth of the mysterious Colorado. They were following Lieutenant Hardy on ground previously seen only by the Spaniards Alarcon and Ulloa centuries before, and possibly by James Ohio Pattie in 1827. The sounding and survey operations began immediately, and by the 27th they had slipped around a point into the river proper. For several days they inched their way carefully along the meandering channels past Greenhith Point and Pelican Island, to the head of navigation for ocean-going vessels at Howard's Point.

Between January 2 and 11 they made short sallies upriver in a long boat and also spent time studying the Cocopa Indians whose peaceful demeanor gave the lie to the prophets of doom at Guayamas. Derby sent one of the Indians upriver with a message to Major Peter Heintzleman, commandant of the fort. On the eleventh the Lieutenant led a party upriver in a long boat. Two days later they met the Major coming downstream.

He had covered eighty miles of meandering river between the Fort and Derby's advance boat. The ensuing days were spent unloading cargo, an operation made precarious by the loss of the ship's anchors because of the flood-tide waves. It was the first of February before they had finished their work and sailed out into the Gulf on their homeward journey.

Derby's report was accompanied by a map which incorporated his survey of the river and that of Major Heintzleman, to their point of meeting. One decided improvement over Hardy's map was that Derby proved that the mouth of the Gila was not where Hardy and Humboldt had said it was but instead lay 104 miles by water upstream from the mouth of the Colorado. He also provided more complete and accurate soundings, as well as data on the winds and weather. Most important, he concluded: "I have no hesitation in saying that it [the Colorado] may be navigated at any season of the year by a steamboat of 18 or 20 ft. beam drawing 2½ to 3 feet of water" (p. 379). His conclusion was almost a prediction of the events of the following year, when Captain Alonzo Johnson began his steamboat freight line on the lower Colorado.[127] It also commanded official attention, which ultimately resulted in the later upriver voyage of Lieutenant Joseph Christmas Ives to the canyons of the Colorado.[128]

In 1852, after a year's sojourn in the East, Derby again returned to California, where for the next two years he worked on a project for diverting the San Diego River into False Bay.[129] The work was designed to prevent the river from filling up the harbor with silt washed down into the bay. Derby's plan, as executed, required the digging of a short channel toward False Bay and the construction of a levee to divert the water. Unusual spring freshets demolished his first efforts,[130] but eventually he

127. See Woodward, *Feud on the Colorado* (above, p. 161, n. 34), for the best account of Johnson's activities on the lower Colorado. See also Wallace, p. 174, for a briefer mention.

128. Ives, *Report* (above, p. 20, n. 51), p. 20.

129. See Abert to Derby, June 10, 1853, copy, LS, TE 77, which acknowledges receipt of Derby's report and sketches on the San Diego River. See also Derby to Abert, March 20, 1854, enclosing a sketch of work done on the San Diego River; and Derby to Abert, Oct. 15, 1853, Progress Report: LR, TE 77.

130. Derby to Abert, March 20, 1854, LR, TE 77.

got his dam constructed—not across the river but parallel to it.[131] And no matter how correct its basis in engineering principles, it remained as Derby's own ludicrous monument, one which incidentally preserved the harbor from destruction.

During the postwar years the Corps of Topographical Engineers had been of incalculable service to the nation as it acted as a vanguard of settlement in the Southwest, clearing away the Indian barrier and laying out the lines of communication. It had probed deep into the West on its series of small, tedious surveys and monotonous reconnaissances in barren and forbidding territories, and its service had been a necessary one. Always, however, the immediate needs of the local frontier conflicted with—and prevented the execution of—any grand plan for the western country. Colonel Abert's dream of a continental railroad from Vicksburg across Texas, New Mexico, and California to the Pacific was splintered into the fragmented surveys in West Texas and those through the Navaho country and among the gold fields of California. Practical problems of supply and defense took immediate precedence over long-range ideas of continental spansion. Yet, for just a brief interval, Colonels Abert and Johnston had seemed about to realize their dream in Texas, before it crashed on the rocks of expediency and sectional rivalry.

131. Stewart, *John Phoenix, Esq.*, p. 137.

7. THE PACIFIC RAILROAD SURVEYS

> In Congress, with all due respect to my associates, I must say the location of this road will be a political question. It should be a question of engineering, a commercial question, a governmental question—not a question of partisan advantage or of sectional success in a struggle between parties and sections.
>
> If the section of which I am a citizen has the best route, I ask who that looks to the interest of the country has a right to deny it the road?—*Jefferson Davis to the Senate, December 14, 1858*

On the surface, the Pacific railroad surveys were an attempt to break a political and economic deadlock over the proper location of the first transcontinental railroad. They represented a last-minute alternative that kept the railroad measure alive in Congress while it held out the promise of an impartial solution to what had become by 1853 a well-nigh insoluble problem of infinite political complexity. Proposed first by a Northern senator, Brodhead of Pennsylvania, and then taken up by the Southern-minded Gwin of California, the surveys promised to substitute the impartial judgment of science for the passions of the politicos and the promoters.[1] It was not the first time that science had had a role in determining a policy for the West. The expeditions of John C. Frémont, it should be remembered, had helped point out the value of Oregon and California to Congress as well as to the public at large. In 1850 by their staunch opposition to the Bartlett-Conde agreement, the officers of the Topographical Corps provided a scientific buttress to the demands of the Southern railroad expansionists for a Southwestern right-of-way to the Pacific. As far back even as the days of Lewis and Clark, the president had found it useful to rely upon the findings of scientific parties to implement his western plans. It was thus characteristic of federal policy in the trans-Mississippi West when issues of public importance arose to seek recourse in the disin-

1. Russel, *Improvement of Communication*, pp. 100, 102, 107.

terested judgment of science. In a sense, this was a way of letting nature itself decide, not only because it placed the decision beyond the control of mere mortals but also because the decision seemed to depend on the overarching justice of the natural law. Upon such a premise was based the whole idea of the Pacific railroad surveys.

If ever there existed in the American experience a problem which seemed insoluble by political means, it was that concerning the location of the Pacific railroad route. No one could have quite anticipated when Asa Whitney made his first proposal, in 1844, for a transcontinental railroad spanning Lake Michigan and continuing on to the mouth of the Columbia that so many other conflicting railroad interests would arise to demand their share of the government's attention. It was true, however, that two previous stages in the history of American transportation had seen the rise of municipal rivalries over the securing of railroad termini. The seaboard cities—Savannah, Charleston, Baltimore, Philadelphia, New York, and Boston—had competed in the first instance. A few years later the inland cities—Pittsburgh, Wheeling, Cincinnati, Buffalo, Detroit, Chicago, Nashville, Chattanooga, and Atlanta—had entered the skirmish.[2] But when the railroads reached the immense trans-Mississippi country, the whole pattern of rivalries became at once more complex and more intensified. It was obvious to all that the economic condition of the country would permit the construction of only one or, at most, two transcontinental lines. For this reason all the older rival interests in the North and South and those newer ones concentrated in the cities along the Mississippi Valley came into headlong conflict. There was now only a single prize; and if one did not secure it, he seemingly lost everything. It became an important tactic for all those interests apparently losing ground in the struggle to combine temporarily to defeat the dominant group. The result was a series of constantly shifting political alliances based on economic expediency.

Though the sectional rivalry between North and South provided the broadest focus for debate, very often the competition took place within the bounds of one section or within one state.

2. Frank H. Hodder, "The Railroad Background of the Kansas-Nebraska Act," *MVHR, 12* (1925–26), 3–4.

The cities of the North and South vied for the railroad terminus, but with an even greater ferocity the neighbor cities of the Mississippi Valley entered the lists. In the Southwest the issue was further complicated by the fact that those who were proposing a railroad laterally across the country did so because they were interested in diverting the flow of goods away from the Mississippi.[3] Vicksburg, Natchez, and Memphis besides rivaling one another were all rivals of New Orleans. Therefore, despite the broad lines of sectional force, the question could also be considered local and western as well. Each city had its spokesman or railroad promoter who stood for those interest groups which hoped to realize profits from the increased land values and improved markets that would result from the securing of the railroad terminus. Some had even more direct motives in that they hoped to profit from the building of the road itself. And beyond all these immediate considerations, the westerners up and down the Mississippi believed that he who controlled the railroad controlled the whole western country, and that control seemed worth the price of any struggle.

The debate in Congress over the location of the Pacific railroad was the focal point for all these varied interests. In theory it was the task of Congress to decide where the best interests of the whole country lay, but in fact the legislative body stood helpless in the midst of the furious and many-sided debate. In the winter of 1852 the older members of Congress could look back on eight years of continuous deliberation climaxed by the furious debate that had absorbed most of the second session of their own Thirty-Second Congress. One by one, railroad schemes had been proposed and defeated by various stratagems. For a long time it had looked as if a Southern route would win out because its backers were able to achieve the greatest measure of solidarity and because important men in the administration favored it. But with the defection of Lewis Cass and the strict constructionists, the Southern plan lost whatever head start it had had.[4] Thus it was to stave off certain defeat that Senator

3. R. S. Cotterill, "The Beginnings of Railroads in the Southwest," *MVHR*, *8* (1921), 318–26, and passim. See also Cotterill, "Southern Railroads and Western Trade, 1840–1850," *MVHR*, *3* (1916), 427–41.

4. Russel, *Improvement of Communication,* p. 103. The effect of Cass' reversal is considered on pp. 103–7.

Gwin had been forced to agree with Senator Brodhead in calling for a survey by the Army engineers.[5]

At the time the surveys were authorized, the field of competing routes had been narrowed to those with considerable Congressional backing. Asa Whitney's northern route, modified so that its terminus would be at Chicago or the head of Lake Superior, was still a contender. Stephen Douglas represented another group, which called for a road from Chicago westward through Davenport, Council Bluffs, and the South Pass. But Douglas had not confined himself to that route alone; he owned the site of the proposed Lake Superior terminus of the northern route, and in addition any midsouthern line would almost certainly connect with his Illinois Central at Cairo, thus by-passing St. Louis and diverting the commerce of the West into Chicago.[6] The St. Louis interests were championed by Thomas Hart Benton, who demanded that the railroad follow a "great central path" from St. Louis through the Rocky Mountains at the Cochetopa Pass near the 39th parallel.[7] Other Missouri interests were served by Congressman J. S. Phelps, representing the Springfield or southwestern Missouri citizens, who wanted the road to run through Springfield southwestward to Albuquerque, whence it was to proceed along the 35th parallel to the Pacific (p. 43). Still another set of Missourians were for a South Pass route that went by way of Hannibal and St. Joseph (p. 36). With three distinct and powerful groups competing within his own state, Senator David Rice Atchison wisely took no side at all, through his private sympathies undoubtedly lay with the southernmost group and certainly against the Benton Democrats (pp. 160–61).

The Southern interests generally favored three alternatives: (1) a road west from Memphis along the 35th parallel; (2) Gwin's proposed main trunk along the 35th parallel to Fulton on the Red River, with branches to Kansas City, Council Bluffs, the Gulf of Mexico, and Puget Sound; and (3) a route sponsored by Senator Rusk of Texas to run from Vicksburg across Texas and along the 32nd parallel Gila River route.[8] This latter route

5. Ibid., p. 107.

6. Allan Nevins, *Ordeal of the Union* (2 vols. New York, 1947), 2, 86–87, 201. See also Hodder, p. 13.

7. Russel, *Improvement of Communication*, pp. 43, 46.

8. Ibid., pp. 42–43. See also p. 97 for discussion of Gwin's bill.

was the one so strongly advocated by Colonel Abert in letters to the Memphis and New Orleans Railroad Conventions.[9] In addition it was the one favored by Robert J. Walker and the Atlantic and Pacific Railroad Company, a gigantic New York corporation with Southern sympathies, which threatened to go ahead with the building of the road regardless of whether it received federal aid. These eight routes were the most important of the proposals, and it was generally believed that from among them any final choice had to be made. While it is one of the ironies of history that the Union Pacific was eventually built along a line different from any of them, it must be observed that ultimately trans-Mississippi railroads were built along parts of each of the major routes advocated. In the last days of the Thirty-Second Congress, however, it looked as though none of the routes would ever have its road and the nation would be left without adequate defense of its newly won far-western domain. It was from fear of this eventuality that Congress finally agreed upon a measure calling for the Pacific railroad surveys, to be undertaken by the Corps of Topographical Engineers.

Far from clarifying matters, however, it soon became apparent that the projected surveys themselves merely served to add a new dimension of complexity to the already existing problem. To those who looked closely, the surveys fitted a grand pattern of intrigue designed to secure the railroad prize for the Southern interests. The fact that Jefferson Davis as Secretary of War had charge of the survey operation was proof enough for most men that they would be biased. Commentators from Maine to Arkansas were critical of the survey plans, and Davis as Secretary of War was under continual attack. The most outspoken critic of all was Thomas Hart Benton. His salvos proved the most damaging because he had shrewdly observed the chain of circumstances connecting the Mexican Boundary Survey, the Gadsden Purchase, and the Pacific railroad surveys. He directed numerous speeches against these three projects, but the most noteworthy was his attack on the Gadsden Purchase bill in the House of Representatives. Describing the Southwest country under consideration as

9. Abert to J. Loughborough, St. Louis, Sept. 24, 1849, copy; and Abert to Glendy Burke, New Orleans, Dec. 17, 1851, copy: LS, TE 77.

"so utterly desolate, desert, and God-forsaken that Kit Carson says a wolf could not make his living on it," Benton linked the proposed land purchase with the railroad project and the work of the Topographical Corps. He ridiculed the idea of a railroad route through the desolate country so near to the border, saying "it takes a grand national school like West Point to put national roads outside of a country and leave the interior without one." Then he waved aloft a map of San Diego and declared, "It is said to belong to the military—to the scientific corps—and to be divided into many shares, and expected to make fortunes of the shareholders or lot holders as soon as Congress sends the Pacific railroad to it." To clinch his argument Benton linked Major Emory to the scheme by pointing out that the Major was financially interested in the paper city and that he was, moreover, tied in with the Atlantic and Pacific Railroad Company by virtue of the fact that its president, Robert J. Walker, was his brother-in-law. "In fact," Benton glowered, "an immense ramification of official and speculating interest is attributed to it . . ." [10]

Besides expressing his desire to obtain the railroad for the St. Louis interests, Benton's critique was also clearly prejudiced by his personal grudge against Major Emory and the West Point officers who had sided with General Kearny in the Frémont court-martial following the Mexican War.[11] However, his charges demand consideration because they were representative of those leveled at the western operations of the Corps by many other important spokesmen. Was the Corps, or any of its members, unduly motivated by either sectional bias or desire for personal gain?

Major Emory had played an important part in all of the Corps' southwestern projects. Indeed, the report of his reconnaissance with Kearny had first raised the question of a railroad along the 32nd parallel in official circles.[12] It is therefore significant that he was a prime target for Benton's accusations.

10. *Cong. Globe,* 33d Cong., 1st Sess., *23,* Pt. II (1854), 1031–36.

11. Nevins, *Frémont* (above, p. 16, n. 42), pp. 305–42, tells the story of the Frémont court-martial as it arose out of the dispute with Kearny. However, his account is strongly prejudiced against Kearny's officers—see esp. pp. 329, 332.

12. Buchanan to Trist, Wash., July 19, 1847, in Moore, *Buchanan,* pp. 368–69.

From the beginning the Major had shown a pronounced disposition to take any steps necessary to secure a railroad right-of-way along the Gila, from "torturing the treaty" to an outright invasion of Mexico.[13] Moreover, he had shifted ground on several occasions in his evaluation of the Gila River country for a railroad. First he had declared that a route existed along the Gila River itself, which prompted Buchanan to advise Nicholas P. Trist that provision for such a railroad route be included in the peace treaty.[14] Later, Emory pointed out to the Texas congressmen that the only practicable route lay far south of *both* the Bartlett and the Gray boundary lines, and that an additional slice of Mexican land was needed.[15] In spite of this conviction, he supported the Texan opposition to the Bartlett-Conde agreement, which called for the restoration of Gray's line.[16] However, later reports of the Pacific railroad surveys indicated that no suitable road led from the Colorado River into San Diego, and even today the Southern Pacific Railroad passes through a small part of Mexican territory.[17] What this suggests is that Emory was at least overenthusiastic in his desire to promote a southwestern railroad on any terms.

Whatever his motive, his emphatic stand so influenced Colonel Abert that the Colonel had, in effect, given the 32nd parallel route the official endorsement of the Corps in his letters to the various railroad and commercial conventions.[18] In addition, Lieutenant Colonel Graham and Lieutenant Whipple, by their determined opposition to the Bartlett-Conde agreement, tended to commit the Corps even more strongly in favor of the Southern route. If this were not enough, the appointment of the high-ranking Virginian Joseph E. Johnston as Chief Topographical Officer in Texas implied that important projects were planned for the Southwest. That these included the construction of railroads seems clear from Johnston's correspondence with Abert in the winter of 1852.

13. Emory, *Report, 1,* 51; and Emory to Volney Howard, Dec. 18, 1851, EP.
14. Buchanan to Trist (above, n. 12).
15. Emory to Volney Howard, Fort Duncan, Nov. 7, 1853, draft, EP.
16. Ibid.
17. *Pacific Railroad Reports, 11.* See maps by Lts. John G. Parke and G. K. Warren.
18. Abert to Loughborough and to Glendy Burke (above, n. 9).

Of paramount importance but less susceptible of precise evaluation is the relationship of the Corps to the Atlantic and Pacific Railroad Company. Chartered by the State of New York for the capital value of $100,000,000 the Atlantic and Pacific Company was one of the largest financial ventures ever undertaken in the United States up to that time.[19] Its announced aim was to construct a railroad from Vicksburg across Texas to El Paso and then along a 32nd parallel route to California, passing over a portion of Mexican territory through which the Company had high hopes of purchasing an official right-of-way.[20] The president of this huge venture was Robert J. Walker, pint-sized former Senator from Mississippi and one-time Secretary of the Treasury in the Polk administration. Walker's career was full of lights and shadows. He had rendered brilliant service in Polk's cabinet, but other episodes, notably the Dancing Rabbit land scandals and the Mississippi bond repudiation, had caused many observers to consider him America's foremost confidence man.[21] Walker's chief assets were his knowledge of finance and his strong ties with both New York bankers and Southern railroad enthusiasts. One of his political confrères in Mississippi had been William Gwin, in 1852 the powerful prorailroad senator from California. In addition, Walker's friends included George Mifflin Dallas, Polk's vice-president, and Jefferson Davis, whom he had helped to raise to power in Mississippi.[22] The only limitation on Walker's personal enthusiasms was the limitation of his funds. He had very little money in his own right, and indeed most of the original stock subscribers to the Atlantic and Pacific Company fit this category. The list was nevertheless studded with important names: Anson Jones of Texas; Governor Philip F. Thomas of Maryland; Levi Chatfield, Attorney General of the United States; and Thomas Butler King, a well-known Georgia politician and financier.[23] But be-

19. *Charter, By-Laws, and Regulations of the Atlantic and Pacific Railroad Company, Adopted November 4, 1853*, New York, 1853. See also Russel, *Improvement of Communication*, p. 97.

20. Ibid. (*Charter*).

21. Dodd, *Robert J. Walker* (above, p. 129, n. 55). Magdalen Eichert, "Some Implications Arising from Robert J. Walker's Participation in Land Ventures," *Journal of Mississippi History, 13* (1951), 41–46.

22. Dodd, p. 23.

23. *Charter* (above, n. 19).

tween all of the subscribers there was little possibility of raising a hundred million dollars, and it was obvious that they planned either to sell their shares among Southern enthusiasts as the railroad was being constructed or else to erect a huge watered stock company and build the road, using federal subsidies and Texan land grants.[24] Many critics doubted that they intended to build a road at all. Among these, Sam Houston declared that Walker and his cohorts planned to "board" off the money paid in by unsuspecting stockholders.[25] However another line—the Texas Western Railroad, owned by Walker—employed A. B. Gray to make an independent southwestern survey for a proposed route in 1853. Thus it seems safe to say that Walker and his associates did plan to build the road if they could. In December 1852 they had approached an unnamed former United States official in Mexico with an offer to send him as their agent to negotiate the southwestern right-of-way with Santa Anna.[26] In addition, they put up $300,000 worth of stock securities before the State of Texas as a guarantee of good faith, so that they could secure land grants and begin constructing the road.[27] What made people suspicious, however, was the fact that Walker, Jeptha Fowlkes, an unsuccessful Tennessee banker, and T. J. Green, a Texan adventurer, had managed to get themselves made trustees with sole and absolute power over the company, even including the right to bargain away the company's assets and designate

24. Cornelius Glen Peebles, *Exposé of the Atlantic and Pacific Railroad Company (Extraordinary Developments)* (New York, 1854), passim. Subsequent developments tended to confirm Peebles' assertions.

25. Amelia W. Williams and Eugene C. Barker, eds., *The Writings of Sam Houston, 1813–1863* (8 vols. Austin, 1941), *6*, 182. The synopsis of Houston's speech, made at Nacogdoches, Texas, May 11, 1855 (pp. 180–84), reveals the Walker plan and describes the rejection by Governor Pease of the railway company's worthless collateral stock-market securities. In characteristic fashion Houston declared: "I do not believe in Lynch Law, but if a respectable number of citizens of Texas were to take these fellows out and administer a decent number of lashes, accompanied by a coat of tar and feathers, and then turn them loose without injury, I would stand off and say I didn't advise it, but I reckon it was well done."

26. *Charter* (above, n. 19). R. J. Walker, Jeptha Folkes, et al., *Vindication of the Atlantic and Pacific Railroad Company* (New York, June 19, 1854), p. 2.

27. Williams and Barker, p. 182.

which of the stockholders should participate in any profits.[28] The whole plan collapsed suddenly when Governor Pease of Texas found that only $2,000 of the $300,000 security represented honest assets, and he refused to begin making the land grants.[29] Walker eventually offered to convert shares of worthless Atlantic and Pacific stock into shares of his own Texas Western, which had a clear charter.[30] This last maneuver suggests that Walker planned to build the road and then in his capacity as trustee sell it cheaply to the Texas Western Company, which he owned outright. Whatever his financial plans, it seems reasonable to believe that he intended to build the first transcontinental railroad through the Southwest at some other expense than his own.

The importance of the Atlantic and Pacific Company for this study lies in the fact that it has been interpreted as providing the motive for Major Emory's enthusiastic backing of the 32nd parallel route. Benton's suggestion that the Major was tied in with the company is plausible: Walker actually *was* Emory's brother-in-law and the Major *did* own shares in the paper town of New San Diego that depended for their value on the arrival of a railroad.[31] It is also possible that Walker may have conceived his whole railroad scheme as a result of Emory's glowing reports to members of Polk's cabinet in the summer of 1847. But these circumstances constitute all the evidence which links Emory directly to the Walker scheme. On the other hand, it is significant that Emory had been enthusiastic about the Gila River route long before Walker had conceived of his company, and he undoubtedly acquired his land interests in or before 1850, when he was in San Diego, and thus before Walker's scheme was launched. Moreover there is no record of any correspondence between Emory and Walker among the Major's private papers, which suggests that the kinship relation was no stronger between them than between Walker and his other brother-in-law, George Gordon Meade. Emory openly admitted his California land holdings but hotly

28. Peebles, p. 13.

29. Williams and Barker, p. 182.

30. Atlantic and Pacific Railroad Company, *Circular to the Stockholders* (New York, 1855), p. 18, and passim.

31. Emory to the *National Intelligencer,* Wash., April 10, 1855, draft, EP. Emory to the editor of the Washington *Globe,* July 6, 1854, draft, EP.

denied any connection with Walker's company.[32] Most significant is the fact that the Atlantic and Pacific Company based its projected line on the surveys of A. B. Gray, whose conclusions Emory had explicitly repudiated. With his chance for financial glory so obviously dependent on the judgment of one whom the Major considered incompetent, he could hardly be expected to refrain from making his views known to Walker; yet his letter books yield no such evidence. Though it is impossible, with the data at hand, to be definite, it seems more reasonable to conclude that from his own observations Emory genuinely believed the Gila route to be practicable, and that upon the strength of this he had invested in San Diego real estate so as to be certain to capitalize upon a sure thing. In this he behaved no differently than did Stephen Douglas, with his interests in Lake Superior shorelines, or than Pierre Chouteau, who invested in a railroad iron factory near St. Louis while his representative stormed the halls of Congress.[33] Frémont himself held large interests in California at this time.[34]

But though there was no certain monetary motive for Emory's advocacy of the Southern route, there were a number of indications that his strong Southern ties colored his patriotism. Most of his advocates in Washington were Southerners who ranged in their sectional devotion from the moderate James Alfred Pearce of Maryland to the slippery Southern jingoist Pierre Soulé. In his correspondence with the Texan railroad enthusiasts during the boundary dispute Emory indicated on numerous occasions his willingness to serve their cause, and it is of some significance that he always referred to the Gila River line as "the Southern route." It was to the earnest solicitations of Thomas Rusk, Jefferson Davis, and Benjamin Fitzpatrick of Alabama that the Major owed his appointment as Commissioner of the Gadsden Treaty Boundary Survey.[35] This appointment was strategic because it removed him from his post as the controversial head of the Pacific railroad surveys but placed him where he could still have an indirect

32. Ibid. (*National Intelligencer*).

33. John T. Scharf, *History of St. Louis City and County* (2 vols. Phila., 1883), *1*, 183.

34. Nevins, *Frémont*, map facing p. 378.

35. James A. Pearce to Emory [Aug.] 4, 1854, EP.

influence on the location of the proposed railroad. He had already done his work on the Pacific surveys by drawing up the plans for the field operations and organizing the Washington office, and his continued presence as chief of the surveys only offered a bigger target for opponents of the War Department.

Davis himself was Emory's closest personal friend.[36] And in 1855 while surveying the Gadsden boundary the Major was approached by a party clearly in Davis' confidence, if not by the Mississippian himself, with a proposal that he visit the north Mexican provinces in an effort to detach them from Mexico.[37] Though he professed to deplore filibustering, Emory was prepared to do his part for the cause, were it national or sectional. Again, though it is impossible to be conclusive, given Emory's proven Southern sympathies and connections with the leading Southern spokesmen, any association of the Major with the surveys seemed to indicate a desire to support the Southern aspirations if it was at all possible. On these grounds, his initial appointment as chief of the surveys seems in retrospect decidedly suspicious.

Even more suspicion is to be directed toward Jefferson Davis. Was he disposed, as Secretary of War, to use the Army surveys to bolster the Southern railroad cause? It was obvious he favored the building of a Southern road if possible. In 1849 as chairman of the Senate Committee on Military Affairs he had submitted the report calling for wagon-road surveys across Texas, which were to be forerunners of the railroad. It was Davis, too, who was generally accused of having been the master mind behind the Gadsden Purchase, though Senator Rusk was its most ardent advocate.[38] The appointment of General Gadsden was also laid to Davis' influence.[39] This was significant because Gadsden had been an outspoken pioneer supporter of the Southern transcontinental road. As early as 1845 he had proposed a route through Texas and along the Gila River in Mexican territory. In 1851 he was party to a scheme for forming a slave colony in California.[40]

36. Davis to John B. Floyd, Wash., June 15, 1859, copy, EP.

37. Bernard C. Steiner, "Some Letters from Correspondence of James Alfred Pearce," *Maryland Historical Magazine, 16* (1921), 171.

38. Garber, *The Gadsden Treaty* (above, p. 157, n. 16), pp. 112–13.

39. Ibid., pp. 81–82. Actually Gadsden received letters from Davis and Marcy on the same day.

40. Ibid., p. 80.

Davis himself, as previously mentioned, became involved as late as 1855 in a movement to detach the northern provinces from Mexico, a plan that involved the use of the 32nd parallel railroad as the crucial economic attraction. During the Congressional struggle of 1852–53 over the railroad Davis had, of course, favored Rusk's bill for allowing the President to choose the route, for it would have been almost certainly to Davis that Pierce would have turned for advice.[41] Later the Mississippian advocated leaving the choice of the route in the hands of the private contractors.[42] It is clear, therefore, that because of his close identification with the Southern cause Davis was prepared, all things being equal, to give his own section the benefit of the doubt. But though both the Secretary of War and the Corps of Topographical Engineers had at various times been directly connected with Southern railway plans, it did not necessarily follow that they would adopt a partisan interpretation of the Pacific railroad surveys. Even further, if the Southern route were to be singled out as the best, this still did not prove that they were running contrary to the national interests; for it was a distinct possibility that what they stood for, a 32nd parallel route to California, was based on geographical realities and was honestly conceived with the national as well as the sectional interests in mind. Only a closer look at the railroad surveys themselves can resolve these questions.

The Pacific Railroad Survey bill as finally passed by Congress on the second of March 1853 ordered the Secretary of War to achieve the virtually impossible. Within ten months—by the first Monday in January of 1854—he was to submit a full report to Congress on all the practicable railroad routes across the trans-Mississippi West to the Pacific Ocean.[43] It was to be based on field surveys made by parties under the supervision of the Topographical Corps. There were to be as many distinct parties

41. For an idea of Davis' influence on Pierce see ibid., pp. 66–67.

42. Speech of Davis in the Senate, Dec. 14, 1858, published in Dunbar Rowland, ed., *Jefferson Davis, Constitutionalist* (10 vols. Jackson, Miss., 1923), *3*, 364.

43. *Cong. Globe*, 32d Cong., 2d Sess., *26* (1853), 841.

as there were feasible routes, so that all might operate simultaneously and complete the work in the time allotted. Fortunately for the Topographical Bureau, the nature of the surveys was such as to make them, in fact, reconnaissances rather than the exact laying out, mile by mile, of a railroad line. The operation was to be a general topographical survey aimed at determining the relative merits of the competing routes rather than minute projections of actual rights-of-way. This was to be accompanied, however, by data on the exact elevation and grades of the mountain passes, and on the climate and resources of the regions through which the proposed routes would pass. Because the task called for such a broad collection of information, there was included a contingent of expert scientists with each of the field parties who were to compile reports on the various aspects of natural history that were in any way relevant to the construction of the railroad. The role of theoretical science was to provide a backlog of basic knowledge concerning the resources of the new country and its potential for supporting a railroad with its accompanying population. Here, as never before, was a chance to compile a great scientific inventory on all levels and at the same time to make that data relevant to the national problem at hand. The opportunity for science to serve as the positive instrument of public policy had never been greater.

At the outset, four main parties were ordered into the field: one to operate between the 47th and 49th parallels from St. Paul via the Great Bend of the Missouri; another to follow a line between the 38th and 39th parallels from the headwaters of the Arkansas through the Cochetopa Pass to the Salt Lake; a third to operate along the 35th parallel from Fort Smith via Albuquerque and Zuñi to California; and the fourth to explore the Tulare and San Joaquin valleys for passes that connected with the 35th and 32nd parallel routes. The total appropriation to cover these surveys was $150,000, of which the first three groups received $40,000 each and the last $30,000.[44]

There were certain notable omissions in the routes chosen for exploration. Most obvious of these was the much-discussed 32nd parallel route across Texas and along the Gila River. Abert and

44. Russel, *Improvement of Communication*, pp. 168–71.

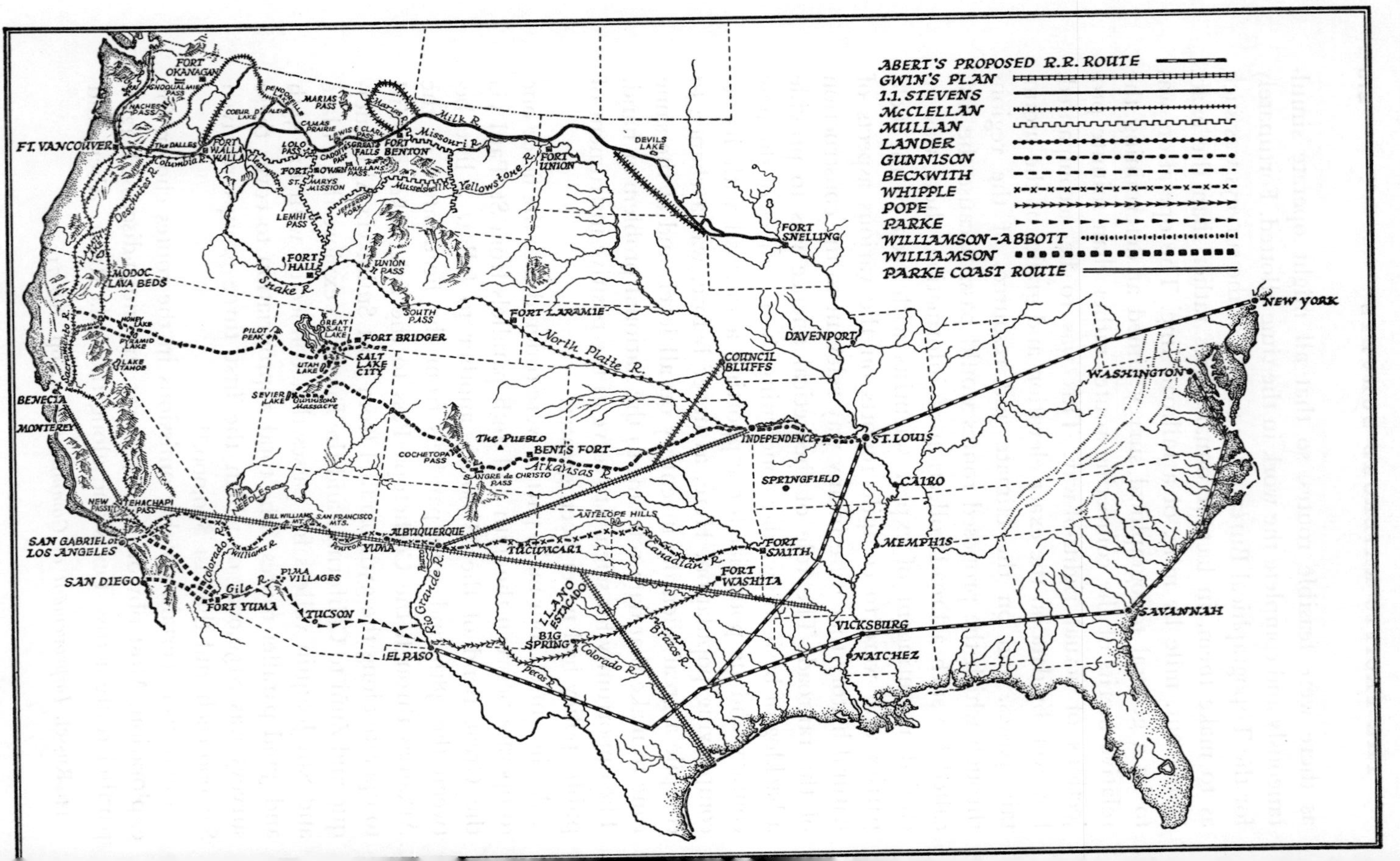
ABERT'S PROPOSED R.R. ROUTE
GWIN'S PLAN
I.I. STEVENS
McCLELLAN
MULLAN
LANDER
GUNNISON
BECKWITH
WHIPPLE
POPE
PARKE
WILLIAMSON-ABBOTT
WILLIAMSON
PARKE COAST ROUTE
FORT OKANAGAN
SNOQUALMIE PASS
NACHES PASS
FT. VANCOUVER
The Dalles
Columbia R.
FORT WALLA WALLA
Deschutes R.
MARIAS PASS
CAMAS PRAIRIE
LOLO PASS
FORT BOWEN
ST. MARYS MISSION
LEWIS & CLARK PASS
GREAT FALLS
FORT BENTON
Marias R.
Milk R.
Missouri R.
Yellowstone R.
Musselshell R.
FORT UNION
DEVILS LAKE
FORT SNELLING
LEMHI PASS
FORT HALL
Snake R.
UNION PASS
SOUTH PASS
FORT LARAMIE
North Platte R.
MODOC LAVA BEDS
HONEY LAKE
PYRAMID LAKE
LAKE TAHOE
Sacramento R.
PILOT PEAK
GREAT SALT LAKE
FORT BRIDGER
SALT LAKE CITY
UTAH LAKE
SEVIER LAKE
Gunnison's Massacre
BENECIA
MONTEREY
The Pueblo
BENT'S FORT
COCHETOPA PASS
SANGRE de CHRISTO PASS
Arkansas R.
COUNCIL BLUFFS
DAVENPORT
INDEPENDENCE
ST. LOUIS
SPRINGFIELD
CAIRO
WASHINGTON
NEW YORK
NEW PASS
TEHACHAPI PASS
NEEDLES
BILL WILLIAMS MT.
SAN FRANCISCO MTS.
ALBUQUERQUE
ANTELOPE HILLS
SAN GABRIEL
LOS ANGELES
Williams R.
Colorado R.
YUMA
TUCUMCARI
Canadian R.
FORT SMITH
MEMPHIS
SAN DIEGO
Gila R.
PIMA VILLAGES
FORT YUMA
TUCSON
Rio Grande R.
LLANO ESTACADO
FORT WASHITA
BIG SPRING
Colorado R.
Brazos R.
Pecos R.
EL PASO
VICKSBURG
NATCHEZ
SAVANNAH

Davis undoubtedly considered the existing data sufficient to demonstrate the possibilities of the road. But soon considerable doubt was raised as to its merit. The lack of water and timber as well as the danger from Indians were undeniable drawbacks, and the Secretary of War eventually saw the need for a further exploration of the more critical sections of the route. In October 1853 he ordered Lieutenant Pope of the Topographical Corps to explore a line across the Llano Estacado from Doña Ana, New Mexico, to Preston on the Red River. Fifteen thousand dollars was allotted to this survey from a contingency fund.[45] At the other end of the Southern line Lt. J. G. Parke was ordered to proceed eastward from California along the Gila River and connect his survey with that of Pope. He was given $5,000 and whatever funds could be spared from the Williamson and Whipple surveys.[46]

A serious limitation was placed on the value of the surveys by the initial failure to provide for any exploration of possible passes in the Sierra Nevadas north of the 35th parallel. Such passes, if located, would have made it possible to construct a road via the Salt Lake settlements to San Francisco on a relatively central line. The ill-fated Warner-Williamson expedition of 1849 had reported a possible railroad pass near Goose Lake, and this should at least have warranted a further investigation of the area. Besides this omission, the regular South Pass route was not surveyed, the Secretary giving as a reason the fact that the previous work of Frémont and Stansbury rendered it unnecessary.[47] But in submitting the reports on the various possibilities for the transcontinental road, very little consideration was given to the Frémont and Stansbury reports, or, consequently, the South Pass route or any nearby alternative. In general it is possible to conclude that the routes selected for survey were those with the most political support. Scientific considerations were relegated to a secondary role. Perhaps it could not have been otherwise, for the Secretary of War was obliged to satisfy as many of the major interest groups as he could, lest he leave himself open to further charges of favoritism and sinister design.

45. Ibid., p. 171.
46. Ibid., p. 170.
47. *Pacific Railroad Reports, 1*, Pt. I, 12.

In choosing the leaders of the various expeditions Davis for the most part showed tact. Most of the officers were Northern men. Only Major Emory and Lieutenant Pope came from states within the slavery orbit; they were from Maryland and Kentucky respectively, though both of them eventually became generals in the Union Army. However, as if to prove the inconclusiveness of any rule based on the relationship of sectional sympathies to place of origin, the case of Lt. Joseph Christmas Ives, assistant to Whipple on the 35th parallel route, should be cited. Ives was born in New York City, lived in New Haven, and attended Yale College, yet he later became the chief aide to Jefferson Davis when the latter was president of the Confederacy.[48] Perhaps the only questionable choice made by Davis, besides that of Emory, was Isaac I. Stevens, commander of the Northern party. Stevens, as the new governor of the Washington Territory, was almost certain to overstate the case for a Northern route. The really significant fact, however, is that Davis was apparently very careful to avoid any direct connection of Southern-minded officers of the Corps with the railroad project, with exception of Major Emory, who was his personal and trusted friend.

The first and most elaborate party to take to the field was the I. I. Stevens expedition, which had been ordered to explore the possibilities of the Northern route so earnestly desired by Asa Whitney and his supporters. Stevens had been a brilliant young lieutenant in the Engineer Corps attached to the Coast Survey before resigning his commission to become governor of the newly formed Washington Territory.[49] His chief attribute was his incredible energy. One observer described the governor as "a smart, active, ubiquitous little man, very come-at-able, [who]

48. *Catalogue of the Officers and Students in Yale College, 1845–46 and 1846–47* (New Haven, 1846–47), pp. 20, 21. *Class List,* Yale Univ., 1845–46 and 1846–47, Memorabilia Room, Sterling Memorial Library, Yale. See also James M. Patten, *New Haven City Directory 1845–6* (1845), p. 76; and T. C. DeLeon, *Belles, Beaux, and Brains of the 60's* (New York, 1907), pp. 116–19.

49. Hazard Stevens, *The Life of Isaac Ingalls Stevens* (2 vols. Boston, 1900), *1,* 278–82. Here he is referred to as Major Stevens, but this was only his brevet rank.

wears a red shirt and helps pull on the rope when we get stuck in a mud hole." [50]

The Northern route party was composed of two main sections, each with a subordinate contingent. Stevens himself commanded the main body, which marched west from St. Paul. He supervised a secondary group, which proceeded by boat up the Missouri River to the initial rendezvous at Fort Union. On the western end of the line Capt. George B. McClellan had charge of a party exploring the Cascade Mountains for feasible railroad passes. One of his advance units under Lieutenant Saxton had orders to hurry eastward and meet the Stevens party somewhere in the vicinity of the Bitterroot Valley.

All of the groups were well staffed with regular Army officers and scientific personnel. Stevens' eastern party included five hand-picked lieutenants, two civilian engineers, a professional artist, a geologist, and surgeon-naturalist, not to mention numerous special scientific assistants.[51] McClellan also managed to secure the service of two noteworthy scientists, Dr. George Gibbs and Dr. Thomas Cooper, as a part of the regular personnel of his party.[52]

Stevens' general instructions, which he wrote himself,[53] specified that the expedition was to

> examine the passes of the several mountain ranges, the geography and meteorology of the whole intermediate region, the character, as avenues of trade and transportation, of the Missouri and Columbia rivers, the rains and snows of the route, especially in the mountain passes, and, in short to collect every species of information bearing upon the question of railroad practicability . . . moreover to give great attention to the Indian tribes, as their friendship was important and bore directly upon the question both of the Pacific railroad and the safety of [the] party.[54]

50. George Suckley to John Suckley, Lightning Lake, Minnesota Terr., June 30, 1853, George Suckley Papers, Yale Collection of Western Americana.

51. *Pacific Railroad Reports, 12,* 33.

52. Ibid., p. 32.

53. Stevens, *The Life of Isaac Ingalls Stevens, 1,* 292.

54. *Pacific Railroad Reports, 12,* 31.

Starting on June 6 from St. Paul on the upper Mississippi, Stevens launched his expedition westward across Minnesota toward the country north of the great bend of the Missouri River.[55] He had already surveyed the possibilities of a route from St. Paul to the shores of Lake Superior; and when he headed west, his main objective was to find passes through the mountain barrier that separated the Missouri River system from that of the Columbia. The progress of the expedition was characterized by numerous side explorations under subordinate civilian engineers and army officers that covered most of the Dakota region as far south as the Black Hills and as far north as the Canadian Border area. All of the parties reassembled at Fort Union near the mouth of the Yellowstone and again at Fort Benton just above the Great Falls of the Missouri, before attacking the main problem of locating passes over the Continental Divide and through the Bitterroot Mountains. Relaying to a large extent on the journals of Lewis and Clark, they located, in all, five passes across the Rocky Mountain divide: the Marias, the Lo-Lo, the Hell-Gate, the Lewis and Clark, and Cadotte's Pass. The latter route was particularly favored by Governor Stevens, and his description indicates that the transition from the Dearborn tributary of the Missouri River to the Clark's fork at the Columbia was a mere matter of crossing a low hill, thus appearing to confirm Jefferson's wild guess of some fifty years earlier when he saw the headwaters of the Missouri and the Columbia separated by only a single range of hills.

When rendezvous was made with advance elements of McClellan's party in the Bitterroot Valley, the next step was to turn the northern flank of the Bitterroot Mountains by way of Lakes Pend d'Oreille and Coeur d'Alene and then strike out across the Columbia Plateau for the passes located in the Cascade Mountains. At this point complications arose, as McClellan and Lt. Andrew Jackson Donelson refused to take their tired horses through the Snoqualmoo [Yakima] and Nachess passes and the party was forced to detour far to the south, via Fort Walla Walla

55. Unless otherwise stated, this account is based on I. I. Stevens, *Narrative and Final Report of Explorations for a Route for a Pacific Railroad near the Forty-Seventh and Forty-Ninth Parallels of North Latitude from St. Paul to Puget Sound,* in *Pacific Railroad Reports,* Vol. 12.

and the Columbia River. Later McClellan also refused to attempt the Snoqualmoo Pass from Puget Sound eastward, because he overestimated the depth of the snow in the mountains.[56] Even though one of the civilian engineers subsequently made the trip through the pass and pronounced the snow only a few feet deep, it remained one of the doubtful factors of the Northern survey. In addition to the movement of the main body, other elements of the Stevens expedition ranged far over the entire Northwest country from the 43rd parallel near Fort Hall all the way to the Kootenay outpost of the Hudson's Bay Company in Canada. Lieutenant Mullan explored the Muscle Shell and Yellowstone River country, penetrating the heart of the Blackfeet territory in search of a connection with the main Oregon Trail route. Doctor George Suckley, the expedition's chief naturalist, made a remarkable canoe trip of 1,049 miles in fifty-nine days, all the way from the Bitterroot Valley to the Pacific Ocean. Only sixty miles of the trip passed over land, and his scientific collections were nearly as extensive as those collected by the whole of the Stansbury expedition of 1850.[57]

Stevens' evaluation of the Northern route was distinctly favorable, as might be expected. In his final report he was able to include the results of a further expedition which he made on his own initiative in 1855, and thus his conclusions were based on an impressive number of personal reconnaissances as well as on those made by his subordinates in both summer and winter. Two main destination points were selected, Seattle and Fort Vancouver, and there were two passes and two overland trails by which these destinations might be reached, making a total of eight possible routes in all to the Pacific Coast (pp. 346–51). The proposed roads all began at Breckinridge, a paper terminal town on the western border of Minnesota, laid out by the promoters of the newly formed Minnesota and Pacific Railroad Company which had followed on the heels of the Stevens Survey (p. 348). The alternate routes either followed a plateau north of the Missouri

56. Ibid., p. 146. For more details on this matter see Philip Henry Overmeyer, "George B. McClellan and the Pacific Northwest," *Pacific Northwest Quarterly, 32* (1941), 3–60.

57. George Suckley to Rutsen Suckley, Fort Vancouver, Dec. 9, 1853, Suckley Papers.

or else along that river and thence via the Sun River to either Cadotte's Pass or the Lewis and Clark Pass. Both turned north to Coeur d'Alene Lake and then either passed over the Snoqualmoo Pass to Seattle or detoured south to Walla-Walla and Fort Vancouver. All variations required extensive improvements, but the Snoqualmoo route particularly called for costly tunneling operations. Stevens' cost estimates ranged from $90,338,649 to $95,927,880, and distances varied from 1,526.6 miles to 1,575.9 miles (p. 351). On the vital question of possible interference from snow, Stevens declared that it "would not present the slightest impediment to the passage of railroad trains" and that in fact the whole area had a milder climate than Wisconsin or Iowa (p. 331). The agricultural capacity of the country he found compared "favorably with the best portions of the empire of Russia for the cultivation of the great staples, and west of the Rocky Mountains far surpasses them, approaching the most productive countries of Europe in character" (p. 331). Viewed as a whole, the Stevens expedition was a remarkable accomplishment because it covered so much unknown territory in such a short time with reasonable efficiency. It was disappointing, however, in that the final report seemed to take on the tone of special pleading, and several important questions were not adequately considered, such as the matter of the Snoqualmoo Pass.

Adverse views of both the conduct of the Stevens expedition and its findings were registered by members of the exploring party itself. The naturalist, Suckley, was particularly explicit in his personal letters to relatives back home, declaring: "There was the greatest amount of disaffection in the command throughout amounting almost to open mutiny—arrests, shooting, kidnapping, and violence were openly breached and everything in the way of short rations, lawlessness, and sour looks was to be seen." [58] Of greater importance was his critique of Stevens' Northern route:

> The general feeling here [Fort Steilacoom, 1854] is in favor of a railroad route through the South Pass having a Y-shaped bifurcation, the one branch to San Francisco, the other to Puget Sound. The extreme northern route to the mind of all who went over it; including that of our railroad estimating

58. Ibid.

> engineer, who were unprejudiced seems *impracticably, expensive.* A road *might* be built over the tops of the Himalayeh [*sic*] mountains—but no reasonable man would undertake it. I think the same of the Northern route. Tunnels of two miles in length are not our only obstacles; gullies, steep grades and deep cuts are bad enough, but the almost innumerable heavy and strong high bridges required, and the large number of short and sudden curves, frequently of less than 1,000 feet radius, are very serious obstacles.[59]

He also pointed out that "The Governor is a very ambitious man and knows very well that his political fortunes are wrapped up in the success of the railroad making its Pacific terminus in his own territory." [60]

So serious did the inhabitants of Washington Territory consider the objections of this kind that the territorial assembly authorized Frederick West Lander, one of the civilian engineers formerly with the expedition, to make a special exploration of the Puget Sound—South Pass bifurcation route.[61] His favorable report was included in the final edition of the *Pacific Railroad Reports,* where it seriously undermined the proposed Far Northern route.[62] Taking this into consideration, as well as the gross understatement by Stevens of the probable costs of construction, the Topographical Officers, in evaluating the governor's report, looked unfavorably upon construction along the Northern route.[63]

The exploration for a central route between the 38th and 39th parallels was placed under the command of Lt. John W. Gunnison, who had served as assistant to Stansbury on the expedition to Salt Lake in 1850. His task was to explore the Cochetopa Pass route so earnestly advocated by Thomas Hart Benton and the aggressive St. Louis interests. The crucial question of the survey was to determine whether it was possible to discover a railroad pass leading out of the San Luis Valley in the vicinity of the much-

59. Suckley to John Suckley, Fort Steilacoom, Wash., Jan. 25, 1854, Suckley Papers.

60. Suckley to Rutsen Suckley (above, n. 57).

61. *Pacific Railroad Reports, 2,* Pt. III, p. 5.

62. Ibid., pp. 5–44.

63. Ibid., *1,* Pt. I, p. 11.

touted Cochetopa Pass. Frémont had tried and failed spectacularly in the winter of 1848.[64] But the failure had not convinced Benton that no route existed in this mountainous area. So convinced was he that his campaign to recoup his political fortunes depended in large measure on promoting a railroad through this region.[65]

Not satisfied that the War Department had seen fit to appropriate $40,000 to explore his route, Benton insisted that Frémont be appointed head of the 38th parallel expedition.[66] When Gunnison received the official command, Benton saw to the promotion of two separate ventures for exploring that route in the same year. The first of these independent parties headed west in the early summer of 1853. It was commanded by the intrepid Edward Fitzgerald Beale, who at Benton's instigation had been appointed Indian agent for all of California and Nevada, with a princely appropriation of $250,000 to facilitate his operation.[67] Beale decided to follow the 38th parallel route as the "shortest and most direct" to California, and he took with him as press agent his kinsman, Gwin Harris Heap, an eastern reporter. It is not surprising that they published a highly favorable report on this route in an attempt to offset any possible negative opinions by Gunnison's official party.[68] The other expedition was financed by eastern capitalists and was led by Frémont himself, who hoped to succeed where he had failed in 1848. Like his previous attempt, this was a winter venture, and again the party suffered severely and produced inconclusive results.[69] Both Benton ventures, however, received maximum publicity, and it was clear that Old Bullion was once again resorting to his favorite political technique of using a scientific expedition as a means of promot-

64. William Brandon, *The Men and the Mountain* (New York, 1955), is a detailed study of this expedition of Frémont and his men.

65. Russel, *Improvement of Communication*, p. 184. William Nisbet Chambers, *Old Bullion Benton, Senator from the New West* (Boston, 1956), pp. 397, 410.

66. Russel, p. 168.

67. Stephen Bonsel, *Edward Fitzgerald Beale* (New York, 1912), pp. 65–66.

68. E. F. Beale and Gwin Harris Heap, *A Central Route to the Pacific . . .* , Phila., 1854.

69. Nevins, *Frémont*, pp. 408–20. S. N. Carvalho, *Incidents of Travel and Adventure in the Far West with Colonel Frémont's Last Expedition*, ed. B. W. Korn, Phila., 1954, first published New York, 1857.

ing a policy he deemed economically and politically desirable.

With a party that included Lt. E. O. Beckwith, Third Artillery, as assistant and R. H. Kern as topographer, along with a geologist, botanist, and astronomer, Lieutenant Gunnison began his march from Fort Leavenworth on June 23, 1853.[70] When they reached the headwaters of the Arkansas, they proceeded up the Apishpa Creek, crossed over to the Huerfano, and finally descended through the Sangre de Christo Pass into the San Luis Valley. A side expedition established a connection between that point and the Taos settlement. Going by way of the controversial Cochetopa Pass, they eventually crossed the Grand and then the Green rivers, and found a passage through the Wasatch and Pavant Mountain barriers down into the Great Basin near Utah Lake. Most of the difficult journey west from the San Luis Valley had been made in the face of a reported uprising by the Utah Indians, but no hostilities had been offered until the party reached the valley of the Sevier River. There, in the early morning of October 26, 1853, Gunnison, Kern, Creuzefeldt the botanist, Potter a Mormon guide, and four other members of the expedition were massacred by Utah Indians.[71] The massacre of Gunnison had an important effect on the promotion of a central Pacific route: it forced the command to postpone, for the winter, the second phase of the survey, which was the Stansbury–Bridger's Pass–41st parallel route, relatively a much more feasible route than that along the 38th parallel (p. 78). When the expediton did take up this survey, in the following spring of 1854, its leader was the inexperienced artilleryman Lieutenant Beckwith, whose report would carry far less weight than that of the better-known Gunnison.

From the 38th parallel survey as far as Utah Lake, Gunnison had achieved what he considered four main results: (1) a new military road to Taos, (2) another southern emigrant wagon

70. This account is based on E. G. Beckwith, *Report of Exploration for a Route for the Pacific Railroad, by Capt. J. W. Gunnison, Topographical Engineers, near the 38th and 39th Parallels of North Latitude, from the Mouth of the Kansas River, Mo., to the Sevier Lake, in the Great Basin,* in *Pacific Railroad Reports,* Vol. 2.

71. Ibid., p. 74. For a more detailed account see Nolie Mumey, *John Williams Gunnison* (Denver, 1955), pp. 113–23, 123–49, 165–78.

road to California, (3) a military road which would enable the Army to penetrate and command Utah, and (4) the knowledge that (p. 70) "for a railroad route it [the 38th parallel route] is far inferior to the Middle Central by Medicine Bow River and Laramie Plains" [the 41st parallel route]. The results of his survey showed plainly that a railroad via the 38th parallel route was unfeasible because of the "enormous expense" of tunneling, bridging, and spanning gullies. So hopeless was it that Gunnison had considered it would be a waste of labor even to go into a detailed estimate of probable costs (p. 56). Though he had not lived to discover the best route to the Pacific, he had at least been able to demonstrate the obvious absurdity of Benton's mythical "great central path to the Pacific."

The second phase of the central surveys began the following spring, when Lieutenant Beckwith explored the Stansbury route as far east as Fort Bridger. He designated both the Weber and the Timpanagos canyons as practicable passes over which the railroad could pass between the Salt Lake Valley and the Laramie Plains. East of Fort Bridger he accepted Stansbury's previous report of the route through Bridger's Pass and down Lodgepole Creek.

On his own initiative Beckwith petitioned the Secretary of War to allow him to continue the 41st parallel survey west to California. In an order of February 21, 1854, the Lieutenant was authorized to continue on to the Pacific (pp. 113–14). He crossed the Great Basin via Pilot Peak and the Humboldt River to the base of the Sierra Nevadas near Mud Lake, where he discovered two suitable passes into the Sacramento Valley, the Madeline Pass, and Nobles' Pass near Honey Lake. Beckwith's final report was extremely favorable toward the 41st parallel route. He emphasized that the line followed a remarkably straight course through fertile territory which would furnish sustenance for settlers along the way. The government could also take advantage of the already existing Mormon community for help in constructing and maintaining the road (p. 61). Despite the obvious advantages of this route, however, the fact that Beckwith had not included an estimate of probable costs of construction caused it to be largely overlooked in the final evaluation of the field reports. Yet in its eastern segment it was roughly the course along which the Union Pacific eventually did build the first transcontinental road.

Lt. Amiel Weeks Whipple, the able assistant astronomer on the Mexican Boundary Survey, was placed in charge of the third major party sent into the field. He was ordered to explore the 35th parallel route via Albuquerque and Zuñi.[72] This was the route previously explored in the summer of 1851 by Captain Sitgreaves.[73] It was also the line proposed by Lieutenant Pope to Congressman Phelps of Missouri, who subsequently became the spokesman for the southwestern interests of that state [74]—interests which in 1852 secured from the state legislature land grants, an exemption from taxation, and a loan of $1,000,000 to facilitate the construction of a railroad across the plains to the Southwest.[75] The 35th parallel route was particularly important because its location provided a possible means of compromise between the southern Missouri group, the Cairo interests (which were tied in with the ubiquitous Senator Douglas), the Memphis faction, and the supporters of Senator Gwin's bill for a railroad through to the Arkansas settlements. Thus this route could command the widest possible base of Southern allegiance and still offer certain advantages to the North-Central groups.

The main body of Whipple's party assembled at Fort Smith, Arkansas, in July 1853.[76] It was well staffed with scientists, including Dr. Jules Marcou, a Swiss geologist, who was the protégé of Louis Agassiz, and Heinrich Baldwin Möllhausen, an artist-naturalist who had been sent to America by the great Humboldt himself. A subordinate party under Lt. Joseph Christmas Ives was directed to join the main command at Albuquerque and act as an auxiliary force through the Indian country on the way to

72. The account is based on A. W. Whipple, *Report of Explorations for a Railway Route near the Thirty-Fifth Parallel of North Latitude from the Mississippi River to the Pacific Ocean,* in *Pacific Railroad Reports, 3,* Pt. II, p. 1.

73. Sitgreaves, *Report of an Expedition down the Zuñi and Colorado Rivers* (above, p. 244, n. 8), passim.

74. Pope to J. S. Phelps, Oct. 28, 1852, copy, LR, TE 77.

75. Grant Foreman, *A Pathfinder in the Southwest* (Norman, Okla., 1941), pp. 5, 6.

76. Whipple, *Report,* p. 4.

California. Perhaps the only deficiency suffered by the 35th parallel expedition was a lack of sufficient instruments caused by the extraordinary demands of the year, which saw, in addition to the Stevens and Gunnison expedition, the departure of Perry for Japan, of Cadwallader Ringgold for the North Pacific, and of Elisha Kent Kane for the Arctic.[77]

The primary objective of Whipple's survey was to examine more carefully than ever before the country between the Zuñi villages and the Colorado River. Previous expeditions had provided information on most other segments of the route, and Lieutenant Williamson was attending to the location of passes in the Sierra Nevadas. Whipple's main contribution was to be his survey of the broken and intricate country around the Bill Williams Fork and the San Francisco Mountains, continuing to the Colorado River and beyond it as far as the Mojave River.

On July 14 they set out and marched along the familiar Canadian River route of Gregg, Marcy, Simpson, and Abert. When they reached Albuquerque, they were joined by Ives' party and proceeded to the Pueblos of Zuñi, where they prepared for the crucial part of the trip. The guide was Antoine Leroux, the mountain man. Leroux had been with Sitgreaves in 1851 and was inclined to favor a retracing of that earlier trail, but Whipple ordered a more southerly course in hopes of following the valley of Bill Williams Fork all the way to the Colorado, and so locating an easier route. As it was, his route proved as difficult as that of Sitgreaves, though he found a pass south of the San Francisco Mountains that he considered an improvement on the previous route. After striking the Colorado near its confluence with Bill Williams Fork, Whipple's party turned north along the river and made a crossing at the Needles, where they were assisted by the previously warlike Mojaves. Setting a course due West, they struck the Mojave River and eventually came upon the Mormon wagon road to San Bernadino that branched off the Old Spanish Trail. From this point their survey duties were confined to the most rapid reconnaissance. They were able, however, to confirm Lieutenant Williamson's report that the famous Cajon Pass was unsuitable for railroads.

Although Whipple's report on the practicability of the 35th

77. Foreman, *Pathfinder,* p. 17.

parallel route was as consciously objective as possible, he could not entirely suppress his enthusiasm: "there is no doubt remaining," he asserted, "that, for the construction of a railway, the route we have passed over is not only practicable but in many respects eminently advantageous." [78] He had found easily negotiable passes through the various mountain ranges, and what was more surprising, he had found the country more fertile and adaptable to agricultural settlement than had previously been reported. At one point he said, "It is believed that in climate, as well as soil, this country far surpasses that of Kansas." [79] Here was at least one important modification of the belief that all the Southwest country was a cactus-filled desert. The influence of Whipple's survey was lessened considerably, however, by the apparent confusion of his cost estimates. Humphreys and Warren placed the cost of Whipple's route at $169,210,265, which was much higher than the others, though they admitted that Whipple had undoubtedly overestimated by a great margin.[80] In the final report Whipple revised his estimates in line with the others and placed the cost at $93,853,605.[81] Because of the lack of water and timber on the Southern route, and because of the more central location of the 35th parallel route, more and more groups began to favor it as the 1850's wore on.

When the Topographical Bureau began its comparison of the relative merits of the various proposed routes, it was soon apparent that despite the many explorations of the area there was inadequate railroad data on the 32nd parallel route. Accordingly, two distinct surveys were sent into the field in the fall and winter of 1853–54 with orders to obtain the required information on grades, roadbeds, passes, and the extent of resources which could support the building of a road. The first of these was commanded by Lt. John G. Parke, who had recently assisted Lt.

78. Whipple, *Report,* p. 132.

79. Ibid.

80. A. A. Humphreys and G. K. Warren, *An Examination by Direction of the Hon. Jefferson Davis, Sec. of War of the Reports of Explorations for Railroad Routes from the Mississippi to the Pacific, Made under the Orders of the War Department in 1853–54 . . . ,* 33d Cong., 1st Sess., H. R. Exec. Doc. 129 (1855), 57.

81. *Pacific Railroad Reports, 3,* Pt. II, 76.

Robert S. Williamson on the California surveys of passes near the 35th and 32nd parallels. He received his orders on December 20, 1853, and by January his expedition, numbering fifty-eight men, was under way.[82]

The object of Parke's expedition was to resurvey the Gila River route between the Pima villages and the Rio Grande, following a cut-off version of the emigrant trail called Nugent's Wagon Road. Before he left San Francisco, Parke conferred with John Nugent himself, and at the outset he was able to correct a number of prevailing errors concerning the actual location of this road. The subsequent course of the expedition took them via Tucson, through the Chiricahua Mountains at the Puerto del Dado, across the salt *playas,* to a junction with Cooke's Wagon Road as it headed south after leaving the Rio Grande. A few days later Parke explored a direct route to the town of Molino just above El Paso, which eliminated the necessity of following the Cooke route. In general, the results of his exploration indicated that there were few obstacles, such as excessive grades or high mountain passes; the level character of the terrain was in fact its strong point. Of greater concern was the lack of timber and water. There were only nine localities along the route where the water supply was permanent (p. 18). In order to make the 32nd parallel route entirely practicable, artesian wells would have to be drilled along the way. Parke recommended immediate experiments of this kind (p. 19).

In the spring of 1855 Parke again explored the 32nd parallel route between the Pima villages and the Rio Grande.[83] His primary achievement on the second survey was the location of another pass between the base of Mount Graham and the Chiricahua Mountains, which reduced the total distance by thirty miles, lessened the number of summits to be crossed by four, and the

82. John G. Parke, *Report of Explorations for That Portion of a Railroad Route, near the Thirty-Second Parallel of North Latitude Lying between Dona Ana, on the Rio Grande, and Pimas Villages, on the Gila,* in *Pacific Railroad Reports, 2,* Pt. V, p. 4. The account is based on this report unless otherwise stated.

83. Parke, *Report of Explorations for Railroad Routes from San Francisco Bay to Los Angeles, California, West of the Coast Range, and from the Pimas Villages on the Gila to the Rio Grande, near the 32nd Parallel of North Latitude,* in *Pacific Railroad Reports, 7,* Pt. I, pp. 19–42.

sum of ascents and descents by 3,500 feet. The new route also lowered the maximum grade to 60.3 feet per mile instead of 93, and was nearly 1,000 feet lower at its greatest elevation than the previous route. In conclusion, Parke asserted that with respect to distance, elevations, and climate, the 32nd parallel route possessed decided advantages over any other. The light grades would facilitate construction, and lack of timber and water were the only drawbacks.

On February 12, 1854, Capt. John Pope with a large party set out from Doña Ana on a survey of the eastern part of the 32nd parallel route between the Rio Grande and Preston on the Red River.[84] The important problems confronting this expedition were the location of a suitable pass through the Guadalupe Mountains and the exploration of the Llano Estacado. Most of the route was generally known from the previous work of Marcy and Michler, both of whom had had the requirements of a railroad in mind.[85] Neither of his two problems caused Pope much difficulty. He easily located a route through the Guadalupe Mountains, and his main command followed a course closely parallel to the well-known emigrant trail via the Horsehead Crossing of the Pecos, Mustang Springs, and Big Springs. Although he passed somewhat north of the regular trail, Pope never risked his command in a venture far out onto the Llano Estacado. Instead he sent two subordinate parties to test its possibilities, one under Capt. C. S. Taplin and another under Lt. K. Garrard of the First Dragoons. From their reports he concluded that the dreaded Llano Estacado presented no obstacle to the road that could not be overcome by the sinking of artesian wells at strategic points. In summing up the findings of this expedition Pope was lavish in his praise of its possibilities. He listed its advantages as follows: (1) there were easy grades along the whole route; (2) construction costs were reasonable; (3) for half the distance, timber and building material could be obtained on the ground; (4) the line passed close to the heads of navigation of the principal Texas rivers; (5) the only obstacle, a lack of water, was easily removed; (6)

84. John Pope, *Report of Exploration of a Route for the Pacific Railroad, near the Thirty-Second Parallel of North Latitude, from the Red River to the Rio Grande,* in *Pacific Railroad Reports,* 2, Pt. IV, p. 51.

85. See above, Chap. 6.

timber had to be transported only a short distance; (7) agricultural and mineral resources were good; (8) the country was suitable for a chain of military posts; and (9) the climate was very mild.[86]

Pope also pointed out that the railroad could tap the rich Santa Fe trade of northern Mexico, and he added further that Texas would contribute land grants covering the cost of 1,200 of the 2,000 miles of road. At the same time he implied that a termination of the road at Fulton, Arkansas, would satisfy the Memphis, Vicksburg, Shreveport, New Orleans, and Cairo interests.[87] It was not necessary to demonstrate further the road's advantages to the citizens of Arkansas and Texas. It was clear from his report that Pope was personally enthusiastic over the 32nd parallel route, but so also had been Emory, Johnston, Abert, Marcy, Simpson, Michler, and, in a more recent day, Lieutenant Parke.

The topographical explorations in California were focused on two basic objectives, the location of suitable passes through the Sierra Nevadas and Coast Range and the determination of a route that would connect California with Oregon and Washington. Early in July of 1853 Lt. R. S. Williamson led an expedition south from Benecia into the San Joaquin and Tulare valleys for the purpose of exploring all of the passes in the southern Sierras.[88] He was to carry his survey into San Diego and out onto the Mojave Desert so as to connect it with the 35th and 32nd parallel surveys. Lieutenant Parke was his chief assistant, but the party also included a naturalist, an artist, a civilian engineer, and the renowned map maker Charles Preuss, who had been with Frémont on three of his five expeditions. Along the way, Williamson also secured the services of another old Frémont hand, Alexis Godey, the mountain man. Preuss and Godey were particularly important to the Williamson survey because they were able to identify the passes through which they had passed in 1845.

86. Pope, *Report,* p. 47.

87. Ibid., pp. 49–50.

88. Williamson, *Report of Explorations in California for Railroad Routes to Connect with the Routes near the 35th and 32nd Parallels of North Latitude,* in *Pacific Railroad Reports,* 5, 10. The account is based on this report unless otherwise stated.

Thus when Williamson delivered his controversial report on Walker's Pass, there could be no doubt that he had explored the right one.

In all, the California expedition explored five passes in the Sierras, of which only two were found practicable, the Tehachapi Pass and the Cañada de las Uvas. The others, including the famous Walker's Pass, were deemed unfeasible, principally because of their steep grades and rugged topography. This was a complete revision of previous opinion, which had looked upon Walker's Pass as the great gateway into California.

The next phase of the survey operation involved the examination of the passes into Los Angeles and San Diego. Here another pass was discovered, and appropriately named New Pass. It connected the desert with the Santa Clara Valley north of Los Angeles. Cajon Pass, which led into Los Angeles, was found suitable if improved by a tunnel, and the San Gorgonio Pass, which was pronounced the best pass in the Coast Range, enabled the party to descend into the San Bernardino Valley. An important phase of the survey was the exploration of one hundred miles of the Mojave Desert, with the consequent conclusion that on all previous maps the Mojave River and the Old Spanish Trail had been represented incorrectly. The most distressing conclusion of the Williamson surveys to adherents of the 32nd parallel route was that no feasible railroad pass existed between the Gila River and San Diego. Both Warner's Pass and Jacum Pass were pronounced impracticable (p. 41).

In his conclusions Williamson seemed reluctant to admit the possibility of a route to California from a point higher up on the Colorado than Fort Yuma, because the intervening territory was largely unknown desert. Such a road, however, he pointed out, if found practicable would have an easy way onto the great interior valleys of California through the Tehachapi Pass (p. 43). The other route that he recommended started at the Gila and passed into Los Angeles and the Santa Clara Valley and thence, via the New Pass and the Tehachapi Pass, into the Tulare Valley, from which it was a comparatively simple matter to reach San Francisco (pp. 41–42). The results of Williamson's surveys did not rule out the 32nd parallel route, but they dimmed the possibilities of San Diego's becoming the Pacific terminus. Because of the fact that the road would almost certainly have to swing northward into San Francisco, the 35th parallel route seemed clearly to be the shorter if not the better of the two southern routes.

A final attempt was made by Lieutenant Parke to trace a route from Los Angeles to San Francisco, west of the Coast Range. His survey took him over much of the country previously examined by Lt. George H. Derby between San Miguel and Suisun Bay, and he was able to report favorably on the existence of such a route.[89] The Southern Pacific Railroad eventually laid its tracks along this coastal route.[90]

The second major California expedition was sent out in the spring of 1855 after most of the previous survey results had been received in Washington. Its objective was to locate a route between San Francisco and the settlements in Washington and Oregon. In the event that a railroad was built to San Francisco, it seemed imperative for defensive as well as economic purposes that a coastal road be built. Lt. R. S. Williamson was placed in command of the expedition, but he fell ill, and his assistant, Lt. H. L. Abbott of the Topographical Corps assumed command of the final phase and saw to the composition of the official reports.

Accompanied by a large escort, the survey party followed up the Sacramento Valley to the Pit River Canyon, and found it practicable for railroads.[91] Then they continued on to the dangerous Klamath country, where the party split into two groups: one, headed by Williamson, explored the Cascades north of Klamath River, the other, under Abbott, headed straight for the Des Chutes River and Fort Walla Walla. Both officers led parties which explored the mountainous country between the Des Chutes and the Willamette valleys for suitable railroad passes heading into Fort Vancouver. Later Lieutenant Abbott made a return trip to San Francisco west of the Cascade Mountains via

89. *Pacific Railroad Reports, 7,* Pt. I, p. 18.

90. George Leslie Albright, "Official Explorations for Pacific Railroads, 1853–55," *University of California Publications in History, 11* (1921), 142 n. This study gives a good outline of the various exploring parties.

91. Henry L. Abbot, *Report upon Explorations for a Railroad Route from the Sacramento Valley to the Columbia River,* in *Pacific Railroad Reports, 6,* 65. The account is based on this report unless otherwise stated.

the Willamette, Umpqua, and Rogue River valleys, a trip that was carried out in the face of dangerous Indian hostilities.

The final results of the surveys indicated that two possible routes existed between California and the Washington settlements, one east and one west of the Cascade Mountains. The main obstacle was the series of ridges between the Sacramento and Des Chutes valleys, which had been successfully circumvented by means of passes that turned their flank in either direction. In addition to their railroad data, the Williamson-Abbott surveys opened new agricultural possibilities in the little-known country between California and Washington. Like most of the other railroad surveys, they presented a much more favorable picture of western climate and resources than had previously been assumed by the Washington policy-makers, who had been conditioned by earlier official descriptions of the Great American Desert.

In the end, the effect of the Pacific railroad surveys proved to be almost exactly the opposite of their intended purpose as expressed by Congress. They did not furnish a conclusive report on the "most practicable and economical route for a railroad from the Mississippi to the Pacific Ocean." Instead, confusion was deepened and competition intensified by the most obvious results of the reconnaissance, which indicated first that not one but several extremely practicable routes existed, and second that because of this the far-western country was possibly more valuable than anyone had previously imagined.[92] Because of miscalculations in their conception, execution, and evaluation, the surveys in fact ultimately became the final stroke of doom to any plan for a federally sponsored transcontinental railroad before the Civil War.

The responsibility for this failure to provide a solution to the railroad problem does not belong to the Topographical Corps alone, however. Both Congress and the Secretary of War must assume a share of the burden. When the final results of the Pacific surveys were compiled, perhaps the most surprised parties in the country were the high-ranking officers of the Topographi-

92. For an adverse opinion see "A Review of the Pacific Railroad Surveys," *North American Review, 82* (1856), 235–36.

cal Corps and Jefferson Davis himself. For nearly eight years most of the Corps' attention had been focused on the Southwest. In the expeditions immediately prior to the Mexican War, in the campaigns of the War itself, in the postwar Mexican boundary surveys, and even in the extensive wagon-road operations across Texas and New Mexico, the official gaze of the Topographical Corps had been fixed on the Southwest. First Emory, then Johnston, and finally Abert had become convinced that the progress of national destiny was inevitably linked to the possibility of constructing a transcontinental railroad along the 32nd parallel to California. All during the postwar years data had been accumulating in the Topographical Bureau that amounted to innumerable rational arguments in support of a 32nd parallel project. Of all the Topographical officers who served in the West during this time only Simpson had registered an adverse opinion, and he stood opposed only upon the advisability of constructing any railroad so far in advance of the tide of civilized settlement. Yet almost by accident, the Pacific railroad surveys seriously qualified this western experience by implying that if all factors were properly considered, several routes existed that were perhaps better than that of the 32nd parallel.

On the other hand, to Southern political leaders the annexation of Texas and the Mexican cession had raised the possibility of a new era for the South. There was a chance to expand as far as the Pacific. As the Topographical Corps gathered its data on the Southwest, the means of expansion became more and more apparent. Every commercially minded Southerner believed that the Southwest country contained the only ice-free, mountain-free route for a railroad. And they could rejoice at the further natural advantage of numerous north-south flowing rivers which would enable the steamboats from the Gulf to meet the railroad running laterally across the country. Because of this apparent endowment of nature, the South always seemed to lead in the race to begin construction of the road. Frequent railroad conventions were held in the South, and its statesmen were the most aggressive in advancing their cause in Congress. Projects like Robert Walker's Atlantic and Pacific Company made the Southern transcontinental road seem just around the corner; and when Texas offered to grant its land to any bona fide railroad project, the battle seemed virtually won. Only the die-hard strict-constructionists hung back, and they were mostly from Southern seaboard states that would gain little advantage from a government-sponsored policy of internal development. These men were overshadowed by new Southern leaders like Rusk of Texas, Borland of Arkansas, Atchison of Missouri, and, above all, Davis of Mississippi.

Jefferson Davis was in a unique position to appreciate fully the value of the extensive army surveys in the Southwest. He had served on the Senate Committee for Military Affairs from 1848 to 1851, and in 1853 he was appointed Secretary of War. Only Senator Benton had more inside information on western exploration projects and their results. Because he knew well the views of the Topographical Corps on the feasibility of the Southern route, it was easy for Davis to be positive that his section possessed the key to Manifest Destiny in the West. Had not geographic science made this an indisputable fact?[93] Those in opposition had little in the way of scientific findings to buttress their convictions. Stansbury's Salt Lake reconnaissance had gone unattended. Frémont's Colorado expedition had ended in a disaster that hurt the St. Louis cause more than it helped, and nobody had explored the northern Rockies since Lewis and Clark. Thus the Northern cause seemed based solely on a selfish desire for increased commercial and political power that ignored the unbiased findings of science. By 1855 it was a simple matter for Davis to see *all* the other interests in this light, for only the 32nd parallel route had been truly endorsed by the government scientists. He could say, as he did in 1858, "If the section of which I am a citizen has the best route, I ask who that looks to the interest of the country has a right to deny it the road?"[94] That he did see things this way was undoubtedly the cause of his failure to make the Pacific surveys serve the whole country. More than

93. Jefferson Davis, "Report to 33d Cong., 1st Sess.," in Rowland, *Jefferson Davis, Constitutionalist* (above n. 42), *2*, 317. See also Davis to Humphreys or G. K. Warren, Portland, July 14, 1858, LR, BES 48. This letter illustrates the perfect accord that existed between Davis and the officers of the Bureau of Exploration and Surveys on the question of the railroad route, and also suggests that the evaluations were based on scientific considerations.

94. Jefferson Davis, "Remarks on Pacific Railroad Bill, Dec. 14, 1858," in Rowland, *3*, 364.

anything else, his failure semed due to a certain rigidity of mind, an inability to appreciate the nature of existing reality. His attention was too narrowly confined to the scientific findings of earlier years, and hence upon the good fortune of his own section. This caused him, as it did most Southerners, to look upon the railroad surveys as a ritual that had to be undergone before the rest of the country could perceive the scientific advisability of the 32nd parallel route. Because of this notion, the field parties were sent out strictly in response to the loudest demands by political pressure groups. It was as if their mission were to report back the impracticality of all the other heavily backed plans, so that in the end the selection of the 32nd parallel route would be inevitable.

Some Northern senators may have gone along with this situation; for when the Survey bill was drafted, so little time was allotted for the field work that the impossibility of a really thorough railroad survey was practically assured. Under these circumstances any result was open to criticism. Yet the railroad question had not been allowed to die completely. When he drew up the over-all plan for the surveys, the overconfident Davis played into the hands of the opposition by making the reconnaissances of a general nature and by relying to a large extent on the results of previous expeditions that had not been specifically railroad expeditions.[95] In its very conception, therefore, the reconnaissance was virtually doomed to failure if it did not deliver a report that pleased the majority of political representatives.

Again, at the outset, Congressional pressure prevailed over cooler scientific judgment in the selection of the routes to be explored. For example, because of his powerful following, Benton was able to secure an expedition on the 38th parallel route, while the more feasible one via Lodgepole Creek and the Cheyenne Pass, near the 41st parallel, was not taken seriously. Perhaps the Secretary of War hoped the surveys would prove Benton wrong rather than discovering a new route.[96] At any rate, the whole project suffered because not enough attention was given to the

95. For example, data from Emory's reconnaissance of 1846 were included. See *Pacific Railroad Reports, 2,* Pt. VI. See also ibid., *1,* Pt. I, p. 12.

96. See R. H. Kern to J. S. Phelps, Pittsburgh, May 29, 1853, Yale Collection of Western Americana, which implies that this is Davis' wish.

important line along the 41st parallel, in both its eastern and its western extremities. Captain Humphreys later expressed his unwillingness to project a line through the potentially hostile Mormon community, but this reluctance seemed merely a later rationalization.

In addition to the illogical choice of routes to be explored, the actual method of conducting the surveys, with respect to both the kind of data collected and the various sources used, made them of dubious value for the actual selection of a railroad route. Only the roughest estimates of grades, curves, ascents, altitudes of passes, etc. was submitted, and the actual terrain to be crossed was only generally characterized. In their announced aim they were not to be precise railroad projections. But, as one House Committee noted, the estimate of cost admittedly varied as much as $35,000,000 on a single route, and Captain Whipple had overestimated the costs of his route by over $75,000,000.[97] On other occasions data from earlier reconnaissances, such as those of Frémont, Stansbury, and Emory, was introduced to establish the practicability of a certain route, yet none of these men had made specific calculations of the kind needed for railroad engineering. Zedekiah Kidwell's minority report in the House of Representatives pointed out, for example, that Frémont, although an experienced railroad engineer, had erred badly when he said that there was scarcely "a perceptible rise" from river to river through the Sangre de Christo Pass, for an instrumental survey showed that the grade exceeded 340 feet to the mile.[98] A part of Emory's reconnaissance of 1846 was used to characterize the 32nd parallel route between the Pima Villages and the junction of the Gila and Colorado; yet at the time that survey was made, Emory had neither the time nor the inclination to make the specific observations needed for railroad engineering. Nowhere in his report do any data on grades and curves appear.

But if the conception and execution of the surveys were vul-

97. Zedekiah Kidwell, *Supplementary Report in Reply to the Comments of the Sec. of War,* 34th Cong., 3d Sess., H. R. Misc. Doc. 44 (1857), 7. See also A. A. Humphreys, *Report . . . upon the Progress of the Pacific Railroad Explorations and Surveys,* 34th Cong., 1st Sess., H. R. Exec. Doc. 1 (1855–56), 94.

98. Kidwell, *Supplementary Report,* p. 4.

nerable, the chief storm of criticism was directed toward the final evaluation of the data by Capt. A. A. Humphreys of the Topographical Engineers, and by Jefferson Davis himself. Since both of the reports agreed, and since Humphreys supplied most of the analysis for Davis' report, a critique of Davis' summary should characterize the position of both. The Secretary's conclusion was, to say the least, predictable. He declared with certainty that "the route of the thirty-second parallel is, of those surveyed, 'the most practicable and economical route for a railroad from the Mississippi River to the Pacific Ocean.' "[99] In his detailed analysis of the individual routes he gave the appearance of fairness, but the scales were so weighted that any adverse factors counted very heavily against the other routes, while such things as lack of water and timber on the Southern route were dismissed as mere trifles. In general, the Secretary assumed that all the land west of the 99th meridian formed a sterile belt, with the possible exception of the Southern route, where Lieutenant Pope had reported fertile, watered country as far as the 102nd meridian.[100] Thus all the lines were placed on equal footing as far west as the mountain barrier, an assumption which, in its too-broad application of the Great American Desert theory, overlooked the Missouri River Valley and much of the present-day wheat belt. It was true that, given the level of technology at the time, the land appeared to have far less potential than it has today, but "sterile belt" and "desert" were harsh terms to describe that entire country. Again and again in his report Davis stressed the sterility of all the mountain area, in strict contrast to the findings of the various field parties.[101] When he had to acknowledge the existence of valuable timber or farm lands, he declared it too little to make any difference in the choice of a route. Yet in most of the reports the individual parties found surprisingly large tracts of valuable land and possibilities for irrigation and improvement of the country by man-made methods.

Climate, too, was stressed by Davis as a general factor which made Northern routes prohibitive; yet all the parties, including that of Stevens, saw either the climate in general as mild enough

99. *Pacific Railroad Reports, 1*, Pt. I, p. 29.

100. Ibid., p. 25.

101. See, e.g., ibid., pp. 11, 16, 21.

for a railroad or the snowfall as insufficient to provide an obstacle. Only Stansbury's report, which described the existence of snow in August in the Uinta Mountains, tended to reinforce the Davis-Humphreys line. But to seasoned railroad engineers snowfall rarely presented a problem, because it never fell enough at one time to prevent prompt clearance. Even the drifts could be cleared by engines with plows in a brief time. The only time climate was an important factor was during the construction period, when it was necessary to maintain large parties of men in the field.

In considering the Stevens route, the Secretary stressed the long and expensive tunnels that were needed, the severely cold climate (in contradiction of Stevens' data), and the proximity of the route to a powerful foreign power.[102] He also accepted McClellan's exaggerated account of the depth of snow in the crucial Snoqualmoo (or Yakima) Pass when it was evident from the report that McClellan had never seen the Pass and had no reliable data concerning it, while qualified experts who had traversed it had given the level of snow as only a few feet. Davis and Humphreys advanced Stevens' over-all cost calculations from $117,121,000 to $140,871,000, but this was probably justified when comparing it to estimates along the other lines.[103] Though Stevens' report undoubtedly deserved a skeptical analysis, it is evident that both Humphreys and Davis were somewhat overzealous in their demonstration of its bad features. That they fastened on the wrong factors, rather than that they delivered an adverse criticism, seems most significant.

For the 41st, or emigrant trail, route the Secretary unfairly took refuge in the fact that the Lodgepole Creek—Cheyenne Pass route had not been surveyed, without saying why he had not authorized its exploration.[104] From this position it was a relatively easy matter to demonstrate the impracticality of constructing a road through the Devil's Gate and along the broken terrain of the Sweetwater Valley to the South Pass. All the cost

102. Ibid., pp. 9, 11.

103. Ibid., p. 11. Though Hazard Stevens claimed that his father's estimates were altered, hence falsified, the alterations appear to have been done fairly and in line with the criteria for making cost estimates on other routes.

104. Ibid., p. 12.

estimates were based on the South Pass trail; yet the Union Pacific engineers preferred the Lodgepole Creek route across the Laramie Plains. Lieutenant Beckwith's comments on the climate tended to controvert Stansbury's data on the August snow of the Uinta Mountains. At the other end of the line the Madeline Pass in the Sierras was the only pass considered, and this required expensive construction in two places along the rugged upper Sacramento Valley. Colonel Steptoe's new route, which crossed the Sierras via Carson River and avoided this rugged stretch, was mentioned but not seriously considered in the final evaluation; yet it would undoubtedly have lowered the $116,095,000 cost estimate by a substantial amount. The Secretary did, however, grudgingly admit that the difficulties of the 41st parallel route were "already known to be less than on any other route except that of the thirty-second parallel." [105]

The 38th parallel route, the one advocated by Benton, was obviously impractical according to Gunnison's report, and Davis seemed justified in quickly rejecting it. Some observers questioned his motives in exploring it at all.[106]

The biggest surprise came in the 35th parallel route, which was found to be extremely favorable in all respects except in its cost estimate, which was an astronomical $169,210,205. The Secretary declared he believed it to be too high, "but no data had been furnished for its correction as yet." [107] In November 1855 Captain Humphreys reported that a closer inspection of Whipple's data had enabled them to revise the cost estimate to $94,720,000.[108] This estimate did not make it as cheap as the 32nd parallel route, but its other advantages in timber and water, as well as its easy connection with San Francisco via the Tehachapi Pass, clearly made it a desirable route. That it would have satisfied both the St. Louis interests and the middle-Southern interests as well as, perhaps, even the Douglas faction made it even more desirable.

Most of the attention, then, was given to the 32nd parallel route, and the language of both summaries made the selection

105. Ibid., p. 16.
106. Kidwell, *Supplementary Report,* p. 4.
107. *Pacific Railroad Reports, 1,* Pt. I, p. 22.
108. Humphreys, *Report* (above, n. 97), p. 94.

of this route seem almost a foregone conclusion, which it apparently was to Davis and Humphreys. The formidable obstacles presented by the lack of any pass into San Diego and the complicated series of ascents and descents required for the road to reach San Francisco via San Gorgonio, New Pass, and Tehachapi were glossed over. Timber, though scarce, could be hauled by the train as it made its way along.[109] Water was available in artesian wells. And as if to prove that the Secretary always intended to select the 32nd parallel route, in early 1855, even before the results of the surveys were all submitted and digested, Lieutenant Pope was sent out onto the Llano Estacado to begin drilling experimental wells.[110] Even the importation of camels at this time suggests that the Secretary saw a sudden extraordinary need for beasts of burden adapted to the arid Southwest.[111]

From the general slant of their summary of the *Railroad Reports,* the conclusion is inescapable that Davis and Humphreys were biased in favor of the 32nd parallel route, the latter because ten years of experience in the exploration of the West had undoubtedly built up a picture of the country which was difficult to revise overnight, and Davis because he depended on the Topographical Corps and because he saw the combination of scientific testimony and the demands of his own section irreproachable in the face of obvious Northern political and commercial pressures.

But as Kidwell of Virginia had pointed out, Davis had not only failed to serve the interests of the whole nation, he had betrayed the South he sought to serve.[112] Because of his inflexible approach, he failed to see that the 35th parallel route actually had the best chance of uniting all the various political groups, particularly if the terminus were placed far enough West to allow a fork to run to St. Louis and one to Memphis and Fort Smith. It had been found that Whipple's route was as good in all respects as the 32nd parallel route. Moreover, it fitted the realities of the

109. *Pacific Railroad Reports, 1,* Pt. I, p. 26.

110. Humphreys, *Report of the Office of the Pacific Railroad Explorations and Surveys, Nov. 29, 1856,* 34th Cong., 3d Sess., H. R. Exec. Doc. 1 (1856–57), 212.

111. This charge was actually leveled at Davis by Senator Henry Wilson of Massachusetts. See Rowland, *Jefferson Davis Constitutionalist, 3,* 376.

112. Kidwell, *Supplementary Report,* p. 6.

political situation far better than the Texas route, which had no chance of success at all after the surveys focused all the opposition on it. Davis had hitched national and sectional fortunes to the scientific experience of the Topographical Corps, and both he and the Corps were unable to adapt to the exigencies of the moment. The Corps, dominated by a kind of institutional inertia, was unable, when confronted with the evidence, to reappraise its efforts of the previous ten years. Likewise, both Davis and Humphreys were unwilling to revise their opinion between the first and second versions of the railroad report even though they admitted the new-found merits of Whipple's route.

The result was failure. Controversy resumed where it had left off, with little hope of ever producing a transcontinental railroad. Science and politics had had their chance, but the Corps in its professional pride and the Secretary in his sectional prejudice had ignored reality. In the end, though nature had offered the alternatives and science had revealed them, it was still the passions of men that governed their relevance to the course of national progress.

8. THE SAVANTS AND THE SURVEYS

> Roads and canals, by multiplying and facilitating the communications and intercourse between distant regions and multitudes of men, are among the most important means of improvement. But moral, political, intellectual improvement are duties assigned by the Author of Our Existence to social no less than to individual man. . . . Among the first, perhaps the very first instrument for the improvement of the condition of men is knowledge . . .—*John Quincy Adams, 1825*

IF, IN THE PACIFIC RAILROAD SURVEYS, science had served as the instrument of public policy, it was also true that public policy had been the handmaid of science. For, though the members of the Thirty-Second Congress had authorized the surveys for the practical purpose of settling the railroad question, the administrators of the project conceived its objectives in much broader terms. All aspects of trans-Mississippi geography were to be legitimate fields of inquiry. Thus the Democrats, traditionally committed to "wise and frugal government" and strongly opposed to any program such as that of John Quincy Adams, which advocated subsidies for knowledge and education, were nevertheless induced to spend $500,000 for the assembling and printing of a huge scientific compendium which drew, for the first time, the clear outlines of the trans-Mississippi West.

The massive volumes of the *Pacific Railroad Reports* represented the combined efforts of the Topographical Engineers and a sizable contingent of the country's foremost scientists. Not since Napoleon had taken his company of savants into Egypt had the world seen such an assemblage of scientists and technicians marshaled under one banner. And like Napoleon's own learned corps, these scientists, too, were an implement of conquest, with the enemy in this case being the unknown reaches of the western continent. The immense quantity of data collected by these government scientists constituted a plateau from which it was possible at last to view the intricacies of western geography.

As a project, the Pacific surveys were representative of the weaknesses and strengths of the nineteenth-century intellect in America. They suggest some of its limitless curiosity about the mysteries of the natural universe, but they also reveal the inherent superficiality of such a broad approach to science. In their indefatigable cataloguing and their relentless chronicling of experience, the surveys reveal something of the quest for the unique and the marvelous that dominated a nineteenth century dedicated to the picturesque in architecture and the romantic in literature. They are part of the same naive curiosity which made P. T. Barnum's freaks the wonder of the day and which saw in the chambered nautilus or the common snowflake some representation of the mysterious forces of life. Philosophically speaking, every new face was a new image of the Diety. Louis Agassiz described the work of the naturalist as that of classification through which he could approach "the thoughts of the Creator, reading his conceptions, interpreting a system that is his and not ours." [1] Even though, as the 1850's progressed, the scientists became more specialized and further removed from metaphysical speculation, the one great problem confronting them was that of order, or, as most scientists still believed, to "find a meaning in all these plans that will prove them to be the parts of one great conception and the work of one mind." [2] But before they could find this order, the scientists, in contrast to the metaphysicians, had first to seek out the facts of nature in all their variety. This was what Charles Darwin had done when he cruised round the world aboard the *Beagle*. A similar necessity had called Humboldt and Bonpland to the green world of the Amazon Basin. In America it was a time when science was not quite ready for an ultimate generalization because of the sheer abundance of the new data encountered every day. For this reason, an evaluation of the scientific results of the railroad surveys and of all such efforts of the Topographical Corps must involve questions on two levels. What was the extent and significance of the new information they brought back, and what was the nature of the order that they brought to this abundant new data?

One hundred and six scientifically trained men, assisted by a small army of "chainbearers," "rodmen," and part-time soldier-

1. Agassiz, *Methods of Study in Natural History* (above, p. 18, n. 47), p. 64.
2. Ibid., p. 14.

naturalists, took part in the surveys either as field collectors or as museum classifiers.[3] All the operations were under the direct supervision of the Secretary of War and his special assistants, Major Emory, and Captain Humphreys, chief of the newly created Bureau of Western Explorations and Surveys, a section of the Topographical Corps directly responsible to Secretary Davis. The organizational problems were so complex and the correspondence relating to the surveys alone was so large that efficiency demanded the creation of a special staff to handle it, so as not to disturb the normal functioning of the Corps as a whole. Applications for positions on the surveys formed a never-ending stream of mail from scientists, politicians, friends of the president, and even foreign ambassadors. The civilian personnel of each of the parties was usually chosen by the individual expedition commanders after consultation with Davis and Emory. Because the important civilian appointees were scientific men, the Smithsonian Institution, the country's leading scientists, and various learned organizations had an important part in determining who would go on the expeditions. Spencer F. Baird, Assistant Secretary of the Smithsonian Institution, worked dilligently to see that the surveys were supplied with the proper scientific collectors. As might be expected, a number of his own protégés were appointed. It was appropriate, of course, that the national scientific institution be directly represented in such a national project. In addition the Smithsonian Institution supplied detailed advice on collecting techniques and furnished instruments when the army engineers found their own resources inadequate.[4] In accordance with its official policy, however, the Institution limited its activities to advice and technical assistance, leaving Congress to supply necessary funds.

James Hall of Albany and John Torrey of Princeton also wielded considerable influence in the selection of personnel. For example, John Strong Newberry, geologist of the Williamson-Abbott Survey, was a protégé of Hall.[5] Torrey controlled the appointment of

3. It should be made clear that the museum men did their work in the eastern museums and academies; they did not accompany the expeditions into the field.

4. George Brown Goode, *The Smithsonian Institution, 1846–1896* (Wash., 1897), pp. 467–68.

5. Merrill, *First One Hundred Years of American Geology* (above, p. 58, n. 83), p. 363.

nearly all the botanical collectors, and even some of the geologists, including the talented Scotsman James Antisell.[6] Louis Agassiz' friend Jules Marcou also managed to get attached to the Survey as chief geologist to the Whipple expedition.[7] The total effect of this system of advice and recommendation was the creation of a powerful scientific lobby that not only controlled individual appointments but was actually instrumental in persuading Secretary Davis to embark on his ambitious scientific project to the extent that he did. For years there had been a reciprocal arrangement between the officers of the Topographical Corps and the country's leading scientists in which the officers received credit in the scientific world for their findings in the field while the museum men were assured of a constant flow of new specimens, the opportunity of securing employment for their young protégés, and government contracts for evaluating the scientific results of the explorations. Thus within the framework of a simple Jacksonian democracy there existed an unofficial federal patronage of science that was indissolubly linked to the practical development of the country. The Pacific railroad surveys constituted the most remarkable evidence of this arrangement, and the eventual cost of the surveys made it a sticking-point in future Congressional sessions devoted to a consideration of scientific projects. It would be too cynical, perhaps, to suggest as some senators did that the Pacific surveys were an attempt by the scientists and the public printers to derive a profit from the public treasury by leading the government into activity far beyond its normal scope. It is true, nevertheless, that public printing was a time-honored means of political patronage and that in terms of actual results federal contracts were one of the few means of support for scientists in the days before the creation of land-grant colleges.

More important, however, was the fact that the scientific world was able to use the federal government as a means of securing the kinds of data it needed to advance the cause of knowledge. Because they offered advice and determined the choice of field collectors, the scientific arbiters were able to govern the kinds of data collected and the form in which it was organized. In many cases they were even able to determine the choice of problems to

6. Rodgers, *John Torrey* (above, p. 16, n. 38), p. 241.

7. Merrill, p. 315; see pp. 272, 276, for Marcou's earlier work with Agassiz.

be considered. This perhaps partially accounts for the fact that it was an age of classification, in contrast to the post-Civil War era under the domination of John Wesley Powell, which was dedicated to the solution of specific scientific problems of wide-spread implications. While Timothy Conrad and James Hall made their lists of fossils and minerals before the war, in the 1870's and 1880's Powell and Clarence Dutton worked on volcanism and mountain-making, using such case-study examples as the Hawaiian volcanoes and the Uinta Mountains.[8] This distinction in approaches is fundamental because it illustrates the impossibility of a direct comparison of final scientific results between these two periods, in the same way that it is impossible to measure the findings of the untutored mountain men against those of the scientific cartographers of the succeeding "great reconnaissance" period. While scientific knowledge is generally considered cumulative from age to age, there is a sense in which it is not, for it is obvious that each age asks different questions of science, and these very often render the older data irrelevant if not entirely obsolete. The questions asked during the pre-Civil War period in America were to some extent governed by the institutional context in which they arose, for the community of science was closely bound together under the guidance of a few leaders. What interested these leaders generally guided all researchers, whereas in more recent times there exists an infinite number of researchers working independently in universities, foundations, and the laboratories of private companies. That the American scientists of the 1840's and 1850's were so little concerned with inference and so much concerned with pure classification was therefore partly due to its leadership and partly to the aforementioned necessity of determining the total extent of the data before generalizing about it.

Still another aspect of the Pacific surveys was their relation to the whole community of scientists in both Europe and America. The field parties included a sizable number of Europeans, and the survey results in the form of specimens and reports were made

8. Stegner, *Beyond the Hundredth Meridian* (above, p. 20, n. 52), pp. 160–61. Thomas Manning, unpublished history of the United States Geologic Survey. Professor Manning retains the manuscript of this work at Texas Technological College, Lubbock, Texas.

available to the leading scientists of Europe. Many of the outstanding figures in the surveys were Germans. These included Baron F. W. von Egloffstein, a Prussian who executed the awe-inspiring illustrations of Utah landscape that accompanied Beckwith's report and who assisted Edwin Freyhold in the actual drawing of G. K. Warren's master map of the West. Frederick Creuzefeldt was another, a botanist who lost his life in the Gunnison massacre, of which James Schiel, a German geologist on the same expedition, was one of the survivors. Charles Preuss made his last trip into the West as cartographer to the Williamson Survey, and his map of California was his final contribution to the geography of the West before he ended his own life.[9] Most colorful of the German scientists was Heinrich Baldwin Möllhausen, mentioned above.[10] He joined the survey upon the recommendation of Humboldt and Baron Gerolt, the Prussian ambassador.[11] Having had previous experience on the frontier with Duke Paul of Wurttemberg's expedition to the Rocky Mountains in 1851,[12] Möllhausen proved to be a valuable addition to Whipple's party. He made sketches of the topography and drew most of the illustrations for the final report. When he returned to Germany, he published a two-volume account of his western labors that was one of the best travel books of an age devoted to that literary form. In fact, though he made one more trip to America, his first travel book marked the beginning of a literary career in which he drew on his western experiences to write some fifty novels that earned him the well-deserved title of "the German Fenimore Cooper." [13]

Also important among the European scientists was Louis Agassiz' protégé Jules Marcou. One of the famous Neuchatel group of natural scientists, Marcou never quite achieved the status of

9. *Library of Congress Information Bulletin, 13,* No. 44, Nov. 1, 1954.

10. Preston Barba, *Baldwin Möllhausen, the German Cooper* (Phila., 1914), pp. 37–45. See also Baldwin Möllhausen, *Diary of a Journey from the Mississippi to the Coasts of the Pacific with a United States Government Expedition,* trans. Mrs. Percy Sinnett, 2 vols. London, 1858. This diary devotes considerable space to a recounting of Möllhausen's life before joining the Pacific railroad surveys.

11. Barba, p. 46.

12. Ibid., pp. 39–43.

13. Ibid.: note the title of Barba's book.

his better-known colleagues, Agassiz, Guyot, and Lesquereaux.[14] However, on the Pacific railroad surveys he achieved the distinction of being the first professional geologist to run a survey across the whole continent. He also published the first complete geologic map of the West, which made him a controversial figure in American scientific circles for most of his later career. The direct participation of the European scientists in all phases of these western surveys underscores the fact that although the work was essentially a national project in a remote section of the country, it had valuable results which accrued to western culture as a whole. The scientific labors of museum men in Paris and Potsdam, London and Leipzig were directly affected in some measure by data derived as a result of the American experience in settling the far-western frontier.

In the United States the scientific results of the expeditions were made explicit through the publication beween 1855 and 1860 of seventeen volumes of official reports and at least twenty-three papers of importance read before various learned societies and published under their auspices.[15] Many of the significant scientific results of the surveys were published in the transactions of these independent learned societies before they came out as government documents, and the impact of the official reports was therefore perhaps less startling than it might otherwise have been. Nevertheless, because they represented the total achievement of the surveys, the *Pacific Railroad Reports* deserve attention in any attempt to assess the importance of these military-scientific expeditions.

The *Reports* were published in two distinct editions. In 1855, almost a year after the specified deadline, Secretary Davis rendered the preliminary report in three octavo volumes with an extra folio of maps.[16] They consisted of accounts of all the principal

14. Leonard C. Jones, "The Neuchâtel Group and Science in the United States," from the *American Swiss Gazette,* Nov. 18—Dec. 30, 1931.

15. Meisel, *Bibliography,* pp. 189–221, lists all the papers in Society transactions.

16. *Report of the Secretary of War on the Several Pacific Railroad Explorations,* 33d Cong., 1st Sess., H. R. Doc. 129, 1855.

surveys except the Williamson-Abbott Pacific Coast Surveys, the second Stevens survey, and F. W. Lander's independent reconnaissance. There were also the two crucial reports, one by Captain Humphreys, and one by Secretary Davis, which evaluated the results with respect to the possibilities for the railroad. No material of a specifically scientific nature was included in the octavo edition, and there were no illustrations. The maps, for the most part, were hastily compiled, since they were included only to indicate, in general terms, the routes taken by the exploring parties. G. K. Warren's map was a mere sketch bearing an apologetic legend: "This map is a hurried compilation of all the authentic surveys and is designed to exhibit the relations of the different routes to each other. An elaborate map on a scale of 1 : 3,000,000 is being compiled and is in an advanced state." [17]

Late in 1855 the second edition of the *Reports* began to be issued in a series of expensive quarto volumes which eventually were to run to thirteen massive tomes. Two were published in '59, and a final volume in '60. Besides the change in format there was also a marked difference in the railroad data between the first and second editions. Whipple's cost estimates were cut in half, and a more accurate description of the entire route was included. The second Stevens report and Lander's dissenting opinion was also published. Neither the Davis nor the Humphreys evaluations were changed, however.[18]

The thirteen-volume *Report* was a monumental achievement, but the conditions which governed its publication were such as to partially limit its practical utility for working scientists. Its most distinctive feature was the inclusion of all the scientific data collected, accompanied by hundreds of illustrations of Indians, plants, animals, birds, and land forms. One entire volume was devoted to a résumé of previous official western explorations after Lewis and Clark, and it contained a series of twenty-four maps and profiles, plus four maps of older vintage to point up the discoveries of prior decades of topographical exploration. Nevertheless, because of the magnitude of the whole undertaking and the number of separate groups at work on the surveys, the reports were highly disorganized, with results from a single expedition

17. Ibid., map in Vol. 4.
18. Ibid., Vol. 1; cf. *Pacific Railroad Reports, 1*, Pts. I, II.

scattered throughout the various volumes. Separate botanical and geological essays were included with each expedition, while three of the later volumes were devoted to a résumé of zoology. Data from other sources, such as the valuable collection made by Lt. D. N. Couch and Dr. Luis Berlandier in Texas, were included to round out the geographical field.[19] Even the cacti and rock specimens collected as a hobby by Major George H. Thomas (who was to receive the nickname "The Rock of Chickamauga") at Fort Yuma were incorporated into the report.[20] Unfortunately, there was no general index or even a comprehensive table of contents. The pages were not numbered consecutively from the beginning to the end of each volume, and different printers saw fit to add or subtract maps and illustrations at will. As a result, the *Pacific Railroad Reports,* though one of the most impressive publications of the time, were a little like the country they were intended to describe: trackless, forbidding, and often nearly incomprehensible.

The most important achievement of the surveys was Lt. G. K. Warren's map of the trans-Mississippi West. An event comparable in importance to the publication of Lewis and Clark's first reports, Warren's map marked the culmination of six decades of effort to comprehend the outlines of western geography. Though there were still vast areas marked unexplored on its surface and not all of the features were correctly laid down, Warren's map, nevertheless, was a landmark in American cartography. One eminent authority has correctly asserted that "subsequent efforts in the way of maps may properly be deemed merely the filling in of detail." [21]

Published in Volume *11* of the *Reports,* which was issued in 1859, the map actually bears the terminal date of May 1, 1857. It incorporated all of the most trustworthy data up to that year, including the results of the Topographical Engineer expeditions over the preceding fifteen years. Both Emory and Humphreys had supervised Warren in his task, and he also acknowledged the assistance of Edwin Freyhold and F. W. Von Egloffstein, who did the actual drawing.

19. *Pacific Railroad Reports, 8–10,* passim.
20. Ibid., Vol. 8.
21. Wheat, "Mapping the American West," p. 103.

The general map was drawn to a scale of 1 : 3,000,000, which made it a single very large sheet over four feet in both dimensions. Such a scale, as Warren admitted, was more useful for showing an over-all view than it was for indicating detail. In some cases important streams and landmarks had to be exaggerated out of proportion so as to be visible on the map.[22] Warren's method of compilation was also open to some criticism, since he based his views on compromises between what he considered the most trustworthy sources. He recognized, of course, that some sources were more accurate than others, and he analyzed the techniques used and the instruments available to each observer before he made his comparisons. Still, in many instances he was forced to depend on a relatively unreliable source because it was the best available for the particular locale. The map was therefore of uneven accuracy in its portrayal of various topics or localities. Furthermore, when two relatively reliable sources disagreed, Warren followed the risky course of taking an intermediate position. Although great advances had taken place in the technique of celestial observation to determine terrestrial position, the points on Warren's map were therefore still only approximate locations.

It must be said in defense of the map, however, that in most cases errors of this type were inconsequential, and even the most modern determinations of position are not absolute but only exceedingly close approximations. Compared to Warren's map, all previous works of a general nature on the trans-Mississippi West are mere sketches. Then, too, when he could he used the careful observations of the Coast surveys and the Lake surveys, which were to become a model of technical accuracy throughout the world. The detailed work of the United States Land Office surveys was also used when it applied.[23] While it would be wrong to insist that Warren's map was absolutely correct on the western country, it is clear from an analysis of his sources and method as well as from a comparison with previous works that the 1857 map was of fundamental importance in the progress of geographic knowledge in the United States.

Included on the map were all the existing and projected roads,

22. Warren, "Method of Compiling the Map," *11*, 92. See below, Appendix C.

23. Ibid., p. 94.

the forts and towns, and the hunting grounds of the numerous Indian tribes. The last mystery of the Great Basin was solved by Whipple's report, which showed that it did not terminate at the Mojave River, since the Mojave had no connection with the Colorado. Instead, the Basin area continued south to the Gulf of California as if through a vast lagoon at its southern end. In contrast to Emory's general map accompanying the Mexican Boundary Survey *Report,* Warren's map had the Northwest country filled in in greater detail than ever before, though much of the area east of the Three Forks of the Missouri remained unknown. There were other important unexplored areas evident on the map: the Yellowstone country, the area south of the Salmon River, parts of the Snake River Plateau, the Grand Canyon country, and what John Wesley Powell was to call the "Plateau Province," which extended all across southern Utah, northern Arizona, and northwestern New Mexico. Even large sections of the Great Basin and the Llano Estacado were still imperfectly known. All these would not be entirely filled in until the end of the nineteenth century. In addition to his unavoidable omissions, Warren also erred somewhat on his understanding of the Colorado River country above the junction of the Green and Grand. This was principally because he followed Lieutenant Beckwith's map, which contained the original error. Beckwith had mistaken the present-day Gunnison River for the main channel of the Colorado and called it the Grand. The present main channel he indicated as a separate tributary and named it the Blue.

In the post-Civil War jurisdictional conflicts between the Army and John Wesley Powell, the Warren map was often attacked as being either inaccurate or too large in scale to be of value.[24] Powell advocated detailed, quadrant-by-quadrant section maps that would allow all geological data, however minute, to be included.[25] Given his objective, Powell was undoubtedly correct in calling for such maps as a preliminary to his geological survey. But in attacking the Warren map he was on less certain ground, for a knowledge of the whole outline of the West was

24. J. D. Whitney, "Geographical and Geological Surveys," in *Notes Relating to Surveys in the Western Territory of the United States,* 43d Cong., 2d Sess., H. R. Exec. Doc. 109 (1874–75), 61.

25. Stegner, *Beyond the Hundredth Meridian,* pp. 278–79.

a more urgent need in the 1850's than were the small detailed surveys. Indeed, there remains some doubt today whether the United States Geological Survey mapping project will ever complete its topographical survey of the West. To have awaited this event would have been as disappointing and frustrating to western settlement as awaiting the millennium has been to the anxious followers of William Miller. Moreover, with the rapidly changing demands for new minerals, like uranium, much of the earlier Geological Survey work is now as obsolete as Abert's old map of New Mexico. The lesson is clear. Until the cartographic problem could be viewed as a whole, not even an intelligent beginning could have been made toward any meaningful refinement of the data. At long last, Warren's map had made that beginning possible.

Because the fundamental problem confronting the Topographical Engineers was one of geography, Warren's map necessarily was the basic document of the Survey *Reports*. The project had been organized as a series of expeditions which probed the West in isolated reconnaissances along a line of march 2,000 miles long. Any generalization or correlation of results between these parties depended first on the creation of a master map on which could be entered all the details of land forms, plant distribution, geological strata, Indian trails, and mineral deposits. That he was able to provide this base was the measure of Warren's success. But if the cartographers could be said to have succeeded, there were other groups of scientists who found that the rapid linear surveys placed a severe limitation on what they could contribute. Most of them found it difficult to study particular problems in detail, and it was virtually impossible to form an accurate picture of the entire region. The geologists in particular suffered under these conditions. The best ones admitted the limitations, and restricted their generalizations accordingly. James Schiel explicitly declared that since his geological explorations had been confined to the "immediate neighborhood" of the road, he had not "attempted to found unwarrantable generalizations on restricted, and from their very nature, insufficient observations." [26] William P. Blake, though he covered more territory on his several expeditions, also admitted: "In a rapid reconnaissance

26. *Pacific Railroad Reports*, 2, Pt. II, p. 96.

of any region in a direct line, it is impossible to bestow that attention upon the phenomenon presented by the disturbed and metamorphosed rocks which their obscured condition demands."[27] For the geologists of the expeditions, then, the form which the surveys took was far less conducive to spectacular results than it was for the topographers. In this sense the strength of the cartographer's report is the strength of the surveys, and the limitations of the geological report are a measure of their weakness.

Six geologists accompanied the various expeditions. James Schiel went with Gunnison, Jules Marcou with Whipple, William P. Blake with the Williamson surveys, Dr. Thomas Antisell with Parke's, John Strong Newberry with the Williamson-Abbott, and Dr. George Gibbs with Isaac I. Stevens on the 47th parallel expedition. Almost all these men were protégés of some prominent scientist in an eastern citadel of learning. Antisell, who secured his appointment through John Torrey,[28] was an Irish surgeon whose amateur interest in geology had caused him to publish in 1846 a treatise on the geology of Ireland. He had come to America for political reasons in 1848, and while practicing medicine had been informally attached to the staff of a number of colleges and learned institutions. His Pacific railroad report was his first and last geological work in America.[29] George Gibbs was already a resident of Oregon when Captain McClellan secured his services. Afterward, Gibbs became one of the founders of scientific studies in the Far West. Along with Doctors Cooper and Suckley, who were stationed at Forts Vancouver and Steilacoom, Gibbs formed part of a respectable far-western scientific triumverate. His contributions to the Pacific surveys in geology were, however, lamentably slight, and those of his colleague Elwood Evans not much more impressive. W. P. Blake first became known through his work on the Pacific surveys, though he had previously studied with James Hall. In 1865 he became professor of geology at the new University of California, and finished his distinguished career as director of the famous Arizona School of Mines.[30] Newberry had been inspired to take up a scientific career by James Hall, and he gradu-

27. Ibid.
28. Rodgers, *John Torrey*, p. 241.
29. Merrill, *First One Hundred Years*, p. 313.
30. Ibid., p. 314.

ated from Western Reserve College in 1846, took his M.D. in 1848, and studied science abroad until 1851. He practiced medicine in Cleveland, but he worked closely with Hall in the study of geology and paleontology.[31] Newberry became one of the important figures in western geology and also one of the few men to work on both the Topographical Engineer surveys and the later United States Geological Surveys under John Wesley Powell. Schiel and Marcou were, of course, two of the Survey's European representatives previously mentioned.

The primary task of these men was to locate and describe the geological factors that would be relevant to the construction of the railroad—such things as the relative hardness of the rock where tunnels were to be constructed, or the strength of the roadbeds whether through canyons or along the sides of mountains. They were also to report on the economic possibilities of their particular areas. Precious and semiprecious minerals and the various kinds of building stone available were important objects of their search. W. P. Blake made an extensive analysis of the California gold regions, in which he described not only the locations of the gold veins but the actual processes for extracting the gold from the earth. He pointed out that California gold was generally found in four kinds of deposits—alluvial drift, ancient river beds, the alluvial fans from these river beds, and lacrustine deposits, "found in extensive basin-shaped depressions that were once filled with water and clay and volcanic ashes." [32] From his observations of the gold regions Blake agreed with the English geologist Sir Roderick Murchison, explorer of the Ural Mountains, that "gold is, geologically speaking, very modern . . . the rocks being probably impregnated with it after the Miocene period." [33]

Thomas Antisell, who also worked in California, made a study of the famous New Almaden quicksilver mines, which dated back to Spanish times, though in 1855 they were owned and operated by Americans. His most striking observations were not strictly confined to geology, for he described in vivid terms

31. John S. Newberry to James Hall, March 2, 1853, Box 5, James Hall Papers, New York State Museum, Albany, N.Y.

32. *Pacific Railroad Reports, 6,* Pt. II, pp. 276–77.

33. Ibid., p. 279.

the ruthless exploitation of natural and human resources that characterized the New Almaden operation. Though production was doubling every year, and soaring well past one million dollars in export value, the process used to extract the mercury from the ore wasted 155,000 pounds of mercury in 1854 alone.[34] Moreover, the poisonous vapors from the inefficient ore furnaces took such a toll of men that although they were put on short two-week shifts, the symptoms of mercury poisoning appeared daily: first "salivating," then "paralytic trembling," and finally "disease of the brain terminating in insanity."[35] The descriptions by Blake and Antisell thus indicated two aspects of the American commercial occupation of the new western domain.

Though they dutifully made their economic surveys, the geologists were basically interested in theoretical problems. And though the surveys made it difficult to generalize, they did consider an astonishing range of respectable theoretical problems. But perhaps this was not so astonishing, since before their eyes was continually spread a tremendous natural geological laboratory, infinite in variety, fantastic in appearance, and comparatively unmodified by the hand of man. As might be expected, they excelled at describing the land forms and in determining their true nature. In California, Antisell emphasized the fact that four overlapping mountains separated by interior valleys made up the "Coast Range," and he even deplored the use of that single inclusive term (p. 15). On the other hand, his colleague John Strong Newberry insisted that the Coast Range in Oregon and California, like the Sierra Nevadas and Cascades in the interior, formed a single chain.[36]

All the geologists agreed that the Great Basin had been an inland sea. Antisell believed that the Pacific Ocean had washed against the western face of the Wasatch Mountains on the far side of the Basin.[37] Blake examined the Great Basin terrain more closely and noted that much of its surface indicated a series of secondary inundations. He saw the huge alluvial fans and the evidences of ancient beaches: "In view of these facts it becomes

34. Ibid., *7*, Pt. II, p. 36.
35. Ibid., p. 35.
36. Ibid., *6*, Pt. II, p. 57.
37. Ibid., *7*, Pt. II, p. 21.

interesting to inquire how far the present condition of the surface is due to oceanic action or to subsequent aqueous modifications." [38] Then he turned to the Colorado River, still overflowing onto its flood plain, and theorized that the Great Basin as it stood then was perhaps all that was left of a great arm of the sea that had extended north from the vicinity of the Gulf of California. Adopting a uniformitarian position, he reasoned that the very process of piling up silt that characterized the lower Colorado was the final phase of the process that had ultimately sealed off the Great Basin. As final evidence he pointed out for the first time that much of the Basin area was below sea level (p. 232). These questions were not answered by Blake and Antisell. It was left to the United States Geological Survey's Grove Karl Gilbert to reveal finally all the scientific mysteries of the Great Basin, in his classic *Lake Bonneville,* published as an official government monograph in 1890. But something of the complexity of the Basin's geologic history had begun to be understood.

Perhaps the best geologic work by survey men was their description of the forces at work upon the land. No place in the world offered a better opportunity to observe the work of erosion, abrasion, weathering, volcanic action, etc. than did the barren, naked contours of the Basin and Range region. Schiel had observed, "It is a remarkable feature in the character of the country between the Rocky Mountains and the Sierra Nevadas, that whole formations disappear, as it were, before our eyes. The wearing and washing away of mountains takes place here on an immense scale, and is the more easily observed, as no vegetation of any account covers the country, hiding the destruction from the eye." [39]

Again it was Blake who led the way in describing these geological phenomena. He noted first how the prevailing westerly winds were deprived of their moisture by the Sierras before they reached the Basin, thus causing its dryness.[40] Then he made a comprehensive study of the southwestern deserts, noting how the wind caused the sand to pile up around solid objects to form dunes, and how blown sand acted as an abrasive to groove and

38. Ibid., 5, Pt. II, p. 220.
39. Ibid., 2, Pt. II, p. 102.
40. Ibid., 5, Pt. II, p. 221.

polish the rock formations (p. 242). His paper, read before the American Association for the Advancement of Science and entitled "On the Grooving and Polishing of Hard Rocks and Minerals by Dry Sand" (August 1855), was an early recognition of the fact that water and ice were not the only agents of erosion.[41]

The evidences of erosion were everywhere apparent on such a fantastic scale that Antisell was unable to believe that water alone provided the shaping force. He asserted that the great rivers of the west, the Klamath, Columbia, Gila, and Humboldt, followed "a great depression or chasm [formed] across the strike of these ranges by the exertion of volcanic forces acting after they were elevated."[42] Speaking of the Gila specifically, he argued: "It is difficult to imagine that the river could have formed this course for itself by wearing its passage silently for ages through this overflow; it would rather appear as if there was a valley or gap in the flow, produced by some other cause, which the river now occupies" (p. 134). It was with extreme reluctance that Antisell abandoned this catastrophic position to accept the idea that a river could cut laterally across a mountain range; yet by 1855 most geologists in the United States had agreed that this was indeed how river valleys were often formed. When Powell later added a comparison of a log being pushed toward a saw, its chief significance was as a metaphor which helped to explain the truly fantastic erosion of the Grand Canyon country as it had been slowly uplifted. Blake, in his report, mentioned the Grand Canyon as an example of massive erosion: "The course of this river [the Colorado] is marked by one of the most stupendous valleys of erosion known to geologists. . . . What a mine of fossils from different chapters of the world's history must be exposed here in readiness for the student!" But he had to add with disappointment that his knowledge of the Canyon was based on "vague reports" and that it yet remained "to gratify the sight of some future explorer."[43]

Blake's most spectacular observation of erosion was in connection with the familiar Antelope or Boundary buttes which lay on the 100th meridian near the upper Canadian River. "These

41. Merrill, pp. 313–14.
42. *Pacific Railroad Reports, 7,* Pt. II, p. 16.
43. Ibid., *3,* Pt. II, p. 42.

mounds," he wrote, "were originally connected together by a continuation of their horizontal strata so as to form a plain or table-land. By the action of streams and drainage water, deep ravines have been excavated in various directions, and a large part of the plain has been washed away, leaving a remnant of the strata, the flat-topped mounds or columns here and there" (p. 18). He added that the Antelope Hills were probably once part of the Llano Estacado. Still other instances of processes at work shaping the earth were found by Antisell and Newberry. Antisell pointed out what had been equally evident to the Mexican Boundary geologists, namely the volcanic and igneous nature of much of the southwestern country. He noted three distinct volcanic outpourings in the Peloncillo Range alone (p. 153). In California he called attention to the numerous earthquakes (p. 19). Newberry's contribution was his discovery of evidences of glacial action in the Cascade Mountains.[44] If they did nothing else, the railroad expeditions, in making it clear that there were many processes at work all simultaneously shaping the earth's surface, took science a considerable distance past the doctrines of catastrophism.

A final phase of geologic endeavor to which the survey scientists paid attention was the attempt to reconstruct the various time sequences, and to deduce some idea of what each geologic horizon was like. All agreed, from their fossil evidence, that the California Mountains had been recently uplifted. Miocene and Eocene fossils abounded, and Blake reconstructed an entire horizon from fossils of charcoal. "These little fragments," he wrote, "not only show the presence of adjoining dry land covered with vegetation at that distant period, when the whole inhabitable part of California was submerged beneath a tertiary sea, but they, together with the volcanic ashes in which they were entombed, assure us of then existing volcanoes in full activity, sending out streams of lava and producing conflagrations in forests long since passed away."[45] Blake also insisted that the Aztec and Aquarius Mountains of Arizona were older than the Sierra Nevadas.[46] Antisell, in comparing the relative ages of the Coast Range and

44. Ibid., *6*, Pt. II, pp. 41–42.
45. Ibid., *5*, Pt. II, p. 173.
46. Ibid., *3*, Pt. II, p. 59.

the Sierra Nevadas, described the latter range as being uplifted in the Miocene era while the Coast Range was still resting as quiescent strata below the surface of the sea, not to emerge until long afterward toward the close of the Quaternary period.[47] He believed that California was still being uplifted. His most sweeping generalization, perhaps, was his assertion that during the Eocene period the Atlantic and Pacific Oceans were connected (p. 21). Yet in his summary Antisell pointed to a flaw in scientific reasoning that had corrupted many American geologists who were eager to match their fossil findings with the standard stratigraphic columns of Europe. Speaking of California, he declared: "The tertiary deposits are but local and cannot, on that very account, be over any extent of the globe synchronous. Their periods of formation and duration bear a certain relation of time to the strata upon which they lie; but it is not by any means certain that their periods of formation were to any extent contemporary with congeneric beds in distant continents" (p. 30). This was a fundamental truth for American geologists, not yet perfectly understood, though James Hall, in his monumental *Paleontology of New York State,* had recognized the fact and created his own stratigraphic column for purposes of immediate regional comparison.

There arose two international controversies in connection with these western geologic surveys. Both of them involved Jules Marcou, who had served as Whipple's geologist. One had to do with matters of proper procedure. The other concerned a question of geologic history. Of all the western geologists Marcou had had the best chance to make a continuous cross-section observation of the Far West, and much was expected of his final report. However, when his survey work was finished he pleaded ill health, and taking his notes and collections prepared to sail for Paris, where he could continue his work in a "better climate."[48] This infuriated Secretary Davis, who insisted that the notes and collections were the property of the United States and must not leave the country. Marcou was detained and forced to write a hasty sketch of his labors before he was allowed to sail. When he got to Paris, the French geologist gained his revenge. He never

47. Ibid., 7, Pt. II, p. 19.

48. Merrill, pp. 315–16; see also his appendix, pp. 675–81.

contributed a full-length report but used his notes to write a private report which accompanied his first complete geologic map of the United States. Moreover, he distributed the carefully hoarded rock collections piecemeal among his European scientific friends. That he was ever allowed to return to the United States was perhaps only due to the subsequent reaction against Jefferson Davis in the Civil War. Even in his later career Marcou was continually embroiled in conflicts, and he remained critical of the Topographical Engineer surveys to the end.

The other, more theoretical, international controversy arose when Blake's description of the Llano Estacado strata specifically denied the validity of Marcou's earlier description.[49] The French scientist had designated the Llano Estacado as being basically a Triassic formation covered over with Jurassic strata.[50] He based his conclusion on the appearance of a gypsum bed which he compared with similar European and Canadian strata thought to be of the Triassic period (p. 166). There were no fossils which could be used as evidence, so his generalization was all based upon a mineral comparison. As a result of his inference that the Llano Estacado was as old as the Triassic age, Marcou also concluded that the table lands had been uplifted by the intrusion of the Sierra Madre Mountains. Blake's critique was assured, though like Marcou he based his generalizations on far too little evidence ever to be conclusive. He refuted the idea that the Llano Estacado was Triassic or Jurassic, declaring that the gypsum beds were hardly acceptable evidence, since "it is a widely diffused mineral, being found from the upper Tertiary down to the lower Carboniferous" (p. 78). He added emphatically, "The gypsum is by no means to be regarded as laid down at the time of the deposition of the strata, but is a more modern formation, the result of decomposition and recomposition of the materials present in the strata or supplied from without. . . . We also find that the strata which the formation was thought to resemble, the gypseous strata of Windsor, Nova Scotia, and Plaister Cove, are not Triassic, but Carboniferous" (p. 78). Thus he concluded that the Llano formations were of the Cretaceous period, with Carboniferous the most characteristic strata, and moreover that the

49. *Pacific Railroad Surveys, 3,* Pt. II, pp. 25, 59, 81, and passim.
50. Ibid., p. 81. See also Marcou's report, p. 166.

Sierra Madre's uplift had preceded the deposition of the Llano Estacado because there was no evidence of metamorphism or disturbance, only uniform horizontal beds extending out from either side.

Although he had been positive in his attack on Marcou, Blake himself had been as eager as any to generalize about the vast plains area from the two hasty reconnaissances that he had made. Unfortunately, though his contemporaries were unaware of it, Blake was wrong in his critique. Much of the Llano Estacado is made up of Triassic formations, with Cretaceous rocks forming only a partial cover. Moreover, modern geologists would also agree with Marcou that the formation of the Sierra Madres had come after the deposition of the Llano Estacado—that these high plains had been uplifted by the process of mountain-making that took place on their western margin.[51]

The dispute between Blake and Marcou became national when Marcou published his geologic map of the United States, an act of unlimited audacity if not sheer foolhardiness, since he had made only one trip across the continent and but one to Lake Superior. James Hall, the Sage of Albany, was furious, partially because Marcou seemed so evidently trying by unfair means to steal a march on the American scientists.[52] Blake was also outraged, and for similar reasons.[53] Hall expressed the opinion of most American geologists when he coolly termed Marcou a "scientific quack." [54] Blake was given the job of reviewing Marcou's works in the *American Journal of Science,* and he gave the vindictive Frenchman what he thought was an intellectual thrashing for all the American geologists to applaud.[55] Point by

51. W. S. Adkins, "The Mesozoic Systems in Texas," *The Geology of Texas,* University of Texas Bulletin 3282, Vol. 1, Pt. II (Aug. 22, 1932), 239–40, and passim.

52. Merrill, pp. 674–75. At this time Hall was at work on his geological map for the Mexican Boundary Survey and Marcou's map anticipated his map.

53. Blake was making a geologic map, which eventually was published with the *Pacific Railroad Reports.* See Vol. 3.

54. C. C. Parry to Emory, Sandy Hill, Feb. 15, 1854, EP.

55. William P. Blake, "Review of the Geological Map of the United States and British Provinces by Jules Marcou," *American Journal of Science,* 2d ser. 22, 1856.

point, Blake showed that Marcou had invented formations when he had not seen them personally. Marcou had carefully described the Black Hills (the present Laramie Range) as being adjacent to the Wind River Mountains, but, Blake pointed out, Warren's reconnaissances indicated that these mountains didn't exist at all north of the Laramie Fork of the Platte. The Wind River range of Wyoming and the Raton Mountains of New Mexico Marcou had called volcanoes, while Frémont and Abert had shown them to be respectively granite and sedimentary deposits. With evident relish Blake took Marcou to task for the latter's Llano Estacado thesis once again, concluding that Marcou's description resulted in making the Jurassic younger than the Cretaceous. In a tone not far different from Emerson's Phi Beta Kappa oration, he concluded with a reprimand for the "courtly muses" of Europe: "The fact that Mr. Marcou's map is widely circulating in Europe just such American Geology as this has made it the duty of the science of the country to protest against its being accepted abroad, notwithstanding its publication under the sanction of the Geological Society of France."[56] A further ironic conclusion to the affair was rendered by Marcou's publication of still another map[57] while Hall and Blake were quarreling between themselves over their own geologic maps, thus affording periods of relief for the beleaguered Frenchman.[58] Out of all their study and controversy the geologists had produced remarkably little, and two lessons were obvious. First, it was impossible to project anything like a comprehensive geologic map of the West from the data of such brief reconnaissances, and secondly, their audacity notwithstanding, the geologists had come to have a better idea of the immense complexity of the trans-Mississippi geology and the unparalleled opportunities it offered for the further study of the earth in all phases of its development.

The work of the botanists seemed even less spectacular as they continued to add to their immense lists of genera and species. Because of the constant activity of previous years, Torrey and Gray

56. Ibid., p. 388.
57. Merrill, p. 309.
58. See correspondence between Hall and Blake, 1856–57, Boxes 7, 9, James Hall Papers.

found that there were few new species left to discover in the West. Almost single-handed they had classified the botanical results of all the western expeditions up to 1853, and by the time the surveys were ended, most of the basic descriptive classification of American flora had been accomplished. Neither of them seemed interested at this time in problems of causation or distribution. Torrey set the pattern for botanists of the era. A minute, painstaking description of each plant was, for him, the fundamental work to be done. Gray, his younger protégé, followed in this line, though he was one of the first to accept Darwin's hypothesis when it reached this country.[59] In fact, he later became one of Darwin's staunchest defenders against the attacks of conservatives like Louis Agassiz, his friend and colleague at Harvard.[60]

Each of the individual expedition reports included a descriptive catalogue of specimens by Torrey and Gray. On the Stevens Survey, however, most of the work was done by Doctor Thomas Cooper, with Gray classifying only the plants east of the Rocky Mountains. Specialists like Sullivant and Bailey and Engelmann contributed data on their interests—mosses and liverworts, fresh water infusoria, and cactaceae. Only two other problems besides that of classification were considered by any of the survey botanists. One was the Humboldtean thesis of plant distribution according to altitude and locality. That is, they attempted to determine some relationship between the plants and the topography. Altitude, as Humboldt had pointed out, was a prime determinant of the type of plant life. Being a geologist, John Strong Newberry attempted to relate plant growth to the geologic formations while undertaking most of his own botanical analysis along with his geological work. Doctor Cooper of the Stevens Survey achieved a limited kind of generalization by listing the plants on either side of the Cascade Mountains and indicating their differences. But most of the botanical reports were cautious and attempted little more than the cataloguing of specimens collected.

59. W. G. Farlow, "Asa Gray," *Biographical Memoir of the National Academy of Sciences, 3* (1895), 171, 172.

60. Ibid. See also Richard Hofstadter, *Social Darwinism in American Thought* (Phila., 1944), p. 18.

One exception to this procedure was J. M. Bigelow's essay on the distribution of plants along the route traversed by Whipple's survey party. Besides making his report in the form of an essay in plant geography, Bigelow made a study of the forest trees and their distribution. His data was displayed on a curious profile chart, similar to a geological profile except that it was covered with dozens of colored symbols representing kinds of trees instead of rock strata.[61] His report, like Cooper's on the Northern survey, was nothing more than a unique application of the principle laid down by Humboldt many years before.

As compared to the earlier results of Nuttall's exploration, or even of Stansbury's expedition, and certainly as compared with the Mexican Boundary Survey, the botanical results of the Pacific railroad expeditions were unimpressive. In this instance the researchers were too conservative at a time when new questions needed to be asked in order to account for the tremendous variety of specimens lately found in the West. Darwin had asked himself such a question after many years of similar labor as a collector in the field, and he was able to bring a kind of order to the mass of collected data that the world came to know as the theory of evolution. No such questions were asked by Torrey and Gray, and only one of the field scientists even hinted that he was aware that any problem existed. This was John Strong Newberry in whose report on the plant geography of the Williamson-Abbott Survey appeared the only inkling in all the thirteen volumes of the *Railroad Reports* of anything like a theory. "To these causes," wrote Newberry, "which are very appreciable in their action, and which have produced by far the most striking phenomena presented by the vegetation of the west, another should be added, *that which has controlled the radiation of species from their original centers of creation.*"[62] This was as close as the Pacific railroad scientists came to the important scientific question of the age.

Three separate volumes were devoted to the zoological reports of the western surveys. They included four monographs—on mammals, birds, reptiles, and fishes—plus short accounts of the individual expeditions, and numerous illustrations. The individ-

61. *Pacific Railroad Reports, 3.*

62. Ibid., *6,* Pt. III, p. 9. Italics are mine.

ual accounts were included to show which animals were characteristic of each of the routes, while the monographs were intended to be résumés of most of the new zoological data accumulated on all of North America over the past twenty years. They resembled John Torrey's botanical reports in that they were huge classified lists which described all of the new species and indicated the relationship of each animal to the whole order. The accent was strictly on classification, with no thought given to any other kind of generalization.

All four monographs came under the supervision of Spencer F. Baird of the Smithsonian Institution, though he was personally responsible for the writing of only three of them. Charles Girard, his long-time colleague, did the report on fishes, while Baird wrote on the mammals and reptiles and worked with John Cassin and George N. Lawrence in the compilation of the report on birds. Cassin had taken over from Titian Peale and completed the final report on the birds of the Wilkes expedition. He had also done the ornithological reports on the Gilliss expedition to Chile, and Perry's expedition to Japan.[63] Lawrence was a lesser-known New York ornithologist.[64] It was fitting that Baird should do the reports on mammals and birds, not only because he was the best qualified but because as the protégé of Audubon he was compiling the works that were to be the scientific successors to those of the great naturalist.[65]

Baird's reports on the mammals and birds were of monumental importance in the history of American science. They were more than compilations of western phenomena collected on the railroad surveys, since they included notice of all specimens of North American mammals and birds. Baird wrote in his preface that "it soon became evident that none of the published descriptions of the old and standard species were sufficiently minute and detailed to furnish the necessary means of comparison. . . . It became necessary therefore to redescribe as far as they could be procured, all such species, which, in fact, proved finally to be nearly all previously known." [66]

Because of their comprehensive nature, the mammal and bird

63. Robert Henry Welker, *Birds and Men* (Cambridge, 1955), p. 168.
64. Ibid., p. 171.
65. Ibid., p. 92.
66. *Pacific Railroad Reports, 8,* Pt. I, p. xxvi.

reports were published separately as private ventures in 1859 and 1860 respectively, entitled *Mammals of North America* and *Birds of North America.* According to Baird's preface, he actually thought of them as being the successors to Audubon's *Birds of America* and Audubon and Bachman's *Viviparous Quadrupeds of North America.*[67] In making the comparison he pointed out that his report on mammals added seventy new species to that of Audubon and Bachman.[68] A later writer, comparing Baird, Cassin, and Lawrence's *Birds of North America* with the earlier work of Alexander Wilson and John J. Audubon, has found that Wilson described 262 species, Audubon 506, and Baird 738. The same author termed Baird's *General Report* "the most important ornithological work issued by the federal government in the nineteenth century." [69] The naturalist Elliot Coues went even further in his praise: "The appearance of so great a work, from the hands of a most methodical, learned, and sagacious naturalist, aided by two leading ornithologists of America, exerted an influence stronger and more widely felt than that of any of its predecessors, Audubon's and Wilson's not excepted, and marked an epoch in the history of American ornithology. . . . Such a monument of original research is like to remain for an indefinite period a source of inspiration to lesser writers, while its authority as a work of reference will always endure." [70] Some of Coues' enthusiasm for Baird's work can doubtless be explained by his having been Baird's own student; yet his evaluation does not seem much of an exaggeration.

In summary it must be said that the *General Reports* on birds and mammals were particularly important for at least three reasons. They were based on the immense quantity of new data collected by government expeditions which had not been available to earlier scientists. They were based, for the first time, on collections in a local American museum, the Smithsonian, and thus the author was able to make constant studies at first hand instead of accepting second-hand accounts from European museums. Finally, the *General Reports* were the work of men who

67. Ibid., p. xxix.
68. Ibid.
69. Welker, pp. 171, 172.
70. Paul H. Oehser, *Sons of Science* (New York, 1949), pp. 74–75.

had received intensive training in new scientific techniques and who had the benefit of cooperative scholarship, unlike Audubon, who was "an artist with a talent for ornithology," or Wilson and Bachman, who were self-taught and relatively isolated figures. Though they were not spectacular pictorially, the Baird *Reports* undoubtedly marked the emergence of a sophisticated American science dependent on Europe only for the basic techniques of classification which had been formulated in other contexts. The *Reports,* like Warren's map, were typical of the best results of the Pacific railroad surveys in that they were the first general view of their respective fields as they embraced the present continental limits of the United States.

In addition to the data collected by the zoologists and botanists and geologists, there were several other important fields in which significant scientific returns were made. Each of the survey parties made careful observations of the weather along the line of march. This was done with an eye to the feasibility of railroad construction, but the accumulated information, similar to that of the cartographers, represented a comprehensive picture of far-western weather conditions. Taken in conjunction with the monthly meteorological reports of the army surgeons at frontier outposts, this information helped to present a more complete idea of the practical limitations of settlement in the new regions. Insofar as they portrayed, in measurable terms, such realities as the lack of rainfall and the depths of winter snows, the weather reports underscored the problems facing not only the railroad builders but all would-be settlers.

In a more theoretical vein, Lieutenant Whipple's scientific party made observations for the measurement of terrestrial magnetism, just as the Mexican Boundary Survey scientists had done. This kind of information helped to establish and confirm such current theories as Humboldt's aforementioned one of declining magnetic intensity between the poles.

The study of Indians was relatively neglected. Only the Whipple and Stevens expeditions contributed reports on the redmen. The Gunnison debacle, however, provided the most realistic footnote, for it implied that the building of the railroad would not be unattended by dangers from savage attacks. Of the written

Indian reports, Whipple's was more significant than Gibbs' all-too-brief account of the northern Indians. Whipple, assisted by W. W. Turner and Thomas Eubanks, wrote a lengthy essay on the southwestern Indians that he had seen.[71] His essay followed in the tradition of Schoolcraft in that it was really a compendium of all varieties of information concerning the Indians rather than a systematic, definitive study. Like Schoolcraft, he collected all the myths, legends, and accounts of tribal rituals that he could in an attempt to understand the savage mind. The report made a sincere attempt to illustrate the Indians as members of unique cultures with respectable art, ideals, and customs of their own. As such, it was in sharp contrast to the common views of the Indian as wild animal or noble savage that prevailed generally in the United States. Eubanks made color lithograph illustrations of the important Indian artifacts, and Whipple's text described their probable significance. Turner classified and described the twenty-one separate tribal vocabularies that Whipple had compiled. The tribes were divided into six linguistic groups, Algonkin, Pawnee, Shoshonee, Apache, Keres, and Yuma, which provided a means of basic classification still in use today. Turner also claimed credit for having noted the linguistic ties between the Apaches of the Southwest and the Athapascans of Canada, a link that suggested the line of Indian migration over the Continent.[72]

Möllhausen provided the woodcut and lithograph illustrations of the Indians and their habitations. Whipple's text indicates he was dissatisfied with the accuracy of Möllhausen's drawings, which tended to be more stylized than scientific. Navaho warriors, described by Whipple as bright-eyed and enthusiastic, were drawn by the whimsical German artist with eyes half closed and slumped over their tired mounts. The only accuracy in his picture, according to Whipple, was their ever-present Navaho blanket.[73] This illustrates the difficulty that existed for the artist-naturalist who had not quite abandoned his aesthetic instincts when he approached his scientific task.

There was nothing definitive about Whipple's essay, and it

71. *Pacific Railroad Reports, 3,* Pt. III.
72. Ibid., p. 84.
73. Ibid., p. 31.

was really only a collection of useful facts about the tribes encountered, valuable principally for its vocabularies, and because Whipple would include nothing as fact that he had not verified himself. Like most of the information on the Far West frontier, the Indian data belonged in the realm of the exotic. These were new people—the Mojaves with their grass skirts and mud-daubed bodies, the locust-eating Pai-ute from the painted deserts, and the semicivilized cloud-dwellers of Zuñi and Acoma—people who were as curious to Americans of the 1850's as were the nomads of Asia or the wild tribes of Africa, also being revealed for the first time, by European explorers like Paul du Chaillu and David Livingstone.

A final source of knowledge was the series of 147 lithographs that illustrated the volumes of the *Reports*. It was a kind of knowledge that particularly epitomized the half-scientific, half-literary approach to natural history that was so typical of the Humboldtean scientific tradition. First premises founded in semireligious aprioristic assumptions lay always just below the surface of those sublime representations of the western landscape, stretching over the horizon toward infinity.

The magnificent set of lithographs were the work of eleven artists: R. H. Kern, John M. Stanley, F. W. von Egloffstein, H. B. Möllhausen, Lt. Joseph Tidball, Albert H. Campbell, Charles Koppel, W. P. Blake, John Young, Gustave Sohon, and Dr. Thomas Cooper.[74] Some of them were scientists, others were professional artists and veteran frontiersmen. Two, and possibly three, were Germans. Tidball was a lieutenant in the Artillery, Sohon a private in the Infantry. Albert H. Campbell became head of the Interior Department's Pacific wagon-road office and later chief topographical engineer of all the Confederate Armies. John Young still remains a shadowy and imperfectly known figure.

By far the majority of their drawings were landscapes, for the obvious reason that they were meant to illustrate the terrain over which a proposed railroad would have to pass. The accuracy varied from the twisted and exaggerated views by Möllhausen to

74. Taft, *Artists and Illustrators of the Old West* (above, p. 131, n. 61), pp. 255–70. These notes give biographical data on the survey artists that are available nowhere else.

the precisely drawn panoramas by Egloffstein and John Mix Stanley. There was a conflict for most of the artists between the desire to paint the country as realistically as possible and the desire to express the impressions of grandeur and sublimity that the fantastic forms of the new domain inevitably presented. Most of the artists were stunned by the variety and profusion of everything they saw. Mountains were higher, deserts sandier, canyons steeper, streams swifter, and, most of all, the distances more immense and overpowering than any the artists had previously known. F. B. Meek, who sketched the Dakota landscape from a steamer on the Missouri in 1853, recorded this impression as it struck him: "I am taking sketches as we go along, but these views are so vast and the objects generally so distant that the drawing has to be made on a very small scale so that it's very difficult to produce that peculiar mingling and contrast of light and shade so pleasing to the eye when we look upon the landscape itself."[75] If they were to have significance for the *Railroad Reports,* the drawings had to be based on a new sense of scale adapted to the vast distances over which the exploring parties marched on their way to the Pacific. A sense of form is therefore apparent in many of the drawings based upon devices which were perhaps familiar but which when employed in these landscape drawings made them almost a distinctive genre. Space was all-important, but so was accuracy, and in the expression of the former only the props afforded by nature could be used, plus points of view from the tops of mountain eminences, and the use of figures and buildings to give a sense of scale. Horizontal lines of valleys, mountain ridges, skylines, oceans, inland seas, desert floors, terraces, monoclines, and massive ragged escarpments were juxtaposed in layers across the paper to indicate distance and space. One of Stanley's best executed drawings showed a huge herd of buffalo stretching for miles and miles over the rolling Dakota landscape. It was one of the best scenes of a buffalo herd ever done, and the animals and rolling contours were used to indicate scale and distance. Other Stanley drawings showed rock strata in horizontal bands with so much detail that they could serve as geologic illustrations.

75. F. B. Meek to James Hall, Missouri River, June 2, 1853, Box 5, James Hall Papers.

The best landscape work was done by Von Egloffstein, whose steel engravings of the Beckwith expedition were a perfect exploitation of the tension between geographical accuracy and the "stunned imagination." He showed the jagged cliffs of the Weber Canyon, with the river winding away like the Hudson below West Point. He sketched his party encamped for the night on the Porcupine Terraces, with wave after wave of horizontal terrain stretching off to the white and distant peaks of the Uinta Mountains. The men in the foreground were mere dots on the landscape but they did convey the sense of perspective. Four of his engravings were huge folding panoramas of seventy to one hundred miles of landscape observed from a promontory. These bore legends identifying passes far in the distance, or peaks, like Mount Shasta, just above the horizon. They provided a kind of orderly review, like that of a relief map, of where the exploring party had gone. Even the exact time that the drawing was made is recorded, and the pictures are dovetailed into Beckwith's map by a system of corresponding symbols and directional descriptions. One engraving of Franklin Valley betrays Egloffstein's essentially romantic point of view in dramatic fashion.[76] His drawing, made "on May 24 at 10 A.M. from a spur of the Humboldt Mountains," shows the jagged rocks of the Humboldt chain, then a vast, silent, empty valley with Franklin Lake and the Goshoot Pass in the distance, just below a range of far-off hills and low-hanging clouds. Blacks and whites and grays form a pattern of light and shade; and, above all, the impression of infinite distance is conveyed. But in the foreground reclines a large figure of an Indian, bow and arrow in readiness, dog crouched at his feet —an allegorical nature god looking down over all that empty landscape. Thomas Hart Benton's "fabled god Terminus," which he wished to erect in the Rocky Mountains, could never have had a more faithful portrayal.

Along with the landscapes the artists included scenes with the figures and the structures of civilization. Stanley drew numerous scenes of parleys with the northern Indians, and he also managed to take some of the first daguerreotypes of the Rocky Mountain peoples. His "Camp of the Red River Hunters" was perhaps his most interesting portrayal of a unique northern group. He

76. *Pacific Railroad Reports, II*, 30.

also sketched such outposts of civilization as St. Paul, Fort Vancouver, St. Mary's in the Bitterroot Valley, and Old Fort Walla Walla. Other artists like Blake and Koppel sketched southwestern scenes; Mojaves helping the wagon train cross the Colorado, the mission of San Xavier del Bac, the town of Los Angeles as it looked in 1853, the military post at Benecia. All of these, besides portraying the landscape, provided a kind of historical record. They arrested the frantic motion of Manifest Destiny for a brief moment and caught, as if on a single slide, all of the aspects of far-western settlement in 1853. Nature was overpowering, the sublime reality. The progress of man was as a figure in the foreground, just beginning to turn the tide in favor of the forces of civilization. That was what the pictures showed, and that was what the Pacific railroad surveys were all about.

The *Pacific Railroad Reports* were thus an American encyclopedia of western experience. They were meant to be a résumé of all the information gained by the Topographical Corps and its scientific partners up to 1857. They were a broad view, in every sense of the word a reconnaissance, which means that they were somewhat superficial. All of the strengths and weaknesses of the cosmic approach characteristic of Humboldtean science are evident. They included an immense amount of knowledge, took note of countless phenomena, and brought back specimens that made the Smithsonian one of the world's great museums. They produced a map which made a context in which it was possible for later explorers to record their data. They represented, on an elevated level, the enthusiasm of an age which was just opening out onto the world and its natural mysteries, one in which every known phenomenon was being collected so that civilization could digest and account for them all.

But the basic problem then, became one of creating order out of all that variety. For the federal administrators it was a simple matter to do this. Either the data showed the line feasible for a railroad or it did not. The findings of science had a pragmatic function that was to serve the concrete interests of Manifest Destiny, national defense, and economic exploitation. For the pure scientists, however, the problem was not so simple. The whole report represented a cooperative enterprise that made generalization difficult. There was no Darwin to ruminate over all the data and make the grand generalization. The result was order on a lower level. No attempt had been made to apply the findings to the solution of an ultimate problem. Instead the data was classified, grouped, filed, and pigeonholed for future reference. Later scientists could speculate. The men of the Survey were interested only in seeing, from some sublime scientific vantage point, what they had learned and what they had yet to discover.

PART THREE
1854–1863

9. THE WAGON ROAD PROGRAM

Time has become important to us . . . we want the road and that at once.—*Senator John B. Weller, 1856*

AFTER 1855 the prestige of the Topographical Corps began to wane. In part this was due to the failure of the Pacific railroad project and the suspicion of sectional bias that became attached to the Corps as a result of its official evaluation of the Survey findings. But though the surveys were perhaps the most conspicuous turning point, there were other signs of gradual erosion.

Some of these came from within the War Department itself. As early as December 4, 1854, in his report to the Second Session of the Thirty-Third Congress, Jefferson Davis had written, "Topographical services being included in the functions of the corps of engineers, and by officers of the general staff, it is not deemed expedient to retain a separate organization for the topographical corps." [1] In the summer of 1854 he had appointed Capt. A. A. Humphreys, fourth-ranking captain of the Topographical Corps, to be chief of the newly created Office of Western Explorations and Surveys. Besides administering the railroad surveys, this office assumed charge of all the western exploration projects formerly assigned directly to the Topographical Corps as such. Captain Humphreys was accountable only to the Secretary of War, and thus his office achieved almost a staff corps status, by-passing the Chief of Topographical Engineers.[2] It was a process similar to that by which Colonel Abert had won independence for the Topographical Bureau from the Corps of Engineers between 1834 and 1838. Another evolutionary step was made in the summer of 1855 by the establishment of the Pacific Wagon Road

1. *Annual Report of the Secretary of War,* 33d Cong., 2d Sess., H. R. Exec. Doc. 1 (1854–55), 15.

2. It was not until April 3, 1858, that Colonel Abert began protesting the usurpation of his authority. When he did, Humphreys coolly referred him to the Secretary of War. See Abert to Floyd, April 3, 1858, copy, LS; and Humphreys to Abert, April 2, 1858, LR: TE 77.

Office in San Francisco under Major Hartman Bache of the Corps. This was also by direct order of Secretary Davis, though in this case the Wagon Road Office continued to function as a subordinate bureau of the Topographical Corps.[3]

That Davis had any specific plan behind these moves is not certain. He was interested in reorganizing the Army to make it more effective in its defense of the frontier, and to this end he organized two new cavalry regiments in 1855 and staffed them with the best field officers in the Army, including his old friend Major Emory.[4] An experiment involving the use of camels on the western plains which Davis initiated was also part of his plan for making the Army a more effective frontier force by solving the difficult problem of supply.[5] In his last report to Congress in 1856 Davis advocated a policy of retrenchment that would abandon the scattered frontier outposts and concentrate the forces in larger garrisons on the fringe of civilization, maintaining peace among the Indians by annual cavalry forays into their country. It was the same policy recommended by Col. Stephen Watts Kearny following his reconnaissance of 1845.[6] In this context of Army reorganization it is possible to interpret Davis' suggested abolition of the Topographical Corps as part of a retrenchment in those parts of the Army committed to civilian tasks in favor of an expansion of the actual fighting units. By 1854 it was obvious that the demand for public works in the new territories was becoming so great as to make it extremely difficult to answer the demand with a Corps limited by law to only thirty-six officers. If they were merged with the Engineer Corps perhaps a larger authority would result, or else all civilian projects would be relegated to some other department.

About this time, too, the Corps began to come under severe attack from Western men in Congress. The most decisive of these attacks was made by Senator John B. Weller of California on May 28, 1856. He rose in the Senate and ordered two huge folios,

3. Bache submitted monthly reports to Colonel Abert. For example, see Bache to Abert, Sept. 15, 1856, and Oct. 17, 1856: LR, TE 77.

4. John Kerr and Edward S. Wallace, *The Story of the U. S. Cavalry* (Boston, 1953), pp. 73–78, esp. 75.

5. *Annual Report of the Secretary of War,* 34th Cong., 3d Sess., H. R. Exec. Doc. 1 (1856–57), 22–23.

6. See above, pp. 113–15.

bound in fine leather and stamped with California gold leaf, to be placed before the assembly. "I have," he grandly proclaimed, "a memorial to present to the Senate this morning signed by a much larger number of persons than any petition which has ever before been presented to the Senate. . . . It contains the signatures of *seventy-five thousand freemen* residing in the State of California."[7] Weller's memorial called for the immediate construction of a wagon road between the frontier of Missouri and that of California, following the general route of the old emigrant road through Salt Lake to the Carson Valley Settlement at the base of the Sierra Nevadas. The citizens of California demanded the road, he declared, to facilitate immigration into the state, to aid in its defense, and to open up a postal communication with the rest of the country. Weller submitted a resolution calling for $300,000 to be appropriated for the road. At the same time he also sponsored two further road bills, one for $200,000 to build a Southern wagon road from a point opposite El Paso to Fort Yuma on the California border, and another for $50,000 to survey a line from Fort Ridgely in Minnesota via the South Pass to California. Most important for the Corps of Topographical Engineers, he called for the roads to be constructed under the supervision of the Secretary of the Interior, a new departure in road-building procedure. When pressed for his reasons in ignoring the military, he answered:

> I am willing to leave it [the road construction] to any Department of the Government in preference to the military—not certainly from a want of confidence in the head of that Department . . . but because it will be placed in the hands of topographical engineers and in my judgment, they are not as good road makers as civilians. If any Senator would go to the State which I have the honor to represent on this floor, he would find all the roads made by practical men; they are made by stage contractors, who, instead of taking instruments to ascertain the altitude of mountains take their shovels and spades and go to work and they overcome the difficulties of the mountain, while an engineer, perhaps, is surveying the altitude of a neighboring hill.[8]

7. *Cong. Globe,* 34th Cong., 1st and 2d Sess., *25* (1855–56), 1297–98.
8. Ibid.

Weller's rebuke of the Corps was indicative of a frontier self-assertiveness that conveniently forgot the past services of the Army topographers when there were future stakes to be gained without them. In this case, the great California road was an attempt to secure, at federal expense, the national highway that would be the forerunner of a transcontinental railroad. It was similar in conception to the all-purpose highway and line of protecting garrisons that Benton had called for in 1845 before Congressional debates arose over the more immediate projects for a railroad. Now, after the railroad project had failed, Weller undertook to break the impasse by starting more slowly with a wagon-road program. However, its railroad implications were clear. To assure the success of his project, Weller had proposed a Southern wagon road as well as a central one, and thereby gained the support of the Southwestern senators on a *quid pro quo* basis.[9] Likewise he secured the support of the Northwestern men by including the plan for the Fort Ridgely road. It had to be clear, of course, that these projects were not to be connected with the discredited Southern-oriented Pacific railroad surveys and the suspect Corps of Topographical Engineers. Then, too, there were personal motives involved. A sharp disagreement had arisen between the Minnesota territorial delegate and Lt. James Hervey Simpson of the Topographical Corps over the expenditures for roads in Minnesota, and delegate Henry M. Rice refused to have anything more entrusted to the Corps until Simpson was removed.[10] That there might also have been a better chance for Northern control of the projects under the Department of the Interior is suggested by the fact that Senator Charles Stuart of

9. Ibid., p. 1632; the vote on the Fort Ridgely bill gives indication of the alliance between the Western and Southwestern senators. See also Weller's exchange with Senator A. G. Brown of Mississippi, p. 1632, which gives an idea of the proposed horse trading.

10. Jackson, *Wagon Roads,* p. 61. The structure and many of the facts of this chapter derive from this book on federal wagon-road policy. Having examined Jackson's sources in the National Archives, I concluded that his organization of the subject is not only the proper one but indeed the only one to which these sources legitimately lend themselves. For this reason, the source indicated is in most cases Jackson. It should also be noted, however, that new material has been added here, and the interpretation greatly changed and influenced by Howard R. Lamar, *Dakota Territory 1861–1889,* New Haven, 1956.

Michigan backed Weller on the weak proposition that since the Fort Ridgely road ran through Indian territory the Interior Department could effect its construction more easily.[11] The fact that Senator Stuart and Secretary of the Interior Robert McClelland were both Michigan men, as well as that Senator Cass, also of Michigan, overcame his strict constructionist scruples to speak on behalf of the bill, strongly suggests that if the railroad surveys had been under Southern domination, the new wagon roads were almost certainly marked for Northern control. Weller assured Congress that the Secretary of the Interior would not employ Topographical Officers to build the roads, for "He is a western man and he is a practical man, and will make the best selection for the Territories."[12]

The effect of the shift of Western confidence from the Topographical Corps to the Interior Department would have been to throw the entire roadbuilding administration into a civilian agency where requests would not have to be made under the constricting guise of petitions for national defense. That is, the senators were clearly setting a new precedent that would admit, once and for all, the constitutionality of building roads through the territories purely as aids to the settlement of those territories. Thus they could refute the narrower strict-constructionist view that saw roads in the territories as justified only by the exigencies of national defense. The successful passage of all three bills under these circumstances actually cleared the way for territorial delegates to demand unlimited road construction for their territories. It also opened the way to decentralized control of the road construction by territorial Indian agents and temporary civilian appointees like the explorer-politician from Minnesota, William H. Nobles. Decentralized control meant, of course, a greater degree of control by the political oligarchies out in the territories, the kind of control that Rice attempted to exercise when he secured the extension, in Minnesota, of the St. Louis River Road to the point on the Lake Superior shoreline which was owned by his own syndicate.[13]

The passage of Weller's bills constituted a turning point in the

11. *Cong. Globe* (above, n. 8), p. 1632.
12. Ibid., p. 1631.
13. Jackson, p. 60.

trans-Mississippi operations of the Topographical Engineers, for it represented a vote of no confidence by the Western men. Particularly is this evident in the division of the vote on the Fort Ridgely bill, where the yeas included all of the Northern and most of the Southwestern men, including Sam Houston of Texas, John Slidell of Louisiana, and William Sebastian of Arkansas, while the nays were only the die-hard strict-constructionists of the older South.[14] There had been a series of trades between Westerners, north and south, to facilitate the road building which involved the temporary abandonment of support for the Topographical Corps. The end result was the assignment of the largest road projects to the Interior Department, and the eventual creation of a separate Pacific Wagon Road Office under the Department's jurisdiction. Ironically enough, in 1857 a staunch Southerner, Jacob Thompson of Mississippi, became Secretary of the Interior, and when he established the Pacific Wagon Road Office he selected Albert H. Campbell, another Southerner recommended by Jefferson Davis, John B. Floyd, and Thomas Rusk, to be its chief.[15] Neither the patronage nor the control of operations had remained long in Northern hands. The result was chaos. A continual struggle was waged between the Secretary of the Interior and the road builders and territorial officials out on the frontier for control of the various road-building operations. In the new territories there were fortunes to be made from government contracts and speculation in real estate, if the speculators could secure the location of federal roads through their lands. It was little wonder that the Westerners rarely cooperated with the administration when their hard-won victory over the Topographical Corps had failed to gain them the kind of freedom they wanted.

Paradoxically, though the prestige of the Topographical Corps suffered during the mid-fifties, the demand for its services was never greater. Consequently while most territories wanted control of their own improvement projects, the need for roads was so urgent that they were willing to use the Topographical Engineers to get the building started rather than do nothing while

14. *Cong. Globe* (above, n. 8), p. 1632.
15. Jackson, p. 178.

Congress debated over the proper jurisdiction of the public works. During the decade of 1850–60 Topographical Engineers constructed thirty-four separate roads in the far-western territories at a total expenditure of $1,016,000. An additional $100,000 was spent on experiments in the sinking of artesian wells on the Llano Estacado of Texas and the Jornado del Muerto west of the Rio Grande in New Mexico. Besides this, there were at least five other territorial roads, which did not appear as an explicit territorial expense. Viewed in the aggregate, the road-building and well-drilling activities of the Corps constituted one of the major federal subsidies contributed toward the settlement of the trans-Mississippi frontier. In the individual territories the importance of these public works projects had even greater significance if one considers the basic fact that many of these territories were barren and unpromising geographical areas. Until the widespread discovery of precious metals, most of the territories were by no means prosperous even if they managed to be self-sufficient. Thus they were eager for such federal aid as the post office contracts, the wages paid to the territorial legislators, the gift of public buildings, and even the public printing subsidy.[16] Frontier garrisons and the freighting and sutlers' contracts that went with them were especially welcome, and even as late as the 1870's there is evidence that the territorial settlers encouraged occasional Indian difficulties in order to keep the Army in the field buying supplies.[17] One writer has even gone so far as to term the Mormon War "The Contractor's War," because of its obvious benefits to such frontier entrepreneurs as Russell, Majors, and Waddell.[18] Of all these forms of federal aid, the wagon-road program was perhaps the most significant for the early territorial development. Not only did the military engineers lay out the

16. Earl N. Pomeroy, *The Territories and the United States* (Phila., 1947), passim. Though it deals primarily with the period after 1865, Pomeroy's study does indicate the extent to which the territories were dependent on the various forms of federal aid.

17. Lamar, p. 25.

18. E. Cecil McGavin, *U. S. Soldiers Invade Utah* (Boston, 1937), p. 48. Billington, *The Far Western Frontier* (above, p. 120, n. 29), p. 276, indicates that the war did not ultimately redound to the good of Russell, Majors, and Waddell, since it caused them to overinvest in animals and wagons and thus to suffer great losses when the war suddenly collapsed.

basic lines of communication upon which ultimate economic success depended, especially in a country generally devoid of rivers affording transportation facilities, but by this means they also created the real estate values and decided the location of towns and cities and capitals. They made and unmade political factions, since a territorial delegate's or governor's career often depended on securing road appropriations.[19] Moreover, they were a primary means of attracting new settlers into a territory, and of enabling them to push the frontier far beyond the edge of civilization, into the heart of the Indian country. The existence of a good transportation system or even the promise of one was oftentimes enough to attract the first venture capital into a wilderness area. Thus it could be argued that of all the federal subsidies in that vast government-nurtured frontier West of the Mississippi, the road-building subsidies were the most important, because in effect they made it possible to occupy the region rapidly.

The decade of the 1850's saw the inauguration of military road-building activities in the Territories of Minnesota, New Mexico, Oregon, Washington, Kansas, Nebraska, and Utah. In addition, West Texas also received a share of attention from the Topographical Engineers, though most of the main routes had been laid out prior to that time. By 1850 California no longer needed the services of the roadbuilders, as the people of the mining towns and the mail contractors had undertaken to lay out their own trails over the Sierras and along the interior valleys.[20] The Golden State, however, was still dependent on federal action in the territories adjacent to it for its most vital need, a connection with the rest of the country. This was why some 75,000 Californians had shown enough interest to sign Weller's memorial calling for the transcontinental wagon road. It also explained why the news of the imminent coming of the road caused such a frenzied competition between various communities on either side of the Sierra Nevadas, from Sacramento to Carson City. Thus in some measure all of the provinces west of the Mississippi had a stake in the Army wagon roads, to a greater degree, perhaps, than they had in the railroads.

19. Jackson, pp. 64–65.

20. Chester Lee White, "Surmounting the Sierras: The Campaign for a Wagon Road," *California Historical Society Quarterly*, 7 (1928), 3–19.

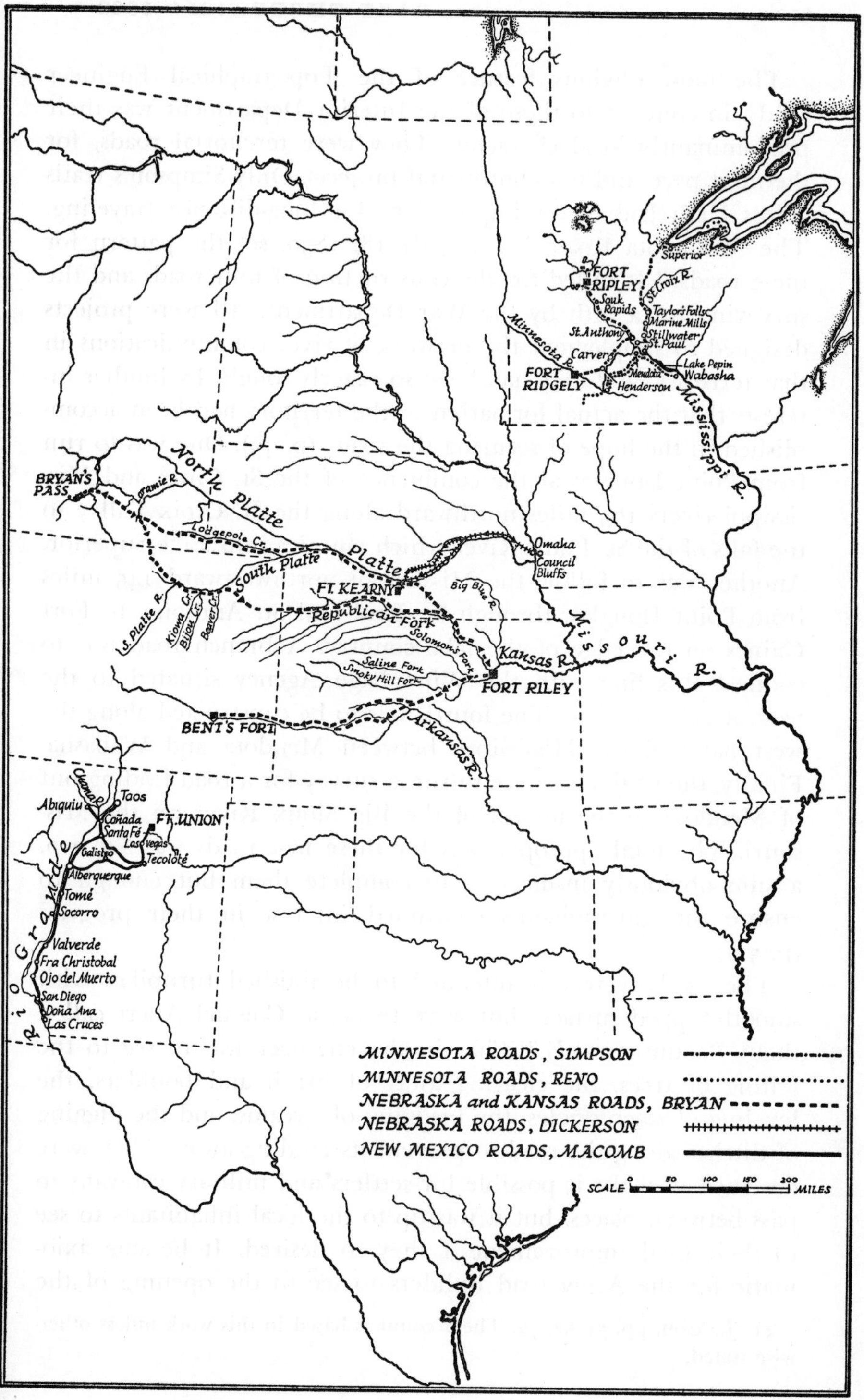

FORT RIPLEY
Superior
St. Croix R.
Souk Rapids
Taylor's Falls
Marine Mills
St. Anthony
Stillwater
St. Paul
Minnesota R.
Carver
FORT RIDGELY
Mendota
Henderson
Lake Pepin
Wabasha
Mississippi R.
North Platte
BRYAN'S PASS
Laramie R.
Lodgepole Cr.
South Platte
Platte
Omaha
Council Bluffs
FT. KEARNY
Big Blue R.
Republican Fork
S. Platte R.
Kiowa Cr.
Bijou Cr.
Beaver Cr.
Solomon's Fork
Saline Fork
Smoky Hill Fork
Kansas R.
Missouri R.
FORT RILEY
BENT'S FORT
Arkansas R.
Chama R.
Taos
Abiquiu
Cañada
Santa Fé
FT. UNION
Las Vegas
Galisteo
Tecoloté
Alberquerque
Tomé
Socorro
Rio Grande
Valverde
Fra Christobal
Ojo del Muerto
San Diego
Doña Ana
Las Cruces
MINNESOTA ROADS, SIMPSON
MINNESOTA ROADS, RENO
NEBRASKA and KANSAS ROADS, BRYAN
NEBRASKA ROADS, DICKERSON
NEW MEXICO ROADS, MACOMB
SCALE 0 50 100 150 200 MILES

MAP 11

The most obvious feature of the Topographical Engineer roads, in contrast to those of the Interior Department was their predominantly local character. They were territorial roads, for the most part, and not continental projects. Only Simpson's trails across Utah had direct implications for long-distance traveling. The Minnesota Road Act of July 18, 1850, set the pattern for these roads.[21] It called for the construction of four roads and the surveying for a fifth by the War Department. All were projects designed to supplement the network of river communications in that territory, and they had been so eagerly sought by lumber interests that the actual formation of the territory had been accomplished in the hope of securing the roads (p. 49). One was to run from Point Douglas at the confluence of the St. Croix and Mississippi rivers 175 miles northward along the St. Croix Valley to the falls of the St. Louis River which empties into Lake Superior. Another was to follow the Mississippi northwestward 145 miles from Point Douglas, through St. Paul and St. Anthony, to Fort Gaines on the edge of the lake country. A branch road was to connect this line with the Winnebago Agency situated to the west at Long Prairie. The fourth was to be constructed along the west bank of the Mississippi between Mendota and Wabasha. Finally, the engineers were to run a survey for a road leading out of Mendota to the mouth of the Big Sioux River on the Missouri. The total appropriation for these first roads was $40,000, a sum obviously insufficient to complete them but enough to ensure the government's continued interest in their progress (p. 51).

The roads were not intended to be finished turnpikes with smooth-topped surfaces but were to be, as Colonel Abert called them, "country roads." That is, the engineer was to see to the felling of trees, the clearing away of brush and boulders, the leveling of steep grades, the bridging of streams, and the digging of ditches along the road to prevent its eroding away. They were designed to make it possible for settlers and military caravans to pass between places, but it was up to the local inhabitants to see to their final improvement if they so desired. It became axiomatic for the Army road builders to see to the opening of the

21. Jackson, pp. 51–52, 72. The account is based in this work unless otherwise stated.

trail over the whole distance first, and then to use what was left of the appropriation to improve the more difficult stretches. By 1855 Jefferson Davis was sending explicit orders to this effect to each engineer assigned to a federal project (p. 73).

Because of a shortage of officers, Colonel Abert assigned a civilian, John S. Potter, to begin work on the Minnesota roads. His work was in the nature of a preliminary reconnaissance of the various lines, but the people of the territory were impatient to begin operations, and in 1851 Lt. James Hervey Simpson was transferred from New Mexico to Minnesota with orders to take charge of the entire project (p. 53). Between 1851 and 1853 Simpson completed the surveys and projected all of the roads on his maps. He also computed an accurate cost estimate for the construction of the roads, which the territorial delegate, Henry H. Sibley, repeatedly submitted to the various sessions of Congress, but to no avail until January 7, 1853, when President Fillmore finally signed a new appropriation for $45,000 (p. 56). Meanwhile, Simpson had to contend with local disputes among the territorial residents as to exactly where the roads should be built. Since vital economic stakes were involved, it was natural that he found it impossible to please all groups. The result was that he was constantly called to work first on one road then on another, or to survey various additional routes in consideration of the claims of the disputing parties.

In addition, he became involved in territorial politics by taking sides against the Democratic party machine and its leader, Henry M. Rice (pp. 56–57). Rice and the Democratic Party were aligned against the older American Fur Company interests represented by Sibley, and when Simpson publicly defended Sibley, he had stepped so far into the local political arena that his usefulness to the territory was virtually ended. It was this dispute between Simpson and Rice that had national implications for the Topographical Corps in 1856. The enmity was not only political between Rice and Simpson, it was also personal; and Rice did everything he could to undermine the Lieutenant, even recommending the appointment of his brother-in-law, Charles L. Emerson, as his replacement. When Rice became territorial delegate, he was able to maneuver in Washington, and while Weller was launching his Congressional attack on the Corps he approached the Topographical Bureau informally, proposing the substitution of Lt. George Thom for Simpson.[22]

In 1853 work was begun on another road along the Minnesota River between St. Peter and St. Paul by Capt. Jesse L. Reno. In 1854 Rice was responsible for getting Congress to extend the St. Louis River road past the falls to the mouth of the river at Lake Superior, where he owned a stretch of land. When it was discovered that a railroad speculating group was behind this proposal, it became obvious that Rice was using his delegate's office for personal profit.[23] It is characteristic of territorial politics that Rice was able to weather the storm of public indignation, and in a counterattack to bring about a jury investigation of Simpson on charges of misappropriation of funds (p. 61). Though the Topographer was easily acquitted, Rice had succeeded in extricating himself from his own difficulties.

In 1854–55 he was able to secure for Minnesota, largely on the basis of Topographical Bureau recommendation, $126,000 in additional road-building appropriations, part of which he caused to be expended by the Commissioner of Indian Affairs on roads in the Chippewa Indian Reservation around Lake Mille Lac. Another road was begun between St. Anthony Falls on the Mississippi and the newly established Fort Ridgely on the Minnesota River, soon to become the starting point for a transcontinental road to South Pass. Still another appropriation of $10,000 was set aside for timber cutting on a new road to the prosperous settlements on the Red River of the North. With the added appropriations, Simpson was able to push the original roads toward completion despite constant interference by local settlers who refused to grant right of way to the road in strategic places, or who demanded that new trails be cut in their neighborhood. Meanwhile, though the Topographical Bureau was responsible for urging further appropriations for the Territory and its suggestions were adopted, the territorial delegate nevertheless claimed the credit, belittling the engineers in order to enhance his own political prestige at home (p. 65). Simpson's experience was thus indicative of the difficulties faced by the federal government in attempting to administer honestly its subsidies to the frontier. So

22. George Thom to Emory, St. Paul, July 26, 1856, EP.

23. Jackson, p. 60.

strong was the settler's desire to gain full control of the dispensation of free government aid that even a well-organized and firmly entrenched agency like the Corps of Topographical Engineers not only was obstructed in its efforts but actually had its very existence threatened.

The Minnesota road-building episode thus hit directly at the fundamental weakness of a democracy—if the people control the government absolutely, what is to prevent that faction which seems to offer them the biggest or the most immediate economic dividend from gaining control? The settlers backed delegate Rice even though his integrity was questionable and though it was apparent he was out for personal gain. Eventually Washington responded, and Capt. George Thom was sent to replace Captain Simpson, in May of 1856. If it was true that he had not built the roads as fast as a private company might have built them, it was also true that as a public officer, he had been forced to respond to any and all conflicting demands.

By 1856 Minnesota, with statehood imminent and the certain termination of federal aid in sight, stepped up its demands for new road appropriations. Delegate Rice's demands were backed by Thom, who estimated that at least $100,000 more was needed to finish all the work that had been started (p. 68). But Congress saw fit to grant only $39,000 as a final appropriation in 1857. The following year Thom was recalled and Captain Howard Stansbury was sent to Minnesota to finish what construction he could with the money available. No further aid was forthcoming, and by June 1861 the office was officially ordered closed. In all, the War Department had expended $312,500 on the roads in Minnesota out of a total federal appropriation of $467,500. The basic transportation network of Minnesota was at least well started, and its future development would thenceforth depend on local initiative.

The Minnesota experience was repeated, with variations due to local geographical conditions, in both Oregon and Washington territories. There was a total of $190,000 appropriated for Army road-building in Oregon during the 1850's, including an initial $20,000 for a road between Fort Steilacoom and Fort Walla Walla, which after 1853 became part of Washington Territory.

In securing the initial Oregon appropriation, delegate Joseph Lane depended on the Minnesota precedent (p. 72). Twenty thousand dollars were granted to cover the cost of the Steilacoom road and an additional road from Camp Stuart in the Rogue River Valley to Myrtle Creek, a tributary of the Umpqua River. In addition, Lane soon secured an appropriation of $20,000 for the continuation of the Myrtle Creek road northward to Scottsburg on the lower Umpqua. He tied this road in with another bill asking a federal reimbursement for the expense incurred in the Rogue River Indian War of 1853.[24] By implication, the road was clearly justified as a military supply route necessary for purposes of defense against the dangerous tribes of Northern California.

The Lieutenant in charge of the Scottsburg road was not a Topographical Engineer but an infantry officer personally selected by Jefferson Davis from the force at Fort Vancouver.[25] He faced difficulties similar to those in Minnesota when competing groups of settlers demanded that the road pass through their neighborhood. One of the factions was led by the famous Jesse Applegate, who had surveyed an alternate route south from Yoncalla over which the California stagecoach passed.[26] After considerable litigation, the Lieutenant was permitted to begin work on the Scottsburg road, and by 1855 it was completed. The southern part of the road, from Myrtle Creek to Camp Stuart, was used as far as Grant's Pass on Louse River near the Rogue, by the regular California stage that ran between the Willamette Valley and San Francisco (p. 75).

In 1855 Major Hartman Bache set up his Pacific Wagon Road Office in San Francisco and assumed command of all the projects in Washington and Oregon. He despatched Lt. George Horatio Derby into the field to begin surveying operations on a new road between Astoria and Salem.[27] Almost immediately Derby became involved in a dispute among Oregonians as to just where the terminus of the road should be located. Some time elapsed before he was able to get official backing for his decision. In the

24. *Cong. Globe,* 33d Cong., 1st Sess., *28* (1853), 46.
25. Jackson, p. 73.
26. Ibid., pp. 73–74, map for the California stagecoach route.
27. Ibid., p. 75.

early part of August, however, Derby led a small surveying party that cut its way 113 miles through the Oregon timber lands to the Tuliatin Plains west of Portland. With the most difficult part of the survey finished, Derby moved north to Fort Vancouver to begin work on roads in Washington Territory. But his work on the Astoria-Salem road was not properly concluded, for his assistant failed to complete the survey before the advent of the rainy season. Thus when Derby ultimately succeeded in getting a contractor to work on the road, Jefferson Davis, who was said to have a personal dislike of "Squibob" on several counts, refused to accept his contracts.[28] In the spring of 1856, Derby was forced to abrogate the existing road contract and supervise the work personally. His superior, Bache, unaware, perhaps, of any dislike of Derby, protested to Colonel Abert that the Secretary of War had canceled the contracts for reasons "unknown to us on the Pacific Coast" (p. 79). Despite this backing from his commanding officer, Derby was relieved of his duties.

Because of strenuous efforts of obstruction by the Whigs John Letcher of Virginia and James Jones of Tennessee, further aid to Oregon roads was not forthcoming until 1857, when Congress granted $30,000 to finish the Astoria-Salem road (pp. 81–82). Lt. George H. Mendell succeeded Derby on this project, and by the beginning of the rainy season had succeeded in completing all but sixteen miles of it. Still the road was not finished (p. 82). Meanwhile, Colonel Joseph Hooker assumed direct supervision of the Camp Stuart road, and by 1858 it was completed. All of these road projects in the later fifties were carried out under great difficulties because of the high prices and labor shortages occasioned by the Colville and Frazer River gold strikes (pp. 76–77, 83). Fortunately, both Derby and Hooker had experienced these same difficulties before in California, and they were able to keep work parties in the field.

In 1858 and 1859 the work of the Topographical Engineers in Oregon consisted of finishing the projects already brought to near completion. Captain Thom replaced Major Bache, and when he became incapacitated with fever, Lt. Junius B. Wheeler, a former cavalry officer turned Topographical Engineer, was ordered to finish the job. But the Oregon roads were never entirely

28. Ibid., p. 79. See also above, pp. 254–55.

completed, for Wheeler was made an instructor at West Point and the work was allowed to lapse until the Civil War.

A final reconnaissance in the Oregon country was undertaken in 1859 by Capt. Henry D. Wallen of the Fourth Infantry, under the orders of Brig. Gen. William S. Harney, military commander of that department.[29] Its objective was to locate a wagon road from the Dalles of the Columbia River to Camp Floyd, the headquarters of Col. Albert Sidney Johnston's Army of Utah, so that the American troops would have more than one supply line. Assigned to the expedition as Topographical Engineer was Lt. Joseph Dixon, a young Tennesseean just out of West Point. Wallen's expedition ultimately failed to locate a practicable wagon road that was an improvement over the older immigrant trail, but it did manage to explore a country previously unknown to Army cartographers.[30] On the outward journey the command of 204 soldiers and Lewis Scholl, a mountain guide, marched south along the Deschutes River and then turned southeastward, skirting the high desert country of central Oregon until they reached a large lake, which they named Lake Harney. At a point 250 miles out, near the western base of the Blue Mountains, Wallen divided his forces, sending half his men back to the Dalles under a competent lieutenant. From Lake Harney the remaining party turned to the northeast and followed the Malheur River to the site of Old Fort Boise. The guide was sent south along the Owyhee River, which ran parallel to the Snake. Eventually, both groups met, and Captain Wallen led a reduced detachment along Raft Creek and around Salt Lake into Camp Floyd.

The return trip followed the conventional Oregon Trail, and the soldiers rescued a number of emigrant parties who, expecting Forts Hall and Boise to be occupied, had miscalculated their supplies. When he submitted his report, Captain Wallen admitted that he had not found a suitable new route because of the barriers raised by the Blue Mountains between Malheur Lake and Fort Boise. Lieutenant Dixon refused to concede defeat, however, and proposed a new reconnaissance for 1860, southeast-

29. Ibid., pp. 85–88. The account is based on this work unless otherwise stated.

30. See, e.g., the blank space in this area in Warren's "General Map," *Pacific Railroad Reports, 11.*

ward from Lake Harney to the Owyhee. This would have passed through the Steens Mountain spur of the Blue Mountains and then descended into Jordan Valley. Congress approved his idea and granted the appropriation, but the Civil War canceled all future plans. Besides its work of basic exploration, Captain Wallen's expedition had managed to shorten and improve the regular emigrant trail, and it had fulfilled an important function by proving that no feasible alternative to the Oregon Trail existed.

The first significant steps toward the establishment of Washington Territory took place at the Cowlitz Convention of 1851. That assembly sent a memorial to Congress asking for separation from Oregon Territory. O. O. Winther has pointed out that "every paragraph contained in the section of reasons why separation should take place, stresses either geographic isolation or inconvenience in travel." [31] Thus, like Minnesota, a new territory was brought into being for the express purpose of securing government aid for its transportation problems. On March 2, 1853, Congress established the Territory of Washington, and the Oregon delegate, Joseph Lane, acting for the new territory, sponsored a bill for its first road, between Fort Steilacoom and Fort Walla Walla.[32]

When Governor Isaac I. Stevens' northern Pacific railroad survey expedition was organized, Capt. George B. McClellan, commander of the western division, was ordered to see to the building of the Walla Walla—Steilacoom road as part of his duties on the Survey.[33] Though he reached the territory in time to make a survey of the Nachess Pass over which the road was to run, McClellan seemed more interested in linking up with the Stevens party and therefore did nothing about the wagon road. The local settlers, by means of volunteer subscriptions and work parties under the leadership of Edward J. Allen, completed a road over the pass by October 15, 1853.[34]

31. "Inland Transportation and Communication in Washington, 1844–59," *Pacific Northwest Quarterly, 30* (1939), 371–72.

32. Jackson, p. 89.

33. Overmeyer, "McClellan" (above, p. 281, n. 56), p. 12.

34. Jackson, p. 95.

The Thirty-Third Congress made a grant to the territory in February 1855 of $55,000, to be expended on two new roads, one from Fort Vancouver to the Dalles and the other from Fort Vancouver to Fort Steilacoom (p. 96). The construction of these was entrusted to Major Bache's Pacific Wagon Road Office, and he, in turn, sent the whimsical Lieutenant Derby to take personal command of the road construction. Though an assistant began work on these roads, it was not until October that Derby arrived to take personal charge, because of the extraordinary situation that delayed him in Oregon. Derby's first work was on the Dalles road, and most of his effort was concentrated in building a portage road around the Cape Horn Mountains, which blocked the path of a direct roadway. In the face of Indian hostilities, gold rushes, desertions, and torrential downpours Derby kept his force at work until the road was completed. At one point, in order to keep his mutinous men on the job, he had to resort to the technique of withholding the workers' wages and persuading the steamboat captain not to take them downriver.

On the Fort Steilacoom route Derby again ran afoul of local competition over the road location, and the work of his assistant, George Gibbs, a resident scientist of the Territory, was called into serious question. In addition, Derby's plans for the road construction called for building it a section at a time instead of opening it for the entire length as he had been ordered to do by Secretary Davis. The work was halted until these questions could be resolved. Once more, Davis' answer was to remove the unfortunate Derby, much to the disgust of his commanding officer, Major Bache, who again wrote in protest that he was "constrained to endorse the views of Derby and express regret that the Secretary of War had not, before implying a censure of the course of action taken, conferred with gentlemen in Washington relative to the country of the Pacific Northwest" (p. 101). Once again in this small matter it seems that Davis was demonstrating that peculiar rigidity of mind that was to cause the failure of the railroad surveys and eventually to do great harm to the cause of the Southern Confederacy.

When Lt. George H. Mendell took over for Derby in October 1856, he found that winter rains had washed away the revetments

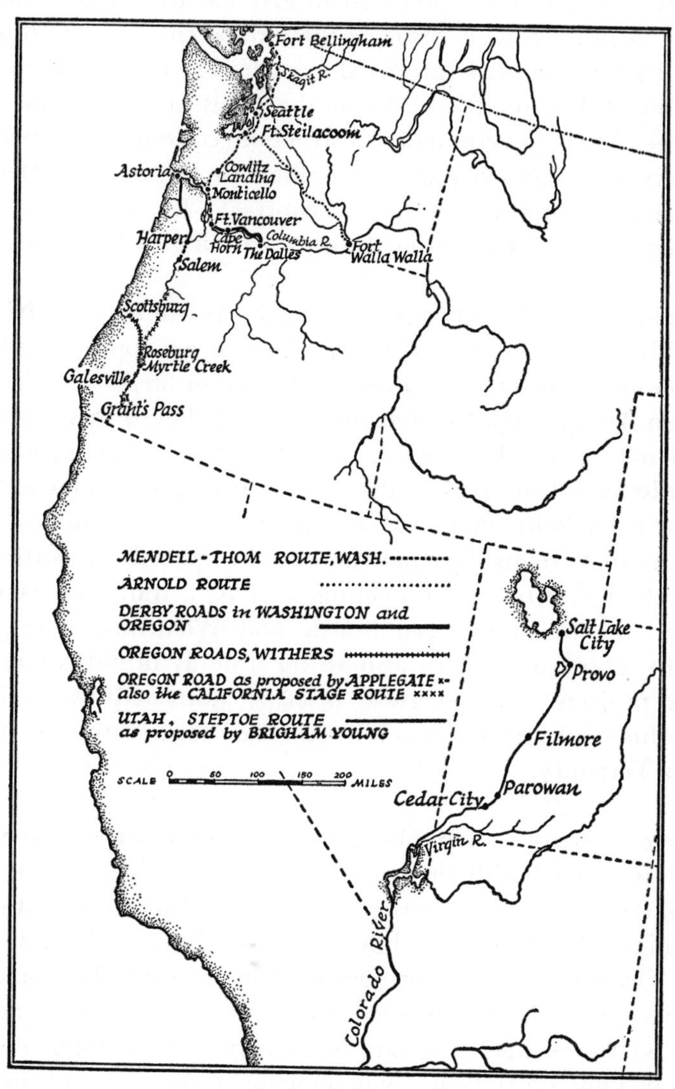

Fort Bellingham
Skagit R.
Seattle
Ft. Steilacoom
Astoria
Cowlitz Landing
Monticello
Ft. Vancouver
Harper
Cape Horn
Columbia R.
The Dalles
Fort Walla Walla
Salem
Scottsburg
Roseburg
Myrtle Creek
Galesville
Grant's Pass
MENDELL-THOM ROUTE, WASH.
ARNOLD ROUTE
DERBY ROADS in WASHINGTON and OREGON
OREGON ROADS, WITHERS
OREGON ROAD as proposed by APPLEGATE
also the CALIFORNIA STAGE ROUTE
UTAH, STEPTOE ROUTE as proposed by BRIGHAM YOUNG
SCALE 0 50 100 150 200 MILES
Salt Lake City
Provo
Filmore
Parowan
Cedar City
Virgin R.
Colorado River

MAP 12

of the portage road and rendered it virtually impassable in winter. It was, however, still an excellent summer road. On the Steilacoom road two factions prepared to give aid to any government project to build a road through their respective neighborhoods. One faction was actually prepared to undertake the road construction itself. Likewise, in each locale there was intense competition over the actual government construction contracts. Ultimately, Secretary Davis resolved all the conflicts by reverting to Derby's original plan for the awarding of contracts. By November 1857 the road was completed from Cowlitz Landing to Steilacoom (p. 102).

In addition to the other projects in the Washington Territory, the Thirty-Fourth Congress had authorized an appropriation of $35,000 for a road around Puget Sound from Steilacoom to Bellingham Bay (p. 103). Lieutenant Mendell believed that this road would not be much traveled, and so ordered construction for short distances from both ends—that is, from Steilacoom to Seattle and from Bellingham Bay to the Whatcom coal mines. The Secretary of War insisted that the road be opened the entire distance, the result being the opening of a pack trail six feet wide through the forest between Seattle and Whatcom. After that, Captain Thom arrived to assume the role as liquidator of the Pacific projects, and Congress, perhaps motivated by sectional bias, refused all further pleas for subsidized construction in Washington Territory.

The construction of public works in the Southwest was more closely connected with the problem of frontier defense than was that in the northern territories. Apaches and Navahoes continued to dominate New Mexico, while the Comanches and Kiowas made West Texas even more forbidding than it normally would be with its tortured, sun-blistered landscape. The physical nature of the Southwest made any large-scale permanent settlement seem unlikely. Only on the narrow floodplains in the valley of the Rio Grande was an agricultural settlement feasible. It was true that as early as 1853 prospectors began to work gold mines on the lower Gila River and in the mountains near Tucson, and that a colony of the choicest adventurers that the frontier could muster was beginning to assemble in the western parts of New Mexico and

Arizona.[35] But among these prospectors, there was, as yet, little demand for government aid or territorial improvement. Most of the pleas for public works came from the older established citizens, or from the military officers themselves, who were having difficulties with the problem of maintaining their isolated garrisons in that unpromising country.[36] Thus the roads constructed were primarily in the interests of defense, but they furnished a network of communication that was vital to civilian commerce.

The first military road appropriations were granted by Congress on July 11, 1854, after an uphill struggle in the House by Representative Philip Phillips of Alabama, who reported the bills.[37] They authorized $20,000 to repair the mail road from Taos to Santa Fe, and $12,000 for the improvement of the trail from that city to Doña Ana near El Paso. These appropriations had been granted on the strength of testimony by the veteran Massachusetts Cavalry leader Col. Edwin Vose Sumner, who declared the roads an absolute military necessity. The Colonel also pointed out that the road to Doña Ana passed over the Jornada del Muerto; hence it would be useless without artesian wells to sustain the travelers, or the cavalry troopers.[38]

Colonel Abert appointed a one-time master of composition at West Point, Capt. Eliakim P. Scammon, to direct the New Mexican road projects.[39] Scammon, who had spent his entire career in civilized surroundings, was reluctant to undertake the duties, and when he did begin operations in the territory he spent $13,000 in one season without commencing work on the roads.[40] There were few controversies between settlers of the sort that impeded progress in other sectors, and Scammon's failure was clearly due to his own incompetence. In 1856 he was cashiered from the

35. Sylvester Mowry, *Arizona and Sonora: The Geography, History, and Resources of the Silver Region of North America* (New York, 1864), pp. 37–39. See also J. Ross Browne, *Adventures in the Apache Country: A Tour through Arizona and Sonora* (New York, 1869), pp. 22, 76, 133–39.

36. *Cong. Globe,* 33d Cong., 1st Sess., *23,* Pt. I (1853–54), 362–63.

37. Ibid.

38. Ibid., p. 563.

39. Jackson, p. 111. Scammon taught French composition to George Horatio Derby at West Point: Stewart, *John Phoenix, Esq.* (above, p. 250, n. 108), pp. 27–28.

40. Jackson, p. 111.

Topographical Corps and the Army because of an irregularity of $350 on his accounts which he was unable to explain.[41] In all the history of the Corps, Scammon was the only officer actually dismissed, though the opportunity and temptation for imitating the acquisitive tactics of the frontiersmen must have been ever present.

In 1855 Congress authorized three more roads in New Mexico and granted a $32,000 appropriation.[42] They were to run from Fort Union to Santa Fe, Albuquerque to Tecolote, and Cañada to Abiquiu. Capt. John Macomb of the Topographical Corps was placed in charge of all the roads in New Mexico, including those previously under Scammon. The Fort Union road was on the main line from Missouri, while that through Cañada and Abiquiu was the beginning of the Old Spanish trail and led into the heart of the Navaho country. Macomb attacked his problems with enthusiasm, but he soon found that most of the appropriation had been wasted by Scammon, and he had to concentrate on strategic sections of the Santa Fe—Taos road, or "Camino Militar," as it was called.[43] Macomb did manage, however, to complete work on the Cañada-Abiquiu road and the Fort Union—Santa Fe road and finish most of the Tecolote-Albuquerque road with the funds allotted him, and also to make some progress on the Doña Ana road. He was able to report to the War Department: "These improvements of the roads in New Mexico are already attracting the favorable notice of the traveling public, and have happened most opportunely to facilitate the very considerable extension of the mail service recently accorded that territory." [44] Before he finished his tour of duty in New Mexico, Macomb was to conduct one more expedition across the contorted Colorado Plateau country, passing along the San Juan River and then turning north almost to the junction of the Green and the Grand.[45] It was an expedition that would place

41. Ibid.

42. Ibid., p. 112.

43. F. F. Cheetham, "El Camino Militar," *New Mexico Historical Review, 15* (1940). 11. See Map 11, above, p. 349.

44. Jackson, p. 116.

45. See John N. Macomb, *Report of the Exploring Expedition from Santa Fe, New Mexico, to the Junction of the Grand and Green Rivers of the Great Colorado of the West in 1859,* Wash., U. S. Engineer Department, 1876.

him among the ranks of important American explorers. In summarizing the achievements of the Topographical Engineers in New Mexico, the foremost student of their road-building activities has declared:

> The routes of the pre-Civil War military roads pointed the way for modern lines of communications. For example, El Camino Militar from Santa Fe to Taos is today a main highway from the New Mexico capital northward into Colorado at Fort Garland. The tracks of the Atchison, Topeka, and Santa Fe Railroad follow in the general route of the old Fort Union military road from Las Vegas across the Sangre de Christo Range into Santa Fe. This railroad's route southward to Albuquerque on down the Rio Grande Valley, across the Jornada del Muerto to El Paso follows the old Doña Ana road.[46]

In West Texas two expeditions took place in 1859–60 which were variations of the kind of surveys conducted by Col. Joseph Johnston and his staff in 1849–50. They were attempts to locate proper supply routes for the isolated Army outposts in the Davis Mountains and the Big Bend country, with the secondary objective of locating a fort site on the Rio Grande near the great Comanche raiding trail. These expeditions were different however. They involved the use of Arabian camels in an experiment to test their possibilities for use as beasts of burden in supplying the frontier garrisons. The first of these surveys, commanded by Lt. William H. Echols of Alabama, took place in the summer of 1859.[47] It was Echols' first independent command. To assist him and lead the escort was Lt. Edward Hartz of the Eighth Infantry. They began at Camp Hudson on the Devil's River near the edge of the Edwards Plateau country. Strung out over the dazzling landscape were twenty-four camels, burdened with packs and water casks weighing up to 500 pounds each. They were tended by special camel drivers, who were unfortunately so inept at loading the beasts that the packs and water casks kept crashing

46. Jackson, p. 120.

47. Ibid., pp. 45–46. See also A. B. Bender, "The Texas Frontier, 1848–61," *Southwestern Historical Quarterly, 38* (1934), 142–46; and Edward L. Hartz, *Diary,* 36th Cong., 1st Sess., Sen. Exec. Doc 2 (1859–60), 424–41.

to the ground. The route led west across the Pecos via San Francisco Springs to Fort Davis, where they were joined by a company of infantry. From this point they improved the rudimentary wagon road leading to Camp Stockton some miles to the east. Out of Camp Stockton, Lieutenant Echols put his exotic cavalry to the test in the Big Bend country before he turned back to Camp Hudson. In his diary of the trip, Lieutenant Hartz reported that the camels had successfully borne their heavy loads every day without causing difficulty, while by contrast the incessant needs of the horses and mules for water rendered them an encumbrance to the command.[48] The chief results of the expedition were to improve the roads between camps Hudson, Davis, and Stockton, and to provide a reconnaissance of the Big Bend region.

The following summer of 1860 Lieutenant Echols took his caravan out again, this time leaving from San Antonio on June 24 with twenty camels, twenty-five pack mules, and an escort of twenty men of the First Infantry commanded by a Lieutenant.[49] At Camp Hudson eleven more men joined the troop as they marched off into the no-man's-land west of the Pecos. Their mission was once again to improve communication and locate a fort site on the Rio Grande. From San Francisco Creek they crossed a *jornada* of 120 miles, during which time they were four days without water. The mules cried piteously and gnawed the canteens, the soldiers slept on their individual water supply, vigilant lest a comrade steal it, and finally the camels began to bellow in hideous fashion, which suggested that even they had reached the limit of endurance. Fortunately, Lieutenant Echols located water just before his command disintegrated in that hostile wasteland.

From Fort Davis they marched directly to Presidio del Norte, a green oasis town on the Rio Grande where American ranches lined the banks. The town itself was a trading post used by the Comanche raiders on their sorties into northern Mexico. After scouting along the Rio Grande for some twenty miles below the Comanche crossing, Echols located an ideal fort site where

48. Hartz, *Diary*, p. 441.

49. William H. Echols, *Report of a Reconnaissance West of Camp Hudson*, 36th Cong., 2d Sess., Sen. Exec. Doc. 1 (1860–61), 36–50. The present account is based on this source, supplemented by Jackson, p. 46, and Bender, pp. 146–48.

the Laguna Lengua emptied into the river forming a small valley. The command then returned to Camp Stockton, improving the existing Indian trails into suitable military roads as they marched along. These road projects in Texas had fewer immediate consequences for settlement than those in other territories because the country was so forbidding that the military outposts would never serve as important nuclei of settlement.[50] But at least these outposts helped to clear away the Indian barrier for those settlers behind on the upper Brazos and Colorado rivers and along the lower Rio Grande. They also helped to check the Indian attacks on those bound across country via the southern route to California.

Still another form of subsidy granted to the arid lands of the Southwest was the $100,000 voted by Congress to pursue experiments in sinking artesian wells on the Llano Estacado and Jornado del Muerto of Texas and New Mexico. The commander of the expedition sent to these inhospitable regions was Capt. John Pope, of whose merits Colonel Abert was still unconvinced. Pope saw important consequences in his experiments: "Fully eight-tenths of the land embraced within the boundaries of New Mexico and the northern and western portions of Texas, are of this desert and unproductive character; and without some means of supplying water by artificial arrangements, a vast region of country equal in extent, to the whole region east of the Mississippi must forever be lost to the government for any useful pur-

50. See *Report of the Secretary of War* (above, n. 5), p. 5, in which the Secretary declared: "The reports of reconnaissances, submitted by the War Department within the last two years, have given such general and detailed accounts of the country between the Mississippi River and the Pacific Ocean as to render here unnecessary its further geographical description. These reports sufficiently show that, with few exceptions, the country lying between the 100th meridian of longitude, and the coast range of mountains overlooking the Pacific Ocean, is not susceptible to cultivation without the aid of artificial means, and that country can probably never be covered by agricultural settlements. A limit has, therefore, been reached beyond which civilization has ceased to follow in the train of advancing military posts, and the service and support of the military establishment is essentially altered. A new post established in the desert region, to which I have referred, does not become the nucleus of a settlement from which, in a short time, the provisions and forage can be drawn . . . but all the heavy articles of subsistence must be procured at a remote market and transported to such frontier posts."

pose whatsoever." He added, "The design of the experiments in artesian well-boring . . . was to obviate, if possible so great a sacrifice, and by furnishing artificial streams such as are familiar from similar experiments in the United States, Europe, and in Algeria, to reclaim all or a large part of this vast region to the uses of man." [51] Captain Pope was thus struggling with aridity, the primary problem of the Southwest, and attempting to apply mechanical ingenuity in conquering it. Long before the windmill would rescue the Great Plains, this earlier generation was hoping that perhaps simple artesian wells might bring prosperity to the southwestern deserts.[52]

On January 5, 1855, Pope received his orders and marched with his command of forty-one laborers, two technical assistants, one geologist (G. G. Shumard), and a military escort onto the Llano Estacado to a point fourteen miles east of the Pecos near the 32nd parallel.[53] They commenced the first boring operation in June 1855, and at the end of three and one-half months the well was 641 feet deep. At 360 feet they had struck pure and clear water which rose 70 feet in the well. Two hundred feet lower they again met water, and upon boring further, a third reservoir of water caved in the entire well, causing the loss of most of their tubing. Pope, however, confidently reported: "Although the practicability of boring artesian wells on this desert was fully tested in the above results which exhibit an abundant and constant supply of water, entirely unaffected by surface rains and easily accessible to pumps . . . I will await further orders." [54]

In November 1855 he shifted operations to a point ten miles from Fort Fillmore, west of the Rio Grande, and in spite of the

51. Pope to Humphreys, June 24, 1859. Report, LR, BES 48.

52. Webb, *The Great Plains* (above, p. 45, n. 64), pp. 337–39, describes and dates the steps in the invention and adaptation of the windmill water-pump for use on the arid plains. Though it was first manufactured in South Coventry, Conn., in 1854 by the Halladay Windmill Co., it was not until the 1870's that Fairbanks, Morse, and Co. began widespread manufacture and distribution throughout the Middle West. Pope's experiment involved the use of a pump powered by a steam engine, which depended on dried mesquite for fuel. For many of the arid regions fuel was as scarce as water, and the steam pump was thus impractical. This explains why the success of Pope's experiment depended on the water overflowing to the surface.

53. Humphreys (above, p. 303, n. 110), pp. 212–16.

54. Pope to Humphreys, Sept. 14, 1855, LR, BES 48.

advice of his geologist began boring again.[55] By February 10 the shaft had been sunk 293 feet with no sign of water.[56] Then the well-diggers moved back to the Pecos and resumed operations five miles east of their test of the previous year, and by April 16 had twenty-five feet of water in the well and no more tubing to probe deeper. When the tubing did arrive, they reached 450 feet before a section collapsed, ruining the well.[57] May 20, 1856, found Pope confidently sinking another shaft. Water was struck at 675 feet. At 830 feet they struck hard sandstone. By 861 feet they ran out of boring rods, being forced to use their ash tent poles before finally abandoning the work. Captain Pope, back in Washington, still reported optimistically, through Captain Humphreys, "there is great probability that a large supply of water overflowing at the surface would have been found . . ." [58]

Pope returned to the field in September 1857 and labored all through that year and the next in a vain attempt to find water.[59] His reports tell of the series of maddening frustrations he encountered month after month in his drilling operations: the winter was unusually severe, the boring apparatus broke down, the pipes sheared off from friction, the cast iron pump broke, the steam boiler filled up with lime secretions, the strata crumbled, and the men grew mutinous. At last, in June 1858, Pope reported: "I am constrained to say after ten months of very severe and unremitted labor that, I fear that, without greater facilities and more extensive preparations than could have been secured under the appropriation . . . it will be impracticable to overcome the mechanical and physical difficulties of the work." [60] Though he hated to admit it, the well-digging experiment had been an unqualified failure. No supply of water of any practicable value was forthcoming. But it was, nevertheless, an admirable failure, for, as he wrote: "Exposed to the extremes of temperature, both in summer and winter on those bleak and unsheltered plains, with no better protection against the weather than the

55. Humphreys (above, n. 53). See also Pope to Humphreys, Doña Ana, Nov. 16, 1855, Report, LR, BES 48.

56. Pope to Humphreys, ibid., Feb. 10, 1856.

57. Humphreys (above, n. 53), p. 214.

58. Ibid., p. 215.

59. See Pope to Humphreys, Reports, 1857–58, LR, BES 48.

60. Pope to Humphreys, June 30, 1858, ibid.

ordinary canvas tent, and frequently reduced to short allowance of bare necessities of subsistence, the men engaged in the work . . . suffered much and endured privation and exposure of the severest character."[61] As for the Captain himself, there was only a dry hole after three long years of disagreeable duty.

Though the formation of the Kansas and Nebraska territories had important implications for the sectional controversy, they also became typical territories in the sense that settlement and the responsibility for their defense was partially undertaken by the federal government. On February 17, 1855, Congress appropriated $50,000 for the improvement of the Old Mormon Trail between Omaha and New Fort Kearney on the Platte River.[62] The primary motive behind this grant was to shorten the supply route to the frontier outposts, but it also aided the progress of settlement. Perhaps, too, it caused a redistribution of wealth from the Fort Leavenworth area, where three to four hundred thousand dollars worth of supply contracts had been let each year to the Omaha and Council Bluffs regions further north on the Mississippi. In March 1855 $50,000 was voted for the construction of a road from Fort Riley to Bridger's Pass through the Medicine Bow Range of the Rocky Mountains.[63] Thus, though they were primarily military supply roads, these constructions would provide easy access by settlers to the farthest reaches of the territory, and at the same time improve the routes to New Mexico and the overland trail of the Rocky Mountains.

The officer appointed to see to the construction of these roads was Lt. F. T. Bryan, who in 1849–50 had helped to survey the cross-country trails in West Texas. He began his survey of the Arkansas River Trail in the spring of 1855, but was delayed until the end of July by a cholera epidemic. His outgoing route was similar to one recommended by Captain Pope in 1849.[64] It followed the north bank of the Kansas River and then ran, via the Pawnee Fork of the Arkansas, to a point on that river above

61. Pope to Humphreys, June 24, 1859, ibid.

62. Jackson, p. 121.

63. Ibid., p. 123.

64. Ibid. See also Pope to Abert, Dec. 2, 1852, LR, TE 77, in which is enclosed Pope to J. S. Phelps, Oct. 28, 1852.

the Cimarron Crossing; thence to its destination at Bent's New Fort in the Big Timbers.[65] The return trip across the plains was made with extreme difficulty along Walnut Creek because of a severe norther which caught the party without firewood. When finally they returned to Fort Riley, Lieutenant Bryan reported the existence of a good wagon trail but recommended that a heavy train be sent over it to mark it more clearly. The major improvements needed were bridges for the three rivers that crossed its path; the Solomon's Fork, the Saline, and the Smokeyhill Fork. When winter descended, Bryan set up his quarters at St. Louis and began work on his maps and reports. The following spring he hired a civilian contractor, James A. Sawyers, to construct the bridges over this road, and the Army reluctantly supplied him with an escort of dragoons to protect him from the hostile Cheyenne Indians. Bryan's assistant, a civilian engineer picturesquely named Coote Lombard, best summed up the effect of the new road: "The bridging of this road has induced settlers to move out at least forty miles beyond the heretofore bounds of civilization, i.e. at and beyond the Saline Bridge. I expect that there will be settlers at the Kaw [Smoky Hill] River Bridge, eighty-five miles west of Fort Riley by next spring—the opening of this road has pushed the settlements beyond where they would be if the road had not been opened." [66]

In June 1856 Bryan left Forty Riley on his expedition to the Rocky Mountains. The expedition included a geologist, a topographer, a barometer expert, several assistants, and two experienced rod carriers.[67] Their course was northwest along the Republican Fork to the Platte River near Fort Kearny. Then they followed the South Platte to Lodgepole Creek, departing from it to follow the Creek into the Medicine Bow Mountains. After searching for several days in the confusing terrain, Bryan failed to locate Bridger's Pass, even with Stansbury's directions.

65. Jackson, p. 124. It should be noticed that in the summer of 1853 William Bent had constructed a new fort near the Big Timbers, thirty-eight miles down the Arkansas River from the more famous Old Fort, which he destroyed with his own hands in August 1849. Lavender, *Bent's Fort* (above, p. 47, n. 66), pp. 315–16, 323–24. See Map 11, p. 349.

66. Quoted in Jackson, p. 126.

67. Ibid., p. 127. See also Bryan to Abert in *Report of the Secretary of War for 1857*, 35th Cong., 1st Sess., H. R. Exec. Doc. 2 (1857–58), 455–520.

Instead, he found an entirely new pass over the mountains which eventually came to be called Bryan's Pass. After traversing this pass, Bryan's party turned back toward Fort Riley, returning by a different route. The return journey followed the Cache-de-la-Poundre and South Platte rivers, and then crossed over to the Republican Fork, which was followed all the way to Fort Riley. In his report Bryan recommended the route taken on the way out as the best, and in 1857 he took a party of laborers and a military escort back over the trail to make it an improved road.[68] In the spring of 1858, however, Bryan made a contract with a local bridge-builder for the construction along that road. When the Secretary of War discovered that the contract offered more money than was left in the appropriation, Bryan was promptly relieved and put on other duty (p. 131). Captain Beckwith, formerly of the Pacific railroad surveys, was sent as his replacement, and he saw to the completion of the road.

In the summer of 1856 Bryan's assistant, Lt. John H. Dickerson, began preliminary work on the Omaha—Fort Kearny road (pp. 132–33). He led a field party out along the Mormon Trail on the north bank of the Platte, and followed part way up the Loup Fork before striking the Platte once again and reaching Fort Kearny. While he was at the Fort, the Lieutenant learned of an alternate route taken by the Mormons, which kept close to the river all the way. Thus on his return survey he was able to shorten the road considerably. Even before he left Omaha, Lieutenant Dickerson was harassed by the conflicting demands of the settlers north and south of the Platte, all of whom insisted that the road should run through their locality. Once again the War Department had to make a decision, and it adhered to the original plan of building north of the river despite the fact that this route necessitated building at least three bridges. When Beckwith replaced Bryan, he also took over supervision of the Dickerson road, and by the end of 1858 the project was completed as far as possible within the appropriation. It was impassable during the spring floods but otherwise was a good road.

After 1858 Congress granted no further appropriations for military roads in either Kansas or Nebraska. The only other projects of importance were Lt. G. K. Warren's series of ex-

68. Jackson, pp. 129–30.

plorations into Dakota Territory and the Interior Department's wagon road built along the Mississippi between the mouths of the Platte and the Niobrara. The Interior Department project was clearly a service to territorial residents and to settlers desirous of pushing out onto the plains toward the Dakotas (p. 238). Lieutenant Warren's expeditions had implications for the scientific understanding of the Far West as well as for the promotion of settlement. For this reason they are considered at greater length in Chapter 11. In Kansas and Nebraska, as in all the other territories, the federal government had been generous in promoting settlement and defending the frontier. Through the Topographical Corps it had expended $175,000 on roads alone.

Even Utah's independent-minded Mormon community was interested in securing government aid. The primary requirements were an improvement of the Mormon Corridor road through Parowan, Cedar City, and Southern Utah to California, and a connection with the road between Fort Bridger and Lodgepole Creek that would make traveling through the canyons of the Wasatch Mountains easier for emigrants and mail stages. In 1854, the Utah delegate, John M. Bernhisel, with the support of Senator Stephen A. Douglas, managed to secure an appropriation for $25,000 to begin improvement on the Cedar City Road.[69] Secretary of War Jefferson Davis assigned the supervision of the road not to a Topographical Engineer but to the experienced Lt. Col. Edward J. Steptoe, who had already been ordered to lead a column of reinforcements to California.[70] Because of a warning from delegate Bernhisel that Steptoe was President Pierce's choice to succeed Brigham Young, the Mormons were wary of his expedition. In addition, Steptoe conducted the inquiry into the circumstances of the Gunnison massacre and its investigation by the Mormons. Steptoe for these various reasons found it impossible to concentrate on actual road work.

The numerous competing groups which besieged him with requests to locate his road to their advantage perhaps indicated the limits of Mormonism's success in fostering an absolutely communitarian spirit. Brigham Young himself applied pressure to

69. Ibid., p. 140. See also *Cong. Globe,* 33d Cong., 1st Sess., *28* (1854), 1341.
70. Ibid., p. 141. See Map 12, p. 359.

persuade Steptoe to expend the entire appropriation between Salt Lake City and Parowan, but the Colonel held to his instructions and refused (p. 143). Ultimately he did exhaust the $25,000 appropriation on improvements along the trail, and the road was opened for travel. There is no evidence, however, that he completed all the improvements necessary to make the road safe for travel. The other road projects of the Utah Territory all came about, paradoxically enough, as a result of the Mormon War and the operations of the Army of Utah. Here Capt. James H. Simpson made his final contributions to the development of far-western communications and the cause of science.

From a consideration of the road-building operations of the Topographical Corps during the 1850's there emerges a picture of the relationship between frontier settlement and the federal government. It indicates to what extent the government had a hand in nurturing and controlling the settlement in that Far West frontier. It also indicates something of the peculiar attitude of the western settler toward the government and its agents in the West. The Corps of Topographical Engineers represented an organized, highly trained, and exceptionally well-intentioned contingent of federal representatives whose official job it was to aid in the defense of the new domain and in the progress of settlement. Considering the obstacles they faced, they performed their task well. Most of the basic roads of the new territories were the product of their surveys, and by laying out these roads they drew the settlers after them into areas previously inaccessible. Where there was a road, there was soon a store and then a freighting service, finally a market for local produce. Outside capital was eventually attracted, for there were fortunes to be made in real estate if not in such things as government freight and mail contracts. Money spent on road construction was multiplied throughout the territory in ever-widening circles at a time when the settlers most needed it. Economically speaking, the time element was an important part of these federal expenditures. They were made when the country itself had not yet begun to produce, and they gave men like the settler-contractors Jesse Applegate and James Leach the capital to get started. It might thus be argued that, basically, the effect of the road-building operation was twofold: it brought in the people to work the land, and it "primed the pump" to get goods and services flowing through the frontier territory.

But where there was money to be made, there was certain to be competition. And among the frontier individualists this took the form of vying for federal improvements in their particular locale, or else attempting by political means to control the expenditure of the federal funds. This was about all a territorial delegate had to offer his constituents, which may perhaps explain the personal character of frontier political feuds. In a situation of this sort, the Corps of Topographical Engineers was caught in the middle. Each officer had to respond to the local demands in some measure lest he and the Corps be censured by the delegate in Congress. But he had also to maintain his professional and personal integrity. Thus much time was consumed by the Topographical Officers in sorting out motives and judging claims made significant by the pressures of current political forces. It was, of course, impossible to satisfy all factions, and though an officer like Simpson or Derby represented the national government, which was supposed to mediate all claims, this was oftentimes scant consolation when a man found himself in a position where he had to make a decision favoring one faction over the other. Thus no matter what happened, delay and dissatisfaction were inevitable. This became important at a time when, in the course of one decade, a whole new domain was being opened up and claimants were increasing yearly. For this reason, perhaps, Jefferson Davis had been unusually far-seeing when he advocated the abolition of the Topographical Corps in 1854. Undoubtedly he believed that it would be better to keep the Army a fighting force and let the Interior Department answer all the supplicants on the frontier—that the demand was increasing far too rapidly for the 36 Topographical Officers thinly distributed over the country to answer the call.

But again, in evaluating their practical efforts, the matter of timing seems especially significant. When the Topographical offices began to close throughout the territories in the late 1850's, the period of dependence was about at an end. Before 1860 the great mineral strikes, like those at the Comstock Lode, Washoe, and Fort Colville, were coming with increasing regularity. From this time on, private capital could afford to build the roads and build them exactly where it wanted without concerning itself with public claims. It made going ahead considerably easier. As one author has said in a later context, after the discovery of exploitable resources, the "starving time" was over.[71] It was thus the contribution of the Corps that it was one of the primary instruments for seeing the earliest western colonists through the "starving time" in the 1850's.

71. Lamar, *Dakota Territory,* p. 94.

10. WAR AND WESTERN EXPLORATION

> To us, however, as to all the civilized world, it was a *terra incognita*, and was viewed with eager interest, both as the scene of our future explorations, and as the possible repository of truth, which we might gather and add to the sum total of human knowledge.—*John Strong Newberry, 1860*

IN 1857 the possibility of a Mormon War caused the attention of the Topographical Corps to be directed toward a region which had been relatively neglected during the Pacific railroad surveys—the Basin and Plateau Province extending over parts of Utah, Colorado, New Mexico, and Arizona. The subsequent Utah campaign and the disastrous operations of the field army under Colonel Albert Sidney Johnston caused the general staff and field commanders to initiate a number of exploring expeditions designed to locate new supply routes into the Great Basin. The sudden end of the rebellion by no means saw the conclusion of this exploring activity, and before the close of the decade a series of careful reconnaissances had been completed that converged in all directions upon the valley of the Great Salt Lake. Though in many cases the reports of these explorations were not published until after the Civil War, the results were nevertheless known and acted upon by the incoming settlers and by enterprising entrepreneurs. Thus in a marked sense, the Mormon War, like the Mexican War, served to draw increased attention to its particular locale, stimulating commercial activity and eventually facilitating settlement, while at the same time adding to the stock of theoretical knowledge.

The Mormon War was the first open wound in the American body politic. When President Buchanan heard of the western uprising, he declared gravely, "This is the first rebellion which has existed in our territories and humanity itself requires that we should put it down in such a manner that it shall be the last." [1] He responded to the crisis by sending a substantial portion

1. Billington, *The Far Western Frontier* (above, p. 120, n. 29), p. 216.

of the Army as a *posse comitatus* to accompany Governor Alfred Cumming to his inauguration as chief executive of the Utah Territory.[2] Beyond the Wasatch Mountains, Brigham Young thundered forth his answer in Churchillian phrases, "There shall not be one building, nor one foot of lumber, nor a stick, nor a tree, nor a particle of grass and hay that will burn, left in the reach of our enemies." [3] He was a man of his word, and the military pattern of the war became one of hit-and-run guerrilla activity, which harassed and crippled the extended supply lines of the advancing American Army.[4] For the American field commanders the first months of the campaign were a sorry disaster, and public opinion, once so eager to chastize the desert saints, began to cool in its enthusiasm. People began to believe that in calling out the Army the president might, perhaps, have made a mistake. Buchanan himself seemed to think so, for he soon named Thomas Leiper Kane, a Philadelphian and confidant of the Mormons, his personal emissary whose duty it was to end the "useless conflict." [5] One of the cooler heads in a hotheaded generation, Kane succeeded in bringing peace. The Mormons laid down their arms and the legionaires took to the hills with their families, while Albert Sidney Johnston led the Army of Utah into the deserted city of Salt Lake. It was said that the chivalrous Virginian Lt. Col. Philip St. George Cooke, who had led the Mormon Battalion in the Mexican War, rode bareheaded through the empty streets as a sign of respect for his old comrades-in-arms.[6]

The Utah campaign had represented a staggering problem for military tacticians and logicians. They were called upon to assemble and march an army a thousand miles into an imperfectly known wilderness country devoid of the means of natural forage and peopled with hostile tribes. There they were to engage an enemy who burned everything before him, took advantage of every topographical feature, and used a strategy of defense in depth of the kind that had brought even Napoleon to his knees.

2. Hubert Howe Bancroft, *History of Utah 1540–1886* (San Francisco, 1889), p. 495; see also p. 500, where Bancroft says that Alfred Cumming was the new governor.

3. Billington, p. 214.

4. Bancroft, pp. 511, 515–17.

5. Ibid., p. 524.

6. Wallace, *The Great Reconnaissance* (above, p. 22, n. 1), p. 216.

It was not surprising that by the first week in November the advance units of the Army of Utah were in perilous straits. Winter was fast approaching, supplies were short, and the Army's supply of beef cattle was daily being run off by the Mormon cavalry under Major Lot Smith. It was only the timely arrival of General Johnston that boosted morale and saved the situation.[7] He ordered the army into winter quarters in the valley of the Green River at two separate encampments, and then set about repairing his broken supply lines. Capt. Randolph Barnes Marcy, the infantryman-explorer who had discovered the sources of the Red River in 1852, was sent south for supplies and cavalry remounts to Fort Massachusetts in the San Luis Valley. His line of march took him over the great interior plateau and the rugged San Juan Mountains, where even the Indians refused to act as guides through the deepening winter snows.[8] The troopers took turns crawling on hands and knees through the ten-foot drifts to break a path for those who followed, and as they approached the last barrier, the Cochetopa Pass, the guide lost his way. Luckily a Mexican mule packer, Manuel Aleno, found the pass and led the party through on a rugged ten-day march to safety in the San Luis Valley. They were ragged and starving, but when they met their advance scouts returning with provisions from the Fort, the weary men went delirious with joy. Marcy remembered, "Some of the men laughed, danced and screamed with delight, while others (and I must confess I was not among the former) cried like children." [9] Ordinarily such an expedition would have been the duty of a Topographical Engineer, but Marcy's long experience in the West had made him the logical choice. His journey demonstrated the necessity of further explorations for supply routes into the Great Basin from the South and Southwest. By the time he arrived at Fort Massachusetts, one such expedition was already well under way far to the south on the Colorado River, and in 1859 Capt. John N. Macomb of the Topographical Corps entered the San Juan country on the first formal reconnaissance of that unknown area.

7. Bancroft, pp. 517–20.

8. Randolph Barnes Marcy, *Thirty Years of Army Life on the Border* (New York, 1866), pp. 224–47.

9. Ibid., p. 243.

As far back as 1852 the federal government had been interested in using the Colorado River as an artery of supply for its interior garrisons, particularly at Fort Yuma. In that year Lieutenant George Horatio Derby had been sent to reconnoiter and map the lower river between the Gila and the Gulf of California.[10] In December 1852 the first commercial steamboat, the *Uncle Sam*—sixty-five feet long with a capacity of thirty-five tons—pulled into the ferry boat landing at Fort Yuma.[11] From that time on, the Colorado Steam Navigation Company bore the responsibility for supplying the garrison at Fort Yuma, and conversely derived its existence almost exclusively from its monopoly of government contracts. In 1856 Alonso Johnson, president of the company, had made overtures to Secretary of War Jefferson Davis, suggesting that the War Department subsidize him in an exploring expedition up the Colorado into the unknown canyon country to determine whether a river supply route into the Great Basin was feasible.[12] Senator John B. Weller, the exponent of letting the civilians rather than the military do the job, backed Johnson in his endeavor.[13] When $75,000 was included in the Army appropriation for 1856–57 to cover western geographical exploration, Johnson naturally assumed that most of it was earmarked for his project.[14] However, Congress delayed approval; and when the Army bill finally passed, Lt. G. K. Warren got first call on the exploration fund for his proposed Dakota Survey.[15] By this time Davis had been succeeded by John B. Floyd as Secretary of War and the Bureau of Western Explorations and Surveys had quite naturally assumed control of the exploration fund. The result was that the proposed Colorado exploring expedition was placed in charge of First Lt. Joseph Christmas Ives of the Topographical Corps instead of the civilian Johnson. When he heard of this,

10. See above, pp. 258–59.

11. Woodward, *Feud on the Colorado* (above, p. 161, n. 34), p. 56.

12. Ibid., pp. 61–62.

13. Ibid., p. 61. For Weller's general attitude see above, pp. 342–45.

14. Ibid., pp. 61–62. There is some doubt as to the appropriation. Woodwards says $70,000. G. K. Warren placed the figure at $75,000: Warren to Humphreys, March 25, 1857, LR, BES 77. The records of BES are divided between R.G. 77 and R.G. 48.

15. Warren to Humphreys, ibid. Warren actually recommended that both the Colorado River and the Nebraska surveys get $25,000 apiece.

the indignant Johnson believed he had been a victim of Army favoritism. Some years later he told a friend that Ives had received the appropriation only because he had married a niece of the Secretary of War.[16] This was quite possibly true in part, for in 1855 Ives, a poor New Haven boy, had married Cora Semmes, belle of Washington, niece of John B. Floyd and cousin to the future Confederate blockade runner Capt. Raphael Semmes.[17] But to attribute Ives' good fortune and Johnson's disappointment to this factor alone seems unjust. It is clear that the Weller-Johnson scheme, like the Weller-Rice-Nobles road-building plan, involved an attempt to derive a private profit from a federal expenditure. The Colorado would be explored, but Johnson's company would realize a handsome return on the operation and obtain, at the same time, an access to the lucrative carrying trade of the Great Basin with no entrepreneurial risk to the Navigation Company. Yet the appropriation had been made under an Army bill for western explorations and surveys for which the government already had a well-functioning bureau. In all honesty Captain Humphreys could hardly depart from precedent and by-pass his own trained men, administering to them a rebuke, as it were, in order to assign the task to a profit-minded civilian who had not yet demonstrated his ability for leading a scientific exploring expedition. Therefore, the only quarrel the frustrated Johnson could have with the government was over the selection of the favored Ives rather than some other Topographical officer.

The selection of Ives as leader of the expedition proved to be a good choice. He was enthusiastic, for as even Johnson pointed out, "he talked of the Colorado expedition as 'the event of his life', destined to make fame for his children." [18] He was experienced, having marched over much of the same country previously in 1853 as assistant to Lieutenant Whipple on his Pacific railroad expedition.[19] And he was well educated, at Yale and West Point, so that he could derive a maximum understanding of the new country traversed, in scientific and literary as well as in practical

16. Woodward, p. 70.
17. Wallace, p. 202.
18. Quoted in Woodward, p. 74.
19. See *Pacific Railroad Reports, 3,* Pt. II, title page.

terms.[20] A comparison of his report with that of Lieutenant White of the Third Artillery, who also explored the river, reveals his true qualifications.[21] It is testimony to Ives' reputation that Baldwin Möllhausen came all the way from Berlin to accompany him.[22]

In October 1857 Ives assembled his exploring party in San Francisco. It included as principal officers John Strong Newberry, the eminent geologist who served as surgeon and naturalist; F. W. von Egloffstein, topographer; P. H. Taylor and C. K. Booker, astronomical and meteorological assistants; and Möllhausen, who was to be the official artist. In addition, A. J. Carroll of Philadelphia came along as engineer and master mechanic to his creation, the U.S.S. *Explorer,* a shallow-draft steamboat which Ives had ordered constructed in Philadelphia and had tested on the Delaware River the previous August.[23] It was to be dismantled into sections and reassembled on the Colorado. While the boat seems a possible extravagance, it may well have been in the nature of insurance against the noncooperation of the disgruntled river boat monopolist Alonzo Johnson.

The party was divided into three detachments for the advance to the Colorado. The first was commanded by Newberry, and it proceeded by coastal steamer to San Diego and then overland by the usual route to Fort Yuma. The second, under Taylor, started eastward from San Pedro and marched via Fort Tejon to Fort Yuma. The third, under Ives' personal direction, embarked on November 1, 1857, aboard the schooner *Monterey* bound for the Gulf of California and the mouth of the Colorado. It must have been a voyage memorable for its discomforts, since the pieces of Ives' steamboat were scattered all over the deck, lashed to piles of lumber and to the mast, leaving only a small open space about the helm and at the bow. Moreover, after the ship rounded Cape San Lucas, a week of "dead calms, of burning tropical days and stifling nights" (p. 29) overtook them, and it was three weeks before they had inched their way up the Gulf to

20. See above, Chap. 7, n. 48.

21. J. L. White's report is reprinted in Woodward, pp. 97–104.

22. Barba, *Baldwin Möllhausen* (above, p. 310, n. 10), p. 52.

23. Ives, *Report* (above, p. 20, n. 51), p. 21. Unless otherwise noted, the following account is based on this work.

Ship Rock, which marked the entrance to the River. They entered the River on November 29 and warped the schooner up the shallows, past the interminable sand flats to a point on the western shore opposite the northern tip of Montague's Island. There they landed near a small shack hoisted up on four-foot piles, which constituted the settlement called Robinson's Landing. It was the only sign of civilized life, and its owner, an eccentric river boat pilot who lived there—taking blackfish, making oil, and searching vainly for the lost treasure of the French filibuster, Count Rousset de Boulbon—had departed upriver leaving only a note fluttering on the door.

Several days were spent in maneuvering the schooner into a precarious landing place where the bulky parts of the steamboat could be unloaded. All around for miles in every direction was a barren plain of mud. The wood for the way and the derrick necessary for assembling the boat had to be dragged for nearly two miles across the sticky mud flats. As Ives observed, "a more unpromising place to build a steamboat can scarcely be imagined" (p. 29). But soon, having overcome the initial difficulties, they settled down to work like so many Robinson Crusoes, sweating, struggling, and at last improvising a miniature shipyard. It was a trench lined with logs sloping down to the river, over which the wooden hoist was erected. Mr. Carroll, the engineer, supervised the assembly operations on the boat itself. The damaged metal plates had to be straightened, then pierced by hand with some sixty holes to hold four reinforcing scantlings which were laid lengthwise along the hull. Finally, with infinite care, the heavy boiler was lowered into place amidships. By the end of December, nearly a month after they landed, the boat was ready for launching. During all this time they had been visited by steamers from upriver, and by increasing numbers of curious and hungry Cocopa Indians. The latter would come trotting over the flats and head straight for the cook's fire, where they would sit watching the cook "with an air of mingled wishfulness and veneration" (p. 31). At other times they were in higher spirits, "laughing and talking over the culinary events of the day," or pointing out the ridiculous habits of the explorers to their grinning squaws (pp. 32, 34).

While they had been engaged in unloading the schooner,

Alonzo Johnson had come downstream from Fort Yuma and offered Ives the use of his boat for $3,500 per month, a sum which Ives termed "beyond the limits of the appropriation." [24] Johnson, doubly disappointed, nevertheless agreed to lend his pilot, Capt. D. C. Robinson, to the Ives expedition, but only "to prevent the government from losing face" (and possibly to assure the continuance of the government supply franchise).[25] Then he departed upriver on a vain dash for glory, declaring to Ives, "Regardless of what you do Sir, I am going upstream on the *General Jessup*. My vessel is large enough to take you and your steamer on board and not notice it. If I find the river navigable I will have it published to the world before you can launch your boat and leave tidewater." [26]

But Ives soon had more important matters to consider than his troubles with Johnson. On December 22 Capt. Cadmus Wilcox had steamed downriver bringing word of the Mormon War.[27] He also brought two letters from Humphreys to Ives which warned him of a possible Mormon exodus southward into Sonora.[28] Humphreys directed him to make a rapid preliminary test of the river's navigability and rush his report to Washington before proceeding with his regular survey. "It is important," the letter read, "that the Department should be made acquainted at the earliest day possible with the practicability of and facilities for sending large bodies of troops from Fort Yuma to Great Salt Lake along the Colorado and Virgin Rivers." [29]

The pilot, Captain Robinson, arrived on December 30, and that night at high tide they launched their craft. The next morning, as the explorers surveyed their handiwork, Ives could not suppress his feelings "of mingled admiration and complacency" (p. 36). Though it looked grand to the builders, to modern eyes the *Explorer* was a homely craft. Painted bright red, it was fifty-four feet long with a stern paddlewheel. The hull was left open, and most of the space was occupied by the bulky steam boiler.

24. Woodward, p. 74. Ives, p. 21.
25. Woodward, p. 76.
26. Ibid.
27. Ives, p. 39.
28. Humphreys to Ives, Nov. 18, 1857, copies, LS, BES 48.
29. Ibid.

At the bow, on a little deck, was a four-pound howitzer, and at the stern a small cabin eight feet by seven feet with a roof which formed an observing deck for the pilot and the scientists.

By the ninth of January the entire party was united at Fort Yuma, which was a rough stockaded encampment built on a gravel spur on the west bank of the river. Across the water was Colorado City—one store, a blacksmith shop, and a tavern. Although it was not an impressive sight, the tiny Yuma settlement was not without its excitements, including mass mutinies, outlaw bands, desertions, Indian dangers, and the kindly ministrations of the saloon proprietress, a former Mexican War camp follower named "The Great Western." It was no wonder that Fort Yuma was known throughout the Army as the Botany Bay of military stations.[30]

While the Ives party had been streaming upriver, Captain Johnson was having his revenge. He persuaded Lt. John Winder, temporary commander of the Yuma garrison, to detail Lt. J. L. White and a squad of soldiers to escort him to the head of navigation somewhere up the river and to scout for possible Mormon activity among the Indians.[31] Among the Johnson party were sixteen civilians, including Pascual, the Yuma chief, and the grizzled old trapper Pauline Weaver, who had scouted for Capt. Philip St. George Cooke's Mormon Battalion in the Mexican War.[32] Johnson's party left on December 31 aboard the *General Jessup* and proceeded upriver as far as El Dorado Canyon on the 35th parallel, thirty-four miles above the Needles, which Johnson proclaimed the limit of navigable waters.[33] On their return they had a chance meeting near the Needles with Lt. Edward Fitzgerald Beale's exotic camel caravan, engaged in tracing a cross-country wagon trail to California. Beale was moved by this meeting: "Here in a wild almost unknown country inhabited only by savages, the great river of the west, hitherto declared unnavigable, had for the first time borne upon its bosom that emblem of

30. See also Sylvester Mowry to Bricknell, Fort Yuma, Calif., Oct. 29, 1855, Mowry Papers, Yale Collection of Western Americana, which gives the most vivid picture of life at Fort Yuma that I have seen.

31. Woodward, pp. 80–81.

32. Ibid., p. 83; see also above, p. 134.

33. Ibid., p. 88.

civilization, a steamer."[34] Having achieved his objective, Johnson steamed triumphantly down toward Fort Yuma. Unfortunately he struck a rock in his haste, sinking the vessel and forcing upon the party the indignity of returning home, as one writer put it, by "Foot and Leggit's Line."[35] Lieutenant White's brief report was forwarded through the usual channels and a copy was deposited in the files of the Bureau of Western Explorations and Surveys.[36] It was with understandable human frailty that Lieutenant Ives neglected to celebrate Captain Johnson's achievement in his own more complete report of the Colorado expedition.

On January 11, 1858, Ives' own party pulled away from the landing at Fort Yuma and headed upriver (p. 45). Their boat ran aground within sight of the jeering garrison at the Fort, but they soon learned that this was only the beginning of their difficulties. Clusters of giggling Indians lined the bank looking on with "unqualified delight" whenever the little steamer stuck on a sand bar. However, their curiosity proved a help as the pilot was able to detect the dangerous places by the knots of Indians gathered on the shore eagerly awaiting a marine disaster. In spite of the difficulties, they pushed ahead, past Purple Hill Pass, Canebrake Canyon, and the Red Gates of the Chocolate Mountains, and into the Great Colorado Valley. Every day brought them into more exotic country, wild and striking in its mixture of dazzling colors and rugged topography. Professor Newberry found a paradise for the study of geology as the river cut into the mountain ranges crossing its path. No American geologist had ever before been afforded such an opportunity for studying the exposed layers of rock strata. Near the head of the Colorado Valley they came upon Monument Mountain, a gigantic mass thrown up against the sky in shades of lilac, pearl gray, pink, and white, with a single blood-red prominence in its midst, visible for miles down the quiet avenue of the river. At the base of these mountains was the Bill Williams Fork, reduced to such a mere

34. Quoted ibid., p. 92.

35. Ibid., p. 93.

36. See LR file, BES 48, for a MS copy of White's report, dated Jan. 30, 1858.

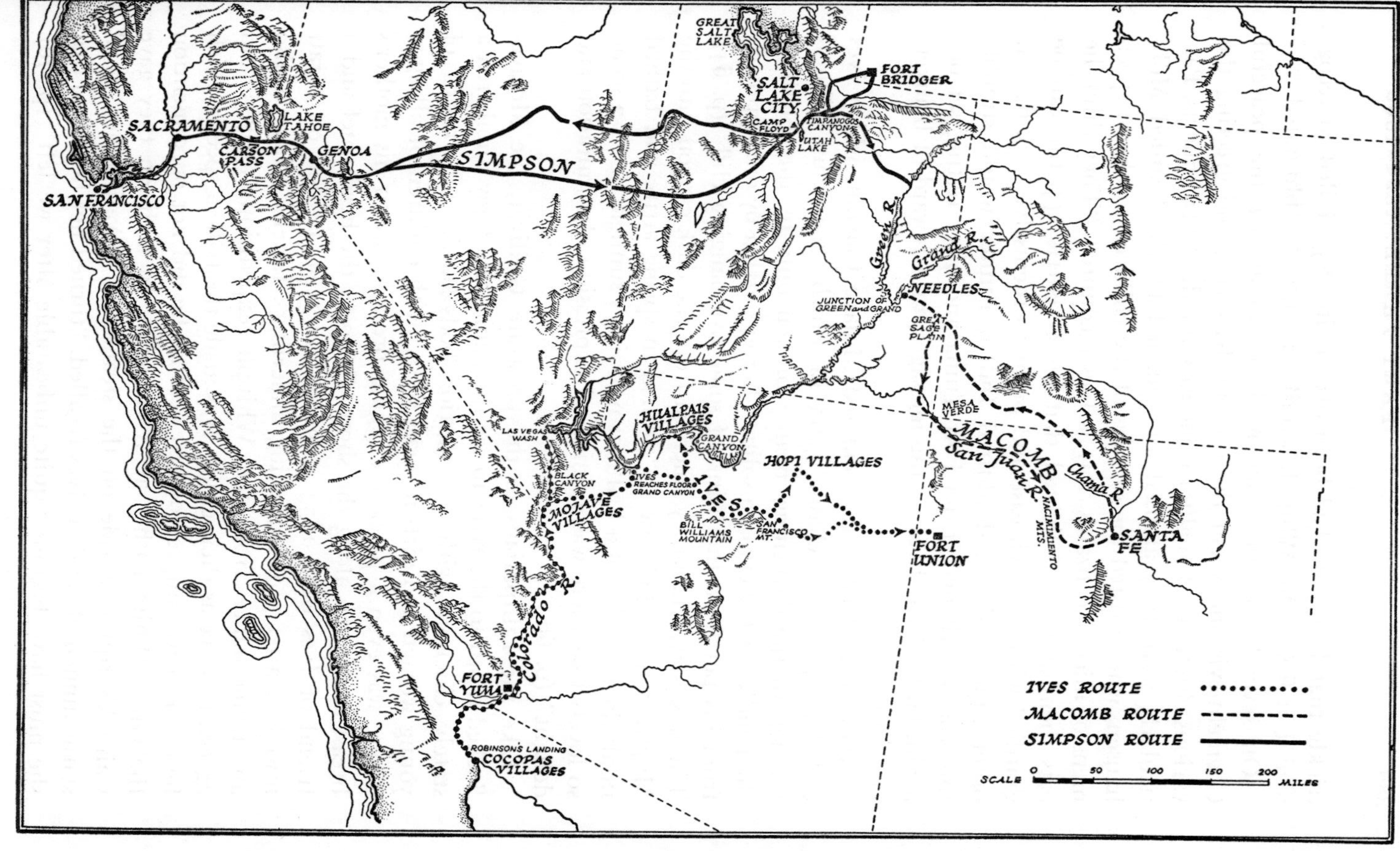

GREAT SALT LAKE
SALT LAKE CITY
FORT BRIDGER
CAMP FLOYD
TIMPANOGOS CANYON
UTAH LAKE
LAKE TAHOE
SACRAMENTO
CARSON PASS
GENOA
SIMPSON
SAN FRANCISCO
Green R.
Grand R.
NEEDLES
JUNCTION OF GREEN and GRAND
GREAT SAGE PLAIN
MESA VERDE
MACOMB
San Juan R.
Chama R.
NACIMIENTO MTS.
SANTA FE
HUALPAIS VILLAGES
GRAND CANYON
LAS VEGAS WASH
BLACK CANYON
IVES REACHES FLOOR GRAND CANYON
IVES
HOPI VILLAGES
MOJAVE VILLAGES
BILL WILLIAMS MOUNTAIN
SAN FRANCISCO MT.
FORT UNION
Colorado R.
FORT YUMA
ROBINSON'S LANDING
COCOPAS VILLAGES
IVES ROUTE
MACOMB ROUTE
SIMPSON ROUTE
SCALE 0 50 100 150 200 MILES

MAP 13

trickle that Ives, who had been over it in 1853, failed to recognize it at first sight. Whipple's trail was entirely obliterated.

On several occasions they made camp among the peaceful Chemehuevis and spent the evening bartering and greeting the various chieftains. Laughter came easy for the Chemehuevis. Particularly were they amused and puzzled by the bearded Möllhausen, who enlisted the services of the children to obtain specimens of mice and lizards, for, as Ives recounted, "They think he eats them and are delighted that his eccentric appetite can be gratified with so much ease and profit to themselves" (p. 62). At other times a dusty, dead-tired Indian runner would stumble into camp with mail from Fort Yuma and after resting set out again, faithfully delivering the messages for a reward of blankets or beads.

Above the Needles they entered Mojave Canyon, which Ives called a "profound chasm," and in which "a solemn stillness reigned in the darkening avenue broken only by the splash of the paddles or the cry of a solitary heron startled by our approach from his perch on the brink of some overhanging cliff" (p. 64). The next day, when they emerged from the dark canyon into the Mojave Valley, they saw it "clothed in spring attire and bathed in all the splendor of a brilliant morning's sunlight. . . . a scene so lovely that there was a universal expression of admiration and delight" (p. 66).

Like the Lilliputians to the prostrate Gulliver, the Mojaves flocked down to the river to see the explorers. They numbered a stately chieftain with his warrior bodyguard, and crowds of young women and girls in grass skirts, with children of all ages. There was even a papoose clinging precariously to his mother's breast as she ran along the shore. Cairook, the head chief and a friend of Ives from 1853, came out in regal fashion on a raft towed by a team of swimming underlings. Ireteba, who was also an acquaintance from the Whipple expedition, arrived and agreed to serve as their guide. Ives made the tribe a speech which he claimed was unprecedented because he did not once mention the Great White Father at Washington. In addition they gave Cairook's squaw a ride on the steamboat, elevating her social status immensely and, as Ives recalled, "turned her head," so that she must have become "quite unbearable after we left" (p. 70).

After leaving the Mojave villages, they streamed upriver into the Cottonwood Valley above the point where Captain Johnson had turned back. At the head of this valley was Pai-ute country and also Black Canyon, the first of the gigantic canyons of the Colorado. On January 8 they reached the Canyon, entered it, and struck a submerged rock. This convinced Ives that he had finally reached the limits of navigation. They made camp, shot up signal rockets, and awaited the arrival of a land supply party under Lt. John Tipton. While they were waiting, Ives, Robinson, and the ship's mate reconnoitered Black Canyon in a skiff. For several days they paddled laboriously through the canyon's mazes, and words almost failed the lieutenant in describing its grandeur: "Stately façades, august cathedrals, amphitheatres, rotundas, castellated walls, and rows of time-stained ruins, surmounted by every form of tower, minaret, dome, and spire have been moulded from the cyclopean masses of rock that form the mighty defile. The solitude, the stillness, the subdued light, and the vastness of every surrounding object, produce an expression of awe that ultimately becomes painful" (p. 86). They rowed upriver as far as a stream which Ives guessed was the Rio Virgin but which was actually Las Vegas Wash.[37] Then they coasted back downstream. He placed the Mormon Road twenty miles west from the river, and saw no difficulty in opening a wagon road connection to it.

While they were camped in the Cottonwood Valley, they were visited by a young Mormon bishop who posed as a lost emigrant. Though he was recognized for a spy and the scouts had already discovered the tracks of four other Mormons along the bank, Ives gave him a bed for the night and sent him on his way. The lieutenant might have been less confident had he known that crouched behind the bushes along the shore on that evening had been the formidable Jacob Hamblin, foremost frontier scout of the Mormons.[38] Generally a peaceful man (he was appalled at the Mountain Meadows massacre), Hamblin and his cohorts were attempting to turn the fickle Mojaves and Pai-utes against the soldiers. They almost succeeded, in fact, in promoting another

37. Wallace, p. 191.

38. Paul Bailey, *Jacob Hamblin, Buckskin Apostle* (Los Angeles, 1948), pp. 181–82.

massacre (pp. 89–90). Only by great persuasion and much present-making was Ives subsequently able to keep the Indians friendly and undo the Indian diplomacy of the Desert Saints.

When Lieutenant Tipton arrived, Ives divided his command, sending half of it back down the river on the steamer; with the other half, including Newberry, Egloffstein, Möllhausen, Tipton, and twenty soldiers, he set off eastward, overland, to discover another connection with the Mormon Road. As they left the river, Ives turned to look back at the Mojave Valley, "enveloped in a delicate blue haze that imparts to it so softened and charming a glow, while the windings of the Colorado could be traced through the bright fields and groves till the river disappeared in the Mojave Canyon" (p. 92). Newberry's impression of the river was that of a geologist. He saw it as a series of basins formed by the mountain ranges which cut across the river and had caused it to overflow over the whole surrounding region. "In the lapse of ages, however," he declared, "its accumulated waters, pouring over the lowest points in the barriers . . . have cut them down from summit to base, forming that remarkable series of deep and narrow canyons through which its turbid waters now flow with rapid and almost unobstructed current from source to mouth" (Pt. II, pp. 19–20). He concluded: "the effect of the removal of the barriers which once checked the flow of the Colorado has been to confine the stream to the channel occupied by its current; to limit its vivifying influence to a narrow margin along the banks, leaving the open areas through which it flows—and which were once lakes and afterwards fertile valleys—arid and sterile wastes" (Pt. II, p. 20). This was the most intelligent theory of the formation of the Colorado, or any western river, that had been made up to that time. But logical as it sounded, John Wesley Powell, in his later study of the Colorado, proved that this was not exactly correct, that, in fact, the river had flowed faster through the mountain areas, cutting through them first as the whole area had been broadly uplifted, like the log to the saw.[39] Newberry and Egloffstein both realized that as they moved inland there was an immense uplift covering hundreds of miles, but they did not connect it with the formation of the river. What Newberry did was point out the volcanic character

39. *DAB.*

of the mountain ranges and the continental uplift, and made a first intelligent guess as to what had happened. For its time this was contribution enough.

On March 23, 1858, Ives' detachment moved eastward generally parallel to Beale's wagon road recently traced through the Black Mountains and the Cerbat Range. Ives confirmed Lieutenant Whipple's guess of 1853 that a good railroad route could be found west of Cactus Pass in the Aquarius Mountains, and he extolled the merits of Railroad Pass in the Cerbat Range. Soon they were in the country of the Hualpais Indians, whom Ives described as "squalid, wretched-looking creatures, with splay feet, large joints and diminutive figures" (p. 97), but with "burning eyes and cunning faces" like the Chemehuevis. The Hualpais lived in an almost untouched state of primitiveness among the rocky crags and deep, silent canyons of the lower Colorado country. They were so poor and their land so valueless that other tribes seldom disturbed them. It was with some difficulty that Ives persuaded two of them to guide his party through the confusing country, and his task was made no easier by Möllhausen's suggestion that they preserve one of the ugliest in a jar of alcohol as a zoological specimen (p. 98). Following the two guides, they approached the lower edge of the Grand Canyon near Diamond Creek, and as they pushed deeper and deeper into the Canyon, Ives reached toward Dante and Doré for his descriptions as he wrote, "the increasing magnitude of the colossal piles that blocked the end of the vista, and the corresponding depth and gloom of the gaping chasms into which we were plunging, imparted an earthly character to a way that might have resembled the portals of the infernal regions. Harsh screams issuing from aerial recesses in the canyon sides, and apparitions of goblin-like figures perched in the rifts and hollows of the impending cliffs, gave an odd reality to the impression" (p. 100). The Hualpais themselves merely added to this impression as they plodded wretchedly about among their scattered grass huts like so many creatures of the underworld.

Near the mouth of Diamond Creek Ives strode out onto the floor of the Grand Canyon proper, probably the first white man ever to do so. Only Cardenas in 1541, Espejo in 1583, Garces in 1776, and perhaps James Ohio Pattie and his fellow trappers in

1823 had even approached the canyon before, and they had not reached its depths. On that April morning of 1858 Ives became part of a sublime moment in the history of American exploration.

From Diamond Creek they wasted two days following an Indian trail which took them along giddy ledges barely wide enough to admit a man or a mule. At times, looking down at the abyss below made the men freeze with fear, and some groped their way on hands and knees. When they came to a dead end, the whole party was forced to turn around and work its way back over the same terrifying route. The Hualpais guides deserted, and the water supply was nearly exhausted, but they finally emerged out onto the Colorado Plateau, where they made a base camp in an inviting pine forest. Ives and a detachment returned to the Grand Canyon and spent several days attempting another descent into its depths. They followed an Indian trail which brought them up short at a waterfall, but Egloffstein found a small rickety vine ladder and managed to slide forty feet deeper into the canyon, accidentally dragging the ladder with him. The soldiers above could see Yampais huts below, but the Indians, undisturbed for perhaps centuries, seemed unwilling to help the Prussian topographer out of their valley. Finally, the troopers made a long rope of their rifle slings and hoisted Egloffstein to safety. After that, they abandoned the attempt at the canyon and returned to the main camp. The barometers indicated that at Diamond Creek and Cataract Canyon the floor of the Grand Canyon was over a mile deep into the earth. Looking out across the broken plateau, as few white men had ever done before him, Ives marveled at the "fissures so profound that the eye cannot penetrate their depths," yet which were "separated by walls whose thickness one can almost span," and at the "slender spires that seem tottering upon their bases," shooting up "thousands of feet from the vaults below." It was, he wrote, like "a vast ruin" (p. 109).

April 25 found them at the northern base of the Bill Williams Mountain. By May 2 they had skirted the San Francisco Mountain and reached the deep-cut banks of the Little Colorado River. Here Ives divided his party once again, sending Lieutenant Tipton with the supply train along Whipple's trail southward to Fort Defiance, a lonely army outpost in the Navaho country. With the rest of his party, including Newberry and Egloffstein, Ives crossed the Little Colorado in Buchanan boats made of canvas stretched over a wooden frame, like a Missouri River bullboat. They were headed northeast over the Painted Desert to the Moqui (Hopi) Pueblos, said to be unvisited since the Spanish times. Though they had to put up with oppressive heat, scorpions, spiders, rattlesnakes, centipedes, and a plaguing thirst, the marvelous sights remained a compensation, particularly for the scientists.

Newberry was the first geologist to observe the Grand Canyon and its subsidiary canyons, and though the expedition moved so rapidly that he had to run to pick up rock specimens, still he was able to trace out a typical stratigraphic column that went deep into the earth and far back into the ages. On a high mesa west of the Little Colorado he took his typical section of the Great Colorado. It went from the upper Carboniferous down through the Devonian, Silurian, and Potsdam Sandstone (which Hayden and Meek had recently pointed out as forming the lower Silurian)[40] to the pre-Cambrian granite which underlay the whole region (Pt. II, p. 42). It was a column of fundamental importance in the development of American geology, and its importance was compounded by the fact that it had a clear connection with the findings of Henry Engelmann in the central regions east of the Wasatch Mountains, and with the columns of Hayden and Meek, in Kansas and the Dakotas.[41] The newer generation of geologists was coming closer in every expedition to assembling the kind of comprehensive view of the West that Warren had achieved for cartographers. In addition, the Colorado Plateau itself was a stupendous and unique phenomenon, with its hundreds of miles of giant-step mesas piled one on top of the other and broken here and there by immense igneous or volcanic intrusions. Newberry also had an explanation for this, "like the great canyons of the

40. F. V. Hayden, *Geological Report of the Exploration of the Yellowstone and Missouri Rivers . . . under Direction of Captain* [Lt. Col. and Brevet Brig. Gen.] *W. F. Raynolds, Corps of Engineers, 1859–60* (Wash., 1869), p. 9.

41. Ibid., p. 9. James H. Simpson, *Report of Explorations across the Great Basin of the Territory of Utah for a Direct Wagon-Route from Camp Floyd to Genoa, in Carson Valley, in 1859* (Wash., 1876), appendix I, passim.

Colorado, the broad valleys, bounded by high and perpendicular walls *belong to a vast system of erosion, and are wholly due to the action of water.* Probably nowhere in the world has the action of this agent produced results so surprising both as regards their magnitude and their peculiar character. It is not at all strange," he added, "that a cause, which has given to what was once an immense plain, underlaid by thousands of feet of sedimentary rocks, conformable throughout, a topographical character more complicated than that of any mountain chain; which has made much of it absolutely impassable to man, or to any animal but the winged bird, should be regarded as something out of the course of nature" (Pt. II, p. 45). Finally, he concluded from his survey that "the outlines of the western part of the North American continent were approximately marked out from the earliest Paleozoic times; not simply by areas of shallower water in an almost boundless ocean, but by groups of islands and broad continental surfaces of dry land" (Pt. II, p. 47). By this means he was able to disprove a current theory that the continent formed from a nucleus around Lake Superior, and that during the Tertiary period most of the West was an open sea.

On May 11 the explorers reached the first of the seven Moqui pueblos after crossing the dusty wastes of the Painted Desert. It was to them like entering the court of Kubla Khan. The town, consisting of flat-roofed adobe dwellings, was built like a series of steps into the mesa, and seemed almost a continuation of the land forms that were visible in all directions across the Colorado Plateau. Peach trees grew on garden terraces, brightly dressed Indians dotted the landscape, and everything seemed orderly and secure compared to the wild environs through which they had come. They spent several days among these people, and then, although warned by the chief that they would never be able to cross the arid plains ahead of them, they set off again northward toward the Colorado. After several days they returned, defeated by the desert, and taking another of the trails that radiated in all directions from the Moqui village they began the eastward march back to civilization. On the final stretch of the journey they were forced to pass through the country of the hostile Navahoes and each day the number of mounted Indians following their caravan increased, adding an ominous note to their emergence from the wilderness. Finally on May 23 they trudged onto the parade ground of Fort Defiance and reached what was, for all practical purposes, the end of their grand reconnaissance. It came none too soon, for shortly afterward the whole Navaho nation erupted into open hostility, and the soldier-scientists, worn out and bedraggled from their long journey, would have made easy victims for the raiders.

Lieutenant Tipton and most of the party marched overland to Fort Leavenworth, affording Newberry a chance to continue his geological labors all the way to the Mississippi Valley. Ives returned via the Butterfield Stage to Fort Yuma, sold the *Explorer* for $1,000, and took a steamer out of San Francisco for Washington. So ended one of the most remarkable American explorations of the nineteenth century. The explorers had tested the navigability of the Colorado, made a connection with the Mormon Road into the Great Basin, and had visited most of the wild tribes of the interior. But they had done even more. Newberry's report revealed the fabled canyons of the Colorado and the unknown Plateau Province to the scientific world. He put together a geologic picture of the plateau country and the Kansas plains that linked his work with that of Hayden and Meek as far north as the Dakotas and with Blake and Marcou on the Llano Estacado, so that a geologic picture of the West was beginning to emerge, from the Kansas Permian to the Potsdam Sandstone of the Grand Canyon and the Black Hills.

The topographer, Egloffstein, invented an entirely new process in mapmaking so that he could better set down the results of the expedition. Instead of being flat, two-dimensional hauchures, the mountains and other topographical features now stood represented in sculptured relief like a sand-table model. The process expressed the ruggedness of the country by adding a new illusion of depth and height.[42] The Prussian's process has been incorporated in every geography textbook from that time to the present. His five-section map was, moreover, the first to portray the canyon and plateau country.

Ives also left a lasting monument. Like Frémont he lavished great care on the writing of his report, and in so doing produced one of the representative pieces of nineteenth-century American

42. Ives, *Report,* Pt. I, p. 6.

literature. Though it was a scientific paper, all of the mannerisms of the romantic imagination are there, skillfully handled, so as to present in terms of human experience just what it was like to go where no white man had ever gone before.

In the summer of 1859, though the Mormon War had already ended, another attempt was made to locate a route into the Great Basin from the South. In June 1859 Capt. John N. Macomb, chief topographical officer in New Mexico, was ordered to lead an expedition northward along the Old Spanish Trail in search of the desired military road into Utah.[43] Twenty thousand dollars was appropriated for the exploration, and Macomb was authorized to take along John Strong Newberry and a staff of four assistants.[44] Lt. Milton Cogswell and a detachment of the Eighth Infantry served to guard them against the hostile Indians, while Albert H. Pfeiffer, the Ute agent, provided assistance in guiding and dealing with the peaceful Indians (p. 5). The expedition marched out of Santa Fe in the middle of July 1859 and headed along the Spanish Trail via Abiquiu and the Rio Chama (p. 5). For forty-five miles they followed the Chama, then, crossing the divide between the watersheds of the Gulf of Mexico and the Gulf of California, they struck the headwaters of the San Juan River. From their crossing of the San Juan they headed due west for seventy miles, through rugged mountain foothills and across all the northern tributaries of the San Juan which flowed southward out of the mountains. While skirting the southern edge of the Sierra de La Plata Mountains, they came upon numerous Indian ruins under the shadow of the Mesa Verde. Some stood out on top of the mesa, while others, probably lookout stations and temporary villages, were nestled under great overhanging ledges. It was the sight of present-day Mesa Verde National Park.

Soon they emerged from the mountains onto the Colorado Plateau, which Newberry declared to be "geologically a basin; topographically a great plateau" (Pt. II, p. 53). In his geological report he explained this new definition of the upland country:

43. Macomb to Abert, June 3, 1859, MS, LR, BES 48.

44. Macomb, *Report* (above, p. 362, n. 45), p. 7. The account is based on this work unless otherwise stated.

> Could anyone be elevated to a sufficient height over the center of this region and be gifted with superhuman powers of vision, he would see beneath him what would appear to be a great plain, bounded on every side by mountain ranges, and here and there dotted by isolated mountain masses, rising like islands above its surface. He would see, too, the profound chasm of the Colorado Canyon scoring with tortuous and diagonal course, the plain, throughout the entire length of its greatest diameter for nearly five hundred miles, the stream flowing from 3,000 to 6,000 feet below the general level, and at all points bordered by abrupt, frequently perpendicular crags and precipices [Pt. II, p. 53].

Immediately before them the Colorado Plateau took on the aspect of a great sage plain (which it has since been named), and the Spanish Trail branched off toward the north, while almost due north lay the path followed by Escalante on his way to Utah Lake in 1776. At the Canyon Pintado, halfway across the sage plain, they discovered the petrified bones of a large dinosaur half encased in the gypsum formation. After several hours of digging they were able to secure part of the skeleton for shipment back to Joseph Leidy, the pioneer student of vertebrate paleontology in the country. Two days later they established a depot camp at Ojo Verde where the main detachment rested, while Macomb, Cogswell, Newberry, two of the technical assistants, and three servants made their way for two days across the incredibly tortured landscape toward the junction of the Green and Grand rivers. At one point their view swept over a wide expanse of the country and Newberry wrote that it was "everywhere deeply cut by a tangled maze of canyons, and thickly set with towers, castles, and spires of the most varied and striking forms; the most wonderful monuments of erosion which our eyes, already experienced in objects of this kind, had ever beheld" (Pt. II, p. 94). On August 23 they emerged from the confines of Labyrinth Canyon; stripping off part of their clothing in the 92° heat, they clambered up the side of a great isolated butte, but once there they could go no farther toward the river, which was still some miles away. But there was no need to go on, for from where they stood their eyes could sweep fifty miles in every direction. The strategic junction of the Green and Grand rivers came into view, and they were enabled now to understand the drainage of the whole central part of the Far West region. Newberry wrote:

> A great basin or sunken plain lay stretched before us as on a map. Not a particle of vegetation was anywhere discernible; nothing but bare and barren rocks of rich and varied colors shimmering in the sunlight. Scattered over the plain were thousands of the fantastically formed buttes to which I have so often referred in my notes; pyramids, domes, towers, columns, spires of every conceivable form and size. Among these by far the most remarkable was the forest of Gothic spires, first and imperfectly seen as we issued from the mouth of the Canyon Colorado. . . . Scarcely less striking features in the landscape were the innumerable canyons by which the plain is cut. In every direction they ran and ramified deep, dark, and ragged, impassable to everything but the winged bird. Of these the most stupendous was that of Grand River, which washes two sides of the base of the pinnacle on which we stood, a narrow chasm, as we estimated, full 1,500 feet in depth, into which the sun scarcely seemed to penetrate. . . . Toward the south of the canyon of Grand River was easily traced. Perhaps four miles below our position it is joined by another great chasm coming in from the northwest, said by the Indians to be that of Green River [Pt. II, p. 97].

Six days later, after they had cut directly south across the Sage Plain, they struck the San Juan at a point about fifty miles from its mouth. From there they could look downriver to its junction with the Colorado, or across it to what is now Monument Valley, the country of the Moqui and the Navaho. Then the expedition turned up the San Juan River and followed it for eight days until it reached the Canyon Largo. At this point it turned south past Nacimiento Mountain to the pueblo of Jemez, which had been the point of departure for Simpson's first expedition into the Navaho country as far back as 1849.

In practical terms, the San Juan expedition had few contributions to make. It showed conclusively that no feasible supply route existed leading into the Great Basin from that direction. However, in the realm of geography and geology its implications were considerable. The whole drainage of the San Juan had been traced and the relationship of that river with the Colorado clearly established. More important, they had also established that the Green River united with the Grand to form the Colorado. The entire maze of intricate canyon country had been threaded, and its geography revealed for the first time. In addition, Newberry was able to establish numerous stratigraphic columns, and to trace the Triassic, Jurassic, and Carboniferous strata far out across the Colorado River. Moreover, he was able to link what he saw with his discoveries on the Ives expedition, which extended his geological conception of the country all across the Plateau Province. Newberry, like Hayden and Meek, introduced a new level of sophistication into the study of western geology. He was better trained than his predecessors, and he could generalize from what he saw in a significant fashion. All of his observations built up to a series of conclusions that enabled him to characterize a whole area of the continent, rather than merely to catalogue its peculiarities. Then, too, he called attention to the value of specialized or key studies of a single mountain chain or a single peak for the purpose of deriving the fundamental principles of its creation (Pt. II, p. 114). His own observations of the Sierra de La Plata, the San Juan, and the Nacimiento mountains led him to believe that the Rocky Mountains had undergone several periods of uplift and inundation but that the great period of uplift had occurred between the close of the Cretaceous period and the opening of the Miocene.[45]

Of Newberry it might be said that more than any other scientist since Frémont he had opened up new and unknown country to the civilized world.

In the Great Basin to the north, the summer of 1858 saw the Army of Utah safely bivouacked at Camp Floyd in Cedar Valley between Salt Lake and Utah Lake and turning from the business of war to the tasks of peace. On August 24 General Johnston ordered his chief Topographical Engineer, Capt. James Hervey Simpson, to make a reconnaissance, via the Timpanogos Canyon, for a wagon road that would connect Camp Floyd with the sup-

45. Merrill, *First One Hundred Years of American Geology* (above, p. 58, n. 83), p. 363.

ply depot at Fort Bridger.[46] The regular road ran through Echo Canyon, but that was so easily blockaded as to completely jeopardize the Army's supply line. On the other hand, the Timpanogos route previously recommended by Stansbury in 1850 had already been improved by the Mormons for part of the distance, making the task of the Army roadmakers considerably lighter.

On August 25, the day after receiving his orders, Simpson set out on his mission, guided by Isaac Bullock of Provo and escorted by an Infantry lieutenant and twenty troopers (pp. 4–5). They marched northeast out of the Cedar Valley into the Valley of the Jordan, where they crossed the River by a Mormon toll bridge sixty feet long. From this point they passed north of Utah Lake and eastward, via the settlements at Lake City and Pleasant Grove, to the mouth of the Timpanogos Canyon. In his report Simpson described the appearance and economy of this section, pointing out that wheat was the great staple but that garden vegetables grew luxuriously. However, he concluded that the cultivable land was but a fraction of the total, and it was likely to become barren from overuse. Provo, the metropolis of the region, he described as a rectilinear town of some 400 adobe houses and 4,200 inhabitants with a single large building called the Tabernacle which was used for religious and secular purposes.

Their route up the Timpanogos took them through the Wasatch Mountain barrier over another toll bridge, and for twelve miles over the already existing Mormon Road, which Simpson pronounced excellent but somewhat narrow in places (pp. 7–8). From the end of this road they marched through Round Prairie and over a small divide between the Timpanogos and Silver Creek, a tributary of the Weber River. Then they threaded their way to the Weber River and down it to White Clay Creek, the Bear River, and thence over the Divide to Fort Bridger. The stretch along White Clay Creek proved to be the most difficult section of the road. After organizing a work party to improve the road as surveyed, Simpson proceeded back along the trail to Camp Floyd. He brought with him the geologist

46. *Report of the Secretary of War Communicating . . . Captain Simpson's Report and Map of Wagon Roads in Utah Territory,* 35th Cong., 2d Sess., Sen. Exec. Doc. 40 (1859–60), 3. The account is based on Simpson, *Report* (n. 41) unless otherwise noted.

Henry Engelmann, who had been with Lieutenant Bryan on his surveys through Bryan Pass to the Laramie Plain. Engelmann, a younger brother of the great botanist George Engelmann of St. Louis, assembled a series of comprehensive reports based on Simpson's surveys and those of Bryan, which described the geology of the whole central region from the Sierra Nevadas across the Great Basin and the Unita Mountains to the Mississippi. He was able to link his findings with those of Hayden in the Dakotas and Newberry on the Colorado Plateau, and thus fill in a huge section of the western geologic picture.

When he returned to Camp Floyd, Simpson was ordered into the field again immediately by General Johnston. This time he was to make a survey into the Basin west of Camp Floyd as far as he was able during the season in an effort to locate a new route to California. The General's immediate objective was also to locate a possible site for a fort part way across the Basin (p. 24).

The exploring party of dragoons, laborers, interpreters, and scientists left Camp Floyd on October 19, 1858, and ranged south through Rush Valley to Johnson's Settlement near Reynolds' Pass. Very soon they found that the Basin was not one large, flat desert but consisted of numerous isolated mountains and parallel ranges. It was thus necessary to make detours in order to skirt these ranges, or locate passes through them. When they had entered Skull Valley, they turned southward for two days' march to Pleasant Spring, and then southwest to Short-Cut Pass in the Thomas Range. At this point, with water nearly two days' march ahead and the winter season fast descending, Simpson decided to turn back for Camp Floyd. On the return trip he found a new pass between Rush and Skull valleys, which he named for General Johnston. Back at Camp Floyd he explained his route to George Chorpenning, the overland mail contractor, and Chorpenning sent a party over the trail to test its possibilities for winter operations in preference to the northern route via the Humboldt River (p. 35).

During the winter of 1858–59 Captain Simpson submitted a project for future explorations across the Great Basin to Secretary of War John B. Floyd. In part it read: "It is believed that a direct route from this post to Carson Valley in Utah can be obtained which would avoid the detour by the Humboldt to the right and that by the Las Vegas and Los Angeles route to the left and that it could be obtained so as to make the distance to San Francisco less than 800 miles . . . 260 miles shorter than the Humboldt River route and 390 miles shorter than the Los Angeles route." In addition, he proposed that another expedition be sent to open a route from Camp Floyd to the headwaters of the Arkansas River, where it would continue via Bent's Fort to Fort Leavenworth (p. 41).

The Secretary of War approved the plan (p. 42). In April, Captain Simpson received his orders, and on May 2, at 7:45 A.M., he led a party of forty-four officers and men due west out of Camp Floyd into the Great Basin. He had as assistants two young officers of the Topographical Corps, Lt. J. L. Kirby Smith and Lt. Haldiman L. Putnam. Henry Engelmann was his geologist, and there was also a taxidermist, a meteorologist, and an artist, one H. V. A. von Beckh. John Reese and a Ute Indian named "Ute Pete" served as scouts. The escort of twenty-two men was commanded by Lt. Alexander Murray of the Tenth Infantry. Their course led them slightly south of due west through Rush Valley, where they passed the federal mail stations, and the great cattle herds of Russell, Majors, and Waddell, to Johnston's Pass in Guyot's Range. From there they moved into Skull Valley and the Salt Lake Desert, which Simpson described as "a somber, dreary waste, where neither man nor beast can live" (p. 47). Along the way, however, they did see numbers of wretched-looking Goshoot Indians, who seemed perpetually hungry and just short of actual starvation.

When they reached the isolated mountain ranges which afforded comparative oases, they passed the half-finished mail stations which the enterprising Chorpenning had strung out across the Basin toward the regular immigrant trail. The most prominent of these were at Pleasant Valley, Ruby Valley, and Hastings Pass in the Humboldt Mountains. The latter was at the point where the mail route linked up with the Hastings Cut-Off and the regular emigrant route. Beyond this point, which the expedition reached on May 12, Captain Simpson turned toward the southwest to blaze his new trail to California. This led through a number of mountains and valleys which the Captain christened with the names of his friends and admired superiors. There were the Cooper Mountains and Cooper Pass (after Adj. Gen. Samuel Cooper), Reese Valley, Simpson Park, and Engelmann Creek. Gradually they worked their way south and west about half a degree of latitude and headed toward Carson Lake. At times, small bands of Digger Indians came into their camp, displaying lively and jocose spirits. But Simpson's description of their struggle for food revealed another side of their primitive life. They say, he recorded, "two rats make a meal. Like rabbits better than rats, and antelope better than either, but cannot get the latter. Have no guns; use bows and arrows" (p. 75). In spite of this, one old Indian philosophically declared that he liked this country "a good deal better than any other," because at least it had "a great many rats" (p. 76).

Near Smith's Creek their guide John Reese stumbled into the caravan, ragged and exhausted after having been lost for several days without food, water, or matches. He had been forced to walk over the mountain range alone through Indian country to regain the exploring party. Fortunately the Diggers were all friendly, even offering to share three fat rats with him. But even in his starving condition Reese declined this rigorous diet.

At the north end of the Black Mountains they struck Carson Lake and turned south to Walker's River, then north again, where they crossed Carson River on a raft made of logs from the Pleasant Grove Mail Station, the first outpost of civilization on the eastern slopes of the Sierras. On June 11 they entered the curious settlement of Chinatown, so called because of its population of fifty hard-living, opium-smoking, gambling, Chinese prospectors. The town had two stores and twelve houses, and whiskey sold for three dollars a gallon.

The expedition did not pause long at this mining camp, and by sundown they had reached Carson City, which also had only twelve houses, but at least it had two ladies. After an overnight stop at Carson City, the soldiers continued on through the wide-open Washoe country, with the lure of easy fortune everywhere at hand. Before they reached Genoa, however, they passed a gallows where hung a victim of easy fortune, one "Lucky Bill," hanged by the vigilance committee. At Genoa, which had been a Mormon settlement, they were greeted by a thirteen-gun salute and the running up of the national flag in honor of their having opened up the much-needed mail and emigrant route that promised to make the town a future metropolis. At that time Genoa counted twenty-eight houses, two stores, two hotels, one printing establishment, and one telegraph office, with a population of between 150 and 200 people.

Leaving the command at Genoa, Simpson took a stage over the Sierras via Dagget's Trail to Placerville. Along the way he noticed the wires of the Placerville and St. Joseph Telegraph Company strung through the branches of living trees as it reached out toward Genoa and the Basin beyond. When he reached Placerville (population 3,500), his companion, Col. Fred A. Bee, owner of the mail and telegraph company, assured him that he could consider his recently blazed trail as adopted by the company. At Folsum the Captain could take railroad cars for Sacramento and perhaps travel the same routes ridden over by Frémont and his wild mountain men some thirteen years before, or the line taken by Lt. George Horatio Derby as he laid out his wagon road up the Sacramento Valley. A sure sign of the incredible progress of civilization was the fancy river steamboat *Eclipse,* which took him to San Francisco from Sacramento. Moreover, as he steamed downriver he could observe that the farmers were using windmills to irrigate their fields, although the pump windmill had only been invented some five years before and would not come into wide use in the Midwest until the 1870's. San Francisco itself was already a metropolis with valid pretensions to culture.

Having accomplished his business, Simpson returned to Placerville and after a wild ride over the Sierras with a drunken stagecoach driver rejoined his men. As a result of this harrowing experience, he recommended that the government appropriate at least $30,000 for the improvement of the road (p. 103). On June 24, 1859, the party began its return march to Camp Floyd. Coming back, it swung approximately forty miles south of the outgoing trail near the Antelope Mountains, and skirting south of Steptoe Valley passed via the White Valley and the Good Indian Spring through Oak Pass in the Guyot Range and then back to Camp Floyd. Lt. J. L. Kirby Smith was then sent over the last 100 miles with a construction crew to improve the route and erect markers to guide prospective emigrants. Within days after his return Simpson supplied parties of California emigrants with a description of the route, and Russell, Majors, and Waddell began laying plans to drive a thousand head of cattle over the road to California (pp. 133–34).

At Camp Floyd, Captain Simpson's orders were modified; he was to find a pass through the Uinta Mountains to the Green River and then return to Fort Leavenworth via Fort Bridger (p. 133). On August 9 he left with a party of fifty-four men to carry out this mission. His new trail followed up the Timpanogos and Coal Creek Canyon to the summit of the Uinta Mountain Divide, then down Potts Fork to the Duchesne, and thence to the Uinta River. It was extraordinarily rough country, but Simpson found a practicable pass, and he reported that his discovery made possible a wagon road all the way from Camp Floyd to the new mining town of Denver City (p. 141). On his return trip to Fort Leavenworth he improved the old route to Fort Bridger by cutting out the difficult stretch along White Clay Creek. When he reached Fort Laramie, the rest of the road was almost a civilized highway.

The explorations in the Great Basin and Wasatch Mountain region were the last ones conducted by Simpson before the Civil War. Unfortunately his final wagon-road report was not published until 1875, because of the Civil War, but it was a capstone to his brilliant career as an Army explorer. From the time he first entered the West on the Marcy–Canadian River expedition of 1849, until 1859, when he concluded his field explorations, Simpson had marched over more of the western country than any of the other Topographers. Always conservative in his judgments and unswervingly scrupulous in his road-building duties, he ran counter to the popular enthusiasms of both the individualistic territorial officials and members of his own Corps, who were always urging headlong progress. In his final report he bluntly pronounced the southwestern prairie country an "unmitigated desert," and yet, he wrote, "notwithstanding all this, annually you will see bills brought forward in Congress in which the land along the route figures as a very important element in the ways and means to construct the [rail]road" (p. 236). He remained a wagon-road man, and believed (like Benton, curiously enough) that the government should first build local roads and postal routes, then populate the country and develop its resources before attempting to construct a transcontinental railroad. In practical terms he had done his part to bring this about. The Pony Express followed his northern route. The Chorpenning Mail Company used his southern route. The telegraph also followed close to this line. Russell, Majors, and Waddell drove their wagons and stock over it, and emigrants passed over it every day on their way to California.[47]

When his wagon-road report was finally published in 1875, it included a complete survey of the botany, zoology, and meteorology of the central region. Though almost all this data had been anticipated by 1875 in papers read before scientific societies, nevertheless Henry Engelmann's geological report remained important as a general picture of the region, which attempted to locate the limits of the various geologic horizons and to line them up with the stratigraphic columns defined by Hayden and Meek. Moreover, combining his discoveries on the Bryan expedition with those of the Simpson expedition, he was able to get a cross section of the entire tran-Mississippi West. He also located numerous sites for the discovery of vertebrate fossils of the kind that would later aid O. C. Marsh in his greater work in paleontology.[48]

In the realm of purer knowledge Simpson also had his say. He conceptualized the Great Basin with an air of finality: it "should be conceived as an elevated central region . . . sloping toward the sub-basins bordering the circumference." He added, "It is preeminently a basin of mountains and valleys." [49]

In his devotion to the increase of knowledge, for both practical and theoretical purposes, there was something typical of the whole Corps about Simpson. He was a rugged explorer, yet he appreciated the subtle speculations of Prof. Arnold Guyot of Princeton, even naming a mountain range after him. And half-

47. Jackson, *Wagon Roads,* p. 156.

48. Simpson, *Report,* pp. 262, 264–65. Charles Schuchert and Clara Mae Le Vene, *O. C. Marsh, Pioneer in Paleontology* (New Haven, 1940), p. 106 (map), and passim.

49. Simpson, *Report,* p. 33.

way up the western slope of Cho-kup's Pass in central Utah, he could pause to wax metaphysical. "These distant views," he wrote, "have, at least to my mind a decidedly moral and religious effect; and I cannot but believe that they are not less productive of emotions of value in this respect than they are of use in accustoming the mind to large conceptions, and thus giving it power and capacity. The mysterious property of nature to develop the whole man, including the mind, soul, and body, is a subject which I think has not received the attention from philosophers which its importance demands." [50]

50. Ibid., p. 69.

11. THE SIOUX COUNTRY

> In making this occupation we should look to the future. Agricultural settlements have now nearly reached their western limits on our great plains; the tracts beyond must ever be occupied by a pastoral people, whether civilized or savage. If the Indian is not doomed to speedy extirpation, if he is to have a permanent home, here is where it must be located.—*G. K. Warren, 1855*

THE INITIAL IMPETUS to military exploration in the high plains and mountain area of the present-day Dakotas, Montana, and Wyoming was the threat of a general Indian uprising by discontented bands of Sioux Indians being pushed ever westward toward the hunting grounds of their traditional enemies, the Crows, by the increasing pressure of white emigration into the northern plains and Rockies. With the massacre of Lt. J. L. Grattan and twenty-nine men of the Sixth Infantry on August 19, 1854, the Great Sioux War, which lasted until the 1890's, can be said to have officially begun. As a result of the massacre the veteran cavalryman Gen. William H. Harney was ordered to lead a punitive expedition into the Sioux country in the following summer of 1855.[1] It was the hope of the high command that a sudden and terrifying retaliation would stop the Sioux before they could unite, as one nation, in mass attacks on the settlers moving across the plains. Despite the ravages of smallpox, the Sioux were steadily increasing in numbers.[2] This fact, together with their mounting belligerence and their strategic position in the imperfectly known badlands country between the North Platte and the Upper Missouri on the flank of the advancing emigrants, made them a definite threat to western settlement. Therefore, the War Department in sending a mounted striking

1. Emerson Gifford Taylor, *Gouverneur Kemble Warren* (Boston, 1932), pp. 21–22. See also G. K. Warren, "Journal" (Warren Papers, New York State Library), p. 2.

2. G. K. Warren, *Explorations in the Dacota Country in the Year 1855*, 34th Cong., 1st Sess., Sen. Exec. Doc. 76 (1856), 17.

force into the Indian country was resorting to the cavalry leader's strategy previously advocated by Kearny and Jefferson Davis.

Accompanying the expedition was Lt. G. K. Warren, who received orders to suspend his work on the General Map of the trans-Mississippi country and report to Fort Kearny as the chief Topographical officer in General Harney's command. Poised and striking in appearance, with black mustaches and his hair flowing Custer style, Gouverneur Kemble Warren was only twenty-five years old, yet he was rapidly establishing a reputation as one of the brilliant young men of his time. He had graduated second in the class of 1850 at West Point, and almost immediately was assigned to duty on the Mississippi Delta project under Captain Humphreys, where he learned the exacting profession of the civil engineer.[3] From this position he had been appointed assistant in the office of the Pacific railroad surveys under Major Emory, where he worked at compiling his master map of the West.[4] More than any other officer of the Corps, he resembled Frémont. Like the Pathfinder he was much in the eye of his superiors, from his boyhood when he used to be present at the gatherings of military heroes at his uncle's house in Cold Spring, just across the Hudson from West Point, to the period of his duties at the Office of Explorations and Surveys on Capitol Hill. Like Frémont, too, he was handsome, ambitious, and daring in the extreme, willing to take chances in the interests of success. He liked the West with its outdoor life of the scientist-explorer, and the camaraderie of the half-civilized mountain men. As with Frémont, his western duties were to be among the solid achievements of his lifetime.

On June 7 he left St. Louis on an American Fur Company steamer for Fort Pierre on the Upper Missouri, where before joining General Harney's Sioux expedition, he was ordered to complete a survey of the military reservation.[5] It took until the sixteenth of July to reach Fort Pierre and then the rest of the month to finish the survey work. He grew apprehensive lest he miss the departure of Harney's command altogether, and after several days of reflection decided to form a small party and

3. Taylor, pp. 8–10.
4. Ibid., p. 19.
5. Warren, *Explorations,* p. 5.

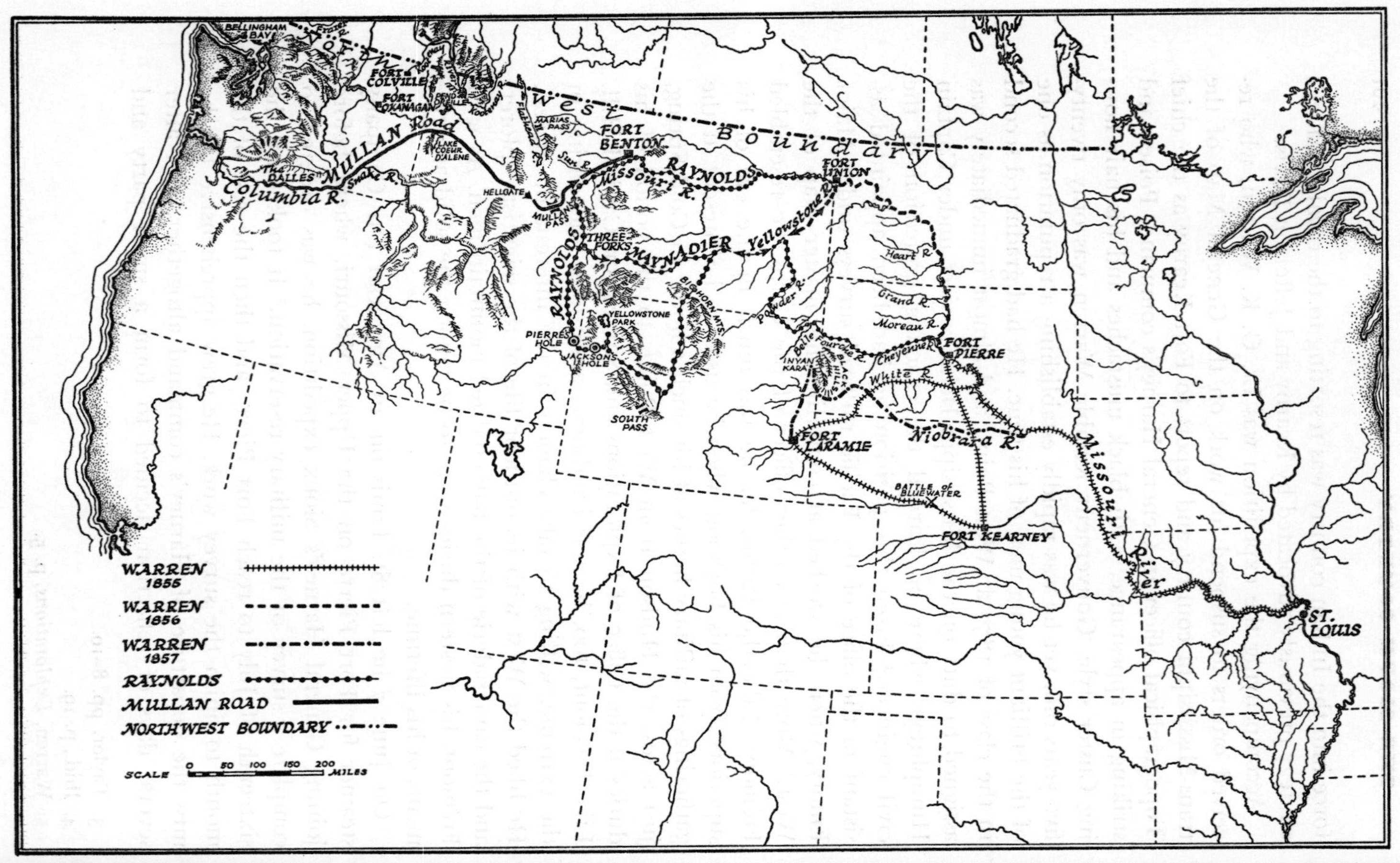
BELLINGHAM BAY
FORT COLVILLE
FORT OKANAGAN
PEND D'OREILLE
North West Boundary
MULLAN Road
LAKE COEUR D'ALENE
MARIAS PASS
FORT BENTON
Sun R.
Flathead R.
THE DALLES
Columbia R.
Snake R.
HELLGATE
MULLAN PASS
Missouri R.
RAYNOLDS
FORT UNION
Yellowstone R.
THREE FORKS
MAYNADIER
BIGHORN MTS.
YELLOWSTONE PARK
PIERRES HOLE
JACKSONS HOLE
SOUTH PASS
Powder R.
Heart R.
Grand R.
Moreau R.
Cheyenne R.
Belle Fourche R.
FORT PIERRE
INYAN KARA
BLACK HILLS
White R.
Niobrara R.
FORT LARAMIE
BATTLE of BLUEWATER
FORT KEARNEY
Missouri River
ST. LOUIS
WARREN 1855
WARREN 1856
WARREN 1857
RAYNOLDS
MULLAN ROAD
NORTHWEST BOUNDARY
SCALE 0 50 100 150 200 MILES

march overland to Fort Kearny in time to make his connection.[6] Major Montgomery and the other officers of the fort warned the tenderfoot lieutenant that he faced massacre in attempting his overland trek directly through the heart of the hostile country.[7] Warren coolly recorded in his journal that "My intention . . . had not been formed without due consideration of those things, and careful conversation with men of the country." [8] So saying, he took seven mountain men and set out on August 8 (p. 20). They were well armed and alert, traveling at night with no tents and no fires. Their route took them south across the Little Missouri and White rivers and through the Sand Hills to the Loup Fork of the Platte. Along the way they saw fresh Indian trails, but managed to avoid all contact with war parties. As a practical result of his daring feat, Warren was able to assert positively that because of the large streams and sand hills, no practicable supply route existed between Forts Pierre and Kearny (p. 14).

The Lieutenant arrived at Fort Kearny two days before Harney's scheduled departure, and was thus in time to undertake the march west to Fort Laramie and participate in the battle of Blue Water Creek on September 3, 1856. The battle first began when some emigrants riding back along the trail warned General Harney that the band of Brulé Sioux responsible for the Grattan massacre was camped near Ash Hollow, just off the main trail. On September 2 the General sent Philip St. George Cooke with elements of the Second Dragoons, the Fourth Artillery, and the Tenth Infantry, all mounted as cavalry, around to the rear of the Indian camp, and then prepared to attack with the main force on the next day. The element of surprise was lost, however, when the Indians discovered their advance and began a rapid retreat up the valley of the Blue Water.[9] Fearing that they would escape before Cooke's cavalry came up, Harney rode forward under a white flag for a delaying parley with the chief, Little Thunder.[10] Warren climbed up a low hill on the right and

6. Ibid., p. 21.

7. Ibid. See also Taylor, p. 23, and Warren, "Journal," July 21–30, 1855.

8. Warren, *Explorations,* p. 21.

9. Warren, "Journal," Sept. 2, 3, 1855.

10. Ibid. See William H. Harney, *Report of the Battle of Blue Water,* 34th Cong., 1st Sess., H. R. Exec. Doc. 1 (1855–56), 49, for another version of the parley.

looked in vain for the cavalry. However, when the Indians began to panic and stir, they knew Cooke was in position. When this happened, according to Warren, "General Harney told him [Little Thunder] to go and tell his young men that they must fight. He mounted and was off like an arrow." [11] Then the fight began, with a cavalry charge driving the Indians in confusion across the valley and scattering them among the bluffs on the eastern side. There many of them dug holes and like cornered animals fought to the death, squaws and children as well as braves. The rest, including the chief, were pursued by the cavalry for miles over the hills, where many were killed like rabbits as they ran. According to Harney, it was "a brilliant charge of cavalry" supported by the whole body of infantry, "who were eager from the first for a fray with the butchers of their comrades of Lieutenant Grattan's party." [12] However, his official report did not quite jibe with Lieutenant Warren's account of the battle, which revealed Harney's dishonorable delaying tactics and which recalled the details of the conflict in terms of the "wounded women and children crying and moaning, horribly mangled by the bullets." [13] In all, eighty-six Indians were killed, while the soldiers lost only five men.[14]

From the Blue Water the Sioux expedition marched in triumph to Fort Laramie. From September 16 to September 29 they lingered at the Fort. During this time Warren had long conversations with the mountain men, and they drew him detailed maps of the Sioux country all the way from the Yellowstone to the Missouri. These were a remarkable series of crude sketch maps by Jim Baker, Joseph Jewitt, Michael Desomet, James Bordeaux, Alexander Culbertson, Colin Campbell, and Joe Merrivale, which form perhaps the only remaining concrete evidence of the mountain man's grasp of the West. One drew the Missouri without its Great Bend. Baker's map leaves a blank space at the headwaters of the Yellowstone, where Jim Bridger claimed to have seen the marvelous sights of "Colter's Hell" (now Yellowstone Park). These maps represented knowledge gained through experience and the

11. Warren (above, n. 9).
12. Harney, *Report,* pp. 49–50.
13. Warren, "Journal," Sept. 3, 1855.
14. Harney, p. 51.

sixth sense developed by these particular trappers which had kept them alive in that hostile country as late as 1855. Most important of these mapmakers was Alexander Culbertson, the highly intelligent factor of the American Fur Company's northern posts at Forts Benton and Union. It requires only a brief comparison between these mountain men's maps and Lieutenant Warren's finished productions, however, to see the difference between two great eras of western exploration.

The rest of the march of the Sioux expedition consisted of a great circle north to Raw Hide Creek; the White River, north of Wounded Knee Creek; then along that river past Sage Creek and the Grindstone Buttes to Fort Pierre; thence down the Missouri to Sioux City, where they arrived on the ninth of November. Lieutenant Warren wasted no space in setting down the conclusions he had drawn from the summer's activity:

> That the portion of Nebraska (which I have visited) lying north of White River is mostly of a clay formation and that south of it is mainly of sand; that but a small portion of it is susceptible of cultivation west of the ninety-seventh meridian; that the territory is occupied by powerful tribes of roving savages, and is only adapted to a mode of life such as theirs; that the Indians should be made to feel the power of the United States; that the military posts, in consequence, should contemplate permanency; that Forts Laramie and Pierre are the most important positions yet occupied; that the latter can always be supplied by steamboat on the Missouri; that the former must be supplied by way of the valley of the Platte; that a great deal yet remains to be learned of this vast territory; and that it is of the utmost importance to acquire a thorough knowledge of it without delay.[15]

Warren spent the winter in Washington, writing a report of the summer's exploration and working on the General Map in the Office of Explorations and Surveys.[16] By the end of April, however, he was in St. Louis preparing to rejoin General Harney on the Upper Missouri.[17] Included in Warren's scientific party

15. Warren, *Explorations,* pp. 21–22.
16. Taylor, *Warren,* p. 30.
17. G. K. Warren to W. Warren, Fort Pierre, May 24, 1856, Warren Papers.

were two topographers, W. H. Hutton and J. H. Snowden. The most important member, however, was Ferdinand V. Hayden, a young geologist who had spent the years 1853 and 1854 in making geological collections through much of the Dakota country.[18] Hayden's first Dakota expedition (1853) had been in partnership with F. B. Meek, a paleontologist, when they had both been subsidized agents of James Hall.[19] An unpleasant competition had arisen with the Culbertson-Evans railroad survey party of that year, and only through the good offices of George Engelmann and Louis Agassiz, in St. Louis, had the dispute been settled.[20] In 1854, having split with Hall, Hayden returned to the Dakotas as an independent and made collections as far north as Fort Benton and the Yellowstone River.[21] F. B. Meek collaborated with him in presenting his early results to the Philadelphia Academy of Natural Sciences, while Joseph Leidy, at the University of Pennsylvania, published an analysis of his vertebrate fossil specimens.[22] Thus by 1856 Hayden had a fast-rising reputation in the world of science, and Warren was eager to have him associated with his own proposed Dakota expedition.[23]

By May 24 Warren had arrived at Fort Pierre after a harrowing trip of thirty-four days by steamer and on foot, during part of which their provisions were nearly exhausted and they had to live off the country.[24] When they arrived at the Fort, General Harney was just completing a treaty which was intended to terminate the Sioux War but which proved to be an uneasy armistice. On June 3 the General ordered Warren to ascend by steamer to a point on the Missouri above the mouth of the Yellowstone River and there to connect his survey with I. I. Stevens' northern Pacific railroad survey. He was to examine all possible

18. G. K. Warren, *Preliminary Report of Explorations in Nebraska and Dakota in the years 1855–56–57* (Wash., 1875), p. 14. For Hayden's previous work in the Dakotas see Merrill, *First One Hundred Years of American Geology* (above, p. 58, n. 83), pp. 501–3.

19. Merrill, p. 501.

20. F. B. Meek to James Hall, St. Louis, May 19, 1853, Box 5, James Hall Papers, New York State Museum, Albany, N.Y.

21. Merrill, p. 502.

22. Ibid., p. 503.

23. See Warren to Hayden, Wash., Feb. 15, 1856, in Merrill, p. 711.

24. Warren, *Preliminary Report,* pp. 14–15.

sites for military posts and assemble general scientific data on the country (p. 15).

The 1856 expedition was largely uneventful. They left Fort Pierre on June 28, reached Fort Union at the mouth of the Yellowstone on July 10, and steamed sixty miles further up the river toward a connection with any possible wagon road over the mountains from the West. Back at Fort Union, Warren hired Jim Bridger as his guide, purchased wagons and mules from a British sportsman, Sir George Gore, and proceeded to ascend the Yellowstone River for one hundred miles. Leaving his wagons, Warren and his scientific party went by mule back as far as the entrance to the Powder River. Then they floated downstream in bullboats, sketching the topography of the river all the way to Fort Union. They left that Fort in a Mackinac boat on September 1 and floated down the Missouri while a land party followed along the shore. This was hardly new country to a geographer, but for Hayden, a paleontologist, it offered numerous opportunities for observation and collection. Warren himself took an active part in catching and preserving zoological specimens. They reached Fort Pierre on October 2 and Sioux City on November 15. When they arrived at St. Louis, they hurried to Washington to begin analyzing the extensive scientific collections. The 1856 expedition had little or no practical value for the operation of the field army or for the road-building program.

On May 7, 1857, Lieutenant Warren received orders from Secretary of War John B. Floyd to take the field again.[25] His objective was to locate a link with the Fort Snelling–Big Sioux Road that would connect it, via the Loup Fork, with Fort Laramie and the South Pass. He was then to explore the Loup Fork of the Platte and the Niobrara, and in the time remaining to ascend to the Black Hills and examine them in detail.[26] His party again included F. V. Hayden and J. H. Snowden, as well as various other assistants and an escort of thirty men of the Second Infantry commanded by Lt. James McMillan.

The main party set out on June 27 from Omaha and marched

25. Ibid., p. 16.

26. Ibid., p. 17. The Fort Snelling–Big Sioux Road is the same as the Mendota–Big Sioux Road.

to a rendezvous with Lieutenant Warren at Sioux City.[27] At this point twelve of the soldiers deserted. Nevertheless, they marched west toward the Loup Fork of the Platte, and striking it followed its course until they reached its source in the sand hills. From there they crossed over to the Niobrara and by an easy route continued on to Fort Laramie. They found this route in no sense, however, a substitute for the regular Platte River Road (pp. 17–18).

At Fort Laramie outfitting took a long time because of the scarcity created by the Utah expedition. When he left the Fort, in order to accomplish his whole mission Lieutenant Warren divided his party. Mr. Snowden, Lieutenant McMillan, and the escort were to proceed down the Niobrara, mapping its course, while Warren, Hayden, two topographers, and seventeen men, together with Morin, the guide, headed north for the Black Hills. Their line of march was due north, via Raw Hide Butte, Old Woman Creek, the South Fork of the Cheyenne, and Beaver Creek. It was along a branch of the latter that they entered the Black Hills. They continued as far north as Inyan Kara, a high basalt dome, from which they could look off to the prairie beyond. Near here, Warren recorded, they met "a large force of the Dakotas who made such earnest remonstrances and threats against our proceeding into their country that I did not think it prudent for us, as a scientific expedition, to venture further in that direction" (pp. 18–19).

After a long and earnest parley with the Indians, Lieutenant Warren agreed to respect Harney's treaty and turn back from his survey of the Black Hills. Accordingly they returned forty miles and then headed eastward, apprehensive lest the large parties of Minneconjous, Sihasipas, and Unkpapas decide to attack them in revenge for the action at Blue Water. After two days, Bear's Rib, head chief of the Sioux, overtook them and agreed to accompany them to Bear Butte to assure their safety. Their retreat from the Black Hills took them by way of the South Fork of the Cheyenne and the French Creek, through the Bad Lands on the White River, to the Niobrara at longitude 102° 3′, where they made contact with Lieutenant McMillan and his party.

27. Ibid. Unless otherwise noted, the account that follows is based on this source.

While Warren was coming near to disaster in the Black Hills, Lieutenant McMillan was fending off the Brulés under Little Thunder, who were spoiling for revenge. Once, twenty-two braves charged the camp and then quickly retreated, doing no damage. It was fortunate that the parties were able to join forces before another massacre occurred. By November 1, however, the reconnaissance was over and the entire command reached Fort Randall on the Missouri River. The difficulty of the country, the ravages of disease, and the inordinate belligerence of the Indians had made the summer's reconnaissance a trying one.

In contrast to the fur traders, Lieutenant Warren devoted much of his attention to problems of settlement in the Dakota region. His first concern was with the extension of military roads between the Missouri River and the Rocky Mountains. Though he had explored as far north as Fort Benton, he had found no route that surpassed the valley of the Platte; consequently he recommended bridging it and making other improvements in the interest of overland traffic (p. 43). There were several other inferior but practicable routes. The Mendota–Big Sioux Road, he thought, should connect with the Platte route by way of Sioux City and the mouth of the Loup Fork of the Platte. A short cut to the north, via the Niobrara and the upper reaches of the Loup, was to be avoided because of the rugged Sand Hills country. Another conceivable route would be by way of the north bank of the White River between either Fort Pierre or Old Fort Lookout and Fort Laramie. For a railroad west from St. Paul he favored following William H. Nobles' wagon route (the Fort Ridgely Road) to Old Fort Lookout, the White River, and Fort Laramie. But of all the routes, whether for wagon or railroad, the lieutenant preferred the valley of the Platte, "which offers a route not surpassed for natural gradients by any in the world" (p. 46).

For the agriculturalist he saw dim prospects: "An irreclaimable desert of two hundred to four hundred miles in width separates the points capable of settlement in the east from those of the mountains in the west" (p. 46). And even though the mountains were destined for great population, the industry would be largely confined to mining and pastoral pursuits (pp. 30–31). Nearly to a man, every Topographical Officer from Stephen H. Long onward had described the plains west of the 100th meridian as being of little value to a civilization largely agrarian in its basic economic activity. To them the plains country formed a barrier to progress. In spite of this, however, the lieutenant saw a bright commercial future for the towns of the Nebraska frontier. In a lengthy prophecy he declared:

> They are, as it were, on the shores of a sea, up to which population and agriculture may advance, and no further. But this gives them much of the value of places along the Atlantic frontier, in view of the future settlements to be formed in the mountains between which and the present frontier, a most valuable trade would exist. The western frontier has always been looking to the east for a market, but as soon as the wave of emigration has passed over the desert portion of the plains . . . then will the present frontier of Kansas and Nebraska become the starting point for all the products of the Mississippi Valley which the population of the mountains will require. We see the effects of it in the benefits which the western frontier of Missouri has received from the Santa Fe trade, and still more plainly in the impetus given to Leavenworth by the operations of the Army of Utah in the interior region. The flow of products has, in the last instance, been only in one direction, but when those mountains become settled, as they eventually must, then there will be a reciprocal trade materially beneficial to both [p. 31].

At one time, western visionaries like Gilpin and Benton had looked upon the towns of the Mississippi Valley as gateways to India. In less than ten years the field of vision had narrowed, but the future looked equally promising. Omaha and Sioux City might well stand like Venice and Genoa as rivals for the rich commerce of an inland empire based on mining and cattle raising. By 1858 the region between the Sierras and the Great Plains was already giving evidence of its future potential.

But if the "Great American Desert" was an easily surmountable barrier for the march of empire, the human barrier was not. Lieutenant Warren considered the warlike and powerful Dakota tribes as the great obstacle to progress. He wrote in alarm, "There are so many inevitable causes at work to produce a war with the Dakotas before many years, that I regard the greatest fruit of the explorations I have conducted to be the knowledge of the proper routes by which to invade their country and conquer them" (p. 53). Yet in his consideration of the Indian problem he attempted to be fair, admitting that he believed "many of the causes of war with them might be removed by timely action in relation to the treaties . . . and a prompt fulfillment of our own part of the stipulations." He added, "I have always found the Dakotas exceedingly reasonable beings, with a very proper appreciation of what are their own rights" (p. 54). At the same time he concluded: "The advance of the settlements is universally acknowledged to be a necessity of our national development, and is justifiable in displacing the native races on that ground alone" (p. 52). The government had only to pursue a wise policy of clearing the way by purchase of the lands, conclusion of just treaties, and seeing to it that the rights of the Indians were protected. There was no evil inherent in the occupation of the western hunting grounds. There was only inefficiency and bad handling in the way it was done. In the end, he came to the only conclusion possible for a believer in American destiny: "the western settlers are now fighting the battle of civilization exactly as our forefathers did on the Atlantic shores, and under circumstances that command an equal amount of our admiration and approval" (p. 52).

The last major exploration conducted by the Topographical Engineers in the West was the Yellowstone expedition of 1859–60. In his reports on the Dakota country Lieutenant Warren had recommended a further reconnaissance beyond the Big Horn Mountains into the upper Yellowstone and Powder River country (p. 7). Accordingly, $60,000 was appropriated for the work, and an expedition sent into the field in the summer of 1859. Lieutenant Warren was not its leader, however, for he had been inexplicably transferred from the Bureau of Explorations and Surveys to a post as instructor at West Point, thus ending his career as a scientific explorer.[28] The man appointed to lead the expedition was Capt. William F. Raynolds, a newcomer to the field of western exploration.

28. Taylor, *Warren,* p. 43.

Captain Raynold's orders were to ascertain the "numbers, habits, and disposition" of the Indians, as well as the climate and resources of the whole region, which according to the Captain's estimate was about 250,000 square miles, or "more than double the area of Great Britain." He was to search out four possible wagon-road routes—the first from Fort Laramie to the Yellowstone, in the direction of Fort Union on the Missouri; the second, from Fort Laramie northwesterly along the base of the Big Horn Mountains toward Fort Benton and the Bitterroot Valley (this to connect with Lieutenant Mullan's road coming east from Washington Territory); the third from the Yellowstone to the South Pass; and the fourth between the sources of the Wind River and those of the Missouri.[29] From these orders it is clear that the War Department as early as 1859 was planning a network of roads that would stretch across the northern regions and open the last stronghold of the Sioux and the Blackfeet to the advance of white settlers.

The Raynolds expedition was elaborate. His staff included Lt. H. E. Maynadier, assistant; J. M. Hutton and J. H. Snowden, topographers; a meteorologist and astronomer; a timekeeper and computer; Antoine Schoenborn, the artist; and the indefatigable F. V. Hayden as geologist. In addition, the Secretary of War had ordered Raynolds to take along four Virginians, one Washingtonian, and two citizens of Illinois "without any special duty being assigned to them." [30] There was also an escort of thirty infantrymen, commanded by Lt. Caleb B. Smith. Jim Bridger served as guide.

Two steamboats of Pierre Chouteau's American Fur Company carried them upriver to Fort Pierre, which they reached about noon on June 18 (p. 19). This was to be the starting point of their trek west to the Yellowstone. Here they were first forced to bargain with the Indians for permission to cross their territory. Threats prevailed where persuasion did not. All the way across the Dakota country, however, they were carefully watched by Indian sentinels. Only when they reached the valley of the Pow-

29. Raynolds, *Report* (above, p. 25, n. 12), pp. 4–5. See p. 6 for Raynolds' estimate of the size of the area he was to explore.

30. Ibid., p. 18. Unless otherwise noted, the following account is based on this source.

der River were they out of the Sioux country. At Fort Pierre the tenderfoot Captain had his first view of the Indians. It was disillusioning. He visited the trading house where he saw them

> lounging about the room literally *au naturel.* They had discarded their gaudy vestments and barbaric trappings and with these their glory had departed. A filthy cloth about the loins, a worn buffalo robe, or a greasy blanket, constituted the only covering to their nakedness. They were lying about on the floor in all conceivable postures, their whole air and appearance indicating ignorance and indolence, while the inevitable pipe was being passed from hand to hand. Dirt and degradation were the inseparable accompaniments of this scene, which produced an ineffaceable impression on my mind, banishing all ideas of dignity in the Indian character and leaving a vividly realizing sense of the fact that the red men are savages [p. 21].

On Tuesday, June 28, they marched westward out of Fort Pierre to the Cheyenne River and headed toward Fort Laramie. Raynolds pronounced the country "totally unfit for agricultural purposes," as the wind sweeping over the "parched and heated soil" struck them "like a blast from a furnace" (pp. 24–25). On the Fourth of July, however, their labors were lightened by a celebration and the consumption of a basket of champagne given them by Pierre Chouteau. Seven days later they reached Bear Butte and the Black Hills, which Raynolds believed was fit only for the savages. July 21 found them at the Powder River, then the boundary line between the Sioux country and that of the friendly Crow Indians on the West. Bridger was at last in familiar country. At this point they decided to head for Fort Sarpy, a fur-trading post on the Yellowstone River thirty miles below the mouth of the Bighorn River. From there they moved southward along the upper reaches of the Bighorn and Powder rivers toward the Oregon Trail, which they reached on October 11, 1859. According to Raynolds, the road was "marked as any turnpike in the east. It is hard, dry, and dusty, and gave evidence of the immense amount of travel that passes over it" (p. 70). They also reached the temptations of civilization. At Richard's Trading Houses near the Platte River Bridge the whole command got uproariously drunk and Raynolds, himself a teetotaler, lost control of them. Lieutenant Smith and the escort mutinied, leaving leaving the Captain and what was left of his command to move into winter quarters at an abandoned Mormon village near the Upper Platte Indian Agency (p. 71). During the winter, time was consumed by Lieutenant Smith's court-martial and by long earnest conversations between Raynolds, who was religious almost to the point of fanaticism, and F. V. Hayden, who despite all of Raynolds' missionary efforts steadfastly pursued the paths of material success.[31] The Pony Express was opened that winter, too, and Raynolds recalled it as being among "*the* events of the age, and the most striking triumphs of American energy" (pp. 76–77).

Early in May the expedition, minus Lieutenant Smith who had been acquitted of the charges and sent on other duties, resumed its field operations. It was divided into two parties. Lieutenant Maynadier led one detachment up the Bighorn to the Greybull River and westward to the Clark Fork of the Yellowstone. Then he followed the Clark Fork to the Yellowstone itself and crossed over the mountains into the Gallatin Valley, where, near the Three Forks, he awaited the arrival of Raynolds' party (pp. 130–45).

Raynolds' contingent headed westward toward Wind River and attempted to cross the mountains into the valley of the Upper Yellowstone (today's Park area). However, their efforts were baffled by mountain ridges and deep snows. Raynolds sadly recorded that they "were compelled to content [themselves] with listening to marvellous tales of burning plains, immense lakes, and boiling springs, without being able to verify these words" (p. 10). It was a keen disappointment to Raynolds, as both Bridger and Robert Meldrum, the only men ever to gaze upon these marvels, convinced him that the upper Yellowstone was "the most interesting unexplored district in our widely expanded country" (p. 10). If the expedition had started a few weeks later in the summer of 1860, they might have reached the Park area, and Captain Raynolds would thus have achieved greater importance in the public eye.

31. W. F. Raynolds, "Journal," Feb. 6, 18, 1860, Raynolds Papers, Yale Collection of Western Americana.

As it was, they turned due west and marched around the Park area, via Pierre's Hole and the Grand Tetons, across the Continental Divide to the Three Forks rendezvous. The march required great labor. On one occasion even Bridger had given up hope of proceeding further; but Raynolds floundered and crawled, face down, through the snow drifts and across the icy surfaces to lead the party to the very summit of the Continental Divide. It was a personal triumph for the tenderfoot over the already almost legendary mountain hero.

At the Three Forks the party divided again, with Lieutenant Maynadier taking the Yellowstone Route to Fort Union while Raynolds marched down the Missouri to Fort Benton and a rendezvous with Major George Blake, who was setting out with the first party of troops to cross over Lieutenant Mullan's wagon road to Oregon. From this point they followed the Missouri to Fort Union, Fort Pierre, Fort Randall, and St. Louis. Their two-year reconnaissance had given them at least an idea of the broken country that lay between the Missouri and the Bitterroot Valley. However, no road had been located that would stretch across the Dakotas and make a direct link with the strategic Mullan Road. In fact, if anything, the impression gained from Captain Raynolds' *Report* was that such a trail did not exist because of the ruggedness of the country and the existence of numerous broad rivers, like the Big Horn and the Yellowstone. But in spite of this, and in spite of the disappointment on the Upper Yellowstone, the Raynolds' expedition was important, because it brought the government scientists into the last major unexplored region of the Far West. What the Ives and Macomb surveys had been to the unknown Plateau Province, the Warren and Raynolds surveys were to the Dakota-Wyoming region. When the Army resumed operations against the Sioux after the Civil War, it was to the Warren and Raynolds reports that they turned for information. Their reports were printed and distributed by the Engineer Office much as had been the old Congressional Documents.[32]

Beyond this it is difficult to measure the value of these northern

32. The reports of the Warren and Raynolds expeditions, both made before the Civil War, were printed in 1875 and 1868 respectively; even after the war they were the principal source of information on that country.

explorations precisely. They did not locate a definite route across the country to Washington Territory, though they did indicate ways of penetrating the Sioux country. Raynolds' men managed to link up with the advanced scouts of the Mullan Road party which, in 1860, was just completing two years of grueling labor on a wagon road that stretched between Fort Walla Walla and Fort Benton, via Lake Coeur d'Alene, the Bitterroot Valley, and Hell Gate River.[33] The Mullan Road, though it never became the important thoroughfare for settlers that its builders hoped it would be, nevertheless formed one of the important arteries of transportation by which the miners moved into the gold regions in Idaho and Montana. It also provided an avenue of trade between the inland diggings and the seacoast settlements in Washington, thus channeling the trade away from California. But it was not until 1862 that a private contractor, John M. Bozeman, laid out a trail to the Montana gold diggings, and not until 1865 that James A. Sawyers made a road between Yankton and Virginia City, via the Powder River and the Bozeman Pass.[34] As far as locating wagon roads was concerned, the Raynolds and even the Warren expedition can be considered practical failures.

On the other hand, they helped to complete the scientific picture of the West. Geographically speaking, their maps were important. Most significant of all was the effect of these expeditions on the fast-maturing science of geology. Here, thanks to the labors of F. V. Hayden and his collaborators, F. B. Meek and Joseph Leidy, an almost revolutionary advance was made in the study of western geology.

Neither Hayden nor Meek could be said to belong to the Humboldtean tradition. They were not interested in cosmology or idealistic metaphysics. Unlike Captain Simpson, Carl Ritter (the German geographer), or Louis Agassiz, they did not much care whether the natural phenomena they observed presented evidences of an overarching Intelligence. Instead, they frankly concentrated on observation for its own sake, and for the achievement of a limited kind of truth. They were satisfied, for example, if they could prove that true Permian beds, comparable to those in Europe, did, in fact, exist in Kansas, and they did not question

33. Jackson, *Wagon Roads,* pp. 257–78, esp. 266.
34. Ibid., pp. 281–96.

either the meaning of this fact or its relation to every other aspect of nature. In retrospect the shift in approach may not seem startling, particularly since many of the contemporary scientists, like Newberry, Engelmann, and Hall, implicitly had something of this same point of view. Yet the nature of the resistance to evolution—on the grounds of special creation—is one index of the prevailing idealistic climate of scientific opinion. To note a contrast with the works of Hayden and Meek one had only to listen to Arnold Guyot as he asserted before the American Geographical and Statistical Society on February 16, 1860, that "a science of the globe which excludes the spirit world represented by man, is a beautiful body without a soul." [35] But in a sense, as the experience of the Topographical Corps and its scientific partners shows, the very enthusiasms of the Humboldtean scientist led to the change in the scientific approach. If the Humboldtean was to comprehend the cosmos, he had first to account for every phenomenon in it. But the search after all these pieces of data of infinite variety and exotic appeal eventually engulfed the searcher in a multitude of natural facts—enough so that the very abundance made him stop and construct his limited pattern of order. This was what Hayden's work represented for the study of western geology.

Most important of the Hayden and Meek contributions was the determination of a typical stratigraphic column with which the other geologists could make their comparisons. There were nine layers:

1. Metamorphosed Azoic rocks, including coarse granite
2. Lower Silurian (Potsdam Sandstone)
3. Devonian
4. Carboniferous
5. Permian
6. Jurassic
7. Cretaceous, Upper, Middle, and Lower
8. Tertiary
9. Post Pliocene or Quarternary [36]

This presented a measuring stick, and each of the various epochs was assigned the name of the prominent locales where it could be

35. Quoted in Simpson, *Report* (above, p. 391, n. 41), p. 70 n.
36. Warren, *Preliminary Report,* p. 63.

observed, such as "the Fort Pierre Group." James Hall had followed this procedure in his section on the paleontology of New York, while Newberry related his Grand Canyon section to that of Hayden and Meek.[37] The column's greatest effectiveness resulted from the precision with which each formation was determined, and this, in turn, depended on a careful analysis and classification of the fossils discovered in it. Here F. B. Meek excelled, and while Hayden collected the specimens and placed them in field diagrams, Meek, back in an eastern museum, sorted and classified them into a system that was really useful for identification purposes. His work on the Cretaceous beds was the most complete.

Then, too, as a result of their labors in this direction, Hayden and Meek were able to identify the important Potsdam Sandstone formation for the first time in the West, and figuratively speaking give a floor to all the other layers.[38] They also identified numerous fresh-water fossils which they interpreted as estuary and lake deposits, thus indicating periods where dry land stood out above the continental seas.[39] Most of their fossil discoveries were revealed in papers read before the Philadelphia Academy of Natural Science or in articles in the *American Journal of Science,* but they often bore titles that linked them to the Warren or Raynolds expeditions.[40] In addition, the preliminary reports of the Army Topographers included reports by Hayden and Meek. In 1857 the first Warren report included Hayden's geological map of the West, which he later insisted both antedated and was more accurate than those by Blake in the *Pacific Railroad Reports,* Hall in the Mexican Boundary Survey *Report,* and Marcou in his private report on the West.[41] With each report Hayden was able to correct his map, until in his final *Geological Report of the Yellowstone and Missouri Rivers,* published in 1869, he presented a completely colored geological map of the Dakota-Montana-Idaho region.[42] In many respects this 1869 report was the

37. Ives, *Report* (above, p. 20, n. 51), Pt. II, pp. 56–57.
38. Warren, *Preliminary Report,* pp. 7, 63.
39. Ibid., p. 65. See also Merrill, *First One Hundred Years,* p. 508.
40. Ibid., pp. 61–62.
41. Hayden, *Geological Report* (above, p. 391, n. 40), p. ix.
42. Ibid., geological map.

most important geological work of the Topographical Engineer period, because it was a résumé of all Hayden had found by the end of this phase of his western labors.

In addition to his careful work in paleontology and geologic mapping, Hayden developed a theory of mountain-making which began by accepting the idea of huge igneous upthrusts from below but which eventually included some idea of lateral crustal displacement and folding.[43] If Dana's *Manual of Geology* of 1862 was the first in this country to propound the syncline-anticline thesis, the terms had been used by Hayden years before.

Not the least of Hayden and Meek's achievements was the collection of countless specimens of extinct vertebrates that they brought back for classification by Joseph Leidy of Philadelphia. Shy, self-effacing, one of the authentic geniuses of his time, Leidy stood alone, pre-eminent in his field of comparative anatomy. For years the Pennsylvania professor pursued the study of vertebrate paleontology as a hobby, and all western discoveries came to him for classification.[44] The Evans expedition of 1849 had brought back the first specimens from the Dakota Badlands, but from 1853 onward Hayden kept him busy classifying specimens, and Leidy's papers before the Philadelphia Academy came to be a regular event.[45] It was the specimens from the Dakota country and Leidy's incredible labors that really established the science of vertebrate paleontology in the United States. Though most of Leidy's papers bore dry, matter-of-fact, titles, one of his later works, "The Ancient Fauna of Nebraska," indicated that paleontology could be a profound, exciting, and almost artistic branch of scientific endeavor. One of the results of all this labor in classifying vertebrate fossils was to establish the fact that there were animals on this continent that are now extinct. This, of course, eventually led to a proof for evolution, and though it was O. C. Marsh who made explicit the importance of the horse cycle of evolution, it was Leidy who during these earlier years had put together the first horse cycle, and, in fact, first called at-

43. Merrill, p. 509.

44. Henry Fairfield Osborn, "Joseph Leidy, 1823–1891," *National Academy of Sciences, Biographical Memoirs, 8* (1913), 358.

45. Ibid., p. 360. Leidy classified and described virtually all of Hayden's vertebrate specimens.

tention to the existence of a horse native to the American continent.[46] The existence of the elephant, the camel, and the rhinoceros similar to corresponding species of present-day Asia and Africa, suggested that the American Continent might well be older, not (as previously suspected) younger, than Europe.[47] Perhaps human migrations across the Atlantic were really reversing the first spread of creation outward from its center. Infinite possibilities for speculation were fast being opened. All these steps in the progress of science were owing, in part, to the Army expeditions into the West that gave Hayden his chance to collect and observe with government sponsorship and protection from the Indians. It was the opening of a new era in western exploration, which was interrupted by the Civil War but which in the postwar years would see the increasing predominance of scientific over practical reconnaissances.

Though the Raynolds expedition was the last of the explorations conducted by the Topographical Corps, it was somehow an appropriate one. It included nearly all the figures who had dominated that particular age of exploration. There was Raynolds, the soldier-scientist, just entering upon the conquest of the wilderness. There was also the fur-trade entrepreneur Pierre Chouteau and his agent Alexander Culbertson. There was the Indian—variously noble savage, indolent beggar, and hostile warrior. And there was Jim Bridger whose retirement from the life of a trapper back in 1842 dates the end of one era of exploration. Bridger had thus spanned two ages of western exploration, and he remained as a symbol of the white man's struggle with nature at its wildest. Still another figure belongs to the cast—F. V. Hayden, who represented, in a sense, the difference between the mountain man's West and the engineer's West, but who, like Bridger, was to span two eras. And finally, waiting in the wings as the all-important silent partners, were the settlers who would take full possession of the Continent as a result of these labors in western exploration.

46. Ibid., pp. 357–58.
47. Ibid., pp. 358–59.

EPILOGUE

THE LAST TOPOGRAPHICAL ENGINEER to leave the West was Lt. John G. Parke. Between June 1857 and the closing days of 1861, Lieutenant Parke was in the field along the 49th parallel, serving as chief astronomer and surveyor to the Northwest Boundary Commission. As in the Mexican Boundary Survey, the work in the Northwest was performed by a mixed commission operating under the authority of the State Department. The task of the Commission was to cooperate with Great Britain in the running and marking of the international boundary along the 49th parallel from the summit of the Rocky Mountains to the Straits of Juan de Fuca. Since the terms of the Treaty of 1846 were clear in their specification of the Northwest land boundary along the 49th parallel, the only dispute that arose was over the water boundary, and this matter was eventually settled by international arbitration in 1871.[1] This dispute did not concern the Topographical Bureau, since Lieutenant Parke's duty was confined to the land boundary. In contrast to the experience of the Mexican Survey, no sectional or political interests were attached to this operation, and as a consequence its history is largely one of routine activity.

The actual survey work was begun by the American party, which worked alone through 1857 and the spring of 1858, after which a British party under Col. J. S. Hawkins of the Royal Engineers, finally entered the field (p. 15). By the end of 1858 the line had been run from the initial point at Camp Simiahmoo on the Gulf of Georgia ninety miles eastward through the wilderness to the valley of the Skagit River (p. 16). In the working season of 1859 the line was advanced as far as the Columbia, an additional distance of 150 miles, which carried them past the difficult Cas-

1. Marcus Baker, "Survey of the Northwestern Boundary of the United States, 1857–61," *United States Geological Survey,* Bulletin 174 (Wash., 1900), p. 9.

cade Range. The method of procedure was to send a reconnoitering party ahead to blaze a rough trail over the mountains and through the dense forests. Then teams of astronomers and surveyors would follow, setting up stations along the way for making exact astronomical observations and tracing the line with a laborious chain and compass survey. To mark the boundary long slashes twenty feet wide were made in the forests near the astronomical stations, in the vicinity of settlements, and at the crossings of rivers and streams. The chief problems that arose were the difficulty of the terrain, which made the supplying of the field parties a laborious process, and the rising costs of mules and equipment caused by the Frazier River Gold Rush.[2] Only once did the British and American parties disagree over the location of the line itself, and later conferences over the drafting table soon satisfied both parties.[3] In the spring of 1861 the work was completed and the parties disbanded and returned to Washington for the final phase of compiling the maps and official reports. An office was set up in Washington at the corner of Pennsylvania Avenue and Twentieth Street NW, where, under the supervision of Archibald Campbell, the commissioner, and Lieutenant Parke, the astronomer, an extensive report on the work of the preceding four years was compiled.[4]

In addition to the making of maps, the usual attention was paid to the various branches of scientific endeavor. F. B. Meek wrote on fossil mollusks, George Suckley on fishes, birds, and mammals, John Strong Newberry on fossil plants, Elliot Coues on birds, John Torrey on plants, and Theodore Gill on fishes.[5] Several of these men reported their findings in separate lectures presented to various learned societies. But ultimately the Civil War interrupted the final phase of the Boundary Survey work, calling its officers to other duties and preventing the publication of the ambitious report. All that remained of the survey were the slashes in the forest marking the line, a number of half-finished maps, a magnificent series of watercolor sketches by James Alden, the artist of the Commission, and a multitude of widely

2. George Clinton Gardner, "Report . . . on the Northwest Boundary Survey, 1857–1861," Yale Collection of Western Americana, p. 34.

3. Ibid., pp. 210–11, 224, 233.

4. Ibid., pp. 228–30. Baker, p. 17.

5. Baker, p. 62.

scattered monographs and field reports, which today remain uncollected and unpublished in the National Archives. Perhaps the most intriguing aspect of the whole project was the disappearance of the final draft of the report. It was borrowed by Commissioner Campbell for his later work on the boundary of northern Minnesota and has never been found.[6]

In a symbolic sense, it may be appropriate that the final report was lost, for in this way the Northwest Boundary Survey can stand for the whole era of the Topographical Engineer, which has likewise dropped from the public memory. A whole cast of heroes, and a long series of explorations and surveys that marked off the present continental limits of the United States, from the Big Bend of the Rio Grande to the Simiahmoo Peninsula, has been largely forgotten, consigned to the moldy calfskins of the public archives. Yet, as the history of the Topographical Engineers has shown, their contributions were numerous and important. As a Corps they functioned as a central institution of the era of Manifest Destiny, reflecting its problems and its achievements.

As has been noted, the problems the Corps faced were peculiar, and yet typical of a branch of the central government having an extensive positive function to fulfill. The Corps was always forced to operate in the midst of the powerful pressures of economic and political factions. It was committed to the principle of national growth, but in aiding the direction of that growth it entered into the realm of partisan sectional politics, and no course which it pursued, could entirely satisfy the numerous factions. Its officers were particularly vulnerable to social pressures and grandiose schemes for expansion, because they had reputations to make and the ideal example of Frémont before them to indicate the path to success. Thus in retrospect it seems almost inevitable that the Corps of Topographical Engineers should follow the course it did—attach itself to the southwestern project for a railroad and, believing in the importance of the project, campaign vigorously in its behalf. Though by the 1850's the Senate and the House were largely responsive to popular control, the Cabinet remained a last rampart of Southern defense. And in the public eye the Topographical Corps was the very creature of such a cabinet.

By the same token, when the West began to develop, in rail-

6. Ibid., pp. 11–12.

roads, in mining, and in homesteading, the local governments began to assume a greater importance, and a national agency which held tight control over federal improvement and expenditure in the territorial communities was extremely vulnerable to their attack. Numerous examples have been presented to indicate the difficulty of engaging in a positive program of public works which would at the same time satisfy the infinite number and variety of popular demands. Thus the difficulty of achieving necessary positive progress was infinitely increased. It was the dissatisfied western entrepreneurs, large and small, who were responsible for the contemporary criticism of the Corps. With the passage of time, perhaps they have been responsible, also, for the creation of a series of myths that have obscured the real services of the Corps to the nation.

In spite of the difficulties, however, the achievements of the Topographical Engineers were considerable. In the realm of practical service they explored the important trails, located passes through the mountains, and supervised the construction of roads (both local and transcontinental). They totaled up the national resources. They prospected for water and minerals. They surveyed the possibilities of agriculture, and they helped to brush aside the Indian barrier. They mapped most of the major rivers and on several occasions supervised their improvement projects. They surveyed the important harbors, built dams, constructed lighthouses, and laid out coastal fortifications. In all of these operations they invested their skills and the extensive federal subsidies in an underdeveloped region at a time when the settlers themselves were unable to do so.

Because of their pragmatic orientation, the line between the practical and the theoretical works of the Corps must remain indistinct. Nevertheless, they served the whole nation as well as the West in making their great inventory of the unknown country. Their extensive collecting activities alone provided an opportunity for harnessing the energies of natural science to the service of the people. Their work also aided the growth of theoretical science by providing employment and opportunities for gaining experience to most of the important American scientists of the time. In collecting, compiling, cataloguing, and organizing all of the brute data of nature, the Army expeditions were performing the basic work of science. On numerous occasions the result was a monumental treatise on some phase of natural science—Torrey's *Botany of the Boundary;* Baird, Cassin, and Lawrence on birds; Hayden's work in geology and paleontology; Newberry's cross section of the Grand Canyon. At other times their contributions led to erroneous conclusions. But this was the scientific method in action, as they focused sharply upon the western environment and with the data at hand groped their way toward a complete picture of the region. In a larger sense, the progressive revelations of these scientific expeditions helped to change the basic assumptions of American culture. As they noted the continuous processes in nature, the doctrine of uniformitarianism became accepted among the scientists of the day. The fossil discoveries of Hayden and Meek and the plant distribution patterns noted by Gray prepared the way for an acceptance of Darwinism and all that it implied. It was not, however, in the realm of revolutionary hypothesis that the Topographical expeditions had their important results. Rather, operating in a context of Romanticism that sought to comprehend and appreciate rather than to rationalize, the scientific expeditions of the Corps served as a means of revelation more than of analysis. The tremendous number of specimens, the long, tedious catalogues, the thousands of pages of mathematical computations, the maps, the narratives, the pictures, and the scientific plates—all added up to a comprehensive picture of the West that was tremendous in size and scope. Though it had gone no further, the scientific work of the Corps had at least provided a solid factual basis upon which, and out of which, the future great hypotheses could be constructed.

The total picture of the Corps operating in the West is, more than anything else, a picture of the cultural mind in action. It represents the collective absorption by a people of new knowledge, and a new appreciation of the complexity of the modern world as the nineteenth century began to see it. Above all it provides a picture of man employing all of his skills to arrive at a kind of ordered knowledge of his environment.

With the outbreak of hostilities in 1861 the rapid disintegration of the Topographical Corps began. Even before that year some of its best officers, like William Hemsley Emory and Joseph E. Johnston, had transferred to other branches of the service. Early in April 1861 Colonel Abert, ill and growing old, began to falter. On the eleventh of that month Major Hartman Bache assumed temporary command of the Topographical Bureau.[7] In August both Colonel Abert and his old friend Lt. Col. James Kearny were placed on the retirement list.[8] Abert was among the last of the old-line soldiers to be retired. On September 28 Major Howard Stansbury, the explorer of the Great Salt Lake, also joined them in retirement. For a brief time in the hectic military reorganization of 1861 the Corps seemed to prosper despite the changes wrought in its personnel. By an act of August 6, 1861, two more lieutenant colonels, four majors, and a company of regular soldiers were added to its complement. But this gain was more than offset by the mass transfer and resignation of its experienced officers. Nine men, including Lieutenants Ives, Dixon, Bryan, and M. L. Smith, resigned to join the Confederacy. Eighteen Topographers became line officers in the Union Army, commanding brigades and divisions. In December 1861, when Stephen H. Long took command as Colonel of the Corps, there were only twenty-eight officers left on its roster.[9] Yet the demand for their services was still widespread. Most of the field commands had a Topographer as staff officer, and both Whipple and Macomb served for a time as commander of John A. Wise's balloon reconnaissance unit.[10] Whipple even made an ascension high over the Confederate lines in what may well be one of the opening chapters in the history of modern aerial warfare in America.[11]

On March 3, 1863, the Corps of Topographical Engineers was legislated into oblivion. In "An Act to promote the efficiency of the Corps of Engineers" the Topographical Corps was once again merged with the Corps of Engineers. Gen. Joseph G. Totten assumed command, and Stephen H. Long became the senior colo-

7. Beers, "History of the U. S. Topographical Engineers," Pt. II (above, p. 8, n. 9), p. 352.

8. Ibid., Major Campbell Graham was also retired.

9. Ibid., pp. 351–52.

10. F. Stansbury Hayden, *Aeronautics in the Union and Confederate Armies* (Baltimore, 1941), pp. 43, 48–49, 61–63, 130, and passim.

11. Ibid., p. 185.

nel.[12] Thus, though it could never erase its two decades of brilliant achievement in the development of the American West, the Civil War had brought the Corps back again to its subordinate status of 1831, where it was to remain.

Though the war caused the destruction of the Corps, its officers played a larger part in the outcome of the hostilities than any other comparable group. There were M. L. Smith and Joseph Johnston at Vicksburg, and Johnston later at Chattanooga and a hundred other battles on the retreat to Atlanta.[13] There was W. B. Franklin, who along with "Bold" Emory saved the army of Nathaniel Banks from certain destruction in the Red River Campaign.[14] Emory it was, too, who served brilliantly as a cavalry commander at Hanover Courthouse, and later under Sheridan in the Shenandoah Valley.[15] Joseph Christmas Ives joined Jefferson Davis' personal staff, where he and his wife, Cora Semmes Ives, became important figures in the society of the beleagered Confederacy.[16] From the poor boarding-house boy of New Haven he had come a long way to a dominant position in the Confederate aristocracy. Amiel Weeks Whipple was killed instantly at Chancellorsville as he led his men in a desperate resistance to Stonewall Jackson's sudden onslaught.[17] John Pope continued to be his own press agent, and from his "headquarters in the saddle" he directed the disastrous battle of the Second Manassas.[18] He was not, however, entirely unsuccessful as a soldier, for it was Pope who captured Island Number Ten in the Mississippi, which had been fortified by the Texan engineer A. B. Gray.[19] But the high point of the Civil War, so far as the former Topographers were concerned, came at Gettysburg. There, George Gordon Meade was the Union commander, and G. K. Warren was his chief engineer. Down on the first line was

12. Beers, p. 352.
13. *DAB.*
14. *DAB.*
15. *DAB.*
16. DeLeon, *Belles, Beaux, and Brains of the 60's* (above, p. 278, n. 48), pp. 116–18.
17. *DAB.*
18. *DAB.*
19. W. P. Webb and H. B. Carroll, eds., *The Handbook of Texas* (2 vols. Austin, 1952), *1*, 722.

the former desk soldier A. A. Humphreys, leading a brigade in Dan Sickles' Corps.[20] It was his brigade that received the full force of the Confederate charge, and sober, dignified Humphreys earned himself the nickname of "the fighting fool of Gettysburg." G. K. Warren, however, performed the most decisive service. With his topographer's eye trained on the plains of Nebraska and in the chart rooms of the Topographical Bureau, he immediately grasped the importance of Little Round Top, commandeered some men, and led them to its summit—just in time to prevent the Confederates from taking it.[21] His action meant the difference between victory and defeat. Today these officers are remembered, if at all, for their services in the great Civil War. Warren stands immortalized in bronze, gazing down across the quiet fields of Gettysburg. But a far better memorial for these soldier-explorers lies in the rivers and the mountains of the Far West which they helped to discover and which still bear their names.

20. W. A. Swanberg, *Sickles the Incredible* (New York, 1956), p. 215.
21. Taylor, *Warren* (above, p. 406, n. 1), pp. 126–30.

APPENDIX A

ROSTER OF THE CORPS OF TOPOGRAPHICAL ENGINEERS [1]

ORIGINAL COMPLEMENT OF THE CORPS UPON ITS FORMATION, JULY 7, 1838

Col. J. J. Abert
Lt. Col. James Kearny

MAJORS

Stephen H. Long *
Hartman Bache
James D. Graham
William Turnbull

CAPTAINS

William Swift
Augustus Canfield
John Mackay
George W. Hughes *
John McClellan
William G. Williams
Campbell Graham
Walter B. Guion *
Thomas J. Cram
Washington Hood

FIRST LIEUTENANTS

Thomas B. Linnard
James H. Simpson
Augustus P. Allen
Joseph E. Johnston
Andrew A. Humphreys
John N. Macomb
Jacob E. Blake
Howard Stansbury *
Thomas J. Lee
William H. Emory

SECOND LIEUTENANTS

Lorenzo Sitgreaves
Israel Woodruff
Eliakim P. Scammon
Charles N. Hagner *
John C. Frémont *
William R. Palmer *
Joseph D. Webster *
William H. Warner
John W. Gunnison
Robert M. McLane

1. Adapted and corrected from Henry Putney Beers, "A History of the U. S. Topographical Engineers, 1813–1863," Pt. I, *The Military Engineer, 34* (1942), 291. Asterisks indicate men who did not attend West Point.

Changes in the Corps prior to the Civil War

July 31, 1839 George Thom appointed Brevet Second Lieutenant
July 17, 1840 Washington Hood, died
July 1, 1841 Amiel W. Whipple, Second Lieutenant, transferred from the Artillery
Sept. 1, 1841 Augustus P. Allen, died
March 31, 1842 Walter B. Guion, resigned
May 19, 1842 George G. Meade, appointed Brevet Second Lieutenant
John Pope, appointed Brevet Second Lieutenant
James W. Abert, appointed Brevet Second Lieutenant
July 1, 1843 W. B. Franklin, appointed Brevet Second Lieutenant
William F. Raynolds, appointed Brevet Second Lieutenant
M. L. Smith, appointed Brevet Second Lieutenant
July 1, 1844 William G. Peck, appointed Brevet Second Lieutenant
July 1, 1845 William F. Smith, appointed Brevet Second Lieutenant
Thomas J. Wood, appointed Brevet Second Lieutenant
May 9, 1846 Jacob Blake, killed (Mexican War)
July 1, 1846 Edmund L. F. Hardcastle, appointed Brevet Second Lieutenant
Francis T. Bryan, appointed Brevet Second Lieutenant
George H. Derby, appointed Brevet Second Lieutenant
Oct. 19, 1846 Thomas J. Wood, transferred to Second Dragoons
March 15, 1848 John C. Frémont, resigned
July 1, 1848 Robert S. Williamson, appointed Brevet Second Lieutenant
Nathaniel Michler, appointed Brevet Second Lieutenant
July 1, 1849 John G. Parke, appointed Brevet Second Lieutenant
July 14, 1849 Charles N. Hagner, died
July 31, 1849 W. H. Swift, resigned
Sept. 26, 1849 William H. Warner, killed
July 1, 1850 G. K. Warren, appointed Brevet Second Lieutenant
Aug. 4, 1851 George W. Hughes, resigned
July 1, 1852 George H. Mendell, appointed Brevet Second Lieutenant
July 1, 1852 George W. Rose, appointed Brevet Second Lieutenant
Joseph C. Ives, appointed Brevet Second Lieutenant
July 1, 1853 William R. Boggs, appointed Brevet Second Lieutenant
April 7, 1854 Joseph D. Webster, resigned
April 18, 1854 Augustus Canfield, died
June 28, 1854 William R. Boggs, transferred to Ordnance
July 1, 1854 Henry L. Abbott, appointed Brevet Second Lieutenant
Charles N. Turnbull, appointed Brevet Second Lieutenant

Sept. 1, 1854 John McClellan, died
March 3, 1855 William H. Emory, transferred to 2nd Cavalry
March 3, 1855 Joseph E. Johnston, transferred to 1st Cavalry
April 30, 1855 Thomas J. Lee, died
Oct. 2, 1855 William G. Peck, resigned
April 30, 1855 Edmund L. F. Hardcastle, resigned
June 4, 1856 Eliakim P. Scammon, dismissed
June 27, 1856 Junius B. Wheeler, transferred from the Cavalry
July 1, 1856 Orlando M. Poe, appointed Brevet Second Lieutenant
Oct. 7, 1856 George M. Rose, resigned
July 1, 1857 J. L. Kirby Smith, appointed Brevet Second Lieutenant
Haldemund S. Putnam, appointed Brevet Second Lieutenant
William P. Smith, appointed Brevet Second Lieutenant
Dec. 9, 1857 William Turnbull, died
July 1, 1858 William H. Echols, appointed Brevet Second Lieutenant
July 1, 1859 Charles R. Collins, appointed Brevet Second Lieutenant
Orlando G. Wagner, appointed Brevet Second Lieutenant
Robert T. Beckham, appointed Brevet Second Lieutenant
July 1, 1860 Nicholas Bowen, appointed Brevet Second Lieutenant
James H. Wilson, appointed Brevet Second Lieutenant
May 15, 1861 George H. Derby, died
June 24, 1861 Alfred Mordecai, appointed Brevet Second Lieutenant
Oct. 23, 1861 Alfred Mordecai, transferred to Ordnance

APPENDIX B

NOTE ON MAPPING TECHNIQUES

THE MAPPING and geodetic works of the Topographical Engineers varied widely in quality. In some cases it was not the task of the topographer to make accurate surveys of his line of march, but merely to make observations of the nature of the topographical features that governed the possibilities for constructing railroads or wagon roads. Elaborate scientific equipment was rarely furnished to such parties. At their best, however, the Topographical Engineers were capable of making extremely competent surveys based upon a series of careful astronomical observations whose results were often computed by leading mathematicians in America and abroad. The following material (which retains the wording of Emory's report) is included as a sample of the instruments used and the reasoning behind one of the best of the surveys, Major William H. Emory's survey of the Mexican boundary.

INSTRUMENTS USED

Transits	3	(Troughton and Semmes, and Estel)
Theodolites	5	(Estel, Gambey)
Azimuth instrument	1	
Surveyor's compasses	4	
Schmalcalder's prismatic compasses	13	
Astronomic telescope of four-foot focal length	1	(Troughton and Semmes)
Equatorial stand for telescope	1	
Sextants	4	
Artificial horizons	3	
Barometers	23	
Daniel's hygrometer	1	
Horizontal intensity instrument		
Pocket chronometers		
Box chronometers		
Telescope with micrometer		
Acromatic telescope		

Raspile telescope
Altitude and azimuth instrument
Fox-dip circle
Circumferentors or goniometers

In his personal review of the astronomical labors of the Boundary Commission Major Emory described his work (here lightly edited) as follows:

"The entire length of the line stretching from ocean to ocean, following the sinuosities of the River is about ——— When it is considered that this vast space is harassed nearly at all points by hostile bands of Indians it will be seen at a glance not only from its extent, but from the inconvenience of the savages that a trigonometric survey was out of the question. The next most accurate method was that of linear surveys checked by astronomical observations. Nine or ten principal points were selected for primary stations and determined by elaborate observations for longitude on the moon and moon-culminating stars and for latitude by observation of stars near zenith with 46-inch telescopes by Troughton and Semmes. Intermediate points were determined by transmission of chronometers, occultations, eclipses of the satellites, and all the means resorted to which give results secondary in accuracy. In tracing the parallels, latitude was determined every 15 or 30 miles and ordinates to the parallel measured from the prime vertical which was determined by measurements of the elongations of Polaris made with the best Gambey Theodolites.

"The reductions for longitude were made in all cases when practicable from corresponding observations, most of which were furnished by Professor Airy of Greenwich Observatory and for which Maj. Emory gratefully acknowledged his obligations before a meeting of the American Association for the Advancement of Science. . . . Among the results made he stated the determinations of 208 points in latitude and longitude extending entirely across the continent and most of them not heretofore determined.

"As an evidence of the truth with which the astronomical work has been conducted it may be stated that the results in latitude obtained by using the zenith telescope developes very distinctly the errors in the declination of many stars as given in the British Association catalogue. . . . It was concluded to determine the latitude and longitude of each point by direct observation on the heavenly bodies and compute the azimuth of the line connecting them. So nicely were the observations made that when the parties charged with tracing the first line on the face of the earth, met in the desert north of the Colorado, they were within one hundred feet of each other."

APPENDIX C

G. K. WARREN'S METHOD OF COMPILING THE MAP OF 1857[1]

THE COMPILATION of a map exhibiting the present state of our knowledge of the topography and hydrography of the territory of the United States, from the Mississippi River to the Pacific Ocean, is attended with two perplexing difficulties. First, the determination of what is reliable information; and second, the reconcilement of those discrepancies which are found to exist even in maps of reliable explorers. Comparatively few points in this large area have their latitudes and longitudes determined with precision, and the surveys and explorations vary in accuracy, by almost insensible degrees, from the determinations of a boundary line to the crude information of the Indian, or the still more vague representations of the imaginative adventurer.

In some large sections we possess no information, except from uncertain sources. In these parts the rule was adopted to leave the map blank, or to faintly indicate such information as is probably correct.

Where discrepancies are found on comparing the maps of reliable explorations, especially in relation to geographical positions, the principle has been carried out of considering that explorer's map the most accurate whose experience and means of observation were the most perfect. Where these advantages appeared equal, a mean of the results was adopted. In other cases, a less proportionate value was given to the inferior, and in some cases it was even rejected. It is evident that the combination of the materials of different maps in one has necessarily required some distortion of the originals; but, in all cases, much caution was observed to make this distortion as little as possible.

The scale on which the general map was drawn and engraved is that of 1 to 3,000,000 or 47.35 miles to an inch. This is too small to adequately represent the topography and character of the country, except in a very general way, and exacts either a sacrifice of many important

1. From "Memoir of Lieut. G. K. Warren, Corps Topographical Engineers, upon the Material Used and Methods Employed in Compiling the General Map to Illustrate the Reports of Surveys for Railroad Routes from the Mississippi River to the Pacific Ocean," *Pacific Railroad Reports, 11,* 87–102 (lightly edited).

details, or a deviation from the adopted scale. Many streams are laid down that would not, in their proper proportions, have a width greater than the one-hundred-thousandth part of an inch. It is thought, however, that the map will answer the purposes for which it was intended, and its size (four feet by three feet ten inches) renders it more convenient for reference than if it were drawn upon a larger scale.

The projection of the meridians and parallels of latitude has been made from the tables published in the annual report of Professor A. D. Bache, Superintendent United States Coast Survey, for 1854, and is known as the "Polyconic method." This projection admits of a correct application of the scale of distance to all parts of the map, in directions east and west, and also along the middle meridian. But as we recede from the middle meridian, the length of miles on the scale are somewhat too small. This difference is greatest on the northeast and northwest corners of the map. Thus the length of two degrees on the one hundred and twenty-fourth meridian is about three miles greater than on the one hundred and sixth or middle meridian. This distortion is, however, so small that distances are practically correct for all azimuths.

The compilation was begun at the eastern portion, the valley of the Mississippi. Here the surveys of the United States lands furnish a great amount of accurate material, but as they do not generally depend upon astronomical determinations, it is necessary to seek elsewhere for the means of fixing them in correct geographical position. I have, perhaps, attached more than the usual value to these surveys, and feel that it is needful, in order to sustain the accuracy of the compilation, to give my reasons for so doing.

The first operation of land surveying, according to the principles adopted in the United States General Land Office, is to mark out and carefully measure a principal meridian. A principal base line is then established and measured along a parallel of latitude. Sometimes this line is run first. "Standard parallels are established at stated intervals, to provide for or counteract the error that otherwise would result from the convergency of the meridians." Some of these lines are measured several times; and the numerous checks which the system presents in the subsequent subdivision makes the measurements between any two meridians or parallels very reliable. The error in the difference of longitude between any two points near the same parallel, or in the difference of latitude near the same meridian, as determined by the Land Office plots, will not probably exceed one minute of arc in a distance of 500 miles. Any slight deviation which may be made in the establishment of the meridian will not materially affect such differences of longitude; but it will affect the relative longitude of points along the meridian. It will be seen hereafter that there is reason to think that errors of deviation from the true meridian have been made in running the land survey meridians.

The first step made in compiling the Land Office maps was to fix upon the geographical positions of the different principal meridians.

The fourth principal meridian runs north from the mouth of the Illinois River through Illinois and Wisconsin, and, according to the land surveys, is about 134 miles east of the mouth of the Minnesota River. This point, as determined by Mr. Colhoun of Major Long's expedition in 1823, and subsequently verified by Mr. Nicollet (see page 116 of his report), is about longitude 93° 05′, and is undoubtedly the best determined point, by astronomical observations, on the Upper Mississippi. It would place the fourth principal meridian in longitude 90° 20′, which is the position I have assigned it in the State of Wisconsin. The longitude of St. Louis, quite well established by the observation of Mr. Nicollet, is about 90° 15′ 10″. The fourth meridian is about twelve miles to the westward, making it here in longitude about 90° 30′. If both of these are correct, an error of about one degree deviation to the east was made in running this meridian—an error which I felt obliged to assume in locating it.

The fifth principal meridian, in Missouri, lies about 144 miles west of St. Louis, making its longitude there 92° 13′. This meridian, in Louisiana, lies about 146 miles west of New Orleans, whose longitude (Nicollet's Report, p. 121) is 89° 59′. It is therefore in this latitude in about longitude 92° 23′. But the longitude of Nut Cape, at the mouth of the Sabine, is about ninety miles west of the sixth principal meridian, as referred to New Orleans and Cape Nut, amounts to three minutes, which is probably within the limit of error in these astronomical results. I have therefore given the sixth principal meridian, in Louisiana, the position obtained from a mean of these two references, that is, in longitude 92° 21′ 30″. Here, therefore, with the sixth principal meridian, as with the fourth, we find a difference in the longitude of its northern and southern extremities of 8′ 30″, requiring a deviation from the true meridian of one degree to the east.

The positions of the fourth and sixth principal meridians having been fixed thus, the surveys made with reference to them established the longitudes approximately of all points of the Land Office surveys from Lake Superior to the Gulf of Mexico; of the whole western frontier; of the west boundaries of the states; and of the starting points of all the expeditions from that region. Previous astronomical determinations placed these points from twelve to fifteen minutes too far to the east.

The adoption of the determinations of positions for the mouth of the Minnesota River, for St. Louis, for New Orleans, and for Cape Nut, to the exclusion of all others, was not made without careful investigation and comparisons.

Mr. Warner Lewis, surveyor general of Iowa, furnished me with several measurements along the base lines in that state, and the gentlemen in the General Land Office in Washington afforded me every facility for investigation and comparison.

The longitudes of places thus determined on the general map will, probably, not be found in error by more than 5 of arc. All astronomical determinations of latitude were used, when carefully made, and they generally agreed with the land surveys. The eastern portion of the map was compiled and engraved in 1854, since which time several good determinations of longitude have been obtained, and compare as follows with those upon this compilation:

Point Seul Choix, 85° 48′, general map; 85° 50′, *Captain J. N. Macomb, T.E.*
Chicago, 87° 40′, general map; 87° 38′, *Major J. D. Graham, T.E.*
Lyons, Illinois, 90° 14′, general map; 90° 14′, *Major J. D. Graham, T.E.*
West Boundary Missouri, 94° 38′, general map; 94° 40′, *J. H. Clark*

The land surveys have been reduced on the bases thus established as far east as the map extends, and as far west as these surveys have been made.

These surveyed lands are bounded on the west by an irregular line extending from the Upper Mississippi, southwest by the St. Peter's River, across the northwest corner of Iowa to the Big Sioux River, and thence south, through the eastern parts of Nebraska and Kansas (passing near the mouth of Loup Fork and Fort Riley), and thence along the west boundaries of Missouri, Arkansas, and Louisiana, to the Gulf of Mexico. These surveys, therefore, determine the geographical position of the eastern portion of most of the lines of exploration with much more precision than the few hasty and imperfect astronomical observations which the parties were enabled to make. This method of reducing the Land Office surveys has also located the Mississippi River with a geographical accuracy probably not before equaled by any map.

The land surveys in Utah furnish us with a map of a considerable area along the western foot of the Wasatch Mountains, near the Great Salt Lake, their geographical position being determined by the results of Captain Frémont's astronomical observations near the site of Great Salt Lake City, in 1845.

The land surveys in New Mexico are as yet confined mainly to the valley of the Rio Grande, but in the latitude of Santa Fé have been extended east to the sources of the Canadian river. These surveys connect the Mexican Boundary surveys with those near the thirty-fifth parallel.

The land surveys of California, Oregon, and Washington Territories also afford much reliable information. The *San Bernardino meridian* passes through the summit of the peak of that name, in the southern part of the State of California, and, as referred to the astronomical determinations of the United States Coast Survey, is in about longitude 116° 55′. The *Monte Diabolo meridian* passes through the summit of Monte Diabolo, about twenty-seven miles east of San Francisco, making its longitude, by the Coast Survey determinations, about 123° 53′. Work in the vicinity of this meridian has been extended northward far enough to fix the longitude of Fort Reading at about 122° 11′ 09″. At the time of constructing this portion of the general map, the best determination of this point which we possessed was that of Capt. J. C. Frémont, published in his Geographical Memoir of Oregon and Upper California. This places it in longitude 122° 6′ 50″. The determinations of Lieutenants Williamson and Abbot place it in longitude 122° 10′ 50″, closely agreeing with the Land Office work referred to the Coast Survey.

In Oregon and Washington territories, *the principal meridian* of the Land Office surveys passes through the point of land formed by the junction of the Willamette and Columbia Rivers. Its longitude has been determined by measurement between it and several points of the United States Coast Survey, and is about 122° 47′. The meridian through Mount Pierce has not as yet determined any points of particular value.

The United States coast surveys on the shores of the Pacific and Gulf of Mexico are copied on the general map wherever they have been extended. The work, however, is just beginning—large portions of the coast being only fixed by preliminary reconnaissances; the outlines of the shore on their maps are therefore frequently changed as their surveys progress.

By means of the United States Land Office surveys, and a few carefully determined astronomical positions, the longitude of most of the starting points of the different exploring expeditions on the east have now been geographically fixed; and by means of the Land Office and Coast surveys, the termini of many of them on the west. The maps of the surveys of the boundary between Mexico and the United States have been reduced to the general map as received from the office of those surveys; the work forming the southern border of the compilation. From this line I shall proceed north in describing the manner in which the map has been filled in, and in so doing shall take up the different surveys without regard to the date of their prosecution, selecting the most reliable first. In doing this the strict order of relative position must occasionally be abandoned, in order to settle the longitudes of some points common to several explorations.

Texas first claims attention. Colonel Johnston's published map (Senate Exec. Doc. 64, Thirty-First Congress, First Session), as well as the manuscript maps of his subsequent explorations, are all made under the supposition that the longitude of San Antonio de Bexar is 98° 40′. But his subsequent observations with a transit gave for this longitude 98° 25′, or 15′ east of that on the map. This would seem to require that the reconnaissances represented on that map should all be moved 15′ toward the east. The surveys of the Mexican boundary, however, show that El Paso and the mouth of Devil's River were only about 10′ too far west on Colonel Johnston's map. I have therefore moved the eastern part of Colonel Johnston's map 15′ to the east, and the western portions but 10′, and reduced the intervening routes of reconnaissance accordingly. The longitude of Preston then becomes 96° 38′. On Colonel Johnston's map it is 96° 53′; on Captain Marcy's, 96° 20′.

Captain Pope's preliminary map, published with his Pacific Railroad Report, 8vo edition, differs very materially, in some of the positions, from those thus obtained from Colonel Johnston's map, especially along the route of the survey of Lieutenant Michler, T.C.; but, after careful examination, I have adopted Colonel Johnston's work. Captain Pope's railroad reconnaissance route has been reduced conformably to the positions thus obtained. The portions of Texas south and west of Colonel Johnston's map have been reduced from J. DeCordova's map of Texas, dated 1849, which was the last edition available at the time of my compilation.

The map of Lieutenant Parke's exploration for a railroad route between El Paso and the Pimas villages, in 1855, has been adopted and reduced without change. His survey was very carefully checked by a nearly continuous system of compass triangulations from peak to peak. His line was located by an odometer and compass survey, corrected by astronomical observations, adopted as given by the United States Mexican Boundary Commission.

Lieutenant Parke's map of his surveys for a railroad route in California, in 1854–55, has also been reduced without change on the general map. The following note appears on his map:

"The entire coast line, with the exception of that portion lying between Point San Luis and Santa Barbara, and also the position of Picacho de Gavilan, were obtained from charts of the United States

Coast Survey. The eastern limits of the Coast range; the position of the Tulare, Buenavista, and Kern lakes; a portion of the Mojave Valley; the Los Angeles and San Bernardino plains; the Santa Aña River, and the foothills of the Sierra Nevada, were obtained from the surveys of the United States General Land Office. The lower portion of the Mojave Valley and the south end of Soda Lake were taken from the surveys of Lts. A. W. Whipple and R. S. Williamson, United States Topographical Engineers."

The portion of the Coast mountains of California lying between the limits of Lieutenant Parke's and the Mexican boundary maps and the country extending as far east as Soda Lake, are reduced partly from the Land Office maps, partly from Lieutenant Williamson's map of surveys in 1853 and 1854, and partly from Lieutenant Whipple's survey of a railroad route near the thirty-fifth parallel. The San Bernardino meridian, placed in longitude 116° 55′ by referring it to the Coast Survey longitude of San Diego and San Pedro, is considered to determine the longitude of other points where the Land Office surveys have been carried with more accuracy than either Lieutenant Whipple's or Lieutenant Williamson's surveys. The longitude of the eastern entrance of the Cajon Pass is thus fixed at 117° 29′; Lieutenant Whipple having it 117° 25′, and Lieutenant Williamson 117° 32′ 40″. Los Angeles is placed in longitude 118° 14′; being on Lieutenant Whipple's map 118° 10′, and on Lieutenant Williamson's 118° 13′ 20″. The maps of Lieutenants Whipple and Williamson have been altered in the reduction to agree with these positions. The mouth of the Mojave Canyon, west of Soda Lake, is placed by Lieutenant Whipple in longitude 116° 11′ 35″, and by Lieutenant Williamson in longitude 116° 18′. As Lieutenant Whipple had the benefit of Lieutenant Williamson's determination in making his own, and was, moreover, supplied with an astronomical transit, his longitude has been adopted. However, as his longitude of Cajon Pass was four-minutes too far east, the same error probably affects his location of the point under consideration, and it would, perhaps, be more accurate to assume a median position between Lieutenants Williamson and Whipple's for the mouth of the Mojave Canyon, viz: 116° 15′. By taking Lieutenant Whipple's determination, I was enabled to reduce his map without change from this point to near its eastern or starting point at Fort Smith.

The longitude of Fort Smith, Arkansas, as determined by the Land Office maps in the manner already stated, is 94° 25′. This result receives confirmation from the determination of the longitude of Fort Gibson, 95° 15′, by Lieutenant Woodruff. For, by the road survey made by R. Richardson in 1826, the difference of longitude between Fort Gibson and Fort Smith is fifty-one minutes, agreeing almost exactly with these two independent locations. The following positions in longitude have been given Fort Smith on different maps:

	degrees	*min.*
Major Long's map of explorations to Rocky Mountains in 1820	95	5
Lieutenant Simpson's survey of Canadian in 1849	94	23
Captain R. B. Marcy's map of his routes in 1849	94	14
Map compiled in Topographical Bureau in 1850	94	3
Captain Marcy's map of explorations to sources of Red river in 1852	94	7
Lieutenant Whipple's map of survey for Pacific railroad route in 1853 and 1854	94	29
Adapted longitude	94	25

The meridian which passes "100 paces west of Fort Smith" forms the west boundary of Arkansas between the Arkansas and Red rivers. There being four minutes difference in longitude between Lieutenant Whipple's position of Fort Smith and the one adopted by me, the discrepancy has been distributed along his route between Fort Smith and the branch of Topofki creek, which is in longitude 96° 57′ 37″, this distance being practically enough to reduce the difference within the limit of error of such reconnaissance. From this branch of Topofki creek to Albuquerque his map is reduced without change. This portion of Lieutenant Whipple's map, forming sheet No. 1, as carefully revised by him, does not differ materially in its geographical positions from that published in the House Exec. Doc. No. 129, Thirty-third Congress, First Session. The following changes were made by him in the names: Camp No. 31, Washita River, to Camp No. 31, Comet Creek; Camp No. 32 to Camp No. 32, Silver Creek; Camp No. 33, Washita River, to Camp No. 33, Oak Creek; Camp No. 42, Antelope Creek, to Camp No. 42, White Sandy Creek. Lieutenant Whipple's longitude of Albuquerque, 106° 37′ 52″, is six minutes east of Major Emory's position for it.

From Albuquerque west to Soda Lake Lieutenant Whipple's revision of his work changed the longitudes of nearly all his points, at first published in House Doc. No. 129, Thirty-third Congress, First Session. The first edition of the general map was compiled and engraved from his preliminary map. The second edition contains his work in its revised form. As Lieutenant Whipple's longitudes were, in some instances, determined by means of observations with an astronomical transit, his geographical positions were adopted in preference to those of Lieutenant Simpson on his expedition to the Navaho country in 1849, or of Captain Sitgreaves in his expedition along the Zuñi and Colorado rivers in 1851. . . .

The latitudes of these different surveys agree almost exactly. The route of Captain Sitgreaves was compiled both times to fit the longitudes determined by Lieutenant Whipple, sometimes requiring elongation and sometimes contraction. Captain Sitgreaves' route down the Colorado, from William's River to Fort Yuma, is made to accord with Lieutenant Whipple's determination for the mouth of Williams' River, and that of the United States Mexican Boundary Commission for Fort Yuma. Lieutenant Whipple, in revising his sheet No. 2, made the following changes in the names of places:

Camp No. 76, Rio Puerco of the West, to Camp No. 76, near Lithodendron Creek
Camp No. 77, Lithodendron Creek, to Camp No. 77, Rio Puerco of the West
Camp No. 104, Pueblo Creek, to Camp No. 104, Aztec Pass
Camp No. 105, Pueblo Creek, to Camp No. 105, Williams's River
Camp No. 106, Cañon Creek, to Camp No. 106, Williams's River
Camp No. 107, Cañon Creek, to Camp No. 107, Williams's River
Camp No. 108, Cañon Creek, to Camp No. 108, Williams's River
Camp No. 109, Cañon Creek, to Camp No. 109, White Cliff Creek
Camp No. 113, mouth of Cañon Creek, to Camp No. 113, Williams's River
Camp No. 114, Big Sandy Creek, to Camp No. 114, Williams's River
Camp No. 115, Big Sandy Creek, to Camp No. 115, Williams's River
Camp No. 116, Big Sandy Creek, to Camp No. 116, Williams's River
Camp No. 117, Big Sandy Creek, to Camp No. 117, Williams's River
Camp No. 118, Big Sandy Creek, to Camp No. 118, Williams's River
Camp No. 119, Big Sandy Creek, to Camp No. 119, Williams's River
Camp No. 120, Big Sandy Creek, to Camp No. 120, Williams's River
Camp No. 121, Rio Santa Maria, to Camp No. 121, Williams's River
Camp No. 122, Rio Santa Maria, to Camp No. 122, Williams's River
Camp No. 123, Rio Santa Maria, to Camp No. 123, Williams's River
Camp No. 124, Rio Santa Maria, to Camp No. 124, Williams's River
Camp No. 125, Rio Santa Maria, to Camp No. 125, Williams's River
Camp No. 126, Rio Santa Maria, to Camp No. 126, Williams's River

Lieutenant Simpson, in his map of the route of the expedition to the Navaho country in 1849, bases all his astronomical determinations upon the longitude of Santa Fé, determined by Major Emory in 1846, viz: 106° 2′ 30″. In this way he determined the longitude of his station, "two miles northwest from the mouth of the Cañon de Chelly" (his most western station), to be 109° 42′ 30″. Cañon Cito Bonito (near Fort Defiance) to be 109° 15′ 30″; Zuñi to be 108° 56′. According to Lieutenant Whipple, Zuñi is 13′ too far west. Lieutenant Whipple's revised position for Fort Defiance is in longitude 108° 59′, making Lieutenant

Simpson's position for it 16′ 30″ too far west; but this determination of Lieutenant Whipple depends upon a side reconnaissance, and cannot be considered as accurate as the main line of his route. I have, however, considered the determinations of Lieutenant Whipple, where they have tested Lieutenant Simpson's work, as sufficient authority for moving the latter's position of the most western part of Canyon de Chelly 13′ to the east, thus placing it in longitude 109° 2′. Lieutenant Simpson's trail was reduced between this assumed position and Santa Fé, adopting Major Emory's longitude for the latter. The error in position which Lieutenant Simpson's work shows, according to Lieutenant Whipple's, is not greater than is liable to the method employed, viz. chronometric differences by chronometers transported over rough and mountainous country.

Lieutenant Simpson's survey along the Canadian in 1849, agrees with the positions adopted by Lieutenant Whipple.

I have experienced not a little difficulty in bringing in Captain Marcy's map of the expedition to the sources of the Red River in 1852. Astronomical observation with a sextant and watch were occasionally made on this exploration by Captain G. B. McClellan, Corps of Engineers. Captain McClellan has no report thereon in the printed document, and no observations are given, the results being mentioned through the journal or report of Captain Marcy. The latitudes of points, as thus given, differ sometimes considerably from the map, and I have adopted the latter, thinking it most probable that the discrepancy grew out of error in copying the manuscript or printing the report. . . .

The longitude of the camp on Otter creek was found by lunar distances to be 100° 0′ 45″. It is not stated how many observations were taken, but the expedition arrived at the point May 22, and by May 29 the observations had been made and calculated, and Captain McClellan started on this day, traced the one-hundredth meridian south to its intersection with Red River, and marked a cottonwood tree to indicate the point. The longitude of the mouth of the Little Witchita, 98°, and of Fort Washita, 96° 38′, I have already determined, the difference being 1° 22′. On Captain Marcy's map of 1852, the first is in longitude 98° 30′ (thirty minutes too far west), and the second is 96° 20′ (eighteen minutes too far east), the difference being 2° 10′. Fort Arbuckle is placed by Captain Marcy in longitude 97° 7′. The position it assumes, by reducing Captain Marcy's trail between the mouth of the Little Witchita and Fort Washita to the general map, is 97° 8′, and this has been adopted. If the longitudes I have adopted for Fort Washita, Fort Arbuckle, and the mouth of the Little Witchita are correct, Captain

Marcy's map of 1852 contains a relative error between the two last points of thirty minutes of longitude. Captain Marcy, in his map of 1849, places the mouth of the Little Witchita in longitude 97° 25', and in the one of 1852, in longitude 98° 30'. When at or near the head of the North Fork of Red River, he made an excursion of about thirty miles direct to the Canadian River, striking it at the mouth of *Sandy Creek,* where he marked a tree, in longitude 101° 55', according to his map. Lieutenant Whipple's exploring party, in 1853, did not know of this, and it is not positively certain that the creek called by Lieutenant Whipple *White Sandy* Creek, is that visited by Captain Marcy. If, however, it is the same, its longitude, according to Lieutenant Whipple, is 101° 35', being twenty minutes east of the position given it by Captain Marcy. This and other reasons lead me to think that Captain Marcy's map places the eastern front of the Llano Estacado and the sources of the Red River at least twenty minutes too far west; for, if Captain Marcy's latitudes be assumed correct, as I have done, and his position of the source of the North Fork of the Red River be plotted, it falls in the immediate valley of the Canadian, as determined by Lieutenant Whipple, and only about ten miles from the main stream, instead of thirty, which Captain Marcy found to be the case. The only way to preserve this distance between the streams, without changing the latitudes, is to move the positions of Captain Marcy east to the amount of twenty minutes. This, again, is the only way of making his survey of the North Fork agree with the position determined for it by Lieutenant Abert's survey in 1845, as will be explained further on.

I have therefore moved the sources of Red River twenty minutes east of Captain Marcy's position, the mouth of the Little Witchita thirty minutes to the east, and, in order to subject his map to the least distortion which the changes require, the camp at Otter Tail Creek twenty-five minutes to the east, placing it in longitude 99° 35'. By moving this point with the other parts of the map, I have been enabled to represent the routes of this expedition in nearly the same relative positions as on the original map. The errors I have supposed, for the purpose of representing this information, are within the limits of error of determination of longitude by the means employed.

On Captain Marcy's map of the sources of the Brazos and Big Witchita, made in 1854, Fort Belknap is placed in longitude 98° 47'; the mouth of Panther Creek 100; Large spring, near the Big Wachita, 98° 48'; on the general map these same points are respectively: 98° 36'; 99° 50', and 99° 35'. These are the only points I can recognize to be nearly common; although the last two are not certain, they go to show that the whole of the positions on the map are from ten to twelve minutes too far west, and that the different parts are relatively correct.

As reduced on our map, the routes appear about eleven minutes east of the geographical positions given on the original.

The survey of the southern boundary of Kansas, by Lt. Col. J. E. Johnston, in 1857, has been adopted on our map without any change, as it was made by means superior to those possessed by any other surveyor or explorer whose lines are crossed by his.

The survey of the road from Old Fort Osage, through to San Fernando de Taos, in 1825, 1826, and 1827, by J. C. Brown, C.E., has also been adopted as given by him, with the following modifications: This survey was made with chain and compass, corrected by astronomical observations, with a sextant for latitude. The longitudes were fixed by assuming, from the previous determinations of others, that Old Fort Osage was in longitude 93° 51′. According to the position I have assigned Fort Osage, it is in longitude 94° 14′, requiring an addition of twenty-three minutes of longitude to all points of the survey. The point on this route where the southern boundary of Kansas strikes the Cimarron, is determined on our map, by Colonel Johnston's survey, to be in longitude 102° 10′. On Brown's map it is in longitude 101° 52′; showing that his work at this point requires to be moved eighteen minutes west. Brown's survey between this point and Fort Osage is consequently adapted to the general map by shortening it five minutes in longitude. West of this point, on the Cimarron, Brown's map is nearly copied, all points being moved eighteen minutes westward. Taos thus comes to be located in longitude 105° 30′, which is nearly ten minutes east of its position on Major Emory's map.

Major Emory's determination of the longitude of Santa Fé (106° 4′ by lunar distances, see p. 266 of his Report of Mil. Recon.) is given on his map at 106° 2′. The Land Office connections with the Mexican Boundary Survey and Lieutenant Whipple's determinations of Albuquerque agree; and applying this same connection to Santa Fé, its longitude would be about 106° 2′, agreeing with Major Emory's map. This longitude has been adopted. The position of Albuquerque and Isletta having been moved six minutes to the east of Major Emory's position, the portion of his map between these points and Santa Fé was shortened in longitude to this amount. The longitude of the Copper Mines, as given on the Mexican Boundary map, is 108° 6′; on Major Emory's reconnaissance map it is 108° 12′. This position has therefore been moved to the east just the amount which Lieutenant Whipple moved Albuquerque. Major Emory's reconnaissance in 1846 has therefore been moved entire between these points six minutes to the east, and thus reduced to the general map. West of Mount Graham the Gila River has been taken from the maps of the surveys under the Boundary Commission.

Major Emory's route in 1846, from the place where he struck the Santa Fé Trail to Choteau's Island, on the Arkansas, is nearly that of the road surveyed by Mr. Brown in 1825, 1826, and 1827. The longitude and latitude of the mouth of Walnut creek and of Choteau's Island, and the survey of the river between them, being almost precisely the same. This position of Choteau's Island on our map, as obtained from Brown's survey in the manner explained, is about nineteen minutes farther west than that given by him, and nineteen minutes farther west than that given by Major Emory. In Major Emory's report (p. 223), his determination of longitude of Bent's Old Fort, by seven observations of the distance of Aquilae from the moon, is 102° 27′ 19.9″, and by four observations for the distance of Spica, 103° 26′ 2″; mean of all, 102° 56′ 40″. In the list of geographical positions given (p. 176 of his report), this longitude is given 103° 1′, and it is so represented on the map. On Captain Frémont's map of routes in 1842, 1843, and 1844, the longitude of Bent's Old Fort is given at 103° 45′, and the difference between it and the mouth of Fontaine qui Bouit Creek, 1° 15′. This last point, as determined by Captain Frémont in 1845, is in longitude 104° 42′; substracting this difference from it, places Bent's Old Fort in longitude 103° 27′ (in the table of positions in his memoir it is given as 103° 33′ 20″). As this difference of longitude between the Fort and the mouth of the Fontaine qui Bouit Creek, a distance of about eighty miles, depends upon the topographical reconnaissance with estimated distances, it cannot be considered very exact; still its near coincidence to Major Emory's determination by the moon's distance from Spica renders its correctness more probable. Taking now the map of Captain Gunnison's route up the Arkansas, as prepared by Mr. Egloffstein, we find he places Choteau Island in 101° 21′, being nearly the same as that on the general map (101° 20′), as obtained from Brown's survey. Captain Gunnison's map places Bent's Old Fort in longitude 103° 24′ 30″; and as the adoption of this saved any change in embodying this map, and does not differ materially from my deduction from Captain Frémont and Major Emory's work, I have done so.

In reducing Major Emory's reconnaissance from Bent's Fort to Santa Fé, it would seem that as the position of the fort has been moved west, while that of Santa Fé has remained the same, the position of the Raton Pass should also be moved to the west. I have, however, retained it as given by him: First, because the Spanish Peaks, which must have been fixed in position by bearings along his route, were placed farther *east* by Captain Gunnison than by Major Emory; and second, because by taking the position of the crossing of the Canadian as fixed by Brown's survey, and connecting the Pass with it by Lieutenant Abert and Peck's reconnaissance, it would be necessary to move it to the *east*. Major Emory's position for the Raton Pass has therefore been retained as being a mean of all the other requirements. Lieutenant Peck's reconnaissance of the Cimarron route, as given on Major Emory's map, makes the position of the "Point of Rocks" somewhat east of that obtained from Brown's survey, which it has been made to conform with.

In reducing Lieutenants Abert and Peck's reconnaissance of the Canadian in 1845, the trail between the Raton Pass and the Cimarron crossing of the Canadian is made to correspond with the position of those points as already adopted, and this moves his position for the latter point fourteen minutes to the east. His position for his camp of September 9, 1845, on the Canadian, is the same as on Lieutenant Whipple's map. His route in reducing had thus to be shortened fourteen minutes in longitude between that point and the Cimarron crossing of the Canadian.

Lieutenant Abert's longitude of the point where he left the Canadian (as nearly as I can recognize it on Whipple's map) seems to correspond, in position, with Lieutenant Whipple's, as does also the crossing of the North Fork of the Washita. They have therefore been adopted. Lieutenant Abert's positions are retained as far east as Old Fort Edwards, at the mouth of Little River.

Lieutenant Abert's map of explorations in New Mexico, in 1846, has been reduced to the general map, by making the points of his trail correspond, in position, with those of the other explorers, reduced, as already stated, wherever they intersect.

In Mr. R. H. Kern's reconnaissance of the Pecos he assumed the longitude of Anton Chico to be 105° 25′. According to Lieutenant Whipple it is 105° 9′, being sixteen minutes to the east of Mr. Kern's position, whose work has therefore been moved sixteen minutes to the east for that portion of the Pecos below Anton Chico.

The boundary of the country lying between the upper part of the Pecos and the Rio Grande having now been determined, the map of Lt. I. N. Moore was used to fill in the intervening space, his positions being made to conform to those previously adopted.

The map of the survey of the boundary of the Creek country by Sitgreaves and Woodruff, and of the North Fork of the Canadian, &c., has been reduced to the general map without any change.

Major Long's map of his expedition to the Rocky Mountains has been used for his route between the Arkansas and Canadian rivers. The point where he left the Arkansas I believe to be about half way between the mouths of the Apishpa and Timpas creeks, in longitude 103° 27′, by the general map; on his map it is in longitude 103° 46′.

We have therefore moved his trail between this point and the Canadian nineteen minutes to the east, which makes the mouth of the branch of the Canadian down which he traveled correspond to the mouth of one represented on Lieutenant Abert's map. The route of Major Bell (who conducted the detachment of Major Long's expedition along the Arkansas) is used to put in that stream between Walnut Creek and Fort Gibson.

The map of the reconnaissance of Captain Boone between the Arkansas and Canadian rivers has been reduced to correspond with the positions already determined, wherever they are common to his routes.

The reconnaissance of Lieutenant Amory between Fort Gibson and the Santa Fé Road, to Independence; of Major Merrill between Fort Belknap and Council Grove; and of Captain Pope, from the Cimarron to the Arkansas, have been reduced to our map, by making the points common to the explorations previously reduced to conform therewith.

As before stated, the longitudes of all points along the west boundary of Missouri are determined by reference to the land surveys, the longitude of them being determined by that of St. Louis. The longitude of Westport, the starting point of Captain Frémont's first two expeditions, is thus determined to be 94° 37′, instead of 94° 22′, as adopted by him; that of Fort Leavenworth to be 94° 58′, instead of 94° 44′, as determined by Mr. Nicollet, and adopted by Major Emory and Captain Stansbury. Captain Frémont, in a note preceding the list of astronomical positions in his report of his second expedition (p. 321) says: "The course of the ensuing expeditions will intersect the line established by our previous operations at various points, which it is proposed to correct, in longitude, by lunar culminations, and such absolute observations as may be conveniently obtained. Such a position at the mouth of Fontaine qui Bouit, on the Arkansas River, will be a good point of reference for the longitudes along the foot of the mountains. In passing by the Utah to the southern portion of the Great Salt Lake, we shall have an opportunity to verify our longitudes in that quarter; and as, in the course of our exploration, we shall touch upon several points previously determined along the western limit of our recent journey, we shall probably be able to form a reasonably correct frame on which to base the construction of a general map of the country."

In Captain Frémont's memoir and map on Oregon and Lower California will be found the astronomical results of this expedition from the mouth of Fontaine qui Bouit Creek, westward. No topographical explorer has since visited points along his routes with means capable of detecting any errors in his determinations, and they have been generally adopted. The mouth of the Fontaine qui Bouit Creek was placed on the first map in longitude 105°; on the second, according to moon culminations, in 104° 42′ 41″. The longitude determined at Great Salt Lake, and at Lassen's farm, on Deer Creek, California, by moon culminations, confirmed his first determinations of positions in these regions as given on his previous map. The position for Lassen's is only about five minutes too far east, as since determined. The correction which Captain Frémont found at Fontaine qui Bouit, namely, seventeen minutes east, if used to correct the "longitudes along the foot of the mountains, as given on the map of explorations in 1842, 1843, and 1844, would place St. Vrain's fort in longitude 104° 55′, and Fort Laramie in longitude 104° 30′; and this last agrees nearly with that adopted on Stanbury's map." (See note of Lieutenant Gunnison, p. 302, Stanbury's Report.) But Mr. Preuss, in constructing the map of 1848, puts Fort Laramie still farther east, namely, in longitude 104° 25′, and St. Vrain's Fort in longitude 104° 47′, moving these points farther east, it seems to me, than the correction at the mouth of Fontaine qui Bouit Creek demanded. I have taken Fort Laramie in longitude 104° 30′, and St. Vrain's Fort in longitude 104° 55′. Captain Frémont's route, in 1843, from St. Vrain's Fort west to his station of September 13, on Bear River, had to be elongated from what it is represented on the map of 1844, and shortened from what it is on the one of 1848. I retained the position of the crossing of the north of the Platte (longitude 107° 10′) as given on the map of 1848, Lieutenant Gunnison having adopted it in constructing Stanbury's map. This is nearly the position it would have by distributing the correction which I have applied to St. Vrain's Fort between that point and Frémont's station of September 13, 1843. This station of September 13 depends for its longitude on an occultation of τ Arietes, and to it all the points of the route along Snake River, and the Columbia as far as the Dalles, are referred by chronometric differences. Captain Frémont's routes south of Lieutenant Beckwith's trail, in Utah, have all been reduced to our map as given on his map of 1848, his position for the point where the Santa Fé Trail leaves the Mojave, agreeing with the best recent determinations. In putting down Captain Frémont's route from Bent's Old Fort east along the Smoky Hill Fork of the Kansas, as given on his map of routes in 1842, 1843, and 1844, I have moved his position of Bent's Old Fort from 103° 45′ to 103° 24′ 30″, and of the point where he struck the Santa Fé Road from 96° 58′ to 97° 12′, thus shortening this portion of his route by thirty-four minutes in longitude. St. Vrain's Fort having been moved seventeen minutes east, and the mouth of the Republican Fork fourteen minutes west (Fort Riley from 96° 30′ to 96° 44′), the intervening portion of his route, *via* the Republican Fork, was thirty-one minutes shorter in longitude than represented on his map of routes in 1843–44.

The Kansas River, as far west as Fort Riley, has been reduced from the Land Office surveys. Captain Gunnison's survey for a railroad route has, therefore, not been used west of that point. His map, as constructed by Mr. Egloffstein, places Fort Riley in longitude 96° 50′, being six minutes too far west, and of the mouth of Walnut Creek 98° 49′, instead of 98° 42′. The work between these two points has been moved six minutes to the west. From Walnut Creek to Choteau Island Brown's survey was used in the compilation, and from that point (which coincides in position with that from Captain Gunnison's survey) westward, the maps prepared by Mr. Egloffstein from Captains Gunnison and Beckwith's surveys, have been exactly copied, except for the position of Fort Reading, which was assumed by Mr. Egloffstein as 1′ 42″ eastward of Colonel Frémont's location, or about six minutes too far east. This error in Captain Beckwith's map was distributed through his work in the Sierra Nevada.

Captain Stansbury's routes have all been copied on our map nearly as given by him west of the meridian of Fort Laramie, subject only to such slight changes as Captain Beckwith and Lieutenant Bryan's surveys showed to be necessary. He, however, adopted from Mr. Nicollet the longitude of Fort Leavenworth (94° 45′) instead of 94° 58′, which required his route to be shortened thirteen minutes between this fort and Fort Laramie. Fort Kearny had thus to be moved eight minutes west of its position on Captain Stansbury's map, that is, from 98° 58′ to 99° 6′. The chain and compass survey made between Fort Kearny and Omaha by Captain Dickerson, in 1856, showed the difference of longitude between them to be very nearly the same as I had adopted, the longitude of Omaha being determined by the Land Office surveys, as before explained. Lieutenant Bryan, on his map of explorations to Bridger's Pass, adopted the position of Fort Kearny as given by Captain Stansbury, although he changed Fort Leavenworth, upon which Captain Stansbury's determination depended by his compass survey, no astronomical observations having been made for its longitude. The longitude of the mouth of the Platte being determined from the Land Office surveys, this stream has been laid down from Colonel Frémont's and Captain Stansbury's maps, to conform to the longitudes of the points I have enumerated.

The mouth of the Big Sioux, according to the Land Office surveys, referred to the meridians determined as already described, is about twelve minutes west of what it is as given by Mr. Nicollet. The position of Lake Jessie, according to Governor Stevens's map, is also twelve minutes west of Mr. Nicollet's determination; and, as Mr. Nicollet's work is uniformly from twelve to fifteen minutes too far east along the Missouri, wherever checked, I have thought it best to move it entire from the mouth of the Big Sioux to Fort Pierre, and thence to Devil's Lake, twelve minutes to the west. Fort Pierre then becomes in longitude 100° 24′ 30″, instead of 100° 12′ 30″.

The longitude of the mouth of the St. Peter's River having been adopted from Mr. Nicollet, and the route to Devil's Lake having been moved twelve minutes west, Mr. Nicollet's routes between the meridians through these points have so been put down as to proportion this difference throughout.

In my map of "Reconnaissance in the Dakota Country," I assumed the positions adopted on the general map. In my explorations on the Missouri and Yellowstone, in 1856, I determined the longitude of Fort Union, by two sets of moon-culminating stars, to be 104° 2′ 7″, corresponding nearly with that adopted by Governor Stevens. The Missouri River has been put in from my map from the mouth of the Big Muddy to the Big Nemaha. Below that it is taken from the Land Office surveys. From the Big Muddy to Fort Benton it is from reconnaissances made under Governor Stevens.

On Governor Stevens' explorations, in 1853, no observations were made for longitude. The route was determined by compass courses and odometer distances, checked by observations for latitude between the mouth of the St. Peter's River and Fort Walla-Walla. The longitude of Fort Walla-Walla, according to Colonel Frémont, is 118° 32′; but he made no astronomical observations at this point. According to Captain Wilkes, it is 118° 47′ 45″. The means by which this was obtained will be found in the following letter, which Captain Wilkes was kind enough to send me, in answer to certain inquiries. His determination, as given in his letter to me, was adopted.

Washington City, *July* 5, 1854

Dear Sir: Your letter of June 29 would have been answered sooner if I could have found the observation by which the position of Walla-Walla was determined.

The position I assign to it is, latitude 46° 2′ 48″ N., longitude 118° 47′ 45″ W. The result of three-days' observation deduced from chronometer. These were made by Lieutenant Johnson, of the expedition, who had charge of the party, and were calculated out under my own examination of the notes. The position was also determined by bearings or angles on three mountain peaks, which gave a very near accordance in the result. I have always felt great confidence in the result. I gave them at the time a very careful examination, and think Lieutenant Johnson made them under favorable circumstances. Mr. Drayton, who also visited Walla-Walla, on the survey of the river up to that point, agrees in his determination with Lieutenant Johnson at this point. Their observations were intended to serve as checks upon each other.

I am, very respectfully, your obedient servant,
CHARLES WILKES

Lieutenant G. K. Warren,
Topographical Engineers, Washington.

The determination of Captain Wilkes was also adopted by Mr. Lambert (Governor Stevens' topographer), who constructed his map in this office. He says of the route of the main line of Governor Stevens's survey, in his report on topography, (*Pacific Railroad Surveys,* quarto edition, Volume 1, p. 176, Governor Stevens' Report): "It is satisfactory to know that the survey, as it was first plotted, independent of correction by astronomical points, but connected by those of Captain Wilkes and Professor Nicollet, was only ten miles in error, being in excess." As far west as Walla-Walla, Governor Stevens' route, as mapped, is, therefore, copied on the general map; but west of this, along the Columbia, it has been subjected to some modifications by the Land Office surveys and the reconnaisance by Lieutenants Williamson and Abbot, in 1855.

The Yellowstone River, as far up as the mouth of Powder River, was taken from my reconnaissance in 1856. Powder River is the same as the Warharsa on Lewis and Clarke's map. Any one will, I think, be convinced, who examines the maps and reads Lieutenant Mullan's description of the Muscle Shell River in Governor Stevens' report, and Captain Clarke's description of the Yellowstone in chapter 33 of *Lewis and Clarke's Travels,* that they are the same river; and also that the branch up which Lieutenant Mullan traveled when he left the Yellowstone, is the one Captain Clarke calls Shield's River. I have so taken them. The route of Captain Clarke from the source of the Jefferson Fork of the Missouri to the Yellowstone, and down the latter, has been put in so as to conform to the points of his route determined by Lieutenant Mullan's and my own reconnaissances.

The survey of Captain Reno, from Big Sioux River to Mendota, was reduced so as to conform to the Land Office work. The reconnaissance of Captain Sully, in 1855, from Fort Ridgely to Fort Pierre, was made to conform to the positions obtained from Mr. Nicollet.

Captain Pope adopted Major Long's position of the Pembina settlement on the Red River of the North, but he moved the position of the junction of the Red River and the Bois des Sioux about twelve minutes to the east of it. Governor Stevens and Captain Simpson's surveys indicate that Captain Pope's work, between the Red River and the Mississippi, is crowded by at least twelve minutes more than it should be. I have, therefore, retained Major Long's position of Red River, and of his route to Lake Winnepeg, and thence to Lake Superior. Captain Pope's map was reduced so as to make his route agree in longitude with that of Major Long wherever they crossed. From Mr. Nicollet's map has been taken the sources of the Mississippi, and the lakes, &c., between it and the Crow Wing River; which latter was taken from Captain Simpson's survey. The position of many of the lakes given by Mr. Nicollet in this neighborhood must have been derived in some uncertain way from the Indians, as many of them cannot now be recognized. The attempt has been made to retain for these lakes the names of the eminent scientific men with which he adorned the map of this region; but it is probable that, as the country becomes inhabited by white men, these names will have to be replaced on our maps by the more common ones of the country. Mr. Nicollet's map (I know not on what grounds) put Red Lake considerably to the west of the position given it by Major Long; but the latter I have adopted, as recent examinations show it to be more probably correct.

The boundary between the United States and British Possessions has been taken from the maps of the surveys of the Northwestern Boundary Commission, from Lake Superior to Rainy Lake.

Lieutenant Abbot's Pacific railroad maps of Oregon and northern California I have adopted exactly as prepared by him.

Fort Vancouver was placed by Wilkes in longitude 123° 19′ 30″; and this was adopted by Captain Frémont on his map of 1848. In Frémont's map of 1842, 1843, and 1844, the longitude of this point is taken at 122° 41′ 30″; Captain McClellan adopted 122° 19′ 30″ on his map of explorations in the Cascade mountains. Mr. Lambert, on making Governor Stevens' map, took it 122° 40′. But the Land Office surveys, in connection with the Coast Survey, show the longitude of Fort Vancouver to be 122° 32′ 30″, which we have adopted. This position is near a mean between that first given it by Captain Frémont and that by Captain Wilkes. Lieutenant Abbot's position for the Dalles is 120° 58′. Governor Stevens' map has it 120° 53′, which is the same as on Wilkes' and Frémont's maps. Lieutenant Abbot places the Cascades in about longitude 121° 42′; Frémont, 121° 36′; Wilkes, 121° 57′; which last was adopted by McClellan and Stevens. Lieutenant Abbot's observations place Mount Adams in latitude 46° 12′, longitude 121° 19′ (being two minutes south and fifteen minutes west of its position on Captain McClellan's map;) Mount St. Helen's in latitude 46° 11′ 30″, and longitude 122° 5′ (being ten minutes south and four minutes west of Captain McClellan's determination). Both Wilkes and Frémont confounded these peaks. A note on Lieutenant Abbott's Oregon maps shows that, by his compass bearings, Captain McClellan placed Mount Rainier about fifteen minutes too far east; Captain McClellan placing it in longitude 121° 25′, and Nachess Pass in longitude 121° 25′.

Lieutenant Arnold's survey, in 1854, through the Nachess Pass, after correcting his longitude of Walla-Walla (which he took at 118° 55′, or eight minutes too far west), places the summit of the Nachess Pass in longitude 121° 9′; Mount Rainier he puts in longitude 121° 25′, probably taking it from Captain McClellan. Lieutenant Arnold's position of the Nachess Pass is some six minutes north of that on Captain McClellan's map, and differs also in being sixteen minutes in longitude to the east. To represent Lieutenant Arnold's survey would require much of Captain McClellan's work to be changed; but as the latter had already been engraved before the former was received, it was not possible to make the change for the first edition of the general map. The additional examinations now being made in this neighborhood will require much of the Cascade Range of mountains in Washington Territory to be re-engraved.

The numerous small reconnaissances not mentioned in this explanation of the manner of compiling the general map, have all been reduced to it according to the geographical positions determined by the other reconnaissances and surveys, the compilation of which I have discussed.

BIBLIOGRAPHICAL ESSAY

THE MOST IMPORTANT materials for a study of the Corps of Topographical Engineers can be found in the departmental letter files of the National Archives and in the long series of Public Documents printed for the Senate and the House of Representatives. In addition to these official repositories, a number of private libraries contain relevant manuscript resources to such an extent that they can be considered a third major source of information on the Topographical Corps. This study began, in fact, with the William Hemsley Emory Papers of the Yale Collection of Western Americana.

The following bibliography, as it relates to the manscript resources used, is complete. For reasons of brevity, however, only the most important printed materials have been listed. Full references to these and to many supplementary citations will be found in the footnotes or in the short title list.

MANUSCRIPTS

In the National Archives, the departmental record groups that proved the most valuable were the Old Army Section, Record Group 77; the Department of the Interior, Record Group 48; the Department of State, Record Group 59; and the Cartographic Records Section. The Old Army Section contains the major bulk of the records of the Topographical Corps. Most important of these materials are:

1. The document file, consisting of eighty-eight boxes of letters and documents received from 1830 to 1865.

2. The letters-issued books consisting of twenty-four volumes of copies of letters sent out by the Topographical Bureau between 1829 and 1867. There are also index volumes to this series.

3. The letters-received books from Jan. 31, 1829, to March 1, 1866. These contain relevant materials only from about 1850 to 1866, and are much less useful than the actual file of documents received. There is an index volume for the period 1864–65.

4. The letters-issued book, internal improvements, May 5, 1824, to May 1, 1827, which contains significant materials on Isaac Roberdeau and Stephen H. Long.

5. The letters-received book from May 14, 1824, to June 16, 1831,

a special register of letters transferred from the files of the Corps of Engineers to the Topographical Bureau in 1831. It contains only résumés of the full texts of the letters.

6. The letters issued to the Secretary of War, Dec. 6, 1843, to Jan. 21, 1867. These are in ten volumes, and contain the full texts of the letters. All of the annual reports are reproduced here.

7. The records of the Office of Explorations and Surveys, 1857–61, which consists of four boxes of folded documents. The records of this office are divided between the Old Army Section, Record Group 77, and the Department of the Interior, Record Group 48. (See below.)

8. Catalogue of the books of the library of the Office of Explorations and Surveys. The books themselves provide insight into the geographic and scientific knowledge available to the officers of the Corps.

9. Contracts, from Sept. 6, 1841, to Aug. 10, 1863; and Aug. 27, 1866, to June 8, 1867.

Of lesser importance are:

1. Deed book, Nov. 3, 1842, to Nov. 3, 1846.

2. Returns of the Topographical Engineers, 1839–63.

3. Capt. T. J. Cram, "Military Topographical Memoir—Fort Dalles on the Columbia to Fort Boise on the Salmon River, 1857"; and idem, "Military Topographical Memoir on Routes Connecting Oregon and California to Utah, 1857." Both of these are bound manuscript volumes. They received no mention in the text of this study because they represent a compilation from existing sources rather than any original work on the part of Captain Cram. His reputation suffered accordingly.

4. Lt. J. C. Ives, "Exploration and Survey of the Colorado River, 1857–58," bound MS volume (two copies).

5. Captain John N. Macomb, "Exploration from Santa Fe, New Mexico to the Junction of the Green and Grand Rivers, 1859." MS copy of his original report. This is valuable because Macomb's published report is very brief.

6. Field Notes, occupying sixty drawers, and accompanied by DeGrange's Index. These are less valuable than might be expected, since they are mostly small notebooks full of sketches of the topographical details used to compile the printed maps.

The Department of the Interior Records, Record Group 48, also contain valuable materials, the most important of which are:

1. The letterbooks of correspondence from the Pacific Railroad surveys. These fill seven drawers.

2. The letters received by the Office of Explorations, supplementing those mentioned above in Record Group 77. Among the most im-

portant are the reports of Lieutenant Pope's artesian well experiments.

3. Correspondence relating to the Mexican Boundary Survey.

4. Register of letters received on the Mexican Boundary Survey, July 12, 1858, to Sept. 9, 1862.

5. One volume of letters sent in relation to the Mexican Boundary Survey, 1858.

6. The Records of the Wagon Roads Office. This was not a Topographical Engineer operation, but it throws light on the Army's wagon-road program.

The State Department Archives were primarily concerned with the operations on the Northwest Boundary and the Mexican Boundary Survey. Since the official report of the Northwest Boundary Survey has never come to light, the thirty-eight envelopes of correspondence concerning the Survey remain the only source of material for a study of this operation. Fourteen of these envelopes contain only meteorological data and are of little value. The rest include the reports of the field parties and subordinate officers to the Commissioner, Archibald Campbell, and are thus more important. For the Mexican Boundary Survey there are fifteen envelopes, three of which contain correspondence by Major William H. Emory.

The Cartographic Records Division contains materials which were indispensable for the present study. The originals of most of the printed maps that accompanied the official reports of exploration can be found here. Many contain notations or markings by the cartographers. *The Catalogue of the Exhibition of Geographical Exploration and Topographic Mapping by the United States Government,* National Archives Publication No. 53-2 (Washington, 1952), gives a good description of some of the important maps in this collection. It should be observed, too, that the originals of many of the paintings and drawings made by the exploring parties can be found in this Records Division. Particularly noteworthy are the drawings made to accompany James H. Simpson's "Wagon Road Report" on Utah, which never appeared with his original report, and the beautiful series of watercolor paintings by James Alden, made to accompany the report on the Northwest Boundary Survey, which, was, of course, never published.

There are other groups of archival records that have a bearing on the operations of the Corps, such as the records of the Corps of Engineers, and of the Adjutant General's office, as well as some of the materials in the Office of Indian Affairs, but these have only a tangential value. The real heart of the study, as far as archival records are concerned, lies in the four above-mentioned groups.

The manuscripts division of the Library of Congress also contains collections of papers that proved useful. Of these, by far the most important are the Nicholas P. Trist Papers, principally because they provide insight in the true meaning of Article V of the Treaty of Guadalupe Hidalgo. Of lesser importance were the William B. Franklin Papers; the James Buchanan Papers; the John N. Macomb Papers; the Dr. William Lee Papers; and the Journals of Titian Peale. A unique set of documents, which were used to only a limited extent, were the diaries of Charles Preuss, Frémont's topographer. Written in German, these diaries cover the periods June 4, 1842—Oct. 2, 1842; May 30, 1843—July 5, 1844; and Dec. 1848—Feb. 10, 1849. Thus they give an account of Frémont's first, second, and fourth expeditions into the West. These diaries are important because they present a less flattering view of Frémont by one of his closest associates. No attempt was made to canvass all the papers of the political figures of the period that are in the Library of Congress. I consulted the papers of the Topographical Engineers and referred to the other collections only in response to specific problems.

Pertinent manuscript collections are widely scattered in various libraries. Among the most important of these are:

1. The Pennsylvania Historical Society, which contains:
   a. The A. A. Humphreys Papers, important because he was chief of the Bureau of Explorations and Surveys, but somewhat disappointing in their yield of information
   b. The George Gordon Meade Papers
   c. The Isaac Roberdeau Papers
   d. The James Buchanan Papers
   e. Scattered items from the Simon Gratz Autograph Collection
   f. The Daniel Parker Papers, important because they contain the only sizable number of personal letters by Colonel Abert that I was able to find
2. The John Carter Brown Library, containing the papers of John Russell Bartlett. This is a highly important collection for the light it casts on the Mexican Boundary Survey. It includes a complete series of letterbooks, a manuscript journal of Bartlett's experiences as Boundary Commissioner, a manuscript autobiography, a scrapbook of newspaper clippings relating to the Boundary Survey, and a portfolio of paintings and drawings by Bartlett, Henry Pratt, and Seth Eastman.
3. The New York Public Library, which contains some papers by George Gibbs on the geology of the Northwest country, and some letters of Henry D. Mansfield discussing the Mesilla valley crisis.

4. The New York State Library at Albany, which contains the extensive papers of Gouverneur Kemble Warren. These include a manuscript journal of his Nebraska-Dakota expedition of 1855, some correspondence with his family, the journal of his assistant, J. Hudson Snowden, and seven manuscript sketch maps made on the spot from data derived from the mountain men.
5. The New York State Museum at Albany, in which are to be found the Papers of James Hall. This is a large and important collection, particularly so because of the picture of nineteenth-century science reflected in the correspondence. Hall also worked closely with the government scientists.
6. The New York Botanical Gardens, for the papers of John Torrey. His extensive correspondence contains a number of letters from Frémont, Emory, and other Topographical Engineers, and in addition, provides an important picture of the status of nineteenth-century botanical studies in America.
7. The Bancroft Library furnishes a small collection of the George Horatio Derby Papers, and the Narrative of Thomas Salathiel Martin, who accompanied Frémont in 1845 and 1848.
8. The Huntington Library, with a small collection of the John W. Gunnison Papers and the James Hervey Simpson Papers.
9. The Maryland Historical Society, for the James A. Pearce Papers and the Brantz Mayer Papers. These were examined at my request by Jerry E. Patterson of the Yale Historical Manuscripts Collection.
10. The Texas State Historical Society Library, for the Thomas Rusk papers. These also were searched by Mr. Patterson.
11. The Yale Historical Manuscripts Collection, for the papers of Daniel Cady Eaton. They yielded scattered letters by Frémont, Arthur Schott, and others; and for the Barna Upton papers, which give the best possible presentation of the life of the common soldier in the Mexican War.
12. The Yale Collection of Western Americana, which contains:
    a. The William H. Emory Papers, approximately 4,000 items on details of his early career, essential for an understanding of the Mexican Boundary Controversy. This collection is of fundamental importance. It contains letterbooks and an archival file of letters to and from Emory during the Boundary Survey period. Its one weakness is that it includes only a few personal letters to his family and relatives.
    b. The Elwood Evans Papers, especially his "Journal and Notes Kept . . . while a Member of the Northern Pacific Railroad

Exploration and Survey under the Command of Governor I. I. Stevens."

c. The I. I. Stevens Papers.
d. The George Suckley Papers—small number but extremely valuable for the insight they afford on the Stevens expedition.
e. The W. F. Raynolds Papers, which includes Raynolds' field journals from his Yellowstone Expedition of 1859–60, the reports by his assistants Henry R. Maynadier, and J. Hudson Snowden, and a portfolio of original paintings and sketches by J. D. Hutton and Antoin Schoenborn.
f. The Clinton Gardner Papers, consisting of his journal while on the Northwest Boundary Survey, and some personal correspondence.
g. The George Foster Emmons journals, which contain an account of his exploration from Vancouver to San Francisco Aug.–Oct. 1841, while serving as an officer in the Wilkes Expedition.
h. The Henry Eld Journal, which also deals with the Oregon explorations conducted by Commander Wilkes.
i. The Paul Max Engle papers—maps and sketches while on Lt. G. K. Warren's Dakota Expedition of 1857.
j. The George Gibbs papers: which contains only a few letters to Suckley.

Because the papers of Amiel Weeks Whipple are at the Oklahoma State Historical Society and have been published in *The Chronicles of Oklahoma,* it did not seem necessary to consult the documents themselves. Another important collection, the James W. Abert Papers, are now in the possession of Mr. Rosenstock of Denver, Colorado, who did not feel that he could make them available at this time. A fire at the Smithsonian Institution in 1865 destroyed much that might otherwise have been crucial to this study. Not the least of this loss was the large collection of Indian paintings made by John Mix Stanley on his various trips to the West. Despite its promise, therefore, the Smithsonian Institution did not figure very importantly as a source.

Public Documents, Printed

Much of the record of the Topographical Corps and its western activities is embodied in the reports submitted to the Houses of Congress and printed as public documents. *The Annual Report of the Secretary of War* for the years 1839–61 included the "Annual Report of the Chief of Topographical Engineers." Before 1839 the reports of projects under the Topographical Bureau were included in the annual reports of the Chief of Engineers. These reports, along with the general remarks of the Secretary of War, are important because they constitute an over-all view of the work of the Corps and its place in the entire military approach to the trans-Mississippi West. In addition, they illustrate the wide range of projects undertaken by the Army throughout the country. Of all the secretaries of war in the period 1839–61, Jefferson Davis stood out as the one most interested in improving the quality and changing the character of the Army. He was also the only one who addressed himself to forming an explicit program for the trans-Mississippi West. For this reason, his annual reports for the years 1853–56 are extremely interesting and important.

Most of the official reports of the field-exploring expeditions were published as individual public documents. Usually they were written in the form of a detailed, day-by-day journal, with a series of appendixes constituting various scientific reports and tables of statistical data. Almost every report included a map. The maps, as well as the reports, varied widely in quality. The models for most of the Topographical Engineer reports were those of John Charles Frémont. His *Report on an Exploration of the Country Lying between the Missouri River and the Rocky Mountains, on the Line of the Kansas and Great Platte Rivers* (1843) and his later, more inclusive work, the *Report of the Exploring Expedition to the Rocky Mountains in the year 1842, and to Oregon and North California in the years 1843–44* (1845) were representative examples of the nineteenth-century scientific report written in the style of literary romanticism. The style has been generally attributed to Jessie Benton Frémont, but later Topographical Engineer reports use this style often enough to indicate that it may well be merely typical of the time. Less lyrical in style and somewhat less important was Frémont's *Geographical Memoir upon Upper California in Illustration of His Map of Oregon and California,* published in 1848 with Charles Preuss' map. This was not a journal but a scientific essay obviously patterned after J. N. Nicollet's *Report Intended to Illustrate a Map of the Hydrographical Basin of the Upper Mississippi River* (1843).

Several of the earlier reports were made as a result of the field operations of the Mexican War. Of these, the most significant is William H. Emory's *Notes of a Military Reconnaissance from Fort Leavenworth, in Missouri, to San Diego, in California* (1847–48). This report was accompanied by the subreports of Philip St. George Cooke, A. R. Johnston, and James W. Abert, which gave the first scientific picture of the Southwest since Humboldt's "New Spain" of 1811.

Some of the reports were brief accounts or journals of wagon-road surveys and included very little scientific data. Typical of these was James H. Simpson's *Report of the Exploration and Survey of a Route from Fort Smith, Arkansas, to Santa Fe, New Mexico,* or George Horatio Derby's *Topographical Memoir Accompanying Maps of the Sacramento Valley.* Other reports were on a more elaborate scale, such as Howard Stansbury's *Exploration and Survey of the Valley of the Great Salt Lake of Utah, Including a Reconnaissance of a New Route through the Rocky Mountains,* which included many illustrations, scientific subreports, and a separate atlas of maps. The best by far of these individual reports was Joseph C. Ives' *Report upon the Colorado River of the West* (1861). It is a long, carefully written journal, consciously literary but with a maximum amount of attention to scientific observation. John Strong Newberry's geological report, which accompanied Ives' narrative, is one of the best of the government geological reports. It is the first such report on the Grand Canyon. Newberry also wrote most of John N. Macomb's *Exploring Expedition from Santa Fe, New Mexico to the Junction of the Grand and Green Rivers of the Great Colorado of the West in 1859* (1876) in the form of an extended geological résumé. One other set of individual reports is very important, namely G. K. Warren's series of explorations in the Dakotas. They derive their principal value from the geological reports by F. V. Hayden and F. B. Meek that accompany them.

The outstanding production of the Topographical Corps was the thirteen-volume series of Pacific Railroad reports entitled *Reports of Explorations and Surveys to Ascertain the Most Practicable and Economical Route for a Railroad from the Mississippi River to the Pacific Ocean.* A quarto set, it contains the correspondence and field journals of the various railroad exploring parties of 1853–55. Also included is Frederick West Lander's report on his exploration of a line from Fort Vancouver to the regular emigrant route that was sponsored by the territorial legislature of Oregon. In addition to the journals, Volumes 7, 9, and 10 are devoted exclusively to scientific reports on botany and zoology. These are among the most important American scientific productions of the nineteenth-century. Volume 1 contains the controversial résumé and evaluation of the railroad routes by A. A. Humphreys and Jefferson Davis. Extremely important is Volume 11, which is made up of G. K. Warren's *Memoir* and the various maps compiled, including Warren's monumental "General Map" of the trans-Mississippi West. Though they present formidable obstacles to convenient use because of their disorganized arrangement and lack of consecutive page numbering, the Pacific Railroad surveys are nevertheless a monumental work, of the greatest importance in understanding the methods and achievements of the Corps in the West.

Another group of public documents deal with the Mexican Boundary Survey. Emory's *Report on the United States and Mexican Boundary Survey* is the final résumé of the boundary survey work and contains the scientific reports. The account of the operations is heavily slanted by Emory, and often appears to be an argument for his own position rather than a balanced account. Though the report was authorized by the 34th Congress, it was actually published in 1857 (Vol. 1) and 1859 (Vol. 2). The public documents on the Boundary Survey consist mostly of correspondence, arguments, and details of charges preferred against various members of the Commission. Of great importance are Senate Executive Documents 60, 89, 119, 120, 121, and 131 of the 32d Congress, 1st Session (1851–52); Senate Executive Document No. 41, 32d Congress 2d Session; and Senate Executive Document No. 55, 33d Congress, 2d Session (1854–55).

In addition to these public documents, relevant material on science in the trans-Mississippi West may be found in the annual reports of the Board of Regents of the Smithsonian Institution, published as part of the serial set of documents, and in the separate volumes of the *Smithsonian Contributions to Knowledge.* The latter volumes include such important essays as Joseph Leidy's "The Ancient Fauna of Nebraska," F. B. Meek's and F. V. Hayden's "Paleontology of the Upper Missouri," and John Torrey's "Plantae Fremontianae." The *U. S. Statutes at Large* for the period 1838–65 furnish an index to laws passed, although they are often not much help in breaking down the aggregate appropriations for military and deficiency bills. For debates and speeches see the *Congressional Globe,* 1838–65. A useful guide to the progress of laws and various petitions is the *Senate Journal* that accompanies each session of Congressional documents. The most complete official source of information on the Northwest Boundary Survey is Marcus Baker's "Survey of the Northwestern Boundary of the United States, 1857–61," *Bulletin of the United States Geological Survey,* 174, Washington, D.C., 1900. This includes the full texts of reports by Lieutenant Parke and Commissioner Campbell. For an idea of the performance of the Topographical officers in the Mexican War see the *Report of the Secretary of War,* 30th Congress, 1st Session, Senate Executive Document 1, Vol. 1 (1847), 45–718. These official reports of the Mexican War should be used with caution, since most of the field commanders appear to have written with more attention to their reputation than to the task of providing information.

Other Printed Sources

Since in the course of its western activities the Topographical Corps touched upon many aspects of American life—politics, science, diplomacy, the process of settlement, and the techniques of military conquest—a wide range of contemporary literature becomes relevant in the writing of its history. An attempt is made here not to include all the sources used but only to suggest the kinds of materials that proved most useful.

Travel Books and Accounts of Explorations

For the earlier period up to 1846 many of the important accounts are published in Reuben Gold Thwaites' series, *Early Western Travels, 1748–1846,* 32 vols. Cleveland, 1805–07. These include Thomas Nuttall's *A Journal of Travels into the Arkansas Territory during the year 1819* (Vol. 13), Edwin James' *Account of an Expedition from Pittsburg to the Rocky Mountains, Performed in the Years 1819 and '20* (Vol. 14), James Ohio Pattie's *The Personal Narrative of James Ohio Pattie* (Vol. 18), and several others of importance for this period. Two rare but significant documents are Thomas Jefferson, *Message from the President of the United States Communicating Discoveries Made in Exploring the Missouri, Red River, and Washita by Captains Lewis and Clarke, Doctor Sibley, and Mr. Dunbar; with a Statistical Account of the Countries Adjacent, Feb. 19, 1806,* Washington, D.C., 1806; and Thomas Freeman and Peter Custis, *An Account of the Red River in Louisiana Drawn Up from the Returns of Messrs. Freeman and Custis to the War Office of the United States, Who Explored the Same in the Year, 1806,* Washington, D.C., 1807. Zebulon Pike, *Expedition to the Headwaters of the Mississippi River, through Louisiana Territory and in New Spain during the Years 1805–6–7* (New York, 1895) is also important, and typical of the kinds of materials available for the period immediately preceding that of the Topographical Engineers.

Of the most direct utility is John Russell Bartlett, *Personal Narrative of Explorations and Incidents in Texas, New Mexico, California, Sonora, and Chihuahua. Connected with the United States and Mexican Boundary Commission,* 2 vols. New York, 1854, a travel book in the tradition of John Lloyd Stephens, E. G. Squier, and Brantz Mayer. It is important because it illustrates the romantic and literary approach to the West, used by the ethnologists and anthropologists of the time. It is even more important as a detailed and well-written chronicle of Bartlett's Quixotic adventures as Boundary Commissioner. John C.

Cremony's *Life among the Apaches* (San Francisco, 1868) contains supplementary material on separate parties on the survey. Josiah Gregg, *Commerce of the Prairies,* ed. Max L. Moorhead (Norman, Oklahoma, 1954), is a classic and indispensable guide to an understanding of the Santa Fe trade. Gregg was an intelligent observer, and he made the first investigation into Southwestern anthropology since the days of Humboldt. Seymour Dunbar, ed., *The Fort Sutter Papers* (New York, 1923), adds material on Frémont's third expedition. Frémont's *Memoirs* (New York and Chicago, 1887) contain accounts of his expeditions, and are the principal source of information on his third expedition, which went West in 1845. Charles H. Corey, ed., *The Journals of Theodore Talbot* (Portland, Oregon, 1931), is another source of material on Frémont's expeditions by one of his trusted lieutenants. William H. Emory, "Extracts from His Journal while with the Army of the West," *Niles National Register, 71* (Oct. 31, 1846), is a little-known version of Emory's first western reconnaissance, which differs from the regular report. José Salazar Yllarregui, *Datos de los trabajos astronomicos y topograficos, despues en forma de un diario, practicados durante el ano de 1849 y principio de 1850 par la Comision de Limites Mexicana* (Mexico, 1850), is the only Mexican version of the Boundary Survey, and it has a limited value because it covers only the period to 1850. Edward F. Beale and Gwin Harris Heap, *Central Route to the Pacific, from the Valley of the Mississippi to California* (Philadelphia, 1854), and A. B. Gray, *Survey of a Route for the Southern Pacific Railroad on the 32nd Parallel . . . for the Texas Western Railroad Company* (Cincinnati, 1855), are typical of the private surveys made to discover and promote transcontinental railroads. In general, it can be concluded that the travel literature of this type is so abundant as to be almost the characteristic literature of the times.

Technical Books and Treatises

In geology, James Dwight Dana's *Manual of Geology* (New York, 1862) and Charles Lyell's *Principles of Geology, Being an Attempt to Explain the Former Changes of the Earth's Surface by Reference to Causes Now in Operation* (London, 1830–33) are the most important texts of the time. James Hall's *Paleontology of New York State* (Vol. 1, Albany, 1847, other volumes published 1852–94), was a model of paleontological investigation that was imitated by F. V. Hayden and F. B. Meek when they made their investigations in the Dakotas and in Kansas. Hayden's most important work for this period was his

Geological Report of the Exploration of the Yellowstone and Missouri Rivers, Washington, D.C., 1869. This embodied his discoveries of the Potsdam Sandstone, and Meek's careful discussion of Cretaceous fossils. Other reports of Hayden and Meek, as well as those of Joseph Leidy, can be found in the *Proceedings of the Philadelphia Academy of Natural Sciences.* Important essays on geology by Say, Morton, Conrad, and others appeared in *The American Journal of Science,* published by Benjamin Silliman in New Haven, beginning in 1818.

In botany, Gray's *Manual of Botany* (Boston and London, 1848) and John Lindley's *An Introduction to the Natural System of Botany* (New York, 1831) are key works. The latter has an appendix by John Torrey, who first introduced the natural system of plant classification into the United States and became its champion. Most of Torrey's own works were concrete reports like his *Botany of the Boundary,* which was thought by Gray to be the most important botanical work published in America. *The Proceedings of the St. Louis Academy of Science* provide insight into George Engelmann's investigations of cactaceae, and also of the status of organized science in the principal western cities.

Geography was the queen of early nineteenth-century sciences, and nowhere were its concepts better epitomized than in the studies of Alexander von Humboldt. His major works are available in English translation. The most important for me is the *Political Essay on the Kingdom of New Spain . . . with Physical Sections and Maps . . .* (1811), which included a survey of what is now the American West, and his important map of the Southwest country, as well as his famous profile cross-section of Mexico and a description of one of the earliest uses of the barometer to determine altitude. Also significant was his *Aspects of Nature* (Philadelphia, 1849), which mentioned the work of Frémont in the West, and *Cosmos* (London, 1847), the first volume in a series published down to 1870, which embodied Humboldt's philosophy and his general approach to geography. William Gilpin in *The Central Gold Region* (Philadelphia and St. Louis, 1860) and *Mission of the North American People* (Philadelphia, 1873) borrowed heavily from Humboldt's ideas. The other significant geographical thinker of the time was Karl Ritter, whose *Erdkunde* was published in 1818. This dealt more with people than it did with the environment, and was influenced by Humboldt's approach, though it differs in emphasis.

Ethnology and anthropology were still primitive studies, and were a branch of knowledge subordinate to geography. Anthropological studies were also strongly tinged with literary mannerisms. Henry

Rowe Schoolcraft, *Information Respecting the History, Condition, and Prospects of the Indian Tribes of the United States* (6 vols. 1851–60), was the major work of the time, and embodied the twin techniques of linguistic classification and the investigation of primitive beliefs and myths. Albert Gallatin's "Synopsis of the Indian Tribes within the United States," published in *Transactions of the American Antiquarian Society* as Vol. 2 of *Archaeologica Americana* (Cambridge, 1836), is also a significant pioneer work in this field. The *Proceedings of the American Ethnological Society* became a source of information after 1845.

In zoology Louis Agassiz, *Methods of Study in Natural History* (17th ed. Boston, 1886) provided insight into the pre-Darwinian scientific mind. The book was first published in 1863, as an answer to Darwin's *Origin of the Species* (1859). Another idea of Agassiz' approach to natural history can be gained from his "Essay on Classification," *Contributions to the Natural History of the United States of America* (4 vols. Boston, 1857) Vol. 1. Elizabeth Cory Agassiz, ed., *Louis Agassiz: His Life and Correspondence* (2 vols. Boston, 1886) furnishes the details of Agassiz' career and indicates something of his relations with Humboldt. Spencer F. Baird's best work was in classification, and his zoological reports for the *Pacific Railroad Reports,* Vols. 8 and 9, embody his general approach to zoology.

For engineering, the key book is D. H. Mahan, *An Elementary Course of Civil Engineering for the Use of Cadets of the United States Military Academy,* 6th ed. New York, 1852. It was first published in 1846 and served as the standard American engineering treatise for many years. European books of importance are Guy De Vernon, *A Treatise on the Science of War and Fortifications,* 2 vols. transl. from the French by John M. O'Connor, New York, 1818; M. L. Sganzin, *An Elementary Course of Civil Engineering,* trans. from the French, Boston, 1837; and J. N. P. Hachette, *Traité élémentaire des machines,* Paris, 1819. Among the significant American works were Stephen H. Long, *Railroad Manual . . .* (Baltimore, 1829), an early treatise on the methods of railroad construction; and A. A. Humphreys and Henry L. Abbott, *Report upon the Physics and Hydraulics of the Mississippi River* (Washington, D.C., 1861), a classic in engineering literature. Lieutenant R. S. Smith, instructor at West Point, published a *Manual of Topographical Drawing* in 1856, embodying the essentials of Robert Walker Weir's course in drawing at West Point, which was of the greatest importance to the Topographical Engineers.

Finally, in any list of scientific books for this period must be included Charles Darwin's *Journal of Researches into the Geology and*

Natural History of Various Countries Visited during the Voyage of H.M.S. Beagle round the World, 2d ed. London, 1845. The edition used here is Everyman's, London, 1930. Also Darwin's *Of the Origin of Species by Means of Natural Selection, or the Preservation of Favored Races in the Struggle for Life,* London, 1859, 1860.

Collected Works, Memoirs, and Controversial Pamphlets

Here the materials available are almost infinite. Among the most important for this study are Thomas Hart Benton, *Thirty Years' View . . .* (New York, 1854–56) and his various other writings and speeches published as pamphlets and in the *Congressional Globe;* Milo M. Quaife, ed., *The Diary of James K. Polk,* 4 vols. Chicago, 1940; James Richardson, ed., *Compilations of the Messages and Papers of the Presidents, 1789–1897,* 10 vols. Washington, D.C., 1907; Maurice G. Fulton, ed., *The Diary and Letters of Josiah Gregg,* 2 vols. Norman, Oklahoma, 1941–44; and Dunbar Rowland, ed., *Jefferson Davis, Constitutionalist; His Letters, Papers, and Speeches,* 10 vols. Jackson, Mississippi, 1923. This latter collection of works is not entirely satisfactory since it does not include all of Davis' writings, and reprints many things which are already available in the public documents. *The Writings of Thomas Jefferson* (10 vols. New York, 1892–99), edited by Paul L. Ford, are still indispensable for an understanding of Jefferson's plans for the West, though they are, of course, highly selective.

Pamphlet materials proved to be of some importance in this study. Particularly significant are Cornelius Glen Peebles' *Exposé of the Atlantic and Pacific Railroad Company* (*Extraordinary Developments*), New York, 1854; and Robert J. Walker, *Vindication of the Atlantic and Pacific Railroad Company,* New York, 1854. These pamphlets are, of course, controversial and must be used with caution, but they do provide clues to Walker's plans for his Texas railroad, and they indicate the important men interested in promoting the scheme. *The Charter, By-Laws, and Regulations of the Atlantic and Pacific Railroad Co., Adopted Nov. 4, 1853* (New York, 1853) and the *Atlantic and Pacific Railroad Co. Circular to the Stockholders* (New York, 1855) provide additional information. A. A. Humphreys' *Letter to the Hon. William M. Gwin, in Relation to the Railroad to the Pacific by the Thirty-Fifth and Thirty-Second Parallels* (Washington, D.C., 1858) and *A Reply to Certain Portions of the Minority Report of the Hon. Z. Kidwell of the House of Representatives, Member of the Select Committee upon the Pacific Railroad* (Washington, D.C.,

1856) are two pamphlets in which Humphreys defends the Bureau of Explorations and Surveys and the War Department from charges of sectional favoritism in the analysis of the Pacific railroad surveys.

Zedekiah Kidwell's "Report on the Impracticability of Building a Railroad from the Mississippi River to the Pacific Ocean . . ." published as part of the 34th Congress, 1st Session, House of Representatives, *Report* 274 (1856), and his "Supplementary Report in Reply to the Comments of the Secretary of War upon the Minority Report Submitted by Mr. Kidwell of the Select Committee on the Pacific Railroad . . ." 34th Congress, 3d Session, House of Representatives, *Miscellaneous Document 44* (1857) are incisive criticisms of the Pacific railroad surveys. The Minority Reports were composed only of Kidwell's opinions, but his comments are nevertheless important for any historian who wishes to evaluate the surveys.

Secondary Materials

Among the most useful are the various guides and biographical directories. For a bibliography of original narratives of western travel see Henry R. Wagner and Charles Camp, *The Plains and the Rockies,* San Francisco, 1921, and the revised and considerably enlarged edition of 1953. It is a basic research book for anyone working in western history. Of almost equal significance for my study is Max Meisel, *A Bibliography of American Natural History* (2 vols. New York, 1924), which lists all the Topographical Engineer expeditions and catalogues the numerous publications that resulted. Adelaide Hasse, *Reports of Explorations Printed in the Documents of the United States Government* (1899), is also a useful guide to pertinent materials. More specialized is Mary C. Withington, *A Catalogue of Manuscripts in the Collection of Western Americana Founded by William Robertson Coe, Yale University Library,* New Haven, 1952. A study of the topographical Corps could not be written without the *Dictionary of American Biography* and G. W. Cullum's *Biographical Register of the Officers and Graduates of the United States Military Academy,* 2 vols. Boston and New York, 1891. Also of great value are the *National Academy of Science Biographical Memoirs,* 28 vols., 1877–1956.

In the field of military history and government for this period the materials are surprisingly meager. Much has been written on the Mexican War, but as yet no book has surpassed Justin Smith's *The War with Mexico,* 2 vols. New York, 1919. The most important source of information on the Corps of Topographical Engineers is Henry Putney Beers, "A History of the Corps of Topographical Engineers,

1813–1863," *The Military Engineer, 34* (1842), 287–91, 348–52, an account of the essential steps in the history of the Corps, including a roster of the men who served as Topographers (see above, pp. 435–37). This roster is not perfectly accurate. Another important article is that of Lt. T. W. Symons, "The Army and the Exploration of the West," *Journal of the Military Service Institution of the United States, 4* (New York and London, 1883), 205–49. Raphael P. Thian, *Legislative History of the General Staff of the United States Army* . . . (Washington, D.C., 1901), gives the texts of various laws that relate to the formation of the General Staff and thereby furnishes a particularly good outline for the history of the Topographical Corps. Less valuable is W. Stull Holt, *The Office of the Chief of Engineers of the Army; Its Non-Military History, Activities and Organization,* Baltimore, 1923. A recent and important general study of the relation of science to the federal government is A. Hunter Dupree, *Science in the Federal Government,* Boston, 1957; it is, however, strictly institutional and devotes only three pages to the western explorations conducted by the Army. George Brown Goode, *The Smithsonian Institution, 1846–1896* (Washington, D.C., 1897) provides an impressionistic account of the relation of the Institution to western exploration. The works of Leonard D. White, *The Jeffersonians* (New York, 1951) and *The Jacksonians* (New York, 1954), are of less help than might be expected, because they move so rapidly and superficially over the vast subject of governmental organization, which, even in a period of "wise and frugal government" was nevertheless extensive. The best study of West Point is Sidney Forman's *West Point: A History of the United States Military Academy* (New York, 1950), but it leaves much to be done on that subject. Thomas Manning's unpublished *History of the United States Geological Survey* is the best work on that subject. Less informative and highly subjective is Wallace Stegner's *Beyond the Hundredth Meridian* (Boston, 1954), which sacrifices the story of the United States Geological Survey to special pleading for John Wesley Powell, with a corresponding derogation of other scientists. Henry Putney Beers, *The Western Military Frontier* (Philadelphia, 1935), is uninspired. More imaginative is F. P. Prucha, *Broadaxe and Bayonet* (Madison, 1953), which studies the role of the army garrisons in the Minnesota-Wisconsin region. Averam B. Bender's *The March of Empire* (Lawrence, Kansas, 1952) is based on immense research but is unimaginative in dealing with the role of the Army in the West. Its chief value perhaps lies in its footnotes. By far, the best study of the Army on the frontier for the present work is William Turrentine Jackson's *Wagon Roads West,* Berkeley and Los Angeles,

1952. A pioneer work on the Corps in the West is Edward S. Wallace, *The Great Reconnaissance* (Boston, 1955), which catches the flavor of the time but is not intended to be scholarly or definitive. An important book on a central topic of the period is Robert R. Russel's *Improvement of Communication with the Pacific Coast as an Issue in American Politics,* Cedar Rapids, Iowa, 1948. It is not the final word but attempts a balanced and judicious survey of a vast subject. George Leslie Allright's *Official Explorations for Pacific Railroads, 1853–1855* (Berkeley, 1921) is a convenient outline guide to the itineraries of the various exploration parties but is very deficient in interpretation. Paul Neff Garber's *The Gadsden Treaty* (Philadelphia, 1923) is still a good book on the subject, though several of his citations seem a bit puzzling. Two specialized studies relating to the government and the Corps are Edgar E. Hume's *Ornithologists of the United States Army Medical Corps* (Baltimore, 1942), a series of biographical sketches of some of the men who accompanied the Topographical expeditions; and F. Stansbury Hayden, *Aeronautics in the Union and Confederate Armies* (Baltimore, 1941), which chronicles the activities of the Topographical Corps in the early Civil War balloon experiments. Two books dealing with post-Civil War relations between the government and the frontier provide valuable insight into the pre-Civil War period: Earl S. Pomeroy, *The Territories and the United States, 1861–1890,* Philadelphia, 1947; and Howard R. Lamar, *Dakota Territory, 1861–1889: A Study of Frontier Politics,* New Haven, 1956.

In approaching technical problems in the various fields, the usual practice was to turn to standard texts and to more simplified treatises that the layman-historian can comprehend. In geology the basic text used for reference has been Chester Longwell and R. T. Flint et al., *Outlines of Geology,* New York, 1947; it includes historical as well as physical geology. Most valuable of all is George P. Merrill's *The First One Hundred Years of American Geology,* New Haven, 1924. This indispensable book gives brief résumés of all the work in western geology for this period, as well as thumbnail biographies of the geologists, both obscure and famous. Less valuable but also significant are Charles Schuchert and Clara Mae Le Vene, *O. C. Marsh, Pioneer in Paleontology,* New Haven, 1940; and Wallace Atwood, *Physiographic Provinces of North America,* Boston and New York, 1940. For references in paleontology Merrill's book again provided the main guide, but two texts are significant introductions to the subject: Edward W. Berry, *Paleontology,* New York, 1929; and Alfred S. Romer, *Vertebrate Paleontology,* Chicago, 1933. Also of value is Leonard C. Jones, "The Neuchatel Group and Science in the United States," *American-Swiss Gazette,* Nov. 18 to Dec. 30, 1931.

In the field of geography and cartography the two most pertinent works are E. W. Gilbert, *The Exploration of Western America, 1800–1850: An Historical Geography,* Cambridge, England, 1933; and Carl I. Wheat, "Mapping the American West, 1540 to 1857," *Proceedings of the American Antiquarian Society, 64* (1954), 19–194. Wheat has also collaborated with Dale L. Morgan in writing *Jedediah Smith and his Maps* (San Francisco, 1954), which is another valuable cartographic study. Lawrence Martin, *Disturnell's Map* (Washington, D.C., 1937) gives the cartographic background behind the Mexican Boundary Survey. For general works see Griffeth Taylor, *Geography in the Twentieth Century,* New York, 1951; R. E. Dickinson and O. J. R. Howorth, *The Making of Geography,* Oxford, 1933; and Richard Hartshorn, "The Nature of Geography," *Annals of the Association of American Geographers, 29,* Nos. 3, 4, Lancaster, Penn., 1939. Also deserving of notice is Ellen C. Semple and Clarence F. Jones, *American History and Its Geographic Conditions,* Boston, 1933.

On natural history in general, some few books are Erik Nordenskiold, *The History of Biology,* New York, 1928; Andrew Denny Rodgers, III, *John Torrey, A Story of North American Botany,* Princeton, 1942; and Robert H. Welker's *Birds and Men,* Cambridge, 1955. The latter is an excellent and imaginative survey of ornithology as it relates to the American scene. Samuel Woods Geiser, *Naturalists of the Frontier* (Dallas, 1937) and Joseph Ewan, *Rocky Mountain Naturalists* (Denver, 1950) are both valuable collections of biographical chapters on important and obscure western naturalists. Ewan's book has an extensive biographical directory that is particularly valuable.

For Indians, the first book is Frederick W. Hodge, *Handbook of American Indians North of Mexico,* 2 vols. Washington, D.C., 1907. This can be supplemented by numerous tribal studies, such as George Bird Grinnell's *The Fighting Cheyennes,* New York, 1915; or Frank C. Lockwood's *The Apache Indians,* New York, 1938. An important study of Southwestern archaeological remains is Adolph Bandelier's "Final Report of Investigations among the Indians of the Southwestern United States Carried on Mainly in the Years from 1880 to 1885," *Papers of the Archaeological Institute of America,* American Series 4, Pt. II, Cambridge, Mass., 1892. An interesting modern attempt at recreating the life of the Pueblos is in Vol. 1 of Paul Horgan's *Great River,* 2 vols. New York, 1955. His approach is through religion and myth, much as was Schoolcraft's. It is highly imaginative and thus not always admissible as "scientific" history. Among the most interesting and useful studies of the Southwestern cultures and the men who studied them is Vol. 1 of Justin Winsor, ed., *Narrative and Critical History of America,* 8 vols. Boston, 1889, especially chapters 3 and 4.

The number of miscellaneous books tangential to the subject of this study is very substantial. Biographies of most of the leading scientific figures are available, but they are frequently out-of-date and anecdotal rather than analytical. Typical is James M. Clarke, *James Hall of Albany, Geologist and Paleontologist,* Albany, 1921. One of the pressing needs in American historiography is a reassessment in biographic terms of the leading scientific figures of the nineteenth century.

Books on the West form a whole literature unto themselves. Frederick Jackson Turner's *The Frontier in American History* (New York, 1920) is inescapable and infinitely suggestive. The works of H. H. Bancroft contain material that can be found nowhere else, and cover the whole West in such detail that they can never be overlooked. W. P. Webb's *The Great Plains* (Boston, 1931) deals with many of the problems of this thesis and has been useful. *The Great Frontier* (Boston, 1952), by the same author, calls for a new assessment of the influence of the frontier on American scientific thinking. The works of Bernard DeVoto, especially *Year of Decision* (Boston, 1942) and *Across the Wide Missouri* (Boston, 1947), are also valuable in their peculiarly vivid way. David Lavender's *Bent's Fort* (New York, 1954) has opened up the Southwest to students of the fur trade. Arthur Woodward, in *The Lancers at San Pascual* (San Francisco, 1948) and *Feud on the Colorado* (Los Angeles, 1955), has contributed two detailed studies on minor points that are extremely able and helpful, although they exhibit a characteristic western bias against the "boys in blue." Robert E. Riegal, *The Story of Western Railroads* (New York, 1926), is a standard work but by no means definitive. Robert A. Taft, *Artists and Illustrators of the Old West, 1850–1900* (New York, 1953), is a mine of information on the early western artists but does not really deal with them as artists, relating their forms and techniques to their aims and problems; instead it comments on the comparative accuracy of their pictures. The same author's *Photography and the American Scene* (New York, 1938) also gives valuable factual data on photographers in the West. Henry Nash Smith's *Virgin Land* (Cambridge, Mass., 1950) is particularly good for relating the romantic tone of the times to the progress of western settlement. He leaves out the Topographical Engineer Frémont as a western hero type, however. Hiram M. Chittenden, *The American Fur Trade of the Far*

West (3 vols. New York, 1902), is also biased strongly in favor of the local western hero, the mountain man, but it remains the most comprehensive book on the subject. An interesting attempt at a new interpretation of Manifest Destiny is Norman Graebner's *Empire on the Pacific,* New York, 1955. It is useful for seeing the connection between maritime expansion and overland expansion, but Graebner overstates his case and presents a minimum of evidence to support it. For political background on the period, in addition to the numerous, fashionable, multivolume biographies, see Allan Nevins, *Ordeal of the Union* (2 vols. New York, 1947) and *The Emergence of Lincoln* (2 vols. New York, 1950), which are surprisingly comprehensive in their scope despite the fact that their narrative line is distorted by too much emphasis on the Civil War. The most recent survey of the history of the trans-Mississippi West is Roy Allen Billington, *The Far Western Frontier, 1830–1860* (New York, 1956), a well-written and valuable book, which however epitomizes perfectly the great oversight of most western historians in minimizing the role of government on the frontier.

Colonel John James Abert, Chief of the Topographical Corps.

The Stephen H. Long expedition, 1819–20; a view near the base of the Rocky Mountains.

An imagined reconstruction of the pueblo, Hungo Pawie, Chaco Canyon, New Mexico drawn by R. H. Kern while accompanying the James H. Simpson expedition to the Navaho Country in 1849.

The Pueblo of Zuñi as it looked to Capt. Lorenzo Sitgreaves in 1851.

tah Indian prisoners at Fort Utah, as seen by Captain Howard Stansbury in the winter 1850.

Apache Indians attacking the United States Boundary Commission, Oct. 18, 1852.

United States Boundary Commission train under attack by a herd of stampeding wil horses, Dec. 31, 1852.

The Chelly Canyon in northeastern Arizona, stronghold of the Navaho Indians visited by Lt. James H. Simpson in 1849.

The Santa Rita Copper Mines, headquarters of the United States Boundary Commission under John Russell Bartlett.

A herd of buffaloes near Lake Jessie in North Dakota as seen by the artist John Mix Stanley, who accompanied the Isaac I. Stevens Northern Pacific railroad survey in 1853

Members of the Isaac I. Stevens survey party meeting with the Assiniboin Indians nea Fort Union at the junction of the Yellowstone and Missouri rivers.

Lt. E. G. Beckwith's Pacific railroad survey party encamped on the Porcupine Terraces near Bear River looking south toward the Uinta Mountains.

. W. von Egloffstein's view of the Franklin Valley from a spur of the Humboldt Mountains, drawn while accompanying the Beckwith Pacific railroad survey expedition in 1854.

Mojave Indians assisting Lt. Amiel W. Whipple's Pacific railroad survey party across the Colorado River in 1853.

Fort Vancouver, American outpost on the Columbia River, 1859.

A Mojave Indian admiring his squaw, drawn by H. B. Möllhausen in 1853.

Navaho warriors mounted for battle, drawn by H. B. Möllhausen while accompanying Lt. Amiel W. Whipple's Pacific railroad survey expedition in 1853.

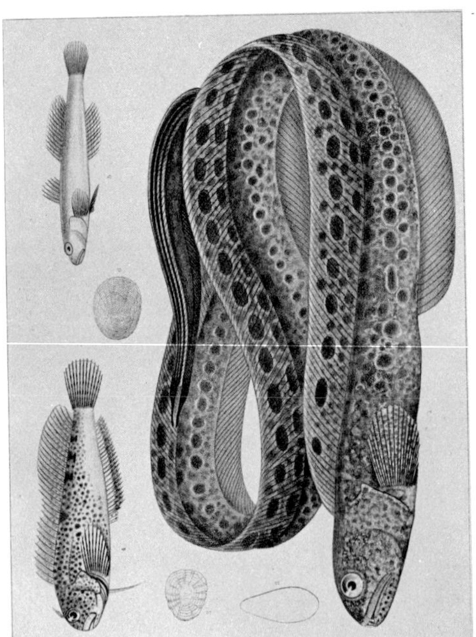

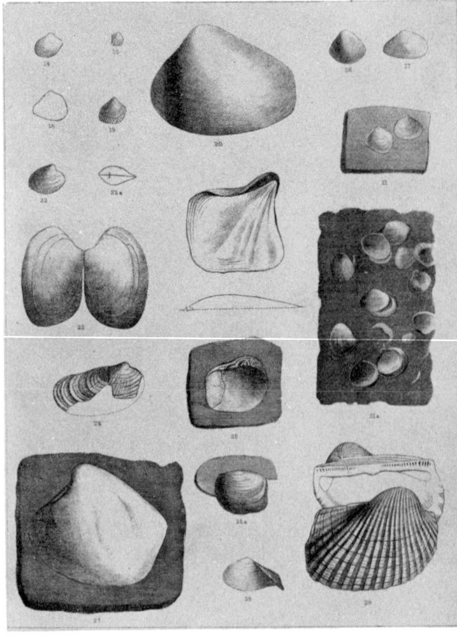

Examples of scientific illustrations published in the *Pacific Railroad Reports,* 1853–59.

Camp Floyd, Utah, headquarters of the United States Army in the Mormon War.

Yellow Creek Camp of the United States Army in the Mormon War.

Capt. James Hervey Simpson's expedition setting out westward across the Great Basin in 1857.

Capt. James Hervey Simpson's expedition arriving at Genoa, a Mormon settlement on the eastern slopes of the Sierra Nevadas near Lake Tahoe.

irst view of the Grand Canyon, drawn by F. W. von Egloffstein in 1857, from the floor
f the Canyon near Diamond Creek.

Capt. W. F. Raynolds' Yellowstone expedition of 1859 sketched by the artist, Antoine Schoenborn.

Above: A topographical engineer at work. Capt. Darrah of the Royal Engineers taking a sighting with his Zenith telescope, Northwest Boundary Survey.

Left: Part of the United States Northwest Boundary Commission Camp on San Juan Island, Nov. 4, 1859.

These and the photograph on the following page are among the earliest of Western photographs and perhaps the only surviving photographic record of the Northwest Boundary Survey. They were taken by British photographers who accompanied the Royal Engineers on the Boundary Survey.

Cutting a swath through the forest to mark the Northwest Boundary near the Moorjie River.

INDEX